P9-CRH-495

Improving Academic Management

A Handbook of Planning and Institutional Research

Paul Jedamus
Marvin W. Peterson
and Associates

Improving Academic Management

Jossey-Bass Publishers

San Francisco • Washington • London • 1980

IMPROVING ACADEMIC MANAGEMENT
A Handbook of Planning and Institutional Research
by Paul Jedamus, Marvin W. Peterson, and Associates

Library of Congress Cataloging in Publication Data

Main entry under title:
Improving academic management.

Includes bibliographical references and indexes.
1. Universities and colleges—United States—Adminis-
tration.   2. Universities and colleges—United States
—Planning.   3. Higher education and state—United
States.   I. Jedamus, Paul   II. Peterson,
Marvin W.
LB2341.I43   378.73   80-8009
ISBN 0-87589-477-1

Manufactured in the United States of America

JACKET DESIGN BY WILLI BAUM

FIRST EDITION

Code 8033

The Jossey-Bass
Series in Higher Education

Preface

This book is addressed to everyone concerned with the effective management and efficient operation of institutions of higher education. In particular, it is designed for those directly responsible for institutional planning and institutional research: chief administrative officers and their associates, vice-presidents and other central administrative officers, directors of offices of institutional research and planning, and the staff members of these offices. It seeks to be useful to decision makers at every type of postsecondary institution, from junior colleges through complex university systems, as well as to policy makers in government and private agencies concerned with academic management.

We hope the volume will serve these readers as a definitive and comprehensive guide to the practice of institutional research and planning in American higher education for the 1980s. As we see it, these critical management functions are now entering the third and potentially most significant period in their history.

The first period, extending into the 1940s and World War II, was marked by a strong sense of shared purpose in higher education. A homogeneous constituency understood and supported the goals of institutions, whether liberal arts

colleges or land-grant universities; it equated college education with social progress; and it endorsed institutional methods of achieving this purpose. During this
period, the locus of institutional planning remained with strong administrative
leaders who were dedicated both to particular ideals and to a particular institution. Presidents such as Robert Maynard Hutchins shaped not only departments
but entire institutions to their vision. In this period, institutional research had its
beginnings, emerging as an outgrowth of educational research at universities,
such as Minnesota, and as a means for measuring and comparing institutional
performance, as in the work of John Dale Russell at Chicago.

World War II began the second period, which lasted into the 1970s. New
constituencies led to a fragmentation of purpose except for the general consensus that universal education required explosive growth; state systems of higher
education and formal coordinating agencies developed to accomplish this
growth; and entrepreneurship and grantsmanship became operating principles.
Professional administrators, even more mobile than peripatetic professors, were
judged by how many buildings they built during their brief tenure. Planning, by
and large, focused on physical plant needs. The new planning offices, established along with offices of institutional research, were often staffed by architects
and space planners and characterized by master plans and space studies, while
those of institutional research, borrowing much from wartime government
agencies and an epidemic of macro-models, data elements, and program classification structures, increasingly associated themselves with the narrow measurement of efficiency.

The present era is marked by not only diverse but often conflicting
agendas for higher education—among them, greater access despite retrenchment and tougher standards despite remediation. Federal, state, and private
largess is being replaced by budget cutbacks and closer scrutiny of expenditures;
inflation is eroding endowment and eating up maintenance and library reserves;
and shifts in student demand for courses are causing grossly uneven allocation
of resources in the face of less flexible budgets. Administrators are faced with
resolving conflicts over institutional purposes and practices—not only with wary
faculty but also with a variety of special interest constituencies, each expecting to
participate in institutional decision making.

In this context, institutional research and planning must take on new
meaning and new responsibilities. Planning must help ensure the institution's
future by anticipating likely changes in its environment, by building consensus
on institutional goals and missions that will link the institution to its environment, and by devising ways to accomplish these goals and missions. Institutional
research must support faculty in their efforts to improve the quality of teaching,
research, and the learning environment in the face of continued budgetary constraints, and it must learn how to take advantage of the incipient information
revolution rather than be overwhelmed by it. Most important (and what is thus
the central organizing concept for this book), institutional planning and institutional research must be *integrated into one interrelated management function* rather
than being conducted separately. The planning process must be research-based
to have validity and utility, while institutional research must be both future-
oriented and related to institutional options in achieving institutional goals and
objectives if it is not to be meaningless.

This book is dedicated to these tasks. It aims at improving academic management by advancing the state of the art of institutional research and planning in light of the foreseeable pressures on colleges and universities.

Part One deals with the impact of current changes in the external environment on higher education and with implications of these changes for institutional research and planning. Chapters identify national issues crucial to the future of higher education; the likely consequences of specific demographic, economic, social, and political trends; the possible effect of changing policies and priorities of the federal and state governments; and the evolving influence of various types of coordinating agencies.

Part Two focuses on facets of what has come to be called "strategic" (as opposed to "tactical") planning—that is, examining potential relations of the institution with its environment rather than merely focusing on factors within the institution. Chapters point to promising approaches of strategic planning and the development of master plans; they illustrate how institutional research and planning help articulate institutional goals and assess "alternative futures" for the institution; and they evaluate techniques in two critical areas of strategic planning for colleges and universities—forecasting enrollments and identifying community and regional education needs.

Part Three demonstrates the uses of institutional research and "tactical" or internally oriented planning on such academic problems as assessing students' needs, improving the teaching/learning environment of the campus, planning new programs and reassessing old ones, and identifying the resources required by these programs.

Part Four concerns resource allocation, including ways of setting financial priorities, selecting appropriate budget strategies, and determining the needs of the institution for faculty, administrative staff, and physical plant.

Part Five shows how to measure the effectiveness of resource allocation in achieving institutional goals and meeting academic needs, not only at the total institutional level but also at the level of individual academic programs and in terms of both faculty and administrative performance.

Part Six examines the relation between offices of institutional research and planning and other management units (including the president's office, the administrative data system, and the academic governance structure) and suggests where these offices should be located within the administrative structure and the role they should play in the decision-making system.

Finally, because institutional research and planning responsibilities of necessity vary among different types of institutions, the chapters in Part Seven recommend organizational and operational modes appropriate for four major kinds of institutions: community colleges, small four-year colleges, medium-sized colleges and universities, and complex universities.

Some chapters and parts of the book will clearly be of greater interest to top-level administrators or faculty leaders than to, say, data-processing staff—but the authors have sought to make their chapters relevant and understandable to all readers. For example, the chapters on master planning and on setting institutional goals will be useful both to decision makers in administrative and faculty ranks and to staff officers responsible for conceiving and implementing the "plan for planning." Similarly, the chapter on assessing alternative futures speaks both to technical staff responsible for collecting data and building models from them and to chief administrative officers, who may be alerted by such models to otherwise unforeseen problems or unanticipated opportunities.

Five years ago, a book of this nature would not have been possible for this range of readers. Institutional research and planning were seldom related; institutional research was less future-oriented; and planning was overcommitted to the manipulation of simulation techniques. Now, however, the questions for improving institutional management go beyond issues of efficiency to broad strategic issues of institutional direction and priorities. As editors, we are grateful to our authors for showing how institutional research and planning can jointly address these issues.

We wish to express our debt to two men who have helped shape the profession of institutional research and planning: James I. Doi and Sidney Suslow (1926–1977). Both in their own way shared three traits: They were our good friends and mentors; they were pioneers in both the historical and the innovative development of the profession; and they exemplified the highest standards of research and scholarship. We, the editors, and the profession in general owe them much.

October 1980

PAUL JEDAMUS
Boulder, Colorado

MARVIN W. PETERSON
Ann Arbor, Michigan

Contents

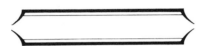

Part Two: Strategic Planning and Research

Part Four: Allocating Resources

Part Five: Assessing Performance

institutional management by clarifying responsibilities,
refining rewards, and improving performance.

Part Six: Increasing Campus Involvement

Part Seven: Current Institutional Practices

strategies of planning and institutional research and
suggests critical factors for making them more effective.

The Authors

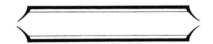

PAUL JEDAMUS is professor of management science at the University of Colorado, Boulder. He received a B.S. degree in chemical engineering in 1944, an M.B.A. degree in 1949, and a Ph.D. degree in commerce in 1955, all from the University of Wisconsin, Madison. Jedamus has taught at the University of Colorado since 1953 and has been a consultant in higher education management since 1956. From 1964 to 1968 he served the University of Colorado as director of Institutional Research.

Jedamus is coauthor of *Business Decision Theory* (with R. Frame, 1969) and *Statistical Analysis for Business Decisions* (with R. Frame and R. Taylor, 1976). He was co-editor with Sidney Suslow and subsequently editor-in-chief of *New Directions for Institutional Research* from its inception in 1974 through 1978. He has served the Association for Institutional Research in many capacities, including membership on the executive, program, and publications committees.

MARVIN W. PETERSON is professor of higher education and director of the Center for the Study of Higher Education at the University of Michigan. He received his B.S. degree in engineering science in 1960 from Trinity College (Hartford, Connecticut), his M.B.A. degree in 1962 from the Harvard Graduate School of Business Administration, and his Ph.D. degree in 1968 from the University of Michigan. From 1962–1966, Peterson served as an assistant dean at Harvard's Graduate School of Business Administration. Since 1968, he has been a faculty member in higher education and a faculty associate at the Institute for Social Research.

Peterson is coauthor of *Black Students on White Campuses* (with R. Blackburn and Z. Gamson, 1978), editor of *Benefitting from Interinstitutional Research* (1976), and editor-in-chief of *New Directions for Institutional Research.* He has served on the executive committees of the Association for Institutional Research, Association for the Study of Higher Education, and the Society for College and University Planning and is currently a member of the Education Commission of the States' task force on "State-Wide Coordination for the 1980's" and the Southern Regional Education Board's task force on "State Responses to Enrollment Decline."

J. Victor Baldridge, senior research sociologist, Higher Education Research Institute

Robert T. Blackburn, professor of higher education, University of Michigan

Foster S. Buchtel, assistant to the president, University of Akron

J. Kent Caruthers, vice-president and director, Educational Management Division, MGT of America

John E. Corbally, president emeritus and distinguished professor of education, University of Illinois

Joseph P. Cosand, professor of higher education, University of Michigan

Eugene Craven, assistant vice-president, University of Wisconsin System

Paul L. Dressel, professor of university research, Michigan State University

Robert H. Fenske, professor of higher education, Arizona State University

John K. Folger, associate executive director for policy and planning, Education Commission of the States

Carol Frances, chief economist and director, Division of Policy Analysis and Research, American Council on Education

Meredith A. Gonyea, president, Center for Studies in Health Policy

Raymond M. Haas, vice-president for administration, West Virginia University

Fred F. Harcleroad, director, Department of Higher Education, University of Arizona

RICHARD B. HEYDINGER, assistant to the vice-president of academic affairs, University of Minnesota

HAROLD L. HODGKINSON, president, National Training Laboratories

KRISTEN HOLMBERG-WRIGHT, research assistant to the president, Indiana University

VAUGHN E. HUCKFELDT, director, National Policy Analysis Center

WAYNE R. KIRSCHLING, deputy commissioner for higher education, Indiana Commission for Higher Education

DOROTHY M. KNOELL, higher education specialist, California Postsecondary Education Commission

OSCAR T. LENNING, senior associate, National Center for Higher Education Management Systems

JACK LINDQUIST, director, Institute for Academic Improvement, Memphis State University

JOHN A. LUCAS, director of planning and research, William Rainey Harper College

RICHARD M. MILLARD, director, Postsecondary Education Department, Education Commission of the States

RICHARD I. MILLER, vice-president for educational services, State University of New York, Brockport

JOHN D. MILLETT, executive vice-president, Academy for Educational Development

BARRY MUNITZ, chancellor, University of Houston

COLMAN O'CONNELL, director of planning, College of St. Benedict

MELVIN D. ORWIG, senior vice-president, Higher Education Assistance Foundation

GLENN PELLINO, research associate, Center for the Study of Higher Education, University of Michigan

NICK L. POULTON, director of university planning, Western Michigan University

JON H. REGNIER, director of physical planning and development, California State University, Long Beach

Bernard S. Sheehan, director, Office of Institutional Research, University of Calgary

Irving J. Spitzberg, Jr., general secretary, American Association of University Professors

Michael L. Tierney, assistant professor and research associate, Center for the Study of Higher Education, Pennsylvania State University

Robert A. Wallhaus, deputy director of academic and health affairs, Illinois Board of Higher Education

Paul Wing, director, Office of Postsecondary Research, Information Systems, and Institutional Aid, New York State Education Department

Improving Academic Management

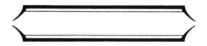

A Handbook of Planning and Institutional Research

1

Harold L. Hodgkinson

Impact of
National Issues

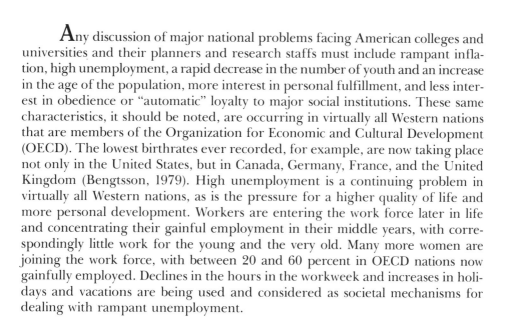

Any discussion of major national problems facing American colleges and universities and their planners and research staffs must include rampant inflation, high unemployment, a rapid decrease in the number of youth and an increase in the age of the population, more interest in personal fulfillment, and less interest in obedience or "automatic" loyalty to major social institutions. These same characteristics, it should be noted, are occurring in virtually all Western nations that are members of the Organization for Economic and Cultural Development (OECD). The lowest birthrates ever recorded, for example, are now taking place not only in the United States, but in Canada, Germany, France, and the United Kingdom (Bengtsson, 1979). High unemployment is a continuing problem in virtually all Western nations, as is the pressure for a higher quality of life and more personal development. Workers are entering the work force later in life and concentrating their gainful employment in their middle years, with correspondingly little work for the young and the very old. Many more women are joining the work force, with between 20 and 60 percent in OECD nations now gainfully employed. Declines in the hours in the workweek and increases in holidays and vacations are being used and considered as societal mechanisms for dealing with rampant unemployment.

At the same time that our population is aging and holding a steady state in terms of births, the astronomical number of children being born in India, the People's Republic of China, and other Asian and African nations will cause the world population to more than double in thirty years—from 3.6 billion in 1970 to a projected 7.5 billion in the year 2000 (Brown, 1979; Ross, 1977). As a result, the West is growing old quickly while the East is becoming even more youthful. As the Western nations age, we will have to seek cooperation and accommodation with nations suffering the ravages of disease, poverty, and malnutrition. The world is becoming very interdependent, perhaps before we are ready for it. The consequences for American life and American higher education are considerable.

Of all these trends, the consequences of three of them warrant detailed consideration in this chapter by institutional planners and researchers: inflation, demographic change, and what can best be called the "disaggregation" of higher education.

Educational Implications of Inflation

Although inflation is a problem in virtually all countries, the United States may be more sensitive to certain inflationary pressures than other nations that have a higher inflationary rate than ours—including the South American countries that, according to the International Monetary Fund, averaged 75 percent inflation in 1976 alone. Education costs always increase faster than the consumer price index because education is extremely labor intensive (*National Comparison Local School Costs,* 1977). Over the next decade, the American people will have to be convinced that, despite a declining number of college-eligible students of "conventional" age, the cost per student and the overall bill for higher education in the United States will continue to rise. This will be an extremely difficult case for educational leaders to make. Our ability to tell citizens what they are getting for their inflated dollar is limited by a lack of adequate measures of productivity in higher education, and citizens are not likely to vote for additional bond revenues for higher education, given the declining purchasing power of the dollar.

A second important impact of high levels of inflation concerns the rapid and consistent decline since 1967 in the faith we Americans express for our major social institutions, from Congress and the military to business and education. Not only does it seem that all these social institutions are conspiring against us economically, making it difficult for us to attain our personal objectives of increased material well-being. In addition, inflation seems to be affecting our own values. Until recently, central to Americans' value system has been a commitment to the Protestant Ethic, loosely meaning that we were ready to deny ourselves things today in order to save up for more of them in the future. Thus, we have saved our money, assuming it will be worth more tomorrow than today.

Unfortunately, most members of the American middle class now sense this value system no longer works. Putting money in a savings account at 5 or 6 percent interest when inflation is running at 13 percent a year means that saved money declines in purchasing power and savers get punished. In contrast, borrowers allow other people's money to decline in value and can come out ahead of savers. As a result, many of the ethical virtues associated with the Protestant Ethic lose their potency. We seem less loyal to our major social institutions, and we seem more concerned with having a good time in the present.

For many people, higher education has had some resemblance to a savings plan. We have worked hard as students in order to increase our future prestige and status. But if the "savings ethic" no longer works, and if people lose their faith in working hard today for increased well-being tomorrow, the consequences for higher education will be quite severe. Some potential students may decide college attendance is not worth the investment. Inflationary pressures will cause many potential consumers of higher education to "shop around" until they can get the best value for their limited dollars. And much more effective institutional planning and research will be called for as the tolerance for error in institutional decisions decreases. Institutional planners and researchers will have to get used to short-term, rapid turnaround studies, with higher anticipated fluctuations in economic variables than has been the case, and federal sources of institutional reporting such as HEGIS will have to increase the rapidity of their turnaround time or their value to institutions and to the Congress will be virtually nothing.

Consequences of Demographic Change

Because of the post–World War II baby boom, American society has been virtually controlled by an enormous "age lump." This group passed through college in the late 1960s, is now employed, and will continue to be a major social concern because of its size. Following the boom came the "bust," with rapid declines in the U.S. birthrate. One consequence for elementary education was the closing of many elementary schools. By 1978, chief state school officers were reporting high school closings as well. And in the 1980s, colleges will probably have to engage in similar reductions in force or seek new markets for their services (*American Demographics,* 1979).

Those born soon after the Second World War are now in child-bearing years. However, thus far, the second baby boom (or echo) has not yet developed. Birthrates are beginning to inch up, but they are a long way from those suggested by the very large number of women in the child-bearing years.

As the "age lump" created by the World War II baby boom moves out of college and into the world of work, we can expect a reduction in youth-oriented social change in the United States and a greater concern for the problems of those in early middle age.

We are still overwhelmingly a nation of nuclear families, but the number of families with children has been declining. A reassertion of traditional family values will probably characterize the 1980s, given the large number of people getting married and establishing families. According to Paul Glick of the Census Bureau (personal communication), only 2 percent of married people get divorced each year, compared to 1 percent several decades ago. But if the current rate continues for forty years, half the population may be divorced.

Given the end of the surplus of young people for the employment market, it will become easier for youth to find jobs. It will be virtually impossible to run a volunteer army on this number of young people, but violent crime will likely be reduced in the United States by 1985 because it is usually committed by unemployed youth, a cohort that will diminish by the mid 1980s.

Most of the U.S. birthrate decline has been among Caucasians; birthrates among racial or religious minority groups, such as Mormons or Seventh Day Adventists, have not declined significantly (*Social Indicators 1976,* 1977). This phenomenon seems to be based on social class, although the data are not clear. Apparently, middle-class blacks are as eager as middle-class whites to limit family size. The overall result, however, will be a pronounced decline in the percentage of Caucasians in the youth population and an increase in the proportions of various minority groups. As minorities come to constitute 30 percent of young people of college age, higher education policies will have to be altered if the institutions are to meet the needs of post–high school youth.

There are obvious contrasts between the baby boom generation and the much smaller cohorts that have been entering kindergarten for the last ten years. The baby boom group will live a life of relative scarcity. There will never be enough resources available to meet the needs of this greatly expanded age group. There will not be enough jobs; there will be a major housing shortage; there will be only a limited number of possible mid-career changes; and occupational and professional mobility will be difficult. As members of this group reach old age, there will not be enough specialized housing, recreation, and other facilities to meet their needs, and the number of people paying into the social security tax system will most likely be smaller than the number trying to collect from it. All in all, we lack the ability to expand services quickly enough for this particular age group.

In contrast, those born more recently will be recognized as a scarce resource. There will not be enough of them to do all the work we would like. They will find more goods and services available to them because the country will have stretched to meet the needs of the baby boom. Thus, college applicants of the 1980s will be able to select from a wide array of institutions that fifteen or twenty years ago might very well have rejected them. As they approach middle age, there will be more than enough housing available because of the housing built to meet the needs of those who came before them. They will be in great demand in the job market and may parlay this increased demand to higher wages and better working conditions.

Effects of the Disaggregation of Higher Education

The most striking trend in higher education over the last decade has been the increase in noneducational organizations in the United States offering education programs past the secondary level. Recent estimates from the College Board indicate that over fifty million American adults are currently engaged in systematic study, with about twelve million studying in college or university settings and some forty-six million studying elsewhere.

For example, the American military runs one of the world's largest education and training organizations for those past high school. The federal government runs a program that provided federal employees thirty-seven million hours of education in 1977. American businesses have, in large numbers, decided to make their own higher education instead of buying it from colleges and universities. Over five hundred business firms now run their own education programs, and several thousand businesses have their own assessment centers where job specifications and performance are analyzed based on specific skills and competencies. Estimates of U.S. industry's annual in-house educational expenditures range from $2 billion (Lusterman, 1977, p. 30ff) to $100 billion (*ASTD National Report,* 1979), and most likely the figure is at least $20 billion a year, not including tuition reimbursements when workers take courses at local colleges and universities.

Probably the most important aspect of this trend is that many businesses and the military no longer consider an additional college degree a prerequisite for promotion. Their self-contained educational systems now provide their own promotion criteria. Moreover, in the state of New York, twelve hundred courses offered by businesses, the military, government, and social agencies are now accepted for course credit by the State University of New York (*Supplemental Listing of Approved Courses,* 1979). The consequences of this trend for higher education are revolutionary. It has always been the academic degree, obtainable only through college and university study, that allowed one to become occupationally mobile. That "monopoly" has clearly given way. Some business firms are even offering their own degrees.

One of the major decisions higher education institutions will have to make about these developments is whether to consider these new education sources allies or adversaries. For example, AT&T had an educational budget of over $1.8 billion in 1979 and employed more than 2,000 PhDs at educating its almost one million workers. Whether as enemy or as source of potential alliance, college educators can no longer ignore the existence of such educational programs, and responsibilities of institutional research are likely to shift drastically as a result. Rather than counting credit hours, institutional research offices of the future may well be charged with assessing the "cost-benefit" consequences for the institution of short-term and long-term alliances with other organizations also engaged in education.

Other new institutional research skills will be required as well. Marketing skills, only a decade ago reserved for the business community, are now widely used by institutions of higher education. Institutions as prestigious and exclusive as Carleton College and Carnegie-Mellon have engaged in very sophisticated market studies, and other four-year colleges and universities are following suit (*American Demographics,* 1979). Community colleges, meanwhile, have several years lead, having begun to use marketing seriously by 1975. Clearly, institutional research will play a large role in the development of marketing skills and the analytical capability that goes with marketing.

Marketing is not selling. Rather, it involves identifying clienteles and service areas, rigorously assessing the kinds of services the organization offers, gauging the competition's strengths and weaknesses, and positioning the organization in a desirable niche, given the competition. The skills of all the social sciences are very relevant to marketing, particularly for higher education institutions.

This emphasis on marketing will lead to shorter cycle planning and to planning processes that include activities of other educational organizations in the service area that may or may not be colleges or universities. Again, the challenge for institutional research offices will be great. For many institutions, the next decade will involve a search for new clienteles and the development of new services, some of them noninstructional. The role of institutional research will be crucial in establishing whether new groups of clients are likely to develop as a "market."

There are more than enough Americans currently studying past high school to make up for most of the decline that will take place in the college-age student population. The problem is that forty-six million of them are now happily studying somewhere else, and the techniques to lure them from where they are to college and university campuses are not yet well developed. Institutions will have to be responsible in their advertising and clear in their statements of objectives if the increasingly sophisticated adult education population is to be drawn into college and university settings. Institutional research responsibilities here will be significant.

The 1970s were primarily a time of developing new and innovative *institutions* of higher education. The 1980s, with a different approach to finance, will see many developing *networks* of existing institutions, as opposed to new institutions. In the long run, the innovative networks may be far more effective in creating a hospitable environment for educational change. There will be many more part-time students, who will be increasingly older than "conventional" students. This trend, particularly strong in community colleges, will develop as well in a number of other kinds of institutions during the 1980s.

A major financial problem here is that the administrative cost per student remains constant, whether the student takes three credit hours or twenty, because all students need student records, parking, counseling, and other services regardless of the number of credits they earn.

Conclusion

A key issue in higher education in the 1980s will be competition versus collaboration. As student registration declines, many colleges and universities may become highly competitive, making false promises to lure students to the campus. This is the worst possible response in terms of public credibility for the education system as a whole. The competition in this decade will also involve proprietary institutions and "external" agencies (businesses and the military), all dealing with the same potential students.

Continuing education legislation in most states virtually guarantees that twelve to fifteen million Americans will be forced to go back to some sort of further education to maintain their occupational credentials. Such legislation applies not only to doctors and lawyers but to real estate agents, nursing home operators, and other occupations. The competition for these twelve million students will be severe because the legislation almost never indicates what is to be taught or who is to do the teaching. It is a virtually open market.

One of the most interesting developments in higher education may be increasing communication between institutional research and planning personnel in academia and people who do similar analytical tasks elsewhere. Every good sized business, for example, employs a number of people who undertake research and planning comparable to, if not more sophisticated than, that in most colleges or universities. Institutional research as a profession will probably come of age in the 1980s, and we may begin to see sharing between those who handle analytical data needs for business and industry, the military, and government as well as higher education.

Given all these trends, institutional research in higher education is clearly going to be more analytical and less concerned with descriptive studies. As one president recently put it to the campus institutional research director, "now that we know what is happening, the questions for you are why is it happening and what can be done about it?" This president was reflecting a relatively new style in dealing with institutional research: a concern for the quality of analysis by institutional research offices so that data can be more directly useful in the decision-making process. As higher education becomes more involved with other kinds of institutions in the future, given the end of the monopoly of post-secondary activities by colleges and universities, institutional research will have to develop sophistication in areas of analysis beyond descriptive statistics. This means the profession will come of age, although for many, it will appear to be both a threat and an opportunity.

Bibliographical Essay

Almost unknown to most educators are a variety of information sources outside of the formal publishing media in higher education:

The Conference Board publishes a variety of excellent surveys and analyses in areas relevant to higher education, including demographics, management, economic and social trends, international business developments, technological innovations, consumer markets, and planning techniques. The quality of their data is first rate.

The U.S. Census Bureau is getting much more interested in serving institutional data needs. A large number of special studies are now available through the Bureau, and lists of these studies are obtainable from it. For institutional planning, the Standard Metropolitan Statistical Area data base of the census is an excellent free source of information, especially for those institutions that limit their student "draw" to a city or region of a state.

The Department of Agriculture, the Department of Labor, and the Public Health Service all publish very good data on matters immediately relevant to higher education.

A variety of associations provide excellent information on educational matters. For example, the American Association of Retired Persons is doing a fine job in providing information on lifelong learning opportunities for senior citizens, and the American Speech and Hearing Association has good material on the developmental problems of aging as they relate to teaching.

In the international area, the publications of the Organization for Economic and Cultural Development (OECD), headquartered in Paris, are some of the best around. A part of OECD is the Council on Educational Research and Innovation (CERI), which does some fine analyses on the educational issues in CERI-OECD member nations. About one half of their studies concern higher education.

In addition to the materials provided by the various higher education organizations, such as the American Council on Education, the Council for the Advancement of Small Colleges, the Education Commission of the States, the National Association of College and University Business Officers, the National Association of Independent Colleges and Universities, and the National Center for Higher Education Management Systems, to name but a few, one should be aware of the many excellent studies of the public schools that are often prophetic of the future of higher education. (The recent study of enrollment declines at the kindergarten to twelfth grade level, published by the National Institute of Education, is a good example—the implications for higher education from this analysis of school problems and solutions is striking [Abramowitz and Rosenfeld, 1978].)

In my opinion, the work of the various futurist "think tanks" has not proven very useful for people who have to deal with middle-range projections (those over the next ten years). A number of their predictions have turned out not to be accurate. Similarly, most linear prediction models are helpful only in a most general way. Whatever else the future is, it is interactive and multivariate. (As someone put it, "Events do not grow up, get married, and give birth to little events.") Most of the future is walking around with us at this very moment, if we can only learn to focus on the things we cannot see. In this regard, I foresee a major shift from quantitative analysis to qualitative analysis in most institutional research and planning efforts. This may involve such data sources as clinical observations, testimonials, field studies, interviews, and group dynamics exercises. The human resource development movement will come to higher education as it has to business and industry, and organizations active in this movement will be sources of publications and information on these techniques.

References

Abramowitz, S., and Rosenfeld, S. (Eds.). *Declining Enrollments: The Challenge of the Coming Decade.* Washington, D.C.: National Institute of Education, 1978.

American Demographics. June 1979.

ASTD National Report, January 5, 1979.

Bengtsson, J. *The Future of the Work Place.* Paris: Organization for Economic and Cultural Development, 1979.

Brown, G. H. "Population." *Across the Board,* 1979, pp. 6–11.

Lusterman, S. *Education in Industry.* New York: The Conference Board, 1977.

National Comparison Local School Costs. (3rd ed.) Westport, Conn.: Market Data Retrieval, 1977.

Ross, D. *Population Trends and Implications.* New York: The Conference Board, 1977.

Social Indicators 1976. Washington, D.C.: Office of Management and Budget, 1977.

Supplemental Listing of Approved Courses. Albany, N.Y.: State Education Department, 1979.

2

Irving J. Spitzberg, Jr.

Monitoring Social and Political Changes

The tension in planning lies between the "is" of the reality one must face and the "ought" of the vision one wishes to achieve. Like weather forecasting, it attempts to understand underlying forces in order to predict changes, which one can then approach strategically. But unlike weather prediction, institutional planning necessarily involves understanding the hopes and visions of individuals and developing strategies that will guide change consistent with these ideals.

This chapter identifies hopes and visions arising in the sociopolitical environment that impact on the planning process, provides some judgments about

Note: I would like to acknowledge the help of six graduate students from the Center for Policy Studies of SUNY/Buffalo. They shared their extensive expertise with me and provided research assistance: Stewart Brecher, Farouk Yagmour, Kathleen Curtin-Glose, Bruce Corning, Michele Twomey, and Leslie Ford. Robert Berdahl of the Department of Higher Education at SUNY/Buffalo and Paul Jedamus, an editor of this volume, have provided helpful critical comments on a draft of this chapter.

the evolving political context within which planning must operate in the foreseeable future, and offers recommendations for strategic planning in a future that will be characterized by significant social and political uncertainty.

The Social Context

In the previous chapter, Harold Hodgkinson identified three important features of society, posing important substantive issues for universities, colleges, and other postsecondary institutions—inflation, demographic change, and the disaggregation of higher education. Other issues the sociopolitical system will pose for higher education will include unemployment, racism, sexism, consumer exploitation, political conflict, energy limits, environmental degradation, and continued concern for social justice.

In this period of rapid social change, when knowledge is important, when the economy is moving from one dominated by the industrial system to one characterized by service employment, and when the culture is built around some sensitivity to social justice but with very inegalitarian distribution of power, we must develop a policy analysis and planning system that guarantees flexibility, responsiveness, and sophistication in the assessment of the future implications of these present issues. Consider several social trends affecting them.

Population Distribution. Changing population distributions among various sectors of the United States have been dramatized by movement from the cold North to the Sunbelt. Population in the Northeast industrial states, particularly the urban centers of these states, declined significantly in the 1970s in a manner not yet fully documented in the 1980 census, while the population grew rapidly in the Southeast and Southwest. The significance of this change for institutional research and planning is heightened by the fact that shifts in the eighteen-to-twenty-four age group may have been even greater than that of the population as a whole (Magarell, 1978). Thus, potential enrollment declines at the postsecondary level in the Northeast and Midwest may be greater than the overall population declines in these areas as well as significantly greater than those to be expected in the far West, Southwest, and Southeast (Magarell, 1978). In addition, the economic dislocation associated with population shift and decline will probably be significantly greater in the Northeast and Midwest than elsewhere in the United States.

Socioeconomic Class. Here the most important trend is the change in distribution of the class structure geographically from rural poverty in earlier decades to today's concentration of the lower socioeconomic classes in the cities. The scale of unemployment in the central cities has created an urban proletariat likely to continue to grow, particularly in Northeast and upper Midwest urban centers. And insofar as the industrial sector of the economy diminishes in importance in comparison to the service sector, areas of the country with very highly capital intensive industrial sectors will undoubtedly become locations of more of the poor and the unemployed—thereby presenting higher education in these regions with renewed curricular and financial challenges.

Economic Trends. Changes in the price of energy have recently provided the most dramatic lesson about the sensitivity of postsecondary institutions to the economic structure, but higher education resource availability is directly related to the health of the overall economy. The expanded rate of new development of industry in the service sector and the light industrial and high technology sectors in the West and Southwest with the continuing movement of resources away from the urban Northeast and North Central part of the United States presents an economic pattern of great significance for the postsecondary institutions in those areas. The shifting of economic resources will be affected by other factors, such as energy and environmental limitations, which are difficult to assess right now. But there is no evidence that in the next decade or two this shift will come to a halt (*Digest of Educational Statistics*, 1978). The significance of this shift for institutions of postsecondary education will be the need for increased capacity for postsecondary education in the Southwest and South with excess capacity in the Northeast (*Digest of Educational Statistics*, 1978).

Both the movement of industry to areas of cheap labor outside the continental United States and the fluctuation of prices according to commodity markets in the Third World and cartel decisions in the Middle East will become matters not just of interest to economists in universities but directly relevant to decisions about the future made by institutions of postsecondary education.

The Political Context

Central to the process of planning in institutions of postsecondary education is the task of developing strategic responses to such economic, social, and demographic trends of our societal setting that are consistent with the political realities of the larger system. When we try to do so, we often focus on political facts that are easily quantified and modeled, despite the softness of the data and the inability of surrogate and secondary measures to communicate important value issues. The elegance of planning models often misses the structure of political bargaining that provides the environment within which all important decisions are made and the constraints around the choices offered at any moment. Therefore, we need to canvass changes in the political environment and make educated guesses about the implications of these changes for postsecondary institutions.

Public Perceptions of Postsecondary Education. One of the most important environmental factors affecting the political agenda is the overall view of postsecondary education people hold. We know something about this from the work of those who undertake large-scale public opinion surveys as well as from electoral results as they affect candidates who hold specific positions. The substance of the mood from the 1960s to the 1970s documented by these data has been one of significant public disillusionment with postsecondary education at the end of the 1960s and a slight moderation in its disillusionment by the end of the 1970s (Rowland, 1977). But the most central point is public apathy toward postsecondary education; the public for the most part had no significant view of postsecondary education. That is, higher education is very low on the public agenda.

One lesson of these facts for university planning is that we cannot rely on hopes for significant positive improvement of the public perception of higher education but must be prepared to deal with remaining skepticism, hope at least for benign neglect, and develop strategies for educating the public about postsecondary education in order to affect public perceptions.

Fiscal Restraint. The passing of Proposition 13 in California has highlighted efforts throughout the United States to restrict taxes and hold down the growth of the public sector. There is no reason to think that in the foreseeable future this mood of stringency in regard to the public sector will change, although there is some indication this fiscal conservatism may be more a demand for clear value from both public and private sectors than a limit-at-all-cost attitude. The political challenge of this public mood will undoubtedly be one of developing ways for both the public and private sectors of postsecondary education to demonstrate that all expenditures are efficient and effective and not unreasoned demands on disposable income. There will be greater consumer resistance to tuition increases and other techniques for passing on the cost of postsecondary education to the student, and techniques are needed not only for calculating institutional efficiency and effectiveness but also for communicating the fact that postsecondary education is providing value for money. This fiscal conservatism will set tight parameters on all increases in a way that does not necessarily match the rate of inflation. In addition, internal demands for assessment of value for money will become part of any planning process so that justification of requests for money to both public and private sources will be readily available.

Social Justice. Ever since the mid nineteenth century, issues of social justice have never been far below the surface of American politics. The 1960s saw the elevation of social justice issues to the top of the agenda; the 1970s have shown these issues to be less politically important. But the underlying problems social justice issues address have not abated in the 1970s. Therefore, there is every reason to expect the social justice issues to continue to be on the political agenda of the 1980s and 1990s, and their importance will depend very much upon the value perspective of those assessing political issues.

Social justice issues in regard to postsecondary institutions will emerge in terms of access for admissions (for example, open admissions demands), the performance of persons from various ethnic and socioeconomic groups in postsecondary institutions, and the composition of faculty and staffs of postsecondary institutions. The rights of other categories of persons—women, the handicapped, and senior citizens—will also create social justice issues.

All these claims will impact on postsecondary institutions through at least four forums: the acts of state legislatures and the Congress, the invocation of court implementation of state and federal policy as well as constitutional rights, the political presentation of these claims within local political communities, and the pressing of these demands in all the constituent forums of postsecondary institutions.

The disputes about these issues in the larger political system will often affect, and indeed emerge from, the political deliberations about them in the postsecondary institutions. For example, we can see the importance of *Bakke*, with its tenuous holding that race was an appropriate consideration in admission but that the category of race as a sole criterion was unacceptable. This ruling has been debated at length and will be part of an emerging refinement of manner of legal implementation of social justice values.

The 1980s will undoubtedly see a continuing evolution of the way American society discusses social justice issues and the approaches implementing policies in a variety of settings, including those of postsecondary education. The challenge for purposes of our planning will be to consider the enhancement of social justice in all procedures of postsecondary institutions and not to leave these issues to the afterthought of ad hoc action in response to political pressure. A number of postsecondary institutions (such as the University of North Carolina, see Middleton, 1979, p. 7) have already been challenged by the federal government to include the demands of social justice in their internal planning; thus, there is a body of experience emerging that can assist institutions in drawing on the values and policies of the larger society in their own institutional planning and development.

Consumer Demands. Consumers of postsecondary services, whether students or community users of knowledge produced by postsecondary institutions, have historically made and will continue to make demands through a market system. But in addition, in recent years, the consumer demand for quality postsecondary educational services has also been voiced through political forums. This trend should continue and, indeed, along with the increased political visibility of the consumer movement, will undoubtedly become a more important force in political decisions about postsecondary institutions. The major implication of this societal respect for the rights of consumers will be to set new standards of care by which quality of all forms of postsecondary performance will be measured. And insofar as postsecondary institutions do not measure up to the claims consumers place on them, there will undoubtedly be a number of political actions taken, ranging from penalties in the distribution of resources to actual legal liability of postsecondary institutions for the quality of the services they provide both to students and the society at large.

Problems of Accountability. In a period of declining resources, the use to which any single dollar or other resource is put becomes of great interest to those within and without an institution. Throughout society, there is likely to be ever-increasing interest in the way all sectors use resources. This sensitivity will lead to more formalized modes of accountability. In the 1960s and 1970s, we have seen the development in the public sector of a number of formal ways of increasing the accountability of those who use the public dollar—in the postsecondary sector, more sophisticated line-item program planning budgeting systems have increased accountability. A number of legislative units have developed program auditing systems in order to assess effectiveness (Berdahl, 1977). Given the ever-tightening public sector budget, these institutional mechanisms for auditing and assessing will undoubtedly be refined in order to increase the public accountability of those who use the public dollar.

In the private sector, the internal constituencies of the university as well as donors have become more sensitive to the use institutions put their dollars to in general, not just in terms of the specific donation or the specific unit in which a person works. Again, the sensitivity to declining resources has been directly linked to a demand for accountability in the use of all resources.

Accountability in terms of the ethical character of decision making is another sector of social sensitivity. Ever since Watergate, Americans' interest in institutional truthfulness and standards of ethical behavior has increased. The Carnegie Council study of fair practices in postsecondary education is an indication of this social interest communicated through policy issues in postsecondary education (Carnegie Council, 1979). This manifestation of social accountability will play the role in the 1980s of encouraging, perhaps even forcing, postsecondary institutions to maintain the integrity of their programs unless they wish to suffer the intervention of other institutions (particularly legislatures) in their internal operations.

Conflicting with these societal demands for accountability will always be commitments to individual academic freedom and institutional autonomy. The challenge to postsecondary education in developing its policies in the 1980s will be to maintain both sorts of integrity—that of individual freedom and institutional autonomy on the one hand and the integrity of ethical practices and rational allocation in use of resources in response to societal demands on the other.

Urban and Rural Policies. Society as a whole will continue to form judgments about complexes of issues it faces. A recent manifestation of the social evolution of policies in the United States is the development of a national health system. Both state and federal positions in regard to the operation of the overall system are emerging. Similar moves are occurring in two major social settings for postindustrial life—cities and the countryside. The development of urban and rural policies by the larger society will undoubtedly have significant impact on postsecondary institutions, as will these institutions on the evolution of these policies.

In the late 1970s, the United States self-consciously attempted to evolve an urban policy. The Carter administration prepared packages of legislation and executive orders designed to cohere the urban impact of federal programs. This move to create consistent governmental policies in regard to urban problems has a special meaning for postsecondary institutions in urban settings. Postsecondary institutions will undoubtedly be viewed as important forums for addressing many of the problems through service delivery and analysis. The challenge to urban postsecondary institutions will be to participate creatively in developing coherent urban policies and to maintain the integrity of their academic missions by not becoming urban service stations.

Rural policy development also offers opportunities to postsecondary institutions. Through the land-grant colleges and the development of the cooperative extension services, American postsecondary education has been an international model of how postsecondary institutions can serve the development of rural societies (Hanson, 1962). But it was only in the last part of the 1970s that the United States as a society once again turned to the problem of developing coherent rural development policies. In the 1980s and 1990s, because of migration back to rural areas, the need to develop coherent policy will become ever more important and will undoubtedly have greater visibility on the American decision-making agenda. Therefore, postsecondary institutions will have an opportunity to take the lead in developing creative initiatives in the area of rural development, this time drawing upon lessons from other developing societies. The role of postsecondary institutions in rural settings in postindustrial societies will be matter for important role definition in the 1980s and 1990s.

Issues for Planning and Institutional Research. If the preceding analysis has correctly identified important social and political trends on the postsecondary horizon for the 1980s and 1990s, the storm clouds seem to be gathering. It is very important that we develop the capability not only of making best guesses about the future but also of developing our own strategic relationship with the future so we may, to some degree, control it. It is with this goal in mind that we must turn to an examination of the planning process for institutions of postsecondary education, so they may respond to and understand the trends and challenges emerging from the sociopolitical environment and chart an appropriate course. We must understand the tools for collecting data and modeling reality so we may make our judgments with the best information possible. Next, we must consider the alternatives open for institutionalizing planning in postsecondary institutions. And finally, we must consider how we can best use alternative analytical perspectives to make judgments.

Organizing Data for Planning. All trend statements made earlier in this chapter were based upon general judgments drawn from the display of macrosocial data. Much planning effort in the past two decades has gone into developing technical models that use such trend data to project enrollments and then from enrollment data extrapolate probable resource and personnel needs. There exist a number of relatively sophisticated models for making enrollment projections and determining the impact of alternative enrollment futures, but few of them have actually informed detailed decision making in institutions of postsecondary education. And they have seldom been communicated in a way that allows them to test the future implications of alternative present decisions. The challenge to those who wish to become more sophisticated in creating, organizing, and using data for purposes of testing the future implications of present decisions is to devise more inexpensive ways to collect hard data, to draw on a number of preexisting data banks, and to translate the information into models that can be used at the moment of possible decision. Because of the expense of creating models, the exercise of data presentation and analysis has been at the same time technocratic and complicated, yet simple in terms of sophistication (Mason, 1976).

Data analysis depends upon the particular use to which data will be put. Decision makers have to play a role in guiding the development of alternative data bases and the models to be used to analyze them. To make this observation is not just to suggest a particular decision maker (a university president, for example) must have a say in the way data are organized and displayed. Instead it is to suggest all those whose interests are at stake in decisions—that is, particularly the "citizens" inside postsecondary institutions—should play a role in establishing the parameters of analysis. There are some experiences of large-scale participation in establishing analytical parameters and then actually using the data for purposes of political decision making (Brown and Healey, 1976). Although these examples are rare, they provide the paradigm for the future development of data bases and their use in the planning process of postsecondary institutions.

Alternative Planning Units within Postsecondary Institutions. If one wishes to enlarge the number of those making decisions and having adequate information for making them, it will be necessary to develop new modes of research and dissemination within postsecondary institutions. These alternative forms of research and planning will have to draw a direct connection between the generation of knowledge and its application through decision making. One of the roadblocks to reform of governance in postsecondary institutions has been the inability to develop ways of providing relevant data in a cost-effective manner to collegial decision-making units. Although many institutions have offices of institutional research, they are usually understaffed and provide timely information to the central administration only. If persons in larger institutions are to carry on creative dialogues about the factual base for projections, there must be alternative locations in these institutions where there is the technical capability to serve decision making and to challenge decisions made by others. Although an adversarial model is not guaranteed to provide "the truth," testing of alternative assessments of reality has a way of guaranteeing justification and explanation.

Another reason to develop decentralized research capabilities and planning responsibility is that the value element inherent in all planning demands explicit articulation of value positions so the value perspective may self-consciously guide the interpretation of factual data. The major virtue of planning processes is that they force people to express their values as they make judgments about what the future will and ought to look like.

Another reason to have local, decentralized research capabilities and value responsibility is that this skill to generate relevant information needs to be shared broadly if all decision-making interests are to be respected. There are a number of efforts in Western Europe and Third World countries to establish a movement toward participatory research, which allows input from those whose lives are affected by research results (Hall, 1978). Because research knowledge gives power, it is critical that those over whom power is to be exercised are able to generate their own information. In the context of postsecondary institutions, this means all constituencies need to develop their own capability to generate knowledge and participate in planning processes.

Alternative Analytical Perspectives. The formal writing on planning and policy analysis clearly documents the importance of decision makers' sensitivity to the impact of diverse analytical perspectives. For example, if one wishes to develop a strategic position in regard to the continuing conflict between the public and private sectors of postsecondary education, one must understand the following factors: (1) There are political personalities involved bargaining for different power relationships. (2) There are institutions whose economic survival will be at stake. (3) There are standard operating procedures encapsulated in legislative and budgetary processes in the public sector and tax laws influencing private philanthropy that provide critical constraints and must be addressed if there are to be changes in the public and private relationship. If one wishes to change a political bargaining relationship, the way institutions pursue self-interests, or the standard operating procedures, one must assess present and future implications of such a move. One must combine in the planning and analytical process the bit (incremental) and long-term scanning envisaged by Etzioni (1968). The individual institution's stance in relation to the ongoing flow of events in the larger political environment must be strategic, that is, one that looks to the long-term relationship between the particular institutions and the society and adjusts its relationship to environmental changes.

The practical implication of using alternative analytical perspectives is that one must have the analytical and disciplinary skills necessary to highlight the central issues from each perspective and to communicate them through the political process to decision makers. Planning must not be viewed as a technocratic undertaking of feeding quantifiable data into the equations of a model. Quantifiable data must serve, not determine, the judgment-making function. Planning is a process of having a polity decide its own future; this is irreducibly a value judgment. Therefore, there must be a structured political forum allowing all those with an interest to have adequate information to present their own position for judgment by the larger political system.

Once planning is viewed as a political process, there are many structures that can be developed to enhance decentralization and provision of large-scale aggregative data. Some public sector innovations may help improve the planning process: First, sunset laws may allow regular review of total systems for purposes of deciding whether they should continue and, if they should, what changes should be made in their operation. Second, regular review cycles with adequate information for both the reviewer and the reviewed seem to be a valuable approach to planning that clearly recognizes its political character.

If we are to understand the alternative analytical perspectives necessary and the value judgments entailed in decision making, we must move past the attempt to create technical models, even though they are important; to an understanding of the dynamics of planning as they affect postsecondary institutions individually and as a total sector. In order to provide this information, we need detailed case studies clearly focused upon the interaction between value and fact in postsecondary planning. Until these case studies are available and systematically analyzed, we can only identify certain features of the planning and policy analysis process as it relates to the larger sociopolitical environment.

If postsecondary institutions are to be sensitive to their sociopolitical environment, planning must evolve in such a way that all decision makers can draw on information about the environment as well as about the particular institution. Most of us have a great deal of knowledge about the postindustrial world, but the planning process should force us to articulate it and compare it with other versions of reality provided by the sophisticated analysis of complex data.

Conclusion

Successful strategic planning in the context of changing sociopolitical environments demands a planning and analysis process that recognizes its political nature and the need for the broad dissemination and sharing of knowledge. If planning is understanding the future implications of present decisions, then we all have an equal right to the knowledge necessary to make those judgments. Therefore, only if planning is viewed as a participatory process that consistently provides information to all with something at stake does it become a useful exercise that serves the political interests not only of postsecondary education institutions but also of the larger society. Insofar as we in postsecondary institutions create a sophisticated planning process that allows broad-based participation, we will be meeting our goals in that we will be providing an occasion for learning as educational as any structured curriculum. We will also create an opportunity to generate new knowledge about how institutions in postindustrial societies should go about planning—and this knowledge is sorely needed by our total polity.

Bibliographical Essay

The National Institute of Education has published a useful critical bibliography that reports a number of experts' conclusions about the most recent and best sources of higher education planning (Halstead, 1979). The three works most useful to the planner of higher education interested in the impact of the sociopolitical environment on the task of postsecondary planning are Allison (1971), Etzioni (1968), and Lindblom (1977). Allison's work is a brilliant case study that transcends its case to explore the metaphysics of policy analysis. Etzioni's work is long and rather tough reading, but the conceptual framework and practical suggestions deserve attention. Lindblom's treatise is lengthy as well but reads clearly and offers an analytical framework that will be helpful to all involved with leadership in contemporary societies.

An area of critical writing about planning often overlooked by those in postsecondary education is that of national planning in developing countries. The literature in this field is critical of the rationalistic approaches taken over wholeheartedly these days by planners in postsecondary institutions. I especially commend Leys (1974), Court (1972), and Nyerere (1968).

References

Allison, G. T. *Essence of Decision: Explaining the Cuban Missile Crisis.* Boston: Little, Brown, 1971.

Berdahl, R. "Legislative Program Evaluation." In J. K. Folger (Ed.), *New Directions for Institutional Research: Increasing the Public Accountability of Higher Education,* no. 16. San Francisco: Jossey-Bass, 1977.

Brown, D., and Healey, M. "Fire and Ice: Rational Decision-Making and College Politics in the Resource Allocation Arena." Paper presented at the Educational Sciences Section, joint meeting of the Institute of Management Sciences and Operations Research Society of America, Miami, 1976.

Carnegie Council on Policy Studies in Higher Education. *Fair Practices in Higher Education: Rights and Responsibilities of Students and Their Colleges in a Period of Intensified Competition for Enrollments.* San Francisco: Jossey-Bass, 1979.

Court, D., and Ghai, D. P. (Eds.). *Education, Society, and Development: New Perspectives from Kenya.* New York: Oxford University Press, 1972.

Digest of Educational Statistics. National Center for Educational Statistics. Washington, D.C.: U.S. Government Printing Office, 1978.

Etzioni, A. *The Active Society.* New York: Free Press, 1968.

Hall, B. *Participatory Research Project.* Toronto: International Council for Adult Education, 1978.

Halstead, D. K. (Ed.). *Higher Education Planning: A Bibliographic Handbook.* Washington, D.C.: National Institute of Education, 1979.

Hanson, J. "The Land Grant Philosophy and African Higher Ed." *West African Journal of Education,* 1962, *6,* 80–84.

Jacobson, R. L. "Colleges Try to Move in on Vocational Education." *Chronicle of Higher Education,* 1977, *15,* 3–4.

Leys, C. *Underdevelopment in Kenya.* Berkeley: University of California Press, 1974.

Lindblom, C. *Politics and Markets.* New York: Basic Books, 1977.

Magarell, J. "The Enrollment Roller Coaster: Colleges Fear the Big Dip." *Chronicle of Higher Education,* 1978, *17* (1), 1.

Mason, T. R. (Ed.). *New Directions for Institutional Research: Assessing Computer-Based Systems Models,* no. 9. San Francisco: Jossey-Bass, 1976.

Middleton, L. "University of North Carolina System Threatened with Loss of $90 Million." *Chronicle of Higher Education,* 1979, *18* (6), 7.

Nyerere, J. *Freedom and Development.* London: Oxford University Press, 1968.

Rowland, A. W. (Ed.). *Handbook of Institutional Advancement: A Practical Guide to College and University Relations, Fund Raising, Alumni Relations, Government Relations, Publications, and Executive Management for Continued Advancement.* San Francisco: Jossey-Bass, 1977.

3

Carol Frances

Influence of Federal Programs

On October 17, 1979, President Carter signed legislation creating a new cabinet-level Department of Education—the latest milestone in a 192-year relationship between the federal government and higher education. This chapter traces the evolution of this relationship, examines the major areas where current federal initiatives affect institutional operations, and identifies in each of these areas specific implications for the work of institutional researchers and planners.

Evolution of the Federal Role

Ever since the American states formed a new nation, the appropriate federal role in higher education has been a subject of debate. George Washington proposed to the first Congress the establishment of a national university; but after sharp disagreements, Congress rejected the centralized approach to education in favor of a truly federal system in which the primary responsibility for public education, including higher education, was at the state level.

Note: The discussion of "Self-Regulation" benefited extensively from discussions with Elaine El-Khawas, director of ACE's Office of Self-Regulation Initiatives, and Kenneth Young, president of the Council on Postsecondary Accreditation.

Table 1 lists significant dates in the relationship between higher education and the federal government. As the federal role has evolved, it became a changing mix of five or six different functions, each of them ascendant in succeeding epochs and each identifiable by an event symbolizing the dominant activity.

1787: Stimulation of the Establishment of Institutions. In 1787, the Constitution was ratified and the Northwest Ordinance was enacted, authorizing land grants for the creation of educational institutions in the new territories. Thus, from the earliest period of our history, the federal government stimulated the establishment of educational institutions through the grants of public lands.

Then in 1862, close to the beginning of the Industrial Revolution in this country, Congress passed the First Morrill Act, which donated public lands to the states and territories to establish the "land-grant" colleges. These became the flagship institutions in each state, created originally to promote the study of agriculture and mechanical arts.

Virtually all higher education institutions in the United States, both public and private, are chartered by the individual states. The only institutions chartered by the federal government are the services academies: U.S. Military Academy (1802); U.S. Coast Guard Academy (1876); U.S. Merchant Marine Academy (1936); and U.S. Air Force Academy (1954). The federal government also supports institutions in the District of Columbia, including Howard University; but they are not regarded as federal institutions.

1890: Support for Instruction. With the passage of the Second Morrill Act in 1890, the federal government expanded its support of higher education by providing federal funds for instruction at the land-grant institutions. Subsequently, the federal government supported vocational education, first, in 1917, below the college level and then, in 1946, at the college level.

The objective of this federal support for instruction was not to promote general education but to meet specific economic needs, first in agriculture and industry and more recently to meet specific shortages of trained workers, for example, in education and in the health professions.

1944: Expansion of Access to Higher Education. The most massive expansion of access to higher education was actually the result of a federal program created to avoid unemployment. In 1944, the Servicemen's Readjustment Act, the GI Bill, was passed. Besides home financing and many other benefits, it provided federal support for World War II veterans to pursue their education. The intent of Congress was to smooth the transition to the postwar economy and to avoid the massive unemployment and political unrest of returning veterans that had occurred after World War I, when only a modest program of vocational rehabilitation and job training was offered.

The GI Bill led to a tremendous expansion of college enrollment; and as higher education responded to the new students' educational needs, the GI Bill helped to undergird the development of the two-year college system.

Arguably, the federal role in higher education was greater than it is now. With the GI benefits, the federal government played a comparatively greater role in the expansion of educational opportunity—at least for men—in the years just after World War II than it does today, considering all the federal need-based student aid plus the educational entitlements to veterans and social security benefits. In 1947–1948, one of every two young men enrolled in college had financial support from the federal government; far fewer receive

Table 1. Chronology of Significant Dates in the Relationship Between Higher Education and the Federal Government

Year	Title	Citation	Description
1787	Northwest Ordinance		Provided land for education
1802	U.S. Military Academy, West Point	(21 Stat. 34)	Provided training for military leadership
1819	Dartmouth Case		Provided the basis for federal support of private education
1830	Franklin Institute Contract		Awarded the first federal "research contract"
1845	U.S. Naval Academy, Annapolis		Provided naval officer training
1862	Morrill Act I	(12 Stat. 503)	Donated land to the states to establish institutions to teach agriculture and mechanical arts
1867	Department of Education	(14 Stat. 434)	Established an agency to collect and disseminate information on education
1874	Nautical Training Grants		Provided first federal matching grants
1876	U.S. Coast Guard Academy		Trained men for the Coast Guard
1879	Howard University		Granted the first federal money to Howard University in Washington, D.C.
1887	Hatch Act	(26 Stat. 417)	Established a system of agricultural experiment stations
1890	Morrill Act II		Provided instructional grants to land-grant institutions
1911	State Marine School Act		Authorized funds for nautical schools in eleven seaport cities
1914	Smith-Lever Act		Established agricultural and home economics extensions
1917	Vocational Education Act	(P.L. 64-347)	Provided grants for vocational training below the college level
1918	Vocational Rehabilitation Act		Provided job training grants for World War I veterans
1919	First Surplus Property Disposal		Gave surplus government property to educational institutions
1920	Smith-Bankhead Act		Authorized grants to states for vocational-rehabilitation programs
	Reserve Officer Training Corps		Established ROTC on college campuses
1936	Merchant Marine Academy	(P.L. 84-415)	Established the U.S. Merchant Marine Academy
1937	Public Health Service Fellowships		Created fellowships for the public health service
1940	Engineering, Science, Management War Training Program		Established a war training program in engineering, science, and management

Year	Act	P.L.	Description
	National Defense Research Committee		Changed to Office of Scientific Research and Development
1944	Servicemen's Readjustment Act	(P.L. 78-346)	Provided federal education benefits for World War II veterans
1945	Fulbright Act	(P.L. 79-584)	Established the Board of Foreign Scholarships to finance the exchange of scholars
1946	George-Border Act	(P.L. 79-586)	Expanded the Vocational Education Act
1946–48	Federal Surplus Property Program		Broadened the surplus property disposal program
1946	Atomic Energy Commission Fellowships		Awarded the first Atomic Energy Fellowships
1948	Information and Educational Exchange Act	(P.L. 80-402)	Established the international exchange of persons, knowledge, and skills
1950	School Construction in Areas Affected by Federal Activities Act	(P.L. 81-815)	Provided funds for school construction in areas affected by federal activities
	College Housing Loan Program		Loaned federal monies to colleges for dormitory construction
1952	National Science Foundation		Created the National Science Foundation (NSF)
	National Science Foundation Scholarships		Awarded the first NSF scholarships
1954	Air Force Academy	(P.L. 83-325)	Established the training academy for air force officers
	Cooperative Research Act	(P.L. 83-531)	Authorized contracts between the U.S. Office of Education and colleges and universities
	National Advisory Committee on Education	(P.L. 83-532)	Established the National Advisory Committee on Education to recommend studies needed in education
	Brown v. Board of Education		Proclaimed "separate is not equal"
1956	Health Research Facilities Act		Provided funds to build health research facilities
1957	Practical Nurse Training Act		Made grants to states for training practical nurses
1958	National Defense Education Act		Provided funds to train people in critical areas (including science and math) to meet national defense needs
	Education of Mentally Retarded Children Act	(P.L. 85-926)	Authorized federal funds to train teachers for the mentally retarded
1961	Area Redevelopment Act	(P.L. 87-27)	Provided assistance to state vocational education agencies

Table 1. Chronology of Significant Dates in the Relationship Between Higher Education and the Federal Government
(Continued)

Year	Title	Citation	Description
1961	Peace Corps Fulbright-Hayes Act Agency for International Development		Provided assistance to underdeveloped countries for vocational training and development of natural resources
1962	Manpower Development and Training Act	(P.L. 87-415)	Provided training for unemployed and underemployed persons
1963	Health Professions Educational Assistance Act	(P.L. 88-129)	Provided funds to expand tracking facilities and loans for students in health professions
	Higher Education Facilities Act	(P.L. 88-204)	Provided financial assistance for building classrooms, libraries, and laboratories
	Vocational Education Act	(P.L. 88-210)	Increased federal support for residential vocational schools, work-study programs, and research and training in vocational education
1964	Civil Rights Act Under Title IX	(P.L. 88-352)	Mandated desegregation of public educational institutions; declared racial and ethnic discrimination to be illegal in federally assisted programs
1965	Economic Opportunity Act	(P.L. 88-452)	Made available grants for college work-study
	Health Professions Educational Assistance Act	(P.L. 89-290)	Provided scholarships for needy students in health professions and grants to improve the quality of instruction in professional schools
	Social Security Amendments		Extended benefits to children of covered workers, who are full-time students and between eighteen and twenty-two years of age
1965	Higher Education Act	(P.L. 89-329)	Authorized funding for community service, continuing education, cooperative education, and libraries; established the teacher corps and offered support for graduate education; established Educational Opportunity Grants
	National Foundation on the Arts and Humanities	(P.L. 89-209)	Established grants and loans for projects in creative performing arts and research, training, and publication in the humanities
	National Vocational Student Loan Insurance Program	(P.L. 89-287)	Encouraged state and nonprofit institutions to establish loan insurance programs to assist students

Year	Act	Public Law	Description
1966	International Education Act	(P.L. 89-698)	Made grants to higher education institutions for graduate and undergraduate international study centers
	National Sea-Grant College and Program Act	(P.L. 89-688)	Authorized sea-grant colleges and programs of education and research in marine resources
1968	Higher Education Amendments	(P.L. 90-575)	Authorized new programs for disadvantaged college students and clinical experience for law students
	Vocational Education Amendments	(P.L. 90-576)	Authorized grants to states for vocational education and part-time employment for persons of all ages
	Health Manpower Act		
1972	The Education Amendments	(P.L. 93-318)	Established the Education Division and the National Institute of Education; authorized Basic and Supplemental Educational Opportunity Grant programs and other student financial aid; established the Student Loan Marketing Association; prohibits discrimination on the basis of sex in any program receiving federal funds (Title IX); required state post-secondary education commissions (Title XII)
1974	Education Amendments	(P.L. 93-380)	Consolidated programs and established the National Center for Education Statistics
1976	Education Amendments	(P.L. 94-482)	Provided federal assistance to the states for career development and educational programs and guidance and counseling services
1978	Middle-Income Students Acts	(P.L. 95-566)	Extended BEOG's program to students from families earning up to $25,000 and made it easier for independent students to obtain funds
	Tribally Controlled Community Colleges Assistance Act	(P.L. 95-471)	Provided federal funds for tribally controlled community colleges for Indian students
1979	Department of Education Organization Act	(P.L. 96-88)	Created a cabinet-level Department of Education consolidating 152 programs

Source: Compiled by Judith Stich, Economics and Finance Unit, American Council on Education.

federal aid today. And in 1947–1948, the federal support constituted a larger share of the total costs of going to college than it does now, even after the enormous increase since 1972 in the dollars of student aid, including the extension of aid to middle-income students with the enactment in 1978 of the Middle Income Student Assistance Act.

1950: Underwriting Basic Research. More than half the basic research in the United States is performed by colleges and universities rather than by government bureaus, private research institutes, or industrial laboratories, as in other countries. Thus, research and development has been an area of significant interrelationships between higher education and the federal government, particularly since the Second World War. Their mutual dependence was strengthened by the creation in 1950 of the National Science Foundation.

Since the early 1950s, the federal share of support for separately funded college and university research grew from a little over half all research funds to almost three quarters in the middle 1960s before declining to two thirds in the late 1970s. In 1966, when the federal share of support peaked, each dollar of investment in research by the institutions was matched by $4.20 from the federal government. By 1975, this ratio had dropped to $2.80 government funds for every dollar of institutional investment in research.

Currently, colleges and universities themselves fund approximately three fourths of a billion dollars of the nation's research and development; federal purchases of research and development from colleges and universities amount to close to $3 billion. Consistent with patterns of support of recent years, the Department of Health, Education and Welfare currently accounts for about half the total federal research and development support to higher education institutions. Second in importance as a source of support is the National Science Foundation, whose share has increased to almost one fifth of the total federal support. Third is the Department of Defense, whose share has declined to about one tenth. The new Department of Energy is fourth, now ahead of the Department of Agriculture, which is fifth.

When the nation was concentrating its effort on winning the race into space and maintaining military strength during the cold war in the 1950s and early 1960s, higher education could help achieve much of the technological advance needed to meet these national objectives. Commensurately, a large share of the nation's research resources were invested in higher education. In the mid 1960s and early 1970s, the nation's highest public priorities shifted out of the scientific domain into the social domain of equal opportunity and affirmative action. In supporting social change, higher education could not, or at least did not, offer as great promise; and research support declined over this era. Now, without significant achievement in reaching the country's social objectives, the nation is shifting again to technological objectives. Increasing productivity, energy independence, and environmental quality are all goals, though they have critical political dimensions, for which it is within the realm of technology to create the solutions to the national problems. And once again, as the nation shifts out of social and into technological objectives, higher education can expect to play a far greater, perhaps indispensable, role. Federal support of higher education research and development may be the growth area of the 1980s.

1965: Promoting Equal Educational Opportunity. The federal government role of promoting equal educational opportunity through need-based student financial aid in higher education evolved out of the "Great Society" programs of the 1960s. Beyond expanding access generally, the federal government sought to remove financial barriers to further education of the low-income and disadvantaged minorities. Up to this time, the federal role had been defined in terms of meeting national needs rather than advancing individual citizens' rights to an education.

The first of these new programs to create greater access by expanding educational opportunities was the College Work Study enacted in 1965 as part of President Johnson's antipoverty program. Two other college-based student aid programs were enacted thereafter, the National Direct Student Loan (1965) and the Supplemental Educational Opportunity Grants (1972). Federal effort to create greater access was intensified and expanded with the major new programs, the Basic Educational Opportunity Grants, enacted in 1972, to channel need-based student aid directly to students. Since 1972, the federal government has concentrated almost all its direct financial support on expanding student access—93 percent of Office of Education funds as budgeted in fiscal year 1980 are channeled to students and 7 percent to institutions.

1978: Middle Income Student Assistance Act. Originally, the need-based student financial aid was targeted on the lowest-income students with the argument that it was more effective and efficient to use federal funds to support those students whose enrollment decisions would be most affected by the aid. Over several years, however, concern emerged over the financial plight of middle-income students, and the politically arresting phrase "middle-income crunch" was coined. Basically, the administration argued that the ability to pay for college as measured by median family income was growing as fast as tuition and consequently no expensive government program was needed to help middle-income students and their families. But these families complained of their financial difficulties and Congress listened and determined to try to do something for them. The question then became whether the better approach was to expand eligibility for the student aid programs that had been targeted on the low-income families or to enact a new program of tax credits, using the tax system to aid the middle-income students. Tax credits were introduced, as they had been for years, but this time with increasing chances of successful passage. The administration was bitterly opposed to using the tax system for yet another social program and countered by proposing the Middle Income Student Assistance Act, which extended the eligibility for basic grants up into the middle ranges of income, effectively from $12,000 to $25,000. There were arguments over the official statistics, however, and critics of the "no crunch" position pointed out that the trends in *average* tuition used in the comparison with family income were confounded by the changing composition of enrollment because the much faster increases in enrollment in the lower-cost two-year institutions were holding down the average tuition. The tuitions for the separate four-year and two-year sectors were generally growing faster than family incomes, particularly if after-tax incomes were considered.

Current Trends in Federal Support

To assess the current federal role in higher education requires examining recent trends in federal financial support for higher education—both direct and

indirect. Analyses based simply on data for direct support, such as funds designated for higher education in the federal budget, can be very misleading as to
the real total. Thus, institutional researchers and planners should be aware that
although direct support for higher education in the form of student financial aid
has been increasing rapidly in recent years, it has been offset, or even more than
offset, by the decline in indirect support from, among other sources, veterans'
benefits.

Actually, there are four types of federal support for higher education,
and a comprehensive picture of the total requires they all be included:

1. *direct support:* support for students and institutions through programs established to achieve educational or equal opportunity purposes
2. *indirect support:* programs of indirect support that benefit those enrolled in
   higher education but were established to promote other objectives, such as
   the veterans' benefits, created in part to compensate for serving in the armed
   services and to defer entry into the labor force and consequently to hold
   down unemployment (Institutional researchers should note that in the special
   analyses of the federal budget, prepared by the Office of Management and
   Budget (OMB), the classification of programs as to whether the support for
   higher education is direct or indirect is not consistent from year to year.)
3. *research and development spending:* federal government purchases of research
   performed by the colleges and universities
4. *tax expenditures:* revenues not collected by the federal government that in effect reduce the taxes that would otherwise be owed by those paying for higher
   education (These include parental personal exemptions for student depen-
   dents nineteen and over, exclusions of scholarships and fellowships from tax-
   able income, and deductions of contributions to higher education institutions.)

In current dollars, the total federal support for all four components
reached $16 billion in the fiscal 1980 budget (Table 2). This is double the 1972
level, which was just under $8 billion. That year, remember, marks the massive
policy shift embodied in the higher education amendments of 1972 to channel
support through students. Note, however, that a growing federal role in student
financial aid is far from being the same thing as a growing federal role in higher
education. Student financial aid is spent for food, housing, and transportation as
well as education.

Direct student aid is up spectacularly. But indirect support is down—
almost as spectacularly. Research spending continues to increase. Tax expenditures are up modestly from year to year.

In dollars of constant purchasing power, the picture is not nearly as bright
(Table 3). Deflating each of the component series with an appropriate price
index and adding them up again, we discover that, in real terms, as measured in
constant 1976 dollars, the federal support for higher education budgeted for
fiscal year 1980 is only $13.4 billion, which is $1 billion less than the 1976 level of
$14.4 billion.

To calculate the real purchasing power of the federal outlay, three separate price indexes were used, each the best available in terms of being constructed on the basis of relevant spending patterns: the Higher Education Price
Index constructed by Kent Halstead for institutional expenditures; a research

Table 2. Federal Support for Higher Education, Current Dollars
(Millions)

	1972	1973	1974	1975	1976	1977	1978	1979	1980
Direct Outlays									
Aid Channeled to Students	$1,079	$1,291	$1,256	$ 1,757	$ 2,508	$ 2,879	$ 3,167	$ 4,152	$ 4,432
Aid Channeled to Institutions	530	489	377	434	434	492	446	516	540
Subtotal	1,609	1,780	1,633	2,191	2,942	3,371	3,613	4,668	4,972
Indirect Outlays	3,091	3,933	4,173	5,882	6,824	5,490	5,440	4,886	4,584
Federally Funded Research and									
Development	1,671	1,888	2,068	2,228	2,675	2,703	3,069	3,357	3,693
Tax Expenditure	1,499	1,522	1,695	1,820	1,973	2,088	2,274	2,614	2,821
Total Federal Outlays for									
Higher Education	$7,820	$9,123	$9,569	$12,121	$14,414	$13,652	$14,396	$15,525	$16,070

Source: Economics and Finance Unit, American Council on Education, June 1979. Based on data from the *Special Analysis Budget of the United States Government*, FY 1974–1980.

Table 3. Federal Support for Higher Education, Constant Dollars
(Millions)

	1972	1973	1974	1975	1976	1977	1978	1979	1980
Direct Outlays									
Aid Channeled to Students	$ 1,420	$ 1,614	$ 1,495	$ 1,910	$ 2,508	$ 2,768	$ 2,853	$ 3,489	$ 3,603
Aid Channeled to Institutions	688	604	438	462	434	464	391	427	—
Subtotal	2,108	2,218	1,933	2,372	2,942	3,232	3,244	3,916	—
Indirect Outlays	4,067	4,916	4,968	6,394	6,824	5,279	4,901	4,106	3,727
Federally Funded Research and Development	2,228	2,390	2,405	2,370	2,675	2,526	2,669	2,752	2,819
Tax Expenditure	1,907	1,903	2,018	1,978	1,973	2,008	2,049	2,196	2,821
Total Federal Outlays for Higher Education	$10,310	$11,427	$11,324	$13,114	$14,414	$13,045	$12,863	$12,970	$13,392

Source: Economics and Finance Unit, American Council on Education. Based on data from the Special Analysis Budget of the United States Government, FY 1974–1980.

price index developed as part of the University Price Index Calculation System by The Ohio State University and the National Association of College and University Business Officers; and a student cost index constructed by the Economic and Finance Unit of the American Council on Education, weighted by type of enrollment.

The federal role is not measured simply in terms of the number of dollars of support, whether they are current or constant dollars. It has to be measured in comparative terms, showing the percentage share of federal support as compared with the percentage shares of all other sources of support. We need to look, consequently, at trends in relative budget shares. As detailed in Table 4, trends in institutional revenues by source of support show the federal share is declining. Meanwhile, the state share, along with the share of student tuition, is increasing.

Entering the 1980s, what trends can we identify that indicate the possible shape of the future federal role and what will be their impact on the campuses?

Another question open for speculation is what will be the effect on higher education of the creation of the new Department of Education. At the outset, it may not affect the day-to-day operations of the institutions a great deal. The biggest impact of the new department, or perhaps its exclusive impact, initially, may be on the federal bureaucracy itself, where federal officials concerned with higher education may function more effectively as some of the layers of organization are removed between the program administrators and top-level department executives.

In an era of political conservatism and fiscal constraint by both major parties, there will be little interest in new education program initiatives and tougher sledding ahead for added funding for existing programs.

Then, what is there for the new Department of Education to do? We can anticipate these federal activities in higher education: getting more efficient at administering existing programs, along with ferreting out fraud and abuse, trying to coordinate and streamline the plethora of existing programs that have evolved incrementally through the political process over the years, stimulating research and innovation in teaching and learning, and enforcing regulations to assure institutions meet federally mandated social program objectives.

Other federal activities beyond those of the Department of Education may have more implications for institutional researchers and planners during the 1980s. Federal regulations are likely to increase; federal concern with the financial viability of institutions may grow; student aid programs will need review; national educational statistics will improve; and voluntary wage and price standards may become mandatory. Each of these trends deserves attention by

Table 4. Percentage of Current Fund Revenues from Federal Sources, 1975–1977, by Type of Institution

Year	Public Institutions	Private Institutions	All Institutions
1975	3.1	1.2	2.5
1976	2.9	1.0	2.3
1977	2.9	1.1	2.2

Source: Unpublished tabulations, Department of Health, Education and Welfare.

planners and researchers; and each of the following sections of this chapter suggests the role planners and researchers may play regarding them as well as possible data sources and analytical approaches for dealing with them.

Federal Regulation

Since the early 1970s, the federal government's role of regulator has broadened from economic concerns about the marketplace to encompass a range of national issues from social justice to environmental quality. In the vast majority of cases, federal as well as state regulations are not directed specifically at colleges and universities; but they apply to education institutions as employers or federal contractors, as they do to all other enterprises.

The initial reaction to this government onslaught of many of those in academic institutions was to argue they should be exempted or excepted from general regulations on the basis that higher education is special. But pressing the claim of higher education for exemptions and exceptions from the social legislation was, by and large, not successful. In some cases, it was even counterproductive because it generated skepticism about the good faith of the institutions, which were thought to be clothing their own interests with the cloak of public interest, which led to the rejection of more legitimate claims as unjustified special pleading of just another special-interest group.

Higher education was not exempted because, the legislators and agency officials countered, on the relevant points at issue, higher education is *not* different—the safety of the workers in chemistry laboratories is just as important on the university campus as it is in the industrial firm. And in the social domain, higher education could not claim, by any means, a superior record in achieving equal opportunity through affirmative action, which would earn it an exceptional status on the basis of performance.

The next step was for both the institutions and the federal government to recognize that compliance with the regulations involved costs and that added funds are needed to cover these costs. Again, the initial response, particularly among the legislators, was that they were hard pressed to see why higher education institutions should get more money to pay for something they should have been doing all along.

More recently, however, there has been some softening of this hard line when it was recognized that if the added costs are not met by proportionate increases in support from all sources of revenue, then they must be met by more than proportionate increases in tuition—or the result, inexorably, will be cuts in the academic programs or deterioration of their quality, after the opportunities have been exhausted for offsetting the added costs with increases in productivity.

Consequently, some of the added financial burdens on the institutions that result from implementing federally mandated social programs were acknowledged as, for instance, in the 1978 amendments to the Higher Education Facilities Act of 1963, which broadened the program of federal loans and grants for new construction to include renovations and modifications of physical facilities needed to bring them into compliance with federal regulatory requirements.

Now, increasingly, academic administrators perceive that some of the *general* federal regulations have a particularly heavy impact on higher education, as, for example, when the mandatory retirement age was raised from sixty-five to seventy. And more and more federal regulations are designed to apply *specifically* to higher education, such as those relating to the administration of student financial aid, the privacy of school records, the conduct of college athletic programs, medical school admissions, and satisfactory progress of recipients of veterans' benefits enrolled in educational programs. Educators are expressing growing alarm that institutional prerogatives on matters as central to their educational mission and character as admissions, hiring, and curriculum planning are being abridged by legislative, judicial, and bureaucratic interventions.

Self-Regulation

In response, higher education has inaugurated an ambitious program of self-regulation to resist further encroachment of government regulation into the college and university campuses. On the recommendation of the major educational associations, in July 1978, the American Council on Education (ACE) established the Office on Self-Regulation Initiatives, the purpose of which is to foster a commitment to self-regulatory procedures and to coordinate the wide ranging activities in this domain.

Self-regulation on an individual campus might involve, first, the strengthening of existing standards and procedures for investigating problems already characterized as widespread and monitoring progress in meeting the self-imposed performance criteria and, second, identifying emerging problems not yet fully recognized and developing new policies and guidelines delineating what constitutes good practice.

Much of the self-regulatory activity on the campuses is directed toward the protection of the student as a consumer of educational services. Model codes of good practice have been or are being developed, for instance, for college recruitment and admissions, for the award of educational credit and credentialing, for assuring the academic quality of satellite campuses, and for tuition refunds. The ACE office is a source of information on these model codes, which could be helpful to institutional researchers and administrators.

Some of this self-regulatory activity is anticipatory, responding to problems not yet the subject of government regulation in the hope of dealing effectively with the concerns on the initiative of the institutions and obviating the need for government intervention. Problem areas identified as still needing self-regulatory action include relations with those who fund higher education.

Whereas federal regulation is regarded as procrustean in the academic world, self-regulation offers the possibility of greater sensitivity to educational requirements. But concomitantly, this new voluntary approach is viewed with a great deal of knowledgeable skepticism on the part of those the regulations are designed to protect and on the part of the federal enforcement agencies.

As the institutions turn to self-regulation, it is not enough to develop model codes and make pious statements of good intentions; the institutions have to make a thorough self-appraisal of their rate of progress in meeting the nation's social objectives. Appreciable work has been done to assist the institutions in carrying out careful studies designed to assess their performance. Self-analysis kits have been developed, tested, used, and are now widely available to help in evaluating progress toward affirmative action, equal pay, Title IX athletic program opportunities, meeting the needs of the handicapped, and protecting the students as consumers of educational services.

To be effective, self-analysis has to be carried out in a straightforward manner—and the conclusions have to be based on fundamentally honest assessments. Some of the self-studies in higher education, however, have resulted in plain whitewash—either in the way the analyses were performed or in the way the findings were characterized to their constituencies and to the public by the institutional officials. But if self-regulation based on self-analysis is going to be used successfully to deflect still further regulatory encroachments into higher education, that self-analysis has to be credible. On the campus, that means the opposing sides in a controversy both have to agree on the facts. This will test institutional researchers' political acuity and integrity to avoid the risk of becoming canon for the defense of current practices rather than facilitators of timely progress toward meeting social goals.

An ambitious program of self-regulation could extend to designing and carrying out a self-administered comprehensive social audit, undertaken with the same rigor and sense of accountability as a financial audit. Institutional researchers could play important roles in formulating the social goals for higher education, developing the social indicators, and showing how to validate and interpret the measures of progress.

The self-regulation activity can be carried beyond the individual campus by the institutional representatives actively seeking to accelerate progress, through cooperation with other similarly concerned institutions to develop broader consensus on performance standards and to identify the most effective approaches.

Areas subject to regulation in which institutions have already collaborated through their associations in preparing advisory publications and proposing guidelines for compliance include the Buckley privacy amendment, Title IX athletic program requirements, and copyright law.

In addition to helping each other, institutional researchers can actively renew or initiate communication with government agencies on how best to facilitate implementation of federal regulations while being faithful to the social objectives and assuring educational integrity and autonomy.

Concern for Financial Vitality

There are early, but significant, signs that the 1980s will witness an entirely new intensity of federal concern about the financial vitality of the nation's higher education institutions. For example, the General Accounting Office, pursuing a new concept of its mandate to report to Congress not only in its traditional role as the nation's auditors but also as policy analysts, has called for periodic Congressional review of the financial conditions of the higher education institutions. Among educators, however, there is an overwhelming preference that responsibility for such analyses remain within the higher education sector and not be taken up in the public sector.

Still more recently, the Office of Education's Program Planning and Evaluation Office has contracted with the American Council on Education to undertake a major study of higher education financing. It starts with identification of the causes and consequences of financial distress. The students are still at the core of the federal concern, however, because the study then focuses on the effect of financial distress on educational opportunities available to different types of students. Finally, the study will identify, cost, and evaluate possible federal policy responses.

Heightened concern about the financial health of the colleges and universities, both in government and out, and a strong conviction that the responsibility for performing the analyses should remain in the higher education sector itself, creates opportunities for more institutional researchers to be actively involved in analyzing financial conditions and their impacts on other dimensions of institutional vitality, including the academic mission, characteristics of the student body, and the quality of the educational programs.

Work on the financing of higher education institutions will require, for many institutional researchers, getting closer, within the organizational structure, to the financial vice-president and opening fuller communication on financial issues as they affect all aspects of the academic enterprise; gaining a better understanding of nonprofit accounting and of new techniques of financial analysis, including simulation of the financial operations of the institutions; developing good, consistent financial trend data and building analytical models; and developing comparative financial data.

A major question college and university executives often ask after they have finished an analysis of the financial condition of their own institutions is, "How are we doing compared with other institutions?" This leads to an important role for institutional researchers in developing comparative data. To do this, peer institutions have to be identified.

Selection of peer institutions in the past was often based on traditional relationships, geographic proximity, or perceptions of who are the closest competitors in the education markets. This ad hoc process of selecting peer institutions may or may not yield appropriate groups for making financial comparisons and for developing ranges of normative data. Consequently, the selection of the peer institutions should itself be subjected to more rigorous procedures, specifying the relevant dimensions along which to select the institutions for comparison (for instance, academic mission, enrollment size and mix, budget level, revenue sources, expenditure types, educational programs, or selectivity).

Studies should be made to determine the similarity of the institutions that form the basis of the comparison lest diversity be so great the institutions find they are "peerless." And, in any event, the degree of heterogeneity should be expressly taken into account in interpreting the comparison data and assessing whether differences from normative indicator values found for the institution are intended or unintended differences.

After selecting the group of peer institutions to serve as the frame of reference for financial comparisons, the next steps are to secure the cooperation of the others and to develop cross-institutional data standards and normative values for the financial indicators. Although important improvements are being made in developing the conceptual basis for financial indicators for higher education institutions, more data have to be generated to establish the range of values the indicators take and the relationship of these values to particular financial conditions. This is the important next step in the field of financial indicator development in which the institutional researchers could make significant contributions.

Wage and Price Standards

Higher education was exempted from the wage and price controls President Nixon imposed in phases from 1971 to 1974 because state and local governments were not covered so public institutions, as entities of the state, were not covered. Equitable treatment of private institutions required they should be exempted as well. In contrast, the antiinflation program President Carter launched in October 1978 was intended to cover all sectors of the American economy, including both the private enterprises and public agencies. Wage and price standards were drawn up as if we had a two-sector economy. Though the antiinflation program covered the higher education institutions, the third, nonprofit sector was not specifically recognized in the original design of the standards. Consequently, the Council on Wage and Price Stability, which administered the antiinflation program, attempted to stretch the standards designed for the profit-oriented firms to cover the nonprofit institutions, declaring revenues in excess of the expenses of colleges and universities were a reasonable proxy for the profit margin standards for business firms in measuring compliance. But profit in business is computed after allowances for capital costs, and this is not the case for the nonprofit institutions using fund accounting in computing current fund surpluses and deficits. Then the Council tried to stretch the standard evolving for public enterprises to cover the public higher education institutions. The prices of goods and services provided by public enterprises would have to be adjusted for changes in the levels of public subsidies made available to them, as it would be in the public interest to reduce inflationary budget outlays by shifting to revenues secured through increased prices. This would be helpful to public institutions, but both public and private institutions face uncontrollable revenues as well as uncontrollable costs.

Originally, only a very limited number of institutions, approximately twenty to thirty, with either over five thousand employees or over $250 million in revenues, had to meet price reporting requirements. As administration of the antiinflation program is intended to be basically self-enforcing, the rest of the institutions are instructed to be careful to document actions taken. The institutional researchers could be helpful in developing information for management to establish equitable salary adjustment policies and to gain perspectives on the program's impact on the nonprofit higher education sector in evaluating antiinflation efforts. Because the differences in the financial structure of the nonprofit institutions are not fully acknowledged in the antiinflation program, the colleges and universities are often placed in the position of appearing to ask for exceptions. But the exception would not be necessary if federal program design were based on a three-sector economy in the first place. Analysis that leads to a greater understanding of the economics and finance of the nonprofit higher education institutions could be particularly helpful should the voluntary standards become mandatory controls as inflation continues unabated and, indeed, the underlying rate of inflation increases at a faster rate than in the first program year.

Student Financial Aid

A full complement of need-based student aid programs of grants, loans, and work study has been in place since 1972—for nearly two generations of American students. The questions that now arise in Washington, at the state capitals, and on the campuses are what has been the impact of this aid, how much is it benefiting students educationally, which students, and how close is the nation coming to meeting its goals of equal educational opportunity. There are still not solid, comprehensive data sufficient to answer these questions with assurance.

The institutional researchers can try to help generate the needed information about the impact of financial aid by focusing on the student, which is critically important because off-campus analysts frequently have access only to the financial aid program data and cannot get information on how they all fit together for the student. Institutional researchers and planners can help provide this needed information to the student financial aid officers on individual campuses and to the federal program managers for use in evaluating the effectiveness of the aid and the formulation of aid policies.

Concerns relating to student financial aid that are likely to be heightened over the next several years range from student debt, half cost, self-help, needs analysis, campus-based aid allocation formulas, and institutionally funded student aid.

Student Debt. Billions of dollars are being made available to students under several different loan programs, some subsidized and some not; but practically nothing is known about how students are accumulating indebtedness over the course of their college careers and what kinds of total debt burdens they have when they emerge from school. It is important to learn and the institutional researchers could help find out how student debt might be affecting decisions to drop out or stay in school; how debt might affect students' choices of fields or decisions about going to graduate school; and how debt might influence their ultimate career aspirations, their decisions about where and when to get a job, and for whom to work. Debt might constrain students' future living and family formation patterns should a young man with a $20,000 educational debt meet a young woman with an equivalent debt. Heavy debt still outstanding might affect attitudes toward voluntary support of alma maters in the future.

More broadly, the enduring concern is how students are financing their college education. What is the situation of the aided students compared with the unaided, considering the economic circumstances of both the students and their families for the dependent students and trying to be fair in the treatment of independent students as compared with the dependent students?

Half Cost. A feature of the original Basic Grant Program is the half cost rule, under which an award to a student is limited to no more than half the student's cost of education. The intent of the provision was to eliminate the free rider. The half cost rule was supported vigorously by the private institutions, which feared students would shift to the public sector if the Basic Grant Program met most of their costs. But it soon became clear that the half cost rule affected most adversely the predominantly low-income students attending low-cost institutions. The half cost limitation distorts the awards and deflects the program from its objective. Technically, imposition of any cost limitation abridges need as the basis for award determination. A compromise negotiated by educators in 1979 between those who wanted to retain the half cost rule and those who wanted to remove it altogether was to raise the cost limit to three quarters concurrent with increases in the maximum award. Objection on the part of Congress to a compromise which raised the cost of the program, however, has led to resistance to legislative enactment of the compromise.

Self-Help. Proposals are now surfacing to amend the Basic Grant Program to replace the cost limitation with an explicit self-help component in putting the aid package together. Student capability to meet the self-help requirement, whether it is part of a national standard or one particularized campus by campus, will differ for different types of students. Analysis of the students' self-help potential and the potential of colleges to help them (especially in areas of high unemployment) would be important to the administration of the financial aid programs on individual campuses and for providing information for the public policy development process.

Need Analysis. Student need analysis has become refined and standardized over the several decades since it was first developed and used—predominantly in the private sector—to limit, or at least to rationalize, competition among the institutions and among students in the award of student aid grants. Need is defined as the cost of education minus any expected family contribution, which leaves a need gap to be met by some combination of grants, loans, and work study.

Need then became the basis of the award of funds to students under the federal financial aid programs. An anomaly was soon recognized, however, in that huge sums of public money were being allocated on the basis of a private determination of need. In sharp reaction to this apparent breach of public finance principle, there were moves to bring government into the need determination, first with Congress approving family contribution schedules developed by the Office of Education and more recently by direct congressional involvement in the actual determination of need by establishing assessment rates on discretionary income and expected family contributions. Need determination by Congress is of necessity broader gauged and far less fine tuned than the assessments of personal circumstances possible with the private procedures developed by the College Scholarship Service and the American College Testing Service or the Uniform Methodology jointly negotiated between the two and the U.S. Office of Education.

Currently, there are two national need analysis systems in use: one in the private sector, the Uniform Methodology, and the other in the public, the schedule for the determination of the family contribution in making the Basic Grant award. In addition, some states have their own systems for state grants. Not only are there two different national need analysis systems, but need as determined by the different schedules is quite different. One essential distinction is that the Basic Grant fixes the family contribution from available resources at a flat rate, but the private Uniform Methodology schedule has a progressive rate of family contribution. The result of this difference is that lower-income students are worse off, that is, their families have to contribute more under the public schedule than under the private, while the reverse is true for the higher-income families, which are worse off under the private schedule. Another distinction is that the private system provides a higher subsistence allowance.

With the conviction in both the public and the private sectors that having two disparate and incompatible systems of need analysis is not workable, there is a growing debate on who should do need analysis. The discussion centers basically on whether need analysis should be public or private. On the one hand, it is argued that public money should not be allocated according to a schedule determined in the private sector. On the other hand, it is argued that although the federal government labels its activity as "need analysis," what it is actually doing is setting program eligibility criteria and determining the amounts of awards within federal budget constraints and is therefore not involved in the determination of actual need. Program eligibility and need analysis are two separate functions, and need analysis should remain in the private sector at least as an independent check on the adequacy of the publicly funded programs.

This current controversy heightens the enduring tensions about the purpose of need analysis. Is it a determination of financial requirements in some absolute dollar sense, based on assumptions of what the students can reasonably be expected to pay and the family to contribute? Or is it restricted in its origins and in practice simply to a rationing device to allocate the funds available for assistance? Because the federal government clearly has the power to determine aid award amounts, this situation is likely to be resolved by moving award level determination to the public sector, where broader criteria will be employed. The determination of need as a complicated and finely tuned process more sensitive to individual students' circumstances would then continue to be done using private need analysis procedures through the packaging process by the student financial aid officers on campuses.

After a number of years during which the federal government through the Basic Grant Program tried to minimize the discretionary role of the student financial aid officers, it is now acknowledged that sensitivity in the award and packaging of aid is necessary in achieving a greater equity among the individual students. This means, however, that the student financial aid officers have to have information about the students in order to make those discretionary decisions. Institutional researchers could be particularly helpful to the student aid officers in the systematic gathering and analysis of the student data, including data on student budgets and student self-help capability.

If the field of need analysis is occupied by the federal government, it may become important to keep running checks of the reasonableness of the need determination as compared with the students' perceptions and the institutions' calculations of need. It is also important to keep in mind to what extent the need analysis is objective and how much of it actually involves value judgments.

Because need analysis has become more or less standardized, it might be thought that determination of need is more or less objective. On closer consideration, it becomes clear that about the only objective information in need analysis is family income, and even that is subject to wide reporting error and technical difference in definitions. Need as derived from ability to pay is not just a matter of measuring resources but is quintessentially a set of value judgments. These value judgments range across questions about whether the appropriate social unit for determining available resources is the individual or the family; about the level of the standard maintenance allowance, which embodies concepts of what standard of living it is reasonable to sustain; and about the provision for retirement, which involves judgments about the appropriate profile of lifetime income. Even if assets can be valued objectively, whether they should be included in the resource base involves subjective choices. Finally, value judgments are involved in setting the rate of family contribution, which functions like a tax rate, and in deciding how progressive to make the contribution rate going up the income scale.

Allocation Formulas. Presently, the allocation of the campus-based student financial aid to institutions is being determined in Washington by a computer-based system combining need formulas, state allotment formulas, and institutional requests, replacing the previous system of panel recommendations. Consequently, it is important on the individual campuses to understand the construction and interaction of the formulas with institutional requests to see how different types of students and different types of institutions are affected by the components in the calculation, to supply accurately the data requested, and to request the maximum funds they could use. "Under-requesting" is a major pattern, particularly in the Supplemental Educational Opportunity Grant Program. Lack of understanding of these processes has already resulted in some institutions securing far less support for their students than they are eligible for. On many campuses, the entire student aid program should be reviewed systematically to determine if all the student aid for which students are eligible is being secured.

The institutions in a particular state should all have an interest in how national student aid policy is affecting their state. They might analyze the share of the total financial aid awarded across the nation which students in their state secure to see if the aid is flowing generally to the regions of greatest need.

Institutionally Funded Student Aid. Institutional researchers should be keenly interested in institutionally funded student aid. Working along with the business officer and the student financial aid officer, they should try to answer the following types of questions, first establishing a context for interpretation of the information by dealing with the impact of all the student aid, then focusing on the use of the institution's own funds to assist students:

1. all student aid
   a. What is the effect of financial aid on student admission, acceptance, retention, and completion?
   b. What is its effect on academic program development and student services?
2. institutionally funded student aid
   a. What are the sources and uses of institutionally funded student aid?
   b. What kinds of students are assisted by the institution as compared with those receiving support from other sources?
   c. Are the policies in awarding institutionally funded student aid concordant with the educational mission of the institution?
   d. What is the effect of the institutionally funded student aid on the overall financial condition of the institution?

An excellent worksheet for assessing the net financial impact of increasing enrollments through increasing student aid awards by calculating the net cash flows has been developed by Hans Jenny, and is illustrated in Figure 1.

Collecting National Education Statistics

For years, education researchers and policy analysts have made careers out of jabbing at the National Center for Education Statistics (NCES), the federal agency responsible for collecting and publishing the information that forms much of our resource material. We have complained vociferously about the inaccuracy and lack of timeliness of the higher education data. But in my judgment, based on several years of working with the national data, the thrusts of the com-

		1972	1973	1974	1975	1976	1977
A.	Revenue from Student Charges:						
	a. Gross Tuition and Fees						
	b. Dormitory Fees						
	c. Food Service Fees						
	Subtotal A.						
B.	Student Aid Income (Restricted)						
	a. Endowments						
	b. Gifts						
	c. State Appropriations—OIG, PHEAA						
	d. Federal Grants—SEOG, BEOG						
	e. Other						
	Subtotal B.						
C.	Expenses for Student Aid Grants						
	a. Funded (Or Restricted)						
	b. Unfunded						
	Subtotal C.						
	Net Total: (A+B) −C =						
D.	Work-Study						
	a. Revenues						
	b. Expenditures						
E.	Loans						
	a. Institutional						
	b. NDSL						
	c. FISL						
	e. Other						
F.	Enrollment						
	a. Body Count						
	b. FTE Academic (On campus only)						
	c. FTE Financial (On campus only)						
G.	Operating Budget						
	a. Current Operating Revenues*						
	b. Current Operating Expenditures*						
	Operating surplus/deficit						

*These should correspond to normal operating budget including interest expense on plant debt and debt amortization payments; exclude capital transfers to/from other funds.

College_____

Respondent_____

Figure 1. Net Cash Flow Analysis from/for Students

Source: Jenny, H. "Improving the Conceptual Framework for Measuring Financial Condition Using Institutional Management Data." In C. Frances and S. Coldren (Eds.), *Measuring Financial Conditions of Colleges and Universities: 1978 Working Conference.* Washington, D.C.: Financial Measures Project, American Council on Education, 1978, p. 10.

plaints are now in the wrong direction. The data NCES can publish are only as good as the data the institutions provide. Basically, it is the institutions, and in some cases, the institutional researchers, who are responsible for originating the bad data. It is now appropriate for the education sector itself to take on greater responsibility for improving the quality of the education statistics.

There is now an opportunity for a cooperative effort led by the institutional researchers working with the education associations and the NCES to mount a combined effort to improve the quality of national higher education statistics—with primary focus on how to assure better reporting by the institutions to the federal statistical agencies. A joint AIR (Association for Institutional Research)-ACE-NCES task force to improve the quality of higher education data could accomplish a great deal. Such a group could encourage top management to commit staff resources to the job of reporting consistent and reliable data. They could stress the importance to the higher education community itself of better data as a basis for making more informed management decisions and for advancing the interests of higher education in public policy arenas.

Especially helpful in improving the quality of the data are the NCES efforts to generate longitudinal data, starting with the enrollment and the financial statistics. In the process of analyzing trends based on the longitudinal data, the inconsistencies become readily apparent, and they can be cleaned up at the institutional level. Fortunately, improvements in data quality will occur simply because the more the data are used, the better the quality will become; and the better the quality, the more the data will be used.

NCES is trying to be as responsive to the needs of higher education as funds and staff resources permit. Plans are being discussed, for instance, for publications of national statistics for institutions grouped by educational mission, which are more relevant for many types of analysis than the standard six-way classification by type and control (public and private universities, four-year and two-year institutions).

NCES also invites knowledgeable suggestions about ways they can be even more responsive to educators' information needs. The institutional researchers might assume special responsibilities on behalf of the higher education community for systematic reviews and periodic reports on how well the sector's information needs are being met and on what areas should be improved.

Participation in the Federal Policy Development Process

Educators, and particularly institutional researchers, have often accepted a comparatively passive role in the federal policy development process in simply analyzing available data to draw conclusions about the effects of events *after* they happen to the education sector. The 1980s present opportunities for a much more active role for institutional researchers and planners to participate in education policy development. One possibility is to expand the capability of analyzing the impact of proposed federal policies on the institutions, both to provide information to legislators and their staffs on the probable outcomes of proposed actions and to help the education sector develop informed positions on issues.

Case Studies. Some of the most important inputs into policy deliberations are carefully documented case studies providing good hard data interpreted with a sensitivity to the complexities of academic enterprises. This is precisely what the institutional researchers can do especially well.

A basic question a member of Congress will ask is, "How will the proposed legislations affect the institutions in my district?" The researchers associated with the institution in a particular district might work cooperatively to provide information to their representatives. Legislators hesitate to generalize from a single case. Consequently, a task force approach, in which a lead institution may coordinate the work of a number of study participants, may be more effective. Special attention might be paid to the information needs of legislators on the key education authorizing and appropriations committees.

Pressures will mount in the course of using the results of institutionally based case studies to extrapolate from the narrow data base to make national estimates of the impacts on higher education. But this is extremely hazardous, and the temptation to draw conclusions beyond those the data base can fully substantiate should be resisted. The most important consideration for educators seeking to shape federal policy development is to earn and maintain public credibility. In the policy process, the greatest resource higher education has is information. The information has to be absolutely consistent in its reliability. Institutional researchers play potentially significant roles in assuring the quality of the information generated to feed into the policy process.

Anticipation of Future Issues. A still more aggressive role for the education researchers and planners to take in the policy process is to try to anticipate future issues and influence the selection of major concerns on which to concentrate public attention. This means the basic orientation of the institutional researcher and planner has to be transformed from a responsive to an anticipatory stance. Two techniques can enhance their ability to anticipate issues. One is to track federal legislative and budget cycles. The other is environmental scanning.

Anticipation of federal issues might be facilitated by recognizing the federal legislative and budgetary cycles. These cycles structure the time frame that orders some of the important relationships between higher education and the federal government. A legislative cycle of roughly four years operates now because of the periodicity of the basic higher education program authorizing legislation. Major amendments to the Higher Education Act were passed in 1972 authorizing new programs, primarily student aid programs, for four years. When these authorizations expired, new legislative initiatives were considered, and new programs were enacted for another four years. Thus, there were major legislative programs enacted in 1972 and 1976 and we can expect similar new initiatives about 1980 and then again in 1985 because of the five-year extension of the authorizing legislation in the last go around. In the years just before the authorizing legislation expires, new ideas are tested; and in the years just after new programs are enacted, the congressional oversight functions predominate. The primary concerns then shift to the effectiveness of the existing programs and away from new initiatives. Likewise, there is an annual federal budget cycle, from the President's introduction of the budget in January to the first and second budget resolutions over the course of the year.

Awareness of these cycles and their possible influence on what will be uppermost on legislators' agendas at different times in the cycles can be helpful to institutional researchers in preparing relevant, timely information for effective participation in the policy process. Missing those cycles and consequently rendering their conclusions and recommendations out of phase and after the fact is a major shortcoming of some of the otherwise excellent policy analysis in higher education, even some done by national study commissions.

Anticipating issues that will be debated not today but one, two, or more years in the future requires a very different type of scanning. We have to survey not only the familiar territory inside higher education but also the far less traveled terrain outside higher education to pick up early warning signals of impending but now altogether unanticipated changes that will shape the environment in which higher education will operate in the future.

The way much of the policy analysis is done today, the data are available after the decisions have already been made. With the more effective anticipatory approach to policy analysis, the data should be ready for consideration before the decisions are made. The improvements needed to make the participation of educators in the policy process more effective are illustrated in the model of the process depicted in Figure 2.

In summary, ten steps to successful federal policy analysis for institutional researchers and planners can be capsuled in the following checklist:

1. Anticipate issues.
2. Make sure you have the best data.
3. Keep the statistics simple.
4. Be rigorous in drawing conclusions, being clear about the role of values in making recommendations.
5. Anticipate counterarguments and be ready to meet them.
6. Build your credibility with quality controls and technical reviews of your analysis.
7. Identify your friends and your enemies—that is, those who agree with you and those who do not. Toughen your arguments by interacting with those who do not agree, starting with your easiest and ending with your sharpest critics.
8. Explain your findings very briefly and be prepared to interpret the implications.
9. Get your information into the hands of people who can use it. Work directly with legislative staff and executive agency executives, and provide information to the local and national media.
10. Above all, maintain your identity and your integrity.

Conclusion

The 1980s will be a decade of stress and opportunity when higher education must heighten its vigilance about the consequences of asking for and possibly receiving federal funds to achieve worthy objectives—but in ways that smother higher education. The role of institutional researchers and planners in this process can be to help establish the agenda of major issues their institution will confront in its relations with the federal government in the 1980s—and to help work out appropriate ways to deal with them, balancing federal fiscal support and accountability with academic integrity and autonomy.

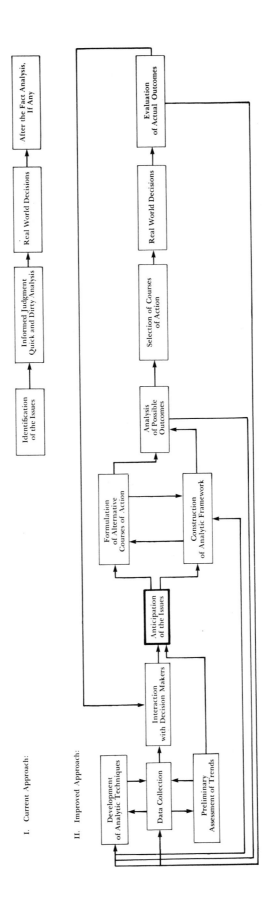

Figure 2. Federal Policy Analysis Models

Further Readings

Recent publications on the topics discussed are cited here under the headings listed:

The Federal Role

Breneman, D. W., and Finn, C. E., Jr. *Public Policy and Private Higher Education.* Washington, D.C.: Brookings Institution, 1978.

Furniss, W. T., and Gardner, D. P. *Higher Education and Government: An Uneasy Alliance.* Washington, D.C.: American Council on Education, 1979.

National Academy of Education. *The Appropriate Federal Role in Education: Some Guiding Principles.* Report of a Committee of the National Academy of Education, Stephen K. Bailey, Chairman, Harry Marmion, Rapporteur, April 1979.

Sloan Commission on the Government and Higher Education. *Government and Private Higher Education.* Cambridge, Mass.: Sloan Commission, 1980.

Federal Regulation

Bender, L. *Federal Regulation and Higher Education.* ERIC/Higher Education Research Report No. 1. Washington, D.C.: American Association for Higher Education, 1977.

Frances, C., and Coldren, S. L. *The Costs of Implementing Federally Mandated Social Programs at Colleges and Universities.* Policy Analysis Service Special Report, June. Washington, D.C.: American Council on Education, 1976.

Hobbs, W. C. (Ed.). *Government Regulation of Higher Education.* Cambridge, Mass.: Ballinger, 1978.

Hook, S., Kurts, P., and Todorovich, M. (Eds.). *The University and the State: What Role for Government in Higher Education?* Buffalo, N.Y.: Prometheus Books, 1978.

"The Impact of Federal Retirement-Age Legislation on Higher Education." A Report of the Social Committee on Age Discrimination and Retirement, *AAUP Bulletin,* September 1978.

Institutional Self-Regulation

El-Khawas, E. H. "Solving Problems Through Self-Regulation." *Educational Record,* 1978, *59,* 323–331.

El-Khawas, E. H. "To Assure Fair Practice Toward Students a Proposed Code for Colleges and Universities." Office of SRI-ACE, 1979.

Institutional Self-Evaluation Handbooks

Regarding *Title IX,* see Commission on Women in Higher Education, American Council on Education, *Institutional Self-Evaluation: The Title IX Requirements,* October 1975.

Regarding *Equal Pay,* see Scott, E. L., *Higher Education Salary Evaluation Kit,* American Association of University Professors, undated.

Regarding *Access for the Handicapped,* see Biehl, G. R., *Guide to the Section 504 Self-Evaluation for Colleges and Universities,* National Association of College and University Business Officers, Washington, D.C., undated.

Financial Self-Assessment

Bowen, H. R., and Minter, W. *Private Higher Education; Financial and Educational Trends in the Private Sector of American Higher Education.* Washington, D.C.: Association of American Colleges, Annual Reports, 1975, 1976, 1977, 1978.

Dickmeyer, N., and Hughes, K. *Self-Assessment of Financial Condition: A Preliminary Edition of a Workbook For Small Independent Institutions.* Washington, D.C.: American Council on Education and National Association of College and University Business Officers, 1979.

Economics and Finance Unit, American Council on Education and National Association of College and University Business Officers. *Financial Measures Project—Measuring Financial Conditions of Colleges and Universities.* 1977, 1978 Working Conference, 1979 Working Conference. Washington, D.C.: American Council on Education and National Association of College and University Business Officers, forthcoming.

4

John K. Folger

Implications of
State Government
Changes

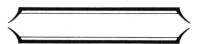

Previous chapters have documented the changing demographic and economic conditions that are affecting higher education and the federal policies that are influencing institutional planning and research. This chapter describes the changes in state government likely to affect higher education in the 1980s and the kinds of research and policy analysis that will be needed as a result.

Changes in State Government

At least four trends are affecting the state context for higher education: changes in public attitudes, the political environment, state organization and procedures, and state responsibilities.

Public Attitudes. Changes in state government in a democracy reflect, and grow out of, changes in public attitudes. Several attitudes are of particular importance in shaping state government's approach to higher education (see Cantril, 1978; Folger, 1978).

First, the public is not confident about government's ability to deal effectively with problems in general. The public has more confidence in state government than in the federal government, but all levels of government get lower general ratings than they did ten years ago.

Second, elected public officials and legislators have a relatively low rating with the public on the job they are doing. The public's view is of critical importance to any elected official, and state legislators and other elected state officials have been trying to improve their image with the public by managing public services, including education, in a more businesslike way and by exercising more oversight and control over higher education.

Third, although education as a whole and higher education in particular get a higher performance rating than most other public services, like welfare and crime control, the rating of the job that education is doing has declined, too.

Fourth, citizens believe education is an essential service, but they do not believe it is doing as good a job as it could or should. The public believes that the quality of schooling has slipped, as indicated by declining test scores, and that parts of higher education have lowered standards to keep their enrollments up.

Fifth, parents rate the schools their children attend higher than schools in general. College students generally give good marks to their own educational experiences and rate their own college experience higher than the quality of colleges in general. The media and the polls reflect a lower rating of education than the ratings given by those in direct contact with education, both at the elementary-secondary and higher education levels.

Political Environment. Changing public attitudes are having a direct impact on state government. The most immediate impact is a higher turnover rate among legislators, governors, and other elected officials. Public dissatisfaction is reflected at the polls. In a number of states, more than a third of the legislature turns over at each election. The problems these short-term public servants must understand and deal with, including education, are getting more complex and difficult; and it is harder to get continuity of attention to issues.

A second factor is that political parties are becoming less influential in elections; public officials run more as individuals; and the media, especially television, have more influence on the outcome of elections than party workers.

The decreasing importance of the party carries over to the formation of public policy through legislation. Special-interest groups and local constituencies are making it more difficult for both governors and legislative leaders to develop a statewide perspective on policy issues or to get a statewide plan enacted.

A related development in many states is the increasing independence of the legislature from the governor's office and the governor's program. Even where the governor and a majority of the legislature are of the same political party, the governor may have difficulty in getting programs and budgets enacted without substantial legislative revision.

Another consequence of critical public opinion is the increased attention of both governors and legislators to the accountability of public agencies and to the oversight of the performance of all agencies that receive state funds. This increased concern for accountability is reflected in several ways. More than two thirds of the states have enacted some form of "sunset legislation," which provides a specific termination date for each agency unless it is reauthorized. More than thirty of the states have expanded their fiscal audit procedures to include some form of performance audit for state government agencies. In over twenty of the states, the state agency for higher education is involved in review and evaluation of existing higher education programs; and in over three fourths of the states new programs must be approved by the state higher education agency (Education Commission of the States Task Force on Accountability, 1979, appendix B). In these diverse ways, states are expanding their interest in accountability.

A fourth change in the state political environment is the increased concern for the level of spending and taxes. There has always been a conflict between the desire for more and better services through government and the desire to keep taxes down. Lately, the pressure for lower taxes appears to be stronger, and the support for expanded services appears to be weaker. A conservative fiscal mood exists in all parts of the country, although a number of states have rejected tax and spending limitations of the California type (Odden, 1979).

Doing a better job with what you have is the emerging theme, and the coalitions of interest groups that were effective in expanding budgets at all levels of government will have a much harder job in the 1980s as they face a broad middle-class pressure to keep spending at current or reduced levels.

A fifth political theme in education is increased state concern about, and opposition to, federal regulation and requirements attached to federal funds. There has always been some tension between government levels about power, influence, and responsibility; but the substantial increase in the federal role in education in the last twenty years has led to increased state concern about the extent to which the state role is being affected by federal actions. As long as federal funds were increasing rapidly, states were willing to accept the funds and the federal requirements; now that funds are leveling off and decreasing, while the amount of federal regulation is still increasing, the states are increasingly concerned about the erosion of their primary role.

Organization and Procedures. State government, like the federal government, is getting bigger, more formal and bureaucratic, and more involved with legal and regulatory processes. The size of governors' and legislators' staffs has increased; state agencies concerned with both elementary-secondary and postsecondary education have also grown in size, although state postsecondary agencies are generally much smaller than the staffs of state departments of education. Twenty-eight of the state higher education agencies have fewer than twenty professionals, and only six large states have more than fifty professional staff.

Two decades ago only a few large states had much staff for their legislatures. Now nearly all states have professional staff for their legislative budget functions, and a growing number have professional staff for education committees as well. The 1970s saw further increases in legislative staff, more legislative committee action on a year-round basis, and a generally increased legislative role in both policy and oversight activities.

The biggest change in state organization, however, has been the increasing scope and recognition of state postsecondary agencies as important regulatory and policy recommending groups. Most of the states had created a state agency of some sort by 1970; but in a number of states, their role and responsibilities were unclear, and their influence was limited. In both a formal and informal sense, their role expanded during the 1970s and is likely to be even more important during the 1980s. The next chapter describes these changes in detail.

The net effect of changes in state organization and staffing has been to create more formal procedures in most states for policymaking and to increase state regulation of higher education, in both budgetary and program areas.

State government in most small and medium-sized states is still operated in a personal and relatively informal manner. Technical and rational systems for budget development and policymaking, which are the bureaucrats' stock in trade, still count for less than personal acquaintance and trust in most state decisions about higher education.

However, the importance of formal and technical procedures for planning and policymaking is increasing, particularly in intergovernmental areas of activity and in budget development. In general, the larger, more urbanized states use formal processes more than the smaller, rural states; but all states are increasing the use of formal and legal procedures for conducting business.

State Responsibilities. The expanding role of state government in higher education has focused attention again on the proper relationships between state government and the colleges and universities. How much autonomy should higher education have from state or federal regulation, and in what areas is state regulation necessary? To what extent should the executive and legislative branch operate directly to regulate higher education, and to what extent should a state-level agency for higher education be charged with these responsibilities?

These issues are not new; they have been examined and reexamined during the entire twentieth century as successive generations of politicians and college administrators have negotiated with each other. The discussion of roles used to be stated in terms of how much autonomy higher education should have from political decision making, with college and university representatives arguing for almost complete independence of higher education (Moos and Rourke, 1959). In recent years, as the expansion of higher education has greatly increased its costs and the attention it gets, there have been efforts to define those areas of legitimate state involvement and oversight and those areas where institutions should be left decision-making responsibility (American Association of State Colleges and Universities, 1971; Carnegie Commission on Higher Education, 1973). The Carnegie Commission divided decision-making responsibility into the three major areas of governance, fiscal affairs, and academic affairs. One problem is the areas overlap. Budget decisions inevitably affect personnel and academic decisions, and academic decisions impact budgetary decisions. The areas of responsibility of institutions can be separated from the areas of responsibility of state government in theory; but in practice, this has proved very difficult. In some states, legislatures have confined their attention to the general level of budget support provided; in other states, they have gotten directly involved in institutional role and scope delineation, the location of particular programs, and curricular issues of what will be taught. In still other states, detailed budget regulations have had the effect of controlling management, personnel, and academic decision making. Gubernatorial and legislative involvement in budget details has generally been much greater than direct involvement in academic or programmatic decision making.

Recently, the Sloan Foundation established a commission on government and higher education headed by Carl Kaysen to look at the impact of governmental regulation on higher education. Although their principal focus has been on the impact of federal regulation on colleges and universities, they commissioned a number of studies of individual states and their governance and regulatory activity. In the California study, the issue was clearly stated, "A strong case can be made that intensive state regulation of universities is counterproductive; it costs money, stifles creativity and diversity, defeats effective administration, and at its extremes, intrudes on academic freedom. . . . But the other elements necessary to substitute a policy of delegation for one of ever advancing regulation are only now being developed. Mission statements and evaluation techniques must be devised and adopted that will create sufficient official and public confidence to sustain pleas for a special relationship between universities and state governments, turning on delegated authority and program accountability" (Adamany, 1978, pp. 190–191).

The Education Commission of the States Task Force on Accountability (1979, p. 1), headed by Governor Byrne of New Jersey, had similar observations: "Additional centralization of responsibility for the management of higher education at the state level is likely in the future unless an effective accountability process is developed. Further centralization of management and decision making may not lead to more effective institutional management or better achievement of state educational objectives. The evidence indicates that institutional diversity and achievement of state education goals can be facilitated by assigning responsibility to institutions and holding them accountable for achieving state objectives. When accountability is partial or incomplete, expansion of direct controls through the budget and increase in regulations are likely."

A prerequisite to an effective decentralization of responsibility and development of new planning and accountability procedures is a stable set of relationships and expectations between state government and higher education. If each succeeding governor and each new legislature have a different policy approach to higher education, and if the state higher education agency frequently gets changed responsibilities, it will be hard to plan, implement budget system improvements, or make effective policy for higher education.

The 1980s are likely to bring a number of fluctuations in economic conditions, enrollment, and demand for graduates; these factors, as well as political shifts, will make it difficult to have a stable basis for planning, budgeting, or program review. Political, economic, and demographic shifts will make it particularly difficult for the state higher education agency to maintain a consistent relationship to institutions and do effective planning. Institutional activities will be affected too, and the effectiveness of their planning and policy actions will be reduced if they are constantly being questioned and changed.

Changes in State Involvement

The relation of state government to higher education is evolving at different rates in different states; but in almost all states, colleges and universities are likely to be expected to do more planning, develop new kinds of budget justifications, and develop more evaluative information about their programs and other activities. In states with a statewide board with major responsibility for planning, program review, and budget review, the public colleges and universities will be interacting primarily with the state higher education agency in developing and conducting new planning, program review, and budget review procedures. In other states, the primary initiative for new planning and budgeting procedures will come from the legislature or the state budget office. Regardless of the state source, there will be an emphasis on more specific and realistic planning, more attention to effective management procedures, better control of program duplication, and more accountability. Budget formulas are also likely to be modified to put less emphasis on enrollment factors and more emphasis on reallocating limited resources. The following sections will review briefly the changes that are likely in program review, accountability procedures, budget analysis, and state-level planning.

Program Review. Historically, program review has been primarily an institutional self-assessment for internal improvement. Much of this "formative evaluation" has been done as part of periodic accreditation reviews. State agencies have not been involved in the process; and only in marginal institutions does the accreditation process carry the threat of sanctions, in the form of loss of accredited status.

New state and institutional purposes are emerging for program review. The first is reallocation of resources (faculty and dollars) among programs so the institution can do more with the available resources. The collegial nature of academic government within institutions makes resource reallocation difficult to achieve. Because institutions have difficulty with academic reallocation, state agencies have increasingly had to initiate the process. A second state purpose for program review is to increase the quality of educational offerings and to eliminate substandard and marginal programs.

Most states conduct program review through the state agency for higher education. Currently, more than twenty state agencies have some role in reviews of existing institutional programs (Barak and Berdahl, 1978), and the number is expanding each year. Over three fourths of the state agencies review and approve or disapprove proposals for new programs. States are taking several different approaches to program review. Some are approaching it from the evaluation model of peer review that has been used by accrediting associations. New York, Louisiana, and Florida are examples of this approach. Out-of-state experts are used to review specific institutional programs; and judgments are made about program continuation, program improvement to eliminate deficiencies, or program termination by the state agency.

A second state approach is to expect the institution or sector of institutions to develop its own program review process and report on the outcome of its reviews. In this model, the institutional board or sector board makes the decision about the future of the program. California and Wisconsin are examples of this approach. A third state approach is to collect periodic information about the productivity and cost of programs, which is reported to the institution and to the legislature. Institutions are then asked to review and report on planned action to improve or terminate programs that do not meet certain objective criteria. Institutions take action partly to avoid unfavorable reactions of the public and the legislature.

Institutions and faculty have a difficult time with program reviews that are conducted to increase efficiency or reallocate resources. Faculty members support program review as a means of quality improvement, but they generally believe that improvement costs money. The major faculty motivation for program review is to document the need for additional resources, which is in opposition to a state motivation to use program review as a basis for using existing resources more effectively. These differing motives have the potential of making program review a center of conflict between institutions and state agencies in the 1980s.

If quality improvement is a key state objective, then program review in traditional academic terms may have an important role to play; but if the major objective is resource reallocation, then the budget may be a simpler and more appropriate place to bring about the necessary changes.

Another problem is that a field-by-field or program-by-program review of academic programs is an expensive and time-consuming process. A modest-sized university will usually have more than fifty different program areas, and a large university may have more than a hundred. When fields are reviewed by degree level as well (bachelor's, master's, professional, and doctorate), the process becomes very complex.

Examination of the details of individual program quality, need for each program, and costs of each program focuses attention on one small part of a total institutional program but gives little information about the extent to which broader institutional objectives are being achieved. To what extent are graduates gaining the desired competencies? To what extent are student needs being met, and are all eligible students benefiting from the program? Review of specific subject areas does not give the kind of overview of institutional performance that may be most important to the improvement of the educational program. Institutional accreditation shifted away from collecting details about program and departmental operations two or three decades ago and now evaluates institutions against their own goals and objectives. If the states are interested in encouraging quality improvement, they should consider moving away from detailed program review to a broader assessment of the way institutions are performing their missions within the state system (Western Interstate Commission on Higher Education, forthcoming).

There is general agreement that the states should define the broad areas of program offerings of each institution (role and mission), but there is considerable disagreement that the state should try to evaluate specific programs in all institutions. A middle ground seems to be that the state could require each institution to have a process to review programs and to assure they meet standards of effective operation.

Some states will probably continue and expand their review of existing programs while others will not get involved in existing program review; still others may develop broader evaluation programs as part of an overall emphasis on greater public accountability. The specific approach the state takes will depend in part on the extent of legislative and/or gubernatorial interests, the existing state-level governance structure, and the state's history and traditions in higher education.

At present, interest in state review of both new and existing programs seems to be on the increase; but this may level off or decrease in the future. If the primary motivation is control of costs, there are easier ways to reallocate resources; and there are broader and more comprehensive ways of assessing quality than through a program-by-program review.

Accountability Expectations. In the past decade, about half the states have expanded their fiscal audit procedures to include some kind of program or management audit. Legislation to provide sunset reviews has been enacted by about two thirds of the states. Either all or part of higher education has been involved in performance audits in about half a dozen states. Program audits and sunset legislation are means legislatures are using to respond to public expectations that government should operate more effectively and that the legislature should exercise more oversight over governmental operations (Berdahl, 1977).

A fiscal audit is an examination of fiscal practices against specific criteria for acceptable fiscal operations. Similarly, a program audit should be made in relation to explicit educational or management standards; but standards of effective educational practice have not been defined. The audit of all institutions by uniform standards would inhibit diversity and would not reflect the different purposes of community colleges, research universities, urban universities, and liberal arts colleges.

"The main problems of performance audits are the lack of appropriate performance indicators . . . and there may be a failure to establish standards and procedures prior to the audit" (Education Commission of the States Task Force on Accountability, 1979, p. 11). Without standards, the audit becomes a judgmental matter. The Education Commission of the States'(ECS) report on accountability suggests an accountability process could be operated without developing uniform standards for education in all institutions by assessing each institution's achievement of its own goals and objectives. This is the approach taken by the federal General Accounting Office, which has had more experience with program auditing than any of the states. Program audits in higher education are too new to say with any certainty the extent to which they will follow the suggestion of the ECS task force and evaluate each institution and system against its own goals and objectives, whether they will try to establish some general standards for management and education as the basis of audit reviews, or the extent to which they will rely on the auditors' judgments.

Regardless of how program audits are carried out, institutions will have to supply more evaluative information about their operations. Probably the greatest increase in requests for information about the institution will be performance data. Where did the graduates go, and how well did they do? What is happening to the dropout rate? How much are students learning, and how do they do on licensing exams? Is the institution competing effectively for research funds, and what are the trends in external research support?

Sunset legislation has been one of the most popular accountability procedures with state legislatures in recent years. It is too early to assess its impact, but the skeptics who think it will be of limited value seem to have the most evidence on their side. First, it is not likely that major public functions like education, health, consumer protection, or welfare will be terminated. They may need to be improved in function, but the threat of termination is not realistic. Second, even when the agency is relatively small, like the student aid board or the licensing board for cosmetology, it will probably have a lobbying group that will pressure the legislature into renewing it. Limited state experience and the analogy of federal reauthorization of legislation suggests the political process makes it very hard to kill any program, even when there is a specific positive action required to retain it.

If states follow the federal pattern and begin to enact more enabling legislation for specific time periods, there will be a substantial impact on both institutions and state higher education agencies. They will have to supply more information and program justification, and there will be much more interaction between colleges and universities and the legislatures on the substance of legislation in addition to the annual or biennial interaction over budget appropriation.

In most states, enabling legislation for higher education is very general, may be included in the state constitution, and does not have a specific termination date. The formal interaction between higher education and the legislature has generally been centered on the appropriations and budget cycle. In some states, the budget has been used to regulate colleges and universities by including a variety of limits or requirements on higher education in the budget bill language.

Sunset legislation, periodic reauthorization of higher education enabling legislation, and the enactment of more detailed statutes affecting higher education are all part of the increasing legislative regulation of higher education. The development of a more effective accountability process may slow the expansion of the legal framework within which higher education must operate, but it is not likely to reverse the trend. Institutions and state agencies are likely to find that more state evaluations of their activities will occur, they will have to justify their programs and management procedures more frequently, and they will have to supply more reports about their activities. This may be valuable if it improves the communication between colleges, legislature, and state officials and if it results in better legislation and state policy in higher education.

One type of report that may become more important in the future as a means of communication is that on the condition of education. The federal government has produced an annual national condition of education report for five years. Several states have begun to produce state condition of education reports; they synthesize available information and indicators of the cost, programs, outputs, quality, and types of students served. A condition of education report serves as one kind of accountability report, giving largely quantitative indicators and trends that indicate in a general way how well higher education is operating. The choice of appropriate indicators for a condition of education report and the provision of comparably defined information will be largely an institutional and state higher education agency responsibility, and it is potentially helpful in improving communication with the public and the legislature.

State Budgeting. The budget has always been the primary means of state influence on higher education. "Schick observed that the governmental budget serves three principal purposes; it controls spending, it enables management of activities, and it determines objectives" (Caruthers and Orwig, 1979, p. 25). Caruthers and Orwig point out that the central emphases in budgeting shift as the state's policy interests change. Incremental, object-of-expenditure budgets were the dominant type of state budgets two decades ago. These are designed to control spending, and some states expanded the number of line items to achieve more detailed control. In the 1960s, more states began to develop objective criteria that allow them to relate appropriations to enrollments and other indexes of activity to achieve more equity. This development is called "formula budgeting." By the early 1970s, at least half the states had some form of formula budgeting (Gross, 1973; Meisinger, 1976).

During the 1960s and early 1970s, a number of states also attempted to link planning and budgeting more closely and to develop budgets based on goals and objectives. The purpose in these budget reforms was to have the budget determine state program and policy objectives. These new budget systems had various names. One was planning, programming, and budgeting (PPB), and a later reform with similar objectives was called zero-based budgeting (ZBB). Another approach to budgeting that has been tried, first in the 1950s and again in the 1970s, is to base some budget allocations on performance criteria. These efforts are described by Caruthers and Orwig (1979, pp. 35–59) and by Peterson, Erwin, and Wilson (1977, p. 134). Wildavsky (1975) has been very critical of the PPB-related "reforms," which he believes have failed to change the basically political nature of budget decision making.

Caruthers and Orwig (1979) provide a comprehensive analysis of budgetary approaches and purposes and the strengths and weaknesses of various approaches. Glenny and his colleagues studied the processes of state budgeting for higher education in detail in eighteen states (Bowen, Ruyle, and Glenny, 1976; Glenny, 1976; Schmidtlein and Glenny, 1977) and analyzed it from both a technical and a political point of view. Although there are a number of common elements to state budgeting, there is also a great deal of diversity across the fifty states in the controls they exercise, the extent to which the budget is the primary instrument of state policymaking in higher education, the decentralization of budget management, the emphasis on formulas and other objective guidelines in developing the budget, and budget links to planning and evaluation.

Even though states develop detailed procedures for reviewing budget requests according to objective criteria, the final decision process is basically a political negotiation. The objective and detailed justifications for the budget, whether formula, PPB, ZBB, or some other acronym, may shape the decision process and focus it; but technical factors do not supplant legislative judgment.

One reason students of budget systems have developed a healthy skepticism about the impact of these new "systems" is that they are frequently abridged or ignored during recession periods or at times when a new political group takes over decision-making responsibility. Recessions and political turnovers occur rather frequently, so budget systems lack the stability needed to have a lasting impact on state policy and program objectives. For example, when a recession cuts state revenues, higher education budgets may receive a simple across-the-board percentage cut, without reference to any of the analysis and budget justification that had gone into preparation of the budget request.

Despite the skepticism about new systems, there are several changes in budget processes that may occur in the next few years. Frequently mentioned is the desire on the part of colleges and universities to change budget formulas and budget criteria so there is less weight given to enrollment in determining appropriations. Because a majority of public colleges and universities will probably lose some enrollment in the next decade, they want to cushion the revenue loss associated with the loss of enrollment. Costs do not go down proportionately with enrollment losses.

There is a similar state interest in reducing the fiscal pressure to compete for students at any cost, which may have lowered standards and led to a proliferation of weak off-campus programs. States have used a number of adjustments to reduce the importance of enrollment. First, some states have developed marginal cost, rather than average cost, funding formulas; so the addition or loss of a student only adds or subtracts part of the average cost per student. Second, states have appropriated funds for a particular enrollment level at each institution, for example, five thousand students. If the actual enrollment is within two hundred students plus or minus of the budgeted level, then no adjustment is made in the institution's budget. This approach is called a "corridor" concept, and the corridor can be set at a percentage width or a numerical width. The corridor can be wide or small. Still another approach is to use the average enrollment level for the last three years as the basis for funding. In this method, no adjustment is made if the institution is under or over enrollment for the year; but the new enrollment figure is part of the next three-year average. These are only three examples of variations in funding criteria that can be used to deemphasize enrollment changes in the appropriations process.

Another interest in a number of states is to find a basis for funding quality improvement in higher education. If enrollment is not increasing, it should be possible to provide some resources for quality improvement. The Tennessee Higher Education Commission has had a multiyear project in which it has tried to develop a basis in its formulas for funding qualitative, performance criteria (Bogue and Troutt, 1978). The Tennessee commission is proposing the inclusion of a "performance" formula factor for the 1980 budget that would be based on several different criteria, including accreditation of professional programs, student scores on standardized exams, and percentage of graduates who pass licensing exams. Although only a small part of the budget would be based on these quality indexes, it would provide an incentive for institutions to be more concerned about qualitative factors.

Another approach is represented by the Florida Board of Regents, which has identified areas of the university system that need qualitative improvement (libraries, teaching and research equipment) and has also identified a limited number of "programs of emphasis" that will receive special funding to enable them to gain national distinction. The programs of emphasis approach is similar in concept to several other states' programs that have identified a limited number of areas that would get special funding; it is also similar in concept to the National Science Foundation's Science Development Grant Program, which in the 1960s provided funds to a number of universities to strengthen selected science and social science departments.

Building up the quality of a department or school in a university is a lengthy process, especially if quality is defined in traditional terms of the graduate teaching and research reputation of the faculty; so these programs will require funding for a number of years. They also are designed for the comprehensive research universities, and broader definitions of quality will be needed if the other public institutions are to participate.

Neither the efforts to fund quality nor the changes in the appropriations process that deemphasize enrollment factors deals with the central fiscal problem of higher education, which is the impact of inflation. Over the past decade, expenditures per student have not kept up with the rate of inflation. If expenditures per student in constant dollars in 1967 are taken as an index value of 100, by 1973, the index had declined to 95; and by 1978, it had declined to 90 (National Center for Education Statistics, 1979, p. 134). The decline has occurred in both the public and private sector. Between 1973 and 1978, per-student expenditures for the public sector, in constant dollars, declined about 7 percent. There have been substantial state variations around this national trend. The Sunbelt and the energy-rich states have generally done better, and the Northeast and Midwest have done worse than the national average.

As long as the support of higher education per student is decreasing in real-dollar terms, the introduction of more equitable formulas that cushion the impact of declining enrollment, the addition of qualitative criteria to funding formulas, or the closer linkage of the budget to goals and objectives of the state will have a limited impact. Between 1971 and 1978, enrollment in higher education grew about 32 percent; and the consumer price index increased 58 percent (National Center for Education Statistics, 1979, p. 134). If enrollment does not grow or declines by 5 to 15 percent in the next seven years, the chance of keeping up with inflation should be substantially improved. The public schools experienced a slight enrollment decline in the last decade but increased real per-pupil expenditures over 25 percent in that period. The resources to offset the impact of inflation on higher education will be available in most states unless taxes are cut substantially or the share of state revenues going to higher education drops sharply. Greater attention to budget systems that reward quality, cushion enrollment fluctuations, and reflect state policy objectives will be possible in many states.

Statewide Planning. Statewide planning in higher education should provide the framework and sense of direction for program review, evaluation and accountability activities, and budget review. A large majority of states have developed a state higher education plan, but the extent to which the plan is actually a guide for the development of higher education and its financing varies widely from state to state.

The content of state plans varies substantially. Some state plans emphasize broad goals and objectives; others focus on academic plans and role and mission statements for each sector and each public institution. Some plans embody most of the public policy objectives in higher education, including issues of opportunities for minorities, access for all citizens, quality improvement, fiscal policies, academic development, and institutional role and mission. Other plans are more limited in scope.

The federal government has mandated state plans in a number of areas of federal support, including health education, vocational education, and compensatory education for the disadvantaged at the elementary and secondary level; but in higher education, the federal government has taken a low-key approach to planning. The federal government has provided limited encouragement to general statewide planning and has encouraged the participation of all postsecondary sectors in planning, including independent higher education, proprietary vocational education, public higher education, and public vocational education. The federal encouragement has broadened the participation in statewide planning and made more states aware of the interrelationships of the various sectors. (See Chapter Five for a more detailed discussion of the federal role in statewide planning.)

The independent sector has also become better organized politically and has successfully sought state support for student aid and, in some states, for direct grants to independent institutions as well. Independent higher education is much better represented in state planning and policymaking than it was a decade ago, and this higher level of involvement is almost certain to continue for the foreseeable future. Private higher education is affected by state plans, and it wants to be involved in the planning and policy formation (Chronister, 1978).

State government interest in planning in the areas of land use, physical facilities, health programs, transportation, environmental protection, and economic development has been greater and has extended over a longer period of time than interest in higher education planning. Up to about 1960, most states left higher education planning to each individual institution and at most did a statewide "study" of higher education every few years. The state higher education agencies established in the 1960s were all given a broad charge to do statewide planning in higher education without much specific direction or clear expectations by state officials as to what the planning should accomplish. Only a few states developed a specific linkage between state plans and the budget process, and most states did not set up a specific evaluation system for assessing the extent to which state goals and objectives specified in the plan were being achieved. Glenny (1976) found that statewide plans did not have much impact on budget decisions in most of the eighteen states he visited. Statewide plans were effective in California in maintaining differentiation of function between the different sectors and institutions, but there were a number of other states where institutional overexpansion occurred despite a statewide plan. Many of the state plans developed in the late 1960s were plans for further expansion and projected more growth than occurred in the 1970s. As a result, a majority of states are entering the 1980s in an overexpanded state, with more programs, more off-campus operations, and fewer students than are needed for a cost-effective operation. There is a good deal of skepticism about the ability of planning to anticipate the future accurately. In many states, the plan did not have enough political support or enough specificity to guide development; and the present overexpansion is not so much an indictment of planning as an indictment of the failure of state officials and educational leaders to pay attention to the plan.

Despite the uneven experience with state educational planning during a period of growth, it appears there is an even greater need for planning to deal with the stability and decline of the next decade. The consequences of every institution acting for its own short-run interest are predictably bad during a period of retrenchment. Although there is an increased need for planning, the necessary political support for planning will be very difficult to maintain because retrenchment is politically unrewarding. In addition, it is likely there will be substantial fluctuations in enrollment and economic conditions during the next decade, which will result in periodic crises in funding and departures from plans and budget formulas in favor of across-the-board cuts and other crisis management techniques.

The planning techniques that have been most successful during a period of growth have usually involved participation of faculty members, students, alumni, citizens, and college administrators in the planning process. In retrenchment planning, widespread participation may be a formula for political rejection of the plan. If the plan does not embody some faculty and administration aspirations, but instead indicates areas to be cut back or eliminated, faculty members and administrators have little or no motivation to support it. An uncertain future determined through ad hoc political negotiation may seem better than a retrenchment plan.

Despite the political problems involved, there is likely to be more emphasis on planning during the next decade, especially planning closely related to the budgeting process. Legislators and state budget officers will be calling on the colleges to eliminate duplication and weak programs; and in many states, higher education personnel will move forward with planning on the grounds that it is better to deal with the issues themselves than to have solutions handed to them by the legislature, often in response to a temporary crisis.

Conclusion

The preceding analysis presents a very mixed picture for state government-higher education relationships. The country is at a turning point in enrollment, public attitudes, and a number of other environmental factors. Political processes at the state level are also changing; and states are depending more on formal legal procedures in planning, policymaking, budgeting, and evaluating. There is more regulation and at the same time, more support for decentralization of management back to the institutional level. There is also support for giving more weight to student choice as a "market force" in determining which programs and institutions will survive the next decade. The need for more planning to assure better use of scarce resources is also stressed, although enhanced student choice and use of market forces is contrary to the policy that emphasizes planning, budget control, and regulation as the desirable means of controlling higher education. There will be new state budget procedures, new state evaluation procedures, and new state program review procedures for institutions to deal with; but the states will change existing procedures in different ways and at different times. A decade hence we will still have fifty different information systems to deal with fifty different planning, budgeting, program review, and evaluation procedures. There probably will be more uniform definitions of terms, somewhat more comparable data, and more similarity in budgeting and planning systems. But the diversity among the states will still be much more noticeable than the uniformity. Although there are many common problems and similarity of environmental pressures among the states, the diversity of structures, personalities, and political and educational traditions leads each state to devise its own solutions.

Bibliographical Essay

There are many good reviews of state politics. One is Jacob and Vines (1976). The relationships between states and elementary/secondary education provide useful contrasts with the postsecondary relationships. A major study of state-elementary-secondary education relations is Campbell and Mazzoni (1976). Public attitudes about education in general and elementary/secondary education in particular are discussed in the annual Gallup polls of attitudes toward education. The first ten years of these polls are available in book form, *The Gallup Polls of Attitudes Toward Education, 1967–78* (1979). The 1979 poll appeared in the September 1979 *Phi Delta Kappan,* pp. 33–45. A good review of the politics of tax and spending limits can be found in "1978: The Year of the New Populism" (1979). An up-to-date, state-by-state analysis of tax and spending limits can be found in *Tax and Expenditure Limitations, 1978* (1978).

General relationships between state legislatures and higher education are reviewed in practical, nontheoretical terms in a series of conference papers given at the University of Arizona in 1977. Papers are presented by educators, a governor, a legislator, and a state higher education executive.

The general relationships between state government and universities are the subject of two of the Carnegie studies (1971 and 1976). A task force of the Education Commission of the States (1973) also reviewed the general relationships in making recommendations for effective state coordinating agencies. Literature on the more specific topics of planning, program review, budgeting, and management is reviewed in Halstead (1979), a comprehensive, well-annotated bibliography in twenty-two sections that emphasizes books and reports published since 1970 that will serve as a guide to the literature about higher education planning, broadly defined. The review of budgeting in the ERIC higher education series by Caruthers and Orwig (1979) gives an excellent overview and review of the literature about budget systems and issues.

The series of reports on state budgeting for higher education by Lyman Glenny and associates published by the Center for the Study of Higher Education at the University of California, Berkeley, gives a very detailed description of the politics and technical aspects of budgeting. Harcleroad (1976), the Education Commission of the States Task Force on Accountability (1979), and Folger (1977) give an overview of the accountability and evaluation issues in higher education. Halstead (1974) covers the technical issues in detail; Clark and Youn (1976) and Clark (1978) give a more theoretical perspective on the issues in planning.

References

Adamany, D. "State Government Regulation of Higher Education in California." A report prepared for the Sloan Commission on Government and Higher Education, December 1978.

American Association of State Colleges and Universities. *Institutional Rights and Responsibilities.* Washington, D.C.: American Association of State Colleges and Universities, 1971.

Barak, R. J., and Berdahl, R. O. *State Level Academic Program Review in Higher Education.* Denver, Colo.: Education Commission of the States, 1978.

Berdahl, R. O. "Legislative Program Review." In J. K. Folger (Ed.), *New Directions for Institutional Research: Increasing the Public Accountability of Higher Education,* no. 16. San Francisco: Jossey-Bass, 1977.

Bogue, G., and Troutt, W. "Allocation of State Funds on a Performance Criterion: Acting on the Possible While Awaiting Perfection." In R. Fenske and P. Staskey (Eds.), *Research and Planning in Higher Education.* Tallahassee, Fla.: Association for Institutional Research, 1978.

Bowen, F., Ruyle, J., and Glenny, L. *State Budgeting for Higher Education: Budget Processes in the 50 States.* Berkeley: Center for Research and Development in Higher Education, University of California, 1976.

Campbell, R., and Mazzoni, T. *State Policymaking for the Public Schools.* Berkeley, Calif.: McCutchan, 1976.

Cantril, A. "Schools, the Quality of Education, and Taxes, the Public's View." Paper prepared for the Forum of Educational Leaders, November 6, 1978.

Carnegie Commission on Higher Education. *The Capitol and the Campus.* New York: McGraw-Hill, 1971.

Carnegie Commission on Higher Education. *Governance of Higher Education: Six Priority Problems.* New York: McGraw-Hill, 1973.

Carnegie Foundation for the Advancement of Teaching. *The States and Higher Education: A Proud Past and a Vital Future.* San Francisco: Jossey-Bass, 1976.

Caruthers, J., and Orwig, M. *Budgeting in Higher Education.* Washington, D.C.: American Association for Higher Education, 1979.

Chronister, J. *Independent College and University Participation in Statewide Planning for Postsecondary Education.* Washington, D.C.: National Institute of Independent Colleges and Universities, 1978.

Clark, B. *Academic Coordination.* Working Paper YHERG-24. New Haven, Conn.: Yale Higher Education Research Group, 1978.

Clark, B., and Youn, T. *Academic Power in the United States: Comparative, Historical, and Structural Perspectives.* Report No. 3. Washington, D.C.: American Association for Higher Education, 1976.

Education Commission of the States Task Force on Accountability. *Accountability and Academe.* Denver, Colo.: Education Commission of the States, 1979.

Education Commission of the States Task Force on Statewide Coordination. *Coordination or Chaos.* Denver, Colo.: Education Commission of the States, 1973.

Folger, J. *New Directions for Institutional Research: Increasing the Public Accountability of Higher Education,* no. 16. San Francisco: Jossey-Bass, 1977.

Folger, J. *The South's Commitment to Higher Education, Progress and Prospects.* Atlanta, Ga.: Southern Regional Education Board, 1978.

Glenny, L. A. *State Budgeting for Higher Education: Interagency Conflict and Consensus.* Berkeley: Center for Research and Development in Higher Education, University of California, 1976.

Gross, F. *A Comparative Analysis of the Existing Budget Formulas Used for Justifying Budget Requests.* Monograph No. 9. Knoxville: Office of Institutional Research, University of Tennessee, 1973.

Halstead, K. *Statewide Planning in Higher Education.* Washington, D.C.: U.S. Government Printing Office, 1974.

Halstead, K. (Ed.). *Higher Education Planning: A Bibliographic Handbook.* Washington, D.C.: U.S. Government Printing Office, 1979.

Harcleroad, F. *Educational Auditing and Accountability.* Washington, D.C.: Council on Postsecondary Accreditation, 1976.

Jacob, H., and Vines, K. (Eds.). *Politics in the American States.* Boston: Little, Brown, 1976.

Meisinger, R. *State Budgeting for Higher Education: The Use of Formulas.* Berkeley: Center for Research and Development in Higher Education, University of California, 1976.

Moos, M., and Rourke, F. *The Campus and the State.* Baltimore: Johns Hopkins University Press, 1959.

National Center for Education Statistics. *The Condition of Education, 1979.* Washington, D.C.: U.S. Government Printing Office, 1979.

"1978: The Year of the New Populism." *Intergovernmental Perspective,* 1979, 5.

Odden, A. *Voter Attitudes Toward Government and Spending.* Denver, Colo.: Education Finance Center, Education Commission of the States, 1979.

Peterson, M., Erwin, M., and Wilson, R. "State Level Performance Budgeting." In J. Folger (Ed.), *New Directions for Institutional Research: Increasing the Public*

Accountability of Higher Education, no. 16. San Francisco: Jossey-Bass, 1977.

Schmidtlein, F., and Glenny, L. *State Budgeting for Higher Education: The Political Economy of the Process.* Berkeley: Center for Research and Development in Higher Education, University of California, 1977.

Tax and Expenditure Limitations, 1978. Washington, D.C.: National Governors' Association Center for Policy Research, 1978.

The Gallup Polls of Attitudes Toward Education, 1967–78. Bloomington, Ind.: Phi Delta Kappa, 1979.

Western Interstate Commission on Higher Education. *Proceedings of a Conference on Program Review.* June 4–6, 1979. Boulder, Colo.: Western Interstate Commission on Higher Education, forthcoming.

Wildavsky, A. *Budgeting, A Comparative Theory of Budgetary Processes.* Boston: Little, Brown, 1975.

5

Richard M. Millard

Power of State Coordinating Agencies

F_{ew} developments in the last two decades have had more impact on higher education than the creation of statewide coordinating and governing boards. Their relation to public institutions is direct and pervasive, but many of them have responsibilities related to independent and proprietary institutions as well. This chapter briefly traces the history of such agencies, details the variance in their structures among states, and examines their primary functions as mandated by law and executive order or as developed by policy.

Most state coordinating agencies were created to guide the orderly growth of higher education. Currently they, like the institutions with which they deal, are facing changing conditions that will have major impact not only on their functions and operations but also on those of the institutions.

Development of State Boards

Currently, all states except Wyoming have some form of statewide post-secondary or higher education governing, coordinating, or planning board or agency. With two exceptions, such boards or agencies are constitutionally or statutorily created. The exceptions, Delaware and Vermont, are authorized by executive order.

Such boards are not a new phenomenon. The oldest, the New York Board of Regents, was established by the first session of the New York legislature in 1784. Five additional boards were established during the nineteenth century and eleven more before 1950. By far, the majority of these early boards were consolidated governing boards for senior public institutions. The New York Board of Regents (1784), the Florida Board of Education (1885), the Kentucky Council on Public Higher Education (1934), and the Oklahoma Board of Regents (1941) were the coordinating board exceptions. The rest were governing boards some of which were charged aggressively to pursue reduction in duplicate programs. For example, the Georgia Board of Regents, established during the depression of the 1930s, eliminated ten institutions, demonstrating that retrenchment is not just a recent and projected occurrence.

Real pressure for statewide coordination of public higher education began in the 1950s and accelerated in the 1960s. Six new coordinating boards appeared in the 1950s, with twenty-three coordinating agencies and two (Maine and West Virginia) governing boards created since 1960. Moreover, three of the earlier coordinating boards were changed to governing boards; and in Oregon, a coordinating board over all education has been added besides the governing board for senior public institutions.

It is no accident that this major acceleration in the development of state coordination occurred during the most rapid expansion of higher education in the history of the country. Many of the boards created between 1960 and 1975 had written into their authorizing legislation the responsibility to provide for the orderly growth of public higher education. Other relatively common concerns that contributed to these boards' formation and to their functions were keeping increasing rates of expenditure in perspective and balance, providing for budgetary equity among institutions in the light of their different functions, assuring reasonable diversity among institutions within the state in relation to the variety of state needs, avoiding unnecessary duplication of programs not related to demand in the expanding market, and balancing institutional operations with political and social realities as these relate to social and geographical distribution of opportunities. In addition, in many states, governors and legislators wanted to avoid dealing with interinstitutional rivalries directly in the governor's office or in legislative halls and sought a means of ameliorating them beforehand.

Finally, the inclusion in the federal higher education amendments of 1972 of Section 1202 on State Postsecondary Education Commissions changed the scope of statewide planning and of planning agencies in many states and in a few states complicated coordination by leading to the creation of an additional agency. The 1202 legislation was intended to increase the level and intensity of state higher education planning and coordination by broadening the scope of agency responsibilities to include not just public higher education but all segments of the postsecondary educational universe, including nonprofit private, proprietary, and public and private postsecondary vocational schools. In addition, funds were authorized under Section 1203 for general statewide planning in order that resources could be "better coordinated, improved, expanded or altered so that all persons within the state who desire, and can benefit from postsecondary education may have an opportunity to do so." Even though the amounts available to states under Section 1203 have been minimal ($3 to $3.5 million per year since 1974), the legislation has had major impact. To date, forty-eight states have designated existing agencies, augmented existing agencies, or created new agencies as state postsecondary education commissions. (North Carolina and Wisconsin are the two exceptions.) The addition in the last two years of Tennessee and Colorado, which did not originally respond, seems to indicate that expansion of state planning to include all postsecondary education has become a continuing state concern. The major impact of the 1202 legislation has undoubtedly been to extend the scope of statewide planning beyond the public sphere to other segments of postsecondary education, although it must be noted that this has not happened uniformly to all segments or in all states.

State boards are constantly subject to review and change, of course, by the governors and legislatures that created them. Thus, even though the trend over the last twenty years has been in the direction of strengthening them, there are exceptions. Wyoming in 1978 eliminated an essentially weak board, and discussions are currently going on in a number of states about possible reorganization and decentralization, as well as further centralization. The critical question seems to be whether boards created to deal with issues of expansion will be adequate to deal with conditions where expansion is not part of the picture.

Agency Types and Functions

Statewide boards vary considerably from state to state in the number of institutions under their purview, in their powers in relation to institutions, and in the scope or applicability of their responsibilities; but most boards have some responsibility either prescribed by law or developed as policy for planning, program approval, and budget development and review. Some may also be responsible for other activities, such as operating a state student assistance program, authorizing institutions to operate and to grant degrees, and managing various state-based federal programs.

In relation to the three central functions, a state board may have major responsibilities in program approval, including review of existing programs, but no statutory role in the budget process, as in New York. It may have major responsibilities in the budget process, including recommending a consolidated budget, but only advisory responsibilities in relation to program review, as in Alabama. It may have statutory planning responsibilities only for senior public institutions in the state or for the full range of postsecondary education; and beyond these statutory responsibilities, it may or may not extend its functions to other areas by policy decisions.

Boards may be classified in a number of ways (Berdahl, 1971; Carnegie Foundation for the Advancement of Teaching, 1976; Millard, 1976); but for institutional planning and research, a classification based on their major functions is likely to be most useful. The first obvious distinction here is between "governing" boards and "coordinating" boards. Governing boards are legally responsible for the management and operation of the institutions under their governance. They are involved in budget management and operational policies after appropriations are made as well as in developing the budget and submitting it to the governor and legislature. They have regulatory powers in relation to internal institutional operation and management and deal directly with institutional administrators without other mediating boards, except in North Carolina and Utah, where institutional councils or "trustees" exist with delegated and defined, but restricted, powers. In contrast, coordinating boards do not have the legal responsibility for institutional management and operation, even though some coordinating boards may submit consolidated budgets and, in one case (Oklahoma), receive and allocate appropriations, approve and review programs, and plan for the state system of higher education as a whole.

Even among governing board states there are differences in types of institutions included, in structures and in the powers of the central office. Thus, in eleven states, governing board responsibilities extend to all, or most, public two- and four-year collegiate institutions, while in eight states their responsibility covers senior public institutions only. Some governing boards have a strong executive system where the chief executive officer as chancellor or president and his or her staff administer the system, as in Georgia, North Carolina, and Wisconsin. In others, such as Arizona, Iowa, and Kansas, the executive officer plays a less dominant role as executive coordinator, executive secretary, or executive officer to the board. And a few governing boards, including those in North Carolina, Hawaii, Utah, and Idaho, have responsibility for statewide coordination and planning beyond the institutions they govern.

Coordinating boards, although not responsible for the management and operation of institutions, also vary extensively, with some having strong regulatory authority to review and approve new and/or existing programs, to recommend a consolidated or aggregated budget, and to plan for all postsecondary education in the state. At the other end of the spectrum are the advisory boards with neither direct program approval nor budgetary authority and a primary responsibility only in statewide planning. Table 1, adapted from McGuinness (1979) and Millard (1976), illustrates the diversity of board structures and powers as these relate to program review and budgets.

Table 2, adapted from McGuinness (1979), shows the planning responsibilities of boards by source of responsibility, that is, whether authorized by constitution, statute, or executive order or carried out as a matter of board policy. In all states, statewide planning for public senior institutions is mandated by law or constitution, as it is for all public community colleges in the forty-nine states that have them. Except in Arizona, Mississippi, and Wyoming, planning for both senior institutions and community colleges is the responsibility of one agency. By law, in forty-seven states, planning for public postsecondary vocational education is done by an agency also responsible for planning for senior institutions and community colleges; thirty-one states include independent institutions; and twenty-three states include proprietary institutions. If one adds those institutions for which planning is carried out under executive order or by board policy, forty-seven states include postsecondary vocational education, forty-six include independent institutions, and forty-one include proprietary institutions.

Table 1. State Higher Education Boards

		Coordinating Boards						
		With Program Approval Authority			With Program Review and Recommendation Authority Only			
Consolidated Governing Boards—All Public Institutions	Consolidated Governing Boards for Senior Institutions. Separate Agency for Community Colleges	Consolidated or Aggregated Budget	Budget Review and Recommendation	No Statutory Budget Role	Consolidated or Aggregated Budget	Budget Review and Recommendation	No Statutory Budget Role or Program Approval	Executive Appointed Agency
Georgia[b]	Arizona[c]	Connecticut	Colorado	New York[e]	Alabama	Alaska	New Hampshire	Delaware
Hawaii	Iowa[b]	Illinois	Indiana		Arkansas	Oregon[e]	Nebraska	Vermont
Idaho[e]	Kansas[b]	Massachusetts[c]	Kentucky[b]			California	Maine	Wyoming
Montana[ce]	Mississippi[b]	New Jersey	Louisiana			Minnesota	South Dakota[e]	
Nevada[c]	North Carolina	Ohio	Missouri			Washington		
North Dakota[c]	Florida[abe]	Oklahoma	New Mexico			Michigan[e]		
Rhode Island[e]	Oregon[ab]	South Carolina	Tennessee			Florida[ef]		
Utah		Maryland	Texas					
West Virginia			Pennsylvania[de]					
Wisconsin			Virginia					
Alaska[ab]								
Maine[ab]								
New Hampshire[b]								
South Dakota[ab]								

[a]Separate statutory coordinating agency
[b]Separate 1202 commission
[c]Separate 1202 commission staffed by governing board staff
[d]Governing board in relation to state-owned institutions, coordinating board for state-related, and so forth
[e]States with agency responsible for all levels of education
[f]No program review authority

Source: Richard M. Millard, director of Postsecondary Education, Education Commission of the States, adapted from McGuinness, A. "Intergovernmental Relations in Postsecondary Education: The Case of the 1202 Commissions." Unpublished doctoral dissertation, Syracuse University, 1979, Table 23, p. 321.

Table 2. Planning Responsibilities by State

State Agency	Four-Year Public	Two-Year Public	Public Voc. Edu.	Independent	Proprietary
Alabama Commission on Higher Education	S[a]	S	S	E[a]	E
Alaska Postsecondary Education Commission	S	S	S	S	S
Arkansas Board of Higher Education	S	S	S	S	S
Arizona:					
Board of Regents	C[a]				
State Board of Community Colleges	S	S			
Postsecondary Commission	E	E	E	E	E
California Postsecondary Education Commission	S	S	S	S	S
Colorado Commission on Higher Education	S	S	S	E	E
Connecticut Board of Higher Education	S	S	S	S	S
Delaware Postsecondary Education Commission	E	E	E	E	E
Florida Department of Education:					
Commission for Post-High School Edu.	S/E	S/E	S/E	S/E	S/E
Board of Regents	S				
Georgia:					
Board of Regents	C	C			
Postsecondary Commission	E	E	E	E	E
Hawaii Board of Regents	C/S	C/S	S	S	S
Idaho Board of Education	C/S	C/S	P[a]	P	P
Illinois Board of Higher Education	S	S	S	S	P
Indiana Commission for Higher Education	S	S	S	S	S
Iowa:					
Board of Regents	S	S			
College Aid Commission	E	E	E	E	E
Kansas:					
Board of Regents	C/P				
Legislative Education Planning Committee	S	S	S	S	S
Kentucky:					
Council on Higher Education	S	S			
State Advisory Council on Voc. Edu. (1202)		E	E		

[a]Symbol Key: C = constitutional, S = statutory, E = executive order, and P = agency policy.

Table 2. **Planning Responsibilities by State** (*Continued*)

State Agency	Four-Year Public	Two-Year Public	Public Voc. Edu.	Independent	Proprietary
Louisiana Board of Regents	C/S	C/S	E	S/E	E
Maine:					
Board of Trustees	S	S			
Postsecondary Commission	S	S	S	S	S
Maryland Board of Higher Education	S	S	S	S	S
Massachusetts:					
Board of Higher Education	S	S	S	P	S
Postsecondary Education Commission	E	E	E	E	E
Michigan Department of Education	S	S	E	E	E
Minnesota Higher Education Coordinating Board	S	S	S	S	S
Mississippi:					
Board of Trustees	C				
Junior College Commission		S			
Postsecondary Education Planning Board	E	E	E	E	E
Missouri Department of Higher Education	S	S	P	S	P
Montana:					
Board of Regents	C	S			
Committee on Federal Higher Edu. (1202)	E	E		E	
Nebraska Coordinating Commission for Postsecondary Education	S	S	S	S	S
Nevada:					
University of Nevada System	C	C	C		
Higher Education Commission (1202)	E	E	E	E	E
New Hampshire Postsecondary Education Commission	S	S	S	S	S
New Jersey Board of Higher Education	S	S	E	S	E
New Mexico Board of Educational Finance	S	S	S	S	
New York Board of Regents	C/S	C/S	C/S	C/S	C/S
North Carolina:					
Board of Governors	S	S		S	
Board of Education		S	S		
North Dakota:					
Board of Higher Education	C/S	C/S			

[a]Symbol Key: C = constitutional, S = statutory, E = executive order, and P = agency policy.

Table 2. Planning Responsibilities by State *(Continued)*

State Agency	Four-Year Public	Two-Year Public	Public Voc. Edu.	Independent	Proprietary
Postsecondary Education Commission	S	S	S	S	S
Ohio Board of Regents	S	S	S/P	S	S
Oklahoma Board of Regents	S	S	S	S	S
Oregon Educational Coordinating Commission	S	S	S	S	S
Pennsylvania Department of Education	S	S	S	S	S
Rhode Island Board of Regents	S	S	S	E	E
South Carolina Commission on Higher Education	S	S	S	S	E/P
South Dakota:					
Board of Regents	C/S				
Education and Cultural Affairs Planning Commission	S		S	S	S
Tennessee Higher Education Commission	S	S	E	E	E
Texas Coordinating Board	S	S	E	S	E
Utah Board of Regents	S	S	S	S	S
Vermont Education Planning Commission	E	E	E	E	E
Virginia Council on Higher Education	S	S		S	S
Washington Council for Postsecondary Education	S	S	S	S	S
West Virginia Board of Regents	S	S	E	E	E
Wisconsin:					
University of Wisconsin	S	S			
Board of Voc. and Tech Education		S	S		
Wyoming:					
University of Wyoming	S				
Community College Commission		S			

ᵃSymbol Key: C = constitutional, S = statutory, E = executive order, and P = agency policy.

Conditions Affecting State Agencies

The problems facing both state higher education agencies and their institutions during the next decade are likely to be severe and similar. Over the last two decades, both institutions and agencies have planned and operated in a context of expansion. Although there have been minor fluctuations and the expansion rate has declined in recent years, most planning and coordination modes and even board powers and actions have reflected this expansion context. Thus, for example, most state coordinating agencies have program approval or program review authority; but in some cases, this has been limited to new programs. In practice, relatively few state coordinating agencies have undertaken major review of existing programs and those few reviews have been primarily at the graduate level. One of the critical questions is whether, given the changing conditions, existing boards and agencies will be able to deal with these conditions effectively without changes in powers and structures.

A number of factors discussed in previous chapters will affect the general climate in which planning and operations will occur. Among these, some are likely to have major impact on state agency and institutional relations, particularly as they relate to the substance and the form of the planning process. These include enrollment changes, fiscal constraints, increased demand for accountability, social justice issues, and executive/legislative tensions.

Demographic and Enrollment Changes. Although enrollment projections vary with the projectors, enrollments will clearly decline throughout the next decade in most states. Nationally, the number of eighteen- to twenty-two-year-olds, the group that now provides about 75 percent of college students, will decrease about 25 percent by 1993 (Bureau of the Census, 1978). This will vary by geographic area, with the most severe declines in the Northeast. However, no section can expect major increases (Glenny, 1976). Enrollments, in contrast to college-age population, do not depend on the eighteen- to twenty-two-year-old population alone; and the decrease in this group may be offset to some extent by older students. A number of institutions are counting on older students at least to help ameliorate the drop. Between 1970 and 1978, the percentage of twenty-five- to thirty-year-olds has increased by 50 percent and those between thirty and thirty-five have increased from 3.7 percent of the age group in 1970 to 6.5 percent in 1977 or 75 percent (Bureau of the Census, 1978). One in ten students is over thirty-five. In spite of the increasing institutional competition for older students, the assumption that entering older students will continue to increase at the same rate or that, if they do, they will fill the vacant places of the declining eighteen- to twenty-two-year-olds is open to question. Even if more older students enroll, it will take considerably larger numbers to equal current full-time students because most are part-time. There is some evidence to suggest that older students who want traditional college offerings are already enrolled. Thus, in 1976, for the first time, the percentage of older students did not increase.

There will also be shifts within the traditional college-age group. The number of minority students and women is likely to increase while that of white males continues to decrease. An additional reason for concern is that although the peak of eighteen- to twenty-two-year-olds has not yet passed, enrollments dropped .2 percent in the fall of 1978 (Bureau of the Census, 1978). If this indicates a decreasing interest in college attendance that may continue, it may make the current rather bleak enrollment picture considerably worse.

To all of this must be added the probability of year-to-year fluctuations, institution by institution and program by program, that are likely to occur, depending upon the economy and shifting student interests. These may be even more important and disruptive to planning than the general decline. In the period ahead, the emphasis in coordination and planning will clearly have to be on retrenchment, consolidation, and reallocation of resources to meet what may be rapidly changing conditions.

Fiscal Constraints. Assuming state appropriations for higher education remain constant or increase slightly, a reduction in the number of students in theory should provide additional funds on a per-student base, as was the case with elementary/secondary education when enrollments began to decrease in the early 1970s. Unfortunately, a very different climate is likely to make such increases unlikely in higher education in the 1980s. In spite of state surpluses, tax relief and more limited public spending seem to be high priorities in most states. Although few states followed California, the Proposition 13 mentality is widespread. As a result, higher education is likely to be faced with decreasing enrollments, fiscal austerity, and continued inflation. To the extent that states accept the president's antiinflation guidelines, any funding increases will be less than the projected level of inflation, thus resulting in an actual decrease in spending power.

The situation is complicated by the fact that the largest percentage increases in higher education costs have been and are likely to continue to be in areas over which higher education has limited or no management control. These include social security, hospital and medical costs, and energy costs. All of this may call not only for tight budgeting but for the need to rethink and restructure the budgeting process, particularly in states utilizing enrollment-based formulas.

Accountability. Although the public considers higher education an essential service, it, like all other government services and agencies, is increasingly subject to accountability demands. Public higher education institutions have always been held financially accountable; but this aspect has recently taken on new dimensions that relate to educational effectiveness, attainment of educational objectives, and continuing oversight of the educational process. In part, this reflects concern for increased efficiency and more effective management and, in part, for maintenance and improvement of quality in the face of increasing competition. It also reflects a concern that public business be publicly conducted. Finally, increased interest in accountability reflects an uneasiness, present from the days of student unrest, about the relevance of higher education to student interest, which is heightened by unemployment or underemployment of college graduates.

This concern with accountability has taken a number of forms, including increased regulation and oversight; demands for new, more adequate, and better analyzed information from institutions; performance audits; evaluation as a part of the budgeting cycle; review of new and existing programs; and general institutional evaluation. A few states have even imposed "sunset" conditions (time frames within which the agency or program must be reviewed for effectiveness and continued, modified, replaced, or eliminated) on state agencies and particular programs.

Three of these forms affecting accountability in higher education call for special mention. The first is the growth in performance budgeting. The initial accountability line has always been through state budget control. However, traditional budget approaches based on input costs are not particularly useful for accountability purposes. As government budgets have expanded, new methods have been sought to provide assurances that funds are being spent effectively as well as legally. Procedures have been developed as part of the budget development process to provide for evaluation of the need for each activity. These have taken different but related forms, such as PPBE (planning, program, budgeting, and evaluation), zero-based budgeting, priority budgeting, and budgeting by objectives; but all are designed to relate budgets and expenditures to specific goals or objectives and thus obtain more control over the effectiveness of the budgeting process. In practice, these performance budgets have not placed as much emphasis on the evaluation part of the cycle as on other parts. The newly developed systems request new forms, but they usually are evaluated without the measures having been developed and agreed upon in advance.

The second area regarding higher education accountability is performance audit. Performance audits extend beyond both fiscal audits and management audits and raise the question of effectiveness of activities or organizations in achieving their goals or objectives. Following the example of the federal General Accounting Office, some twenty states have developed either legislative or executive performance audit agencies. Although usually not created with higher education in mind, performance audit operations have turned to higher education or some part of it because higher education constitutes an important and flexible part of the state budgets. When performed by a state audit agency, such audits raise serious questions about institutional and program integrity. Who sets the standards and how the evaluation takes place become critical issues. That performance evaluation will become a more frequent and legitimate demand seems clear, and it is incumbent upon higher education to be able to demonstrate its educational effectiveness. However, unless such audits are based on agreed-upon accountability objectives and evaluation procedures are carried out by knowledgeable people, they are likely to be ineffective or even counterproductive.

A third accountability possibility now being explored in some states is the development of an effective accountability system within higher education, possibly under the aegis of the state coordinating agency. Instead of relying on increased regulation and control, such a system involves four steps: (1) agreement on the definition of goals for which higher education should be held accountable; (2) determination of who is responsible for accomplishing these goals; (3) agreement on and use of an evaluation process, including self-evaluation, that will demonstrate achievement of objectives; and (4) the process of reporting to the public, the governor, and the legislature on evaluation results (Education Commission of the States, 1979). Such an accountability system may involve a regional accrediting agency in part of the process. Whatever the form of accountability, the pressure and legitimate demand for it affect both the state higher education agency and the public institutions, as well as their relations to each other.

Social Justice. The 1970s were characterized by major movements to extend educational and economic opportunity to groups who had been disadvantaged in the past—including racial and ethnic minorities, women, the handicapped, and the economically underprivileged. These movements have been reflected in federal and state laws and reinforced by the courts. Progress has been made in educating women, increasing the percentage of minorities in colleges and universities, providing access for handicapped persons, and providing opportunities to low-income students. Achieving such progress has required modifications of state and institutional policies, expenditures of additional funds for student aid, building renovations to accommodate the handicapped, admissions policy changes, and development of special programs. These have called for statewide and institutional planning and action and, in the states affected by the Adams case, major statewide readjustment. In spite of the progress, there is still far to go before equal opportunity becomes a reality.

The projected conditions for the 1980s pose a series of tensions for the area of social justice that will affect institutions and state agencies and are likely to heighten rather than eliminate social justice concerns. Increasing competition for students, plus increasing percentages of minorities in the eighteen- to twenty-two-year-old population, will encourage institutions to include larger numbers of minorities in the college population. However, financial stringency is likely to make costly developmental programs less attractive for institutions, state agencies, legislators, and governors. Affirmative action requires increasing numbers of women and minorities in teaching and administrative positions at a time when faculties will have to shrink and a large portion of the faculty has tenure. Increased emphasis on continuing adult education and lifelong learning to offset the decreasing traditional college student population will tend to appeal to the already best educated, thus furthering the educational gap for minorities and the economically deprived unless special efforts are made to encourage their participation. But such special efforts will require scarce funds that may have to be taken from other programs. Even in student aid, increasing concern with middle-income students and the utilization of institutional and even state aid for recruitment purposes not primarily related to student need pose problems of widening rather than closing gaps. Unless institutions and state agencies take these factors into account in the planning and budgeting process, social justice issues are likely to become more rather than less acute in the decade ahead.

Executive/Legislative Tensions. State higher education boards or agencies, particularly in coordinating board states, are usually considered part of the executive branch of government. Members of such boards are normally appointed by the governor, although there are exceptions, such as New York, where the legislature elects the regents. Executive officers are appointed by their boards, but they generally are considered equivalent to heads of state departments and in some cases have cabinet status (for example, in Arkansas, Colorado, Missouri, New Jersey, and New York).

Legislatures have created state higher education boards; or, in a few cases, they are provided for constitutionally. They report to and work with legislatures in appropriations requests and recommendations of system changes related to planning and carry out such additional programs or duties as legislatures may assign to them. Because the board's primary relations to the institutions are added to these responsibilities, state boards and agencies are in a uniquely vulnerable position.

The natural tensions that exist between the executive and legislative branches of state government have tended to be heightened in recent years. Both legislatures and governors have added capable staffs, and the board must be able to work with both without being perceived by either as the other's captive. The situation is complicated by the variance among states in gubernatorial and legislative powers. In strong-governor states, the governor's budget carries considerable weight; and the governor has line-item veto power. In weak-governor states, the governor's budget is not as important; the governor may not have line-item veto power; and a simple majority can override a veto.

It is in the area of budget review and appropriation requests that the tensions between the governor and the legislature, with their improved staffs, can create problems for both state higher education agencies and institutions. The board, the governor's office, and the legislature all having full review responsibilities leads to increased redundancy. As legislative staffs add capable budget analysts, the staff is less likely to rely on the findings of the board or of the governor and wants to undertake in-depth review on its own. In states where the governor presents a consolidated budget and does not want budget requests to go to the legislature apart from the executive budget, the board may actually be captive by the executive office, regardless of the type and depth of analysis the legislative staff undertakes. The latter may call for additional information from agencies and institutions in different formats and greatly increase the work load of all concerned.

Ideally, the three should work closely together; but in fact, this is seldom the case. Glenny (1976, p. 98) argues, "no phenomenon found in studying state budget practice seems likely to have as much impact on colleges and universities as the growth in number, size, and professional capacity of legislative budget staffs." Consequently, he recommends state postsecondary education agencies, in order to avoid redundancy and being outmaneuvered by such staffs, give up detailed budget review, leave it to the executive budget office and the legislative analysts, direct more of their resources to planning and policy studies, and reserve their budget activities to analyses in relation to long-range plans and policy issues. Particularly in those states where for whatever reason the legislature or the governor feel the higher education agency or the institutions are not sufficiently accountable, the likelihood of direct gubernatorial or legislative intervention tends to increase at the expense of system and institutional autonomy.

Responses to Changing Conditions

The changing conditions in the 1980s are likely to create major strains for statewide agencies and institutions in their relations to each other and to the legislative and executive branches of state government. They are also likely to change the nature, intensity, and forms of the major functions of state agencies, which in turn will require new types of information and responses from institutions. Before examining these functions individually, a brief look at possible general state responses that could have impact on or change the directions, even structures, of state agencies and of institutions is in order.

Increased Reliance on the Market. Following the federal lead of supporting students rather than institutions, states could rely more heavily on the market as a regulatory mechanism. This would involve increasing tuition in public institutions, increasing student aid, decreasing institutional support, and thus letting students determine which institutions survive and which do not. This would eliminate or reduce the role of state agencies to consumer regulatory operations, market forecasts, and possible administration of student aid. It would mean institutional planning would emphasize market forecasting, market development, and program adaptation to market alternatives. Because of heavy investments, states might continue to support some basic institutional maintenance and applied research for the benefit of the state but not instructional costs. The purest form of such a market approach would be a voucher system, such as that proposed in Ohio under Governor Gilligan. Although more reliance on the market may occur in some states, particularly those with large private sectors, the likelihood of a major move in this direction is not great in light of the current level of state investment in public institutions and the political infeasibility of discontinuing public institutions.

Increased Centralization through Consolidated Governing Boards. With emphasis on increased accountability, a number of states may be tempted to increase centralization and regulation. Under difficult circumstances, one solution attractive to legislators and governors is frequently to propose a single governing board or agency with the power and responsibility to bring about essential change. Such a board and its executive can be held directly accountable to the legislature and/or the governor. This also has the advantage of removing the onus of hard decisions from the legislature and the governor while technically leaving decision making to the academic community, within the limits imposed by appropriations and legislative and executive directives. The last states to move from coordinating to consolidated governing boards have been Utah (1974), Wisconsin (1973), and North Carolina (1972). However, legislation has been proposed to create consolidated governing boards in a series of states, including Connecticut, Massachusetts, and Minnesota. Discussions and studies continue; and the possibility of such moves in other states should not be discounted, particularly as the fiscal and enrollment situations tighten.

Strengthening the Role of the Coordinating Agency. Without moving to a consolidated governing board, a number of states have within the last few years further strengthened the role of the state coordinating agency to meet changing conditions. This is the minimal response likely to occur in additional states. Major changes have taken place in Louisiana, where the regents were given constitutional status (1974), Maryland (1976), Connecticut (1977), and South Carolina (1978). Boards have been renamed and strengthened in California (1974), Oregon (1975), and Washington (1976). Changes have included moving from separate to consolidated budgets, extending program review and approval explicitly to existing as well as new programs, extending planning scope and authority, and requiring the board to restructure the internal governance of the system.

Direct Legislative and/or Gubernatorial Intervention. In a few cases, where the legislature or the governor has been dissatisfied with the existing system, the legislature more frequently than the governor has directly intervened to assume functions formerly considered the province of statewide agencies or institutions. In Nebraska, by statute, a legislative committee directly assumed responsibility for determining institutional role and scope and developing a management information system. In Colorado, the legislative joint budget committee not only reduced the coordinating agency staff but reserved to itself the budgetary review functions previously lodged with the board. In Mississippi, the legislature directed a management review of the senior educational system; and the Florida legislature authorized a governance and management review in 1979. Legislatures have attempted by law to regulate faculty work loads in Florida, Michigan, and Washington. Again, as the situation becomes more acute, the probability of increased legislative and gubernatorial intervention in direct system operation may increase.

Other Alternatives. There are other alternatives, some of which involve combinations of those mentioned, under consideration in some states now. One of these involves decentralization of the state agency regulatory role along with regionalization of planning and budget development functions. A second involves eliminating intervening system boards, giving institutions separate boards of trustees but strengthening the central agency's role. A third, which addresses the relation to private higher education, is to provide incentives for consortium arrangements. A fourth, seriously considered in Florida in the 1979 legislative session, is to dissolve the consolidated governing board, replace it with a coordinating board, and establish separate governing boards for each institution. The fact that such alternatives are under consideration points more to instability of governance and structure in some states in the face of anticipated conditions than to alternate answers.

Statewide Planning Operations and Alternatives

Statewide planning may be considerably more difficult in the next decade than it has been in the past because of the uncertainties involved and the difficulties of prediction. The traditional concepts and modes of rational planning, including the ability to identify long-range goals and objectives, present some problems in the current context. Some investigators question whether such goal setting and developing rational means to their achievement are either feasible or desirable under present circumstances (Morgan, 1978). Long-range planning in the classical sense of preparing a master plan may be a less-viable alternative in the future. This is not, however, to suggest that in some situations developing a master plan may not be mandated and essential or that the elements or issues addressed in doing so are not as crucial today as in the past.

In a number of states and institutions, the emphasis has changed from producing master plans to what might be described as developing a continuous or rolling planning process. This may involve a series of different planning processes that are brought together at critical points for review in relation to each other. Such planning involves recognition of different types of goals, some major and some subsidiary. The latter may not be primarily educational but may relate to such issues as survival, retrenchment, and recruitment, which require more administrative implementation or action than programmatic development. Nevertheless, these subsidiary goals may be conditions for the possibility of meeting more encompassing educational goals.

Although the approaches to and/or modes of planning vary and change, the essential components of planning remain fairly constant. Basically, planning involves identification of key problems, accumulation of accurate data about these problems, analysis of their interrelations, extrapolation of future alternatives that might emerge from present conditions, assessment of probable consequences of introducing new variables, and the choice of the most desirable modified alternatives as basic objectives to be obtained. In addition, it includes a sequential plan or plans for implementing the basic objectives and a system for periodically reevaluating the objectives and the means for achieving them.

Traditionally, it was fairly easy to distinguish between what might be called strategic or long-range planning and tactical or short-range, intermediate planning. Strategic planning involved developing the framework that reflected the state's fundamental assumptions about postsecondary education; the long-range societal objectives and goals; and the principal missions, roles, and functions of all postsecondary institutions and agencies. Strategic planning tended to constitute the master plan. In contrast, tactical planning took place within the parameters of strategic planning and dealt with short- and intermediate-range goals, developmental time frames, and step-by-step means for achieving the goals. The functions of strategic and tactical planning are as critical now as at any time in the past, but the distinction between them is blurred. Some states and state agencies require current updates of the master plan or use of a rolling base approach with a three- to five-year plan or projection, modified and developed each year in the light of tactical issues. There are various reasons such flexible planning is needed. One is a recognition of the more rapid rate of change and the possibility that a long-range plan will be outdated by intervening events. Another is a more programmatic approach to planning, in which changing circumstances constantly modify the changing plan. Complexity of goal determination is also a factor, as is the range of issues presently relevant to the planning process and to the need for determining priorities among them.

The goal-setting process is complicated not only by the distinction between primary educational goals and subsidiary administrative goals, which may in some instances take priority, but also by goals only in part determined by the educational and immediate political communities. The latter include social equity goals, which are frequently determined by federal legislation and the courts but must be accommodated in state and institutional planning. Obtaining consensus is perhaps most difficult in connection with such goals as they relate to educational goals and extend beyond the range of federal and court mandates to the interpretation of these in educational terms. In fact, in such areas, the goal-setting process may not be able to move much beyond defining the problem and circumscribing the tolerable limits of action commensurate with educational objectives.

Closely related to the difficulties involved in goal determination is the broadening of the scope of planning on the statewide level for which agencies have become responsible in the last few years as regards both institutions and issues. Whereas during the 1960s and early 1970s the primary planning responsibilities of such agencies related to four- and two-year public institutions, presently by statute, executive order, or board policy, they extend to public postsecondary vocational institutions (forty-seven states), independent nonprofit institutions (forty-six states), and proprietary institutions (forty-one states). (See Table 2.) This means a far wider range of institutions and their constituencies must be involved both in goal determination and in providing information for planning. It also means increased complexity in the types of objectives, in their relation to each other, and in the development of priorities among them as such priorities relate to needs assessment, funding availability, and state educational goals. The situation is further complicated in some states, where the responsibilities for planning for these various types of institutions do not all lie with the same agency. In such cases, interagency communication and cooperation in the planning activities, although essential, may be difficult.

In spite of the difficulties, 93 percent of the state agencies in 1978 reported they are involved in master planning efforts in contrast to 61 percent in 1972 (McGuinness, 1979). These efforts included determination of goals of institution types as follows: senior public, 97 percent; community colleges, 89 percent; postsecondary vocational, 68 percent; independent nonprofit, 82 percent;

and proprietary, 66 percent. In by far the majority of cases, the planning included developing policy recommendations for the types of institutions; and representatives of the various types of institutions were involved in the planning process. Among the types of information required from the institutions or developed in the planning process were current enrollments, enrollment projections, facilities inventories, and program inventories. Given the legal and executive mandates and the degree of state agency involvement in the planning process, some investigators argue, political support from institutions and the legislative and executive branches of state government will erode during the next decade (Folger, 1979). However, there is little evidence to support the belief that this erosion has taken place yet. As systems face retrenchment, this may change.

Among the issues of growing importance that statewide planning must address are the problems of retrenchment, including elimination of duplication, preservation and strengthening of quality, institutional and program consolidation or elimination, staff and faculty reduction, modification of institutional role and scope to meet changing conditions and needs, and readjustment of budgeting procedures to minimize enrollment fluctuations.

At the same time, considerably more attention must be given to adult education, continuing education, lifelong learning, and off-campus operations as institutions seek new clienteles. This is already an area of major interinstitutional competition that is likely to become more severe; but there are also many other players, including community organizations and centers, business, industry, labor, libraries, the military, and federal programs. This will increase the participants and issues even further.

Finally, given restrictions in funds, decreasing enrollments, and other noneducational state priorities, postsecondary education must not find itself in self-defeating competition with elementary/secondary education. It will be progressively important for postsecondary education planning to be articulated with planning for elementary/secondary education in attempting to meet the total educational needs of the state. This is not to suggest that planning or governance of the two segments of education should be merged, but it is to recognize that close communication and some joint planning are essential in areas where the lines of separation are blurred—such as vocational education, adult education, and developmental education.

All these factors have major implications not only for planning on the statewide agency level but on the institutional level as well. If, for example, the next decade were to see a major shift to the market approach to planning, as mentioned earlier, the statewide agency role would decrease or disappear and the institutional role would increase but with primary emphasis on market forecasting, market development, and adapting programs to market conditions. If the movement is to greater centralization and consolidated governing boards, the consolidated governing boards would be faced with all the planning issues but with the disadvantage of having to deal with nonpublic institutions as nonneutral interested parties and competitors. Assuming neither extreme prevails but some increased powers or responsibilities of state agencies to meet the changing conditions occur in some states, what are the implications of or for statewide and institutional planners regardless of whether the state agency operates in a traditional master planning mode or in a rolling or continuous master planning activity?

Analyzing Needs. At both the state and the institutional level, needs analysis will have to be more extensive, more analytical, and more focused. At the state level in particular, this will require more extensive and judicious utilization of manpower information, not to tailor all postsecondary education to manpower needs but to ensure the system as a whole is responsive to these needs, both current and emerging. It will require taking into account in needs analysis a wider range of constituencies, including not only institutions and current students but the adult population, business, industry, labor, the military, and the political community. Such needs analysis will have to be related to changing social and political priorities such as energy and conservation. Shifts among age cohorts will be particularly critical, as will shifts within them in racial and economic composition.

At the institutional level, some of the same factors will apply. Institutional needs will have to be balanced with community needs, which will have to be balanced with available resources. Whether or not a movement in the direction of reliance on the market as a planning device occurs, market analysis will become more important as a condition of institutional viability; and some adaptation of programs to their marketability will be essential. State agencies may require some form of market analysis, not only in determination of role and scope but in approval of new programs.

Setting Goals or Objectives. As noted earlier, setting goals or objectives has become considerably more complicated in the last few years and promises to become more so in the period ahead. This is perhaps more the case on the statewide than on the institutional level; but if so, it is more a matter of degree than of kind for two reasons. First, institutional goals must fit into or even, in the case of independent institutions, be relevant to statewide goals if the institutions are to participate in and benefit from statewide planning efforts. Second, some of the externally generated goals apply as much to the institutions as to the statewide planning efforts, for example, civil rights, occupational safety, and provision for the handicapped. Further, the institutions have a vital role to play in determining statewide goals in terms of their historical functions, their capabilities, and their personnel and facilities resources.

As has always been the case, determination of goals or objectives must be based upon analysis of needs, identification of problems, accumulation of accurate data, extrapolation of alternatives and their consequences, and choice of the most desirable alternatives as objectives. What is new is the range of problems, issues, and alternatives and the difficulties of achieving consensus under conditions of variable enrollments and retrenchment. This will call for recognizing the variety of types of objectives that must be taken into account and the more difficult business of setting priorities among them. Consensus may still not be too difficult on general goals or objectives; but on specific goals, it may be much more difficult to obtain. And yet, development of goal specificity will become essential, not only to system health but to institutional survival. To develop such specific objectives will require probably more information and clearly more targeted information from institutions. This may occur at the same time that funds for developing more effective information systems are curtailed. If this happens, it will become progressively important to consider the cost benefits of the information sought or requested and to set priorities in terms of its usefulness.

On the statewide level, institutional objectives need to be assessed in relation to each other, to overall needs analysis, to legislative and executive mandates and objectives, and to the wider community's expectations. Undoubtedly, the agreed-upon objectives will and should reflect political negotiations as well as reasoned alternatives in the light of information. However, the more adequate the information and thorough the objective formulation process, the more likely the political negotiations are to take place within an educationally relevant context, given the parameters of resources. Whether this takes place will depend not only on the central agency but on institutional cooperation and effective planning. Institutional political support for statewide planning may well decrease under retrenchment conditions in the hope that there are short-range advantages in "going it alone." Nevertheless, in the long run, such a policy could be disastrous both educationally and fiscally.

Determining Role and Scope. Role and scope determination involves translating goals and objectives into specific institutional missions. This is critical to any form of the planning process. To some extent, institutional mission in a broad sense frequently is determined in basic legislation or, in some instances, in the state constitution. However, such legislative mission statements tend to be broad and lack the specificity essential to planning for a period of limited resources. Specifications of role and scope have usually been the central element in state planning documents; but again, in the past, these have tended in many cases toward generalities rather than specifics.

Approaches to role and scope determination have tended to follow two different methods. One is to request the institutions to develop their own mission statements based on their assessment of their resources, capabilities, and aspirations. Traditionally, institutions have considered development of mission statements their own prerogative within boundaries set by law. The role of the state agency in such an approach has been that of developing the composite picture, suggesting some modifications for compatibility. The second approach has been for the state agency, usually with institutional involvement, to develop mission statements with a view toward institutions within the system complementing each other in meeting identified state needs. Although these approaches are not mutually exclusive, changing conditions seem to require a combination of the two. Some institutions may have to change or radically modify their missions in order to survive. The statewide board is frequently charged with the responsibility for preventing unnecessary duplication and overlapping functions where not called for by geographical or service reasons. It is also charged with ensuring effective resource allocation or reallocation to meet real educational needs and to enhance quality. Accordingly, there are dimensions of the planning process, including role and scope determination, that transcend individual institutional concerns. From this standpoint, it is critical that the board and institutions work closely together but that the institutional perspective be balanced by the board's statewide perspective.

Careful analytical self-study becomes crucial if the institution is to play a responsible role in role and scope determination. Without an accurate picture of institutional capabilities, resources, and markets and without a translation of these into specific objectives, either development or contribution to development of role and scope statements is likely to be inadequate and ineffective.

Involving and Legitimizing. The history of statewide planning has made clear the ineffectiveness of statewide plans developed without the full involvement or participation of the affected institutions and communities. This in part explains the lack of enthusiasm for master plans, in contrast to a continuous or rolling planning process. One of the advantages of the planning process is the opportunity to bring together the participant institutions and groups to develop an understanding of the issues, to move toward consensus where possible, and to be apprised fully of the reasons for recommendations and actions, even when consensus may not be possible.

As noted, the process is complicated currently by the number and types of institutions and groups that need to be involved. This may, on the one hand, slow down the process or, on the other, call for more pragmatic planning in which different issues and groups are addressed either on a priority basis or as the situation (including crises) dictates. Regardless of the approach, it is crucial that appropriate institutions and groups, including representatives of the legislature and the executive office, be not only informed but involved in the decision-making process. Whether this be done through advisory groups, task forces, or special working committees is not as important as that it be done. In many instances and on particular issues, public hearings may also be called for. Such involvement is a minimum condition of legitimization of the planning process. From the institutional standpoint, such involvement will require time and effort on the part of the staff and even faculty. But from the standpoint of an institution's future and self-interest, it is time well spent.

Implementing Plans. Planning has far too frequently been carried on as though it were a separate exercise not related to budgeting or program review. Implementation of planning, thus, effective planning, clearly does not take place in a vacuum. The practical implementation of planning beyond legislative changes, if called for, lies in translation of the plan into budget development and appropriation allocation, program review in light of planning objectives, and administrative oversight. From this standpoint, institutional involvement in the planning process and in its implementation is crucial to its effectiveness. Also for this reason, programmatic forms of budgeting have had wide appeal and are likely to increase in the future, even recognizing the limitations of some forms tried in the past or currently being proposed.

Budget Approaches and Issues

Each state, as Glenny points out, adopts its budget methods and practices "to reflect its particular political mores and structures" (1976, p. 30).

Most states with consolidated governing boards for all public higher education or for only senior institutions present *aggregated* or *consolidated* budgets to the governor and the legislature. A consolidated budget request is one in which the primary bases of the request are programs or functions across institutional or campus lines. In most instances, individual campus requests do not appear or, if they do, are subordinated to statewide justification for funding of the group as a whole (Glenny and others, 1975). In an aggregated budget request, individual institution budget requests are assembled into one document, totaled, and presented with or without significant revisions to the state; but individual campus requests retain their own identity. In states where individual campus or segment budgets are forwarded to the legislature, the central board may review and recommend changes; but each campus budget stands as a separate unit request for appropriations.

Regardless of the form or level of aggregation, the budgetary document or documents, both for institutions and state agencies, constitutes the practical planning document. Unless plans are translated into formal budget requests, whether the budgets are in plan relevant form or not, the plans will not be carried out. Some forms of statewide budgeting are more conducive than others to direct relation of the planning process, attempting to incorporate planning as part of the budgeting process. Others require translation of planning into more specific implications. One of the concerns frequently expressed by Glenny and others in the latter case is that the translation does not take place; so planning has little effect on budgeting and thus, in fact, little effect.

Caruthers and Orwig (1979) identify five major approaches to budgeting on a statewide basis: incremental budgeting; formula budgeting; planning, programming, and budgeting systems; zero-based budgeting; and performance budgeting. The various approaches may be mixed; and in some cases, different approaches may be utilized by different state agencies, for example, the state higher education agency, the governor's budget office, and the legislature. When this happens, the information burden on institutions is likely to be overwhelming.

Perhaps still the most widespread and the traditional form of budgeting is *incremental budgeting*, in which the base is the previous year's budget and each line item or budget unit is increased, kept constant, or reduced. A premise of incremental budgeting is that the current base is properly distributed by functions and object of expenditure unless special studies or programmatic changes call for further increment or reduction. During periods of expansion, this approach is rarely questioned and special cases can be made for adjustment above the normal increment. Such budget requests thus can incorporate priorities. Incremental budgeting has some advantages even in a period of decline, for it is also possible to identify fixed costs, which can be incrementally adjusted for new price level requirements. The major difficulty in incremental budgeting is that it does not necessarily reflect program and planning activities. Further, the assumption that a current budget is distributed properly may or may not be correct and may become progressively less so in the future. Such an approach at best tends to perpetuate inequities and to encourage interinstitutional as well as intrainstitutional infighting, end-running, and a "squeaky wheel" approach to budgeting.

Formulas are essentially a mathematical or quasi-mathematical device for distribution of scarce dollars among institutions within the state. Twenty-five states used some form of *formula budgeting* in 1975. The nature and complexity of formulas vary considerably from state to state, as does the extensiveness of their use in relation to various parts of the budget. They appear to be objective; but as Meisinger (1976, p. 2) points out, they usually are a combination of technical judgments and political agreements. Formula budgeting is generally combined with or is a modification of incremental budgeting. In its more elaborate form, formula budgeting may involve separate formulas for various institutional functions along with variable formula applications in institutional areas for type of program and levels of students. The advantages of a formula approach, according to Meisinger (1976, pp. 7–9), are that it (1) tends to lessen the complexity of budgeting standards, (2) serves as a means of accommodation among institutions, (3) establishes the limits for the incremental amount to be added to or subtracted from the budget base, and (4) provides an "objective" base for equity in treatment of institutions.

One of the more serious problems with current formulas is that they are based on average costs by instructional level and field and are enrollment dependent. This worked to the advantage of institutions during the period of expansion, but such formulas create additional problems in periods of decline. Although formulas will probably not disappear, they will need revision to reflect fixed, variable, and marginal costs if they are to be of value in a period with variable or declining enrollments.

Planning, programming, and budgeting systems (PPBS) originated with the federal government and have been adopted or adapted in various states with mixed results. Even the definition of the term is not easy or agreed upon. Caruthers and Orwig (1979, pp. 45–46) define it as follows: "*Planning* involves the selection and identification of the overall long-range objectives of the organization and the systematic analysis of various courses of action in terms of relative costs and benefits. *Programming* requires decisions on the specific courses of action to be followed in carrying out planning decisions. *Budgeting* entails the translation of planning and programming into specific financial plans."

It was devised as a process for uniting the budgeting and planning processes to ensure implementation, but far too frequently it has, where implemented, tended to become a parallel rather than a supplement to traditional budgeting approaches. In its original form, it is not well adapted to departmental programs when programs cut across departments. Perhaps the most serious difficulty lies in the fact that the evaluation parts of the cycle have not received much emphasis and the objectives to be evaluated and the measures of those objectives have not been developed and agreed upon in advance. Many states have adopted forms of budgeting described as program but as Glenny (1976, p. 29) points out "these differ dramatically from one state to another."

Regardless of the particular forms or of the controversy surrounding PPBS, the basic concept of uniting programming, planning, and budgeting is critical in budgeting for changing conditions. Although PPBS will have to be further modified in its applicability to higher education and may disappear in its earlier forms, its concepts will persist until some more satisfactory linkage is established.

Although *zero-based budgeting (ZBB)* has not had as much impact on state-level higher education budgeting as the other forms discussed, it has been tried in some states (for example, Arkansas). In theory, it demands a total rejustification of every activity from a zero base rather than through incremental approaches. In practice, it has usually taken the form of starting from some percentage lower than 100 percent, but not zero, and has tended to be applied to selected rather than all programs. Essentially, it involves developing budgeting units or packages and ranking these in relation to each other. Among the more difficult problems in its use are developing criteria for ordering priorities. It has had limited application to date and may have limited utility in higher education. ZBB may turn out to be most applicable not in instructional but in service areas.

Performance budgeting is related to PPBS and focuses on and elaborates one concept of it. Peterson (1977, p. 2) has described performance budgeting as "*a budgeting structure* that focuses on activities or functions (program structure) which produces results (outcomes or impacts) and for which resources (inputs) are used *and a budgeting process* that attempts to allocate resources on the basis of anticipated or past results." A number of states use a program budgeting structure in higher education, and six states collect and report outcome measures in the budgeting process. Hawaii and Washington have the most extensive experience with it. Ten additional states in addition to the District of Columbia have attempted to use some form of performance indicators in the budgeting process (Peterson, 1977, pp. 3–4).

Performance budgeting attempts to use qualitative as well as quantitative measures of results and to allocate resources on the basis of performance indicators and outcome measures. In part, its appeal lies in its relevance to accountability and its possible use as a basis for identifying ineffective and/or inefficient programs for discontinuance in retrenchment. The major problem with performance budgeting is the difficulty of determining appropriate performance criteria. Qualitative measures are not normally part of management data bases and require special collection efforts and listing procedures, and then the establishment of causal relations between expenditures and qualitative results is difficult. Even in the cases of Hawaii and Washington, performance budgeting has had only limited success because of its complexity. Performance budgeting does not have strong legislative support in its present forms in many states. However, the concern with impact or results continues, and demand for some form of performance measures is likely to increase.

Regardless of budget form, either of presentation or approach, a series of issues is likely to become more rather than less acute in the next decade, for both institutions and state agencies. One of these issues is the degree to which the state agencies will or should become involved in the budgeting process in the light of growing legislative and executive staff involvement and the redundancy this involves. As noted, some redundancy is desirable; but redundancy approaching 100 percent places additional burdens on all concerned, including institutions, in time, effort, and paperwork. Glenny (1976) has suggested state agencies give up detailed budget development and review, devote more of their resources to planning and policy studies, and reserve their budget activities to analyses in relation to long-range plans and policy issues. Even if this were to take place, it is not likely to reduce substantially the information and analysis requirements for institutions. Although it might be advantageous to the agency in removing it from the direct budget negotiations, it would place the institutions in a somewhat more vulnerable position between the executive and legislative branches of government in the political decision-making process on budget. Because of pressure from the legislature and the governor on agencies to take a more active role in assuring retrenchment (where necessary) occurs in an orderly way, the probability that agencies will play a decreased role in budgeting may not be high. Boards may in fact have to become more adept rather than less involved in budgetary consideration.

A second issue relates to possible retrenchment and the role of state agencies in it. Bowen and Glenny (1976, p. 17) have documented the fact that when retrenchment becomes necessary, particularly within a budget cycle, agency and institution response tends to be in terms of across-the-board cuts rather than selective retrenchment. But there are limits to how often this can be done; and the impact, if continued, is likely to be at the expense of quality. Given a longer time frame, retrenchment must become selective and integrally related to the planning process. Although planning for retrenchment is difficult and is not enthusiastically welcomed by institutions, the alternative is likely to be a series of destructive, morale-reducing crises. To avoid this, planning, priority setting, and developing in advance of budgetary implications are crucial. State agencies and institutions need to work closely together at least in developing contingency plans for such retrenchment well ahead of its occurrence.

One aspect of such planning for retrenchment, particularly for those states utilizing formula budgeting, is review and revision of formulas to make sure they are adaptable to conditions of decline. As noted, average cost, primarily enrollment-driven formulas developed for and workable under conditions of expansion, could be disastrous in periods of retraction. Such formulas should be revised to take into account far more clearly fixed, variable, and marginal costs. A major study of formula revision to deal with retrenchment problems is currently underway at the National Center for Higher Education Management Systems and should be available in 1980. In the meantime, formula revision will require close cooperation among institutions, state higher education agencies, and executive and legislative budget analysts in determining fixed and variable costs, the degree to which they are so, and the extent to which marginal costs can be utilized in developing budget requests.

Whether or not one utilizes a formula approach to budgeting, as Caruthers and Orwig (1979, pp. 58–59) point out, various attempts at budget reform are likely to continue: "Beyond the influence of people in leadership positions, the demographic and economic realities of the next decade are likely to demand continued emphasis on rational decision making and, particularly what Morgan terms marginal-utility analysis. . . . We are likely to see procedures that recognize the inflexibility of the base and that minimize paperwork and analysis . . . approaches that provide predictability and rationalization of decision making . . . models that enable the rational evaluation of alternatives at the margin . . . and attempts to change the financial incentive structure through relating performance to the budgetary structure."

Such moves toward budget reform will not necessarily require additional information but frequently information in new forms. When a state changes budget formats, the new data and data structures may require the design of new data collection and accounting systems; and these are likely to be both expensive and time-consuming for institutions at a time when funds are tight and their more effective expenditure is the point at issue (Schmidtlein and Glenny, 1977, p. 183). The necessity of resource reallocation in the face of enrollment decline and the need to deal with changing clienteles (older students) and programs adapted to their needs, which do not fit into traditional budgeting practices, will require closer linkages between budgeting and planning. Budgeting will have to reflect the need to reduce programs and to extend new services at the same time.

It would appear, in other words, that in the next decade, at both institutional and state agency levels, budgets will have to become more rather than less integrally related to planning and program review. In this, they are likely to become the practical, simultaneous instruments for institutional and program evaluation, for program consolidation, for institutional consolidation or elimination in some circumstances, and for expansion of some activities or programs to meet changing markets.

Program Review

Of the various state higher education functions, the most sensitive one from the institutional standpoint is academic program review. This moves to the heart of the academic process, which has traditionally been considered the prerogative of institutions and their faculties. Statewide governing boards have always had such authority, although they have differed in their exercise of it from extensive to very little. As coordinating boards were established, they were frequently charged with reviewing new programs to prevent unnecessary duplication and to assure that added programs fit within the institutional missions. Among coordinating boards, some were given the power to approve or disapprove new programs; others could review and recommend only. Presently, coordinating boards in twenty states have power of approval; seven review and recommend. In a number of states, the original legislation called not only for review and/or approval of new programs but of existing programs as well. The legislation in a number of states has been strengthened to permit or require such review of existing programs in recent years and such strengthening of the legislation in some other states is anticipated because the issue of review of existing programs becomes progressively critical in periods of retrenchment.

Although states vary in how they conduct program assessments, for all states involved in such assessment, at least three questions are basic: (1) Which programs should be reviewed and on what basis? (2) What criteria should be used in the assessment process? (3) How should the evaluation process be implemented? To some extent, the answers vary with the type of program review.

New Programs. Of particular importance during expansion, new program review remains a major concern of most agencies. Even during retrenchment, new programs are proposed—some related to changing missions; some to changing clientele; and some to new, high-priority local or national manpower and other needs. In some states, agencies review only major graduate programs involving requests for new funding. In others, review includes all new academic programs, changes in degree designations, and new majors or minors within degrees, whether or not new funding is involved (Barak and Berdahl, 1978, p. 18). When the legislation calls for approval or review of new units of instruction, the intent usually is establishment of any new college, school, division, institute, department, or degree program. Such approval seldom, if ever, extends to individual courses, which are considered the prerogative of the institutions. Even the question as to when to review new programs is not generally agreed upon. In most cases, review occurs when the program is presented to the board for approval. However, in some states, prior notice is asked for preliminary review in relation to system or statewide goals and institutional mission. In California, institutions are expected to submit projected new major programs two to five years in advance.

In most states, seven factors are called for in the program review process: program description, purposes and objectives, needs analysis, cost analysis, resource analysis, program accreditation (that is, who accredits, requirements for accreditation, and present accreditation of related or expanded programs), and availability of adequate student financial aid (Barak and Berdahl, 1978, p. 26).

The review process may include any or all of a series of steps. First, a number of states require prior notification or approval of planning for a new program, that is, notification as soon as initial planning for a new program begins. This may be as informal as a phone call or a letter of intent; but it has the advantage of avoiding duplicate planning efforts by different institutions, of providing such information for the statewide planning operation, of encouraging cooperation and communication before the formal request for approval is delivered, and of avoiding unnecessary work if there is little or no likelihood the program will be approved. Second, to ensure the program has been thoroughly reviewed by the institution, most boards require a statement of approval by the institution, either its governing board or its chief executive. Third, most states use a prescribed format for program submission to assure some degree of comparability among requests. Fourth, a number of states currently require an interinstitutional review, which may consist of asking each similar institution in the state to comment on the proposal (Washington and Florida) or review by a formal interinstitutional committee (Kansas and Minnesota). Fifth, some states, in addition to or in place of interinstitutional review, utilize a process of outside review. This may be done by formal or informal committees of out-of-state consultants chosen by the board staff or the institution or both. Sixth, any of these steps may be, and usually is, followed by the board staff review or by a review by a committee of the board. Depending upon the state, this may be more or less extensive, from checking to see that the requisite information is present to comprehensive analysis and recommendation. In many states, an institution may informally withdraw the request at any stage during the process if it believes the request will be rejected. The final stage is board action.

Particularly today, proposals for new programs need to be carefully developed by the institutions and their planning staffs, with special attention to needs, cost, and resource analysis. It is incumbent upon the state agency carefully to relate program review to state as well as institutional objectives and thus to the planning process. Although new programs are and will continue to be essential to institutional and system viability, with tightened resources, other programs may have to be given up to fund them. The possibility of adding whatever faculty or students desire without clear documentation of need is probably past.

Existing Programs. Reviewing existing programs is considerably more complex than reviewing new programs. As of 1977, some twenty state higher education agencies were involved in review of some existing programs and others were developing procedures to do so.

Barak and Berdahl (1978, p. 56) list six purposes that may be involved in existing program review: (1) financial (to cut back on expenditures), (2) efficiency (to enable more effective utilization of existing resources), (3) accountability (to assure institutions effectively meet state goals), (4) quality (to upgrade the overall quality of programs by eliminating low-quality programs and reallocating resources to improve others), (5) consumer protection (to protect students from programs of questionable value), and (6) political (to demonstrate agency response to political mandates).

Because of the large number of programs in any system, the selection of programs to be reviewed is critical and may be circumscribed by legal limitations, limited staff and resources, and considerations of how the agency can or should get involved in the review process. As a result, some states confine or have confined such reviews to graduate programs, others to certain types of institutions only, and others to certain subject areas. In most states, a screening device or preaudit for identifying programs for review is essential. Such a device may involve a single criterion, such as low productivity, high cost, quality, need, or a combination of these. Those programs singled out by the criterion then undergo extensive review. Such preselection or audit and review requires as a prerequisite an effective information system and a uniform taxonomy if it is to be effective.

Among the concerns of institutions in some states is the danger of relying wholly on quantitative measures and the difficulties involved in qualitative assessment. A combination of quantitative and qualitative factors is clearly essential. A task force of the Education Commission of the States on Coordination, Governance, and Structure of Postsecondary Education (1973, pp. 51–52) suggested ten factors should be taken into account in program review, particularly as it relates to phasing out or consolidating programs: (1) the number of graduates from the program in each of the last five years; (2) the number of students enrolled in the program (entry and dropout rates); (3) the size of classes and the cost of courses identified as integral elements in the program; (4) cost per program graduate; (5) faculty work load; (6) program quality as reflected by its regional or national reputation, faculty qualification, and level of positions achieved by program graduates; (7) total production of a program's graduates from all institutions in the state, region, and/or nation; (8) the economies or improvements in quality to be achieved by program consolidation and/or elimination; (9) general student interest and demand trends for the program; and (10) program appropriateness to changed institutional role or missions. Each of these is used by some states, although no state uses them all. The most frequently used appear to be number of graduates (fifteen), students enrolled (twelve), student interest and demand (ten), appropriateness to role and scope (ten), program quality (nine), and size of classes and cost of courses (nine) (Barak and Berdahl, 1978, p. 72).

According to Barak and Berdahl (1978, p. 75), the various states' review processes can be grouped into four approaches, based on where the primary responsibility lies: institutionally oriented, intrainstitutionally oriented, agency staff oriented, and outside peer or consultant oriented.

State agencies can utilize incentives to encourage institutions to review their own programs, without any major assessment of statewide needs. Some states coordinate the institutional or segmental reviews through a planning process that also assesses statewide needs. In a few cases (Wisconsin, for example), state agencies monitor the institutional reviews to ensure quality and uniformity. The major difficulty in such an approach is it does not readily provide for interinstitutional comparisons in terms of either quality or duplication.

In some states, an interinstitutional committee assists in developing the guidelines and criteria and may play a continuing role in the review process through jointly reviewing programs, recommending actions to the institutions and statewide board, publishing results, and ensuring the cooperative involvement of the institutions themselves. Unlike the institutional review approach, it makes possible lateral comparisons and review in the light of analysis of statewide needs.

In a few states, the review is undertaken primarily by agency staff. When this is the case, the staff usually identifies programs with (as in Washington) long patterns of low productivity, then requests the institutions involved to develop reviews of these programs and to make recommendations to the board on their continuation or termination. With the institutional reviews in hand, the staff makes specific recommendations for action to the board. One of the dangers of such an approach is the extent to which the staff is considered knowledgeable, sensitive, and mature. If they are not so considered, the end result is likely to be less than satisfactory to all concerned.

Because of the academic community's deeply ingrained reliance on peer group evaluation for quality judgments, careful use of outside consultants is likely to be perceived as the most objective approach to program review. New York, Louisiana, and Illinois, with their Commission of Scholars, have led the way in utilizing the outside consultant approach; and other states are following suit. The choice of the outside consultants is particularly important and must be made with objectivity and preferably with some institutional involvement. The use of consultants tends to increase costs. There are dangers the consultants will work from special biases and be unaware of special problems or statewide needs. But the results of the consultant review go to the board, so these problems can be overcome to some extent, particularly if the board and its staff evaluate the results in relation to the statewide planning framework.

Probably no state fits neatly into any one of these paradigms. Most states use some combination. What is important is that, whatever the approach, the review process is integrally related to the planning process and that systemwide, as well as institutional, objectives be kept in mind. It also is critically important that due process take place. This includes not just approval but effective institutional participation. Barak and Berdahl (1978, p. 86) agree: "First and foremost is the development of a process that generally involves the institutions. This means more than merely [being] allowed. . .an opportunity to appeal an unfavorable state board decision at the conclusion of the review. It ideally includes institutional participation in the very design of the process, in the determination of guidelines and procedures, in the selection of outside consultants (if any are used) and in the deliberations of an interinstitutional advisory committee."

Conclusion

The period ahead will not be easy for either state agencies or institutions. The requirements of state planning, budget review, and program review will be even more closely interrelated than in the past. Institutional planners and state planners will need to work more closely together and will be more rather than less dependent upon each other. Additional demands for information related to budget reform, to review of existing programs, and to a continuous planning cycle will occur, as will the need for more adequate analysis of the information itself. The problems related to retrenchment, increased accountability requirements, fiscal restraint, and social justice will not disappear. Institutions and state agencies must reinforce each other more effectively. The alternative is not likely to be a return to greater institutional autonomy and clearly not to affluence but rather to a Darwinian fight in which few if any institutions will emerge stronger or to direct political intervention that could destroy institutional integrity altogether.

Bibliographical Essay

The general literature on state boards of higher education has increased markedly within the last decade. Glenny's *Autonomy of Public Colleges* (1959) was one of the first major studies of the development of state governing and coordinating boards. Berdahl's *Statewide Coordination of Higher Education* (1971) is still a classic in the field. In 1971, Glenny, Berdahl, Palola, and Paltridge developed a manual for coordinating boards that outlined responsibilities and approaches to carrying these out. Glenny and Daglish added to the literature in 1973. Two Carnegie Commission on Higher Education reports (1971 and 1973) concentrated in whole or in part on statewide coordination and governance issues. The Education Commission of the States established a Task Force on Coordination, Governance, and Structure of Postsecondary Education that issued its report in 1973. Millard (1976) analyzed types of boards and their functions. Also in 1976, the Carnegie Foundation for the Advancement of Teaching issued a report called *The States and Higher Education.* Another task force of the Education Commission of the States on state-level accountability in higher education issued *Accountability and Academe* in 1979. In addition, the commission annually publishes *State Postsecondary Education Profiles Handbook,* which includes current structures in the state, basic statistical information, state higher education publications, and studies underway. Although these do not constitute an exhaustive list, they are basic resource documents on state coordinating and governing boards or agencies, on their diversity, and on some of their problems.

A number of the publications cited also deal with statewide planning or some aspect of it. Halstead (1974) includes a detailed discussion of planning issues and methods. Halstead (1979) is a major annotated bibliography. Although it deals with higher education planning in general, a number of sections are relevant to statewide planning. Chronister (1978) is of special relevance to the involvement of independent institutions in planning. McGuinness (1979) is of particular value in assessing the scope of statewide planning both in terms of types of institutions and issues.

In the area of budgeting, the series of publications from the Center for Research and Development in Higher Education at the University of California, Berkeley, issued from 1975 through 1977 is highly valuable. This series includes Glenny, Bowen, Meisinger, Morgan, Purvis, and Schmidtlein (1975); Glenny (1976); Bowen and Glenny (1976); Bowen, Ruyle, and Glenny (1976); Meisinger (1976); and Schmidtlein and Glenny (1977). On how accountability relates to budgeting, Folger (1977) should be consulted. Finally, an excellent overview of budgeting issues and approaches with special reference to state systems is provided in Caruthers and Orwig (1979). By far the most definitive study of state-level program review to date is Barak and Berdahl (1978).

References

Barak, R., and Berdahl, R.O. *State Level Academic Program Review in Higher Education.* Denver, Colo.: Education Commission of the States, 1978.

Berdahl, R. *Statewide Coordination of Higher Education.* Washington, D.C.: American Council on Higher Education, 1971.

Bowen, F. M., and Glenny, L. A. *State Budgeting for Higher Education: State Fiscal Stringency and Public Higher Education.* Berkeley: Center for Research and Development in Higher Education, University of California, 1976.

Bowen, F. M., Ruyle, J. H., and Glenny, L. A. *State Budgeting for Higher Education: Budgeting Process in the 50 States.* Berkeley: Center for Research and Development in Higher Education, University of California, 1976.

Bureau of the Census. *Current Population Reports.* Series P-20, No. 324. Washington, D.C.: Government Printing Office, 1978.

Carnegie Commission on Higher Education. *The Capitol and the Campus.* New York: McGraw-Hill, 1971.

Carnegie Commission on Higher Education. *Governance of Higher Education: Six Priority Problems.* New York: McGraw-Hill, 1973.

Carnegie Foundation for the Advancement of Teaching. *The States and Higher Education: A Proud Past and a Vital Future.* San Francisco: Jossey-Bass, 1976.

Caruthers, J. K., and Orwig, M. *Budgeting in Higher Education.* ERIC/Higher Education Research Report No. 3. Washington, D.C.: American Association for Higher Education, 1979.

Chronister, J. L. *Independent Colleges and University Participation in Statewide Planning for Postsecondary Education.* Washington, D.C.: National Institute of Independent Colleges and Universities, 1978.

Education Commission of the States. *Coordination or Chaos?* Report of the Task Force on Coordination, Governance and Structure. Report No. 73. Denver, Colo.: Education Commission of the States, 1973.

Education Commission of the States. *Accountability and Academe.* Report of the National Task Force on the Accountability of Higher Education to the State. Report No. 126. Denver, Colo.: Education Commission of the States, 1979.

Folger, J. (Ed.). *New Directions for Institutional Research: Increasing the Public Accountability of Higher Education,* no. 16. San Francisco: Jossey-Bass, 1977.

Folger, J. "Coordination and Governance in an Era of Limits." Unpublished paper, 1979.

Glenny, L. A. *Autonomy of Public Colleges.* New York: McGraw-Hill, 1959.

Glenny, L. A. *State Budgeting for Higher Education: Interagency Conflict and Consensus.* Berkeley: Center for Research and Development in Higher Education, University of California, 1976.

Glenny, L. A., Berdahl, R. O., Palola, E. G., and Paltridge, J. G. *Coordinating Higher Education in the 1970s.* Berkeley: Center for Research and Development in Higher Education, University of California, 1971.

Glenny, L. A., Bowen, F. M., Meisinger, R. J., Morgan, A. W., Purvis, R. A., and Schmidtlein, F. A. *State Budgeting for Higher Education: Data Digest.* Berkeley: Center for Research and Development in Higher Education, University of California, 1975.

Glenny, L. A., and Daglish, T. K. *Public Universities, State Agencies, and the Law: Constitutional Autonomy in Decline.* Berkeley: Center for Research and Development in Higher Education, University of California, 1973.

Halstead, D. K. *Statewide Planning in Higher Education.* Washington, D.C.: U.S. Government Printing Office, 1974.

Halstead, D. K. (Ed.). *Higher Education Planning: A Bibliographic Handbook.* Washington, D.C.: U.S. Government Printing Office, 1979.

McGuinness, A. "State Federal Relations in Higher Education: State Postsecondary Commissions." Unpublished manuscript, 1979.

Meisinger, R. J. *State Budgeting for Higher Education: The Uses of Formulas.* Berkeley: Center for Research and Development in Higher Education, University of California, 1976.

Millard, R. *State Boards of Higher Education.* ERIC/Higher Education Research Report No. 4. Washington, D.C.: American Association for Higher Education, 1976.

Morgan, A. V. "Budgeting Approaches in the 80s." Paper delivered at Conference on the Financing of Postsecondary Education in the 80s, University of Arizona, Tucson; December 5, 1978.

Peterson, M. W., Erwin, M., and Wilson, R. "State-Level Performance Budgeting." In J. Folger (Ed.), *New Directions for Institutional Research: Increasing the Public Accountability of Higher Education,* no. 16. San Francisco: Jossey-Bass, 1977.

Schmidtlein, F. A., and Glenny, L. A. *State Budgeting for Higher Education: The Political Economy of the Process.* Berkeley: Center for Research and Development in Higher Education, University of California, 1977.

State Postsecondary Education Profiles Handbook. Denver, Colo.: Education Commission of the States, National Center for Higher Education Management Systems, State Higher Education Executive Officers, 1976, 1977, 1978.

6

Fred F. Harcleroad

Effects of Regional Agencies and Voluntary Associations

The diverse, pluralistic society of the United States depends on non-government associations to perform thousands of functions necessary for effective operation of social institutions. De Tocqueville recognized this fact in 1835; and as higher education has grown in the years since, the need for such associations has also grown. Colleges and universities, even more than other institutions, cannot rely totally on government to support their operation. The "taxing" and "spending" power of the federal government has resulted in great federal influence, and on an increasing basis, on almost every higher education institution. Current economic stresses and accountability demands are leading to increased federal and state involvement in all aspects of higher education decision making. De Tocqueville's (1946, p. 108) prophetic statement about the tendency toward government takeover emphasizes the need for other voluntary systems or associations: "It is easy to foresee that the time is drawing near when man will be less and less able to produce, by himself alone, the commonest necessaries of life. The task of the governing power will therefore perpetually increase, and its very efforts will extend it every day. The more it stands in the place of associations, the more will individuals, losing the notion of combining together, require its assistance: these are causes and effects that unceasingly create each other."

Voluntary associations and agencies grew in numbers as higher education developed more institutions and increased enrollments. This has been true since the end of the nineteenth century and continues today. An array of interinstitutional organizations, some totally voluntary and some quasi-governmental in nature, influence planning and analytical activities at the institutional level. Their current efforts to stress college and university self-regulation and self-control not only illustrate this influence but indicate their importance vis-à-vis state and federal agencies. This chapter describes four major types of these groups: regional agencies, voluntary consortia, institutional-based associations, and voluntary accrediting associations.

Regional Agencies

Regional interstate compacts have been established by a majority of states since World War II to meet postsecondary education needs that cross state lines. Originally, they concentrated on student exchange programs for the medical field, but their areas of service have now expanded to the point that their indirect effects on institutional planning and research can be very significant. In order of establishment, the three agencies created by these compacts are

- Southern Regional Education Board (1948)
  130 Sixth Street, N.W.
  Atlanta, Georgia 30313
- Western Interstate Commission for Higher Education (1951)
  P.O. Drawer P
  Boulder, Colorado 80302
- New England Board of Higher Education (1955)
  20 Walnut Street
  Wellesley, Massachusetts 02181

These three agencies cover thirty-three states, leaving out the Midwest, New York, Pennsylvania, and Delaware. In the Midwest, when a similar compact was considered, the Big Ten universities and the University of Chicago established their own Committee on Institutional Cooperation (CIC) in 1958. This eleven-institution consortium has a small staff but sponsors dozens of varied projects, including a traveling scholar program, polar studies, external degrees through correspondence, ocean sciences, and a center for historical cartography at the Newberry Library in Chicago. The CIC is an example of an effective consortium, but it does not provide the same type of services as the three interstate agencies. As a result, efforts are once again underway to establish an interstate compact in the Midwest. In 1978, the Minnesota and South Dakota legislatures were the first of fifteen proposed states to approve its establishment. In order to begin operations, six states must adopt the plan by 1981. If established, it will provide for interstate student exchanges at resident tuition rates, cooperative programs in vocational and higher education, and an areawide approach to gathering and reporting information needed for educational planning.

The Southern Regional Education Board (SREB) includes governors, legislators, and key figures from higher education and public life from fourteen states (Alabama, Arkansas, Florida, Georgia, Kentucky, Louisiana, Maryland, Mississippi, North Carolina, South Carolina, Tennessee, Texas, Virginia, and West Virginia). In its thirty years of operation, it has played a major part in the development of such important areas as equal opportunity for all students in higher education and expanded graduate and professional education. Its research and information program has been vital in state and institutional planning. Its regular legislative work conferences, planned by its legislative advisory council, have been very influential in setting policy and funding directions in the region. In 1977–1978, SREB's future directions and functions were set after lengthy study by a high-level task force. Five general functions were outlined: research and information services, forums for discussion and planning, administration of interstate arrangements (for example, student exchange programs), addressing special regional needs, and consultation activities. The report of the special task force stressed the board should provide relevant and helpful information and policy analysis by concentrating on its research, information, and consultation functions and keeping information about these trends before decision and policymakers. Recently, the National Institute of Mental Health provided $350,000 to study the impact of training programs on the distribution of mental health professionals in the South, and the U.S. Public Health Service provided $300,000 to assist in state and regional planning for allied health education. These two current grants indicate the importance of SREB's research efforts as they provide institutional research data and affect institutional planning in vital fields.

The Western Interstate Commission for Higher Education (WICHE) now has members from thirteen states—Alaska, Arizona, California, Colorado, Hawaii, Idaho, Montana, Nevada, New Mexico, Oregon, Utah, Washington, and Wyoming. It was planned originally to pool educational resources, to help the states plan jointly for the preparation of specialized skilled professionals, and to avoid, where feasible, duplication of expensive facilities. The student exchange program in medicine, dentistry, veterinary medicine, dental hygiene, nursing, mental health, and other specialized fields has been a major effort. WICHE regularly conducts regional conferences on critical topics, annual legislative workshops, and extensive research studies and publications. One of its developments, the program in higher education management and information systems, created so much demand for participation in the other thirty-seven states it became the National Center for Higher Education Management Systems. WICHEN, its special council for nursing education, has operated continuously since 1957 and has been a key research, consultation, and planning source for the development of nursing degree programs. In 1978, an extensive study of future needs for nurses and differing types of nursing services was completed. These findings are important for planning nursing programs in most of the western states.

Two current studies are of critical importance to institutional planners.

One study concerned optometry education (there are only three schools of optometry in the thirteen states) and projected shortages of optometrists in twelve of the states. WICHE has a two-year grant from the Carnegie Corporation of New York to study the expansion of regional cooperation in graduate and professional education. Its purpose is to encourage sharing of graduate resources by establishing an information system about such programs. Decision makers will be provided data designed for institutional and state planning based on a regional perspective. The two major planning issues to be addressed are whether western state graduate students have adequate access based on current interstate mobility and whether lower tuitions for out-of-state students can be justified by improved resource sharing of graduate facilities. With decreasing graduate enrollments and a need for programs to assure a reasonable flow of young doctorates into both academic service and newer expanded areas needing doctoral graduates, this latter study is an important one for institutional planners.

The New England Board of Higher Education (NEBHE) serves six states—Connecticut, Maine, Massachusetts, New Hampshire, Rhode Island, and Vermont. It administers such programs as the regional student exchange program, the New England Council on Higher Education for Nursing, a library information network, and an academic science information center. A major study was its analysis of need and recommended location of a school of veterinary medicine.

Clearly, regional interstate compacts provide critical research data for selected areas of institutional planning. In some cases, their findings directly affect the location of an academic program at a particular institution or the source and size of the student body for an existing program. Expansion or contraction of an expensive program is often a critical planning decision. In areas such as this, an external regional compact can greatly affect an individual college or university. Because regional compacts provide a unique blending of legislators, governors, officials of executive agencies, and key officials from institutions of higher education, these organizations will continue to fill a vital communication link in interstate planning.

Voluntary Consortia

Cooperative arrangements between higher education institutions in the United States have been carried on for many decades. The Claremont, California, and Atlanta, Georgia, university centers started in the 1920s and are outstanding among the early successful cooperative group arrangements of this type that grew into institutional federations. Since then, hundreds of institutions have developed informal and increasingly formal arrangements for interinstitutional cooperation. For example, the Washington Metropolitan Area Consortium of Universities (which includes American University, George Washington University, Georgetown University, the Catholic University of America, and Howard University) first started discussions in the 1930s. These discussions finally culminated in a formal set of articles of incorporation in 1966. During that same year, a U.S. Office of Education (USOE) national survey determined there were 1,017 consortia operating in the United States; and the evidence indicated a number of consortia were not reported. The federal study included a number of "statutory" consortia, such as the groups of institutions administered or coordinated by a state coordinating board or governing board. It included those cooperative groups with any interinstitutional plan, program, compact, or other arrangements formalized through correspondence or contrast "for the primary purpose of increasing the effectiveness or influence" of the institutions. This listing included all types of consortia, from simple, bilateral arrangements dealing with a single area of service to large, complex consortia performing many services and contributing in many areas of education (Moore, 1968, p. 4).

Shortly thereafter, the Kansas City Regional Council for Higher Education (KCRCHE) took the leadership in developing communication between consortia and established a plan for keeping records of available consortia. KCRCHE set aside staff time and some funds and founded the national consortium newsletter, *The Acquainter.* The staff chose five criteria to help identify the more substantive, general-purpose consortia to publish in an annual directory. To be included, a consortium had to be a voluntary formal organization, have three or more member institutions, have multiacademic programs, be administered by at least one full-time professional, and have a required annual contribution or other tangible membership support. The first directory, published in 1967, listed 31 consortia. The 1976–1977 directory listed 122 cooperative organizations or arrangements, with a total institutional membership of more than 1,250 institutions. The 1978 list shows a slight drop, to 114 academic consortia listed with two or more member institutions in each one.

In spite of this drop in overall numbers, these consortia represent a major development in American higher education and a significant factor in current institutional planning and development. In 1975–1976, the Council for Interinstitutional Leadership, which now publishes the *Acquainter,* moved to the University of Alabama and became associated with the Institute of Higher Education Research and Services there. The council has performed extensive studies between 1977 and 1980 relating to consortia and their cost savings and effectiveness in helping institutions deal with the current situation.

The big push for the development of consortia in the 1950s and 1960s was based on the need to maximize the use of resources to meet the challenge of increasing enrollments, expanding research efforts, and increasing demands on the higher education community for additional services. The demands of the 1970s and 1980s appear to be just the opposite. Demands for efficiency in plant, facilities, and faculty use again require interinstitutional arrangements in order to make optimum use of the available facilities. O'Dell (1979, p. 6) spelled out the meaning of the "tax revolt" for independent colleges and universities. He listed many possible consequences of the tax revolt for both state-supported colleges and universities and private independent institutions, emphasizing the continuing need for "more cooperation among various types of educational institutions, including independent institutions: shared use of facilities and joint programs."

Areas of Consortium Activity. The importance of voluntary consortia to institutional planning and research becomes evident with the enumeration of their varied activities. An Academy of Educational Development study of twenty-nine consortia (Schwenkmeyer and Goodman, 1972) divides their activities into seven major areas: administrative and business services, enrollment and admissions, academic programs, libraries, student services, faculty, and community services. In each of these areas, they found significant and extensive cooperative efforts that had been carried on by many institutions in several consortia. Because data on these seven research areas provide the basis for most institutional planning, existing consortia arrangements or possible future consortia should be an important factor to consider. In some cases, also, the consortium provides the actual data base for determining trends and potential avenues of effort. Because consortia agreements are both formal and informal, an institution first needs records of each consortium in which it is involved and second needs an evaluation of the value of each one in meeting institutional objectives.

In its 1972 study, the Academy for Educational Development (AED) found numerous geographically widespread examples of cooperative efforts at planning and implementing programs in all seven of the categories. The current list of consortia is three times as great as the AED survey list, and the numbers of involved public and private institutions is over twelve hundred. Consortia have become critically important factors in many institutional plans, and they conduct a great deal of the related institutional research. In addition to providing economic advantages, consortia also perform the following functions (Tollefson, 1977, p. 5):

1. provide new and improved educational program opportunities through the better use of existing faculty, facilities, and services
   a. for new and existing clients
   b. through coordinated, shared, or joined curricular or service programs
2. strengthen self-reliance through freely given allegiance; encourage grass-roots self-direction; facilitate interreliance among faculty and staff
3. advance sense of community which is active and integrated among institutions which share a common purpose and people to be served
4. improve quality and visibility of institutional programs and services
5. draw useful institutional comparisons and contrasts regarding:
   a. curricular offerings
   b. faculty specialties
   c. instructional support services
   d. facilities
   e. student services
   f. administrative services
6. challenge institutional insularity and minimize its effects
7. enhance cultural life of the area or region in educational service

Voluntary consortia have proven to be an ideal planning vehicle for joint programing of public and private colleges and universities or private colleges acting alone. In fact, a recent restudy of McGrath's fifty private college sample (Lepchenske and Harcleroad, 1978, p. 17) found "Interinstitutional cooperative arrangements served as a method of providing new educational programs and as a method of retaining old programs for the least expense. Cooperative efforts were found to provide expanded capabilities while requiring a minimum of resources in faculty, facilities, and money. Cooperation was a management method which provided opportunities for students to participate in high cost programs through the use of shared resources."

Financial Benefits of Consortia. Advocates of consortia activity normally stress the educational advantages that accrue from their programs. However, financial saving is often obtained, and this aspect undoubtedly will become more important. In some cases, existing programs have been able to continue without cutbacks, due to economies based on consortium arrangements. In others, actual saving accrues, and it can be used to meet growth costs in other areas. A few examples from issues of the *Acquainter* illustrate the fiscal and planning importance of consortia.

> The Union of Independent Colleges of Art (nine institutions in the Kansas City area) made a preliminary study of the cost effectiveness in their joint admissions program alone. Direct cash benefits to each institution were found to be more than $62,986 each with each college paying fees of only $8,256 per college.
>
> The Hudson-Mohawk Association of Colleges and Universities (with fifteen members) shared information on fuel oil prices. Three of the members in 1972 reported reduced costs by $20,000 in one year by using this data in their bargaining with suppliers. In February 1978, they reported savings of over $50,000 during the summer of 1977 on fuel oil, paper, and other office supplies.
>
> The Worcester Consortium combined their oil purchases and the single supplier cut 10 percent to get the entire bid. The consortium members (including both public and private, two-year and four-year institutions) saved $30,000 by joint purchasing in a two-and-a-half-year period, much of it from the oil contract.
>
> The Associated Colleges of Central Kansas operate a computer center jointly. Separately, they estimate each institution's cost would be $100,000. Together, members can operate effectively for $20,000 each.
>
> The Council of West Suburban Colleges (four colleges near Lisle, Illinois) consolidated their employee benefit insurance and saved $46,333 from February 1 to July 31, 1977. The Associated Colleges of the Midwest estimate a regular annual saving of 10 percent through cooperative purchase of insurance.
>
> The Washington Metropolitan Area Consortium of Universities in 1978 combined their purchases of liquid helium and liquid nitrogen through the physics department of Georgetown University and reported saving $500,000 from their total research budgets for that period.

Effects of Federal Legislation. Several pieces of federal legislation mention cooperative arrangements. The most critical is the Higher Education Act of 1965, which includes Title III, "Strengthening Developing Institutions," to encourage cooperation among—and thereby raise the academic quality of— "colleges which have the desire and potential to make a substantial contribution to the higher education resources of the Nation but which for financial and other reasons are struggling for survival and are isolated from the main currents of academic life."

Many consortia have been developed as a result of this act, and their impact has gone beyond Title III. A prime example is the ACCTion Consortium. Funded since 1975, this multipurpose "technical assistance organization" by 1978 included 114 private and public community, junior, and technical colleges in thirty-nine states. Member colleges participate for three-year periods in one of four college service areas: community service, instructional services, resource development, or student development services. Four of the colleges receive the grants from USOE and coordinate interinstitutional-type assistance between the various institutions.

Most of these efforts include institutional planning in one of the four areas. In the community service area, for example, it includes community needs assessment. In instructional services, it includes such items as curriculum development, evaluation techniques, and assessing teacher effectiveness. In resource development, it includes the identifying of resource needs (funds and facilities), the analysis of eleven varied sources of funds, and methods of working with them. In student services, emphasis on seventeen functional areas includes planning of student recruitment and admissions, student retention, and follow-up studies. With twenty-five to thirty-five colleges in each of the four areas, this consortium provides an example of the advantages of a large, nationwide consortium making good use of institutional planning and institutional research.

Current Developments and Trends. Liberal arts colleges led the way for several decades in establishing consortia, and Patterson (1975, p. 1) found in 1970 that approximately 75 percent of member colleges were private, nonprofit institutions. By 1975, 40 percent were public. Federal and state support of cooperative ventures of this type increased consortia in numbers and membership. I have discussed the federal impact through Title III, but some states have made significant changes in this area. The Virginia legislature divided the state into six regions for continuing education; and six corresponding consortia were established, funded, and managed by the institutions in each region. The Illinois legislature passed the Higher Education Cooperative Act of 1972, which provided some state support for voluntary combinations of private and public institutions, including some from out of state, which applied for funds on a competitive basis. The Quad-Cities Graduate Center in Rock Island, Illinois, administered by Augustana College, combines the offerings of ten public and private colleges and universities in Iowa and Illinois to provide graduate degree programs to several thousand graduate students. Funding is provided by both states and the result is a major, free-standing graduate school drawing strength from its ten members. Several other states, such as California, Connecticut, Massachusetts, Minnesota, Ohio, Pennsylvania, and Texas, have used the consortium approach for specific, sometimes limited purposes. This trend toward public financing of consortia thus becomes a key factor to consider in future institutional planning.

In the past, consortia have been developed to provide for interinstitutional needs in times of growth and in times of decline. They are uniquely capable of handling mutual problems of public and private institutions and thus provide a powerful deterrent to further governmental incursions into private and sometimes public institutional operation. McKeefery (1978) indicates the extent of such public and private efforts at working together in interinstitutional cooperation. He found three groups or types: the small informal partnership; the regional/urban grouping; and other special-purpose groupings, including multistate groups, international associations, and institutions serving military installations. McKeefery (p. 4) found "the total number of institutions involved in cooperative arrangements is 775, almost equally divided between private and public. Assuming a current count of 2,700 postsecondary institutions in the United States (and a part of Canada), this means about one-fourth (28.7 percent) of them claim substantial private-public cooperative programs. Two or even three times this number could participate before saturation, but this is unlikely. One reason is that public-private groups are outnumbered by like-kind groups which have strong ties through religious affiliation, similar clientele and programs, or professional emphasis." Thus, at various levels of formality, significant numbers of institutions of all types are currently using consortia to adjust to changing curricular and funding necessities. Although governmental controls continue to increase and to affect institutional planning, voluntary consortia provide another way to plan independently for future operations and program development.

Institutional-Based Associations

Colleges and universities combine in a variety of institutional-based national organizations, often for lobbying purposes. Some of them become very important for their aid in institutional research and its effects on institutional planning. A major example is the American Council on Education, which actually serves as an umbrella-type organization for higher education. Other major national organizations of institutions with great legislative and informational significance are the Association of American Colleges, Association of American Universities, American Association of Community and Junior Colleges, American Association of State Colleges and Universities, National Association of Independent Colleges and Universities, National Association of State Universities and Land-Grant Colleges, and numerous associations representing special types of institutions. Another category of national membership associations with important institutional research overtones includes such groups as the American College Testing Program and the College Entrance Examination Board, whose service bureau, the Educational Testing Service, is not itself a membership organization.

In addition, there are many specialized associations with an institutional membership base, representing different administrative functions, such as graduate schools, registrars, business offices, religious affiliations, and academic fields. Each of these affects institutional planning in some way because each directly affects programs. For example, the National Association of College and University Business Officers (NACUBO) had a key role in establishing the agreement for royalty payments for use of copyrighted music by college and university personnel. Knowledgeable institutional officials followed these negotiations very carefully because they had a direct effect on college budgets the next year. And the American Association of State Colleges and Universities (AASCU) has many programs that affect institutional planning at its two hundred fifty member institutions. Its Resource Center for Planned Change may be the most pertinent, encouraging institutions to work together on planning, program evaluation, and innovative programs for new clienteles.

The American Council on Education (ACE) (Suite 800, One Dupont Circle, Washington, D.C. 20036) includes approximately fifteen hundred institutions and associations as members. It studies crucial issues in higher education, develops major reports, conducts conferences, and serves as a central coordinating association for the development of major policy statements. Through its office of educational credit, it provides such national guidebooks as the *Guide to the Evaluation of Educational Experience in the Armed Forces* (published periodically since 1945) and *The National Guide to Credit Recommendations for Non-Collegiate Courses*. These guidebooks provide standard materials to use in institutional decisions on credit toward degrees. By determining allowable academic transfer credit, they directly affect the total credit hours students take at an institution for its degree. Through its policy analysis service and its economics and finance unit, it prepares and distributes key back-up research, which many institutions need for local planning.

The Council for the Advancement of Small Colleges (CASC) (Suite 320, One Dupont Circle, Washington, D.C. 20036) over the past quarter century has had a striking effect on management and operations of literally hundreds of small, independent colleges. Many of these colleges had very limited or no institutional research or planning before joining the council. Some actually had no budgets and only limited accounting records. CASC has developed a number of valuable planning tools plus seminars, conferences, and a consultation service to assist in using them. Its *Handbook for College Administration* reviews and analyzes different management functions, amplified by specific practical case studies, exercises, and helpful illustrations.

The most important CASC activity in the area of institutional research and institutional planning is its comprehensive planning and data system (PDS), developed to improve comprehensive information systems and planning activities in small, private, independent colleges. The system includes nine "hard" data modules (student recruitment, financial aid, student attrition, instructional program analysis, faculty activity, library costs and services, personnel and compensation, fund raising, and college goals and climate) and two "soft" data modules (a marketing approach to program development and student learning outcomes). First, manuals for each module describe each module, its purpose and how the data for each one can best be used. Second, for the first nine modules, there are data collection instruments, data element definitions designed for small colleges, access to a central computer processing center, and a display reporting system to compare one college's data with another's. Third, consultation services are available at relatively modest cost. Finally, any college can contract with CASC for a comprehensive and continuing planning and data system service involving institutional diagnosis, design scheduling, implementation, use, support, and evaluation. Probably no other membership association offers such a complete institutional research and planning system.

The American College Testing Program (ACT) (P.O. Box 168, Iowa City, Iowa 52240) has over twenty-six hundred postsecondary institutions as members and provides a number of valuable research services, mostly critical to the student part of a total data system. In medical and dental education, its reports on students and curricular practices provide basic information for planning by individual schools. The experimental College Outcomes Measures Project currently is providing key data for institutional self-study and future planning by approximately fifty institutions. In South Carolina, the ACT Career Planning Program provides data for a statewide guidance program for the postsecondary technical institutions and later follow-up of student success. The ACT Student Need Analysis Service, in which over thirty-two hundred institutions participate, provides each one with special group statistical data about its applicants. These data on a significant portion of many student bodies indicate trends and help institutions in managing and planning programs.

The most important ACT service for institutional research and planning, however, is the ACT Assessment Program and its follow-up research services. Data are available for close to one million students a year, and each institution receives complete background data for guidance and counseling of each individual student. Three follow-up research services—the Class Profile Service, the Basic Research Service, and the Standard Research Service—provide group data and analyses of each institution's freshman class at no cost. The Class Profile Service describes the entering freshman class as well as those students who sent their scores to the college but did not enroll there. The Basic Research Service analyzes ACT data, standard scores, and high school averages in relation to first-term overall college grades and develops prediction equations for forecasting the performance of prospective students. And the Standard Research Service describes the academic abilities and achievements of the current freshman class and develops prediction equations used in forecasting the performance of future students. (For more information, see ACT, 1979.)

Clearly, institution-based associations such as ACE, CASC, and ACT contribute in many ways and in differing degrees to the data and planning needs of their member institutions. As the accountability demands on institutions grow, all possible sources of help will be put to work; and future trends undoubtedly will be toward increased utilization of such associations.

Voluntary Accrediting Associations

Voluntary accrediting agencies developed originally as private membership associations of secondary schools and colleges to establish uniform college entrance requirements. The six regional institutional accreditation agencies grew from these early associations approximately as follows: (1) New England Association, formed in 1885, accrediting standards for colleges in 1954; (2) Middle States Association, formed in 1887, accrediting standards for colleges in 1921; (3) North Central Association, formed in 1895, accrediting standards for colleges in 1910 (first list of accredited colleges in 1913); (4) Southern Association, formed in 1895, accrediting standards for colleges in 1919; (5) Northwest Association, formed in 1917, accrediting standards for colleges in 1921; and (6) Western Association, formed 1924, accrediting standards for colleges in 1949 (Orlans and others, 1975, p. 9).

Specialized, programmatic accreditation began in the same period, and the Council on Medical Education of the American Medical Association issued its first list of classified medical schools in 1907. Law followed soon after. "By the end of the 1920s, accreditation was initiated in such specialized fields as landscape architecture, library science, music, nursing, optometry, teacher education, and collegiate business education. There followed in the 1930s similar activity in chemistry, dentistry, engineering, forestry, pharmacy, social work, theology, and veterinary medicine. Today, more than fifty fields in postsecondary education are subject to specialized accreditation conducted through the direct or indirect involvement of several times that many national organizations and thousands of individuals" (Selden and Porter, 1977, p. 2).

In addition to regional institutional and specialized programmatic associations, there are a number of national institutional accrediting agencies, such as the American Association of Bible Colleges, the Association of Independent Colleges and Schools, the National Association of Trade and Technical Schools, the National Home Study Council, and the Association of Theological Schools in the United States and Canada. These all continue to be membership associations, requiring institutions be accredited in order to retain membership. For those wishing to continue as accredited members, for whatever reason, there are a number of factors that affect institutional research and aspects of institutional planning.

The major reasons for such concern are the dramatic changes in the purposes and uses of accreditation during recent decades. The Council on Postsecondary Accreditation (COPA) defines accreditation as "a self-improvement self-regulating process. It includes an in-depth self-analysis by an institution or program to evaluate its compliance with mutually agreed-to criteria, followed by an on-site examination by third-party peers to verify whether the institution or program has perceived itself correctly. The granting of accreditation status signifies that an institution or program meets or exceeds a level of educational quality believed to be necessary for that particular institution or program to achieve its stated purposes and, thereby, meet its responsibility to all its publics" (Council on Postsecondary Accreditation, 1976, p. 1).

The Council on Postsecondary Accreditation (1976, pp. 3–4) lists six goals for accreditation. These goals define what accrediting agencies think accreditation is and clearly affect institutional data systems and planning:

1. foster educational excellence by developing criteria and guidelines for assessing educational effectiveness
2. encourage improvement through continuous self-study and planning
3. provide assurance of clearly defined and appropriate objectives and conditions under which they can be achieved
4. provide counsel and aid to established and developing programs and institutions
5. encourage educational diversity
6. protect institutions' educational effectiveness and academic freedom.

The entrance of the federal government into the funding of higher education on a massive basis since World War II has drastically changed the overall uses of accreditation. Reported abuses of the Servicemen's Readjustment Act of 1944 (GI Bill) led to a series of congressional hearings, which led in turn to major additions related to accreditation in Public Law 550, the Veterans Readjustment Act of 1952. Section 253 of that law empowered the commissioner of education to publish a list of accrediting agencies and associations that would be relied upon to assess the quality of training offered by educational institutions. State approving agencies may then "utilize the accreditation of such accrediting associations or agencies for the approval of the courses specifically accredited."

Extensive legal arguments about the resulting powers of the USOE still continue (see Orlans and others, 1975). The important resulting factor for institutional planning is not the arguments but the greater institutional dependence of "eligibility" for funding based on membership in a now much less voluntary accrediting association. Although the courts normally have ruled that accreditation by accrediting agencies is not quasi-governmental action there has grown up an important new concept called the "triad." The triad also has importance for institutional planning because it involves delicate relationships between the federal government and eligibility, the state government and its responsibilities for establishing or chartering institutions and credentialing through certification or licensure (Selden, 1972b, pp. 14–15), and voluntary membership associations that require accreditation for membership.

The most important and current effect of these changes on institutional research and planning is the increased emphasis by the accrediting associations on thorough, institutionwide, carefully documented self-studies coupled with more frequent site visits. Expanded data systems are needed with time series data showing trends in the major self-study subareas, such as student characteristics, faculty experience, teaching loads, program availability, facilities use, graduate placement, funding sources, and expenditures. Eventually, this could lead to more frequent reporting and to educational auditing (Harcleroad, 1976, pp. 18–25).

Another important development is the expansion of specialized accrediting associations. New specialized academic disciplines constantly emerge and soon develop minimum standards, licensure activities, and a new membership association to accredit programs. This is particularly true in the health care field (Selden, 1972a, pp. E-19–E-21) but extends to other fields also. Fieldwork and clinical practice facilities in particular often depend on having an approved (accredited) program. Without these facilities, the program cannot be offered and the institution cannot secure them otherwise. Some prime examples are fieldwork in physical therapy, social work, community health nutrition, music therapy, and occupational therapy. One specific illustration is the need for accredited status expressed by President Noah Langdale of Georgia State University to the Georgia Board of Regents when it changed its B.S. degree concentration in social welfare to the bachelor of social work in January 1979 in order to have its program accredited by the Council on Social Work Education. Institutional program planning in specialized programmatic areas must consider accreditation—and this is a regular consideration in many institutions.

A final critical dimension of accreditation and planning grows from the trend toward the involvement of legislatures and state higher education agencies in accreditation (Pailthorp, 1976, p. 43). Membership is not involved. This type of accreditation is carried on by state regulatory agencies either separately or in cooperation with regional associations. In 1979, nineteen of the state higher education agencies carried on some form of related accrediting activity based primarily on specific legal powers and in a few cases on general powers (Birch, 1979, pp. 127–133). For example, the Oklahoma Regents for Higher Education accredited all new institutions or those desiring initial accreditation. For continuing accreditation, institutional membership in the North Central Association was acceptable. In Maryland, the state board of higher education in 1979 worked out an agreement with the Middle States Association that is just one part of the state board's program of continuing, regular evaluation of institutions and their attainment of the standards of excellence adopted by their board. This last state agency program may be a prototype for future development in this area. If so, it will have a fundamental effect on future institutional data systems, research, and planning.

Conclusion

The four quasi-governmental and voluntary systems described in this chapter are critical to social progress and, as a result of cooperation, valuable to institutional planners and institutional researchers. The voluntary associations and the combined compacts, agencies, and informal organizations continue the important historical tradition of "associations" and the democratic system of group development to take care of individual needs. Increasingly, they are "in the middle" between institutions that do the actual work of education and governmental agencies with increasingly larger roles. The huge sums of money from both the federal and state levels portend even greater movement toward bureaucratic controls of institutions, even to the operational level. Difficult and uneasy though their financing may be, these differing independent systems and associations have an important part to play in future planning in institutions of higher education in the United States.

Bibliographical Essay

Bibliographical materials related to the four "other" systems discussed in this chapter come from four almost totally separate groups of material. References related to the first area, regional agencies or compacts, basically come from the agencies themselves. A major source of information about the compacts is, in each case, the agency's annual report. Each agency also has one or two regular newsletters, and a review of recent issues is the best source of information about their efforts. Persons interested in the work of these agencies normally can obtain these reports and newsletters without charge from the following addresses: New England Board of Higher Education, 20 Walnut Street, Wellesley, Massachusetts 02181; Southern Regional Education Board, 130 Sixth Street, N.W., Atlanta, Georgia 30313; The Western Interstate Commission for Higher Education, P.O. Drawer P, Boulder, Colorado 80302.

Voluntary consortia have been the subject of fairly serious study during the past quarter century. In 1968, the United States Office of Education conducted a definitive national survey of voluntary consortia (Moore, 1968). Two other studies are also of special interest in connection with liberal arts colleges and their use of consortia: Trendler (1967) and Lepchenske and Harcleroad (1978). Fritz H. Grupe has written extensively on consortia, and a good example is *Interinstitutional Cooperation at the Departmental Level*. The most critical and important researcher in this area during the past decade has been Lewis D. Patterson, currently executive director of the Council for Interinstitutional Leadership, associated with the Institute of Higher Education Research and Services at the University of Alabama, P.O. Box 6293, University, Alabama 35486. He has published a number of directories, edited *The Acquainter*, and written many articles and descriptive materials related to the current activities of the various types of consortia. Individual reports from the consortia also provide insight into their many activities; and a key reference is the annual "Fact File" of the *Chronicle of Higher Education*, which lists the names and mailing addresses of voluntary academic consortia in the United States.

Institution-based associations are so numerous that no single listing is available, and good basic reference materials related to the overall area are limited. Two key sources of information regarding such agencies are the section on higher education associations in the *Education Directory, Colleges and Universities,* published annually by the National Center of Education Statistics. This includes many professional associations plus those associations that carry on accreditation activities. Many of the major professional associations are housed on One Dupont Circle at the National Center for Higher Education and Affiliated Associations. The annual *Higher Education Directory* of these organizations, published by the American Council on Education, provides name, address, and descriptive materials about this group of forty to fifty of the key organizations.

The literature on voluntary accrediting associations has recently become voluminous. A highly selective listing includes the following materials. Three important historical documents are Kelly, Frazier, McNeely, and Ratcliffe (1940); Blauch (1959); and Selden (1960). Two useful monographs published by the ERIC Clearinghouse on Higher Education are Harcleroad and Dickey (1975) and Trivett (1976), both available from the American Association for Higher Education, One Dupont Circle, N.W., Suite 780, Washington, D.C. 20036. Selden (1972a, b) completed an important analysis on accreditation in the health sciences. The two major lists of accrediting associations are published by the Council on Postsecondary Accreditation and the Department of Eligibility and Agency Evaluation of the U.S. Office of Education. The COPA list is found in its publication, *The Balance Wheel for Accreditation,* July 1978, One Dupont Circle, N.W., Suite 760, Washington, D.C. 20036 and the DEAE publication, *Nationally Recognized Accrediting Agencies and Associations,* March 1977, the U.S. Office of Education, Washington, D.C. 20036. These latter two publications are updated regularly. Harold Orlans has conducted two major studies of accreditation. The first is by Orlans and others (1975), and the second, emphasizing accreditation and Veterans Administration activity, will be completed and published in 1980. A number of dissertations have dealt with accreditation activity. Two recent ones with considerable influence are Miller (1973) and Birch (1979). The *Journal of Higher Education,* Vol. 50, No. 2, March/April 1979, is devoted entirely to accreditation and current critical problems related to it. Ten articles and one special review essay discuss the current pressures on accreditation, federal relationships, legal decisions, and problems with nontraditional education. Finally, the Council on Postsecondary Accreditation has developed a series of brief monographs on many aspects of accreditation. Examples include Fisk and Duryea (1977), Harcleroad (1976), and Finkin (1978). This selective bibliography will provide initial entry into the extensive accreditation literature.

Although all of the "other agencies" discussed in this chapter have some similarities, their differences are significant. The varied literature of each type is important for institutional planning staffs to know and take into account in overall institutional planning efforts.

References

American College Testing Program. *Using ACT on Campus.* Iowa City, Iowa: American College Testing Program, 1979.
Birch, G. "State Higher Education Agency Responsibility for the Evaluation and

Accreditation of Public Four-Year Institutions of Higher Education." Unpublished doctoral dissertation, Center for the Study of Higher Education, University of Arizona, 1979.

Blauch, L. E. (Ed.). *Accreditation in Higher Education.* Washington, D.C.: U.S. Department of Health, Education, and Welfare, 1959.

Council on Postsecondary Accreditation. *COPA, The Balance Wheel for Accreditation.* Washington, D.C.: Council on Postsecondary Accreditation, 1976.

de Tocqueville, A. *Democracy in America.* Vol. 1. New York: Knopf, 1946.

Finkin, M. W. *Federal Reliance on Educational Accreditation.* Washington, D.C.: Council on Postsecondary Accreditation, U.S. Office of Education, 1978.

Fisk, R. S., and Duryea, E. D. *Academic Collective Bargaining and Regional Accreditation.* Washington, D.C.: Council on Postsecondary Accreditation, 1977.

Grupe, F. H. *Interinstitutional Cooperation at the Departmental Level.* Potsdam: State University of New York, 1972.

Harcleroad, F. F. *Educational Auditing and Accountability.* Washington, D.C.: Council on Postsecondary Accreditation, 1976.

Harcleroad, F. F., and Dickey, F. G. *Educational Auditing and Voluntary Institutional Accrediting.* Washington, D.C.: ERIC Clearinghouse on Higher Education, 1975.

Kelly, F. J., Frazier, B. W., McNeely, J. H., and Ratcliffe, E. B. *College Accreditation by Agencies Within States.* Washington, D.C.: U.S. Office of Education, 1940.

Lepchenske, G. L., and Harcleroad, F. F. "Are Liberal Arts Colleges Professional Schools, A Restudy." Topical Paper No. 11. Tucson: Center for the Study of Higher Education, University of Arizona, 1978.

McKeefery, W. J. *Cooperative Arrangements Between Private and Public Colleges.* Washington, D.C.: American Association of State Colleges and Universities, 1978.

Miller, J. W. "Organizational Structure of Nongovernmental Postsecondary Accreditation: Relationship to Uses of Accreditation." Doctoral dissertation, Catholic University of America, 1973.

Moore, R. S. *Consortiums in American Higher Education: 1965–66.* Washington, D.C.: U.S. Government Printing Office, 1968.

O'Dell, M. "The Tax Revolt: What It Means to Independent Colleges and Universities." *CASC Newsletter, Supplements,* 1978–1979, p. 6.

Orlans, H., and others. *Private Accreditation and Public Eligibility.* Lexington, Mass.: Heath, 1975.

Pailthorp, K. *Regional Accreditation.* Olympia: Council for Postsecondary Education, State of Washington, 1976.

Patterson, L. D. "Evolving Patterns of Cooperation." *ERIC Higher Education Research Currents,* 1975.

Schwenkmeyer, B., and Goodman, M. E. *Putting Cooperation to Work.* Washington, D.C.: Academy for Educational Development, 1972.

Selden, W. K. *Accreditation.* New York: Harper & Row, 1960.

Selden, W. K. *Study of Accreditation of Selected Health Educational Programs.* Part 1: *Working Paper.* Washington, D.C.: National Commission on Accrediting, 1972a.

Selden, W. K. *Study of Accreditation of Selected Health Educational Programs.* Part 2: *Committee Report.* Washington, D.C.: National Commission on Accrediting, 1972b.

Selden, W. K., and Porter, H. V. *Accreditation: Its Purposes and Uses.* Washington, D.C.: Council on Postsecondary Education, 1977.

Tollefson, G. "The Case for Consortia Among American Colleges and Universities." In *The Acquainter.* University: Council for Interinstitutional Leadership, University of Alabama, May 1977.

Trendler, C. A. "Interinstitutional Cooperation for Academic Development Among Small Church Related Liberal Arts Colleges." Unpublished doctoral dissertation, Indiana University, 1967.

Trivett, D. *Accreditation and Institutional Eligibility.* Washington, D.C.: American Association for Higher Education, 1976.

7

Marvin W. Peterson

Analyzing Alternative Approaches to Planning

Because conceptual and pragmatic confusion often inhibits successful institutional planning, this chapter offers a conceptual framework for viewing institutional planning and research, identifies the major organizational issues in designing an integrated planning function, and provides a context for the remaining chapters in this book. Five basic questions guide its organization:

1. What is planning and what are the major concepts that describe it?
2. What are the major theoretical models of or approaches to planning and how do they differ?
3. What is strategic planning and what are its major elements? How do environmental factors and external relationships affect planning?

Note: This chapter was prepared under a grant from the Carnegie Corporation of New York to the University of Michigan.

4. What is tactical planning and its major elements? How are they related to strategic planning and to each other?
5. What are the major institutional issues in developing an institutional planning function?

The authors of other chapters of this book deal implicitly and explicitly with the first two questions, but I present a broad institutional definition and array of theoretical models of planning that encompass the varied perspectives of all the authors of this book. My discussion of strategic planning relating the institution to its environment grows from the chapters in Part One dealing with the implications of major environmental changes and external organizations for institutional planning and research and sets the stage for the other chapters in Part Two, which detail the major elements of strategic planning. My analysis of tactical or intrainstitutional planning serves as a preface to the chapters in Part Three on academic planning and institutional research, in Part Four on allocating resources, and in Part Five on evaluation and assessment. And my description of major organizational issues lays the groundwork for those Part Six and Seven chapters that examine patterns of institutional planning and research in different types of institutions, the process of developing planning and research, and their linkage to governance, leadership, and information systems.

Definition of Planning

Planning can be viewed as emanating from different levels of social behavior: individual (Michael, 1973), organizational (Drucker, 1969), or societal (Etzioni, 1968). At the organizational level, it can be viewed as a separate, analytically oriented institutional function (Ackoff, 1970), as an integral part of the decision-making and control function (Anthony, 1965), or as a more politically oriented policymaking function (Bauer and Gergen, 1968). To analyze and improve college and university planning, a broad institutional perspective is useful. From this perspective, planning can be defined as a conscious process by which an institution assesses its current state and the likely future condition of its environment, identifies possible future states for itself, and then develops organizational strategies, policies, and procedures for selecting and getting to one or more of them. This definition views planning as a key organizational process that may or may not be developed as part of the larger institutional management function; and it assumes (1) that the institution and its members are concerned about future as well as current states of the institution and the means for getting to them, (2) that they choose to develop a conscious planning process to reach these states rather than rely on the whims of key individuals or sporadic responses to unpredictable external events, and (3) that some attempt to assess institutional strengths and weaknesses and to examine the environment for constraints and opportunities can lead to changes that are beneficial to the institution's vitality. This definition says little about how this planning process is conceived, how it can be organized, what subprocesses it includes, and how planning relates to other institutional processes, functions, and structures. However, its focus on planning as *process* emphasizes a dynamic view of planning in contrast to a static view.

Static and Dynamic Views of Planning. A static view of planning is illustrated by the development of a "plan" rather than a "planning process." New institutions that begin with a master plan and other institutions that develop a master plan or complete a self-study by adopting specific recommendations for future directions are engaged in static planning: creating a plan or a sense of future direction. Such occasional or periodic plans may be useful during uneventful times, but recent experience suggests their inadequacy as demands on and conditions affecting institutions change rapidly. The failure of a master plan predicated on false assumptions about clientele is reflected in the Riesman, Gusfield, and Gamson (1970) study of Oakland University; and Ladd's 1970 report on self-studies for the Carnegie Commission describes the weaknesses of periodic self-study in major universities when such study is not linked to ongoing institutional planning or governance processes. Examples of institutional master plans produced for varied reasons and then left to repose on library shelves are numerous. If reassessed and updated regularly, such plans could be an integral part of their institution's planning process. But most experts now agree that development of an effective continuing planning process through a dynamic view of planning is as crucial as creating a master plan.

The development of a planning process does not, of course, preclude varying the regularity or continuity of planning. Ad hoc, intermittent, or continuous planning may all be part of the process. Ad hoc and often short-term planning is frequently necessary when unanticipated events occur, such as an unforeseen drop in resources or the opportunity to acquire or merge with a nearby campus. And some planning activities, such as updating master plans, can often be done most realistically on a periodic basis rather than by expecting the possibility of continuous planning. The balance of ad hoc, intermittent, and continuous planning for different planning activities is a crucial issue in the development of a planning process and needs to be anticipated by those charged with responsibility for it.

Planning as Process, Structure, and Technology. Defining planning as an organizational process does not imply that the formal structure or technology of that process is unimportant; but colleges and universities often introduce formal structures for planning, such as a new office or a prestigious committee, or adopt new techniques, such as resource simulations, Delphi surveys, forecasting, and needs assessments, on the assumption that these themselves are planning. As with the adoption of a static plan, however, formal structures and techniques do not assure that institutional purposes are reviewed or changed or that means of achieving them are adopted. A focus on planning as process reflects the fact that colleges and universities, as human service organizations with labor intensive functions, need to place their primary emphasis on the pattern of activities and relationships among individuals involved in planning. Structures and techniques do make important contributions to planning, but they need to be recognized as parts of the process rather than preeminent or independent of the process. It is useful to think of institutional planning as consisting of three interrelated parts, as depicted in Figure 1.

An institution's *planning process* may be viewed as made up of seven elements arrayed in two broad categories: (1) strategic elements, such as environmental scanning, institutional assessment, values assessment, and master plan-

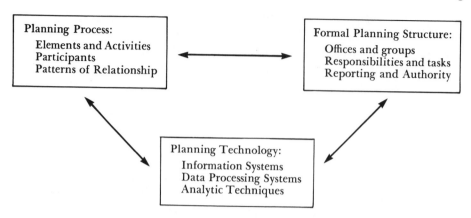

Figure 1. Parts of the Planning Process

ning, which focus on the broadest issues of institutional policy and direction; and (2) tactical elements, such as program planning, priority setting, resource allocation, and program review, which focus on policy implementation—each of the seven elements of course, include a wide array of activities which are described by the participants in the planning process and the patterns of relationship among and between these participants and their activities. The *formal planning structure* involves the organizationally defined offices or positions and groups, their responsibilities and tasks, and their reporting and authority patterns as they participate in the process. And *planning technology* refers to the information systems (institutional and noninstitutional data bases), the data-processing systems (manual and semiautomated as well as computer hardware and software), and the analysis and research techniques that serve the planning function. In practice, the distinction between process, structure, and technique often becomes blurred, yet emphasizing each can lead to very different conceptions of planning. (For example, a formal structure may exist with an unclear process or inadequate techniques.)

   Merely defining planning as a dynamic institutional process which includes formal planning structures and techniques that are easily described does not provide an adequate basis for analyzing or designing one. Additional concepts or variables which can be used to understand the planning process can be organized into three broad categories: those that describe the domain, some process characteristics, and the organizational pattern of planning. The domain and process concepts also serve as a basis for comparing six models of planning to be discussed later. These concepts capture, in large part, the institution's rationale for its planning process. Failure to recognize the distinctions these concepts imply often leads to conflicts among and between planners, administrators, and faculty who do not agree on how to approach the planning process or what it should accomplish.

Domain Concepts of Planning Process

   The Content of Planning. Conceptually there are three dimensions which provide an overview of the content domain of planning. One describes the "planning elements" or subprocesses of planning which may be part of the institutional planning process. These generally include: environmental assessment, institutional assessment, values assessment, master planning (including the establishment of mission, role, and scope; setting goals and objectives; and designing institutional strategies), program planning, priority setting and resource allocation, and program review. Each of these elements often incorporates a variety of more focused planning activities and each is discussed later in the chapter.

Content may also focus on different organizational units or types of resources included in an institution's planning process. Organizationally, planning may occur around structural units, such as colleges, departments, centers, bureaus, and the like, or around various functions, such as the National Center for Higher Education Management Systems (NCHEMS) typology of academic, research, service, and other support functions with its related program and output classification structure. Resource elements on which planning may focus often include physical facilities, fiscal resources (operating and capital), human resources (students, faculty, and staff), and information resources.

Historically, planning in most higher education institutions has included only some of these planning elements, organizational units, and types of resources or has treated them somewhat separately. The current challenge is to integrate them all in the planning process.

Basic Institutional Unit for Planning. Perhaps the most crucial decision in designing the planning process is the planner's perception of the basic units from which the institution is formed, which are the primary focus for planning. To a large degree, this decision shapes the remaining concepts and serves as the basis for the theoretical models of planning discussed later. Planning can emanate from six sets of perceptions about the institutional units, which are the primary building blocks for planning:

1. a set of formally devised responsibilities and offices and well-defined processes and structures for relating to them
2. a collection of individuals and groups with their own needs, abilities, and natural but related activity patterns and interests
3. an array of members' attitudes, opinions, and values, which reflect a set of belief systems
4. a well-defined, quantifiable set of clients, members, and resources organized around tasks, functions, and product or output services
5. a set of interest groups organized around issues that may conflict and/or change
6. a collection of individuals or groups that are autonomous and self-directed

Planning cannot always make such a clear distinction, yet there is often a tendency for planners to stress one of these six different basic sets without examining its appropriateness. Stressing different basic units suggests six different theories or models (Table 2) of the planning process. Is the stress on the formal-rational, natural-human groups, belief systems, tasks and techniques, interest groups, or autonomous professional units?

Institutional Purpose and Motive of Planning. The institution's purpose or motive for engaging in planning in the first place may be the most overlooked dimension in designing a planning process. Aside from the fashionable imperative that institutions should plan, a growing body of literature suggests planning has some positive impacts if done well. It is a legitimate response to external group pressures, fosters an increased awareness of or more clearly defines critical problems facing the institution, increases external perceptions of being well managed, and improves communication and understanding of how interdependent the parts of the institution really are. The question of why any institution engages in planning is rarely answered. Answers may be found by examining the objectives of and expectations for planning; the role of the planning office and the institutional function that planning serves.

The answer is seldom found in a formal institutional document defining planning objectives and only occasionally in a governing or coordinating board's decree or a presidential mandate. Even when they exist, such formal directives are only a part of the picture. Institutions may commence planning because of critical events (a major budget crisis or a sudden enrollment decline or shift) or pressure from external groups (a critical accrediting report or a legislative or state agency) or a key personality (the president, a faculty leader, an influential consultant, or a second-echelon administrator). The concern, however, is to identify the formal directives, events, and personalities involved in initiating planning and to recognize that many sources or events shape their initial expectations of results. These expectations will change over time and must be reassessed periodically to assure that the formal objectives and informal expectations are not in opposition or that widely conflicting and/or unrealistic expectations for planning are not emerging.

Is the role or function of the planning process or of the planners to *identify critical issues* and problems confronting or likely to confront the institution for examination and review by the broader membership or its governance machinery? Is it to *assist others* (deans or department chairs) in incorporating planning activities in their own realms of responsibility? Is it to *coordinate* planning activities that are the responsibility of other administrative and academic units? Is it to *develop plans* and critically to *examine alternatives*? Or is it to prepare for and assist in *implementing action plans* and major institutional changes? In effect, the distinction is the continuum between staff and line planning and objective but neutral planning and advocacy planning. In reality, institutional planning will often adopt different roles or purposes at different times and on different issues. Yet failure to distinguish or recognize this difference or to confront conflicting expectations may subvert a planning process.

A frequently unexamined purpose for planning is the role or function it plays in meeting the needs of the entire institution. Planning can contribute to at least four functional needs of a college or university—the first two more externally oriented and the second two more internally oriented. Planning whose primary function is institutional *adaptation* is concerned with adapting the institution to external changes. As such, its primary concern is with selection and modification of the institutional mission (functions, clientele, and major organizational and resource strategies) to ensure long-term viability. Planning that seeks to accomplish this function is ambitious, threatening, and difficult to manage. A less-ambitious externally oriented function of planning focuses on *problems in boundary relations.* Its primary concern is with improving or maintaining the flow of resources to and from the institutions and with the groups that affect it (for example, identifying new student clienteles or improving the institution's image with the legislature). Such planning activities, which are more fragmented, may eventually affect institutional mission; but they are not as difficult to manage and are not seen as threatening to its entire fabric. A more internally oriented function for planning is one that focuses on the *improvement of institutional management:* making programs more effective or efficient through changing resource allocation, improving their operation, or evaluating them. Planning focused around improving or resolving problems in resource allocation, program functioning, or institutional processes is less likely to change radically an institution's mission but may aid in achieving it. The other internal function for planning is improving or dealing with problems in the *human maintenance* dimension. This focus attempts to maximize institutional procedures and processes that improve faculty and staff morale, commitment, and performance and opportunities for individual (or group) growth and development in ways that serve the institutions. All four of these institutional functions can be addressed by a planning process, and in practice it is difficult to maintain distinctions between them.

The conditions initiating planning will foster some formal purposes and expectations. More rational assessment of institutional needs or environmental pressures may suggest different purposes or desired outcomes for planning. The evolving role of the planning process or office may identify still others. However, the major institutional problems that must be addressed will likely vary over time—sometimes requiring major changes of institutional mission and at other times dealing with more focused problems. These differing purposes for, expectations of, and desired outcomes of planning need to be examined to ensure that the planning effort is focused on the most pressing institutional needs and that the right planning activities and expertise are being utilized (revision of the master plan will not revitalize an outdated faculty and a planner skilled in economic forecasting may not be good at planning an improved faculty incentive system).

Internal or External Orientation. Because planning at any level involves some attempt to balance institutional strengths and weaknesses with environmental limitations and opportunities, a critical planning concept is its external or internal orientation. A major dimension to consider is the institution's *relative control* over environmental trends and groups in determining its resource flow. To the extent external factors dominate, planning must stress outside trends and forces. To the extent the institution feels it can control its key resources and influence or afford to ignore its major external groups, planning can focus on internal institutional concerns. For example, state colleges located in nonpopulous areas have much less control over their future than do larger prestigious universities located near key population areas. In most institutions, planning needs to be sensitive to both internal and external factors.

Future Orientation. Planning is future oriented, so an important concept in the planning process is how the institution or its planners choose to view it. Two dimensions are helpful in clarifying this concept. First, the time perspective on the future can vary: *Short* (two to three years), *middle* (four to five years), and *long* (ten years) seems to be the current institutional time line. It is usually somewhat longer for state agencies. The choice of time frame depends on the predictability of the events being planned for and the feasibility of making the requisite changes. The more certainty with which an event can be predicted far into the future, the more reasonable is a longer-time perspective. The current trend seems to be toward shorter time frames on institutional master plans. As uncertainties about college attendance rates for various groups, competitive factors, and economic conditions increase, master plans seem to become shorter term and require more regular updating. But they are probably more flexible and realistic.

The nature of an institutional future planners choose to focus on is a second dimension that largely reflects their view of the untapped potential of their institution and its control over the environment. Are they choosing to take an *ideal or utopian* view of the future of their institution, reflecting the belief that their institution has the potential to shape its own future and to ignore its environment; a *realistic but feasible* view of their institutional future, which reflects an assessment of how their institution can accommodate to the most likely and dominant environmental trends; or a *potential capability* view, which suggests the institution can develop its own human capacities further and overcome the external trends? A less future-oriented perspective is one that concentrates on improvement in efficiency and/or management effectiveness but will be basically unchanged by either environmental focus or major internal changes.

Concern for the future is even reflected in the debate over the nature of planning decisions. Is planning making decisions about future states, about the future implications of current decisions, or about the implications of foreseeable events or conditions (contingency planning)?

Planning Typologies: Organizational Level, Substance, and Decision Type. Planning typologies are closely related to the level or content of the organizational issue and the type of decisions being dealt with and have implications for the type of evidence (information) considered, the analytical techniques used, and the decision process employed.

A major planning typology distinguishes substantive (ends) and expedient or procedural (means) planning (Palola, Lehmann, and Blischke, 1970). Substantive planning assumes a central role, for planning is developing, assessing, and/or modifying the desired ends of planning: broad statements of institutional mission, goals or objectives, and major functional or programmatic strategies or directions. The key assumption is that clarity of substantive ends will provide direction and improve the probability of attaining these ends. Procedural planning focuses more attention on the institutional means for achieving a plan or objective. It assumes substantive ends are given (by a higher governing body or state agency, for example) or are widely understood. Planning then concentrates on designing processes of resource allocation, operating decision guidelines, evaluating, and other institutional procedures likely either to accomplish the substantive plans or to improve organizational effectiveness and efficiency.

A similar but more concrete typology related to a hierarchical view of the institution is between strategic, tactical, and operational planning (Anthony, 1965; Glenny, and others, 1971). The terminology has the unfortunate connotation of military planning, where the terms were widely used. Strategic planning has a broad focus and deals with substantive issues of purpose and direction; it usually has an external orientation and is primarily concerned with defining an institution's relationship to its larger environment. It addresses the questions of *what business we are in, where we are going.* Tactical planning, like procedural planning, is more limited and intrainstitutional in its orientation. It deals with manipulating resources, programs, and other means of achieving strategic plans or goals. It addresses the question *how do we get there?* Operational planning is concerned with the design of institutional procedures to carry out tactical or strategic plans (such as Program Evaluation and Review Technique [PERT] or CPM techniques). It develops control mechanisms to assure the institution and its resource flows function as planned. This tripartite distinction becomes increasingly useful as higher educational institutions and their leaders become aware of the need to consider external groups, forces, and trends in establishing directions, to understand their institution's capacity to respond, and to assure they use resources efficiently.

Policy planning and contingency planning are quite different typologies. They have as their principal focus major environmental changes or internal problems that suggest a critical future condition, choice, or decision for the institution. Both seek to analyze the factors affecting that condition or choice, to define it and its probability of occurrence more clearly, and to assess the likely impact of alternative policies or decision choices. Clearly, policy and contingency planning, which begins with specific situations rather than broader planning concerns, may deal with strategic or substantive, tactical or procedural, or operational planning issues and may cut across them. Advocates of policy analysis (Weathersby and Balderston, 1973) argue that dealing rationally and analytically with issues as they emerge is more realistic than trying to deal with broad issues of mission, goals, and strategies and leads to a pattern of preferences and precedents that constitutes institutional plans. Contingency advocates stress its realism in facing uncertain situations and say it can be part of any planning approach. These three content focuses of planning may be practiced separately or integrated into a more comprehensive planning process.

The process of planning and these typologies all imply decision making. Two useful decision typologies in planning are those of Anthony (1965) and Simon (1957). Anthony suggests a hierarchy of policy decisions that focus on institutional missions, goals, and strategies; management decisions that are concerned with program selection, resource allocation, and effective goal accomplishment; and operational decisions concerned with routine and day-to-day decisions. This reflects the distinction of substantive or strategic, procedural or tactical, and operational planning. Simon elaborates by distinguishing between value and factual decisions, which has extensive implications for planning and highlights a major problem. Value decisions are ones for which judgments have to be rendered on the goodness or badness, desirability or undesirability, of a decision and where the criteria for it are not easily measurable. Factual decisions can be formulated in terms of a choice based on more quantifiable and measurable criteria. The distinction, though not always operationally clear, is helpful to planners. Value decisions are more difficult. Yet substantive or strategic planning often confronts planners and college and university decision makers with value-laden policy choices: To what extent should we shift our emphasis from liberal to career education? Is it more desirable to reduce costs by eliminating programs or releasing personnel on a seniority basis? Should the college invest in a high-cost marketing program in hopes of attracting students or concentrate funds on program improvement and faculty development to attract them? Such decisions involve substantial value dimensions as well as factual ones. Tactical or operational planning tends to deal with more tangible and factual decision issues: Are programs accomplishing their goals? Are resources being used for purposes allocated and efficiently?

Analytically, the planner hopes to reduce value choices to more factual dimensions, but the fact-value distinction has other implications. Value-loaded policy decisions suggest the collection of more "soft data," such as perceptual measures (opinions, attitudes, and such) of changes in societal values or program quality that may not be as "hard" or objective as that useful to measure the managerial decisions about program goal accomplishment or operational decisions. Hard or objective data, useful in analyzing factual decisions, are more amenable to inclusion in a retrievable management information system than those for value-based decisions. Further, value decisions probably require the participation of more affected parties in exploring the nature of the issue, the implications of alternatives, and the opinions of disparate parties. Thus, the type of decision is related to the type of planning and has implications for the type of data collected for inclusion in an information system, for analyses that can be done, and even for the decision process utilized (Peterson, 1972).

Process Concepts or Characteristics of Planning

Two planning process dynamics (goal centeredness and decision-making and analysis style) and two bases for participation (expertise and representation) are four basic concepts that describe most planning processes.

Planning Process Dynamics. Although our most common views of planning are shaped by rational notions of goals, planning can vary in terms of the goal centeredness of the process. Table 1 contrasts the degree to which an institution stresses single or multiple goals and the formality of their adoption. A *goal-centered* planning process stresses a single goal or highest priority. This type of emphasis is unrealistic in larger, complex institutions and difficult to gain support for even in a small one. Yet, particularly in times of crisis, highly visible goals may serve as a catalyst. In most institutional planning, a multiple set of goals is identified. Because they are often contradictory, they are not useful guides to action unless *prioritized. Consensus-centered* planning with the informally derived

Table 1. Institutional Goal Centeredness

Mode of Adoption	Number of Goals Emphasized	
	Single	*Multiple*
Formalized, Prioritized	Goal Centered	Priority Centered
Informal	Consensus Centered	Pluralistic

single goal or priority is often desired in smaller institutions. However, it is difficult to achieve or may exist and not be realized. There is substantial evidence that consensus goals are strong motivators and may lead to later formal endorsement. Finally, many institutions have multiple goals and have neither formalized them nor established a set of priorities. Such a *pluralistic* set of goals, if identified and accepted, may serve to limit unrelated activities and make the transition to a more formal set of priorities easier to negotiate if resources are constraining.

The second concept combines two interrelated process dimensions: the decision-making and analysis style planners emphasize. Five dynamics describe this concept. The most widely discussed is *neutral, rational analysis* of planning issues typically approached in a criterion-referenced, problem-solving mode (seeking the best comparative solution, for example, accomplishment of goals and objectives). This is appropriate where planning issues and alternatives are clear and where goals are agreed upon. Second, when planning issues, alternatives, and goals are unclear or decisions value laden, analysis and decision making can be approached through *reasoned discussion,* in which varied perspectives, points of view, and modes of analysis are shared in debate format. The emphasis is on the logic of the analysis and the positions stated. In such a situation, a third alternative approach might involve *collaborative learning,* about both the problem and the mode of analysis. This is often appropriate if planning is being introduced to a staff for the first time or in a small institution with limited formal planning and analysis experience. Unfortunately, planning often occurs in situations where there are sharply contrasting and competing perspectives. Here a fourth approach is to encourage *advocacy analysis* (different analysts may discover different data, differing approaches suggest different choices, and differing groups will interpret results differently). Such analysis usually leads to bargaining and negotiations, compromise, or coalition building to resolve planning differences. This may be likely in large institutions with units competing for declining resources or in institution-state agency dealings on planning issues where each has a different perspective. Finally, in highly decentralized or autonomous units, planning efforts may require highly *varied modes* of analysis and decision making that can be only *loosely coordinated.* This is probably most appropriate in the large institution whose units have independent resources and limited dependence on one another—an increasingly uncommon occurrence.

Bases for Participation. Although essentially characteristics describing the dynamics of the planning process, the two dimensions of participation in planning, the nature of the expertise required and the pattern of representation, are too central not to be treated separately. Different planning tasks require different kinds of expertise. The *planning process* expert has a conception of how to organize, marshal resources for, involve participants in, understand the nuances of, and obtain action as a result of planning. The *planning analyst* expert may share expertise with the process expert but is more proficient in technical research and analysis skills and in the use of information systems, research methods, and computer technology. The *organizational design and development* skill suggests another planning expertise. Because much planning involves organizational design or revision, understanding the human needs and interactions, organizational processes, and structural implications of trends, alternatives, and motivational schemes in implementing changes is an appropriate expertise. *Political skills* or knowledge of situations involving conflicting interests may be needed. *Academic* or *administrative* expertise about academic or functional units provides other expert bases for planners.

Planning representation can be limited to an *expert planning staff* if there is enough trust and respect for the planners and those who selected them and if the planning issues are somewhat objective. More often, representation is broadened to include other individuals with technical (information system, simulation modeling, or economic forecasting) and administrative responsibilities. Planning representation then becomes a rationally selected oligarchy of *planners and administrative specialists*. Another pattern of representation is often the self-selected *political oligarchy*, where representation reflects key interest groups (minorities or alumni). An elected or selected *intellectual or leadership elite* (the faculty blue ribbon committee) constitutes another pattern. On occasion in smaller institutions, planning may include a more *egalitarian democracy* involving all interested parties. The expertise stressed in planning and the bases for representation may vary; but the critical issue is for each institution to reflect on its own traditions, approach to planning, and planning problems; balance the expertise that can carry out the planning process; and include respected representatives to ensure legitimacy.

Organization of the Planning Process

The identification of several domain and process concepts that can be used to describe planning suggests seven related organizing concepts for the planning process itself.

Comprehensiveness. The discussion of the content of planning (a domain concept) suggests it might vary in its comprehensiveness. Two dimensions, "comprehensiveness of planning elements" and "of organizational scope," capture this concept.

A planning process is more comprehensive as it includes more of the elements of planning: master planning (including environmental, institutional, and values assessment), program planning, priority setting and resource allocation, and program review. Virtually all institutions have a resource allocation process, which may or may not have a priority setting and a planning perspective; many have some form of organized program review process, which again may not be planning related. The least prevalent major planning elements, but ones that are increasingly being instituted, are master planning or program planning. An institution that has all four and takes a longer-term perspective has a more comprehensive institutional planning process. The literature suggests the desirability of comprehensive planning; but comprehensive planning requires a major commitment of institutional resources and there is, to date, little objective evidence about the greater effectiveness of a fully comprehensive planning process.

Not only can the planning process be more or less comprehensive but so can the scope of organizational functions and programs (academic, research, service, and support), organizational units (colleges and departments), and types of resources (fiscal, human, physical, and information) considered in each of the major planning elements. Earlier planning efforts tended to be very limited in scope, for example, campus and physical facilities planning. More recent master planning attempts, planning-related resource allocation efforts, and some planning simulations, which reflect more constrained resources, have tended to be more comprehensive. Although this may be inevitable, it makes management of the planning process much more complex and difficult.

Planning Element Emphasis. An institution's planning may be comprehensive but choose to emphasize different elements in the planning process. State mandates for planning may argue for master planning. Severe budgetary constraints or work load issues may require greater priority in resource allocation. Concern about quality in outmoded programs may suggest emphasis on evaluation. However, whether one element is more or less superior for institutional redirection or redistribution is unresolved and probably depends on which process has the most trust in a particular institution.

Similarly, planning can emphasize different organizational functions, units, or resources. Academic planning gets greater attention as enrollments shift. Planning in research areas becomes more active in periods of uncertainty about soft funding. Human resource planning becomes more crucial under the countervailing pressures of projected stable and older staff and stress on affirmative action. Comprehensive planning may anticipate some of these and moderate the need for special emphasis, yet planning needs to vary its attention to different planning pressures or needs in the institution.

Integrated-Fragmented Nature of Planning. Although planning may be comprehensive, the major planning elements or the organizational units on which they focus may operate in a highly integrated or very fragmented manner. Rational arguments call for close integration of master planning, program planning, resource allocation, and program review; yet these elements occur on different time cycles (such as ten-year state-mandated master plans, annual budget cycles, and five-year program review cycles) or may be the responsibility of widely separated administrative units. The degree of integration, coordination, or fragmentation of the planning elements required in any institution is one that needs to be carefully examined.

Similarly, planning for the organizational elements (academic programs, physical facilities, human resources, or financial affairs) has often emerged as separate planning activities. Planning for academic programs is often divorced from research planning, yet the interplay of soft and hard funds makes them inseparable. Review of graduate programs is often coordinated under the aegis of the graduate dean while undergraduate programs are reviewed at the college or academic vice-presidential level, yet the two depend on the same staff and common resources at the department level. The degree to which programs and resources need to be integrated at the institutional level in the master plan, in priority setting that guides resource allocation, or in program planning and review or may remain fragmented is a perplexing problem.

Fragmented planning is easier to accomplish and may meet some planning needs. As the pressure for a higher degree of integration of planning elements and among these different organizational units and resource segments increases, planning becomes more complex and needs careful consideration to assure that the varied planning activities are not counterproductive. The problems suggested by the degree of comprehensiveness and integration among the major planning elements and the differing organizational units and resources are the best argument for a carefully designed planning process and a major administrative assignment to coordinate them—particularly in a large institution.

Flexibility. The discussion of comprehensiveness, emphasis, and integration of planning suggests a concern for flexibility in the planning process or in its major elements. Most planning models suggest a highly *regularized* planning process that in practice often becomes rigid. Yet the need for flexibility has already been noted because many planning demands and issues are either unpredictable and/or beyond the institution's control (for example, the first Arab oil crisis with its energy cost, facilities, and scheduling implications). Planning cycles should also allow some flexibility for delays, unforeseen problems, and changing planning emphases. However, it is also important to note the value of deadlines and the need to have planning lead to progress and not just activity. Finally, the desirability of flexibility probably varies among planning elements—clearly, it is less feasible and the negative consequences of too much flexibility may be greater in the resource allocation process than in program evaluation or master planning.

Organizational Penetration. Because there is a tendency to think of planning at an institutional level, it is important to think of it in terms of its level of organizational penetration. Is planning merely an activity engaged in by executive officers, or does it permeate the school and college or even the department? Are the impacts of planning decisions communicated and felt only at the highest level or does it lead to changes further down the organizational chart? If planning is to make a difference, it should be accepted beyond the upper administrative echelons and major planning priorities and policies should be consistently implemented wherever they reasonably apply.

Analytical Sophistication. The initial definition of planning assumed analysis of planning issues and problems was a part of the process. With increased pressures for accountability and effective use of scarce resources, all institutional planning decisions need justification. To some extent, the planning process and its elements are viewed as more sophisticated if they are based on a reliable and comprehensive data base, use modern research and analysis techniques, and can produce complex planning studies. This conception leads to the overdrawn implication that computer-based, retrievable information systems and on-line analytical models are synonymous with analytical sophistication. However, information can be overused; computers can be leased; and analytical models can be inappropriate or misinterpreted. Although analytical sophistication is desirable, it should be judged on *adequacy* of information provided, *appropriateness* of the analyses, and *efficient and timely* preparation—not the systems, models, and machines from which it emanated. Unfortunately, analytical sophistication still implies a good institutional data base, persons skilled in research and analysis, and knowledge of relevant extrainstitutional data and techniques used elsewhere—all expensive technical adjuncts to planning. Fortunately, services and models to increase analytical sophistication are becoming more readily available and less expensive for smaller institutions and are no longer just the province of large or wealthy ones.

Structure of the Planning Group. Probably no concept receives greater attention than this one. Four dimensions always seem to emerge as significant: *selection* (How were they selected and by whom? Was the selection process legitimate in light of institutional traditions?), *composition* (What was the basis of expertise and representation for the members? Is there a good mix of planning and administrative expertise and of functional, affected, or interested parties, as institutional representation patterns would suggest, or a reason for deviating?), *permanence* (Is the planning group intended to have continuity? If so, is that provided for in the selection process?), and *responsibility* (Is it clear that this planning group knows its function as planners and its specific institutional charge?). Clearly, the appropriate structure will vary by institution and may also vary by the major planning element involved. The crucial variables are competence for the task and legitimacy in the wider institution.

Theoretical Models and Approaches to Planning

To be successful, planning must accommodate to the traditions, governance and administrative style, and problems facing the particular institution. If the planning process fits these broader institutional patterns, it is more likely to be legitimately accepted and integrated into the institution. If it contrasts significantly, resistance to or an isolated or ineffectual planning process is likely to result. It is also possible to design a planning process that differs from traditional modes of governance as a mechanism for changing them. However, that introduces two challenges: changing governance *and* the development of an effective planning process. Although there is neither a proven best model of planning nor a pure model, following are six quasi models or approaches to planning that have been identified in the literature. Each is described briefly using the concepts describing the domain and process characteristics identified in the previous section and includes a commentary on the most appropriate institutional settings or conditions (see Table 2).

Formal-Rational Model. A rational view of the planning process is the most complete and widely recognized model of planning in higher education and in other types of organizations. It overlaps considerably with the organizational development and technocratic/empirical models and is the easiest to describe. The basic paradigm, developed in the 1950s (Taylor, 1976), assumes a rational, comprehensive sequence of planning elements and includes formulation of institutional mission based on a situational appraisal, development of goals and objectives, establishment of broad program and resource strategies, selection and design of action programs, implementation, and review. The intent is a completed cycle of activities that then acts to become self-assessing and self-correcting. The process is based on a rational assumption that mission and objectives can be clearly formulated and will guide the other cyclic activities. In effect, because subsequent cycle iterations do not begin in the same initial state, the process is a spiral rather than a repetitive cycle.

Figures 2 and 3 suggest two alternative views of the rational planning process in higher education today. Both highlight the major planning process elements an institution may engage in and in which major planning decisions are made: strategic or master planning (including institutional values, and environmental assessment), priority setting and resource allocation, program planning, implementation, and program evaluation. Both suggest the influence of the larger institution's values, governance patterns, and administrative style. However, Figure 2 views planning as a closed cycle (or spiral) of activities. Strategic planning activities are differentiated from but seen as linked to tactical planning and implementation. The cycle of elements is comprehensive, but it

Table 2. Theoretical Planning Models and Primary Dimensions: Institutional Rationale for Planning Models

Model	Planning Domain					Planning Process	
	Basic Institutional Planning Unit	Planning Orientation	Future Orientation	Institutional Purpose/Function	Planning Typologies	Planning Dynamics	Bases for Participation
Formal—Rational	Formal offices, processes, and structures	Internal, external, or both	Most likely; probable	Adaptation—goal and mission definition and change; managerial—goal achievement	Substantive and procedural; strategic and tactical	Goal-centered; problem solving; rational analysis	Planning process expertise; functional or rational representation
Organizational Development	Natural groups; needs, abilities, attitudes, and activity patterns	Internal	Achieve members' capability	Maintenance—growth and development	Procedural and tactical	Consensus centered; collaborative interaction; learning and problem solving	O.D. expertise; egalitarian community or natural democracy
Technocratic/Empirical	Quantifiable; clients, members, and resources; tasks, functions and outcomes	Internal	Improve current condition	Managerial—improved efficiency and effectiveness	Procedural and tactical	Goal centered; problem solving; rational analysis	Planning technology expertise; technical or administrative oligarchy

Philosophical Synthesis	Member attitudes, opinions, and values; belief systems	Internal	Ideal state	Maintenance—strengthen resolve	Substantive	Consensus oriented; reasoned discussion, debate and persuasion; logic	Intellectual expertise; elite community or oligarchy
Political Advocacy	Interest groups and issues	Internal, external, or both	Feasible state	Boundary—deal with conflicts; Adaptive—accommodate new pressures	Policy and contingency	Priority oriented or pluralistic; bargaining, negotiation, coalition formation; advocacy and analysis	Interest group leadership or political organizing expertise; interest-group representation
Coordinated Anarchy	Autonomous units, groups or individuals	Internal	Achieve autonomous capability	Can vary by unit	Varies by unit	Pluralistic; loosely coordinated; varied analysis	Expertise in units' activity; minimal representation by unit

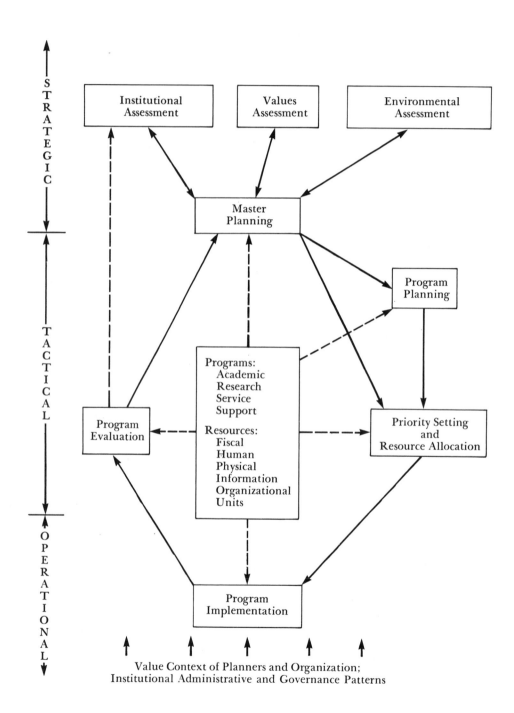

Figure 2. The Rational Planning Cycle

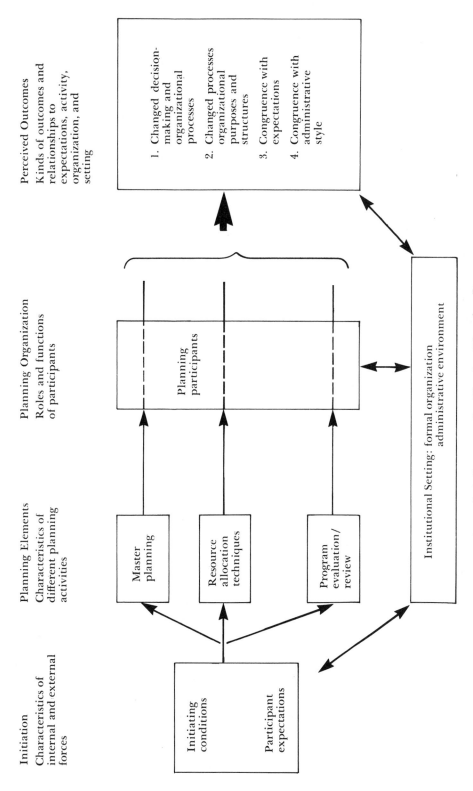

Figure 3. A Structure for Viewing Planning Processes

Source: Poulton, 1979.

highlights the fact that planning may occur for differing types of institutional programs or functions (academic, research, service, and support) or organizational units and may include various types of resources (fiscal—both operating and capital—human, physical, and information processing).

Figure 3 views the planning process from a different perspective (Dror, 1963; Poulton, 1979). Initiating conditions are seen as key forces in establishing expectations for planning. The major planning elements are seen as ongoing but parallel rather than linked in a regular cycle. Each planning element may have its own planning organization of roles, functions, and participants, which may be similar or different and may change over time. The outcomes of planning are seen as changes in four broad areas: decision making and organizational processes; organizational purposes, structure, or programs; expectations for the planning effort; and the institution's administrative style. Figure 3 views planning as an emergent phenomenon and reflects the reality that planning may not be comprehensive, that is, the major planning elements may not be fully developed, closely integrated, or even equally emphasized to have effective institutional planning.

In applying either view of this rational paradigm, administrators and planners often attempt to prescribe the detailed activities within each element, assign responsibilities for them, and formally adopt the process. Not only is the planning process formal and rational, but there is a tendency to view the college or university as that set of formally defined offices, processes, and structures for which or to which the planning process is applied (that is, a college has a formal mission and goal statement developed, has resources allocated and programs implemented in accordance with the plan, and is reviewed and evaluated on the basis of the performance compared to the plan). This process can be applied at the unit level (a department), to an office (the dean), or to an institutional process (admissions). The similarity to program, planning, and budgeting (PPB) and formal management by objectives (MBO) systems, which are central to many institutional planning efforts, is obvious.

The planning orientation can be either internal to the institution's needs and problems or external to the changes or pressures of the environment. The primary purpose of planning can vary, depending on its orientation—an external orientation may lead to an adaptive role by revising or redefining institutional mission and goals or an internal focus will likely lead to a managerial role by seeking to improve goal achievement (efficiency or effectiveness) or programs and processes. This planning model relies on both substantive or strategic and procedural or tactical planning typologies. Because of its rational orientation, the planning focus will probably tend to be on a most likely or probable institutional future state.

The dynamics of formal-rational planning tend to be goal centered— seeking a formal goal or clear set of priorities that will guide other behavior. Decision making reflects a problem-solving mode because each planning element has its own problem focus (define mission, set goals, and so forth), and rational, analytical techniques (including behavioral and soft data) can be utilized. Because of the degree of formalization of the planning process, a high degree of expertise in the process and in analysis is typically valued. The process is applied to formal units of the institution, so functional or administrative representation is likely to be the most valued.

The advantage of this formal-rational model is the high visibility, clarity, and continuity it gives to the planning process. Because it is formalized and focused on formal units, it should not be as subject to whims of personality or internal political squabbles. Its comprehensive set of activities suggests it should be linked to implementation. On the assumption it includes a formal planning staff, there should be expertise for analytical and process skills required for effective planning.

The disadvantages flow from the fact that the processes and governance mechanisms in most colleges and universities are often not as rational as the model presumes. Because each element in the rational cycle can be extensive, the fiscal and human resources required for the planning process are often high—particularly in smaller colleges that lack the resources. The planning elements themselves have different life cycles (budget-annual, reviews-five years, and so forth) and are difficult to coordinate. The added complexity of trying to operate this cycle at several institutional levels at once can become unmanageable. Because of the formalization and rationality, there may be a danger of developing a staff of planners isolated from the real activities of the institution. Finally, there is substantial concern that this highly rational model fosters only incremental, and seldom fundamental, changes and that it may not be responsive enough to meet immediate pressures or entrepreneurial opportunities.

Organizational Development (O.D.) Model. The O.D. model of planning or planned change has its roots in the human relations tradition. It begins with a rational paradigm of the planning process similar to the formal-rational model (that is, the stages or activities are diagnosis, action planning, implementation, and evaluation). However, this model is far less concerned about the formality of the planning process itself and begins with a very different basic assumption about the makeup of the institution for which planning is done. It begins with a focus on the organization as composed of individuals or natural human groups whose needs, abilities, attitudes, and activities make up the social, cultural, and activity patterns of the institution rather than on formal structures and processes. In this model, planning is concerned with innovation and change conducted in an experimental (trial and evaluation) mode. Targets for change are the organization's culture, management style, work structure, decision-making patterns, communication, interaction, and influence. The major planning issue is to understand the institution or group as a human system and to develop its capacity to plan as a means of improving individual, collective, and organizational well-being. Planning (as well as other human organization dynamics) is viewed as a process of learning for all members of the institution (Bennis and others, 1976; Michael, 1973).

Although some organizational development experts have emphasized the role of the extrainstitutional environment (Lawrence and Lorsch, 1969), the primary emphasis of this approach to planning is internal—focusing on the members themselves. There is a strong emphasis on internal institutional change in this approach to planning, but the primary emphasis is on the human maintenance function—improving the performance of and growth and development opportunities for individuals and groups in the organization. The offshoot may be adaptive changes in institutional mission or managerial improvement of the institution or its programs. Because of the nature of the basic unit and internal planning orientation, this type of planning tends to be more procedural and tactical (changing organization culture, processes, and so forth) than substantive or strategic; and the nature of the institutional future planned for is one that seeks to maximize member capabilities.

The dynamics emphasized in an O.D. approach are usually consensus centered—seeking change goals most members will endorse. Decision making emphasizes collaboration, frequent and open interaction around issues and problems, and learning about the issues, the alternatives, and means of analysis. Analysis usually emphasizes rational, problem-solving approaches to achieving consensus, assessing alternatives, and evaluating performance.

The significant advantage of the O.D. approach to planning is the emphasis on change and the strong motivating force it may unleash in individuals if done effectively. Like the rational approach, it is visible, may include a comprehensive set of planning elements, and attempts to link planning to implementation.

The disadvantages of this approach are the tendency to rely on outside, respected change agents to initiate the process, a difficult role for a planning officer to perform. The often internal orientation is also a significant weakness today, although an external perspective can be built in. Critics point out that in large institutions, those where planning requires autonomous or even antagonistic groups to deal with each other or where resources are shrinking, such collaborative, consensus-oriented planning is idealistic or naive. Another concern is the time-consuming nature of the O.D. approach and the uncertainty about whether realistic goals (given external pressures) will emerge.

Technocratic/Empirical Model. Unlike the first two models, the technocratic/empirical model emphasizes planning techniques and is not in a pure sense a process model. However, because of the recent emphasis on planning techniques, it is a useful pseudomodel to consider. It tends to rely on rational process notions (usually systems analysis), but the techniques generally deal with only limited segments of the planning process (for example, Delphi techniques for goal setting or forecasting for resource flows). However, there are planning techniques that attempt to serve all the elements in a comprehensive planning process. One example is the NCHEMS attempt to develop a comprehensive, consistently defined, and integrated management information system that can be aggregated at various levels, arrayed around differing program and outcome structures, and used for analytical techniques and models on specific planning problems. Implicit in the rational PPB process (Schick, 1968) is a set of systems analysis techniques that deal with overall planning, alternative program assessment (and evaluations of selected ones), and budgeting or resource algorithms.

What is important about this quasi model, however, is not its coherence or its comprehensive or segmented character but the fact that it reflects a planning approach that began in the late 1960s, continues today, and emphasizes empirical techniques. Implicit in this approach is the assumption that the basic units of a college or university are quantifiable, measurable resources (the number of important characteristics of fiscal, physical, and human resources) that can be traced through a clearly defined, functionally linked set of tasks, activities, programs, functions, and outcomes. These constitute the basic structure on which empirical techniques can be rationally applied at various stages in the planning process.

Such planning techniques can be either internally or externally oriented.

Environmental scanning, trend analysis, forecasting, simulation modeling, market research, consumer or institutional needs assessment, scenario development, Delphi, budget analysis, cost-benefit techniques, evaluation models, and a myriad of data collection, analysis, and statistical techniques are but a few of the arsenal of techniques. The 1960s focus was on techniques that dealt with internal planning and served a managerial purpose—planning activities aimed at improving efficiency and effectiveness. The type of planning emphasized was more procedural or tactical than strategic, and the future concern was with improving the current condition of the institution. However, more recent large-scale, state-level data bases, awareness of data on environmental trends, market assessment techniques, and such have focused more externally and potentially play an adaptive function—assessing the appropriateness of mission and goals, a strategic planning concern.

Because the technocratic/empirical approach tends to adopt a rational process model of planning and a formal hierarchical view of an institution (for example, the NCHEMS program structure), it adopts rational dynamics and tends to be goal centered or concerned with more formalized priorities. The approach to decision making reflects a problem-solving mode that emphasizes rational analysis of the problems and alternatives. The planner in this approach is assumed to have expertise in the underlying techniques of computer and information systems and research skills. Participation is more likely to be limited to technical planning staff, heads of analytical units (budget, information systems, institutional research, and so forth), and administrative staff with analytical skills.

The advantages of this approach are its greater emphasis on precision and analysis, on the preparation of more quantifiable and rational justifications for plans, and on conveying an image of sophisticated planning and greater accountability. The development of complex analytical techniques (such as resource simulation models) has also provided administrators and planners with greater understanding of the institution.

The disadvantages are often the inability of planners with this emphasis to deal with the many nonrational dimensions of planning (the value-laden choices or the unresolvable conflicts, for instance) and such staff planners' isolation from administrative and governance channels, which renders their work less useful. The fragmented nature of many planning techniques and the tendency to expect too much from an empirical technique often deters the development of a more comprehensive planning process (for example, resource simulations do not set the priorities or make the decisions about where to reduce resources). Finally, the expense of sophisticated information systems, computer facilities, and analytical staff often may not be justified in smaller colleges or in larger institutions where less-sophisticated techniques might suffice.

Philosophical Synthesis. Like the technocratic/empirical model, this is not a well-developed process model of planning. This approach is grand in scope and draws on many disciplines and fields of endeavor. As a planning process, this mode asks fundamental questions about the current and future nature of society, humankind, teaching and learning, and knowledge. The planning concern is to probe beneath these fundamental questions to more basic trends or assumptions about where our political, social, ethical, economic, and educational environments are going and to develop a rationale (a mission) for the institution that guides our institutional decisions and programs. In the 1960s, new institutions founded on the ecology movement (University of Wisconsin-Green Bay and Evergreen State College), with a new educational rationale (University of California-Santa Cruz or Hampshire College), with a new delivery system (Empire State College), and others reflect such a philosophical synthesis in their planning. Existing institutions engage in such planning in debates over general education (Harvard University) or the role of career and occupational versus liberal education. Despite its presence, this process is often not conceived of as planning because these discussions do not occur regularly and their linkage to tactical planning, implementation, or review is unclear at best. However, because this approach is useful in thinking through some of our most complex academic and educational mission issues, it needs to be better understood and refined as an approach to planning.

This approach begins with the members of the institution as its basic planning units. However, unlike the O.D. approach, which focuses on their behavioral and psychological nature, this approach focuses on their intellectual and human traditions—seeking members' common values and belief systems on which to build. The planning debate may range over external and internal institutional patterns, but the common tendency is to seek an internal synthesis and rationale the faculty can support and believe reflects external realities. This approach to planning primarily serves a maintenance function, that is, it gives the faculty a more tangible sense of the rationale for their institution, their approach to the curriculum, their students, or their educational process. In a sense, it serves to focus superordinate goals that may motivate individual performances or collective action. Any adaptive, change-oriented, or managerial-oriented function of this approach is secondary. Despite the internal basis for its rationale, this approach deals with some of the most complex substantive and implicitly strategic planning issues. Because of the heavy emphasis on internal development of a rationale, the concern for the institution's future may often seem to be seeking a utopian or ideal state rather than a feasible or realistic one.

The dynamics of planning are consensus oriented in seeking a common mission and rationale; however, intellectual debates can be heated and divisive if norms of professional behavior do not prevail. The decision dynamics tend to reasoned discussion, debate, and persuasion. Although the complex issues and varied backgrounds of participants allow for varied types of analysis, the stress is on logical argumentation first and analysis second (indeed, formalized analysis of issues that could be part of such debates is often missing). The planner's expertise in this mode is his or her own intellectual expertise—a respected reputation in a field or discipline and ability to deal logically with philosophical debate. The basis for participation is at once broad or narrow, depending on the restrictive or inclusive norms of the institution. It could vary from an oligarchy of respected faculty (and administrators), to an elite community of faculty, to a community of learners.

The advantages of this approach are unclear. The process is often observed in visible and occasionally prestigious institutions with a strong central mission. When it works, it often engenders wide involvement in basic questions of institutional mission. The disadvantages are that it is an intensive, time-consuming (critics would even say inefficient) process that seldom yields fundamental change and is not a comprehensive and well-integrated process. Yet, given our concerns about the need for a strong sense of purpose in many of our institutions, we might learn more about how to utilize this process more efficiently, to integrate appropriate analytical techniques, and to link it to more tactical planning concerns.

Political Advocacy. Like a technical/empirical and philosophical synthesis, this approach is not a well-developed planning model, but it seems to have a somewhat clearer process notion of how major issues are determined in colleges and universities. The notion of process suggests five stages (Baldridge, 1971): (1) social context analysis, in which the problem or issue emerges and the various interest groups concerned with it are identified; (2) interest articulation, in which interest groups develop their positions on the issue and attempt to influence others; (3) policy formulation, in which policy positions are developed, analyzed, and reacted to by the interest groups; (4) legislative transformation, in which a policy is formally enacted or endorsed by a legitimate planning or governance group; and (5) enactment, in which the regulations and guidelines for administrators who enforce and operating units who follow the policy are prepared. Unlike the rational and O.D. models, this one downplays mission and goals and accentuates policy issues as the focal point for planning. Many have suggested institutional master plans are often a compromise set of policy positions developed by such a process rather than a rationally conceived set of missions and goal statements. The major difference is that this approach assumes the basic organizing units of colleges and universities are interest groups and issues the institution must confront and that, whether desirable or not, all planning and decision making needs to begin with this assumption.

Given the basic assumption, planning can be either internally or externally oriented. It will vary by the issue, the internal or external position of the interest group (for example, legislative fiscal agency and institutional groups), and the internal or external concerns of on-campus interest groups. To a greater extent than the other approaches, this model is capable of dealing with boundary conflicts between the institution and its external pressure groups. It can also serve an adaptive role in redirecting the institution as new policies lead to an accommodation with internal and external issues or pressures. This type of planning implicitly focuses on policy issues—these may be either strategic and substantive or tactical and procedural and are not necessarily related. Indeed, the major concern of a planner utilizing this approach is to forge policies that are not mutually inconsistent and that represent a viable picture of the institution's mission and direction. Because the approach is pragmatic, the concern is to develop an institutional future that is a feasible state amidst the varying issues and pressure groups.

Because the political approach focuses on policy, the strategic direction is more likely to be pluralistic, attempting to accommodate diverse missions and goals. At best in a carefully controlled legislative transformation or policy enactment process, one would expect a priority-centered planning process. The decision dynamics in the planning process accentuate bargaining, negotiation, compromise, coalition formation, and the like—rationally oriented problem solving or consensus occurs only when it occurs naturally. This mode encourages advocacy analysis, either analyzing the issue from the perspectives of the interest groups or letting them do their own. This does not mean rational, empirical techniques will not be used but recognizes that even those may lead to the defense of different positions, depending on the nature of the data, the technique used, and the criteria of choice applied.

Planning expertise in interest-group dynamics, political organizing, and policy analysis is more important than in the other models. The basis for representation stressed most often reflects either all the interest groups or at least those with power to influence the policy decision or block its implementation.

The advantages of this process are the practical reality that many institutions seem to operate this way and that, in a period of declining resources, attempts to redirect or reduce them will be focused around explicit and difficult policy choices on which intense interest groups will emerge and need to be dealt with. Given the more stabilizing tendency and function often encountered by the other approaches, the encouragement of conflict and the focus on real issues around which policy choices need to be made may induce more change than the others. The critics, of course, point out that the sense of direction may be lost if issues and policies are dealt with piecemeal. Other disadvantages are potential dominance of large or powerful interest groups, who may advocate policies not in the long-term best interest of the institution. The lack of a clear link to implementation and evaluation processes to assure that plans become reality is a concern. Perhaps the greatest disadvantage is the complex problem the planner or chief administrator has in coalescing a sense of direction while designing a policy-legislating process that is legitimate and prevents abuses, being aware of the differing interests and dynamics on different issues, and knowing which issues are ready for policy formulation.

The political advocacy model, like the philosophical synthesis, offers a pragmatic view of some of our most difficult planning issues. Many planners suggest an understanding of political dynamics is useful within a rational process model.

Coordinated Anarchy. This final planning model is probably the least discussed and hardest to describe. It is not based on a rational process, as were the first three; it lacks the consensus orientation of philosophical synthesis; and it does not have the basic sense of process and policy analysis represented in the political model. This model begins with the view that the basis for organizing a college or university is and should be productive but highly autonomous units (separate colleges and professional schools, departments, specialized research centers or institutes, administrative units, and such). This view of a university was emphasized by Kerr (1963), and its dynamics were described as a process of organized anarchy by Cohen and March (1974). The underlying assumption is that professionals in these autonomous units are best able to foster progress in their area, that spontaneity should be encouraged, and that constraints should be limited. In such a setting, planning is only a loosely coordinated process. The sense of direction is both prospective and retrospective: Areas making great strides, in a burst of spontaneity (biomedicine), or likely to be in great demand (energy-related research or career-oriented fields) will shape priorities for development and receive increased resources; areas that have outlived their usefulness will be reduced; and areas that are valued or unique but currently out of vogue (humanities or Chinese studies five years ago) will be protected. Institutional planning is a continuous attempt to assess where each autonomous unit and its environmental forces are tending, to reformulate that sense of movement or goals within some broader philosophical synthesis of the institutional mission, and to reflect it in the allocation priorities. Planning could be encouraged and facilitated in each unit.

Clearly, the institutional planning orientation in this model depends on the autonomous units. Each unit may vary in its own orientation but is presumed to be both internal and external. The function of planning is an adaptive, change-oriented mode. Yet because the coordination of planning and any centralized sense of direction is limited, the actual function will vary widely, depending on each unit's planning success. Institutional-level planning will generally be limited to substantive issues or strategic planning with less procedural or tactical emphasis. However, it can vary widely in each unit. The nature of the institutional future is conceived as a flexible one as the autonomous units are encouraged to achieve their maximum capability.

Clearly, this planning model is pluralistic, attempting to accommodate and foster diverse goals. Planning decisions among and between units are closely coordinated only where there are strong interdependent relationships or shared resources among units. A varied array of analytical planning techniques could be used by each unit; but at the central institutional level, they would focus most on assessing external trends and monitoring unit progress and resource needs. This mode suggests the need for planners who are knowledgeable about each unit's field or discipline. Representation on planning may vary, depending on each unit's approach, but, at the central level, suggests representation from the units by the key unit administrator or planner and by highly respected academics.

The advantages of this model are the strong emphasis on spontaneity (often criticized in the other models), the incentive for each unit to do its own planning and development, and the argument that units that relate to different, rapidly changing environments (such as law and medicine) are in the best position to respond to them. Some suggest this model is only applicable in large, complex universities or those segments of a university that are nearly self-supporting.

The disadvantages include the suggestion that this model presumes slack or fluid resources, that many units are not in fact autonomous but merely seemed to be during an era of expansion, and that reduced resources increase the interdependence among units. Because this model suggests a pluralistic and loosely coordinated institutional planning process that depends on each unit, there is concern the institution may respond too slowly to declining units, which then drain resources from other stronger and more viable ones, or it may not have developed the capacity to deal with major resource and enrollment reductions.

Radical and Anti-Planning: A Commentary. Colleges ̱ ıd universities have always harbored severe critics of rational planning. President Enarson (1975) of Ohio State defends "intuitive" planning, and Lindblom (1959) suggests we really just "muddle through." However, three of the models described (philosophical synthesis, political advocacy, and coordinated anarchy) incorporate some of the concerns of radical planners who have difficulty accepting the more objective, mission- and goal-directed, and formalized process notions reflected in the first three models (formal-rational, organizational development, and technocratic/empirical). The three more radical planning models also reflect, in different ways, the failure of the rationalists to deal with the intellectual nature of higher education (philosophical synthesis), the reality of interest groups and conflict (political advocacy), and the lack of spontaneity and freedom (coordinated anarchy). The concerns of the antiplanners, those who reject all notions of planning, are not dealt with.

It is important to recognize that in any institutional planning process, a dominant model or approach will probably emerge. It will, no doubt, not be a pure model but rather some combination. This dominant model stands a better chance of success if it takes as its basic planning focus an organizing assumption that reflects the basic tradition of the institution; if the planning orientation, purpose, and content reflect the real planning issues facing the institution; and if the dynamics of planning and participation reflect the governance process and administrative style of the institution. Within the planning process and its elements, variations in approach will occur. Such variation is natural if the planning process is to accommodate to different planning issues and contexts and will likely be tolerated if that rationale is understood and communicated.

Two observations are helpful in organizing the remainder of this chapter. First, despite this discussion and identification of six models or approaches to planning, it is apparent that a rational process notion pervades three of them (the formal-rational, organizational development, and technocratic/empirical approaches). Several recent widely publicized models of comprehensive planning for higher education are compatible with this rational process paradigm (see Casasco, 1970; Fuller, 1976; Parekh, 1975; Sturner, 1974; and those developed by Academy for Educational Development (AED), NCHEMS, American Association of State Colleges and Universities (AASCU), Council for Advancement of Small Colleges (CASC), and other professional associations and consulting or development organizations). The PPB, MBO, Management Information Systems (MIS), and other decision-making and analytical approaches tend to assume the paradigm. Second, the distinction of strategic planning that focuses on an institution's relationship with its large environment and tactical planning that focuses on more internal planning issues is conceptually useful in thinking about two levels of planning.

Therefore, the next two sections of this chapter and Parts Two through Five of the book are organized around the planning elements identified at the strategic and tactical level in the formal-rational model (Figure 2). This organization is to enable a logical order of examination of the different levels and elements of planning, their purposes or functions, and some of the issues in trying to relate them to each other. The intent is not to suggest the formal-rational process is either the most effective or even the best picture of reality. Indeed, as will be suggested later, the overall planning process and that within each element probably will and should depend upon institutional traditions and governance patterns and the nature of the planning problems being dealt with.

Strategic Planning

Although planning serves many functions, the primary purpose of strategic planning is to foster institutional adaptation by assuring congruence between an institution and its relevant and often changing environment, by developing a viable design for the future of the institution, by modifying it as needed, and by devising strategies that facilitate its accomplishment. Strategic and master planning are often considered synonymous; however, they usually encompass four broad elements:

1. environment assessment or scanning (to identify trends or potential changes in the environment and their implications for the institution)
2. institutional assessment (to clarify strengths, weaknesses, problems, and capabilities of the institution)
3. values assessment (to consider values, aspirations, and ideals of various constituencies and responsibilities of the institution to them and the larger public)
4. master plan creation (to devise a strategic pattern, design, or direction for the institution on the basis of the first three elements)

Strategic planning then seeks to establish the fundamental assumptions about the environment, the institution, and the future form of the institution. It involves policy decisions, which are the broadest and most encompassing decisions concerned with a college's or a university's long-term future. Those generally include major assumptions about the environment, its trends, and impacts on the institution; assumptions or conclusions about the institution's current strengths, weaknesses, and problems that need to be considered or addressed in the future; the philosophy and rationale for the institution; the proposed mission, role, and scope of the institution and its objectives and goals; the organizational, administrative, and governance structure for the institution; the major program (academic, research, service, and support) and resource (fiscal, physical, human, and information) strategies or policies to guide the fulfillment of the plan; and a tentative set of priorities. These decisions may or may not reside in a single master planning document. Strategic planning then deals with the organization-environment interface and is intended to provide a framework within which tactical planning occurs. Before examining the elements of strategic planning, a brief discussion of that interface focus is in order.

The Organization/Environment Interface: Concepts and Alternative Approaches. Although strategic planning can be pursued without reference to the environment, one of its major contributions is to provide a framework within which the organization-environment interface can be examined. It assumes an institution's long-term viability depends on a planning process that produces and revises its strategic or master plan either in response to external pressures or to enhance its resources from and position in that environment. This assumption suggests some key concepts that define an institution's environment and help identify an institution's strategy for relating to it.

Because environments are complex, one usually attempts to "segment" them. One general approach (Cope, 1978) begins with a framework for segmenting the environment into four broad sectors or subenvironments, each with its own forecasting methodology. Those are social (including demography), political, economic, and technological environments. Cope proposes ways of incorporating these various forecasts into a force-field analysis and into master planning. A more institutionally specific approach (Peterson, 1977) to segmenting the environment is presented in Figure 4. It begins with the assumption that resource flows or linkages (financial, human, enrollments, program need/demand,

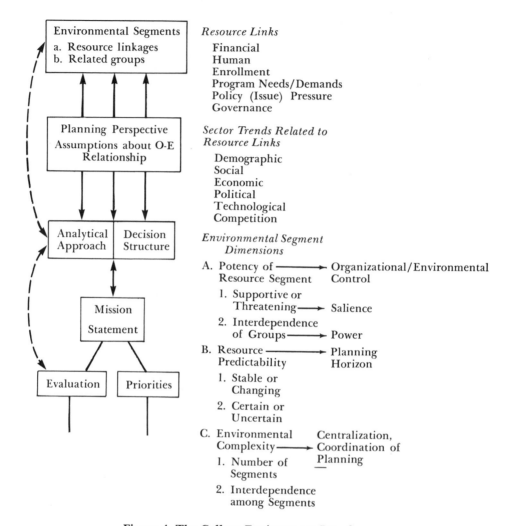

Figure 4. The College-Environment Interface

policy or issue pressures, and external-governance groups) are the basis for segmenting the environment. Key groups related to or potentially affecting each resource link or sublink (for example, various types of operating revenue) are identified as a resource segment. Analysis of the groups forming each resource segment and of basic trends in environmental sectors (for instance, Cope's social, economic, political, technological, plus demographic and competition trends) that might affect resource flows is the focus of this approach. The resource segment view suggests some important concepts on which they can be examined. These concepts further suggest seven strategies or approaches for relating to the environment.

Each resource segment can be distinguished by the *independence* or *interdependence* of the groups that are part of it. Similarly, the groups in the segment can be viewed as basically *supportive* of or *threatening* to the institution. Figure 5 suggests the importance of these two dimensions. As the groups in a segment become increasingly interdependent, they are likely to have more *power* or *po-*

Environmental Segment Is

	Supportive	Threatening
Independent	*Low Potency:* Organization controls resource flow	
Interdependent		*High Potency:* Environmental segment controls resource flow

Groups in Environmental Segment Are (row label)

Figure 5. Potency of Environmental Resource Segment

tency. As they become more antagonistic or threatening, they are likely to use that power to *control* the flow of resources. When the external segment's power is low and the institution controls the resource flow, planning can probably focus on the internal or tactical planning issues; however, under reverse conditions, greater attention has to be given to externally oriented or strategic planning. This dimension of *potency* of the segment and organizational or environmental *focus of control* of the resource flow is helpful in defining an environmental strategy.

Each resource segment can also be characterized by the *degree of change* and *certainty* of its resource flow (or in the underlying sector trends that affect it). Figure 6 suggests that as the segment's resource flow is more changing and uncertain, its *predictability* decreases. This makes long-term planning more difficult. The assessment of the predictability of resource flows also affects the appropriate planning strategy.

Figure 7 identifies seven strategies or approaches an institution may adopt in relating to an environmental segment and suggests how these are related to the degree of resource *predictability* and organization versus environmen-

Amount of Resource Flow Is

	Stable	Changing
Certain	*Highly Predictable:* Long-term planning feasible	
Uncertain		*Highly Unpredictable:* Short-Term planning feasible

Direction Of Resource Flow Is (row label)

Figure 6. The Predictability of the Environmental Resource Flow

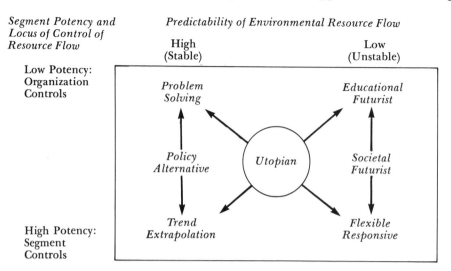

Figure 7. Organizational Planning Approaches for Different Environments

tal *locus of control* over the resource flow. Each approach reflects different assumptions about the resource segment's predictability and its locus of control of the resource flow. In turn, each approach suggests different patterns in the institution's primary *decision motive and process,* the *analytical technique* most closely associated with the approach, and the *benefits* of this approach. Table 3 summarizes each of the approaches. (For a detailed discussion, see Peterson, 1977.)

These approaches to organization-environment relations are of necessity oversimplified and seldom exist in pure form. The environments of higher educational institutions are often extremely complex and suggest conflicts. For example, as resource-related segments increase in number and flow in varying patterns to different units, decentralized planning by units in the institution who understand the resource flow is appropriate. Yet as those resource segments become more interdependent (when one increases, another decreases or one is competed for by several units), more centralized or coordinated planning becomes necessary and extremely complex. Further, there is the political reality that plans to deal with an environmental segment or group often create external reactions or changes in the environment. For example, planned staff reductions to offset enrollment declines may encourage union organizers to intervene, or plans by a public institution to raise private capital funds may deter approvals from the state.

These alternative approaches do, however, imply several things. First, higher education planners need to examine their most important resource links. This could result in a clearer definition of the relevant environment and their service region, in a better understanding of those resource flows in the future and their own assumptions about them, and in foreseeing critical resource issues and identifying alternatives for dealing with them. Second, the need for different approaches for different resource segments and the likelihood that several may be used simultaneously suggest the need for planning groups that can utilize a variety of decision processes, analytical approaches, and external as well as internal data sources. Third, because different organizational units may have somewhat different resource environments, there is a need to design the strategic planning function carefully—the process needs to look at the degree of centralization and/or coordination of planning decisions and the integration of analytical support for those decisions. Fourth, because externally oriented planning is complex and involves decisions based on external dynamics that many college and university personnel may not be aware of, there is a crucial need both to educate those in planning bodies about this external world and to communicate the nature of this planning activity to those whose resources, programs, and jobs may be affected by them.

Environment Assessment or Scanning. This element of strategic planning (see Chapters Nine through Twelve), often developed to a highly sophisticated degree in private industry, is one of the least developed in institutional-level planning, but it is receiving increased emphasis. To date, the emphasis has been primarily on assessing demographic conditions and enrollment potentials, but it is expanding to other resource segments.

The primary purpose of environmental scanning and assessment for strategic planning is to identify opportunities in a college or university's environment that planners may choose to exploit or constraints they may choose to avoid or attempt to circumvent. They attempt to identify underlying sector trends or key characteristics in an institution's environmental segments, to forecast resource flows where possible, and to suggest their institutional implications.

Environmental scanning in higher education today is usually structured in one of three ways: an analytical activity of a staff or an institutionwide planning body of staff; an analytical assignment to a separate institutional research or other administrative group; or a planning group that adopts a less research-oriented focus but includes members knowledgeable about external environments. The strategies or approaches are essentially those discussed in the previous section. The focus is on trends in environmental sectors, on resource segments and flows, on market analysis of needs or demand, and on competitive conditions. The techniques are largely rational: trend analysis, forecasting, simulation modeling of institutional environments, marketing surveys, environmental needs assessment, Delphi and scenario building, and analysis of competitive conditions and even legal-political or governmental controls and constraints or mandates. The range of resources and environmental segments suggests an extensive array of external data sources (census, economic condition, public opinion surveys, or governmental regulations) and a wide array of techniques.

The intent of environmental assessment, however, is not to make plans or set goals but to provide a realistic picture of the external environment within which strategic planning takes place. At a minimum, it allows one to question the underlying resource segment and environmental sector assumptions implicit in an institution's current direction or plan; it can suggest opportunities for and constraints to planning; and it might identify likely impacts of alternative future courses of action. The limits are the difficulties in clearly defining the environment and its segments, the lack of institutional staff knowledgeable in this methodology (or who are too sophisticated), and an array of studies and analyses that are expensive or of little use if not clearly focused by good planning questions.

Institutional Assessment. The purpose of institutional assessment (see Chapter Twenty-One) in strategic planning is to obtain a rational picture of an institution's current functioning: What are the strengths and weaknesses of its various academic, research, service, and support functions; of its staff and other re-

Table 3. Alternative Organization/Environment Planning Approaches

Planning Perspective	Environmental Assumption[a]	Locus of Organizational/ Environmental Control	Major Decision Issue (Motive)	Primary Decision Process[b]	Primary Analytical Approach[c]	Major Benefit or Value
1. Trend extrapolation	Predictable	Environmental	Prepare for impact of the trend (demand usually)	Rational	Forecasting	Consider long-term changes
2. Policy alternatives (organizational or environmental)	Predictable and clear choices	Organizational or environmental	Make or respond to choice (demand/need)	Rational, value, or political	Forecasting and simulation	Forced to face likely choices
3. Societal futurists	Limited predictability; substantial differences likely	Environmental	Select likely future; decide educational meaning (role in society)	Inspired, rational, and value	Scenarios, Delphi	Consider new and radical possibilities
4. Educational futurists	Limited predictability; substantial differences likely	Either or technological	Decide likely future (prepare for radical change)	Inspired, rational, and value	Scenarios, Delphi	Consider new and radical possibilities
5. Utopian	Predictable (at least a segment)	Organizational	Commitment to ideal (perpetuate tradition, achieve ideal)	Value	—	Provides a vision to believe in

| 6. Problem-solving | Stable or very predictable | Organizational | Resolve internal weaknesses (improvement) | Rational | Organizational analysis | Forces internal assessment |
| 7. Flexible, responsive | Very unpredictable | Environmental | Respond to shifts in demand (marketing or political survival) | Political | Market analysis, flexibility | Creates flexible and responsive organization |

---

[a]Planning time perspective depends on time span over which environment is predictable and risk planner is willing to take in going beyond that time span.

[b]*Rational*—information-based decisions; expert or administrative judgment.
Value—value preference decisions; democratic or participatory process.
Political—influence-based decisions; partisan representative process.
Inspired—creative decisions; open solicitation of original or knowledgeable thinkers.

[c]Many techniques in these broad approaches.

sources; of its programs; and of its patterns and processes of governance and administration? This picture is intended to ensure planning addresses major internal problems that need to be resolved, identifies priority areas for development (either to accentuate strengths or to strengthen weaknesses), and assesses the institution's capacity to move in new directions and/or to understand the institutional implications of their planning choices.

Most institutions practice institutional assessment, although it may not be comprehensive or related to planning. Institutional self-assessments have been popular for three decades in different forms. Accreditation constitutes a part of this picture. So do state higher education agencies, executive staff, and legislative groups through planning, budgetary, and review activity, which is extensive and increasing in many states (Folger, 1977). The accumulation of ongoing program reviews supplemented by ad hoc studies and evaluations and the review of institutional operating reports provides another form of institutional self-assessment. These diverse activities may provide a legitimate basis for ongoing institutional assessment but are often piecemeal or require extensive revision to get a useful self-assessment for planning. Most institutionwide strategic planning accepts and incorporates self-assessment, often to the detriment of externally oriented environmental assessment. It may be a carefully structured part of the strategic or master planning activity, a separate function of an institutional research or special study group, or an attempt to provide a broad array of data and reports to a widely representative planning group.

Perhaps more important than the purpose, patterns, and structure of this activity is the need to relate the design, strategy, and analytical techniques of institutional assessment to the needs of planning. First, good institutional evaluation needs to provide a picture of the major resources supplied to (inputs), the activity of (processes), and results (outcomes or impacts) of all major units or programs in an institution (Dressel, 1976). Increasingly sophisticated information and reporting systems make such data readily available (for example, NCHEMS data elements, program and outcomes structures, and reporting formats), which is useful for longitudinal examination of institutional conditions to see if they are improving or worsening and to make comparisons among and between similar units. The stress on common analytical techniques and recent work on information exchange procedures at NCHEMS (Peterson, 1976) make it feasible to have institutional assessment for internal and intrainstitutional comparisons. Second, the assessment of organizational processes, practiced for some time in government and industry, is getting increased emphasis in higher education as planners recognize the need to improve these dimensions of their institution. (Examples include the Educational Testing Service's *Institutional Functioning Inventory* and American Council on Education's recently acquired Higher Education Management Inventory survey.) There is also extensive emphasis on measuring qualitative as well as quantitative performance in assessing results (outcomes and impacts), productivity, or cost-benefit ratios compared to goals or performance standards. These require more sophisticated analyses and/or special studies but are particularly relevant to ongoing planning based on rational notions of goals and objectives. A third notion of institutional assessment is the extensive array of partial (student flow, faculty flow, and so on) or more comprehensive (RRPM, CAMPUS, TOTAL, and so on) resource models used to understand the functioning of the institution, to forecast the impacts of resource changes, or to assess the consequences of substantive (program) or procedural (administrative parameters) plans or changes. Finally, a more complex notion of institutional assessment is to examine its overall functional performance *(productive:* measures of performance of academic, research, and service functions; *human maintenance:* staff quality, morale, and such; *managerial:* efficient and effective use of processes and resources; *boundary:* effective resource acquisition and product or institution image measures; and *adaptive:* capacity to change according to plan or appropriate circumstance).

Strong institutional assessment clearly serves to strengthen the institution's focus on real internal problems, capacities for responding to external conditions, and ability to make changes. It also serves as a basis for later evaluation and assessment of performance. However, the need for a large and/or expensive staff for and the time-consuming nature of elaborate institutional assessment studies must be balanced with the need for useful planning information.

Values Assessment. This element of strategic planning (see Chapters Seven through Nine) is frequently discussed, yet it is perhaps the least understood dimension. Educational institutions in their mission, purposes, and strategies either reflect implicitly or have made explicitly decisions about certain value choices. These constitute a rationale for the institution: a set of decisions about clientele, about institutional functions and responsibilities, and about commitments to society, to the clientele, to the educational process, and to institutional working relationships. Neither the nature of these commitments nor the process by which they were arrived at is clear in most institutional planning. The intent of values assessment, then, is to identify the basic value choices and their implications and to assist in developing a rationale for the institutional plan or planning process.

If it exists, value assessment is likely to be the result of a series of discussions by an institutionwide planning or governance body or an epilogue to the planning process. Some value assessment techniques are beginning to emerge. At the broadest level, societal values can be ascertained by reviewing studies of various sectors or writings of futurists and by using Delphi techniques with either the institutional planning group or a broader array of respondents (Wilson, 1974). On a more focused basis, interviews of key internal and external constituents can be useful in identifying members' perceptions of institutional roles and responsibilities. Analyses of charters, mission statements from higher governing boards, and governmental mandates are another source of these value insights. Another important approach involves surveying constituent groups. The key is to identify potential, as well as current, constituent groups and to develop a values instrument that reflects a particular institution's important value choices. (ETS' *Institutional Goals Inventory* has been used this way and a new scheme developed by the Resource Center for Planned Change at AASCU is another example.)

Raising value questions and obtaining some consensus or agreement that divergent values will be accommodated is acknowledged as important. Failure to do so may lead to future planning conflicts or to lower commitment to the process. Yet this activity is still embryonic and will probably continue to be dealt with through broad representation in planning, by planners' sensitivity to seeing that basic issues surface, and by extensive discussion and debate.

Master Plan Creation. "Master plan" (see Chapter Eight), a term often synonymous with institutionwide or strategic planning, may incorporate the three previous elements (environmental, institutional, and values assessment), draw on them from related administrative units, or utilize them more implicitly. Here it refers to the process that decides how the institutional planning process will function; incorporates environmental, institutional, and values assessment information into a set of planning choices (the seven strategic policy decisions) or plan for the institution; and gets that process and plan accepted and implemented.

How the institutional planning process will be designed is the subject of this entire chapter. However, the decision about how it will function is also crucial. If an ongoing and comprehensive institutionwide strategic or master planning process is selected, that decision will have crucial consequences for the direction of the institution, may affect the regular governance processes, and requires a substantial resource commitment. Decisions to launch strategic or master planning may be made by state or institutional governing boards or by institutional leaders. However, on the basis of institutional experience, it is clear that the design of the process (and its elements) needs careful consideration, review, and approval by internal as well as external governance bodies if it is to function effectively.

Institutional master planning will vary, depending on whether a more rational (or O.D. or technocratic/empirical) or less rational (philosophical synthesis, political advocacy, or controlled anarchy) process model is assumed. The more rational will tend to make greater use of top down, centralized, or highly coordinated and analytically oriented processes with more organized participation. Structures for master planning seem to fit the following modes:

1. the elected "blue ribbon" committee of highly respected institutional leaders (Princeton University initiated this pattern during a budget crisis and has continued it as an effective and legitimate group that revises priorities annually.)
2. the institutional "team leadership" approach with selected leaders of various major constituencies: (faculty senate, student government, executive officers, deans, and board members) (Wichita State University has launched such an approach with a grant from the Kellogg Foundation.)
3. the "administrative team" approach, in which the executive officers, perhaps with board members and an analytical support staff, take on the function as a part of their role (This is consistent with the MBO tradition and, its proponents claim, improves the integration of planning and implementation and clarifies responsibilities. Furman University and Colorado State University, among others, have adopted such an approach.)
4. the "line executive officer-planner" approach, in which a chief executive officer, perhaps with an advisory group of any of the previous types, assumes responsibility for strategic and tactical planning and may oversee the related analytical offices (These plans are usually presented to the key governing board for review and approval.)
5. the "subcommittee" approach, in which a subcommittee, usually with diverse membership of the board or an institutionwide governing body, is assigned the institutional planning task
6. the "combination" approach

Each of these patterns may reflect differences in institutional decision-making style and/or administrative style. They will vary in their reliance on analytical staff for institutional, environmental, and values assessment and for reviewing the implications of alternative goals and strategies. Their mode of selection, composition, permanence, and responsibility can also differ.

For an ongoing strategic master planning group to influence implementation, key responsibilities are to update the environmental trends and assumptions to keep the plan viable, to revise priorities and see that resource allocation decisions reflect them, to review institutional reports and program reviews to assess progress, and to see that the master plan is updated when needed and that the planning process functions in the best interests of the institution. Obtaining acceptance for the master plan suggests the need for a master planning group that is consistent with the tradition and governance structure of the institution, has some continuity of membership, has broad representation, and is coordinated with the major institutional governance body.

The advantages associated with master planning are the insight gained from carefully examining the institutional, environmental, and values contexts of the institution; the sense of wholeness and completeness from a well-documented and organized master plan; and the sense of purpose from one that is legitimately endorsed and enforced. The disadvantages include the extremely difficult and complex nature of the task: conflicting trends; the difficulty of reaching agreement on goals, strategies, and priorities; and the often large numbers of individuals and groups involved. The process can be time-consuming, expensive, and lead to little specific action or change. Streamlining this process once it is in place and incorporating the concept of continuous updating and reranking are essential if it is to become a framework for tactical planning.

Tactical Planning

Tactical planning serves two primary functions: preserve the vitality of institutional units and assure the implementation and achievement of the master plan or some set of institutional priorities. The three planning elements I shall discuss, program planning, priority setting and resource allocation, and program review, have been treated extensively in the literature. As we become more concerned about faculty and administrative redirection and training, staff development is increasingly being considered a subelement of tactical planning, although I shall not discuss it here.

Program Planning. Program planning (academic, research, service, support, or administrative programs) is an element that can be independent of institutional planning and may be a separate process at the program level (see Chapters Thirteen through Sixteen; Heydinger, forthcoming). Our interest in program planning is primarily as an activity that links master planning and resource allocation. Its purpose is twofold: to develop programs that contribute to the accomplishment of institutional goals and that are themselves effective. The distinction between new and existing programs is useful.

The development of new programs when resources are limited and student and/or client demands are changing is a critical activity. The past practice of allowing programs to evolve from other ones, to depend on the interests of faculty entrepreneurs, or to utilize outside funds for development was often in-adequate and unresponsive. In times of constraint, existing programs are con-servative, individual faculty members find their normal work loads heavier and their access to funds more difficult, and external funds are limited. Con-sequently, some institutions are developing a more conscious new program de-velopment process that may occur at the central administrative, school, or de-partment level. The general steps they encourage are clear: set institutional priorities for program development, provide incentive or developmental funds to underwrite developmental activity, establish a review process to identify the resource needs and other institutional impacts of the new program, select pro-grams for further development, and provide assistance in clearing extrainstitu-tional program review and approval processes. The latter step can be especially critical for public institutions in states with new program approval procedures. This element should reflect institutional priorities, suggests the need for a clear process and analytical support, and involves the resource allocation process.

Planning for continuing programs is usually tied more closely to the actual budgetary process. However, attempts are made to develop program plans that go beyond the normal budget cycle and identify program goals and priorities for expansion or reduction with their resource implications. Program planning can adopt a more or less rational process, depending on the approach to planning, and can be done from the bottom up (programs prepare and submit their own goals and plans) or from the top down (they conform to prescribed priorities and guidelines). The former can inundate the planning process with inordinate and irreconcilable paperwork, and the latter is likely to produce resistance or stability rather than change. A major concern is to provide a framework of priorities for continuing program planning, to allow for and reward incentives aimed at new efforts, and to prepare enough background information on program operating data and performance efficiently to accomplish the data-generating aspect of program planning.

In planning for new and continuing programs, needs assessment tech-niques for current and potential clientele, market studies of supply and demand, and the increasing array of program planning and resource models are impor-tant analytical tools. Depending on one's approach to planning, the process may emphasize more or less rational processes and the structure to govern it may be dominated by administrators, faculty, or analytical staff. The key is to relate pro-gram planning, to the extent feasible, to institutional goals and program devel-opment priorities and to assure that the resource allocation process reflects them.

Priority Setting and Resource Allocation. These interrelated activities (see Chapters Seventeen through Twenty) are well developed in the literature, par-ticularly resource allocation and budgeting (Caruthers and Orwig, 1979). In the past, they were often not integrated into the institutional planning process, leav-ing the actual resource allocation process unaffected by planning and reducing the chances of planning redirecting resources or having desired effects. The purpose of these two activities from a planning perspective is to translate plans into shorter-term (two- to three-year) program and resource priorities and to reflect those in the allocation process—providing, along with program planning, the primary linkage of strategic institutional planning to implementation.

The priority-setting activity in most institutions is either not present or very unclear (perhaps deliberately) and is probably the most controversial. Whether done explicitly as a master planning activity, separately, or implicitly in the budget process, priorities affect or reflect real resource distribution. Its importance is highlighted by the fact that experts disagree on the extent to which planning and budgeting can and should be integrated. Some argue the specific budget pressures and time constraints are incompatible with planning (Schmidt-lein and Glenny, 1977), and others contend their separation is a major difficulty (Schick, 1966). Priorities are in the middle.

Priority setting, both for program development and planning and for other resources, is the key interface between planning and resource allocation. It also coincides with the primary interface between longer-term institutional goals and objectives and the current short-term resource constraints, opportunities, and ongoing commitments. Even when it is an explicit activity with rational intent, the process is going to involve nonrational and political dynamics. Priority setting can be the responsibility of an institutionwide planning group (Princeton has made this the primary focus of their planning group annually), a separate budget priorities body (the University of Michigan utilizes this approach), or a responsibility of the budgetary group. The exact locus and structure will probably reflect institutional traditions of planning and budgeting and of administrative or faculty involvement. If priority setting is to have a legitimate impact on budgeting and program development, the group responsible for it needs to be clearly identified and the process by which it occurs needs to be understood. The selection and composition of the group will depend on institutional governance patterns and on the planning model adopted. The authority of this group in relation to program development and budgeting also needs to be understood. Analytical support for assessing the short-term implications of external (for example, economic decline or inflation) and internal (for example, bargaining agreements) impacts on the institutional resource mix and the implications of differing priority choices is required. However, only if priority choices are made prior to specific annual program and resource distribution decisions is there certain to be movement toward institutional goals.

Budgeting, the most common form of resource allocation, is not inherently a planning process. Its primary function is to improve the efficient allocation of resources, often an implicit function of planning. Caruthers and Orwig (1979) discuss the varied purposes and I have already noted its linkage to priority setting and program development. However, it is important to recognize the increasingly wide array of budgeting approaches and their relation to planning (see Chapters Seventeen and Eighteen).

Program Review. Program review (academic, research, service, or administrative programs) has not been widely viewed as a planning element (see Chapters Twenty-Two through Twenty-Four). In the past, it has been associated with specialized accreditation and maintaining minimum quality or standards. More recent concerns that program demand/need is shifting, that across-the-board and other forms of non-program-based resource reductions have reached their limit, that program efficiency or effectiveness may be suffering under these shifts and declines, and that institutions cannot afford all their programs have led to a more visible, planning-oriented role for this activity. State-level program review is now extensive and may even mandate institutional program review activities (Barak and Berdahl, 1978). In a planning setting, program review has four purposes: to determine if program purposes and goals are appropriate in light of institutional objectives (or can be justified as unique); to assess the need and/or demand for a program and its resource requirements; to assess if the program is performing or accomplishing those purposes and goals and how it might improve; and to determine, in light of the program review and institution's program and resource priorities, whether the program should be expanded, continued, reduced, reorganized, or discontinued. Program review that reflects institutional priorities can become a mechanism for program redirection and resource reallocation (either by revising program resource needs or freeing resources through program closure). These planning purposes suggest a far more rigorous notion of program review. It can lead to summative judgments as well as review for minimum standards or formative recommendations for improvement.

Designing a program review system that is responsive to planning needs, provides a means for program change, and supports resource reallocation faces several problems. Structurally, program review may be the province of an institutionwide group, of separate but coordinated review groups (graduate education, undergraduate, extension, or administrative area), of a specialized staff working for an institutionwide planning or governance body, or even of an externally mandated group (state higher education agency or legislative review group). Patterns of selection, composition, permanence, and responsibility vary and need to be clearly defined and understood. The problem in initial design of such groups is the threatening nature of planning-oriented reviews. Prior review practices by different groups and the special interests of various internal (faculty, deans, vice-presidents, or a specialized review staff) and external (accrediting or state board) groups have led to well-staked-out turfs, positions on program review, or fears of this new mode. Thus, it is crucial that program review be designed to build on existing practices where reasonable, develop a structure and a process that is carefully reviewed and approved, and have strong support for its purposes by governance bodies, administrative officers, and the institutionwide planning body.

Approaches to program review, like budgeting, are well documented elsewhere (Dressel, 1976; see also the Jossey-Bass New Directions for Program Evaluation Series). Approaches include input or efficiency models, objective versus goal attainment models, goal-free models, process-oriented models, comprehensive models, and adversarial models (see Craven, 1980). All generally assume a similar set of stages in conducting an evaluation that usually includes a definitional phase for determining issues, participants, purposes, and processes; a data collection and information analysis phase; an interpretation and reporting phase; and a judgment and evaluation phase. These variations suggest the need for a program review group that is not only aware of its planning role but sensitive to issues in designing an evaluation process.

Other major issues in designing a program review process often occur around the following: Are program reviews cyclical or reserved for atypical (or marginal) programs? Does the program conduct an initial review or is it done externally? Are all programs subjected to the same review approach or model—the same process? Because program review is often an extensive and time-consuming process, several institutions (Michigan State University, for example) have devised extensive program- or department-based information and reporting systems for monitoring or auditing the program performance. This requires an extensive data base; but once it is in place, it provides a data base for program planning and budgeting as well as review and a means of identifying problem programs between review cycles.

Although institutions are reluctant to close programs, several have found it useful to establish a second phase in the review—by either an external or internal group. This is especially critical if program closure includes the release of tenured staff. Such decisions are becoming more common and may be a primary reallocation source for future program development. Yet it highlights the need to design review processes that anticipate such circumstances and to devise procedures for resource reallocation and staff release.

Strategic and Tactical Planning—A Comment. For the sake of clarity, this discussion of the elements of strategic and tactical planning has assumed a comprehensive formal-rational approach or model. However, it should be recalled that the institutional planning process (or the major elements) may be more similar to the other five models. Or it may be a combination of the conceptual dimensions of a planning process (see Table 2): institutional planning unit focus; internal/external orientation; purpose for planning; future orientation; planning typologies; and dynamics of goal centeredness, style of decision making and analysis, and bases for participation. The overall planning process may also vary in its organizing dimensions: comprehensiveness, planning element emphasis, integration, process flexibility, organizational penetration, analytical sophistication, or planning group structures. To the extent that the planning elements do exist, the notion of future-oriented priority setting based on internal and external realities and the willingness to reallocate resources is essential to any or all these elements if there is to be an institutional planning process or function that guides or changes the institution.

Contextual and Organizational Fit Issues

Planning is not an isolated process or function. The discussion of the planning process, its concepts and theories, and the major strategic and tactical elements has touched on the relationship of the planning process to the basic concept of organization, to its role or purpose in the institution, and to the larger environment. However, designing a planning process must also entail adapting it more specifically to the institution. The following are some institutional fit issues that will influence the planning process design. They reflect planning's critical interface with the governance, administrative or leadership patterns, and analytical and information-processing segments of the institution.

Linking Planning and Governance. Because planning is designed to influence some of the broadest and most critical decisions an institution can make, it needs to be closely integrated into the governance or decision-making system (see Chapter Twenty-Five), which can be examined along three dimensions.

First, if planning and those participants it attracts reflect the decision-making style of the governance bodies it seeks to influence, it is more likely to be a process they understand and view as *legitimate*. In large part, this will be a reflection of the culture of the institution, which includes patterns of analysis, participation, communication, and influence. The six theoretical models of a planning process are closely analogous to institutional decision-making styles. It is also feasible to adopt one style for master planning (for example, the more bureaucratic formal-rational model to fit a state mandate or reflect executive decision patterns), another for academic program review (a more collegial developmental or philosophical approach to reflect faculty patterns), and another for resource allocation (a representative, political approach reflecting competitive behavior). In reality, these approaches are not simple or easy to gauge. Current governance patterns may be unproductive (for example, highly political budgeting competition), and it may be desirable to approach them differently in the planning process.

Second, the *authority* and *responsibility* relationships of the planning group to the governance bodies or administrators need to be considered. Do institutional goals need approval by the university senate, the board of trustees, or both? Do recommendations on program planning or review decisions go to deans, school executive committees, the academic vice-president, an institution-wide curriculum committee, or the faculty senate? Failure to define these relationships often leads to jurisdictional squabbles or delays and can even undermine the entire planning process. Of course, this does not resolve the situation when groups with different views claim final jurisdiction. The question of who can initiate ideas or alternatives for a planning group's consideration and who is responsible for implementing a recommendation are just as important as who acts on it.

Third, the structural *representation* or participation links with related governance groups and administrative levels have already been discussed but deserve mention. They are especially important when new planning processes that may affect existing patterns are being designed (such as when an institutionwide program planning or review process affects the dean's role or when a group that will have to act on or implement recommendations desires more effective communication).

Leadership and Administrative Style. To the extent that administrators dominate the governance process, allocate resources, or implement planning decisions, it is essential that a planning process and/or a major element have the support and commitment of the president and associated executive officers. This truism from the industrial planning literature is reflected in most higher education experience with planning. It may not be sufficient, but it usually is a necessary condition for effective planning. Support for planning should include staff, resources, and the commitment to utilize its results, as well as encouragement.

A crucial dimension within the planning process is the leadership and administrative style of a planning officer. The purpose of planning differentiates coordinating, supportive, analytical, and advocacy styles of planning leadership. The level of a planner's appointment, expertise, and credentials reflects status that adds or detracts from his or her leadership role. However, the planning officer's external leadership that relates effectively to institutional governance and administration and internal style of administering a planning staff may not necessarily be the same.

Planning Centralization or Decentralization. This issue is partly one of institutional authority and responsibility for planning as it relates to governance and administration. However, it is also an issue in the structure of the planning process. In public institutions, the issue is initially one at the state-institution boundary. To what extent is institutional planning, resource allocation, and program review prescribed by statewide plans for the respective institutions and by the processes of these major planning elements? Within an institution, it is a question of whether the primary responsibility for master planning, priority setting, resource allocation, and program review activities will occur at an institutionwide level, at the school and college level, or at some lower level (and whether it will vary by element). As institutions become larger, have more autonomy, have less-threatening external circumstances, and have more diverse and resource independent units, decentralized planning elements are more feasible and possibly more suitable to the needs of their particular unit. However, many institutions face the reverse or mixed characteristics. There is no easy answer. To the extent that planning elements are more decentralized, the problems of coordinating planning efforts increase.

Coordinating Planning with Analytical and Information Systems. Throughout this chapter, the relationship of planning or its major elements to information resources and analytical techniques has been emphasized (see Chapter Twenty-Six). Information systems development, computing resources, and analytical techniques for use in higher education have grown rapidly in the past decade, have been widely discussed (Lawrence and Service, 1977; Staman, 1979), and will continue to change. The problem for planners is threefold. First, keeping up with changes in these areas as they relate to planning is a professional development task for persons with primary planning responsibility. The second aspect is how to assure that the institution's information, computing, and analytical resources serve the planning function. Solutions are *structural,* giving a high-level planning officer direct responsibility for computer and information systems development and related analytical studies; lie in *staff expertise* provided directly or on an assigned basis to the planning office; or are an *acquired* service from other university offices or external purveyors of such services. These alternatives need to be reviewed in relation to the status and responsibility of the chief planning officer, the centrality of the planning function in the institution, and the demands for information and analytical services by other units.

Figure 8 summarizes the third aspect: the nature of the relationship between type of planning and some broad research and information categories. As one moves from implementation through tactical to strategic planning, the decision issues and the nature of the research design and analytical techniques become more complex, require more nonstandard and external data sources (other institutions, environmental data, and so forth), and use more complicated data collection strategies. However, the value-laden nature of strategic policy issues is also less likely to lead to clear decisions, and the costs of analysis are likely to increase. I have already discussed the nature of this dilemma and the emphasis an institution should give to information and analytical system development.

Administrative Structure of Planning. The structure of the planning group (selection, composition, permanence, and responsibility) and the bases for participation (expertise and representation) were discussed earlier (also see Chapters Twenty-Five through Twenty-Seven). The design of an administrative staff structure for planning (who is responsible and what constitutes the staff) is interwoven with the desired comprehensiveness, emphasis, and intended integration of the planning process and with planning's relation to institutional

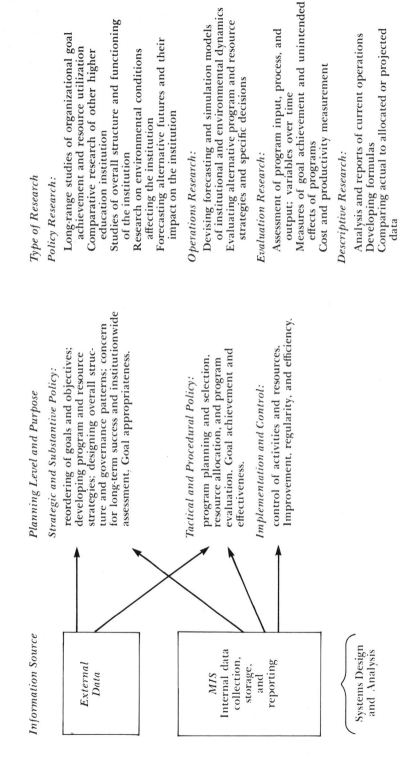

Figure 8. Planning and Analytical Approaches

governance, its pattern of centralization, its coordination with information and analytical systems, and the size of the institution. The issue here is the administrative one. Should planning be part of the line responsibility of all administrators from the president down (an MBO alternative), the part-time assignment of an assistant to an executive officer or president, the responsibility of an expanded institutional research office, a full-time staff director, or the primary responsibility of an executive officer? Clearly, all patterns currently exist and there is little evidence on which to base a choice from among them.

As planning, particularly in larger institutions, becomes more comprehensive (more planning elements and organizational units and resources) and mandated by external governance groups, includes more decentralized patterns among the elements, and is more analytically oriented, the number of planning groups, direct participants, units affected, meetings, and studies to coordinate increases rapidly. Under these circumstances, the argument for a high-level staff or line planning office becomes more convincing. The staffing of such an office is beyond the scope of this discussion but clearly requires some staff with broad planning and organizational expertise (presumably the director), staff with varied research design and evaluation expertise, and staff with programming and information system design expertise.

Planning as Organizational Change. The adaptive or change-oriented function of planning was identified at the start of this chapter, yet much of the criticism of planning is the tendency to rationalize stability. Planning to effect institutional change needs to produce short-range (one- or two-year) results in order to maintain the commitment of executive officers and the involvement of participants and to know that it is working, that is, it needs to have some short-term, viable purposes and expectations, as with any other institutional activity.

Perhaps as critically, the planning process or its director needs to examine strategies of change that might guide the activity. Is it to exert pressure for *incremental* but consistent change, to foster *planned change* (organizational development) efforts, to stress *decisive* and occasionally extensive changes, or to let change *emerge* from the various dynamics of planning? Is change to emphasize directive or *authority-based* methods, *participatory* processes, *rational* solutions, or *conflict* modes? The role of the planning office as initiator, neutral analyst, process coordinator, or advocate was discussed. The concept of a change strategy can shape the work of a planning staff, its relation to others, and its own effectiveness and needs to be examined carefully.

Planning as Education and Communication. Comprehensive planning involves many participants and affects numerous groups. Planning and its elements are processes that may not be fully understood, involve analysis of problems and issues about which most institutional members have little information, and influence decisions that can have wide consequences. Planning—or a planning officer—needs as a primary objective the development of regular and informative means of communication with constituents, participants, and governance links, explaining planning processes, emergent issues and alternatives, and rationales for recommendations.

Similarly, because planning will be a new activity and responsibility for many administrators and has a continuous turnover of participants on planning bodies and planning staff members, education about planning is also a useful objective. In designing an institutionwide planning process, Wichita State

University established a professional development center with training in the various planning activities as part of its program for faculty and administrators.

Planning Evaluation. Information on the outcomes, impacts, and benefits of planning is only beginning to emerge in case studies and a few comparative works (for example, Chapters Twenty-Eight through Thirty-One). Therefore, except to provide examples, it is unlikely such studies will directly help an institution revise and improve its planning process. Designing a planning process is an evolutionary activity. As such, it might benefit from a well-devised evaluation plan that examines how the design issues raised in this chapter have been resolved, the degree to which the purpose or expectations of planning (or its elements) are being met, the reasons for its successes and failures, and the costs and resources utilized.

Conclusion

Implicit in this chapter has been the notion of critical questions an institution can or should ask itself in designing a planning process. I have summarized these.

The Rationale for Planning. What general model or approach to planning (Table 2) is appropriate to our institution—formal-rational, organizational development, technocratic/empirical, philosophical synthesis, political advocacy, or controlled anarchy—or a modification or combination of them? • What is to be included in the content of planning—elements, organizational units, resources? • What assumption about the basic institutional unit for planning best reflects our tradition and self-image? • What primary purpose or institutional function (need) do we want planning to serve—adaptive (major redefinition or changes), managerial (improved effectiveness and efficiency), maintenance (improved capacity for known growth, development, and performance) or boundary (dealing with major problems of external relations)? What is the priority on these functions? And what are the specific planning expectations, desired outcomes, or formal goals under each? • What role is the planning process expected to play in achieving this purpose—1. identify critical issues, 2. assist others in doing studies, 3. coordinate assessments, 4. develop and examine alternatives, or 5. advocate action? • Are the major problems confronting the long-term viability of our institution internal, external, both, or uncertain? • What is the nature of the institutional future that planning should emphasize—most likely or probable, feasible, improvement of current, ideal, or allow members or units to achieve their capability? • What is the planning typology emphasized—substantive (ends) or procedural (means); strategic (master planning), tactical (and implementation); or policy and/or contingency issues? • What are the dynamics of this planning process? Is it goal-centered, consensus-oriented, priority-oriented, or pluralistic? Are planning decision processes likely to be oriented to problem solving; organized learning; reasoned debate and discussion; bargaining, negotiation, compromise, and coalitional; or loosely coordinated? Is analysis likely to emphasize quantitative rationality, qualitative rationality, reasoned logic, collaboration, or advocacy? • What is the basis for participation in planning? Does the planner role emphasize planning process, organizational development, intellectual, rational analysis, or political expertise? Is participation based on representation of administrative units, technical units, functional groups, affected units, interest groups, or elite or egalitarian democratic principles?

Planning Process Overall Design. • The institutional planning process (and its major elements) can be organized along the following dimensions: Is the planning process (or element) intended to be comprehensive or limited in planning elements or subelements; comprehensive or limited in organizational scope—programs (academic, research, service, support) or resources (human, financial, physical, and information)? What is emphasis on process elements and organizational programs and resources; integrated or fragmented view of elements and organizational programs and resources; integrated or fragmented view of elements, programs, and resources; flexibility, regularity, rigidity of planning processes; degree of organizational penetration; degree of analytical sophistication; or structure of the planning group (selection, composition, permanence, and responsibility)? • How is the institutional environment to be viewed? How is the environment delineated—by sectors (political, social, economic, technological, competitive, or other) or segments (resource flows)? How can environmental segments be typified on interdependence, supportiveness, potency or control of resource flow, and predictability? What are the boundaries of the service or resource region for each segment? • What approach to organization-environment interface is appropriate for each segment: trend, policy alternatives, problem solving, societal futurist, educational futurist, flexible responsive, utopian, or a combination? • How do the organization-environment approaches vary on decision motive, decision process, analytical approach, and benefits and limits?

Strategic Planning Elements. Which strategic planning elements are to be developed—environmental assessment, institutional assessment, values assessment, or master planning? • How is each to be organized? • How is each structured in terms of purpose, structure or model, analytical approach, and issues?

Tactical Planning Elements. Which tactical planning elements are to be developed—program planning, priority setting, resource allocation, or program review? • How is each to be organized? • How can each be organized or described in terms of purpose, structure of model, analytical approach, and issues?

Overall Organization. How can the overall planning process be organized in relation to the larger institutional context? • How is it linked to governance in terms of decision-making style (six models), patterns of authority and responsibility, and membership linkages? • What is the institutional leadership's support for, commitment to, and utilization of planning? • What is the leadership style of the planning director—externally and internally? • How centralized or decentralized is each of the major planning elements? • How is planning coordinated with analytical and information systems services in the institution in terms of planning staff updating and development and organizational linkages (authority for, planning staff expertise, or acquired services)? • Where does administrative responsibility for planning rest? • What is the size and expertise of the planning staff, if any? • What is the change strategy employed by planners—incremental, planned, abrupt, emergent or directive, participatory, political? • How does the planning staff develop methods to meet its needs for communication about planning and education about planning? • How does the institution intend to evaluate its planning process and elements? Who is responsible?

References

Ackoff, R. *A Concept of Corporate Planning.* New York: Wiley, 1970.

Anthony, R. *Planning and Control Systems.* Cambridge, Mass.: Harvard Graduate School of Business, 1965.

Baldridge, V. *Power and Conflict in the University.* New York: Wiley, 1971.

Barak, R., and Berdahl, R. *State Level Program Review.* Denver, Colo.: Education Commission of the States, 1978.

Bauer, R., and Gergen, K. (Eds.). *The Study of Policy Formulation.* New York: Free Press, 1968.

Bennis, W., and others. *The Planning of Change.* New York: Holt, Rinehart and Winston, 1976.

Caruthers, J., and Orwig, M. *Budgeting in Higher Education.* ERIC/AAHE Report No.3. Washington, D.C.: American Association for Higher Education, 1979.

Casasco, J. *Planning Techniques for University Management.* Washington, D.C.: American Council on Education, 1970.

Cohen, M., and March, J. *Leadership and Ambiguity.* New York: McGraw-Hill, 1974.

Cope, R. *Strategic Policy Planning.* Littleton, Colo.: Ireland Educational Corporation, 1978.

Craven, E. *New Directions for Institutional Research: Alternative Models of Academic Program Evaluation,* no. 27. San Francisco: Jossey-Bass, 1980.

Dressel, P. L. *Handbook of Academic Evaluation: Assessing Institutional Effectiveness, Student Progress, and Professional Performance for Decision Making in Higher Education.* San Francisco: Jossey-Bass, 1976.

Dror, Y. "The Planning Process: A Facet Design." *International Review of Administrative Sciences,* 1963, *29,* 44–58.

Drucker, P. *The Age of Discontinuity.* New York: Harper & Row, 1969.

Enarson, H. "The Art of Planning." *Educational Record,* 1975, *56,* 170–174.

Etzioni, A. *The Active Society.* New York: Free Press, 1968.

Folger, J. (Ed.). *New Directions for Institutional Research: Increasing the Public Accountability of Higher Education,* no. 16. San Francisco: Jossey-Bass, 1977.

Fuller, B. "A Framework for Academic Planning." *Journal of Higher Education,* 1976, *48,* 65–77.

Glenny, L., and others. *Coordinating Higher Education for the 1970's.* Berkeley, Calif.: Center for Research and Development in Higher Education, University of California, 1971.

Heydinger, R. (Ed.). *New Directions for Institutional Research: Emerging Approaches to Academic Program Planning.* San Francisco: Jossey-Bass, forthcoming.

Kerr, C. *Uses of the University.* Cambridge, Mass.: Harvard University Press, 1963.

Ladd, D. *Change in Educational Policy.* New York: McGraw-Hill, 1970.

Lawrence, G. B., and Service, A. *Quantitative Approaches to Higher Education Management.* Washington, D.C.: ERIC/AAHE, 1977.

Lawrence, P., and Lorsch, J. *Developing Organizations.* Reading, Mass.: Addison-Wesley, 1969.

Lindblom, C. "The Science of Muddling Through." *Public Administration Review,* 1959, *19,* 79–88.

Michael, D. *On Learning to Plan —and Planning to Learn: The Social Psychology of*

Changing Toward Future-Responsive Societal Learning. San Francisco: Jossey-Bass, 1973.

Palola, E., Lehmann, T., and Blischke, W. *Higher Education By Design.* Berkeley: Center for Research and Development in Higher Education, University of California, 1970.

Parekh, S. *Long Range Planning: An Institution Wide Approach to Increasing Academic Vitality.* Washington, D.C.: Change Magazine Press, 1975.

Peterson, M. "Decision Type, Structure, and Process Evaluation." *Higher Education: International Journal of Education and Planning,* 1972, 1.

Peterson, M. *New Directions for Institutional Research: Benefiting from Interinstitutional Research,* no. 12. San Francisco: Jossey-Bass, 1976.

Peterson, M. "Alternative Strategies for Planning the Institution-Environment Interface." In C. Adams (Ed.), *Improving the Processes of Administration in Higher Education.* Washington, D.C.: Association of Instrumental and Decision Sciences, 1977.

Poulton, N. "Impacts of Planning Activities in Research Universities: A Comparative Analysis of Five Institutional Experiences." Unpublished doctoral dissertation, University of Michigan, 1979.

Riesman, D., Gusfield, J., and Gamson, Z. *Academic Values and Mass Education.* New York: Doubleday, 1970.

Schick, A. "The Road to PPB: The Stages of Budget Reform." *Public Administration Review,* 1966, *26,* 243–258.

Schick, A. *Planning, Programming, and Budgeting: A Systems Approach to Management.* Chicago: University of Chicago Press, 1968.

Schmidtlein, F., and Glenny, L. *State Budgeting for Higher Education.* Berkeley: Center for Research and Development in Higher Education, University of California, 1977.

Simon, H. *Administrative Behavior.* New York: Free Press, 1957.

Staman, M. (Ed.). *New Directions for Institutional Research: Examining New Trends in Administrative Computing,* no. 22. San Francisco: Jossey-Bass, 1979.

Sturner, W. *Action Planning on Campus.* Washington, D.C.: American Association of State Colleges and Universities, 1974.

Taylor, B. "New Dimensions in Corporate Planning." *Long Range Planning,* 1976, *9,* 80–106.

Weathersby, G., and Balderston, F. "PPBS in Higher Education Planning and Management." Parts I, II, and III in *Higher Education.* 1972, *2,* 191–205; 1973, *1,* 229–318; 1973, *2,* 33–67.

Wilson, I. "Socio-Political Forecasting." *Michigan Business Review,* July 1974, 15–25.

8

Joseph P. Cosand

Developing an Institutional Master Plan

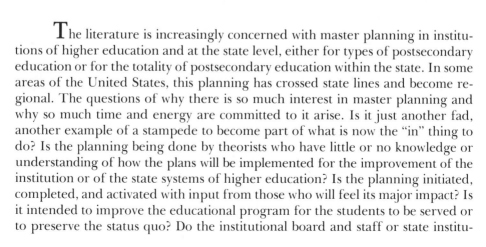

The literature is increasingly concerned with master planning in institutions of higher education and at the state level, either for types of postsecondary education or for the totality of postsecondary education within the state. In some areas of the United States, this planning has crossed state lines and become regional. The questions of why there is so much interest in master planning and why so much time and energy are committed to it arise. Is it just another fad, another example of a stampede to become part of what is now the "in" thing to do? Is the planning being done by theorists who have little or no knowledge or understanding of how the plans will be implemented for the improvement of the institution or of the state systems of higher education? Is the planning initiated, completed, and activated with input from those who will feel its major impact? Is it intended to improve the educational program for the students to be served or to preserve the status quo? Do the institutional board and staff or state institutions to be affected fully understand and support the planning process? Have realistic estimates been made of the funds needed to implement recommendations from the planning conclusions or will this become simply another enervating exercise in futility that contributes further to the accumulated cynicism of college and university faculty and administrators? These questions must be raised and answered prior to initiating the master planning process. There is deep suspicion among the professional staffs of colleges and universities with respect to institutional and state master planning. From my experience, far too much of this suspicion and cynicism is justified.

The Purpose of Master Planning

The questions of why there should be a master plan and what forces are present to initiate interest in it and provide suitable evidence to the appropriate board for approval must be answered and the answers must be made available to those who will be involved in the planning process and those who may be affected by implementation. The time and energy of those participating in the planning process are too valuable to be wasted if the purpose is basically to build the initiator's ego. Institutional autonomy is too highly valued to be jeopardized by a power-hungry state chancellor, board, or governor.

Failure to have institutional and state plans following World War II caused both institutions and states to expand their educational programs and physical facilities haphazardly. Board and administrators' conversations and meetings were dominated by the word *growth*—growth of enrollments, faculties, facilities, and budgets. Perhaps this had to be: Personnel and financial resources were stretched to the limit to provide the necessary educational opportunities for those seeking postsecondary education. We could have planned better if we had planned collectively instead of individually, but each institution and each type of institution functioned independently. In too many instances, separate growth became wasteful and extravagant as we built, expanded, and duplicated one another without much concern for a possible change in the expansion curve or in the public attitude toward higher education with respect to funding priorities.

Although we are well aware of the facts that will affect colleges and universities during the rest of this century, educators could be charged with gross neglect and incompetence if we entered the 1980s without a clear understanding of the essential need for comprehensive educational planning at both the institutional and state levels. The problems higher education will face are serious and cannot be sloughed off. We got by in the 1950s and 1960s because growth covered up our mistakes, as it would in business, industry, and labor. The 1970s were transition years that brought us more into public scrutiny and demanded explanations about cost efficiency, productivity, and accountability. We have been warned and our response will be studied and evaluated.

Creating the Climate for Master Planning

It does not necessarily follow that those affected by the master plan will be involved. Those who are involved in planning must anticipate that any plan imposed upon others without their understanding will probably be doomed to failure. There can only be rumors, false expectations, and likely defiance if there are no clarifications of why the plan is being undertaken. The justifications for master planning that apply in each particular case must be defined to all concerned with the utmost clarity, and those concerned must have the opportunity to challenge the reasons for the plan in open discussion and perhaps debate prior to the initiation of the planning process itself. This philosophy of openness can establish a positive climate in which the planning process can function. It can curtail and possibly eliminate the negative climate of suspicion and cynicism, both of which are prevalent in many planning activities. There cannot be a positive climate within a college or within a state if the planning process and then the plan itself are imposed from the top.

The expectations for a master plan must be defined prior to designing it and must be clearly communicated to the affected parties. The following are illustrations of reasons for planning with corresponding expectations.

Change in College Mission. Colleges of all types are finding their student profiles are changing in age, sex, race, affluence, attendance category, and interests. However, many colleges have been slow to acknowledge these changes and have reluctantly looked for solutions only when faced with serious internal morale problems. The solutions have often been expedient, demonstrating no evidence of problem analysis or of either short-range or long-range planning. The failure has been one of leadership, administrative, faculty, and board, although in too many colleges, the boards have too long been kept ignorant of deteriorating conditions. Expedient actions may well trigger further actions, which will exacerbate an already serious situation concerning the college mission. If the mission is no longer viable, college staff and board must recognize the fact. Their members' expectations would be that the master plan would modify the mission to serve the students now enrolling. This is a difficult task for any institution, most of all for any institution with a long history of a previously adopted and almost sacred mission. However, the staff and board have a right to know and to understand fully what to expect from a master plan designed to change the college's mission.

Change in Recruitment and Admissions Policies. Both public and private colleges sometimes fail to communicate recruitment and admission policy changes to the faculty or board. Such changes are primarily for survival purposes. Added students are expected to replace those who are no longer enrolling. Changes of this type may well modify the quality of the educational program if modifications are not made in the curriculum, teaching methodologies, or the teaching staff itself. Changes of this type may necessitate a change in the college mission. A master plan concerning enrollment and admission changes with resultant effects upon the college mission, curriculum, teaching methodologies, and professional staff must be understood by the board and staff. They must know what to expect if the master plan is designed, developed, and implemented. Changes of this type must not occur through the gradual erosion of the college philosophy. If there is agreement that admission practices must change and that this would result in a change in the educational program, there should be justifiable evidence that a master plan for such change is in order and that the climate for such a plan will be positive, with clear delineation of possible new directions.

A State Master Plan for Higher Education. Reactions to such a plan are mixed, to say the least. They run the gamut from enthusiasm to vehement antagonism. The enthusiasm tends to come from state officials, especially in the offices of higher education. The negativism tends to come from the administrators and faculty. The expressed need for master plans will increase in the coming years due to the pressures of declining enrollments, program duplication, and competition for students and funds. Those supporting the plan will expect it to curtail, if not eliminate altogether, these problems. Those opposing such state planning fear the result will be outright state control of higher education similar to that in most other countries. Institutional autonomy is the major concern of the college and university leadership. The master plan expectations for states are therefore diametrically opposed by those in state offices and those in institutional offices of leadership. Governors and state legislators may be found in either camp or somewhere in the middle of the argument, according to the position of power they see themselves occupying. It is really a question of power, of who makes the decisions in higher education.

Some states exert full control of higher education with little input from the individual institutions. The arguments for such controls are cost efficiency and more conformity of educational opportunity and quality. It is believed service duplication is thus avoided and more uniform student services are provided. College and university presidents and faculty refute these arguments, claiming state controls create homogeneity, stifle creativity, and demand immense amounts of useless paperwork.

State planning for higher education clearly must be understood with respect to its need and use. The extreme positions on expectations are probably for the most part false. The true worth of such planning must be sought out, described, communicated, and made acceptable to all concerned. The expectations from the planning cannot afford to be exaggerated in either direction because the extreme positions are unacceptable. This is a communication and philosophical problem that we in higher education must attack with open minds and full involvement. Such planning should aim to strengthen higher education in the state, improve student services, increase social justice for all potential students, and increase the quality of the overall educational program. We have the right to expect, as do those who provide the funds, that the funds will be expended to the best advantage of the students to be served, whatever the institution. The higher education profession cannot condone wasting funds, duplicating programs, or continuing unnecessary institutions. The profession therefore has the right to expect a state master plan that removes the inadequacies and improves higher education without initiating and establishing controls that destroy the autonomy and creativity of the college staff.

Master Planning for Staff Morale and Creativity. The previous illustrations are specific with respect to program and functions, but they also relate to staff morale and creativity. Colleges throughout the United States are in turmoil about changes taking place without faculty, administration, and board understanding and support. There is open conflict among board members and between boards and presidents and boards and faculties. There is open conflict within faculties and between faculty factions and presidents. Administrative groups are unionizing and are emulating faculty adversarial actions. It is questionable whether these diverse and conflicting groups can expect a master plan to provide a course of action for their college that will improve campus collegiality and overall climate and thus enhance staff morale and creativity. It is also debatable whether the master plan will concern itself with structure, communication, involvement, and implementation. Perhaps there is no need to be concerned with mission, admissions, or state systems, for perhaps these are not the problems. When conflict pervades and respect disappears, program, mission, students, and state policies fade into the background. The destructiveness of present negative climates on too many college and university campuses, some of which is described in detail in higher education publications and in the news media, is damaging to the overall image and health of higher education and in extreme cases can affect institutional viability.

Maintaining the Climate for Planning During Design, Implementation, and Evaluation

The previous four illustrations do not speak to the climate it is desirable and necessary to maintain during plan implementation and evaluation. Everyone concerned may agree on the reasons for and expectations from the plan and enthusiastically support it, but this is only the beginning. Plan design must involve enough staff, both faculty and administration, to allow full communication on the direction the plan is taking. There can be no hidden agendas. If a suspicion develops that the plan is to have an end result other than that agreed upon, the climate will become one of participatory cynicism. Throughout the design stage, there must be communication among the staff and between the staff and board. An increasingly serious problem facing colleges is that of split boards. A thoroughly understood and supported master plan may mend such splits.

As plan design is completed and development progresses, knowledge, understanding, and communication become increasingly important. Relating expectations and design to the realities of day-to-day operations may be difficult. As staff become involved in development, fears and pressures intensify and supporters can become neutral or even antagonistic. Those responsible for plan development must now fully understand the time and energy problems of all staff members involved in the plan. This is the time when leadership must not create bureaucratic obstacles but instead remove them as expeditiously as possible.

The togetherness that has, ideally, persisted through the expectation, design, and development stages is further tested during implementation. As the master plan progresses, more demands are made on the people affected. The management system in use may prove inadequate. Time priorities may have to be rearranged, creating potential conflicts. There is the danger of surfacing the specific demands of the master plan and of avoiding the difficult choices that are needed. Weak supporters or opponents may become active antagonists and openly attempt sabotage. The planning staff will be circumvented if opponents join with board factions to obtain criticism or even withdrawal of board support. Continuing communication during implementation is the key to avoiding such problems. Faculty discussions following presentations and board discussions following staff presentations to the board, full, open discussions of results as measured against expectations, must be regularly scheduled.

A major defect in master plans has been the failure to evaluate results once the plan has been implemented. Too many plans have been initiated, designed, developed, and implemented and then forgotten. This is especially true of the short-range plan, which often is little more than a plan of expediency. The long-range plan can be just as susceptible to abuse if it is followed religiously without regular evaluation and updating. Master plans should include an evaluation section, including specification of who is to do the evaluating, how often it will be scheduled, and who will receive copies of evaluation reports. Perfunctory evaluations are a waste of time and money. Planners' evaluations will be suspect. If reports are not distributed to staff and board members, they will view the plan with cynicism; and rumors will abound.

Correcting and updating must also be designed into the master plan. Updating should follow the scheduled evaluation. The planning team should again involve staff and board members in updating or modifying the master plan. Such changes can be just as threatening as the original master plan to staff. Open communication and discussion within the staff and between the staff and the board must continue.

Maintaining an acceptable climate for an ongoing master plan is vital whether the plan is at the institutional or state level. The concept is the same; the actors are different. The fears, the suspicions and cynicisms, the desire for authority and control, the processes, and the excitement and rewards are all similar. A climate of trust and mutual respect where all are concerned with providing a quality educational program with the resources available is essential.

Approaches to Master Planning

The diversity of institutions, states, and needs precludes adherence to any set pattern of planning. Too often in the past, consultant groups developed a master plan procedure, packaged it, and sold it to a college or state. Although it was not necessarily suitable, the approach was then imposed upon the institution or state, with generally negative results. This is not to say that consultants should not be retained, but consultant packages are not always appropriate for the diversity of needs in master planning. The following approaches to master planning are illustrative and not exhaustive; an approach can be a mixture of them.

Consultant Approach. This approach has the strength of past experience. Consultants are generally experienced planners and can bring to the institution or state a sophistication and background the regular staff generally lacks. There is also the strength of impartiality and lack of emotional involvement. The consultant is able to be objective and to apply procedures without being accused of personal bias. The state or institution can choose between many consulting firms, which provides the opportunity to use the consultant most suited to the special needs of the master planning to be initiated and developed. To utilize these strengths, the institution or state must be knowledgeable about consultants and be prepared to interview several before engaging one. There must be a clear understanding as to the terms of employment, especially with respect to the interaction and responsibilities the consultant has with the staff and board.

The weaknesses of the consultant approach are numerous. The consultant may simply attempt to apply a package procedure developed previously and used on other occasions, regardless of the particular needs of the institution or state. This is a common practice and an unacceptable approach. A master plan must be designed for the institution to be served. A second weakness is the consultant's lack of understanding of the staff's internal networking. Master plans are threats to many staff members. The possibility of change creates uncertainty, especially in those who lack confidence and feel insecure in their positions. The consultant must be ever sensitive to the internal workings of the institution or state, a most difficult demand to meet. However, without such sensitivity, the consultant's progress will be impeded. A third weakness is that the consultant may be viewed as an outsider brought in to do a job the regular staff could have done better. The staff may well transfer its resentment to the consultant and cooperate reluctantly, or not at all, in the planning process. A fourth weakness is that the consultant may impose a master plan with little or no staff involvement in design and development. Such a practice practically guarantees the staff will reject the plan. There are other weaknesses, such as the expenditure of funds that should have been used for other purposes; but these four are the most common.

Presidential Approach. The success of the presidential approach depends on the board and staff's respect for the president. If respect is lacking, the planning process is doomed to failure. The president is expected to have vision and to provide leadership for the future as well as for the present. The president is expected to be sensitive to the needs of the college, as a state chancellor would be expected to be sensitive to the needs of the state. A president is expected to understand the internal networking and the particular insecurities and fears of staff members, which can be exacerbated by a master plan. The president should initiate the master planning process by openly discussing with the staff and board his or her expectations from such a plan and by listening to their comments and suggestions. With this kind of climate, the president can appoint to the master planning team those staff members who will best serve the college. Their appointments will be accepted and respected. With such a beginning, the staff will be calmed and should proceed with the planning process in a positive manner. The president, however, cannot fail to maintain this openness throughout the design, development, implementation, evaluation, and updating of the master plan. Any deviation or withdrawal into secrecy will turn an incipient suspicion or cynicism into active opposition.

The weaknesses of the presidential approach lie in the president's or chancellor's attitude toward the staff and board and in their attitude toward the president. If there is a lack of mutual respect, presidential leadership in the planning process will be a negative factor and may even doom the plan to failure before it gets off the ground. The president cannot impose a master plan upon a staff and expect to obtain positive results. The president cannot enthusiastically initiate a master plan and then withdraw to other activities. If the approach is presidential, it must be presidential through completion. A major weakness in the presidential approach can be the staff appointments. These should be made with the utmost care, for staff activities in plan design and development need to be sensitively handled. Staff members, too, must be aware of the potential suspicions and fears and must function openly and positively. Their attitudes must reflect the president's positive attitude at all times.

Office of Planning and/or Institutional Research Approach. This approach may offer the best chance for a viable master plan design and development. However, plan implementation and evaluation should be the responsibility of other offices. A well-staffed office of planning or institutional research should have the resources to provide a college or a state with a master plan design that fulfills the specific needs and expectations of the college or state. However, the office staff should not proceed with plan design until the office staff fully understands the plan's intent. The strength of this approach is based upon the quality of the research staff, the data available, and the staff's knowledge of the institution's internal operations.

The weaknesses of this approach lie in the exclusivity of offices of planning and institutional research. The knowledge and expertise of research staffs can be weaknesses as well as strengths. Research offices must be an integral part of the institution, serving the total staff and responding to their needs. Where this philosophy exists, there is respect for the research office. Where it does not exist, there is a barrier between the research office and the overall institutional staff. A research staff that lives within itself and for itself cannot expect to be understood or accepted by others. Where such a climate exists, an office of planning and institutional research probably could not design and develop an acceptable master plan. No matter how professional the work might be, it would be viewed with suspicion, as something based on theory rather than reality. It would be similar to a plan prepared by an outside consultant because neither the consultant nor the research staff is part of the institution.

Another weakness in this approach concerns the research staff's capability to design and develop a master plan. Major universities and some other two- and four-year colleges have high-quality research staffs, but these are probably in the minority. The real weakness of the research office approach lies in the quality of the staff resources allotted to the office. If these resources are not sufficient in numbers and expertise, the office should not be assigned the responsibility of designing and developing a master plan. There can be no belief in or support for a master plan if those directing its design and development are unqualified for the task. It is an exercise in futility and can trigger a negative climate in an otherwise positive campus attitude toward administration.

Master Plan Content

An examination of master plans will show that they come in all shapes and sizes and for varied purposes. During the growth years of the 1950s and 1960s, the few institutional-level master plans emphasized design and development of campuses and physical facilities. The term "master plan" was almost coterminous with the architect's master plan for the new campus or with the expansion of an existing campus. At the state level, the master plan referred primarily to the location and development of new campuses. Only occasionally was there evidence of an interest in or concern about a master plan for an institution's or state's total educational program. The California state master plan, designed in the late 1950s and implemented in the following years, did include specifics with respect to admissions, enrollments, and program. But it was an exception.

This limiting philosophy of master planning continues today, and examples where a so-called master plan is a plan for the physical development of the campus abound. Such plans are completed, where resources are available, regardless of changing student needs and interests. Plans of this type are pleasing to look at, can be pointed to with pride, are an achievement. They may also be obsolete and, if completed, result in an extravagant waste of funds. Their relationship to present and future educational demands should be evaluated before construction of further buildings or new campuses is authorized. The evaluation and updating of this type of master planning has been neglected, and many states and campuses have physical evidence of the blind adherence to a no longer viable master plan.

Another type of a limited master plan is one concerned only with enrollment projections based primarily on a head count or full-time-equivalent figure. It pays little or no attention to the interests of the projected enrollees and thus to which programs will attract them. Plans of this type may exemplify the survival syndrome, survival at any cost: Project the enrollments and, where declines are anticipated, recruit the necessary bodies.

The enrollment master plan is often combined with a financial plan in order to merge enrollment and financial needs. Enrollment projections, financial projections, and facility projections can all be combined into a third type of simplified master planning at either the institutional or state level. This type was prevalent during the past growth years and is still popular today, although it will probably not prove useful for the remainder of this century. The following are probably the major ingredients of the broad, inclusive master plan needed in the 1980s.

College Mission. Education for whom, for what purpose, and at which institution are the basic questions a college or a state higher education mission must answer. Doing so is the most difficult part of the master plan because changes in the mission will affect every other segment of the college or the state system. There must be a philosophy and objectives for the higher education program, and they must be dynamic and reflect student needs. The mission must be active, understood and supported by faculty, administration, board, and those who provide the funds on which the college or state system operates.

Students. Who is to be admitted and who is to be served follows from the philosophy, objectives, and mission of the college. The master plan must not equivocate on this essential point. The population that ends up being served can be considerably different from that specified in the mission because there is generally a reluctance to change the mission statement. But such differences must be reconciled because they would invalidate the entire plan.

Curriculum. The mission of the college, its philosophy and objectives, and the students enrolled should certainly be the major forces in curriculum design and development. Therefore, the curriculum must be an integral part of the master plan. As the mission and student profiles change, so must the curriculum change. Unfortunately, this is seldom the case. Plans rarely include a section on curriculum, due perhaps to faculty fear of change. Change may affect the survival of a course, program, department, or even a graduate school or college itself, in the case of a state master plan. A long-term master plan updated annually will show a change in curricular needs. Courses should be added, modified, or deleted. In those institutions where there is a rapid change in student mix, there may be a need for a considerable change in the college curriculum or in the curriculum mix among a regional group of colleges. Curricula tend to be protected with almost a religious fervor by the individual departments or by the institution, regardless of student interests and needs. Well-designed master plans should provide the foundation for curricular change.

This section of the master plan should also include data on time and location for classes in which students wish to enroll. A continuing needs analysis survey of students and potential students will provide the basic data for the master plan. The data should be analyzed and recommendations made for curriculum change. Adherence to obsolete or unneeded curricula wastes physical resources. Failure to initiate and develop needed or expanded curricula wastes human resources. Curricula to serve the needs of both the individual and society must be available. This can become a major goal of the broad-based institutional or state master plan.

Staffing. It is only logical that a master plan include a section on staffing needs when it has already projected enrollments and curricula as they relate to the college mission. This should be done both on a broad, overall basis and by institution and program. Master plans are delinquent when they avoid the difficult task of projecting staff needs. A long-range master plan, updated annually, is a valuable tool in maintaining an optimum student-staff ratio. Lack of planning in this area has created imbalances within the total budget divisions and between the various departments and programs. The cost disparities are obvious and are unacceptable if the college or state is concerned with equity, productivity, and cost efficiency.

Goals will, of necessity, vary according to the type of institution, curriculum, and students enrolled; the size of the institution; and certain other variables. The danger of imposing conformity through state controls is very real and must be avoided. However, gross staffing imbalances cannot be justified because they are reflected in student services, teaching quality, faculty services, and college leadership.

The rapid growth in numbers and percentages of part-time faculty highlights the need for including staffing in a master plan. The presence of such data will bring this rather recent phenomenon to the attention of the professional staff, the boards, and the state officials, as well as the public. The move toward part-time teachers has been rationalized as a move toward increased program flexibility made necessary by the rapid change in the student mix. There is some validity in this argument, but the real reason appears to be more closely related to the financing problems facing higher education. A full-time equivalency of part-time teachers can be funded at from one third to one half the amount that would be required for a full-time teacher.

Staffing is the heart of the college. A master plan should and must identify the needs program by program and compare them with the existing staff. Overstaffing wastes funds and staff time and energy and creates a morale problem. Understaffing wastes student time and energy, which also creates a staff morale problem. The master plan can identify cases of overstaffing and understaffing and help solve both problems.

Facilities. Although facilities planning is not the primary function of a master plan, it must be an integral part of the overall scheme, whether the campus is in the process of development or has been long completed. Construction or remodeling is too often undertaken without fitting into any logical system of priorities. When completed, it is frequently viewed as an expediency and a waste of funds that could and should have been expended elsewhere. The gravest abuse, however, is rigid adherence to a state or institutional master building plan that no longer meets present needs, let alone projected student enrollment or present and projected curricula.

The mission, student enrollment, curricula, and staffing sections of a master plan must precede the facilities section. There are examples of colleges having been completed prior to the enrollment of any students or the establishment of any curricula. I suppose the justification was that someone had a vision. This can be a most wasteful and ignorant method of campus development.

Master planning for facilities must include provision for maximum use and minimum energy and maintenance costs. College facilities are generally grossly underused and, in some cases, are often vacant except between 9 A.M. and 3 P.M. Rooms that could hold thirty to fifty students have classes of from five to fifteen students. Older colleges are especially vulnerable on seat usage, for their classrooms tend to be of an average size. Planning should approach a maximum room utilization of 80 percent from 8 A.M. to 5 P.M. and a seat utilization aimed at 75 percent or higher. Laboratories of necessity have a lower room utilization; but except for those laboratories of a very special type, they should not be the exclusive property of the laboratory teacher. Laboratories such as those for physics, electronics, or botany generally have open table tops free from special equipment. Such laboratories are acceptable for use by any lecture or discussion class. They should be available for other classes as well. The same kind of careful space utilization should be applied to other areas of the campus, such as the library, lounges, and physical educational facilities. The emptiness of many classrooms, laboratories, libraries, dining areas, and gymnasiums creates a museumlike atmosphere. The excuse that students will not attend classes before 9 A.M. or after 2 or 3 P.M. is unacceptable. The problem is being compounded by the increase in evening students at the expense of day students. Perhaps future buildings should be designed for those part-time students who attend classes from 6 to 10 P.M. and let the facilities take care of the fewer numbers of day students. Certainly, this would be the converse of what has been planned in the past.

Campus Location. Colleges and states should have planned campus locations more carefully during the expansion years of the 1950s and 1960s. But there were not the energy problems at that time that we face now and will face increasingly in the coming years. Although it is unlikely many new campuses will be built in the near future, campus location must be a part of the long-range master plan, for its implications are many for both students and overall campus viability. Important concerns are student access, racial mix, population moves, land costs, land preparation, and staff recruitment. The gift of a piece of land is not sufficient reason to accept the land for a campus. Doing so may represent a very small cost saving overall and could be a very costly mistake if it prevents the institution from providing the educational program a needs analysis survey shows is wanted. This is especially true for community colleges.

Student Services. The changing student mix has certainly caused a change in the services to be provided. The rapid increase in part-time students, older students, women students, certain minority students, and less-affluent students creates a far different student profile from that of only a few years ago. Master plans must include this section as a major part of the planning process. Long-range projections updated annually will help the college and/or the state better adjust the services they provide.

A prime example is student financial aid. Even in the most selective and affluent institution, significant numbers and percentages of students are receiving financial assistance from the federal government, the state government, and the institution itself. Colleges were slow to develop quality offices of student financial aid. Inefficiency, mistakes, and an unprofessional climate were the norm, not the exception. Most colleges were unprepared for this activity and responsibility and some still are not prepared. New attitudes toward counseling and advising and toward women's activities are needed. Student personnel administrators must adjust to a rapidly changing world. For these and many other reasons, a master plan will have to include a section on present and projected student services. This is not to be relegated to a lesser level of importance than that given to instruction and business. The leadership in all three areas should be on a peer level in the hierarchy of administrative leadership.

Research. The time is past when a college or a state can ignore the need for the research function in higher education. There are various types of research responsibilities and they vary by institutional type. However, each institution should have a research resource to provide the data needed for the master plan. A successful business, industrial, or professional enterprise is forced to allot a percentage of its budget to research if it is to continue to be a viable entity. Growth industries put their profits into research for further growth. It is difficult to comprehend why institutions of higher learning have been reluctant to support educational research. They have instead either ignored this function or have sought their research funds from foundations or the federal government. Colleges and universities have relied almost solely on "soft" money as it is made available by foundations, the federal government, or by other agencies and organizations.

Improvements in the educational program, be they in instructional methods, curriculum, student services, physical facilities, or management, require research data. Obsolescence is not acceptable in business, industry, or the professions; it is equally unacceptable in our higher education institutions and state systems. The master plan calls for a section on research with annually updated projections of needed research data and services.

Finance. The conclusion to a master plan must be the section on finance, which should be divided into two parts—expenditures and revenue. The college or state leaders are responsible for compiling, analyzing, evaluating, and recommending the total budget to the proper authorizing authority. Such recommendations must be based upon defensible data derived from the planning presented in the previous eight sections of the proposed design for a master plan. Without such defensible data, a budget is more or less based upon unreliable generalizations liberally laced with emotional bias. Management of this type is subject to severe criticism, and it should be. This is probably the major reason board members and citizens with management responsibilities in business and industry frequently have little respect for educational leaders. It may be why some boards are seeking and appointing presidents from business or industry.

This trend toward business management leadership instead of educational leadership for our colleges, universities, and state systems should be of concern to the educational leadership of our country. The wealth of human and physical resources of the 1950s and 1960s in higher education is not apt to be available in the foreseeable future, certainly not in the coming decade. The necessity for intelligent and responsible planning is not new, but there is an increasing urgency for it on both a short- and long-range basis. Educators who are also well prepared to function as managers are increasingly needed. Cost efficiency and productivity combined with enlightened educational planning will be the requisites for tomorrow's educational leaders. The ability to understand and use a master plan will be one of the skills required.

The concluding element in the design, development, and implementation of the master plan is the defined evaluation of the plan. A simplistic evaluation method would consist of annually updating the multiple-year long-range plan. Such updating through research data is factual and should be reliable. However, this cannot be left to chance. The evaluative procedures should be included in the final section of the plan. As with design and development, evaluation should also include involvement of representatives from those staff elements affected by the master plan. Board policies should include one authorizing the master plan process, the date of its submission to the board, and the plan's relationship to the budgetary process.

Master plans are meant to be guidelines for the growth and development of the college or state system as they reflect its mission. They are not meant to be an arbitrary set of regulations. The planning process can be either a positive or negative morale factor for the staff. The manner in which it is initiated, designed, developed, implemented, and evaluated will determine whether it will be a benefit to the college or state on a short- and long-range basis or a destructive force affecting the overall climate of the college or state system of higher education.

Bibliographical Essay

There is no shortage of references on master planning. The major problem is to sift and winnow through the mass of literature to determine what is relevant to a particular institution or state. During the past decade, most states and a large percentage of colleges and universities have developed so-called master plans, and many of these have been distributed as manuscripts or published as articles. An ERIC search for literature under "Master Planning" or on specific aspects of the topic is strongly recommended. The references available from such a search will be far more numerous than can be digested, but some should be examined critically prior to embarking on any master plan.

In addition, the offices of those associations concerned with various aspects of planning can be contacted for examples of different master plan models and the names of institutions that have completed such plans. Among these are the Society for College and University Planning, the National Association of College and University Business Officers, and the eight institutional membership associations—American Association of Community and Junior Colleges, American Association of State Colleges and Universities, American Council on Education, Association of American Colleges, Association of American Universities, Council for the Advancement of Small Colleges, National Association of Independent Colleges and Universities, and National Association of State Universities and Land-Grant Colleges. In addition, the Educational Facilities Laboratories, a division of the Academy for Educational Development located in New York City, the National Center for Higher Education Management Systems in Boulder, Colorado, and the various state boards concerned with higher education can offer suggestions for saving time, energy, and money. But plans of other institutions or states that are not relevant to the needs of a particular institution or state should not be copied: the result will be not only irrelevant but wasteful and worse than no plan at all, leading only to apathy and cynicism about planning in general.

9

Robert H. Fenske

Setting Institutional Goals and Objectives

It is probably poor form to convey a sense of misgiving about the study of institutional goals for a handbook that is intended to be of practical as well as theoretical value. Nonetheless, this chapter registers strong doubts about the efficacy of many present goal studies and the validity of models borrowed from business management to measure academic efficiency in higher education. My concern is not only that "we know not what we do" but that the misapplication of techniques will become legitimate by default and through continued usage may ultimately change the nature of higher education—the genius and characteristics of which have taken centuries to build. I am not alone in these fears. Bailey (1973), Corson (1975), Brandl (1970), and many others have expressed similar fears eloquently, and Richman and Farmer (1974, p. 334), professors of management as well as consultants to higher education and industry on systems

Note: I wish to thank the Wisconsin Vocational Studies Center at the University of Wisconsin in Madison, and especially its director, Merle E. Strong, for providing much needed resources to complete this manuscript during my sabbatical leave. Thanks are also due Lou Attinasi for his editorial assistance. He is a doctoral student in the Department of Higher and Adult Education at Arizona State University.

analysis, have pointed to an ominous future: "If the fundamental problem of goal system operationalization, verification, and restructuring is not handled carefully and effectively during the rest of the 1970s and in the 1980s, much of the vitality, originality, and delight of the modern American higher educational institution may well be destroyed."

Etzioni (1964, p. 9) voiced the general caveat that applies to our present situation: "The desire to establish how we are doing and to find ways of improving if we are not doing as well as we ought to do—often has quite undesired effects from the point of view of organizational goals. Frequent measuring can distort the organizational efforts because, as a rule, some aspects of its output are more measurable than the others. Frequent measuring tends to encourage overproduction of highly measurable items and neglect of the less measurable ones." His concern is inherent in the following discussion which contains, along with the caveats, suggestions about improvements in studying goals in colleges and universities.

Rationale and Definitions

The question: "Why study goals?" is somewhat annoying to most planners and researchers in that the answer seems so obvious, even axiomatic. One of the few things organizational theorists agree on is the necessity of defining and studying goals. Parsons and others (1961, pp. 38–41) indicate that the problem of goals and goal attainment has priority over all other problems in organizations and Hambrick (1976, pp. 45–46) asserts, "No aspect of an organization's strategy, structure, or operation policies can be intelligently discussed or rationalized without a firm understanding and analysis of the unit's goals." In terms of institutions of higher education, Richman and Farmer (1974, p. 335) claim "systematic consideration of the goals problem seems to be the most important thing that an academic manager or administrator should be doing now."

The study of goals is acknowledged to be important because goals not only give an organization a sense of direction, a frame of reference for its activities, and a means by which to evaluate change and progress, they help explain and relate the organization to its publics. But if this is true, why do not all colleges and universities embrace a continual process of setting, revising, and reevaluating goals? Why do relatively few attempt goal setting except when goaded by an external constituency, regulating body, or accrediting agency? Why are goals examined only in response to some crisis? And why do these few attempts have so tepid a reception by faculty, administrators, students, and others? Before answering these questions in the following pages, an explanation of terms and concepts seems essential.

The term *goal* is often used interchangeably with *function, purpose, mission, objective, role, scope,* and *aspiration.* There is no general consensus about these terms but there seems to be a clustering of usage (Corson, 1975; Fincher, 1978; Laughlin and Chamberlin, 1972; Trivett, 1973; among others) that views "goals" as an intermediate concept in a hierarchy between more general "missions" on the one hand and more specific "objectives" on the other. Thus, *mission* is often used to express the aspirations, often unstated, that society has for institutions of higher education. These aspirations are consensual and represent the most general level of hopes and expectations people in general hold for colleges and universities. In this sense, the mission of an institution for higher education is the reason for which society supports it and tolerates it—its very reason for being. Much has been written about the vague generalities published as institutional missions in college and university catalogues. However, in the context of this discussion, they serve their purpose in expressing to external constituencies such as the general citizenry, prospective students, and their parents what the institution hopes to accomplish in response to the support and expectations of society. For example, Lee (1968, p. 1) identifies the three basic missions of American colleges and universities as "to transmit, to extend, and to apply knowledge" and comments that "each of these three missions—teaching, research, and public service—is related to a multitude of programs, intermediate goals, and functions."

Goals usually refer to the aspirations, functions, and purposes of the institution itself as viewed by its internal constituents. They are more specific than missions, and usually include reference to a clientele being served, a process, and an outcome or outcomes. Not all such goals, of course, are stated in the publications or documents of the institution. Some are revealed in what the institution actually does, as represented by its resource allocations and activities—and they may actually be at variance with its stated goals, as Gross and Grambsch illustrate (1974, pp. 16–17). "In the case of the university, there may be strong consensus that a major goal is preparing students for careers as scientists (an intention), but members of the faculty may be observed to be spending much of their time in consulting business firms on practical problems, and a high proportion of the students may end with terminal master's degrees."

Objectives, in this usage, are much more specific than goals, are often characterized by being behaviorally measurable, and as such are of interest to the various management systems that have been developed for application to business corporations and other bureaucratic organizations and that are now being applied to colleges and universities. For example, Carpenter and others (1973, p. 19), in their review of literature on "management by objectives" (MBO), suggest that objectives should be "consistent with the institution's purpose" as well as "concise and specific, measurable and verifiable, understandable by those immediately affected," and capable of specifying "a target date for completion" and "a single result."

Illustrating these three hierarchical levels, one mission of a college might be to teach or to transmit knowledge; a goal related to this mission might be to provide both a liberal arts education and preparation for a career to qualified residents of the state; and a related objective might be: "To ensure that each graduate has acquired subject matter mastery (defined as achieving passing grades in at least four courses) of three different subject matter fields selected among social sciences; natural sciences, fine arts and humanities; and English, literature, and foreign languages and has also acquired a marketable skill or is certifiable for a career or profession as defined by official career or professional certification guidelines. For those careers and professions that do not provide certification guidelines, the criterion shall be that 75 percent of the graduates in a particular field will be hired full-time in that field within two years after graduation. This undergraduate program will be developed and established within three years and will comprise a standard four-year curriculum and one hundred twenty credit hours. This program will be developed within the budget specified by the board for the three-year developmental period."

This chapter focuses on goals but not to the exclusion of missions or objectives. The intermediate level of goals necessarily has important implications for both the more general missions and the more specific objectives; and some analysts, intrigued with the fact that objectives ideally are measurable, are tempted to assume they can be aggregated to equal a specific goal or set of goals. This chapter seeks to show, however, that the concepts of goals and objectives are dichotomous and essentially deal with two different but related issues: goals dealing with values and impact and objectives dealing primarily with administrative efficiency. In so doing, it will focus more on universities than colleges, not only because as Gross and Grambsch (1974, p.1) point out, "universities contain within them much of the variety offered by the remaining institutions" in the postsecondary sector but because universities are of all types of institutions in higher education the most complex, least amenable to formal organizational study, and most typically the "organized anarchy" referred to by Cohen and March (1974). If goal studies can be done at all successfully in universities, they will be no more difficult in less-complex types of higher education institutions.

Institutional Goals and External Pressures

Government, both at the state and federal level, is the most significant of all sources of external pressure on higher education. Probably the most inexorable result of governmental pressure over the past twenty years is the erosion of institutional autonomy. Of the two governmental levels, the federal has led in this process. In the 1950s, the federal government was a passive provider of institutional grants (as for facilities, libraries, and research) which it hoped would encourage or allow the institution to carry out social missions and national policies as stated in the Truman Commission and other reports and as expressed in legislation like the National Defense Education Act. Since then, the movement has been toward a proactive stance involving heavy-handed enforcement of rules and regulations concerning a wide variety of social equity issues, purchase of specific products like research, program and dissemination activities on a competitive grant basis, and most important of all, the move toward the "market model" of support for higher education.

The market model or price system has also been adopted by state governments. Bowen (1973) finds this system ominous: "In this way, higher education would concentrate on those specific activities which someone on the outside would deem worth paying for" (p. 9). A review of current practices indicates that this system is already entrenched in many aspects of higher education. A corollary of the pricing system would be detailed regulation of the purchase and delivery of products and services. This means subjecting institutions to "site visits, inspections, audits, and reports, by placing them under the supervision of public coordinating bodies and by direct legislation affecting programs, tuition, salaries, teaching loads, tenure, and so on" (p. 9).

An interesting analogy to the price system for use *within* the institution was developed recently by Rogers and Van Horn (1976). The model is called *goal-oriented resource allocation*. This system utilizes aspects of both centralized and decentralized allocation processes. Centralized processes are those that have always been used by many institutions for support of academic programs. That is, resources are collected by the central administration and allocations are made to various sub-units according to historic and projected needs. The decentralized resource allocation system is also present in many institutions of higher education for auxiliary enterprises like bookstores, student housing, and food services. Each such unit earns income directly and pays its own operating expenses and purchases services from other areas of the university. Generally, the decentralized unit is required to either earn a profit, break even, or at least not incur a substantial loss. Essentially, goal-oriented resource allocation would generalize the process already used for auxiliary enterprises to units such as academic departments which have never operated this way. Institutional goals would be set up that would govern the operation of this system "to maintain a sense of unity and common purpose in the university" (Rogers and Van Horn, 1976, p. 142). Also, the central administration (president's office) would maintain sufficient central control through the basic operating budget "to determine the overall direction and priorities of the university" (p. 142).

The goal-oriented resource allocation model may or may not prove workable in institutions of higher education. While the model combines elements of common resource allocation practices, it nonetheless contains a basic innovation that lends itself to much controversy. Essentially, it places in the hands of the central administration (the president and those who serve at his pleasure) nearly total power to decide which academic units would be protected from the "profit center" concept for what purposes and to what extent. A president who would choose this model would place himself continually in the position of having to defend his own internalized goal system. On what basis would he select for protection either the department of Hebrew or the department of mathematical physics, both, or neither? If protection was withdrawn completely from all units, questions of institutional goal systems would be avoided—the market model or pricing system would prevail and it is likely that the institution would soon bear little resemblance to present colleges and universities.

While the federal government has pursued the market model most vigorously since the late 1960s, particularly through the competitive research grant programs and through student financial aid programs that are transportable to any institution, the states have also moved in this direction by increasing tuition more rapidly than institutional funding levels, and by more specific methods such as tuition levels differentiated by type of program and graduate level. Since the states are still the largest single source of support for higher education and also grant the legal basis for existence for almost all institutions, their relationship to colleges and universities remains most crucial.

Essentially, the states have always set the missions of their institutions by such means as (1) spelling out those missions in the institution's original charter and in the legal powers of the governing boards, (2) creating or closing out professional schools, and (3) requiring that the state's colleges or universities admit all graduates of the state's high schools. However, historically they have not often intervened directly in the internal educational program goals and priorities of the institution. Those prerogatives have been delegated by the state to the faculty and administration of the institutions through the governing boards.

During the last twenty years, statewide coordinating and planning agencies have increasingly engaged in recommendations and policies that clearly impact educational program goals. A recent document which reported the recommendations of the National Task Force on the Accountability of Higher Education to the State (Education Commission of the States, 1979, p. 48) indicates that "more than three fourths of the states have developed general goal statements, usually as a part of the master planning process." While the Task Force included institutional executives and others, there was a majority of state agency and legislative representatives. Evidently the group did not dally with the question of institutional autonomy, but instead went directly to "the complex question of the appropriate ways in which higher education could best demonstrate its accountability by reporting its effectiveness in meeting statewide goals" (p. vii). State accountability was defined as: *"A concept and process that involves setting goals for higher education, measuring progress in relation to those goals, and reporting to the people of the state, through the responsible state authorities, the degree of attainment of educational objectives"* (p. 2).

It is interesting that the Task Force stated the following as an assumption, not as an issue for debate: *"The recommended accountability process requires the establishment of statewide educational goals.* State goals are different than the sum of institutional goals but in most instances state and institutional goals are closely related. An accountability plan cannot work if there is basic disagreement between a state and the institutions in that state about the primary goals of higher education. For this reason, goal establishment will be most successful if all relevant state and institution representatives are involved in the process" (p. 4).

A point overlooked or simply ignored in such pronouncements is that the state's original charter set institutional goals, and that historically states have delegated goal system review to the governing board. Specifically, states have *not* presumed to involve "all relevant state representatives" in a continual process of reviewing institutional goals. The list of legislative, executive, and even judicial "relevant state representatives" could be very long indeed. Supposedly the U.S. Supreme Court decision in the 1819 Dartmouth College Case had permanently established a buffer between state politics and institutions of higher education. Daniel Webster had successfully argued before Chief Justice Marshall that not only must there be an inviolable sanctuary for criticism of the social order, there should also be recognition that colleges and universities involve *long-term* processes (overlapping four-year careers of students, lifetime careers of professors, and even greater longevity of ideas and educational goals as stated in the institutional charter) that should be protected from the vagaries of two- and four-year state partisan political cycles.

While the Education Commission of the States (ECS) document suggests that state-level goals should be general, many of the states have already developed master plans that call for specific objectives to be pursued by institutions and evaluated by state agencies. Of course, the concepts of evaluation and accountability are empty without at least the threat of punitive action. This sensitive matter is broached with little subtlety: "States should provide adequate rewards and sanctions to encourage achievement of goals. The budget is the primary instrument for state influence on achievement of program objectives" (p. 4). In view of the overall trends toward increased state regulation, it may be fortunate for institutional autonomy and academic freedom that accountability systems adopted by states do not work very well, even to the satisfaction of their strongest advocates.

The Carnegie Foundation for the Advancement of Teaching (1976, p. 15) sounds hopeful in its commentary on *The States and Higher Education* when it states: "There is much opposition to regulation generally, and of higher education in particular." And the Foundation asserted that "we believe that the burden of proof should be on the centralizers and regulators to demonstrate that something can be done better through centralization and regulation" (p. 16). However, such rhetoric by prominent higher education leaders is likely to have little effect on stemming the tide of state regulation.

Richman and Farmer (1974) forthrightly summarize this discussion of institutional goals and external pressures: "Unless universities fall in line with their financial backers, many will be in deep trouble soon. There is no easy way out for any manager or administrator here. Some academic institutions may become unmanageable, because the goal systems of insiders and supporters are so divergent that no compromise is possible. In such situations the outsiders can win— but the cost will be the destruction of the university as we have known it. We may see much of this in the next decade" (p. 224).

Organizational Goal Complexity

In the beginning, setting goals for American institutions of higher education was easy. The statutes of Harvard clearly indicated that "everyone shall consider the main End of his life and studies to know God and Jesus Christ which is Eternal Life" (Hofstadter and Smith, 1961, p. 2), that the two interrelated goals of the college were to educate the community leaders and train orthodox ministers, and that a single curriculum would do well for both purposes. Even though the rules and regulations spelled out by Harvard's founders seemed to describe a theological seminary, such a concept "had no more meaning for them than an engineering school. They did not distinguish sharply between secular and theological learning; and they believed that the college education proper for a minister should be the same as for an educated layman" (Hofstadter and Smith, 1961, p. 2). Every activity and expenditure could be directly related to these two institutional goals, both of them embedded in the overall mission of the institution.

All of this simplicity and compactness in a monolithic religious colony of a few thousand souls, of course, begs the question of goal setting today, with its mosaic of conflicting values among both the internal and external constituencies of a complex multiversity. According to Anderson (1976) modern institutions of higher education exceed all but the military and government in organizational complexity. Unity of purpose and function is gone; seemingly boundless and increasing plurality is the rule. Their system of governance, their organizational structure or lack of it, and their tensions among participants ensure that setting institutional goals is now, and will be for the foreseeable future, a complex, frustrating, and sometimes unrewarding process. Despite these challenges, goal setting continues to be a popular activity in higher education: Governors, state agencies, and governing boards continue to request "role and scope" studies; specification of institutional goals is part of nearly all accreditation studies; the relatively new Institutional Goals Inventory (IGI) has already been used at hundreds of institutions; and its publisher, Educational Testing Service (ETS), has now created two new forms for use at community colleges and small liberal arts colleges. However, this continuing pace of frenetic activity does not necessarily denote either the unification of the goals of the constituencies of higher education or an increase in effectiveness or efficiency in attaining them. Many, if not most, of the reports of goals studies repose undisturbed in file cabinets, while efforts directed at clarifying and attaining measurable objectives seem often to be applied only to the most vulnerable nonacademic offices. I do not mean to imply by this that setting institutional goals is necessarily a useless or hopeless enterprise. Indeed, the purpose of this chapter is to explicate the problems involved, review currently available strategies, and suggest procedures that can enhance success. But to do so requires abandonment of the idea that models of goal setting that work with other complex organizations apply to higher education institutions in a directly useful way. All such models assume a clear line of authority and a consensual set of goals, but neither exists in American institutions of higher education.

Here, the organized anarchy described by Cohen and March (1974) is even more rampant than in the medical clinic—perhaps the closest analogy to a modern college or university. In both cases, the clients tend to be docile recipients of whatever services the professionals offer; the public at large is helpless to regulate effectively the professionals' activities because of the esoteric nature of the service performed; the regulatory agency or board tends to be an advocate of the organization; the professionals decide what services to offer and how to perform them; and administration or management exists to facilitate the professionals' activities and maintain adequate supporting services and financial records.

This analogy of clinic and university is far from perfect, however, because the clinic likely has infinitely simpler goals than the university—probably only one or two, namely, to make a profit and to offer a needed service. Consider, however, the complex tangle of divergent and even opposing goals among university constituencies: Many students want quick certification for a career; faculty cherish learning for its own sake but reward research activities, not teaching; public officials want to see a better match between employment needs and the curriculum; administrators must maximize efficiency of scarce resources but have little control over the vast bulk of expenditures they administer; and trustees have the legal responsibility for the entire institution but find it nearly impossible to do anything but delegate their authority to administrators. Furthermore, on any given issue each of the constituencies is invited and even encouraged to voice its goals and concerns. The student unrest of the 1960s can be traced to the opposing views of students, faculty, trustees, administrators, and public officials on some of the most basic issues of university goals. Their divergence over these goals was never resolved; only the sharpness of the differences have become diffused over time.

Brandl (1970, pp. 84, 87) pointed out that "higher education is many things to many people; it is impossible to compile a self-consistent, yet complete, list of the goals of a university. . . . No wonder, then, that there has been little progress in measuring the outputs of universities. Existing techniques were designed for organizations with an incentive to produce efficiently an agreed-on product. In contrast, a university is in many ways a nonorganization, where there is no agreement on its product, the independence of the individual faculty member is valued highly, and there is surely no inherent goal to maximize. Indeed, a mechanism for maximizing some combination of outputs may be inconsistent with the idea of a university." This situation is made more difficult by the fact that most institutional goals expressed by constituencies are not only vague but are almost without exception socially acceptable, even verging on the "motherhood and apple pie" type of pious wishes. Quarrels over goals among these constituencies are thus over priorities, not over acceptance. Unfortunately for the sake of efficient management and resource allocation, most of the pious wishes involve unlimited expenditure of resources. Universities operate like hospitals and other social institutions in that limited resources are allocated among competing goals; but in the university with relative values about the goals related to the missions of teaching, research, and service and with no absolute value system to rank the various subject matters, the situation amounts to a political free-for-all.

As a result, there are intensely difficult problems of measurement in two spheres: First, it is difficult to measure the degree of consensus or divergence on goals among the main constituencies. For example, in applying one of the standardized instruments of goal setting to a university, one may encounter an equally weighted total score between students who wish to see vocationalism emphasized and the faculty who wish to see basic research emphasized. How is this seeming tie to be interpreted? Does it mean the two goals are equally important as stated aspirations of the institution (implying an equal role and power of goal pursuit to students and faculty) or does it accurately reflect the actual goals according to the activities and resource allocations of the institution?

The second sphere is in measurement of institutional outcomes, impacts, or outputs. A thorough discussion of this difficulty is beyond the scope of this chapter; but such difficulties include short-term versus long-term effects, the value-added concept, and problems of reliability and validity of various measurement instruments. Probably the most crucial problem is that the more highly valued the goal or output, the more difficult it is to measure. Common examples are inquisitiveness, intellectuality, civic responsibility, and ethics or morals. Hambrick (1976, p. 48) summarizes the review of measurement problems: "The nature of university goals makes them quite unmeasurable. To attempt to measure the goals, is to probably mis-measure them."

Perhaps one of the most telling ways to reveal the problems of measuring a university goal system as well as its impact on its clientele is to cite the example of a seemingly spectacular failure. As chronicled in a recent biography, John Steinbeck's frequent contacts with Stanford University were unhappy and unsuccessful both from his point of view and from that of the university (Kiernan, 1979). He was barely admissible on the basis of his high school record (a number of his teachers thought he was quite stupid); he attended classes irregularly, got poor grades, did not involve himself in any of the extracurricular activities the first several times he attended Stanford, and was a five-time dropout. Apparently needing to justify his scholastic boredom, he blamed it on the quality of teaching at Stanford. "Idiots, all of them!" he was known to proclaim. "I can learn more studying on my own" (Kiernan, 1979, p. 51). However, during his fourth try at matriculation, and as a twenty-three-year-old sophomore, he finally encountered a teacher to whom he responded positively. He acknowledged decades later that the intellectual discipline to which that literature professor subjected him was a critical factor in his becoming a major literary figure.

It is almost impossible to conceive of a set of stated goals that would accommodate an academic career like John Steinbeck's. Nowhere in the expressed or unstated goals of Stanford University of the early 1920s would one find a university intention to accept marginal students with low motivation whose college career would include almost continual dropping out and readmission, whose grades were poor, who learned very little in most courses, and who never came anywhere close to earning a degree. His intermittent attendance caused considerable record-keeping problems; his instructors found him obnoxious; his fellow students found him strange; and he responded by being aloof most of the time and affecting bizarre and slovenly attire.

John Steinbeck remained a critic of higher education through most of his life; and except for the one professor, he never acknowledged his academic experience had done him any good whatever. There is little in Steinbeck's contact with Stanford that corresponded to any of the accepted norms or goals of either student learning or university teaching. And yet, if it had not been for that opportunity which brought him in contact with a professor whose intellectual demands taught him what he needed to know, it is unlikely Steinbeck would have persevered in his writing.

It is tempting in formulating and developing institutional goals to conceive of university operation as a rational, orderly process with somewhat homogeneous groups of students entering in unison and emerging four years later as grateful and accomplished graduates. Although this process does apply to many students, the university may succeed most in its most spectacular failures, like Steinbeck. Significantly, such success may not be evident until years or decades later. Can studies of goals overcome these complications and help improve either the effectiveness or efficiency of institutions of higher education? To answer this question, we must examine the evidence from existing studies.

Goals Studies

The 1964 study of institutional goals by Gross and Grambsch, replicated in 1971, was the first empirical survey done on a national basis. These researchers selected a sample of sixty-eight nondenominational "full universities" that offered degrees in many areas for inclusion in the study. They sent specially designed questionnaires to 5,667 administrators and 3,463 faculty members in 1964; in the 1971 survey, these samples were increased to 8,829 and 6,756, respectively. The faculty response rate was about 40 percent in both surveys; about 56 percent of the administrators responded in 1964 and about 51 percent in 1971. The overall purpose of both studies was to determine the goals toward which American universities were moving and how the organized power structure mediated movement toward those goals through resource utilization (Gross and Grambsch, 1974, pp. 27–29). The 1971 replication also reviewed changes over the intervening seven-year period. The authors were especially interested in determining if student unrest had caused goal reorientation. As Clark Kerr remarked in the foreword to their report, what was surprising "is not that the university has changed because of those events, but that it has changed so little" (p. xvii). In an overview of their findings, the authors (p. 3) report:

> Universities remained in 1971 what they had been in 1964; institutions oriented to research and scholarly production, set up to provide comfortable homes for professors and administrators, and according students and their needs a distinctly secondary position. But important changes had also taken place. Professors and administrators both felt a stronger congruence between the actual emphases in their universities and the kind of emphases they felt proper. We found little change since 1964 in the university power structure: higher administration was dominant, with professors occupying a middle position, and students and various "outsiders" (parents, alumni, citizens of the state) at the bottom. Yet, with the exception of department chairmen, all felt they had more power than ever, reflecting a growing confidence in their ability to take charge of their own professional lives. But an ominous cleavage had grown up between outside power holders (regents, legislators, state government, citizens) and "insiders" (chairmen, deans, faculty, students), which very much affected the goals of universities.

As in all empirical surveys, the validity of these findings beyond the time period in which the data are collected is questionable. For example, the high degree of consensus between faculty and administrators in both 1964 and 1971 has probably, according to Richman and Farmer (1974, p. 99), eroded, "given the increased financial problems confronting many academic institutions. It is likely that faculty and administrators now no longer see eye to eye nearly so much, and power conflicts, possibly also differences in goal preferences between them, have likely increased considerably in many cases since the 1971 study."

Several important research strategies Gross and Grambsch developed and used in both surveys became influential on nearly all subsequent goals studies. First, they differentiated between output goals and support goals. They divided output goals into four areas: those that involved changing students in a fundamental way, training students for society, research, and service. They divided support goals into four categories suggested by Parsons' scheme relating to organizational power: adaptation, management, motivation, and position. They measured these eight goal areas in a dual way later used in the Institutional Goals Inventory. Essentially Gross and Grambsch (p. 20) devised a way to measure both goal intentions and goal activities, or, put another way, both the values and the reality of the university. The general form of response for each specific goal was "How important *is* each aim at this university? How important *should* the aim be at this university?"

Beginning in 1969, an ETS research group headed by Richard E. Peterson began developing the IGI. The derivation of conceptual framework from the 1964 Gross and Grambsch study is clear. The IGI gauges the perceived importance of goal statements according to present ("is") and preferred ("should be") importance. The goal statements are of two types, *outcome* and *process,* directly comparable to the "output" and "support" dichotomy Gross and Grambsch used. The general format is as follows: "For each goal statement, the respondent, using a five-point rating scale—(1) of no importance, or not applicable, (2) of low importance, (3) of medium importance, (4) of high importance, (5) of extremely high importance—gives two judgments: how important the goal *is* presently, at the campus; and how important the goal *should be*" (Peterson and Uhl, 1977, p. 5). The Gross and Grambsch studies included forty-seven goal statements; but the general form of the IGI contains ninety statements organized into twenty goal "areas," thirteen of which relate to outcomes and seven of which relate to processes. The thirteen outcome areas are academic development, intellectual orientation, individual personal development, humanism/altruism, cultural/aesthetic awareness, traditional religiousness, vocational preparation, advanced training, research, meeting local needs, public service, social egalitarianism, and social criticism/activism (pp. 6-7). The seven process goal areas are freedom, democratic governance, community, intellectual/aesthetic environment, innovation, off-campus learning, and accountability/efficiency (pp. 7–8). In addition, the IGI permits an option of adding twenty goal statements of local interest. The last page of the questionnaire includes seven questions about the respondent's background (six more can be added as an option) that are used to cross-analyze the pattern of goal responses.

The IGI manual is extraordinarily complete and contains a description of the developmental background of the instrument, full normative data, and detailed procedures on preparation, administration, analysis, and reporting (Peterson and Uhl, 1977). The authors stress the importance of institution-wide involvement in a goals study; all important constituencies should at least be informed about the study and have input about its formulation and results, even if they are not sampled. The extensive bibliography included in the manual is a valuable resource to anyone interested in goals studies as well as to IGI users specifically.

In the fall of 1979, ETS released two new forms of the IGI for specialized application to community colleges and at small (primarily private liberal arts) colleges. The Community College Goals Inventory (CCGI) and Small Colleges Goals Inventory (SCGI) are intended to meet the specific needs of these two types of institutions and were developed in cooperation with the American Association of Community-Junior Colleges and the Council for the Advancement of Small Colleges. In developing goals statements, the IGI drew on a number of studies. One was a project conducted by an ETS group headed by Richard E. Peterson for the California Joint Committee on the Master Plan for Higher Education. It involved samples of administrators, faculty, undergraduate students, members of governing boards, and citizens of the community in which the college or university is located.

The findings are far too massive to summarize here; the reader is urged to consult the final report (Peterson, 1973). However, I discuss the single topic of convergence/divergence among the five main constituencies as an introduction to a major methodological consideration. As an intuitively obvious mode of analysis, determining the extent to which respondents of various types and settings agree or disagree on goals is probably the most appealing. There are a number of ways discrepancies can be summarized statistically into a single score. However, fascinating details are lost by that method. Much can be learned by direct examination of the "is" versus "should be" ranking that each of the five main constituencies grouped by type of institution (university or state, community, or private college) gave each of the twenty goal areas. For example, consider the goal of academic development compared with that of individual personal development. All constituents combined ranked academic development eighth among the twenty goals that "should be" pursued by the one hundred sixteen colleges and universities; their observation of actual practices indicated, however, that it "is" ranked higher than third place (2.6) among the twenty goal areas. Conversely, individual personal development "should be" ranked third according to the total ranking of preferred goals but "is" ranked tenth in the institution's activities. Undergraduate students as a single group ranked individual personal development as second only to "a sense of community for the institution" as a goal that "should be" pursued; however, they perceived that it "is" ranked 12.6 according to their actual observations of the institutions. Within the University of California sector only, all constituents combined perceived that the goal of research "is" ranked first among the twenty goals as a university activity but preferred that it "should be" ranked lower than sixth; undergraduate students at the university preferred that as a goal research "should be" twelfth. These few comparisons are illustrative only and hardly begin to sample the almost unlimited number of relationships.

Since its publication in final form in 1972, the IGI has been used in hundreds of college and university campuses throughout the United States and Canada (Peterson, 1978). It has been translated into French and Spanish and even into Saudi Arabian and Thai. Its popularity is based on several factors: It preempted an unmet need for a nationally standardized instrument; it remains unchallenged by any competitor on a significant scale (which also accounts for its emphasis in this chapter); it evidently not only meets the standard qualitative psychometric tests but is readily adopted and understood by users; it fits nicely into the requirements of accrediting agencies for goals statements, either for initial or reaffirmation of accreditation status (see, for example, North Central Association of Colleges and Schools, 1977); and the fact of its availability has probably created many instances of application.

The California study gave the state committee descriptive data that could be and presumably were used to interpret what certain constituencies perceived about the institution's actual goals and what they felt should have been the goals. The findings were, of course, heavily conditioned by the situations prevailing in the early 1970s. Such goals as "to place no restrictions on off-campus political activities by faculty or students" had a special urgency about them in 1972 that was largely gone five years later. I make this point not only to underscore the temporal limitation of empirical goals studies but to indicate that a purely descriptive use gives the main constituencies only passive input to a decision-making body. Many such bodies must deal with not only what participants at a certain point see "is" and "should be" occurring but what *can* occur in terms of resources, political realities, and other important considerations.

Such limitations on a purely descriptive use of goals studies have led some researchers and planners to develop more active use of the goal-setting process. Such users often involve techniques that encourage convergence of opinions about goals. Uhl, who was involved in early IGI development, has been active in linking the use of Delphi with goal-setting processes (Peterson and Uhl, 1977; Uhl, 1971, 1975, 1978). The Delphi technique avoids the inhibitions and personal influences of face-to-face discussions by circulating repeated anonymous responses among participants, usually by correspondence. Each repetition affords participants an opportunity to revise their opinion, so opinion usually shifts toward convergence (Weaver, 1970). In a 1970 study, Uhl found distinctive patterns of goal understanding among various constituencies, and he found the Delphi process did result in goal convergence. Other institutional researchers (Evans, 1975; Parden, 1975) found it advantageous to modify or otherwise disguise the classic Delphi technique. In the first of the two following case studies, the use of Delphi was both extensive and direct.

In 1977, Uhl conducted a goals study at North Carolina Central University (NCCU) intended to improve communication among university constituencies and produce a set of goals to be used for prospective donors and as criteria in planning and evaluation studies (Uhl, 1978). The institution had undergone a series of metamorphoses since World War II, changing from a teachers college with small liberal arts and graduate program components to a part of the University of North Carolina with professional schools of business, law, and library science. Historically, the institution had served black students almost exclusively; by 1977, about 10 percent of undergraduates and 35 percent of graduate and professional students were nonblack.

The study's general approach was to emphasize wide participation and application of the results to the decision-making process. A preliminary form of the IGI was administered to samples of the university's faculty, students, administrators, alumni, community leaders, and trustees. The Delphi technique was used with three successive administrations of the IGI. A high return rate (73 percent) was achieved from the 252 participants. "While agreement among groups was not always present on the results gathered from the first questionnaire, for most goal areas there was agreement on the last questionnaire" (Uhl, 1978, p. 68). In line with the study's emphasis on practicality, two additional major steps were taken. The first involved comprehensive assessments of both the internal and external environments, with stress on how impending changes would affect reaching the goals defined by the study. The second was intended to employ the results in the planning and decision-making processes. The author observes, "Developing goals is not an end in itself. They are of little value if they cannot be integrated into the institution's decision-making process. This is not likely to happen automatically; a formal process must be developed and monitored to assure such integration" (p. 64).

The process used was to involve units (school, department, or service area) by asking them to develop a five-year schedule of activities that would help them achieve the goals that applied to them. Requests for resources by each unit (budget, personnel, and so forth) were evaluated according to how they related to goal achievement. The source cited gives two detailed examples of the activity and resource listings developed by units (Uhl, 1978, pp.73–76). "The funded activities are monitored and their effects evaluated. The evaluation results become a part of the internal environment which is reassessed yearly, resulting in possible modification of goals and goal activities and thus renewing the cycle" (p. 77). The NCCU experience seems to have not only been a successful joint use of IGI and Delphi but the institution apparently accomplished the rare feat of translating goals into measurable objectives for the decision-making process. The rarity of this accomplishment in a complex university can only be appreciated by a thorough review of the research literature. It is fair to state that several planning and budgeting cycles are probably required to prove the system thoroughly.

The second case study is of interest not only because it illustrates many typicalities of a goals study in a large university but because it involves a Canadian institution and generated a seemingly useful new methodological technique. The University of Ottawa is one of nearly a dozen Canadian colleges and universities that have utilized the IGI in goals studies in recent years. The instrument was "Canadianized" to correspond with terminology familiar to potential respondents, and a French version was available to those who preferred it. The traditions and location of the university evidently made it particularly susceptible to the schisms resulting from the bicultural and separatist movements surrounding it; the need for a goals study was strongly impelled by these pressures.

Personnel from the university's counseling service conducted the study in the spring of 1976 (Piccinin and Joly, 1978). The purpose was to compare the perceptions of existing and desired ("is" and "should be") goals of professors, students, and administrators. Samples of 572 professors, 1,864 students, and 92 administrators were drawn; percentages responding were 59, 44, and 76, respectively. Additional smaller groups of respondents were drawn from student services staff and faculty senators. The three constituent groups generally agreed the university "is" not attaching high or extremely high importance to any of the goals in the questionnaire, including special optional ones dealing with such crucial issues as bilingualism and biculturalism. Moderate importance was observed as being given to traditional academic goals, especially those dealing with institutional prestige (graduate programs and research activities). The three groups also agreed the university "should be" giving high or extremely high importance to such goal areas as intellectual orientation, advanced training, academic development, research, and individual personal development. It should be noted that nearly all IGI studies have a similar pattern in which "should be" goals are generally rated of higher importance than "is" goals. The Ottawa researchers interpreted the variations and agreement in the responses to mean "the respondents do not attach a very high level of importance to the achievement of goal consensus by the university's constituents, yet locate very high the need to group them into a genuine community." Or, put another way, each group could be saying: "There is no need to engage in an exercise intended to achieve goal consensus; all that is required is for the other to adopt *our* list of goals and priorities" (p. 39).

The researchers followed customary modes of analyzing and presenting data by using discrepancy values as recommended in the IGI manual (see Peterson and Uhl, 1977, pp. 20–33). The "is" to "should be" discrepancy values were generally positive, as is usually the case, and discrepancies between faculty, students, and administrators were generally as might be expected, so the researchers sought a statistical answer to the question "where do we go from here?" They developed a "Corrective Action Priority Index" (CAPI) for each goal by simply multiplying the "should be" importance rating by its discrepancy from the "is" rating. "The suggested interpretation of this index is the following: a goal or goal area will produce a high positive CAPI if it is judged important *and* neglected and, as such, most in need of corrective action" (Piccinin and Joly, 1978,

p. 57). A large negative CAPI would indicate current overemphasis as, at Ottawa University, in intercollegiate athletics and "publish or perish" evaluation of teachers. The CAPI presumably helped university planners and administrators take "corrective action," although the researchers were neither prescriptive nor optimistic in the matter (see pp. 64–67).

The University of Ottawa study was in many respects typical of goals studies at complex, multipurpose institutions. It effectively illuminated convergence and discrepancy on goals at a particular time; however, there were no illusions about the study *in itself* affecting priorities or changing attitudes. In particular, the nagging problem of translating descriptive information about goals into action was bothersome: "Goals couched in general, abstract terms constitute unsatisfactory guides for action and inadequate criteria for evaluation; they need to be translated into much more specific, concrete, and unequivocal objectives toward which action can be directed and against which evaluation can be conducted" (Piccinin and Joly, 1978, p. 66). This point will be discussed further in the final section of this chapter.

Both case studies conducted goals studies as their response to specific critical circumstances. Probably the vast majority of goals studies are, however, either in response to mandates from external governing, regulatory, or coordinating agencies or are connected with accreditation studies.

A review of the official guidelines for accreditation published by the regional accrediting agencies indicates they invariably stress studies of goals by institutions wishing to establish or maintain accredited status. The North Central Association of Colleges and Schools (NCA) is an example. Each full cycle of evaluation begins with an examination of institutional goals and a statement of purpose (see North Central Association of Colleges and Schools, 1977, pp. 21–22, 62–66). Traditionally, accreditability evaluation has been done by visiting consultant teams made up of academic and other administrators and faculty experienced in curriculum development, typically through service as departmental chairs. Such team members often demand more of the candidate institution than they could of their own, especially in clarifying goals and linking them to resource allocation. Thus, the accrediting process has developed as academic administrators and professors seeking to satisfy visiting colleagues, with few of the participants having much faith in management systems. The process has as a consequence been characterized as a mutual back-scratching exercise. This type of criticism is almost invariably aimed at a normative process that relies almost completely on a descriptive-historical approach. Scholars of the accrediting process have proposed it is time for a movement toward performance-based models or other means to take advantage of the more objective management systems now available (see, for example, Semrow, 1978, pp. 3, 11–17). It is not yet evident that accrediting will be reoriented in that direction or which of the various management systems will eventually become standard.

Other organizations have developed aids to institutional goal setting. The American Association of State Colleges and Universities (AASCU), under a grant from the Kellogg Foundation, recently published a planning guide that entails a novel approach to goal setting (Alm and others, 1978). Its major thrust is to develop a long-term planning process *for* change *from* change. The complex and detailed paradigm calls for ten interrelated steps. The first four essentially attempt to forecast national and regional trends and societal values through the coming decade and their probable impact on such institutional sectors as students, curricula, and athletics. The fifth stage is formulation of overall institutional goals (also referred to as missions, intents, or purposes), which are value laden, and the more specific objectives, which refer to the goals. The paradigm calls for objectives formulation based on how projected "societal trends and values come together, relate, and interrelate, and create the need to achieve a specific institutional objective" (p. 39). Presumably, unforeseen events as exemplified in the recent past by student unrest and the oil shortage would require the planners to reconstruct the complex planning, goal, and objectives matrices. The ways measurable objectives relate to institutional goals are not spelled out in detail. In this paradigm, it seems clear institutional goal development and the entire planning process are driven by forecasted events, trends, and values as developed by planners rather than in response to either traditional values or consensus of significant constituencies.

In summarizing this section, the excellent overview of methodological considerations in goals studies by Harshman (1975) was a basic resource. There are three basic approaches to analysis of goals data. The first deals with rank ordering a set of goals according to perceptions or opinions. This can involve simple unweighted position ordering of a set of goals or using either ordinal (high, medium, low) or numeric scales in ranking. Gross and Grambsch (1974) ranked respondents' goal data. The second approach analyzes the discrepancies in goal importance among respondents and/or between two perceptions ("is" versus "should be") of the same goal. The University of Ottawa study analyzed both discrepancy scores, as do most studies that use the IGI (Piccinin and Joly, 1978). The third approach involves an attempt at consensus in which respondents consider goals as commonly held abstractions toward which unanimity of opinion is desired. The conduct of the goals study is intended to achieve as much convergence of opinion as possible, even though full consensus is usually impossible. The North Carolina Central University study used a common convergence method, the Delphi (Uhl, 1971).

The statistical techniques commonly used in goals studies include the obvious ones of correlational methods appropriate to ranked, ordinal, or Likert-type scale data, such as Spearman's. If assumptions of interval data are applied, more precise methods such as analysis of variance, t-test, and standard correlational techniques are applicable. Because most goals studies are descriptive, it seems appropriate to use factor analytic methods, such as cluster or discriminant function analysis, to reveal underlying commonalities of values. However, it would be possible in many instances quickly to "lose" the typical goals study steering committee in statistical manipulations, even though they may be meritorious or appropriate. For example, a humanities professor who chairs such a committee may become impatient with data reported in eigenvalues. Perhaps the fact that persons from many disciplines are usually involved in goals studies has kept the methodology plain and simple. Harshman (1975, p. 333) offers a modification for analyzing discrepancy scores that is similar to that developed later in the University of Ottawa study. Called the Resource Reallocation Index, it has the same purpose of discriminating discrepancy scores more accurately. The index is calculated by multiplying the mean of an IGI "should be" goal score by the discrepancy between that mean and the mean of the "is" score. The advantage of thus multiplying rather than simply adding discrepancy scores is that it reduces the additive effect of overemphasizing need resulting from the artifact of "should be" scores being generally higher than "is" scores. Like most others who have studied the problem, Harshman recognizes the difficulty of relating information on abstract, value-laden goals to quantitative data useful in formal management systems (p. 328).

Conclusion

This discussion of studying institutional goals suggests there is a great deal of recent activity in two spheres. One is at the institutional level and is represented by attempts to define what the college or university as a whole is or should be doing. Such considerations necessarily involve abstract and qualitative concepts like intellectuality, creativeness, and responsibility; they express the institution's values and the impacts it hopes or expects to have on society. The other sphere of activity also deals with the institution's goals, but at the level of measurable objectives. Such attempts to measure goal attainment are typically based on those developed for businesses or bureaucracies and deal in such quantifiable concepts as time, money, and supplies; they concern efficient use of resources as well as commonality of purpose.

Most institutional research activity is focused on the second, more quantitative, view of goal setting and institutional efficiency. Indeed, the history and placement in the organizational structure of institutional research suggests that development of operations or systems analysis in the 1950s led to the establishment and growth of the profession. As such, institutional research has been estranged from the goal-setting activities of the academics who actually operate the teaching, research, and service of the research. This separation has perpetuated the duality of qualitative versus operational goals. Corson (1975) has indicated the quantitative approach works well in areas like physical facilities, fund raising, student housing, food services, maintenance, and so forth. "But teaching and research are so little quantifiable and so subject to the varying approaches of different teachers and scholars that institutionwide plans are seldom formulated" (p. 76).

All complex organizations grapple with the problem of improving the efficiency of efforts to reach a goal or goals. However, a university has multiple goals, many of them inconsistent with each other and sometimes even in conflict; furthermore, decision-making power is so widely dispersed as to contradict the line of authority that underlies most management models. Consider one of the systems currently enjoying considerable popularity: management by objectives (MBO), a hierarchical scheme that embraces the most general level of institutional goal to highly specific objectives. The structure is given as "Institutional Purpose Statement, Role Responsibilities, Goals, Terminal Objectives, Enabling Objectives, and Process Objectives" (Carpenter and others, 1973, p. 10). The purpose is "to provide a clear and concise linkage from the most specific action plan element to an institutionally agreed upon purpose or goal" (p. 9). To carry out the process, the assumption is made that a clear line of authority exists from the executive head of the organization to the staff level with least responsibility for making decisions about use of resources. Negotiations are carried out down the line to establish objectives acceptable to the next higher step in the hierarchy. "The development of these objectives is a negotiated process between superior and subordinate and often includes (lateral) peers. . . . After objectives are approved throughout the organizational structure, and the new year begins, the administrator or manager must check each subordinate's progress as promised milestones are reached. Is he meeting his target dates? Time, quantity, cost, and quality must be monitored" (pp. 27–28). Clearly, the less quantifiable the process involved (like teaching and research), the more difficult it becomes to apply MBO meaningfully. To bring the application problem close to home, consider the installation of a MBO system in an office of institutional research at a large university. The routine and recurring tasks, like filling out federal reporting forms, could be amenable to the process. But the continual flow of unpredictable requests for urgent studies and projects would require almost continual renegotiation of process objectives among the administration of the office and the research staff. In a larger context, the hierarchy assumed in the MBO system would be more than a bit strained if not ridiculous when applied to, for example, a Nobel prize-winning physicist engrossed in internationally recognized research on the most esoteric level. What university administrator would such a professor be likely to acknowledge as his "superior" and to whom is he or she "subordinate" in any reasonable sense? Even the community college instructors who teach similar subjects in a large division have dealt with the superior/subordinate question by unionizing. The matter of line of authority is then dealt with collectively in adversarial bargaining; and in many cases, the issue of just who is subordinate is nowhere as clear cut as is assumed in the MBO model.

Thus, the two types of goals studies rarely touch. The IGI type, which deals with abstract educational goals, seldom becomes specific enough to affect efficiency; the management systems are usually operated in the nonacademic areas only because they cannot bridge the gap between the qualitative and quantitative in academic programs. Although there has been intense interest in a goals system for the academic area that would span the hierarchical levels from mission to specific objectives, the few attempts to develop such a system invariably use a most familiar strategy to mediate between effectiveness goals and efficiency goals. Invariably at some point, the interface consists of a dialectical and political process that brings the academician's "infinite resource" approach in touch with the reality of managing limited resources. This negotiation process is indispensable, for there is no standard conversion table linking qualitative goals and quantitative measurement, no "effectiveness to efficiency" concordance or dictionary.

It is true that some researchers and planners assume a linear, unidimensional model exists for the academic area. For example, Laughlin and Chamberlin (1972, p. 103) postulated a model that was depicted by a straight line reaching from "abstract" to "concrete" that spanned the following specific steps: "Mission Statements, General Goals, Degree Goals, Time Reference Objectives, Measurement Objectives, and Cost Objectives." They asserted, "The structure built herein is hierarchical in that an institution could begin by building a mission statement, then, from that statement, build institutionwide goals. Further, the specific schools or colleges within universities could subdivide those goals so that objectives and other goals at a lower level could be obtained. The process could be continued to the specific instructional level within each classroom session and similarly applied within research and public service areas" (p. 105). It is nowhere clear, in this or any other model, exactly how one accomplishes or enhances a valued mission like "creating intellectual curiosity in students" through more efficient resource management. How many pencils and chalk sticks does it take to gain an increment of intellectual curiosity in a student?

The orientation of most state and federal policy makers is toward the popular management systems based on business and bureaucratic models. But as Schmidtlein (1975, p. 116) notes, "Anyone dealing with a faculty knows the traditional, bureaucratic model of top-down decision making does not describe an institution of higher education. . . . Consequently, despite the belief in the efficiency of the (management systems) strategy and the use of planning rhetoric, a high proportion of decisions in higher education continue to be made on a disjointed, incremental, remedial basis."

It is possible that a comprehensive goals system model can be developed someday soon that will bridge the gap between abstract, value-laden goals and measurable, behavioral objectives. Hope resides in the recent development of sound instruments and more sophisticated methodology and, most of all, in sensitivity to the fact that a gap exists and that it may even be conceptually insurmountable. This recognition, rather than blind avoidance of the problem or fogging it over with systems analysis rhetoric, will enlist the best efforts of the best researchers and planners. Some excellent conceptual work has already been done.

Bibliographical Essay

Two of the works cited in this chapter contain excellent bibliographies. Peterson and Uhl (1977) includes general and specific guidelines for studying goals and its bibliography contains 383 entries, including reports of 60 studies using the IGI. It is not only one of the most complete compendiums of strategies, it thoroughly reviews recent studies and conceptual frameworks. I cited Richman and Farmer (1974) extensively because I consider it the most practical and provocative work available on leadership, goals, and power in higher education. It also contains a useful and well-organized annotated bibliography covering the principal recent sources on management systems applied to colleges and universities.

Dobbins and Lee (1968) and Trivett (1973) cover macro-level mission statements well, although both are somewhat dated. In terms of both missions and external pressures, one could do no better than to review the Higher Education Act as amended in 1972 and to follow the current congressional debates concerning its reauthorization. The report of the Education Commission of the States (1979) is a most remarkable document. If any institutional researcher, planner, and especially academician is still optimistic about the prospects for institutional autonomy, a thoughtful reading of this book will soon dispel the notion. It reviews strategies for bringing institutions to heel for fiscal accountability purposes, with little indication (or perhaps awareness) of how this will directly affect the mission, role, and purposes of higher education in the states.

Gross and Grambsch (1974) remains the premier review of the sociological study of organizational goals in higher education. It includes as much theory as most researchers and planners will need as well as valuable material on the conceptual framework for studying goals.

Finally, both Fincher (1978) and Micek and Arney (1974) have contributed significantly to the identification of goals outcomes and criteria or indications of such outcomes. Romney's (1976) national study of measures of progress toward institutional goal achievement has resulted in a useful document published by the National Center for Higher Education Management Systems (Romney, 1978) and an insightful paper (Romney and Micek, 1977) that identifies the goal "translation" problem.

References

Alm, K. G., and others. *A Future Creating Paradigm.* Washington, D.C.: American Association of State Colleges and Universities, 1978.

Anderson, G. L. "The Further Study of Universities as Organizations: Off-Beat Ideas and New Dimensions." In G. L. Anderson and others (Eds.), *Reflections on University Values and the American Scholar.* University Park: Center for the Study of Higher Education, Pennsylvania State University, 1976.

Bailey, S. K. "Combatting the Efficiency Cultists." *Change,* 1973, *5,* pp. 8–9.

Bowen, H. R. "Goals and the Financing of Higher Education." In R. G. Cope (Ed.), *Tomorrow's Imperative Today.* Tallahassee, Fla.: Association for Institutional Research, 1973.

Brandl, J. E. "Public Service Outputs of Higher Education: An Exploratory Essay." In B. Lawrence (Ed.), *The Outputs of Higher Education.* Boulder, Colo.: Western Interstate Commission on Higher Education, 1970.

Carnegie Foundation for the Advancement of Teaching. *The States and Higher Education: A Proud Past and a Vital Future.* San Francisco: Jossey-Bass, 1976.

Carpenter, W. B., and others. *Management By Objectives: An Analysis of Recommendations for Implementation.* Charlottesville: Center for Higher Education, University of Virginia, 1973.

Cohen, M. O., and March, J. G. *Leadership and Ambiguity: The American College President.* New York: McGraw-Hill, 1974.

Corson, J. J. *The Governance of Colleges and Universities.* (Rev. ed.) New York: McGraw-Hill, 1975.

Dobbins, C. G., and Lee, C. B. (Eds.). *Whose Goals for American Higher Education?* Washington, D.C.: American Council on Education, 1968.

Education Commission of the States. *Accountability and Academe: A Report of the National Task Force on the Accountability of Higher Education to the State.* Denver, Colo.: Education Commission of the States, 1979.

Etzioni, A. *Modern Organizations.* Englewood Cliffs, N.J.: Prentice-Hall, 1964.

Evans, W. K. "A Two Time User Looks at the Delphi Technique in Higher Education." In R. G. Cope (Ed.), *Information for Decisions in Postsecondary Education.* Tallahassee, Fla.: Association for Institutional Research, 1975.

Fincher, C. "Importance of Criteria for Institutional Goals." In R. H. Fenske (Ed.), *New Directions for Institutional Research: Using Goals in Research Planning,* no. 19. San Francisco: Jossey-Bass, 1978.

Gross, E., and Grambsch, P. V. *Changes in University Organization.* New York: McGraw-Hill, 1974.

Hambrick, D. C. "The University as an Organization: How is it Different from a Business?" In G. L. Anderson (Ed.), *Reflections on University Values and the American Scholar*. College Park: Center for the Study of Higher Education, Pennsylvania State University, 1976.

Harshman, C. L. "Linking Data to Decisions: Operationalizing Concepts In Institutional Goals Development." In R. G. Cope (Ed.), *Information for Decisions in Postsecondary Education*. Tallahassee, Fla.: Association for Institutional Research, 1975.

Hofstadter, R., and Smith, W. *American Higher Education: A Documentary History*. Vol. 1. Chicago: University of Chicago Press, 1961.

Kiernan, T. *A Biography of John Steinbeck*. Boston: Little, Brown, 1979.

Laughlin, J. S., and Chamberlin, G. D. "Objectives—Goals—Missions: An Institutions Directional Statement for Management and Planning." In C. T. Stewart (Ed.), *Reformation and Reallocation in Higher Education*. Tallahassee, Fla.: Association for Institutional Research, 1972.

Lee, C. B. "Whose Goals for American Higher Education?" In C. G. Dobbins and C. B. Lee (Eds.), *Whose Goals for American Higher Education?* Washington, D.C.: American Council on Education, 1968.

Micek, S. S., and Arney, W. R. *The Higher Education Outcomes Measures Identification Study: A Descriptive Summary*. Boulder, Colo.: Western Interstate Commission on Higher Education, 1974.

North Central Association of Colleges and Schools. *Handbook on Accreditation*. Chicago: North Central Association of Colleges and Schools, 1977.

Parden, R. J. "Delphi Revisited." In R. G. Cope (Ed.), *Information for Decisions in Postsecondary Education*. Tallahassee, Fla.: Association for Institutional Research, 1975.

Parsons, T., and others (Eds.). *Theories of Society*. New York: Free Press, 1961.

Peterson, R. E. *Goals for California Higher Education: A Survey of 116 College Communities*. Sacramento: California State Legislature, 1973.

Peterson, R. E. "The Institutional Goals Inventory in Contemporary Context." In R. H. Fenske (Ed.), *New Directions for Institutional Research: Using Goals in Research and Planning*, no. 19. San Francisco: Jossey-Bass, 1978.

Peterson, R. E., and Uhl, N. P. *Formulating College and University Goals: A Guide for Using the IGI*. Princeton, N.J.: Educational Testing Service, 1977.

Piccinin, S., and Joly, J. *The Goals of the University of Ottawa: What They Are and What They Should Be*. 2 vols. Ottawa: University of Ottawa, 1978.

Richman, B. M., and Farmer, R. N. *Leadership, Goals, and Power in Higher Education: A Contingency and Open-Systems Approach to Effective Management*. San Francisco: Jossey-Bass, 1974.

Rogers, F. A., and Van Horn, R. L. "Goals-Oriented Resource Allocation for University Management." In R. H. Fenske (Ed.), *Conflicting Pressures in Postsecondary Education*. Tallahassee, Fla.: Association for Institutional Research, 1976.

Romney, L. C. "Institutional Goal Achievement: Measures of Progress." Unpublished doctoral dissertation, School of Education, University of Colorado, 1976.

Romney, L. C. *Measures of Institutional Goal Achievement*. Boulder, Colo.: National Center for Higher Education Management Systems, 1978.

Romney, L. C., and Micek, S. S. "Translating Goals into Measurable Objectives: Research Studies and Practical Procedures." In R. H. Fenske (Ed.), *Research and Planning For Higher Education.* Tallahassee, Fla.: Association for Institutional Research, 1977.

Schmidtlein, F. A. "An Analysis of Decision Strategies Employed in the Governance of Higher Education." In R. G. Cope (Ed.), *Information for Decisions in Postsecondary Education.* Tallahassee, Fla.: Association for Institutional Research, 1975.

Semrow, J. J. *The Uses of Accreditation* (mimeo). Boulder, Colo.: North Central Association of Colleges and Schools, 1978.

Trivett, D. A. *Goals for Higher Education: Definitions and Directions.* Washington, D.C.: American Association for Higher Education, 1973.

Uhl, N. P. *Identifying Institutional Goals: Encouraging Convergence of Opinion through the Delphi Technique.* Durham, N.C.: National Laboratory for Higher Education, 1971.

Uhl, N. P. "A Follow-up of a Delphi Study." In R. G. Cope (Ed.), *Information for Decisions in Postsecondary Education.* Tallahassee, Fla.: Association for Institutional Research, 1975.

Uhl, N. P. "A Case Study of Goals-Oriented Research." In R. H. Fenske (Ed.), *New Directions for Institutional Research: Using Goals in Research and Planning,* no. 19. San Francisco: Jossey-Bass, 1978.

Weaver, W. T. *The Delphi Method: Background and Critique.* Syracuse, N.Y.: Educational Policy Research Center, Syracuse University Research Corporation, 1970.

10

Wayne R. Kirschling
Vaughn E. Huckfeldt

Projecting Alternative Futures

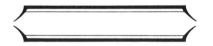

Primitive persons were either futurists or they were dead. Cave son who watched cave dad being mauled by a saber-tooth tiger unanticipated along the path undoubtedly worked a little harder at looking ahead: He probably tried periodically to improve his perspective from the vantage point of the nearest tree or hill. He probably was more inclined to travel in company, even if he did not particularly enjoy it. And he probably became a little more preoccupied with killing tigers, not only because he developed a taste for tiger meat but because he could foresee the day when he and his children could live in peace. Unfortunately, the day he killed the last of the neighborhood tigers, the local volcano erupted.

Today we may be more like primitives than we realize. The comfort of belief in heaven on earth through progress, utopia, or world government seems to glitter less brightly than it once did, while modern-day saber-tooth tigers in the form of nuclear warfare, diminished ozone layers, and widespread famine haunt our consciousness. Our fears, like those of primitive persons, seem to be propelling us into increased concern for anticipating the unexpected.

The Growth of Futurism

In this century, and especially in the last two decades, there has been an explosion of professional interest in the study of the future. This explosion has produced an increased sophistication, if not improved accuracy, in forecasting the future. Among the names that have been suggested for this forecasting are futures research, future studies, futuristics, futurology, prognostics, mellontology, futuribles, and futures analysis; and among definitions of the new field are these five representative examples (Cornish, 1977b, p. 47):

> Futuristics is the systematic study by basically rational or empirical means of the possible alternative futures of human societies and the special problems and opportunities relating to those futures. It is this concern with rational methods and alternative futures which makes modern futuristics different from most earlier attempts at forecasting or prediction. To paraphrase a common definition of politics, futuristics is the art of discovering what is possible. [Draper Kauffman]
>
> For the time being I should like to define this prognostics as the science, which, with advanced methods and instruments, aims at exploring the future and acquiring probable knowledge of the future. It is also the science which tries to control the future, based on this systematic anticipation, by purposively guiding the future by socio-dynamic techniques. It comprises those areas of prognostic reflection, vis. concerning the possible, ideally essential, and actually achievable future developments, in economic, social, technological, political, and cultural areas, and on both a national and a worldwide scale. [Fred Polak]
>
> Futures research is a new discipline concerned with shaping the data and improving the processes on the basis of which policy decisions are made in various fields of human endeavor such as business, government, or education. The purpose of the discipline is to help policy makers to choose wisely—in terms of their purposes and values—among alternative courses of action that are open to leadership at a given time. [Harold Shane]
>
> I define futuristics as the study, forecasting, design, and realization of alternative social values, environments, and organisms for the immediate, intermediate, and distant future. [James Dator]
>
> Any efforts to systematize our assumptions and perceptions about the future . . . fall into three categories: the exploration of possible futures (the art of futurism); the exploration of probable futures (the science of futurism); and the exploration of preferable futures (the politics and psychology of futurism). [Roy Amara]

So far, there is little consensus as to whether the study of the future encompasses a concern about particular time slices of the future, a set of revolutionary attitudes about the future, a schema for treating future probabilities and preferences, a use of images to affect behavior, a collection of future-probing techniques, or a profession with its accouterments of membership, jargon, meetings, and the like. Consensus is emerging, however, about the time period of the future studies field. A futurist worth his or her salt is not likely to be affected by myopia about today, tomorrow, or even next year. As Cornish (1977a, p. 380) puts it: "Futurists tend to focus on the period from five to 50 years ahead. The reason for focusing on this period is that the immediate or near-term future (less than five years) constitutes what might be viewed as the domain of ordinary human concerns (although even five years from now would be regarded by many nonfuturists as a very distant point in time). In addition, one cannot do much to change the world that we will experience in the near-term future; there simply isn't enough time to decide upon and put into effect many basic changes. Nor can we do much useful planning for the period 50 years from now because so many unpredictable events and unknown factors will exert their influence that anything we tried to do would likely be erased in the intervening years." This emphasis on the far off and long range clearly separates futures studies from most planning. It is the rare plan that goes much beyond five years; but for the study of the future, five years hence is but the beginning.

A similar consensus exists about the attitude of futurism. For example, Henchey (n.d., p. 25) observes there is "an attitude (a futuristic outlook) which binds (or should bind) the profession, the discipline, and the movement; this attitude includes an alertness to the future consequences of present policies, an openness to different possibilities, a desire (and ability) to see 'the whole picture' and an acceptance of responsibility for shaping the future. Many activities, then, are recognized as future-oriented. This makes the field rich and exciting, if sometimes ambiguous." Cornish (1977a, p. 380) speaks of "basic principles that typify the thinking of today's futurists." These principles are "(1) the unity or interconnectedness of reality, (2) the critical importance of time, and (3) the importance of ideas, especially ideas of the future." Indeed, the single most important attitude undergirding futurism is a belief that the future can be affected. Probably no futurists place much emphasis on destiny in secular affairs or predestination in religious affairs. Their belief that the future can be shaped is, of course, clearly one of the tenets of planning; and hence in this regard, planners and futurists find themselves standing on the same foundation.

The futurist perspective encompasses intellectual anticipation of many types of futures—probable futures (what likely will be), possible futures (what may be), preferable futures (what should be), nightmare futures (what should not be), plausible futures (what could be), and so forth. To a large degree, the study of the future is a study of probabilities and how those probabilities can and should be manipulated in light of preferences. What makes the study so interesting is that these probabilities must be studied in a situation where the shape of the die, the number of faces, and the rules of the game are rarely knowable with any certainty.

A consistent theme in the futures literature is the use of images to affect behavior. Cornish (1977a, p. 383) has observed, "In social systems, more may depend on what people think will happen than on 'realities.' . . . People think that their actions are based on past events and present realities, but their images of the future may play an even more critical role. Images of the future are the blueprints that we use in constructing our lives, and the blueprints may be more important than the materials we work with (our bodies, families, financial resources, etc.) in determining our success and happiness." If Cornish and other futurists are right on this issue, it brings futurism a lot closer to "the domain of ordinary human concerns." If human behavior is shaped by our sense of the future as well as our sense of the past and present, then it is important that this relationship of thought and behavior be more conscious. This is as true for planners and institutional researchers as it is for presidents, trustees, and faculty.

Futurism has also become a profession and perhaps even an industry. For example, *The Future: A Guide to Information Resources* (1977) notes two hundred and thirty firms or organizations in thirty-five countries, four hundred books and reports, over one hundred periodicals, and more than two hundred courses in schools, colleges, and universities are now devoted to the future. In fact, futurism has become so respectable that even the U.S. Congress has charged itself with identifying emerging issues and gauging the long-term consequences of legislation. To do so, it has formed the Congressional Clearinghouse on the Future, instructed the Congressional Research Service to forecast the "probable results" of legislative proposals and alternatives, and established the Office of Technology Assessment to provide "early indications of the probable, beneficial, and adverse impacts of the applications of technology" (Renfro, 1978, pp. 105, 106).

Futurism has also become identified with the use of various techniques to probe the future. Henchey and Yates (1974) describe fourteen futuristic techniques that can be categorized into three general types, as Popper (1971, p. 1) illustrates:

1. *exploratory* types, which start with past and current trends and make extrapolations that are projected as images of the future (The common exploratory techniques include trend extrapolation, force analysis, technological assessment, Markov chain theory and Monte Carlo techniques as specific types of simulation, and modeling.)
2. *intuitive* types, which are essentially sophisticated variants on the "wise old men" technique that makes speculative projections into the future (The common intuitive techniques include Delphi probes, cross-impact matrices, and scenarios.)
3. *normative* types, which start with future needs and goals and work backward to identify the technology, changes, and decisions required to fill needs and reach goals (The common normative techniques are relevance trees, ariole, decision matrices, morphological analysis, and the application of Bayesian statistics.)

The crystal ball is not specifically mentioned, but one cannot be sure it is not hidden in the list somewhere. Moreover, Henchey and Yates (1974, p. viii) caution, "the fourteen methods . . . were chosen from among the more than one hundred that have been described in the literature." Clearly, futurism in part is a love affair with technique.

In summary, today there is not only something but many things called futurism. For some, it is an attitude; for others, it is a technique or a sharing of interests. Not surprisingly, it is not much more tangible than what it seeks to know—that is, the future. But this pluralism is not unknown either to planning or to institutional research. The following sections will take up three topics: (1) the need for futurism in higher education, (2) the barriers to futurism in higher education, and (3) some suggestions for making futurism usable in institutions of higher education.

The Need for Futurism in Higher Education

Higher education, like American society, is experiencing an increasing rate of change. The implications of this for the larger society have been widely portrayed in both the professional and popular literature. Some attention-grabbing analogies have been made: "McLuhan suggests that we are traveling down a super highway at one hundred miles an hour with our eyes fixed on the rear view mirror" ("A Myth for the Future," 1976, p. 1) and "the American people have been experiencing a series of frightening escalations: an escalation of volume in the world of sound, an escalation of violence on television, an escalation of risks in spectaculars such as auto racing, and an escalation in the hard pornography of books, magazines, and movies" (Bailey, 1976, p. 42). As is becoming painfully obvious, higher education is not immune from this hydra named change. As Bachetti (1977, p. 11) notes, "Change bestows legion opportunities to advance or to stumble (and sometimes to do both together), and higher education today is about as rich in such opportunities as it is ever likely to be."

The question, then, is of what value might futurism be to higher education as it attempts to cope with its deteriorating images of the future and with the aftershocks of larger societal change. Cornish and others (1977, p. 219) may provide the best list of the uses of future studies:

- assisting the decision-making process by (1) providing useful frameworks for decision making, (2) identifying dangers and opportunities, (3) suggesting a variety of possible approaches to solving a problem, (4) helping to assess alternative policies and actions, (5) enabling people to see the present, (6) increasing the degree of choice, and (7) setting goals and devising means to reach them
- preparing people to live in a changing world by (1) providing "preexperience" so the future does not come as a shock, (2) offering a framework for understanding change as a normal process, and (3) making the future an object of conscious study so it becomes more interesting and exciting to contemplate
- offering a framework for reconciliation and cooperation (This applies not only to small organizations and communities but to nations and international communities.)
- contributing to science and thought
- aiding creativity
- helping to motivate people, both young and old, to learn
- providing a perspective for developing a well-integrated personal outlook for philosophy of life
- offering a means for recreation or "fun"

Two important uses of future studies for higher education not highlighted in Cornish's list are encouraging higher education institutions to think in longer terms and providing a form of "social glue" to keep higher education institutions from shattering into a thousand pieces—into countless dreams, special-interest groups, and crises.

As the image of an ever benevolent future fades, higher education institutions are beginning, albeit with painful stops and starts, to look beyond next year's budget. A major impetus for this has been the recent widespread discussion about the enrollment waves of the next two decades. These discussions are apparently convincing some institutions there is no easy way to bandage an enrollment cut that is not going to heal for at least the next twenty years. Moreover, enrollments are not the only future problems. Faculty and facilities are two other notable examples of areas institutions must approach with a wishful view to distant mountain peaks. As the Carnegie Foundation for the Advancement of Teaching (1976, p. 7) notes,

> The next decade of substantial growth will be from 2000 to 2010. This will be a very special period for higher education, and those interested in innovation and improvement and dynamism might well wish that the intervening twenty-five years would disappear. In that first decade of the coming century, at least 40 percent of college and university faculties will be replaced. More than half of all present faculty members were hired in the 1960s, and they will be retiring mostly during the years 2000 to 2010; the opportunity of replacing 40 percent or more of all university faculty in one decade creates enormous possibilities for changing programs, introducing new disciplines, and setting new priorities.
>
> Of all university building space existing today, 55 percent was constructed in the 1960s; it will be extremely difficult to create new plants until these buildings live out their 30 to 40 year period of usefulness. So, after the year 2000, about one-half of higher education facilities will have to be rebuilt or remodeled. This is not the year 2000, however, and we can only hope to make the best of the situation in which we find ourselves.

The second additional important use of future studies is as "social glue." The question of what holds higher education institutions together is especially important as forces that threaten to rule and rip institutional fabric begin to accumulate. It seems reasonable to expect that institutions, like individuals, are held together by a blending of past, present, and future considerations. However, it is only recently that much thought has been given to how past, present, and future images bind together those who create them. Clark's (1972, pp. 178–179) concept of an "organizational saga" is seminal in this area.

> An organizational saga is a collective understanding of unique accomplishment in a formally established group. The group's definition of the accomplishment, intrinsically historical but embellished through retelling and rewriting, links stages of organizational development. The participants have added affect, an emotional loading, which places their conception between the coolness of rational purpose and the warmth of sentiment found in religion and magic. An organizational saga presents some rational explanation of how certain means led to certain ends, but it also includes affect that turns a formal place into a beloved institution, to which participants may be passionately devoted. . . .
>
> The study of organizational sagas highlights nonstructural and nonrational dimensions of organizational life and achievement. Macroorganizational theory has concentrated on the role of structure and technology in organizational effectiveness. . . . A needed corrective is more research on the cultural and expressive

aspects of organizations, particularly on the role of belief and sentiment at broad levels of organization. . . . With a general emphasis on normative bonds, organizational saga refers to a unified set of publicly expressed beliefs about the formal groups that (a) is rooted in history, (b) claims unique accomplishment, and (c) is held with sentiment by the group.

Any institution contemplating its future would do well to begin by articulating (and, if necessary, debating) its organizational saga. Having done this, it should attempt to project this saga forward. Unfortunately, the projection will not be a comfortable one for many institutions. What seems to be needed is an ability in light of old myths (for example, an organizational saga) to select new myths that invigorate institutions and people to move forward. But new myths are not easily created. Amara (1976, p. 98) notes the "collective ability to generate compelling images of the future has diminished, if not disappeared," and we seem unable to utilize the available images.

If we are not getting any better at developing and implementing "compelling images of the future," perhaps one reason is we are getting so good at identifying problems and special interests. One of our major problems is that each of us has discovered our special interests, which are often not our common interests.

There clearly is a need for futurism in higher education. But many things are needed today in higher education, and there is no shortage of solutions being proffered to its dilemmas. Futurism in this regard joins the company of new clientele, curriculum reform, marketing, revised budgeting practices, new financing programs, retention strategies, and the like. Among these efforts, is futurism in the conduct of higher education institutional affairs not only possible but probable?

Barriers to Futurism

Schmidtlein (1975, pp. 111, 112) describes two polar approaches to decision making in higher education: the "Incremental/Remedial" (I/R) strategy and the "Comprehensive/Prescriptive" (C/P) strategy. "In higher education the I/R concept lies behind words like autonomy and pluralism. This view of decision making has contributed to the notion rooted in our past that 'that government governs best that governs least.' . . . Major characteristics of such a decision strategy include: (1) primary concern for the welfare of the individual, (2) uncertainty reduction through rapid, decentralized adaptation to change, (3) social control maintained by a system of checks and balances, and (4) a major focus on process specifications." He contrasts this approach of "muddling through" to the opposite, involving "comprehensive planning, coordination, management science, rational decision making, and, if one is critical, red tape. . . . The principal characteristics of the C/P decision process are (1) primary concern for the welfare of the group; (2) uncertainty reduction through analysis, prediction, and implementation of logically consistent and comprehensive policies; (3) social control through bureaucratic structures and processes; and (4) a major focus on the identification and measurement of outputs."

These two schools of thought clearly embody quite different attitudes about changes and how to adapt to the future. To illustrate these differences, one with a C/P orientation feels when considering rapid rates of change that rapid change intensifies the problem of prediction and thus creates a need to plan. The I/R view is that rapid change makes analysis complex and unreliable and plans are rapidly outdated, so decision making must be remedial. In regard to change technology, the C/P orientation states that critical variables that must be altered are controllable and a control technology is available. This is contrasted to the I/R position that change results from incremental remedial adaptation and invention, so decision processes do not depend on a priori assumptions about the state of change technology.

Each of these schools of decision strategy is represented within the higher education community, sometimes even within the same institution. It is little wonder, then, that higher education response to futurism is uneven. It is sometimes asserted, undoubtedly by I/R types, that planning is what you do if nothing better comes along. Silber (1977, p. 194), most assuredly an I/R type, pokes fun at futurism: "The educators of 1976 peered into the future through an opening flanked by two immense figures. Standing like the pillars of Hercules, Herman Kahn and Colonel Blimp symbolized the durability inherent in planning—pretension and error." Volleys from the other side are just as numerous and snide. Jay Mendell (reported in Cornish and others, 1977, p. 206) writes that "tunnel vision and shortsightedness (the antitheses of future thinking), carefully managed and nurtured, have in the past been positive, not negative, in propelling executives to the top."

In light of the short tenure of many college presidents, it may be asking a great deal to expect them to take the long view when their own purview is so limited. It should also be noted that their role as president may be seriously ensnared not only by relationships within the higher education community (for example, growing roles of state legislators, governors, federal and state agencies, and unions) but also by the considerable momentum of larger changes in society. The best portrait of a college president may not be that of a Dutch boy with his finger in a dike but that of an American boy standing in front of a bursting floodgate. In times of large social change, those in charge may not be.

The Peter Principle might well be expanded so that it proclaims that "work and crises expand to fill and refill the time that is available." For example, Bergquist and Shoemaker (1976, pp. 11–12) call for increased attention to "institutional futures" by use of the Delphi method, scenarios, and other techniques. Yet "institutional futures" is only one of eighteen areas they identify in the first phase of a six-phase process. With enough crises to keep them busy today, few administrators are likely to be drawn to a study of the future, especially when "a future study, almost by definition, is rarely timely for a particular decision" (James Webber and Rebecca Ojala, reported in Cornish and others, 1977, p. 207).

The final major barrier to futurism in academic administration involves skepticism about many futures methodologies. Orlans (1977, p. 34), a member of the Commission on the Year 2000, which met sporadically from 1965 to 1972, notes "the greatest minds—Marx, Freud—trace but a thread of meaning in the fabric of history: And how much of that thread is imagined and how much was really there?" Riesman (1977, p. 24), also a member of the commission, confesses that despite his involvement in a number of attempts to look at the future of higher education, he has "the uncomfortable feeling that even the most imaginative among us can do little more than extrapolate the past into the future, commonly our own most recent past. Whatever the future might be, my sense of historical discontinuity is so strong that I have believed that most of us, myself included, are likely to prove very poor prophets indeed." More specifically, there has been considerable criticism of many of the individual techniques for trying to see or create the future. For example, Boulding (1978, p. 47) reports he is "continually appalled at the influence of think tanks and the scenario writers, people who come up with projections, numbers, and more numbers, in which the more dubious and the less dubious are hopelessly mixed."

On the basis of such criticism, one may be forgiven for at least wondering whether Cornish's list of the eight uses of futurism is not upside down, whether "offering a means for recreation or 'fun' " should come first and "assisting the decision-making process" should come last. If the practice of futurism is to offer more than recreation with an air of science or, as Orlans (1977, p. 31) describes the meetings of the Commission on the Year 2000, an atmosphere of "sherry and Scotch and cigars, short walks around the grounds, new acquaintanceships, other professional business, and gossip," futuristic techniques must be adapted to make their forecasts more usable.

Making Forecasts Usable

So far we have not determined whether futurism is useful in higher education. It seems a good number of institutions could benefit from a long, hard, and systematic examination of futures—both theirs and those of the larger, sustaining society. But there is a real danger that futurism can provide intellectual grist without leaving an action residue of shared visions, policies, and plans. As in so many areas of higher education, quality rather than quantity is apt to be decisive. If futurism is attempted, some delicate balances must be maintained. There is a need to put our heads in the clouds, but end up with our feet on the ground; there is a need to be creative while remaining level headed, to involve the community while recognizing the need for leadership, and to stop the clock long enough to look ahead while somehow dealing with the day-to-day reality, where the clock never stops. To maintain this delicate balance   required in a futures study, the institutional researcher as a futurist must consider several factors. The long-run usefulness of the forecast may be determined to a great extent by the futurist conducting the study. In many ways, the fact that some futures studies receive little use in the decision-making process is due to futurists planting seeds of their own failure at the start of the project. Benveniste (1972, p. 14) summarizes the success rate of planners: "Since 1945 more than twelve hundred national development plans have been elaborated, over one hundred twenty-five central planning offices have been established in both rich and poor countries, and around a hundred specialized training centers give courses in national and regional planning. Yet with twenty-five years of experience behind them, national planners talk more about failures than about successes." Becker (1979, p. 38), with his experience as executive vice-president of the Futures Group, which has performed studies for over five hundred clients, offers this advice to make forecasts usable:

> If the methods used in generating the data are not understandable—and intellectually comfortable—to the boss, the results may immediately become suspect. Indeed, the forecaster's use of sophisticated analytic techniques frequently creates a feeling of intellectual inferiority in the boss, who may begin to feel threatened by his own subordinates.
>
> Too frequently the forecaster is asked for a "number" describing the future. To be truly useful, all forecasts should include estimates of uncertainty. The risks involved in pursuing a given course of action can only be realistically estimated if uncertainties in the parameters upon which we base decisions are also made available.
>
> In the final analysis, planners or forecasters rarely judge the ultimate validity of their own output. Very few forecasters and planners really decide which plan the company will pursue. It is rarer still that a forecaster is given responsibility for carrying out his proposed plan or plans.

One additional clue to the difficulties that inhibit the use of forecasts can be found in the intent of the administration backing the development of the forecast. Benveniste (1972, p. 105) discussed four varieties of planning that can be applied to forecasts: trivial, utopian, imperative, and intentional.

Trivial forecasts have the stamp of expert approval but predict the continuance of the current trend without really considering many difficult issues. The difficult issues that are considered only receive a surface examination, and the presentation of the resulting forecast illustrates the present political choices as favorably as possible. A trivial forecast would be well publicized, with everyone encouraged to participate in its development (with little impact on the final result). Any real opposition to current administration policies is brushed aside because the resulting trivial forecast only provides a technological legitimacy to the current practices.

Utopian forecasting provides a short-term forecast that would please everyone, uses experts to give it a technical foundation, and promotes the political position of the current administration. Examples are forecasts of sufficient funds to support all the necessary programs or a plan that will eliminate illiteracy. Such utopian forecasts may be real in the minds of the experts who assisted in their development, but the required actions on existing policies never occur. The forecast is an administrative hoax to give the appearance that something new will happen.

Both trivial and utopian forecasts are likely to be repeated again and again with new experts involved each time. Thus, such activities hold little promise for the futurist because they are not intended to affect the course of events beyond providing a legitimacy to what will happen anyway.

In contrast, imperative and intentional forecasts are intended to affect the course of events. An imperative forecast relies on existing channels of authority and power to implement action resulting from the forecast. An intentional forecast uses a coalition of supporters for implementation of new policies. One of the main differences in carrying out these changes will be in the amount of publicity the forecast receives in initial stages. The intentional forecast may proceed in some secrecy with limited publicity until the necessary coalitions have been established. In achieving this consensus to establish a coalition, the scope of an intentional forecast may be more limited than that of an imperative forecast.

In higher education, a central, all-powerful administration seldom exists that can develop an imperative forecast. Thus, the following focus of making forecasts useful looks at intentional forecasting rather than the other three alternatives and considers tactics that make intentional forecasting possible.

One of these primary tactics is the establishment of a realistic time frame. Thus, the futurist must determine in advance a schedule that will provide for completion of the forecast at a time when its input on policy issues can be effective. This timing must allow for technical delays and also provide time to build the necessary coalitions. The timing between the technical forecast and the coalition development must be well established to prevent either the development of a forecast without support or the political support being ready without a position paper to go with it.

The issue of the specific time orientation to the future is an important consideration that may provide a different perspective on the other futures issues that follow. Possible time horizons include short-term futures (one to five years), medium-term futures (five to twenty years), and long-term futures (beyond twenty years). Some policy issues are more applicable to one time horizon than another. Issues with different time horizons may be separated into homogeneous groups to provide several studies, rather than one that loses its coalition support because of too broad a spectrum.

Another tactical point to consider when initiating a forecasting project is the selection of the team of experts that will assist the project. When you choose the team members, consider the following: potential team members' external perceptions of the technical and professional competence of the group, actual technical and professional competence of the group, and the team members' ability to work with each other. It is important that the team be able to communicate using familiar language, concepts, and frameworks. The use of technical jargon associated with many futuristic studies may only magnify the distrust potential coalition members may have of the futurist. Communication problems often go deeper than the use of the jargon. If differences exist in the conceptual framework, the futurist may feel he or she is trying to explain celestial navigation to a group that still believes the world is flat.

The futurist who wants to bridge these gaps created by timing, jargon, and conceptual frameworks would be well advised to assemble a list of possible issues about futures projections and communicate it to those sponsors, users, or members of the coalition who will affect the potential use of the results. Clear discussion and agreement on the issues surrounding the forecasting effort should enhance the use of the results. The following should facilitate the construction of such lists:

1. Future projections should build on the facts we know and not obscure the little we know by providing a deluge of questionable information or information overflow.

2. Future projections should make experts' knowledge available to decision makers.

3. Future projections of unexpected events should be fully examined to ensure they are not aberrations of the method used to develop the projection.

4. Future projections should concentrate on the key factors of importance to the decision makers.

5. Future projections may reveal information that can be dangerous to the organizational health of current decision makers.

6. Future projections should contain the assumptions on which the projections are based with a caution to pay as much attention to the assumptions as to the final forecast.

7. Future projections may bring together people with a diverse set of backgrounds, and this expanded dialogue may end with the various parties concluding the others do not understand unless the futurist conducting the project uses modern communication techniques to eliminate communication problems.

8. Future projections should be developed within a time frame that makes them usable to the decision maker who approved the project.

9. Future projections should stimulate decision makers to debate and evaluate the projections, not the method used to develop the projections.

10. The futurist developing the projections should consider the organizational level of the decision maker who is supporting the development of the projections. If sufficient top-level support exists, the results are more likely to be used.

11. The institutional management and the futurist developing the projections should make a specific list of the realistic objectives to be fulfilled by the future projections. The list of objectives might include selections from the following, as well as others:
    a. to satisfy an internal political requirement
    b. to satisfy an external political requirement
    c. to develop better data for improved day-to-day management
    d. to develop better data for responding to external queries
    e. to develop the capability of forecasting significant changes that are likely to occur (Decision makers can then respond with new policies to select the best course of action for their institution in the long run.)
    f. to document a possible future for the purpose of publishing journal articles
    g. to bring together diverse components of the institution, to work together on a nonthreatening effort, thus, promoting improved relationships within the institution
    h. to research and improve a futures methodology

12. The futurist developing the projections must select a methodology to use in developing the futures projections. In making this selection, the futurist should consider a number of different criteria for comparing the possible methods, including some of the following:
    a. the support of key decision makers for a particular method
    b. the cost of acquisition of the methodology
    c. the cost of using the methodology to develop the future projections
    d. the technical complexity or ease of communication of the methodology

e. the availability of funding support as related to the methodology used
f. the futurist's experience with the methodology to be used
g. the relationship between the methodology and the fulfillment of the study objectives
h. the type of information (level of detail, accuracy, or credibility) produced by the method
i. the existence of documented methods or procedures to follow in conducting the futures study using a specific method
j. the availability of national experts to serve as consultants on the use of a specific futures method

Several comments are appropriate concerning the selection of a specific futuristic method to be used in the study. Each of the forecasting technique categories (exploratory, intuitive, and normative) will be considered, with one technique being discussed in each of these categories. Each of these techniques has documented procedures to follow when conducting a futures study. For general details on each of the other alternatives in the fourteen methods, see *Futurism in Education* by Henchey and Yates (1974).

In the category of exploratory methods, the educational modeling techniques available for forecasting are numerous. Yet most of these modeling techniques look at "now" in futures terms or only a short-term forecast for one year ahead. Only generalized modeling techniques, such as the State Planning System (SPS), have the capability of going far into the future. The *State Planning System Design Guide* (Chisholm and others, 1977) and eleven other SPS documents provide a complete set of documents for developing a forecasting model if the futurist knows the educational relationships to be used in the forecast. SPS has the capability to go as far into the future as the futurist would desire. To this date, no example futuristic forecasts using SPS have been documented for use by others; but Halstead and Huckfeldt (1979) are developing a national set of futuristic projections for the National Institute of Education. Before rushing into developing futuristic projections using educational modeling techniques, the futurist should be aware of the reviews applied to educational modeling. An excellent place to start is Mason (1976).

The intuitive techniques have been used to produce a number of forecasts of the future of education. Information on the most recent of these projections can be found in *The Futurist,* a publication of the World Future Society. Special attention should be given to the publications and conferences by the education section of the society. As with the modeling techniques, many of the intuitive techniques are used and the results documented, but few procedures exist that suggest how to proceed in conducting a study. The Delphi is the only known intuitive technique for which procedures have been documented (Huckfeldt and Judd, 1975).

In regard to the normative techniques, a futures process that seems well suited to the needs and temperament of higher education institutions has been developed (Resource Center for Planned Change, 1978). This process consists of the ten stages well documented in the planning guide and intended to help an institution plan for its next decade:

1. trends through the coming decade
2. values through the coming decade

3. a policymaking matrix for trend areas
4. a policymaking matrix for value shifts
5. the formulation of institutional objectives
6. the compatibility of objectives: with institutional purpose, with other objectives, and with value shifts
7. the construction of a futures scenario
8. a history of alternative futures
9. foresight
10. feasibility-evaluating constraints

This process properly begins with a consideration of hard (trends) and soft (values) data. *Trends 2000* is a useful aid to the study of trends (Association of American Colleges, 1970). This handbook covers demography, community assessment, faculty, and programs. Values are the other half of the foundation upon which institutional futures need to be built. This half of the foundation will be both easy and hard for institutions to deal with. It should be easy because higher education institutions typically have prided themselves on being value sensitive and as embodying and expressing clear values. It may be hard because value shifts that will challenge many of the current value foundations of higher education are taking place. As Cornish and others (1977, p. 11) point out, "Change turns the old morality into the new morality. Motherhood, once held in reverence, now is often viewed as wicked, because it contributes to the population problem; patriotism becomes suspect in an increasingly interdependent world." Higher education is not immune from this kind of value flip-flop. It does not take a very active imagination to suggest, for example, that such positive values as tenure, small classes, and attractive campuses will one day in some places become vices to be widely renounced.

Stages 3 through 6 of the paradigm reveal its practical bent. In these stages, an effort is made to translate trends and values into their impacts on the constituent parts and the day-to-day activities of the institution. Then trends, values, and their impacts become the basis for developing a proactive response—namely, for developing institutional objectives. Institutional planners' and researchers' skills are much needed and will be adequately challenged in this phase of the process. To develop these impacts and to suggest objectives will require a feel not only for the parts of an institution but also for how those parts come together to make up the whole of an institution. Synthesis rather than reduction is the challenge.

The construction of scenarios is the business of stages 7, 8, and 9. The first construction takes place in stage 7 with "optimistic" and "pessimistic" scenarios. In effect, these become a form of self-fulfilling and self-denying prophecies. The designers hope their objectives simultaneously will produce the optimistic and deny the pessimistic. These scenarios are images of the future that draw upon the trends, values, impacts, and objectives of the earlier stages. The second phase of construction takes place in stage 8. In this stage, a scenario of how the institution might promote the optimistic scenario and deny the pessimistic scenario is created. The mountain peak is now in sight, as are the chasms, cliffs, ledges, and the traverses. The trick is to find the ways to scale the *last* thousand feet. Having found that, the next step is to find a way to scale the thousand feet before that. The mountain can be climbed if it can be climbed from the top down. Having mentally climbed down the mountain, the climber goes back up the mountain in stage 9. The final scenario to be constructed is what it will mean to have climbed the mountain. If the mountain is a real mountain, it will change those who scale it. The climbers need to decide if this is really what they want. Finally, in stage 10, the climbers become realists. They ask all the right questions about whether this climb really can be made.

Boyer and Kaplan (1977, p. 71) speak of "the tomorrow which, willfully and willy-nilly, is being made today." It is hoped futurism can help higher education institutions increase the willful and decrease the willy-nilly. This hope is both for the institutions and for their students, who soon will leave them to enter the future.

Bibliographical Essay

The references corresponding to the specific forecasting technique, exploratory, intuitive, or normative, are very useful. Additional insight can be gained from Henchey and Yates (1974) and Fowles (1978). Cornish and others (1977) provides extensive information in a full introduction to the study of the future containing not only information on methodology but also views by futurists, case studies, and references to future-oriented organizations and periodicals. The wealth to be found in these volumes is perhaps the future itself.

References

Amara, R. "Education for Survival: Some Necessary Cognitive, Participative, and Perceptual Changes for America's Third Century." *Phi Delta Kappan*, 1976, *58* (1), 91–98.

"A Myth for the Future." *Futures Conditional*, 1976, *4*.

Association of American Colleges. *Trends 2000: Information for Planning. A Handbook for Academic Administrators*. Washington, D.C.: Association of American Colleges, 1970.

Bachetti, R. F. "In Praise of Good Questions." In C. Adams (Ed.), *New Directions for Institutional Research: Appraising Information Needs of Decision Makers*, no. 15. San Francisco: Jossey-Bass, 1977.

Bailey, S. "Educational Purpose and the Pursuit of Happiness." *Phi Delta Kappan*, 1976, *58* (1), 42–47.

Becker, H. S. "Making Forecasts Usable: Some Advice for Practicing Planners and Policy Analysts." *World Future Society Bulletin*, 1979, *13* (1), 37–39.

Benveniste, G. *The Politics of Expertise*. Berkeley, Calif.: Glendessary Press, 1972.

Bergquist, W. H., and Shoemaker, W. A. (Eds.). *New Directions for Higher Education: A Comprehensive Approach to Institutional Development*, no. 15. San Francisco: Jossey-Bass, 1976.

Boulding, K. "In Praise of Inefficiency." *Association of Governing Boards of Universities and Colleges, Reports*, 1978, *20* (1), 44–48.

Boyer, E. L., and Kaplan, M. *Educating for Survival*. New Rochelle, N.Y.: Change Magazine Press, 1977.

Carnegie Foundation for the Advancement of Teaching. *The States and Higher Education: A Proud Past and a Vital Future*. San Francisco: Jossey-Bass, 1976.

Chisholm, M., and others. *State Planning System Design Guide*. Technical Report 92. Boulder, Colo.: National Center for Higher Education Management Systems, 1977.

Clark, B. R. "The Organizational Saga in Higher Education." *Administrative Science Quarterly,* 1972, *17,* 178–184.

Cornish, E. "Towards a Philosophy of Futurism." *The Futurist,* 1977a, *2* (6), 380–383.

Cornish, E. "What Shall We Call the Study of the Future?" *The Futurist,* 1977b, *11* (1), 44–50.

Cornish, E., and others. *The Study of the Future.* Washington, D.C.: World Future Society, 1977.

Fowles, J. *Handbook of Futures Research.* Westport, Conn.: Greenwood Press, 1978.

Halstead, K. D., and Huckfeldt, V. E. *A National Model for Higher Education.* Boulder, Colo.: National Policy Analysis Center, 1979.

Henchey, N. "Making Sense of Future Studies." *Alternatives,* n.d., pp. 24–28.

Henchey, S. D., and Yates, J. R. *Futurism in Education.* Berkeley, Calif.: McCutchan, 1974.

Huckfeldt, V. E., and Judd, R. C. *Methods for Large Scale Delphi Studies.* Boulder, Colo.: National Center for Higher Education Management Systems, 1975.

Mason, T. R. *New Directions for Institutional Research: Assessing Computer-Based Systems Models,* no. 9. San Francisco: Jossey-Bass, 1976.

Orlans, H. "Remembrance of Things Future." *Change,* 1977, *9* (4), 30–36.

Popper, S. H. *The Simulation of a School of the Future: A Report of an Exploratory Study.* Minneapolis, Minn.: University Council for Education Administration, 1971.

Renfro, R. "How Congress is Exploring the Future." *The Futurist,* 1978, *12* (2), 105–112.

Resource Center for Planned Change. *A Futures Creating Paradigm: A Guide to Long-Range Planning from the Future for the Future.* Washington, D.C.: American Association of State Colleges and Universities, 1978.

Riesman, D. "Small Steps to a Larger Future." In *The Third Century.* New Rochelle, N.Y.: Change Magazine Press, 1977.

Schmidtlein, F. A. "An Analysis of Decision Strategies Employed in the Governance of Higher Education." In R. G. Cope (Ed.), *Information for Decisions in Postsecondary Education.* Proceedings of the 15th Annual Association for Institutional Research Forum, St. Louis, April 28–May 1, 1975.

Silber, J. R. "The Rest Was History." In *The Third Century.* New Rochelle, N.Y.: Change Magazine Press, 1977.

The Future: A Guide to Information Resources. Washington, D.C.: World Future Society, 1977.

11

Paul Wing

Forecasting Enrollment and Student Demographic Conditions

The impending decline in college enrollments has been well documented. (See, for example, Carnegie Foundation, 1975; Centra, 1978; Henderson, 1977; Rowse, 1979b.) It is rapidly becoming accepted as one of the basic facts of life in higher education planning for the 1980s. This recognition of the impending decline, however, has not often been translated into appropriate strategies for either systems or individual campuses, where administrators have often assumed their new recruiting efforts and programs for adults will enable them to maintain enrollments.

Given that a decline in enrollments is generally accepted and that institutions have been alerted to the necessity of developing appropriate strategies, one might ask what is more needed from institutional statisticians, analysts, and planners.

This chapter argues that much useful analytical work can be done and,

216

further, that this work holds the prospect of a more effective higher education system. The statistical work required is related to, but goes beyond, enrollment forecasting. It is tied in with important but often overlooked concepts like institutional drawing power (the ability to attract students) and factors related to changes in student demand and student choice of institution (Henderson and Plummer, 1978). The chapter is organized into four sections: (1) a discussion of general concepts related to enrollment forecasting and forecasters; (2) an explanation of forecasting techniques, with special reference to the selection of appropriate procedures for specific forecasting environments; (3) a description of analyses that can supplement and support basic enrollment projections; and (4) suggestions for institutional roles in analyzing enrollments. Its examples and illustrations are based on analyses that have been done in New York State.

Concepts and Responsibilities

The following distinctions among projections, forecasts, predictions, and simulations provide an introduction to the strategies—and their underlying philosophies—open to planners and analysts concerned with future enrollment patterns:

- Forecast—an estimate of future enrollment derived using some systematic procedure or technique
- Projection—an estimate of future enrollment (or other quantity) based on the assumption that the underlying trends and relationships of the past will continue in the future
- Simulation—an estimate of future enrollment obtained by systematically altering one or more of the underlying trends or relationships in the basic forecasting procedure
- Prediction—an estimate of future enrollment, regardless of its derivation, that carries with it a high degree of belief in its accuracy

From these definitions, it may be obvious that the "systematic procedure or technique" used in a forecast need not be a projection model and that the procedure need not involve quantitative techniques, although most forecasting does involve numerical computations of one sort or another. A systematic approach is the critical ingredient, and the major types of approaches to forecasting are described in the next section of this chapter.

Projections are the basis for nearly all current enrollment forecasting efforts. They all share a fundamental weakness, however: Because past underlying trends and relationships are not likely to continue unchanged in the future, the resulting projections are not likely to be 100 percent accurate. Projection models can, however, serve several important purposes. They can provide early warning of significant trends and patterns. They can provide benchmark enrollment estimates that can be compared with future actual enrollments to assess the impact of various changes in policy or environment on student attendance patterns. Differences that exist between projections and actual enrollments are clues that the basic relationships or input data in a model are incorrect or incomplete. Properly designed, a projection model can serve as a vehicle for simulating the impact of a variety of possible changes or variations in the policies and relationships that underlie the projections. A point to note clearly is that projections are generally not expected to be correct; they recognize the uncertainties.

Simulation is probably the most promising approach available for studying and *understanding* future higher education enrollments. Unfortunately, it also is one of the most demanding kinds of analytical tools. Basic computational models must exist to permit rapid calculation of enrollment estimates; and, equally important, data sets and staff resources must be available to quantify the specific assumptions one desires to evaluate. But if data and staff are available, simulation can be extremely useful. It can be used to assess the impact of a wide variety of controllable and uncontrollable changes in the higher education system and its environment. As planners and policymakers are forced to deal with more difficult problems and choices, their need for this kind of capability will increase. The discussion in the third section of this chapter suggests some of the factors and relationships that can be built into existing models to permit useful simulations to be performed.

Predictions, unlike projections, are expected to be correct. They are more in the realm of the gambler or the odds maker than the planner or the analyst. The higher education system is too complex to model in sufficient detail to be able to risk much more than a friendly wager on any enrollment prediction. And because turning points in enrollment patterns are hard to predict (as they are in most forecasting problems), errors can be quite large, particularly for the distant future.

With these basic distinctions in mind, one fundamental question must be explored prior to discussing specific procedures: Who should carry out enrollment forecasting? Among the candidates are institutions, state agencies, and national agencies. Although none of these can or should be arbitrarily excluded from the task, individual colleges are in the least favorable positions to do an adequate job because of the interactions between institutions that occur in the course of recruiting and educating students. When one college is particularly successful in recruiting or retaining students, others will tend to experience declines in their enrollments. This means that for one institution to estimate accurately its own future enrollment levels, it needs to be able also to estimate the enrollment levels of the institutions with which it competes for students. (Those few institutions that have no competition, of course, can develop their own projections independently.) This is not an impossible task, but it requires a larger commitment of resources than many institutions may be willing or able to make. One might hear from a particular institution that it has been very successful in projecting future enrollments accurately. More often than not, however, this can be attributed to an effective admissions system that can accept exactly the number of students required to meet predetermined enrollment targets. When the decline in the pool of potential students begins, most institutions will find that others will start to fish in their pond (Fiske, 1978; Jenkins, 1979). And the fortunes of many institutions will depend on the nature and quality of their bait. In any event, the traditional notion of enrollment targets based on historical trends and attainable through adjustments in admissions strategies is likely to prove inappropriate in these circumstances.

At the state and national levels, it is appropriate, even essential, to deal with groups of institutions. In both cases, it is necessary to trade off detail in terms of geography or classes of institutions against computational and data-handling problems. Recent work by the Western Interstate Commission on Higher Education (WICHE) (McConnell, 1979) suggests undifferentiated national enrollment projections are unlikely to be of much use to local planners and policymakers. This suggests that projection work should either be done at the state level or should result in aggregations that correspond roughly with state boundaries. Differences in financing strategies in different states also call for state-level enrollment studies. States have fewer institutions to deal with and can therefore consider more factors and relationships in developing a projection model. Offsetting this advantage are problems related to interstate migration, which are generally hard to deal with because of lack of data, although these patterns have apparently been relatively stable in recent years. Within a state, the forecaster must consider which institutions should be included in the analysis. In New York State, all degree-granting institutions—public, independent, and proprietary—are included because they are all felt to be competing with each other for students to some extent. In addition, it is relatively easy to develop a comprehensive model for New York because the state education department collects the same information on enrollments and other facets of institutional operations from all institutions. In states where there is little interaction between the public and independent institutions or where insufficient data is available for independent institutions, separate models might be developed for each section or the forecasts might be developed for only the public institutions. The latter option would probably preclude the development of reliable statewide measures of college participation, which could be a drawback.

Of course, other possibilities exist. Groups of institutions that traditionally compete for the same students can establish cooperative enrollment-forecasting ventures. This is already being done in a variety of situations ranging from projections by central offices of multicampus systems to studies by consortia of private colleges. Groups of states could also collaborate, particularly where migration of students across state lines is significant. Ultimately, however, the state level seems to be the most likely focal point. States with large public systems need to know what the prospects are for the public campuses. States with strong public and private sectors must be concerned with diversity and balance. Institutions generally cannot deal with the forecasting problems in a sufficiently broad context, and the federal government does not have a strong incentive to explore institutional interactions and aggregations in sufficient detail to be of general value.

The discussion that follows takes a predominantly statewide perspective for the reasons already outlined and because this is where my primary experience lies. This should not be construed as a suggestion to limit applications of the principles and procedures at the institutional and national levels. Analysts at all levels need to bring to bear all the tools at their disposal on these important issues and problems. In fact, some sort of institutional/state partnership would probably be the best choice.

The effort and expertise required to develop a sound enrollment forecasting model should not be underestimated. Capable analysts supported by effective data systems and computer support are essential. An active dissemination program can help minimize complaints and criticisms about the resulting forecasts. The New York State Education Department maintains a formal enrollment projection advisory committee representing the major institutional sectors and the state division of the budget. The early criticisms of this group led to significant modifications in model structures and even data collection, but the end result was improved models and results that are much more readily accepted as well as enhanced credibility for the department. Publication and distribution to campuses of reports on methodology and results have also contributed to the effectiveness of the New York State efforts. This open approach is possible—even necessary—in large part because enrollment forecasting is a continuing project in New York. Comparisons between actual enrollments and earlier projections are performed regularly, and the results are made available to interested parties.

No matter who in a state handles the enrollment-forecasting chores, sharing ideas and results will almost certainly enhance any serious project. But the question of who is best suited to deal with the problems of enrollment forecasting should not cause one to overlook what is perhaps the critical problem facing higher education planners today. Our understanding about the various aspects and facets of higher education, and particularly the relationships among them, does not provide a solid foundation for many of the important decisions that must be made. We know a lot about some things, a little about others, and nothing about some. Questions about the impact of the installation of a part-time student aid program on full-time enrollments and where students would go if the school were to close are well beyond our reach at the present time. This suggests any state interested in policies and procedures related to institutional enrollments must have more than just an enrollment projection model. Such a model can indicate changes likely in the future, but it cannot provide a basis for developing and evaluating alternative strategies or studying the important but subtle dynamics and interactions within the higher education system. I discuss examples of possible analyses that can be performed later in this chapter.

Forecasting Models

Any forecasting model has several important characteristics or dimensions, each of which must be specified as part of the process of designing the model: structural components, basic relationships, specific forecasting techniques, specific parameters, and an administrative system. The *structural components* are the major building blocks of a forecasting model. They represent the basic elements in the overall structure, such as high school graduates, first-time students, or age groups in the population. They are the boxes in Figure 1. To complete the general description of a forecasting model, it is necessary to identify the *relationships* and *linkages* among the structural components. The relationships are the arrows that connect the boxes in Figure 1. Another critical element in the design of a forecasting model is the *specific forecasting techniques* employed. It is important to note use of the plural in this case because a single model generally involves several forecasting techniques. One usually corresponds to the overall system design specified by the structural components and basic relationships; but others are needed to forecast other aspects of the model, such as participation rates, pools of potential students, or transition coefficients. The *specific parameters* and coefficients define the details of a forecasting model, both within and among the structural components. They identify the specific data elements and characterize the detailed forecasting techniques and other computations

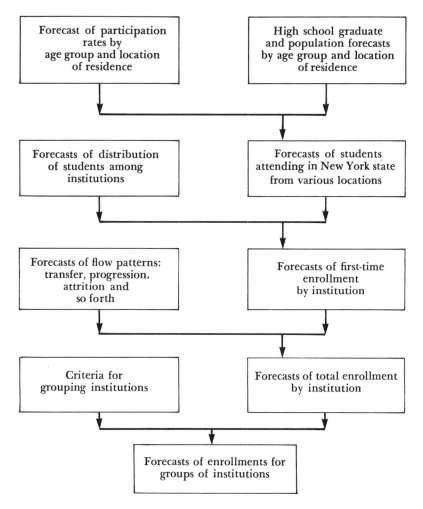

Figure 1. Overall Structure of Enrollment Forecasting Model of New York State Education Department

used in the model. Not every forecasting model needs an *administrative system,* but the effectiveness of a complex model used in a simulation mode can be significantly enhanced by the inclusion of one or more computational support capabilities. These may range from data base management systems to maintain and alter input data, to report generators to create a variety of different summary reports, to procedures to simplify the process of making multiple runs of the model. Before presenting an illustrative design, I shall describe briefly the major forecasting techniques that can be incorporated into the final model.

Specific Forecasting Techniques. There is a variety of specific techniques that can be used in forecasting higher education enrollments. Not all are equally well suited in all situations, and some sort of mixed strategy involving several techniques is typically the most appropriate. In discussing specific techniques, it is convenient to categorize them according to their basic characteristics. A number of classification schemes for forecasting techniques have been proposed in the literature, but I shall use my own (Wing, 1974).

I discuss four broad classes of forecasting techniques, each of which represents a significantly different approach to developing estimates of future enrollments: pattern models, curve-fitting techniques, intentions surveys, and subjective judgment. Because of the nature of the relationships between higher education enrollments and other factors, such as high school graduates, pattern models are almost always the choice for the basic structure of enrollment forecasting models. The other three classes of techniques *can* be used as the basic structure of a model; but in higher education enrollment forecasting, they are generally used only in secondary roles, such as in projecting selected coefficients within the basic pattern model.

In situations where relationship(s) between higher education enrollments and other independent factors (such as high school graduates) can be identified, analysts should seriously consider one or more of the available *pattern models.* If, for example, it is felt that first-time college enrollment is related closely to the number of high school graduates in earlier years, a cohort-survival technique may be appropriate. If a significant and stable proportion of new college enrollees is women between thirty-five and forty-five years old, a ratio method may be appropriate.

Two general considerations should be kept in mind when evaluating pattern models: First, are the independent factors in the model (such as high school graduates and women between thirty-five and forty-five years old) really related to enrollments? Second, is the relationship between the independent factor(s) and enrollments stable and predictable? If these questions can be answered affirmatively, one of the pattern models probably is an appropriate basis for enrollment forecasting.

The same pattern model may not be equally appropriate for all forecasting situations. In one situation, the cohort-survival model may be appropriate for projecting first-time enrollments in four-year colleges and universities, a ratio model may be a better choice for community colleges, and a Markov transition model may be a good choice for estimating persistence patterns of students already admitted. Other techniques, such as multiple correlation and regression, path analysis, or systems of equations, may be more appropriate in other situations.

Enrollment forecasting using *curve-fitting techniques* assumes a particular pattern or trend exists in past enrollments. Projections are made on the assumption that this pattern or trend will continue to hold until the year for which the enrollment projection is desired. Thus, there is an implicit assumption that the past indicates the future. One of the attractive features of curve-fitting procedures is that the only input data they require are historical enrollment statistics.

Despite the fact that curve-fitting techniques require the assumption that past trends will continue in the future, there are two general situations in which it is appropriate to use them: when it is believed past trends will in fact continue in the future and when too little is known about causal relationships affecting enrollments to permit the development of appropriate pattern models. It may be appropriate, for example, to use a curve-fitting technique for forecasting the values of certain parameters in causal models, such as participation rates of high school graduates in higher education. Examples of curve-fitting techniques include simple averages, moving averages, exponential smoothing, polynomial models, exponential models, and spectral analysis.

Pattern models and curve-fitting techniques have one thing in common: They rely on historical data and assume conditions and trends present when the historical data were generated will continue until the time for which the enrollment forecasts are desired. There always are some deviations from historical trends; but if they are small enough, the errors introduced into the projections may fall within tolerable limits. What happens, however, in periods like the mid 1960s, when the Vietnam War broke out, and the early 1970s, when the attitudes of society and potential students toward higher education changed substantially? The impact on enrollment projections was all too obvious: Projections developed for the mid 1960s typically were lower than actual enrollments, and those for the early 1970s typically were higher than the actual enrollments. These are clear cases of shifts in fundamental attitudes that resulted in a violation of the assumptions required by the various techniques employed.

One possible way to avoid or mitigate such a situation is to develop some indicators of the attitudes of potential students toward higher education and of their enrollment intentions. And one way to develop such indicators is to perform an *intentions survey* of potential students: Ask high school seniors or even high school freshmen or sophomores what they intend to do in the future. Running such a survey only once probably will not provide much assistance relative to enrollment forecasting. Only after data have been collected for several years (that is, a longitudinal study made) can attitude and intention trends be compared with participation and enrollment trends to yield more accurate projections. It cannot be guaranteed ahead of time, but it does seem reasonable to suspect such surveys would result in more accurate forecasts.

Using *subjective judgment* in forecasting the future, though not scientific and objective, may sometimes provide a useful complement to other forecasting procedures, especially when objective criteria and measures are lacking. It may be necessary, for example, to rely on experts' judgments to estimate the impact on enrollments of shifts in federal financing patterns, changes in student attitudes, judicial decisions concerning residence status, and such. In all such cases, analysts should apply their intuitions and subjective judgments cautiously because they can be very wrong. It also may be difficult to convince a budget analyst or legislator to accept an enrollment projection based even partly on intuition.

I recommend subjective judgment and intuition only as supplementary procedures, not as a substitute for identifying systematic, quantitative procedures. Armstrong and Grohman (1972) indicate that stock market forecasts improve as technical procedures replace intuitive procedures. This is likely to be true in higher education enrollment forecasting as well.

There are, however, some areas where subjective judgment will be required for some time to come. For example, in selecting the particular polynomial form to be used in a curve-fitting model, it may not be possible to identify a quantitative criterion for making the choice. Or to incorporate the findings of a survey of the future intentions of high school students, an analyst may have to apply his or her judgment in estimating the appropriate quantitative adjustments. Delphi surveys are an example of a subjective procedure.

Developing a Forecasting Model. The development of an adequate projection model takes time. Though it is probably possible to obtain some rough but reliable estimates of future enrollment levels in a week or so, the development of a systematic model in that short time is out of the question. The model I describe suggests one possible structure for an enrollment-forecasting model and outlines some considerations that led to choices made during the design process. The development and implementation of the actual model by the New York State Education Department (Rowse, 1979c) took approximately six staff-years of effort. The basic model, shown in Figure 1, is used to develop projections for the four major classes of students most important for planning and policymaking purposes in New York State: full-time undergraduates, part-time undergraduates, full-time graduates, and part-time graduates. First professional students are also of interest in New York State; but because of the large surplus of applicants for these programs, the model does not deal with them. The capability to develop projections for different groups of institutions (for example, public two-year institutions) and for different levels of students (for example, lower division) has been incorporated to extend the utility of the model as a policy tool.

The decision to enable projections to be generated for different groups of institutions and levels of students is only one of several fundamental choices that must be made in developing the basic structure and capability of any enrollment projection model. Other such choices, identified in the following list, have significant implications for the power and complexity of the model.

- *aggregation levels*
    department/program
    institution/campus
    groups of institutions
    geographic subtotals
    statewide
- *student levels*
    freshman, sophomore, and so forth
    lower division, upper division, and so forth
    undergraduate, graduate, and so forth
    full-time, part-time
- *forecast bases*
    term-by-term
    annual—fall term headcount
    annual—full-time-equivalent average
- *projection time horizons*
    one or two years
    seventeen years or less
    greater than seventeen years
- *student characteristics*
    age
    sex
    race/ethnic background
    income
    ability
    geographic origin
- *institutional characteristics*
    sector/type
    geographic location

    drawing power
    setting (for example, sylvan)
    level of offering (for example, two-year)
- *other considerations*
    degrees awarded
    interinstitutional flows
    retention and stop-outs
    simulation capability

These in turn determine the specifications for the model, that is, the parameters and relationships that need to be included, the data requirements, and the computational procedures. In many cases, technical considerations (for example, data availability and computer capacity) may dictate the structure of the model or at least aspects of it. In New York State, some choices among the options were based on desired outcomes that reflect the basic philosophy and information needs of the state education department; some were based on data availability; and some were based on computational procedures. For example, the choice to work with groups of institutions was based on the perceived need to focus attention on broad planning issues related to the impact of decline of different types of institutions and regions in the state. Even if data had been available at the departmental or program level, it would not have been used. It is important to note, however, that if the state education department had the obligation of reviewing or developing detailed budget recommendations for the public campuses in the state, a different choice might have been made. A number of states prepare short-term enrollment projections involving department/program detail to support their budgeting activities.

The New York choice of a seventeen-year time horizon was dictated by the desire for a relatively long-term perspective, tempered by reluctance to extend the projections beyond the period defined by actual births. Even then, student interstate migration creates uncertainty in the years near the forecasting horizon. The choice of student levels was dictated by the availability of data. The department has felt that the increase in accuracy that might accompany an expansion from a lower division/upper division split to a freshman/sophomore/junior/senior split would be insufficient to justify the increased data collection and maintenance costs. The same is true of the decision to project only fall term headcount enrollment. The choice to limit student characteristics to age and geographic origin was dictated by a combination of data and computational considerations. There is reason to believe the accuracy of the projections would be increased—and certainly the policy relevance of the model would be increased—if sex and racial/ethnic background were incorporated into the model. However, this would also increase by an order of magnitude the size of the basic data sets and the computational requirements of the model, which would tend to restrict its use. In addition, income and ability measures are not available in a form that can be incorporated into the projection model.

After considering these kinds of fundamental choices in light of available data, there still remains the question of model form and structure. Which specific forecasting techniques are going to be used and how will they be incorporated into the overall projection model? In considering the four basic types of techniques, only the pattern models are particularly attractive for overall model structure. The basic relationships that influence enrollments are almost certainly going to change too much to justify use of a curve-fitting technique, and neither intention surveys nor subjective judgment holds much promise as the primary method.

In selecting the specific technique or techniques to be used in the model, it is important to know as much as possible about the determinants of enrollments. Two major factors dominate in most situations: the pools of potential students and the participation rate of these students. In some situations, the number of available openings is also an important factor.

The next step then is to define the pools of potential students based on characteristics of students such as those in the previous list. In practice, one should identify those groups of potential students that have similar participation patterns, subject to data availability. Because college participation varies for different age groups, for men and women, for different racial/ethnic groups, and for different ability and income groups, these are all candidates for distinguishing different pools of potential students. Because different types of institutions tend to draw their students from different geographic areas, geography is also a possible factor. Because nearly all colleges and universities require a high school diploma as a prerequisite for admission, the number of high school graduates in a state or substate region (for example, county) also identifies potential pools of students. In the New York model for full-time undergraduates, high school graduates in each of the eight regents regions are important pools of potential students. To account for the participation of older students in college, the numbers of individuals in the twenty to twenty-four, twenty-five to twenty-nine, thirty to forty-four, and forty-five to fifty-nine age categories are also included as pools of potential students. The participation of each of these groups is estimated by dividing the number of first-time students in each category (for example, twenty to twenty-four) by the total number of such individuals in the population. The model also takes into account the differential participation of each group by region. For example, a separate participation rate is computed for twenty- to twenty-four-year-olds from each regents region to each institution in the state. The part-time undergraduate and graduate models are comparable except that only age categories are used; high school graduates are not included in these models.

This kind of basic model requires a substantial amount of secondary analysis. For example, when projecting first-time enrollments based on the participation of high school graduates in different regions in a state, one must have access to projections of high school graduates in each region of the state. In the New York State model, the analysis that generates these numbers is carried out separately. It is also necessary to have estimates of future participation rates. In the New York State model, a weighted average of the recent participation rates is used. The best results in recent runs of the model for short-term forecasts have been obtained with very high weightings on the most recent year's rates. This suggests that fundamental changes in participation rate patterns are taking place and that a polynomial model or some more sophisticated trend extrapolation model might be more appropriate for projecting the participation rates. Such a modification is currently under consideration, but it will probably await further study and improved understanding of participation rates and the factors that influence them.

After generating estimates of full-time, first-time undergraduate enrollments, there remains the task of translating these into total full-time undergraduate enrollments. This requires some sort of flow model that involves transition probabilities and attrition factors. This aspect of the New York State model is a little complicated because of the use of lower-division and upper-division enrollments as the basic building blocks. The transition statistics generated are sometimes difficult to interpret and are often quite volatile. For example, the ratio of upper-division to lower-division enrollment often fluctuates significantly in response to change in interinstitutional transfer patterns. Similarly, the ratio of lower-division to first-time enrollments varies because of changes in admission policies. It is not necessary to dwell on these vagaries, but anyone seriously contemplating the development of a multiinstitution enrollment projection model should be prepared for some hard-to-interpret results on occasion.

Accuracy. Another important aspect of enrollment forecasting is accuracy (Lewis and Sulkin, 1975). It would be easy *not* to evaluate accuracy. It is time-consuming and can be embarrassing. Anyone serious about forecasting, however, should not succumb to the temptation to sweep questions of accuracy and evaluation under the rug. Comparisons of forecasts with actual enrollments is perhaps the best way to evaluate the suitability of a particular forecasting model or procedure. Differences can suggest aspects of a model that need improvement and may even suggest the kinds of changes that ought to be made. They can also help identify the fact that changes are occurring in the basic relationships that influence enrollments, although simple comparisons probably will not be very useful in defining the specific nature of the changes. Another important reason for devoting attention to accuracy is credibility. This is particularly important for any office or agency interested in using enrollment forecasts as the basis for policy formulation or resource allocation. Administrators will rightfully balk at policies based on inaccurate, unreliable, or uncertain quantitative results. Only by being open about procedures and results, perhaps even to the extent of establishing formal review committees and soliciting suggestions for improving models and input data, can one have any assurance of support or respect.

The extension of an enrollment forecasting model into a simulation tool can often enhance both the utility of the model and the credibility of its user. First, it explicitly recognizes that uncertainties exist and establishes an analytical frame of reference for dealing with them. Second, it provides a basis for exploring policy options and technical alternatives that would otherwise be passed by. And third, it stimulates attention to a host of "secondary" issues that are critical for a thorough understanding of higher education enrollments. This last result, properly handled, should lead to both improvements in the forecasting model and a variety of findings and understandings that evolve rather easily into statements of policy and principle.

Other Enrollment Analyses

The New York State enrollment forecasting model is both powerful and effective. Its basic structure is similar to many others currently in place around the country, varying primarily in level of detail in some aspects. It does have one feature that is unique, however: its ability to deal with the concept of institutional drawing power. In the current version of the model, each institution is categorized as either "higher draw" or "lower draw," based on historical statistics on admissions and geographic origins of students. Roughly speaking, the enrollment decline for the higher-draw institutions is half as great as the overall statewide decline in enrollment. The lower-draw institutions then share the remaining students. Although drawing power is not well understood, it adds conceptual realism to the model and probably enhances its results. It also serves as a tangible reminder that some institutions will fare better than others in the decline. It also helps to remind us how little we really know about higher education.

I have suggested that more than just an enrollment projection model is needed as the basis for effective and credible policies. Ideally, a series of related topics must be dealt with to supplement and support the basic projection work. Institutional drawing power is just one of the possible topics, and the fact that it can be incorporated into a forecasting model illustrates some of the possibilities that exist. An extended set of topics is shown in Figure 2. Most involve analysis of historical descriptive statistics on enrollment patterns, student admissions, student transfer patterns, and student residence and migration. It also involves some more sophisticated supporting analyses of such topics as institutional drawing power, student choice of institution, and groupings of similar institutions. The figure also indicates the basic relationships among these analyses. The emphasis in these projects is on developing improved understanding for planning and coordination purposes. As was the case with the enrollment projection model, the emphasis in New York State is on aggregate, long-term rather than detailed, short-term analyses. Others must decide for themselves the appropriate levels of detail for their own situations.

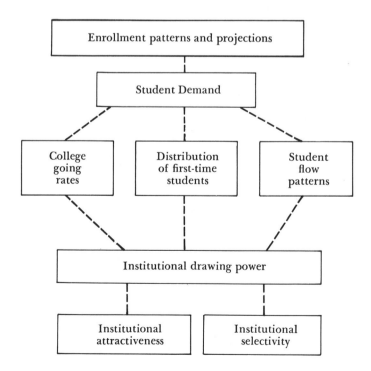

Figure 2. Framework for Analyzing Enrollments

Two types of basic statistics are particularly relevant to developing understanding of higher education enrollment patterns and trends: admissions statistics and enrollment share statistics. They incorporate not only information about enrollments at individual institutions but also about how institutions fare in attracting students. They are interesting in their own right and can also be incorporated into a variety of models to analyze, evaluate, and project institutional behavior. Two major measures of college admissions that are particularly important are the fraction of applications accepted (a measure of selectivity) and the fraction of those accepted that enroll (a measure of admissions yield). Because the two are related in ways that are not completely understood, it is interesting to analyze them jointly using an admissions matrix, as shown in Figure 3. The values of the two fractions for a particular institution (or program) for a particular year (or academic term) define points on the matrix that can be compared either cross-sectionally (for different institutions in the same year) or longitudinally (for the same institution over several years). In general, points in the lower left corner (low selectivity and low yield) are undesirable, and points in the upper right corner (high selectivity and high yield) are desirable.

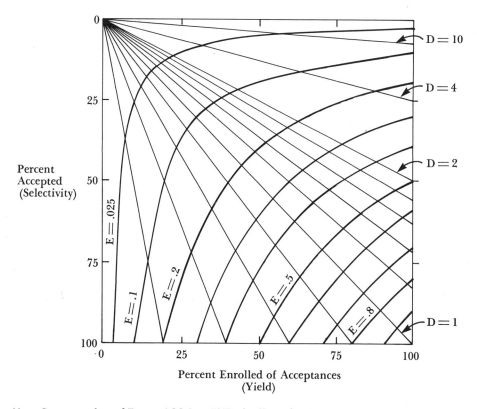

Note: Constant values of **E** = % ACC * % ENR give lines of stable enrollment given stable numbers of applicants (isoens = **E**). These are the curves perpendicular to the lower right corner. One possible measure of drawing power is **D** = % ENR ÷ % ACC; the lines originating in the upper left corner then are lines of equal draw (isodraws = **D**).

Figure 3. The Admissions Matrix

Other points on the chart are harder to evaluate in terms of desirability. The "isodraw" and "isoen" lines on the matrix suggest hypothetical patterns of equal drawing power and equal enrollment levels, respectively. The isoens shown in Figure 3 are based on the products of the values of the ordinate and the abscissa, as is done in a number of situations in the physical sciences. An institution will move along one of these lines when a larger (or smaller) acceptance rate is accompanied by a smaller (or larger) enrollment yield rate. The isodraw lines are based on the quotient of the abscissa and the ordinate. An institution will move along one of these lines when a higher (or lower) acceptance rate is accompanied by a higher (or lower) yield rate. In general, institutions will not move along any particular lines on this matrix over time. Movements toward the upper right corner (toward higher drawing power) are generally desirable; movements toward the lower left corner are undesirable. Movements along isodraw lines toward the upper left corner (toward lower values of E) will result in smaller enrollments. This matrix concept has not been validated experimentally, but it does seem reasonable conceptually.

This admissions matrix can be applied to single institutions or groups of institutions. Plots of the general locations of institutions, though they do not provide conclusive evidence of attractiveness or drawing power, are suggestive, particularly when comparing similar or competing institutions. In New York State, the institutions in each of the four institutional sectors tend to cluster together in broad groups with some overlap among the groups, which may be related to similarities in mission. With some exceptions, large and small institutions tend to be clustered in different portions of the matrix. Whether this phenomenon is inherently related to size is not known at this time.

The stability of these admissions statistics over time is an important consideration if one is considering using them as a basis for evaluating institutional status and performance. Analysis of five years of such statistics for the nineteen types of institutions in New York State indicates they are not very stable, which suggests year-to-year fluctuations in these statistics, even for groups of institutions, should not be used as the sole basis for evaluations of institutional status and performance. Fluctuations for individual institutions are even more severe. The reason for the fluctuations has not yet been carefully studied, but it probably is related to conscious adjustments in admissions strategies to compensate for unexpected successes or failures in earlier years. This seems particularly likely in light of most institutions' ability to fine tune their admissions policies to enroll a precise number of students in any given year.

Another statistic related to admissions of interest to planners and policymakers is the number of multiple applications by students. Significant changes could lead to erroneous conclusions concerning application statistics. This situation has to be looked at for groups of institutions because multiple applications necessarily involve several institutions. Statistics on total applications for admissions for all colleges in New York State divided by total high school graduates in the previous year indicate an increase in multiple applications for the state as a whole. This is another indication that some caution needs to be used in conjunction with these admissions matrices if the results are to be used as the basis for important plans or policies.

It is possible to use the admissions matrix to evaluate the drawing power of an entire state. After adjustment for multiple applications, the position of New York State moved very little on the chart between 1970 and 1977. The fact that enrollments increased significantly over the same period must temper the conclusion that the state has maintained its drawing power, but the admissions statistics do suggest the enrollment increase has not been achieved at the expense of statewide drawing power. How this may relate to future situations is not clear.

The other basic enrollment statistic that needs more attention in the future is the percentage of enrollments at a particular institution or group of institutions, sometimes referred to as "market share." Changes in these statistics over time may be the best overall measure of the success of institutional recruiting and admissions activities. If an institution's share of the total market increases, it is performing well. This conclusion would have to be tempered for any institution that became much less selective in order to achieve this result. This suggests the admissions matrix should be coordinated with analyses of market share. If its share increases, even though the share of its peers decreases, it is performing well. This last possibility raises the important point that *relative* performance is critical. In the decade ahead, it will be important to compare an institution's performance with that of appropriate peers or groups of institutions, particularly of those with which it competes directly for students. It will also be important for an institution that sees its share declining to know why the change is happening and what adjustments it should make to reverse the trend. These latter insights will not appear automatically; they will evolve only out of close attention to student recruiting and willingness to consider changes in goals and procedures.

Similar kinds of analyses could be described for retention rates, graduation rates, transfer patterns, and other basic enrollment-related statistics. Because these are relatively straightforward, however, I shall bypass them in favor of introducing some more sophisticated and potentially more valuable analyses, beginning with the identification of "competing" institutions. This is an extremely important basic problem because unless one knows which institutions are competing with each other for students, it will be very difficult to assess accurately the impact of various actions on enrollment patterns. Knowledge of competition can provide one possible basis for evaluating drawing power; and it can suggest the need for changes in institutional goals, enrollments, targets, and recruiting strategies. There is some evidence that groupings based on student preferences may make possible the comparisons of a variety of basic admissions statistics that would otherwise be meaningless (Rowse, 1979a).

Two basic approaches to identifying groups of competing institutions are possible: One can ask the institution or one can ask the students. This reflects the complementary nature of institutions and students in determining enrollment patterns. Both are involved and both need to be analyzed. The former, of course, is the easier approach; and to the extent that institutions really know their competition, the findings should be reliable. Students can also provide important insights, and a survey of potential students can be very helpful in describing patterns of student interest and evaluating student recruiting. In a pilot study by the New York State Education Department, students were surveyed to identify "natural groups" of institutions based on student statements. The study was based on a survey of recipients of New York State Tuition Assistance Program grants in which students were asked

1. In which institutions were you interested?
2. To which institutions did you apply?

3. By which institutions were you accepted?
4. Which institution did you attend?
5. Which institution would you have attended had it accepted you?

Using counts of institutions that were mentioned together by individual students for questions 1 and 2, groups of "competing" institutions were identified using statistical clustering procedures and factor analysis. The resulting clusters tend to be small (six or fewer institutions per cluster), and they tend to conform to a priori judgments about which institutions are similar to each other. Little overlap was observed between public and private institutions, particularly when using the application patterns.

Although this study is much more complex and expensive than a simple questionnaire to institutions, it has some significant advantages. In particular, this approach permits detailed identification of the groups of students relevant to higher education planning, in addition to the groups of institutions. In the long run, this kind of information could be invaluable to both state and institutional planners, particularly in areas like New York City, where significant changes are anticipated in the racial and income composition of high school graduating classes (Rowse, 1979b). A student survey can also be used to verify the results of an institutional survey. Differences can be brought to the attention of institutional administrators so they can make appropriate adjustments in their plans and strategies.

The relatively small size of the groups of institutions identified in the pilot study deserves a brief discussion. This same result has been observed in several other pilot studies to identify groups of institutions with common characteristics done by the New York Education Department. This finding in a state like New York, with nearly two hundred fifty institutions, has important potential implications for planning, review, and analysis. If fifty or more groups are required to distinguish adequately among all the colleges and universities in the state, the burdens of analysis, display, and interpretation of statistics are greatly increased. The possibilities for meaningful study within the groups are also reduced because of the small sample sizes involved. In fact, individual case studies may be the only acceptable basis for quantitative analysis.

The next topic for discussion, institutional drawing power, grows out of this work on groups of institutions. Actually, there are a number of possible approaches to measuring institutional drawing power: share of total enrollments in a state, share of total enrollments within a group of "competing" institutions, enrollment share within specific groups of potential students, changes in any of these enrollment shares over time, changes in location on the admissions matrix, the "reserve" of students at an institution as measured by the percentage not accepted (particularly of a given ability level), and constructs based on measures as viewed by students (for example, retention, quality, atmosphere, and distinctiveness). The adequacy of any of these approaches is not known with certainty, although all appear to be relevant to the problem. The one I discuss has been pilot tested in New York State (Rowse, 1979a), but it is not sufficiently well understood at this point to be recommended for wider application.

Drawing power is a relative measure of an institution's ability to compete effectively for students. In the New York State Education Department pilot study, the five questions asked of the students, in addition to providing a basis for grouping institutions, can be used to determine whether any significant "dominance patterns" exist. In a situation in which one institution enrolled a significant majority of the students that had been accepted by both it and a second institution, the first would be said to dominate the second. Any *dominated* institutions clearly stand to lose heavily in the decade to come. One of the interesting things about the groups of institutions defined by the students in the pilot study is the possible relationship of these groups to dominance patterns. One hypothesis is that dominance patterns exist within these groups and that there is likely to be one or more dominated institutions in *each* group. This is not startling; but many of the groups identified in the New York State pilot study contain only institutions most people would agree are solid, high-quality colleges and universities. This line of reasoning suggests that, unless they make adjustments, even good schools may lose a disproportionate share of enrollments. Many institutions will make adjustments—some have already begun. In general, the effect of these changes will be either to enable an institution to compete more effectively in the group it is in or to switch all or part of its recruiting emphasis to another group of students and institutions, thus moving the institution to another group. The result of these adjustments cannot be determined with certainty in advance, although one would generally expect that a "better" institution lowering its admissions standards to compete with "lesser" institutions would have at least some success in maintaining its enrollment share. Whether this would be sufficient to maintain actual enrollment levels or even whether such an action would best serve the long-term interests of a college is something that deserves a great deal of scrutiny by campus-level planners. Some research has shown the long-term consequences of such actions can be undesirable in some cases (Anderson, 1977).

Another class of analyses that can be performed relates to issues not directly related to higher education itself but nevertheless important to college and university enrollment. Prime examples of these topics are the effect of competency exams on high school graduation rates, the need for and availability of remedial instruction for underprepared students, and the changing income and racial/ethnic mix of high school graduates due to differential birth rates, particularly in major urban centers. It would be virtually impossible to deal with these types of problems directly in an enrollment-forecasting model. In fact, the questions these kinds of topics raise tend not to be quantitative and technical but qualitative and normative. How should we deal with these situations? What can colleges and universities do to help? The first step in dealing with these questions is to identify the issues. The New York State Education Department has identified a series of factors and situations that may impact higher education (Rowse, 1978). These have been examined briefly to determine whether further effort is possible and profitable, and selected topics have been pursued more thoroughly where the issues are important and data exist (as in Rowse, 1979b).

Institutional Roles

The emphasis in this discussion has been on multiinstitution analyses, not because the subject is irrelevant at the campus level but simply because the situations at an individual campus depend in part on the situations at other campuses.

Many suggestions for campus planners are explicit in the discussion, and the discussion suggests several principles for campus planners and analysts to follow:

- Know your own institution and what it has to offer.
- Know your students and what they want and need.
- Know your competition and how well they are competing with what they are offering.
- Be prepared to make adjustments if your current programs are not succeeding.

Actually, these are good marketing principles that are relevant in any business or industry (Johnson, 1979; Kotler, 1975; Krachenberg, 1972; Leister, 1975). And just as in any other enterprise, long-term success and prosperity will come to those institutions that can find a niche in the market and give their customers value and satisfaction for their money. This implies marketing that goes far beyond simple advertising. It means solid understanding of programs being offered and their value to prospective students; it means seeking out those students the institution can serve effectively; it means maintaining adequate program quality; and it means being able to recognize and respond to changes in the competition, whether in terms of program, cost, or service. Marketing in this context certainly relates to much of the discussion in this chapter. The kinds of information and relationships described will become increasingly important for campus planners in the future. Those who have the information are certainly not guaranteed success, and those who do not are not guaranteed failure; but the information is likely to be a critical element in the survival of a number of institutions.

Obtaining these insights may require an individual campus to get into more detail than the institutional totals described earlier in this chapter. For example, it may be possible for some institutions to develop detailed discipline-by-discipline enrollment forecasts. If accurate, these could be critical elements in institutional planning, faculty hiring, and such. Data requirements for such detailed forecasts would be beyond the capacities of many state agencies. However, very few institutions would be able to develop reliable detailed forecasts for themselves without developing similar forecasts for their competition. An institution willing to accept the aggregate forecasts of a state agency might focus on the *distribution* of students among the programs on campus. Regardless of the approach taken, caution should be used in any attempt to develop detailed projections. The same resources might produce better results in a more general marketing effort.

It is not sufficient for a campus to have just an effective marketing program; it must also be able to use the information effectively. In other words, it must have good management as well. Flexibility, that is, the ability to deal with a variety of contingencies, is going to be the key to success or failure for many institutions. Administrators will have to be able to interpret the situations they face to determine how to respond; and equally important, they must be able to make the necessary adjustments. The solutions will never be easy; but to the extent that a wide range of possibilities has been considered and thought through in a careful, dispassionate way, the ultimate decisions and their implementation will be made easier.

Conclusion

For agencies and organizations concerned with the long-range prospects for higher education, the bottom line is better understanding, which should lead to more effective planning and thereby better higher education. The fact that some institutions will be forced to close should not drive everyone into defensive positions and cutthroat competition. There is more need for vision and positive leadership now than ever before.

It is not enough simply to project enrollments. In the first place, projections are likely to be wrong because of public attitudes or other factors that could not be anticipated. More important, an approach to enrollment analysis geared totally to projecting enrollments will not support the formulation of policies and strategies to deal with a changing environment.

There is a need to understand the impact on both institutions and students of different factors and situations, ranging from student aid programs to competition for human resources with organizations like the military to the job market. Only this kind of broad understanding can serve as the basis for justifying or evaluating particular programs and actions.

State agencies and other organizations dealing with numbers of institutions must be prepared to deal with problems of coordination, priority setting, and "orchestration" when enrollments decline. Many institutions will be tempted to compromise their ideals in the interest of survival. This will increase the importance of monitoring functions by state agencies, accrediting groups, and others to protect the interests of the students and to maintain the status and image of higher education as a whole.

Institutions should look to state agencies for information that can help them deal effectively—or at least knowledgeably—with the declining enrollment. Particularly important will be information that defines the status and performance of individual campuses vis-à-vis their peers and competitors.

Bibliographical Essay

For readers interested in further exploration of these topics, any of the references cited in the text are recommended. Those interested in designing an enrollment projection model should find the reports by Wing and Rowse particularly valuable. Wing (1974) has provided detailed descriptions of specific forecasting techniques along with actual calculations and comparisons of results. His discussions about constructing forecasting procedures and estimating errors are also relevant. Whereas Wing deals with illustrative data constructed primarily to illustrate data computational procedures, Rowse (1979c) deals with the actual forecasting model used in New York State. His report is thorough, discussing methodology, factors influencing enrollments, numerical projections, and accuracy. It also provides much of the input data necessary to support the New York State model. A less technical and more policy oriented discussion of enrollment forecasts can be found in another report by Rowse (1979b). Although this report deals with situations in New York State, the general approach, findings, and conclusions are relevant elsewhere as well. He pays particular attention to the participation of minorities and adults in higher education.

For institutional planners, two reports of particular interest are those by

Kotler (1975) and Frank (1979). Kotler is extremely valuable, discussing many aspects of the general problem of recruiting students and building constituencies. Frank attempts to identify the actions institutions might take in anticipation of or in response to a decline in enrollments. She has synthesized and summarized a wide variety of books, articles, and reports, many of which are related to marketing and the analysis of enrollment patterns and trends at the institutional level. Using a rather different approach, Anderson (1977) has also examined responses of colleges—in this case, small private colleges—to external pressures. Although he does not emphasize enrollment analysis, he does suggest the kind of comprehensive, multidimensional approach that will undoubtedly be a critical element of effective institutional planning in the future. Those seriously interested in campus-level enrollment projections should also review the work of Salley (1979). He has shown that correlations between business cycles and enrollment cycles can be translated into adjustment procedures to improve the accuracy of short-term projections.

References

Anderson, R. E. *Strategic Policy Changes at Private Colleges.* New York: Teachers College Press, 1977.

Armstrong, J. S., and Grohman, M. C. "A Comparative Study of Methods of Long-Range Market Forecasting." *Management Science,* 1972, *19,* 211–221.

Carnegie Foundation for the Advancement of Teaching. *More than Survival: Prospects for Higher Education in a Period of Uncertainty.* San Francisco: Jossey-Bass, 1975.

Centra, J. A. *College Enrollment in the 1980's: Projections and Possibilities.* Princeton, N.J.: College Entrance Examination Board, 1978.

Fiske, E. B. "Hard-Hit Schools Turn to Marketers." *Business Officer,* 1978, *12,* 26–27.

Frank, J. C. *College and University Responses to Declining Enrollment.* Albany: New York State Education Department, 1979.

Henderson, C. *Changes in Enrollment by 1985.* Policy Analysis Service Report 3, No. 1. Washington, D.C.: American Council on Education, 1977.

Henderson, C., and Plummer, J. C. *Adapting to Changes in Characteristics of College Age Youth.* Policy Analysis Service Report 4, No. 2. Washington, D.C.: American Council on Education, 1978.

Jenkins, C. "Promo or Bromo? Marketing Higher Education." *Universitas,* 1979, *21,* 16–19.

Johnson, D. L. "The Researcher and Nonprofit Marketing: Is Anyone Listening?" In J. Lucas (Ed.), *New Directions for Institutional Research: Developing a Total Marketing Plan,* no. 21. San Francisco: Jossey-Bass, 1979.

Kotler, P. *Marketing for Nonprofit Organizations.* Englewood Cliffs, N.J.: Prentice-Hall, 1975.

Krachenberg, A. R. "Bringing the Concept of Marketing to Higher Education." *Journal of Higher Education,* 1972, *43,* 369–380.

Leister, D. V. "Identifying Institutional Clientele." *Journal of Higher Education,* 1975, *46,* 381–398.

Lewis, J., and Sulkin, N. *Estimating Higher Education Enrollment and Degrees.*

Washington, D.C.: Science Education Studies Group, Division of Science Resources, National Science Foundation, 1975.

McConnell, W. *Projections of High School Graduates in the West.* Boulder, Colo.: Western Interstate Commission on Higher Education, 1979.

Rowse, G. L. *College Participation in New York State.* Albany: New York State Education Department, 1978.

Rowse, G. L. "An Approach to the Measurement of the Drawing Power of Colleges and Universities" (draft). Albany: New York State Education Department, 1979a.

Rowse, G. L. *College Enrollments and Student Access in New York State: Prospects for the Future.* Albany: New York State Education Department, 1979b.

Rowse, G. L. *New York State Higher Education Enrollment Forecasts, 1978–1994.* Albany: New York State Education Department, 1979c.

Salley, C. D. "Short-Term Enrollment Forecasting for Accurate Budget Planning."*Journal of Higher Education,* 1979, *50,* 323–333.

Wing, P. *Higher Education Enrollment Forecasting.* Boulder, Colo.: National Center for Higher Education Management Systems at WICHE, 1974.

12

John A. Lucas

Identifying Regional and Community Markets

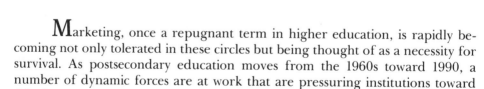

Marketing, once a repugnant term in higher education, is rapidly becoming not only tolerated in these circles but being thought of as a necessity for survival. As postsecondary education moves from the 1960s toward 1990, a number of dynamic forces are at work that are pressuring institutions toward this change.

First, officials are looking with increasing alarm at enrollment projections that become gloomier each fall. Since 1975, enrollment in higher education has leveled off and decreased. The fall of 1978 and the spring of 1979 produced enrollments substantially lower than what had been projected. This recent trend has been caused by lower unemployment rates and lower participation rates of high school graduates. However, the worst is yet to come. Projections now call for the high school graduating classes to be reduced by 18 to 40 percent by 1990. Centra (1979) projects college enrollment will drop 8 to 9 percent by 1985 and decline by a lesser amount in the following five years. This decline will lead not only to severe interinstitutional competition but also to competition with the job market and the armed forces, which are pledged to recruit one-third of the eighteen-year-olds in the early 1980s.

Second, rapid technological changes and sharp fluctuations in the economy place considerable strain on the relevance and stability of the curriculum. While career education and continuing education enrollment have been on the rise, science and engineering have been fluctuating and education and social sciences have been declining. In addition to these fluctuations, a number of new interdisciplinary fields, such as health psychology, bioengineering, and futurism, have emerged; and new home delivery systems, including minicomputers, videodiscs, and cassettes, have developed. The central question is how colleges can monitor and adapt their curricula to rapidly changing pressures.

A third force at work is the slowly dwindling support base for higher education. Referenda are failing; "Proposition 13" attitudes abound; higher education is no longer among the high priorities of legislators; and the terms "educators" and "education" are not held in the same high esteem they once were. All these factors are propelling postsecondary education toward developing a total marketing plan. *Total marketing* refers to a comprehensive two-way process that includes not only traditional student recruitment activities but also market research involving employer and potential student need surveys, image analysis, scheduling and tuition analysis, targeting, admissions analysis, understanding of demand cycles, community and student profile studies, program evaluation, and retention surveys.

Despite the pressures, many barriers impede the development of marketing in higher education. Although some faculty members and administrators still consider marketing a distasteful word linking higher education to the world of business, more of them mistakenly view it as a one-way communication process. Thus, a considerable widening of horizons must take place among staff and faculty before any substantial progress can be made toward developing a total marketing plan. In addition, marketing expertise must be deepened. When most staffs were hired for institutions, marketing skills were not considered an important attribute for selection or for development. Moreover, many administrators, accustomed to following crisis management principles with a short-run outlook, lack the commitment to future investment a total marketing plan requires.

If higher education is to overcome these barriers and move toward a total marketing concept, it will need to integrate a number of skills and programs into a total marketing plan that in turn must be a part of the larger institutional plan. This chapter discusses research techniques regarding employer needs, targeting, community educational needs, curriculum evaluation, class scheduling, retention, and external institutional communication. It explores ways to evaluate the effectiveness of marketing strategies, describes the organization of the total marketing effort, and suggests how this marketing effort can be incorporated in the total institutional planning process.

Determining Employer Needs

The most obvious approach to employer needs is to consider job openings among existing positions and job descriptions. The Bureau of Labor Statistics, along with various state employment services, provides a wealth of information here. The bureau publishes the most useful data through its Employment Projections Program. These projections list some four hundred fifty occupational titles, showing job openings due to growth, job openings due to separation, and total annual job openings. The report provides current data plus projections ten years into the future for the whole nation, by state and by standard metropolitan statistical area. These data are useful, but they leave many deficiencies. For example, educational needs cannot be tied in exactly to job openings. Many graduates of educational programs do not remain in their field when choosing a career; and many replacement openings will be filled by persons already in the field who are in a job transition stage. Another problem is that the mobility patterns of the institution's graduates may not conform to the geographic reporting areas of the Bureau of Labor Statistics. Still another drawback to these projections in terms of their usefulness to education is that they deal only with existing jobs and not with new emerging career fields.

A second approach in determining employers' educational needs is to survey them as to their needs and the probability of hiring graduates from specific institutions. There are several philosophies prevalent in conceptualizing employer need surveys. One thought is to conduct a massive, comprehensive employer needs survey that would result in a rank ordering of career fields by the number of job openings for a given geographic area (in some cases, this area may be nationwide). If done properly, this method provides the most logical framework for making decisions concerning reduction, deletion, expansion, or addition of various curricula in higher education. Many North Carolina community colleges serve so small an area that they can personally interview all their employers. Prince George's County in Maryland maintains a cooperative arrangement with the state employment commission, which surveys all employers in the county. Kansas Metropolitan Community College conducted a massive employer survey of its area, using almost all its available staff, but some had mixed feelings about the value of the study when it was completed. The disadvantages of doing such a massive study are the time and money required. In addition, it is very difficult for employers to respond intelligently to a general request to forecast all employment needs. Many simply do not know.

The other philosophical approach is to conduct limited surveys of specific employers, asking them about their reaction to adding, deleting, reducing, or expanding one specific curriculum. This makes the survey task more manageable, and employers are better able to respond to a specific proposal than to a general forecast of all their employment needs. The disadvantage of this method is that the specific proposals must be obtained in a less than systematic manner in that there is no way to know in advance the priority order of the various program ideas. Good proposals depend upon good two-way communication with the external environment through advisory committees or other means and upon good communication within the institution, which promotes new-idea generation by internal staff.

Where institutions serve a statewide or national employment market, these colleges probably would have to use existing personnel studies done on a broad geographic basis. These institutions might then want to become involved in nationwide or statewide advisory committees of major employers and other colleges. Knowing statewide or nationwide trends or demands, these educational organizations could then determine whether to flow with or buck these trends.

Boardman and Mendenhall (1979) describe an occupational needs assessment program in a community college district in Nebraska where job opportunities are related to program planning. Allen and Gutteridge (1978) compared the job placement of two-year career students with the placement of community college transfer students who continued on to four-year colleges and earned a bachelor's degree. In this particular study, the four-year graduates had an easier time in the marketplace than the two-year graduates. At the other end of the education spectrum, Ochsner and Solmon (1979) examined personnel studies and employment forecasts for highly educated university graduates, primarily Ph.Ds. Heist and Warren (1975) discuss the relationship between curriculum and program planning with personnel need data. They also examined the effect of vocationalism on curriculum development.

Personnel educational needs are not only a function of job openings but are also dependent on the needs of the employees themselves. Growing numbers of license requirements are forcing employees to continue their education while on the job. Even without license requirements, the need to keep current and the desire for promotion are supplementing the demand for career-related education. Employee surveys can sometimes be conducted as part of the employer survey described previously. Using this method, employers can be asked to estimate what they consider job-related educational needs. This is a very efficient way of handling this informational need problem; and in many cases, employers are in a very good position to make useful judgments. Surveying employees individually, either in their job setting or at their residence, can result in an enormous effort; and employees do not always know what educational programs would best suit their career goals. Sometimes specific employee surveys can very profitably be conducted through the cooperation of professional associations. Somewhat related to employee educational needs are the requirements of nonemployees, such as trustees or volunteers in various organizations.

One of the simplest means of assessing personnel educational needs is through external advisory committees. Many states and regulatory agencies require such an advisory committee for every career program offered. These committees are composed of professionals in the field or employers of graduates of the particular career program. These advisory committees are primarily used to review curricula, but they often are a good source for assessing personnel requirements. Their judgments are especially valuable when considering new educational programs in emerging fields where there is a scarcity of other personnel requirement data.

A continuing problem higher educational institutions face is responding to job opening data that change dramatically in cycles. The engineering profession, investigated by Yale (1978), vividly exemplifies this phenomenon. In order to understand the cyclical supply and demand of engineering students, he developed a systems dynamics simulation model and tested its sensitivity to decision variables and policy alternatives. The model considers a number of student decision variables from the time of the decision to enter the field of engineering in high school through high school graduation, college, entering the field, and staying in the field. It also includes decisions to drop out or in along the way and college decisions like recruiting strategy and decisions to restrict or expand enrollment. The model is driven by job openings.

Yale found that when high school sophomores were recruited into engineering on the basis of high pay, high status, and the present job market, the model became unstable or the oscillations in job openings became greater. If there was a large demand for job openings now and many went into the field, six years later, when these students graduated from college, the job market for engineers might be very tight. If there were currently many stories around about big layoffs of engineers and fewer high school sophomores decided to enter engineering, six years later, after their graduation, there might be a shortage of engineers. Thus, the best tool for recruiting engineers among high school sophomores might be an accurate job opening picture in six years.

Similarly, colleges tend to make decisions based on the current job market, which also makes the model unstable. For example, a decision by a college to restrict engineering enrollment on the basis of a current tight job market might lead to a shortage of engineers in four years. Compounding the problem is the fact that a substantial percentage of engineering graduates take jobs outside the field. Many colleges do not realize this and try to equate the graduates to the job supply, thus making the engineer shortage in this case even more severe. If colleges used a good four-year engineering graduate requirement forecast based on the variables discussed previously to make their enrollment decision, the oscillations in engineering job openings would be smoothed dramatically.

Kuh (1978) explores Ph.D. employment cycles and the relationship between the time from a bachelor's degree to the attaining of a Ph.D. with the job market. As the demand increases, this time period shortens and vice versa.

Probably the most difficult task in determining employers' educational needs is that of forecasting demand for new and emerging fields. There is no existing job opening or personnel data available because the field does not exist. The information cannot be obtained from employers yet because in many cases they have to be convinced to use these new potential graduates. For example, the demand for physician aides and legal technicians depends on legislation and the speed with which physicians and lawyers can be motivated and educated in how to use these new paraprofessionals. Larkin (1979) discusses testing the feasibility of new programs at the community college level and Lee and Gilmour (1977) propose a procedure for developing new programs at senior institutions. Facing the reality of today's scarce resources, viable new program development may depend on the weeding out of ineffective or low-need programs. Gilmour and Berk (1977) outline a procedure for abandoning such academic programs.

Targeting

Targeting allows an organization to focus on a specific segment of its potential clients rather than on the general population. Higher educational institutions can, through market analysis, identify a specific target population they want to develop and then design a specific program to attract these potential students. One means of market analysis is to compare the profile of existing students with the profile of the population. Such characteristics as geography of residence, age, economic indexes, enrollment by discipline, student goals, physical disabilities, racial or ethnic background, or student achievement level might be used in the market analysis. This process of separating prospective college students into subgroups with similar characteristics is sometimes referred to as market segmentation (see Spiro, 1978).

Most colleges show a distribution of their enrollment by high school attended, although this is just the beginning because the institution must then decide whether to concentrate mainly on those high schools where they already have success or on those where they have low penetration rates. They must analyze what could be gained in each situation. For example, political considerations may dictate concentrating on low-penetration high schools.

Mapping techniques have come into prominence lately. There are several of these; but the most useful for colleges are probably those that use zip code groupings, as exemplified by a package computer program, Synographic Computer Mapping (SYMAP). Information on SYMAP is available from the Laboratory for Computer Graphics and Spatial Analysis, Harvard University, 520 Gund Hall, 48 Quincy Street, Cambridge, Massachusetts 02138. Such maps use a symbol (plus sign, dot, circle, or square) to represent each zip code area. The symbols become progressively darker as the student population in these areas increases. This type of graphic representation allows decision makers to determine at a glance from where their students are coming.

Probably the most useful information for college officials is penetration analysis. In this method the most relevant sized population tracts (townships, zip codes, counties, and so forth) are selected for the institution. Then student population is matched to the total population over age seventeen in each tract and a penetration rate is determined. This kind of analysis allows a college to know the geographic areas in which it is achieving the best marketing results and the areas where its marketing effort is yielding the poorest outcomes.

As student bodies become older, it will become more important to know the age distribution of a college's enrollment. Age analysis can be combined with geographic penetration analysis so that one could determine, for example, the percentage between twenty-five and thirty-four in a particular population tract enrolled at the college. The major problem with age analysis is that it is difficult to know what percentage of the older populations a college should be enrolling. However, colleges could observe trends over time at their institution or compare age distributions to see if they match the institution's objectives.

Enrollment categorized by curriculum can be the most useful data of all. Different disciplines or programs serve different clientele and markets. Geography of residences, age, and student goals and achievement levels can be unique for each curriculum. Each department or discipline can and should have distinct market goals that should match their individual educational goals. Likewise, each educational unit can analyze its student profile to see if there are gaps they are not serving or examine the student profile to see if it matches the departmental or program educational philosophy.

Although in the past, achievement levels of the entering student have been the chief student characteristic colleges have been concerned about, in the new marketing era it is important to examine many other student body attributes. A college may investigate whether there are gaps in the economic, racial, physical disability, or student goal profile of the student body the institution is not serving. They may want also to explore whether this complete student body profile reflects the institutional philosophy. There are many examples of specific student subgroups focus by institutions cited in the literature. For example, Baskin (1974) discusses institutional focus on nontraditional students and students following a nontraditional pattern of study. Lanter and Howe (1978) look at the impact of the women's movement on the campus and on curriculum. Tittle and Denker (1977) examine reentry women, and Trivett (1977) examines continuing education for the professions.

Federal regulations, state policies, public opinion, or social trends often force higher education institutions to focus on target populations in their marketing efforts. There may be government pressures to serve physically handicapped students or students of lower ability. Because of federal guidelines, employers may be looking for women and minority groups in certain professions, which in turn encourages colleges to look for such individuals for the corresponding educational programs. Some communities might bring pressure to bear on local colleges to provide programs for senior citizens.

Looking at targeting in a different way, an institution might first examine its own image and then explore target groups of students who might respond to that image. The interrelationships between institutional images and place in the student market are called "institutional positioning." Gaither (1979) thoroughly examines this strategy.

Determining Community Educational Needs

There are purposes for postsecondary education other than preparing students for careers. It is important for institutions to identify and understand potential and existing students' noncareer needs and demands. Just as important is the need for these colleges to know clearly the impact they make on their students during their stay in higher education.

Student expectations are estimated in a number of ways. One method is to conduct goals inventory studies measuring what students, potential students, community members, faculty, staff, and board members feel the college should be about. There are a number of packaged surveys on the market, the most notable being the Educational Testing Service's Institutional Goals Inventory. In addition, many colleges conduct their own. William Rainey Harper College (Lucas, 1979c) conducted such a goal perception survey among seven different constituent groups as a part of the college's planning process. Packaged surveys have the advantage of considerable expertise in building the forms and comparing results with relevant national norms. They have the disadvantage that nationally developed goals inventories are not always relevant to one college's particular data needs.

Student expectations can also be estimated by using image analyses. Thus, an institution can know what image potential students or the community hold for them. This image may be accurate or inaccurate and will greatly affect a student's expectations of a college education there. More colleges are beginning to look at their mission to see if it needs to be shifted to meet student expectations and needs. Many small liberal arts colleges are at a crossroads. Jonsen (1978) explains the difficulty these colleges will have in surviving if they attempt to change their historical purpose. He cites an example, Marylhurst College in Portland, Oregon, that did successfully change its mission. Similarly, Loring and others (1978) discuss adapting institutions to the adult learner. The question of whether a liberal arts college can change to accommodate vocational education and still retain its most worthwhile liberal arts goals is raised by Carpenter (1979).

Also important is the need for a college to measure the impact it makes upon its students. Here again there are many packaged impact instruments on the market but also many opportunities for institutions to develop their own measure of change among their students. University of Tennessee (Lucas, 1969) measured the environmental impact it made on its students using a perceptual instrument before entry and after the freshman year. Solmon and Ochsner (1978) reviewed research that measured the effects college had on students. When a college can identify the difference it makes in a student's life, it can communicate this to potential students, thus giving them more realistic expectations of the institution.

In addition to job openings, a college must be able to respond to many other general educational needs of the community, especially in the times ahead, when there will be a scarcity of traditional college students. Although a college could do a random survey of the general public to try to determine its educational needs, such an effort would probably be not too helpful. Most potential students in the general population probably would not know their educational needs; thus, a survey would yield few useful results. Better results might be obtained with a survey of specific proposed educational offerings that asks respondents to indicate whether they would attend for a specific price. Although better results can be obtained to responses to specific proposals, the problem arises as to where a college can obtain good educational offering proposals.

One possible source of proposals is community advisory committees, perhaps composed of community leaders representing a variety of interests who brainstorm feasible offerings to propose to the general public. An offshoot of the advisory committee might work with college alumni to identify relevant continuing educational needs of higher education graduates. A more involved process would be to engage in community development, which involves working with such special-interest groups as senior citizens, homeowners, science fiction buffs, residents of a specific geographic location, or governmental groups. Each special-interest group might develop a priority listing of educational offerings in which their constituency would like to participate and would also help plan these educational offerings. Howard (1979) and Moore (1977) describe this community development process in greater detail.

A description of the effect of the college on the community can be an effective tool in relating to various community groups. Dennison and others (1975) and Cooper, Armijo, and Micek (1978) describe measuring such community impact. Another useful community relations tool is the use of a community needs survey, which Anderson (1977) examines. The ultimate in community development occurs when academic planning is able to respond to expressed community needs. Such a model is explored by Gilbert, Greenbert, and Lewis (1978). Even though many colleges and universities see themselves serving national or statewide constituencies, all have some responsibility and relationship to their local community.

Evaluating Academic Programs

A prime factor in determining the success of any marketing campaign is the quality or acceptance of the product, in this case, the academic program. In order to monitor and be assured of a quality academic program, each institution of higher education must maintain an ongoing faculty and curriculum evaluation.

Most colleges maintain some sort of end-of-term student evaluation process of courses and faculty members. These might be of the quality judgment, trait, or behavioral checklist type. There are several nationally developed instruments, but many institutions develop their own. But having an evaluation instrument does not mean an institution has a meaningful evaluation system. Some of the key issues to be dealt with are who analyzes the data, who sees the data, how the data are used, and whether anyone follows through to see if anything changes as a result of faculty or course evaluation.

For many colleges and universities, evaluation is a perfunctory task to be carried out each year; no analysis is made of the data and the results are buried in some closet. At other institutions, evaluation is too controversial to be carried out even in a perfunctory manner.

If handled correctly, immediate evaluation processes can be a valuable addition to the whole marketing project. Students may be able to identify deficiencies in the course or in teaching styles that disrupt the learning process or cause students to lose interest or withdraw, which in turn would discourage future enrollments. In the right environment, courses could be modified or teaching styles adjusted to reduce these problems. But students taking a course may lack the long-term perspective to make a meaningful judgment about the long-run benefits of the educational offering. Thus, immediate student evaluations must be weighed along with other evaluative data.

The most popular long-term evaluation method is follow-up studies of graduates or former students. These studies might examine the effect of education on the student's present career, continuing education, community involvement, or life-style. These studies might also ask former students to evaluate the benefits of specific courses or specific services, but few colleges conduct such studies by specific discipline. When studies become discipline specific, they can relate specific job descriptions or graduate school requirements to the curriculum at the target college. Students can estimate how well they were prepared in specific skill, cognitive, or leadership areas. Although specific discipline follow-up studies are more useful, they require more research resources to carry out. Lucas (1976) compares institutionwide versus specific discipline follow-up studies in detail.

A less used long-term method of evaluating the academic program is to survey employers who have hired former students or graduate schools where former students are enrolled. These surveys ask employers or graduate schools to rate how well students were prepared for their present situation and to identify strengths and weaknesses of the target college's academic program based on the performances of their former students. A problem with these surveys is that in many cases it is difficult to obtain an acceptable return rate of the survey instruments. There is a limit as to how much colleges can harass employers or graduate schools about returning these survey forms. An advantage of this survey method is that it provides an additional independent assessment of the academic program. Again, these employer and graduate school follow-up studies can be institutionwide surveys or they can be specific discipline based. The advantages and disadvantages are the same as those discussed previously for former student follow-up studies.

The most obvious means of evaluating the academic program is through the faculty. Although this is the most popular method, it is seldom used in a comprehensive, systematic manner. Each department often evaluates its curriculum in an ad hoc manner with little or no resources. A comprehensive faculty development program can deal with academic program evaluation in a very systematic way. This might include faculty orientation, in-service professional development workshops or seminars, innovative travel, sabbaticals, external grants, large institutional grants, small institutional grants, released time, faculty exchange programs, or faculty professional work experience programs. All of these need to be coordinated into a positive cohesive force in the institution. If all these motivational forces are brought together, faculty can do a very effective job of evaluating the curriculum and their teaching styles—thus keeping the product current and attractive to potential students. An example of a very systematic method of handling curriculum development is through the use of the Delphi technique (Reeves, 1978) among relevant faculty and staff.

Most of the literature on curriculum development deals with the need for change and the need to become relevant to student needs. Mayhew (1969) asserts that curriculum is based on tradition and faculty interests. Millet (1968) talks about reconstructing the university and moving the curriculum and teaching process toward a model more relevant to students' expectations. Pressing on for more change, Milton (1972) examines alternative teaching and learning styles. One alternative for change is to allow more interdisciplinary teaching and learning opportunities, as suggested by Assimpoloulos and Belanger (1978) and Mayville (1978). Smith (1978) describes the newest technologies and their possible future impact on curriculum development.

It is often difficult to evaluate the effectiveness of courses or teaching styles without comparing them to alternatives. There is a wealth of educational research comparing structure of courses, teaching styles, and how they interact with individual student learning styles. However, most projects are conducted as scholarly research to be published and seldom find their way to the decision-making matrix of the institution.

Evaluating Scheduling and Tuition

Class scheduling is probably the single most overlooked aspect of a total marketing plan. Scheduling includes the number of courses offered, the times they are offered, the location at which they are offered, and the decision process concerning whether course sections are offered or withdrawn. This process has long been thought of as an isolated task of a college carried on by each academic department, which jealously guards its autonomy.

Over the years, departments have become adept at knowing the sequence of courses their students take and planning schedules that minimize the number of potential conflicts. But as more nontraditional students enter college, these old predictable sequences break down. Many students are not pursuing degrees but just courses; many students switch fields or drop in and out of the institution. Studies at William Rainey Harper College showed course sequences quite different from the sequence shown in catalogue degree sequence. Jobs and family constraints become more of a conflict than other courses. Therefore, it is no longer a simple task to create a low-conflict schedule at most colleges.

The best way to minimize conflicts is to offer as many courses and sections as possible. But there are limits on this strategy because an institution must stay within its financial constraints in terms of an allowable average class size. Offering too many courses and sections may spread enrollment out too thin, thus lowering average class size to an unacceptable level. It is now known that as the number of offerings increase, enrollment increases. William Rainey Harper College (Lucas, 1977a) conducted studies of students going through general registration and found that the number of student credit hours would have increased by a fourth had students been able to enroll in all the courses they desired at the time they wanted. Moreover, this study did not even consider students who did not appear at registration because the courses or times desired were not available. The ultimate situation cannot exist, but the study did show the relationship between the number of offerings and enrollment. The key decisions lie in the balancing of increased enrollment desires through increased numbers of offerings with a reasonable average class size that meets financial constraints. Obviously, the impact of this relationship between offerings and enrollments depends on whether the institution charges a fixed tuition rate per credit hour or a flat tuition amount for all full-time students regardless of the load they carry.

Other constraints against offering large numbers of courses and sections to enhance the marketing effort are space limitations and the off-hour phenomenon. Almost all faculty and traditional students want courses offered between nine and twelve weekday mornings. Most nontraditional students prefer courses on weeknights. At most colleges, space constraints would limit the number of sections offered in the morning or evening. Few students or faculty members prefer afternoons or weekends. However, studies of weekend students at William Rainey Harper College (Lucas, 1977b) show that most weekend enrollments are additional enrollments that cannot be consolidated into other time periods. Even with these additional enrollments, small class sizes make it hard to justify these offerings, especially when support services must be provided. Thus, to make off-hour offerings feasible, additional enrollments must be found. One way to accomplish this might be to offer reduced tuition for classes offered during off-hour periods. Very few colleges have tried this, so it is not known how much of a tuition reduction would be required to move sufficient numbers of students to these off-hour periods.

Tuition in general is another major decision area that affects enrollment. As tuition keeps rising, potential students examine other educational institutions or alternatives to higher education much more closely. Research shows increases in tuition affect older students more than traditional students. Each institution must closely watch its tuition level and determine at what point enrollment is affected substantially so that a raise in student tuition becomes counterproductive.

Tilton and Turrisi (1978) indicate different fee schedules can significantly affect the course load students carry during any one term. Generally, students under block fee conditions (so much per semester for full-time students) will carry a heavier load than students under a per-credit hour fee structure.

Proximity of educational offerings to potential students' residences is directly related to probability of enrollment. Thus, generally speaking, where there is a concentration of colleges, the percentage of the population going to college is higher than in areas where there are no colleges. A key issue is how close institutions have to be before proximity ceases to be a factor. Studies at William Rainey Harper College (Lucas, 1979d) show that even in a community college district twenty miles by twenty miles with a campus in the center, there are substantial differences in the percentage of the population enrolled between those living close by and those living farther away. It is estimated that enrollment might be increased 5 to 10 percent if campuses could be created within three miles of all residents. But there are many problems associated with multiple locations. A college incurs additional security and maintenance costs and additional efforts are required to provide support services, if they can be provided at all. Even more students are inconvenienced because to get the schedule they want, they will travel back and forth between the many locations. Thus, each institution must weigh the benefits from the addition of new students provided by extending their educational offerings into the community versus additional costs and less convenience for existing students.

During their general registration process, all colleges face decisions about whether to drop existing sections or add new sections. These decisions are often made on irrelevant data; a college may try to maintain a certain overall class average or demand additional sections cover costs that are already fixed. The only costs relevant to the decision of offering or withdrawing a section at general registration are those that would be out-of-pocket expenses incurred if the section were offered or that would not be incurred if the section were withdrawn. These costs would be of a part-time faculty teaching the course or overload payment for existing faculty plus small expenses for clerical work (typing exams), class materials, and minor utility costs. These costs need to be balanced by the additional revenue produced by offering these sections, such as tuition, fees, and state reimbursement, if any. However, it must be remembered that this is additional revenue; so a college must know what percentage of the students dropped by withdrawing a section do indeed transfer to another section or take the course the next semester. Only that revenue that would otherwise be lost if the section were withdrawn can be considered additional revenue. In many cases, when institutions determine realistic breakeven points, the requirements in class size for survival of existing sections or for adding new sections are lowered from existing standards. Thus, a realistic decision-making process allows the institution to reach out more effectively and attract more clients and a greater student load. It is acknowledged that in some cases, an institution cannot vary its class size because of certain outside constraints, such as specific accrediting requirements.

Retaining Students

Marketing plans have recognized in recent years that retaining existing students is as important as attracting new ones and thus try to incorporate a comprehensive retention plan in their overall enrollment promotion program.

There are several ways to examine retention. Students may withdraw or stop attending specific classes or may withdraw totally from the institution. Some withdraw or stop attending in the middle of a term; others simply do not return and never finish their degree program. Terenzini (1978) classifies attrition studies into three types: autopsy, cross-sectional, and longitudinal.

For community colleges on funding formulas, withdrawals or nonattendance during a term contribute to substantial reduction of state reimbursement. For other colleges or universities, withdrawals or nonattendance may have no immediate effect on revenues but may lead to total withdrawal from the institution later.

Generally, withdrawal or nonattendance rates in courses are considered local data and there are few examples comparing them across institutions. Studies can examine the data for the whole institution or categorize them by division, by department or discipline, by individual faculty member, or by course. As the data become categorized more specifically, the analysis becomes more politically sensitive, and it becomes imperative to use these data very carefully.

There are several strategies a college can adopt when handling course withdrawal and nonattendance rates. One is to target those courses or faculty with extremely high withdrawal or nonattendance rates, which sometimes leads to defensive postures by those targeted. Another is to implement an institution-wide emphasis on increasing retention. In this case, only aggregate data are shown; and each division or department develops its own plan to increase retention. Faculty members could find out the retention rate for their course on their own. An even more nonthreatening approach is to make retention only one part of a much larger improvement program. Bakersfield College and Los Angeles Community College both instituted Project Renewal in response to Proposition 13. (For more information, contact David C. Scott, Assistant Dean, Research and Development, Bakersfield College, 1801 Panorama Drive, Bakersfield, California 93305.) In order to improve the financial situation, this program focuses on staffing, teaching load, examination of course and program effectiveness, cost-cutting measures, and retention. All areas submit specific objectives they will try to achieve in coming years.

The reasons students withdraw from specific courses are often different from those for which they withdraw from the total institution. A withdrawal study at Harper College (Lucas and Fojo, 1979) found that two-thirds of the students withdrawing from single courses did so because of dissatisfaction with the instructor or the course. Only one-fourth of the students leaving the college before graduating did so because of dissatisfaction with the college. In the final analysis, the faculty must weigh the consequences of the current attrition rate against the possible consequences of reducing attrition.

Withdrawal from institutions of higher education is an area that has produced an abundance of research and publications. Some projects focus on longitudinal studies. Another group of articles tries to predict withdrawal through achievement, perceptual, attitudinal, or biographical measures. Many publications treat the subject of why students leave before graduating; others describe and evaluate specific programs colleges and universities have undertaken to increase retention.

Eckland (1964) produced a fine example of a longitudinal study showing student progress over time. He followed a class of students beginning at the

University of Illinois for ten years. Although only 40 percent graduated in the traditional four-year period, two-thirds finally earned a bachelor's degree within ten years at some college. He also pioneered in long-term follow-up techniques and demonstrated the importance of a high percentage return on follow-up studies. William Rainey Harper College (Lucas, 1979b) conducted longitudinal studies that monitored the performance of a sample of its students over a ten-year period. This study provided a measure of probability for entering full-time and part-time students as to their eventual progression at William Rainey Harper College.

Princeton University (Pervin, 1966) and the University of Tennessee conducted studies to predict attrition and performance among incoming and current students. These studies used biographical data plus an instrument that compared students' perception of self with their perception of the institution.

Withdrawal studies have been conducted at Harper College (Lucas and Fojo, 1979) that track samples of students who fail to return to the college before graduating. The purpose of the study is both to track their current progress and to evaluate why the student left Harper. Three-fourths of the reasons center on personal circumstances or transferring to another college. In other types of predictive studies, Stork and Berger (1978) examined preadmission variables that relate to attrition at a liberal arts college; and Ott (1978) explored factors that affect retention of men and women engineering students.

Communicating to the Target Population

Many of the components of a total marketing plan have been practiced in higher education for years; but until recently, they were never referred to as marketing and were never integrated into a total package. Most of the activities discussed in this section have been an integral part of college life for some time, but they have been handled in different departments with little relationship developed between them. This section deals with the more traditional aspects of marketing, such as recruiting high school students, outreach to high school counselors and faculty, advertising, admissions, mail outs, general community outreach, and employer relations. A good overview of this total communication process is provided by Barton (1978), who describes each of these areas in detail.

The most traditional of all marketing strategies is the recruiting of high school students for the target college. The more standard methods are participating in college days (staffing a table or booth at a high school sponsored event) and leaving appropriate literature in the counseling offices. Many colleges hold parents night to explain to the fathers and mothers of prospective students the many benefits of their institution. Institutions hold open houses or host prospective students on their campus. Variations of this are to stage band days, math competition, or speech contests for high school students on the campus. Another approach is to provide academic services to high schools such as college faculty speaking to high school classes or videotape or computer packages for the classroom. All these approaches are designed to make the prospective student familiar with the college, its benefits, and its personnel, thus making the decision to attend that institution a more comfortable one. Depending on the prerequisites, some disciplines, such as engineering, must concentrate on recruiting younger high school students.

Some colleges adopt indirect recruiting methods by developing relationships with high school counselors or faculty. They might host open houses or demonstrations or professional activities on their campuses. Colleges also might sponsor professional newsletters or publications for high school counselors and faculty. Higher educational institutions might also concentrate on attracting high school faculty on campus for summer workshops or graduate programs.

Educational advertising might be ads placed in local or regional newspapers, radio stations, or television inviting potential students to register at the target college. However, as much publicity can be generated through feature articles in these media. To be successful in this area, an institution must identify unique programs or services offered, interesting individuals serving on the faculty or staff or in the student body, or newsworthy events occurring at the college. Then it must make the media aware of these feature story opportunities. Beyond these obvious strategies, a college can improve its outreach by targeting specific subpopulation groups upon which to focus. If the institution can identify the specific media to reach this target population, the total public relations effort will be more effective. Thus, a college might advertise on billboards, community signs, high school newspapers, union newsletters, company newsletters, senior citizen newsletters, library displays, or whatever specific media would have the most impact on its target clientele.

The admissions process itself can be a very important part of the total marketing plan and, if handled right, can be a source of additional enrollments. There are two key ingredients that can make admissions an effective recruiting tool. One is to keep good records of students from the time they first inquire to the time they actually enroll. The records should include all correspondence both ways between the student and the college. In addition, the records should be ordered so they are easily accessible for evaluation and follow-up. One way to improve the follow-up effort is to order the record by admissions status and date of last contact.

The second important element of an effective admissions process is to maintain a vigorous follow-up program. For example, if after answering an initial inquiry, the college does not receive a response in four weeks, it could send a follow-up letter. This would show that the college is still interested in the student and that the admissions office would be glad to help with any problem related to enrollment.

If the student has been rejected for a particular program, a follow-up letter might indicate alternative programs or alternative entering dates, such as spring or summer. Even if students have been admitted, it is good to correspond with them each month. This lets them know the college is maintaining its interest in them and maximizes the chances that an admitted student will be an enrolled student.

As an extension of the admissions process, all colleges mail out material to prospective students. This material might be bulletins, general brochures about the college, brochures about specific colleges or programs, term schedules, housing information, or student service and financial aid booklets or letters providing specific information requested or inviting prospective students to specific recruitment events. Again it is important to identify target groups in the population upon which the college may want to focus. A college could develop specific brochures or letters for such diverse groups as employers, high school students' parents, senior citizens, the physically disadvantaged, women, musicians and artists, or alumni. In each case, the mail out would educate recipients about specific educational programs or services offered and either urge them to enroll directly or urge them to influence others they come in contact with to enroll.

There are wide variations among institutions of higher learning with regard to community outreach. Many colleges do not consider this a high priority because they focus on the high school student. However, more and more institutions are looking to the general public to supplement enrollment. Faculty and staff actively organized in a speaker's bureau could reach a wide variety of community groups. Many times effective outreach can be achieved through staffed display booths at public events or major shopping areas. Such public events might include major sporting events, fairs, major concert or theater events, parades, holiday celebrations, or other special occasions.

A method growing in popularity is the recruitment van, which is staffed with counselors or paraprofessionals and equipped to distribute literature, provide academic advising services, and, in some cases, register students. The van has the advantages of being mobile and flexible, of being very visible in the community, and of being capable of offering a wide variety of services.

Open houses are a means of attracting the community to the campus, but special events must be planned to motivate adults to come. Special events such as health fairs, career fairs or science fairs have their own built-in attractions. Regional and local colleges can make real estate agents and newcomers' organizations aware of their programs and services and have them in turn relay the message to new families moving into the area.

Evaluating the Marketing Plans

In order to ensure that a total marketing plan is implemented and runs effectively, each component must be periodically evaluated. In this way, the plan can be modified when needed so that it remains consistent with the original objective. Several types of evaluation address these various marketing components. A basic method is to survey current students about how they heard about the college and what caused them to attend. Another is to examine enrollment trends for the whole institution, by discipline or by student characteristics, to determine if new marketing strategies have made an impact. Particularly important is the examination of the progress of new programs. Analyses of the admission process and of registration are also needed. Follow-up studies of former students and evaluations of specific marketing strategies round out the evaluation program needed.

Surveys of current students can identify how students heard about the target college and the principal reason students enroll. In many cases, this survey can help pinpoint the most effective marketing strategies. It must be noted, however, that indirect marketing strategies could not be evaluated by this survey method without follow-up surveys. For example, if the target college developed a supermarket campaign to motivate parents to persuade their children to attend this college, this survey technique would only show students attended because of their parents. These parents would have to be followed up with a survey to determine if the supermarket campaign had any effect on their decision to convince their children to enroll at the target college.

In determining sample size, one would first have to determine how many unique college subgroups there are. For example, programs that enroll more older or part-time students might attract them for quite different reasons than programs enrolling more traditional students. Even among disciplines enrolling traditional students, there might be differences in the principal factors that attract their student body. Usually, one hundred to two hundred students per unique subgroup is an adequate sample, and the study could simply use a short mail out survey instrument. There are generally too many possible reasons for attending to conduct the survey over the telephone.

To a limited extent, analyses of enrollment trends can aid in evaluating marketing strategies. If good enrollment data by discipline and by student characteristics have been kept, some gross inferences can be made about the effects of specific marketing programs. If an intense effort has been launched, for example, to increase enrollment among mathematicians, among students over twenty-five, or among unemployed women, the enrollments in these categories can be examined over time to see if abnormal enrollment increases followed the specific marketing activity. Enrollments are a product of many factors; therefore, it is even more helpful to analyze enrollments of the target college against the same type of enrollment data at comparable institutions. This type of comparative analysis allows a college to separate out the effects of the economy or general college-going patterns.

A very important part of any marketing evaluation is the analysis of the admissions process from the initial contact through actual enrollment. There are several ways of evaluating this admissions process; one is to examine the enrollment results. This could be done by looking at the percentage of all initial contacts, the percentage of all those applying, and the percentage of all those accepted who actually enroll. Obviously, these kinds of analyses would require good records. Comparisons could be made with other institutions or could be made over time to determine partially how effective each step of the admissions process is.

A second method is to examine closely the internal processes in admissions. The written correspondence could be sampled and examined to determine response time in answering inquiries or the patterns of written communication to prospective students who have applied or who have been accepted. Observers outside the admissions office might look at samples of correspondence to see if it is clear, if it answers the questions asked, or if it sets the atmosphere desired for the prospective students. The institution might retain trained outside observers to make telephone calls to the admissions office. These sample calls might determine response time in answering the phone, quality and clarity of the information given over the telephone, and the effectiveness of any referrals made. Although this method might sound devious, if handled in a problem-solving manner, it could be very helpful.

A third approach in evaluating the admissions process is to conduct follow-up mail surveys of inquirers, applicants, or those accepted who fail to register for classes. These persons could be asked why they decided against the target college and how they would evaluate the admissions process they went through. A number of evaluative studies of the admissions process are cited in the literature. For example, Gilmour and others (1977) illustrate a package of data and research that supports the admissions and recruitment process. In samples of specific studies, Bailey and Anton (1978) followed up no-shows and Ramist (1978) analyzed the profile of students who applied against the profile of those who did not apply and those who were accepted against those who were rejected. Farago and Weinman (1978) examined why applications declined at the City University of New York.

Another key element in the evaluation of a total marketing plan is the examination of the effectiveness of student schedules. If a college charges a fixed tuition rate per credit hour, the following might be tried. A sample of students could be surveyed either during registration (written) or after (telephone) to determine how many additional courses or what additional load they would have taken if they could have enrolled in all the courses they desired at the times they desired. The survey could also ask them to articulate the specific conflict that prevented them from enrolling in these additional sections. Those conflicts that arise with great frequency could be examined in detail to see if modifications could be made the following term.

Occasionally, the general population might be surveyed, if feasible, to determine how many persons attempted to register but failed to enroll in any courses because they were unable to find them at the time they could attend. Another means of evaluation is to use trained observers in a simulated role playing situation. Each observer is given a mock schedule and blocks out times he or she cannot attend. Then they go through the registration process and evaluate it afterwards.

Evaluation data such as this can be compared across time to see if there are any trends emerging or can be compared across the institution to identify problem areas.

A follow-up study of graduates or program completers can be a very important part of the evaluation of any total marketing plan. It can be used to evaluate whether a new program met its placement objectives and the degree to which it prepared students for employment or further education. It can also be an aid to curriculum or program size evaluation. If most graduates are leaving the field they prepared for or are underpaid, the college might consider reducing the size of the program. If a very high percentage of graduates is remaining in the field and is starting at very high salaries, the program may be an excellent candidate for expansion.

Such follow-up studies are also excellent sources for promotional material. Mobility patterns and graduates' starting salaries or the percentage of graduates being employed or continuing their education in the same field are extremely useful data for any recruiting strategies. In addition, a detailed description of fields in which graduates are employed can be very valuable information for potential students considering a specific career. For example, the architecture technology program at Harper College (Lucas and Yohanan, 1978) used a follow-up study of its graduates as the principal information disseminated in its recruiting visits to the high schools. Another excellent example is Rossman's (1978) multiinstitutional study of career patterns among liberal arts college graduates, in which he studied the achievements of samples of graduates of 1960, 1965, 1970, and 1975.

Colleges often conduct image analyses and goal inventories, which allow them to compare how outside constituency groups perceive the college and determine if those views differ substantially from internal constituent groups' perceptions. If any significant differences between these two groups' images or goals of the college are identified, the marketing plan might address these issues.

Pilot studies or a laboratory situation might be created to evaluate the effectiveness of various marketing strategies in advance of the implementation. A small panel of judges might rate various alternative promotional efforts in terms of their personal reaction. A complete evaluation can be made on the promotional strategy selected after the fact using one of the methods described earlier.

Other Uses for the Total Marketing Process

In some cases, institutions may not be seeking additional enrollments or higher retention. They may be seeking more support (financial or agreement with educational objectives) from the state legislature or from the general public. In this case, there would be a need to communicate the institutional process, including accurate descriptions of what faculty actually do, what the life of a student is really like, how student services are used, or how academic support services are used. In addition, student outcomes, that is, what happens to students as a result of the educational process at that institution, need to be communicated. Here research must focus on specific person profiles the public can identify with rather than on large sample aggregate data. Finally, community impact study data and image analysis data can be very helpful in generating support when communicated to the general public.

Organizing the Total Marketing Effort

In order for any total marketing plan to be developed, an effective organizational plan must be built. First, there must be a staffing plan and *one* person must be assigned the overall responsibility for developing and implementing this total marketing plan. Depending on the size and the complexity of the whole marketing effort, different organizational structures might emerge. Some institutions might prefer independent marketing plans to develop from within the different colleges or divisions. In this case, each unit would have its own structure under the total institutional structure. For many others, there would be only one primary institutional thrust. The institution may or may not want a number of advisory committees serving the various parts of the marketing effort. However, it is very important that each function described in this chapter be assigned specifically to an individual. It is evident that the marketing organization would cut across total organizational lines.

A second element needed in organizing the total marketing effort is training. The staff assigned the principal tasks in developing the total marketing plan need to take the time to attend, as a team, some nonprofit marketing seminars and spend some time together in a workshop setting for team building, horizon lifting, brainstorming, goal setting, and action planning. In addition, in-service programs need to be developed for faculty, administrators, and other key staff. This may involve bringing in marketing consultants from the outside to put on a seminar or it may involve a workshop conducted by those central core individuals assigned the principal marketing tasks. The objectives of this effort would be to gain acceptance and understanding of the concept of marketing, convince persons of the institutional need for marketing, and motivate these individuals to participate in the marketing plan. Johnson (1979) outlines a similar pattern for organizing the marketing effort of an educational institution.

For the marketing plan to get off the ground, a budget must be developed and must be under the jurisdiction of the person in charge of the total marketing plan. Funds buried in a variety of suborganizational budgets will not be effective in promoting the marketing effort. This is risk capital in that the institution is spending funds now in hopes of a payoff several years in the future. A key question every college or university faces is how much it is willing to risk.

Finally, the marketing plan must be an integral part of the institutional plan. A typical structure for the organization of institutional program plans is instruction, organized research, public service, academic support, student services, institutional support, independent operations, and student access. I propose adding another major component: marketing. The person in charge of developing the total marketing plan would then be an integral part of the institutional central planning committee, and marketing would become an integral part of the college environment.

One possible organizational structure for accommodating the marketing structure is shown in Figure 1.

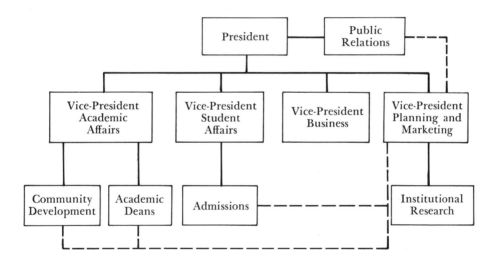

Figure 1. Organizational Structure, Including Marketing

The Office of Institutional Research provides the market research needed to carry out the marketing function. Although a formal process of implementing marketing is just getting under way at Harper College in Palatine, Illinois, the office of institutional research has in the past carried out enrollment projections, enrollment and student profile analyses, student follow-up studies, curriculum and program evaluations, feasibility studies for proposed new programs, community needs analyses, and impact and goal studies that could have been invaluable to the marketing process. Many other offices of institutional research around the country have also provided marketing support for their institutions.

With the function of marketing and planning integrated, the institution can assure itself that policies necessary to carry out the marketing function will be addressed and that goals and objectives set by different units of the organization will include appropriate marketing goals. Finally, there is assurance an operational plan that will implement and monitor the marketing task will be developed.

Consequences of Poor Marketing

If institutions fail to support or invest adequately in the marketing process, through an insufficient budget, failure to provide a trained and competent staff, or lack of cooperation by members of the institution, enrollments may decline and/or public support may diminish. In the extreme, some institutions will fail completely and will cease to exist. More commonly, colleges will become "bare bones" institutions. They will offer less variety in their curriculum and fewer electives and support services. A lower percentage of the public will have access to higher education because of this lack of support services, because a relevant curriculum is not offered for them, or because they are unaware of the fewer educational and support services available.

Bibliographical Essay

Kotler (1975) has produced the "bible" in market planning for nonprofit institutions. Lucas (1979a), in another comprehensive view of developing a total marketing plan, blends the perspectives of a market consultant, a community college researcher, a senior college researcher, and a community developer.

Although it is important to gain an overall view of total marketing before beginning to plan, it is just as important to arrive at a philosophical base for such planning. There are many essays that challenge marketers to develop an aggressive plan, but I can cite only a few. Theobald, Lucey, and Wirtz (1977) produced many challenges in their three articles. Theobald feels there are four fundamental changes needed in education and society. We need a communication society; we need diversity, not conformity; we need to stop thinking that more is better; and we need to make some fundamental value changes. Wirtz asserts the United States is educating more people than the job market can absorb. He cites Sweden as an example of one society facing the overtrained syndrome and choosing higher education rationing as a solution. Wirtz feels we may have to take similar drastic action and suggests focusing on adult continuing education as one alternative.

Bunting, Moon, and Peterson (1978) describe such a lifelong learning alternative and raise five basic questions: Who will be served? What specific next steps justify public investment? What services should be provided? What mix of providers will provide the opportunities? What innovations will likely take root? Zusman (1978), however, raises another sobering issue about adult lifelong learning at the community college level. She notes that while demand for adult lifelong learning environments is growing, legislative support for such programs is weakening. Given such a bleak picture for higher education in the next ten years, Cartter (1975) asks how we can achieve academic progress and pursue a vigorous marketing program while facing a no-growth future. If an institution can grapple with philosophical issues such as these first, its horizons will be lifted; and it will be in a better position to develop a more meaningful total marketing plan.

References

Allen, R., and Gutteridge, T. "The Effects of Additional Education on the Labor Market Experiences of Two-Year College Alumni." *Research in Higher Education,* 1978, *8* (4), 357–372.

Anderson, R. "The Community Survey: An Effective Tool for Administrative Planning and Decision Making." *Community/Junior College Research Quarterly,* 1977, *2* (1), 1–10.

Assimpoloulos, N., and Belanger, C. "Interdisciplinarity: Policies and Practices." Paper presented at Association for Institutional Research Forum, Houston, May 1978.

Bailey, R., and Anton, K. "No Shows and Why." Paper presented at Association for Institutional Research Forum, Houston, May 1978.

Barton, D., Jr. (Ed.). *New Directions for Higher Education: Marketing Higher Education,* no. 21. San Francisco: Jossey-Bass, 1978.

Baskin, S. (Ed.). *New Directions for Institutional Research: Organizing Nontraditional Study,* no. 4. San Francisco: Jossey-Bass, 1974.

Boardman, G., and Mendenhall, E. "Occupational Needs Assessment in Program Planning." *Community College Review,* 1979, *6* (3), 6–12.

Bunting, C., Moon, R., and Peterson, R. *Next Steps Toward Lifelong Learning: Views from Three National Projects.* Washington, D.C.: American Association for Higher Education, 1978.

Carpenter, D. "Bridging the Gap Between Vocational Education and the Liberal Arts." *Community College Review,* 1979, *6* (3), 12–23.

Cartter, A. *New Directions for Institutional Research: Assuring Academic Progress Without Growth,* no. 6. San Francisco: Jossey-Bass, 1975.

Centra, J. "Reading the Enrollment Barometer." *Change,* 1979, *11* (3), 50–51.

Cooper, E., Armijo, J., and Micek, S. "Assessing Community Impact—Some Conceptual Considerations and Field Experience." Paper delivered at Association for Institutional Research Forum, Houston, May 1978.

Dennison, J., and others. *Measuring Impact of Community Colleges.* Vancouver: British Columbia Research, November 1975.

Eckland, B. "College Dropouts Who Came Back." *Harvard Educational Review,* 1964, *34,* 402–420.

Farago, J., and Weinman, J. "The Decline in CUNY Applications: Who and Why." *Research in Higher Education,* 1978, *8* (3), 193–203.

Gaither, G. "Some Tools and Techniques of Market Research for Students." In J. Lucas (Ed.), *New Directions for Institutional Research: Developing a Total Marketing Plan,* no. 21. San Francisco: Jossey-Bass, 1979.

Gilbert, G., Greenbert, B., and Lewis, R. "Academic Planning in Response to Community Needs." *Planning for Higher Education,* 1978, 7 (3), 24–29.

Gilmour, J., Jr., and Berk, L. *A Model for Review and Abandonment of Academic Programs in Post Secondary Education.* University Park: Pennsylvania State University, 1977.

Gilmour, J., Jr., and others. *Research in Support of Admissions and Recruitment at*

Pennsylvania State University. University Park: Office of Budget and Planning, Pennsylvania State University, 1977.

Heist, P., and Warren, J. (Eds.). *New Directions for Institutional Research: Responding to Changing Human Resource Needs,* no. 7. San Francisco: Jossey-Bass, 1975.

Howard, W. "Community Transactions and the Marketing Process." In J. A. Lucas (Ed.), *New Directions for Institutional Research: Developing a Total Marketing Plan,* no. 21. San Francisco: Jossey-Bass, 1979.

Johnson, D. "The Researcher and Nonprofit Marketing. Is Anyone Listening?" In J. A. Lucas (Ed.), *New Directions for Institutional Research: Developing a Total Marketing Plan,* no. 21. San Francisco: Jossey-Bass, 1979.

Jonsen, R. "Small Liberal Arts Colleges: Diversity at the Crossroads?" AAHE-ERIC/Higher Education Research Report No. 4. Washington, D.C.: American Association for Higher Education, 1978.

Kotler, P. *Marketing for Nonprofit Organizations.* Englewood Cliffs, N.J. Prentice-Hall, 1975.

Kuh, C. "Time to Ph.D. and the Labor Market." Paper delivered at Association for Institutional Research Forum, Houston, Tex., May 1978.

Lanter, P., and Howe, F. "The Women's Movement." In *Current Issues in Higher Education.* Washington, D.C.: American Association for Higher Education, 1978.

Larkin, P. "Market Research Methods for Improving College Responsiveness." In J. Lucas (Ed.), *New Directions for Institutional Research: Developing a Total Marketing Plan,* no. 21. San Francisco: Jossey-Bass, 1979.

Lee, W., and Gilmour, J., Jr. "A Procedure for the Development of New Programs in Post Secondary Education." *Journal of Higher Education,* 1977, *48* (3), 304–320.

Loring, R., and others. "Adapting Institutions to the Adult Learner." In *Current Issues in Higher Education.* Washington, D.C.: American Association for Higher Education, 1978.

Lucas, J. *The Environmental Impact on College Students as Measured by TAPE.* Knoxville: Office of Institutional Research, University of Tennessee, 1969.

Lucas, J. "Conflict in Student Output Studies: National and State versus Local Need." *Conflicting Pressures in Postsecondary Education,* Association for Institutional Research Forum Proceedings, 1976.

Lucas, J. "Evaluation of Student Schedules for Those Registering During General Open Fall Registration." *Office of Planning and Research Series,* William Rainey Harper College, Vol. 9, No. 5, September 6, 1977a.

Lucas, J. "Evaluation of the Weekend College." *Office of Planning and Research Series,* William Rainey Harper College, Vol. 8, No. 6, January 25, 1977b.

Lucas, J. (Ed.). *New Directions for Institutional Research: Developing a Total Marketing Plan,* no. 21. San Francisco: Jossey-Bass, 1979a.

Lucas, J. "Longitudinal Study of Performance of Students Entering Harper College—Years—1967–1977." *Office of Planning and Research Series,* William Rainey Harper College, Vol. 10, No. 7, August 1, 1979b.

Lucas, J. "Survey of Goals and Impact of Harper College as Perceived by Seven Harper Constituent Groups." *Office of Planning and Research Series,* William Rainey Harper College, Vol. 10, No. 3, January 25, 1979c.

Lucas, J. "Student Characteristics as Compared to the Community Profile." *Office of Planning and Research Series,* William Rainey Harper College, Vol. 10, No. 7, July 1, 1979d.

Lucas, J., and Fojo, N. "Follow-Up Study of Students Not Returning to Harper Fall of 1978." *Office of Planning and Research Series,* William Rainey Harper College, Vol. 10, No. 8, August 1, 1979.

Lucas, J., and Yohanan, J. "Student Characteristics Compared to the Community Profile." *Office of Planning and Research Series,* William Rainey Harper College, Vol. 10, No. 7, July 1, 1978.

Mayhew, L. "Contemporary College Students and the Curriculum." *SREB Research Monograph,* No. 14, 1969.

Mayville, W. "Interdisciplinary: The Mutable Paradigm." AAHE-ERIC/Higher Education Research Report No. 9. Washington, D.C.: American Association for Higher Education, 1978.

Millet, J. "Reconstruction of the University." Seminar Presentation at the Institute for Research and Training in Higher Education, University of Cincinnati, 1968.

Milton, O. *Alternatives to the Traditional: How Professors Teach and How Students Learn.* San Francisco: Jossey-Bass, 1972.

Moore, N., Jr. "The Role of the Community College in Community Development." *Community/Junior College Research Quarterly,* 1977, *2* (1), 21–30.

Ochsner, N., and Solmon, L. "Forecasting the Labor Market for Highly Educated Workers." *Review of Higher Education,* 1979, *2* (2), 23–46.

Ott, M. "Retention of Men and Women Engineering Students." *Research in Higher Education,* 1978, *9* (2), 137–150.

Pervin, L. *Dissatisfaction with College and the College Dropout: A Transactional Approach.* Princeton, N.J.: University Health Service, Princeton University, 1966.

Ramist, L. "Admissions Yield and Persistence Analysis." Paper presented at Association for Institutional Research Forum, Houston, May 1978.

Reeves, G. "Curriculum Development Through Delphi." *Research in Higher Education,* 1978, *8* (2), 157–168.

Rossman, J. "A Multi-Institutional Study of Career Patterns Among Recent Liberal Arts College Graduates." Paper presented at Association for Institutional Research Forum, Houston, May 1978.

Smith, R. "A Telecommunications Primer for College Presidents." Part 1: "The Technologies Define." *Planning for Higher Education,* 1978, *7* (3), 7–11.

Solmon, L., and Ochsner, N. "New Findings on the Effects of College." In *Current Issues in Higher Education.* Washington, D.C.: American Association for Higher Education, 1978.

Spiro, L. "The Uses of Student Market Segmentation Techniques in College Recruitment." Paper presented at Association for Institutional Research Forum, Houston, May 1978.

Stork, D., and Berger, P. "Attrition in the Liberal Arts College of a Major Metropolitan University." *Research in Higher Education,* 1978, *9* (4), 281–289.

Terenzini, P. "An Evaluation of Three Basic Designs for Studying Attrition." Paper presented at Association for Institutional Research Forum, Houston, May 1978.

Theobald, R., Lucey, P., and Wirtz, W. "Creating Our Future." Three presentations delivered at Society for College and University Planning Conference, Seattle, Wash., August 1977.

Tilton, B., and Turrisi, I. "Impact of Fee Schedule on Average Student Credit Hour Load." Paper presented at Association for Institutional Research Forum, Houston, May 1978.

Tittle, C., and Denker, E. "Re-Entry Women: A Selective Review of the Educational Process, Career Choice, and Interest Measurement." *Review of Educational Research,* 1977, *27* (4), 531–584.

Trivett, D. "Continuing Education for the Professions." In *Research Currents.* Washington, D.C.: ERIC Clearinghouse on Higher Education and American Association for Higher Education, February, 1977.

Yale, D. "An Investigation by Simulation of the Dynamic Instability of Engineering Enrollment." Unpublished doctoral dissertation, Graduate School of Business, University of Colorado, 1978.

Zusman, A. "State Policy Making for Community College Adult Education." *Journal of Higher Education,* 1978, *49* (4), 337–357.

13

Oscar T. Lenning

Assessing Student Program Needs

The concept of need is an integral part of our culture. Satisfying important human needs is the central theme of almost all educational effort, political lobbying, social advocacy, and commercial advertising. As unmet needs become more and more severe or prevalent, they tend to be expressed as increasingly incessant and more vocal demands. However, demands are merely indications of probable need; they are not needs in and of themselves. In fact, demands may sometimes point to surface needs rather than underlying problems; and in certain cases, they may only be intended to arouse attention or promote self-aggrandizement, rather than fulfill other needs.

Given this distinction between need and demand, how can we tell when a demand is indicative of a need, which needs and demands are important and deserve attention, which are feasible to meet concerning our situation and the constraints facing us, and how to order and set priorities with respect to needs and demands? Once such questions are answered, we can decide how to allocate available funds and other resources for meeting needs and demands. During a period of enrollment decline and probable financial retrenchment, an objective and comprehensive analysis of needs and demands for programs and program restructuring becomes especially important for deciding which areas to main-

263

tain, cut back, restructure, or possibly expand. Without the ability to gather and assess relevant information about needs and integrate this information effectively with information about resources, program planning becomes primarily a guessing game or an art. Therefore, this chapter summarizes and synthesizes what is currently known about the assessment and application of information regarding needs and demands for programs and program restructuring, particularly as they relate to current students, and provides some guidelines for administrative and institutional research practice in this area. (Chapter Twelve contains information about the needs of prospective students, including their need for market information.)

The Concept of Educational Need

In the education needs assessment literature, "need" has generally been considered synonymous with a discrepancy between what is and what should be the case. (For a discussion of how "what should be" might be determined, see Fenske's discussion of goal and objective setting in Chapter Nine.) Process and procedural discrepancies between the actual and the ideal—for example, a need for more student-teacher interaction, for computer-assisted instruction, or for peer tutoring—were usually included in this definition during the 1960s. Since Kaufman, Corrigan, and Johnson (1969) published their needs model, however, educational needs have tended to be limited in concept by needs assessment theorists and practitioners to discrepancies in results, that is, discrepancies in outcomes. The classic concept as defined by Kaufman (1972, p. 492) is that "an educational *need* is a measurable outcome discrepancy between what is and what should be . . . if there is no difference between where we are and where we should be, then we have no need." Three years later, English and Kaufman (1975, p. 64) reworded this definition and referred to educational need as "a gap in educational outcomes or results. It is the discrepancy between the current results (not procedures or processes) and the desired or required results."

"Gaps in learner performance" is a more meaningful concept than is "learner outcome discrepancies" to an instructor, a curriculum developer, or a program coordinator. Yet there have been educators who felt that always talking in terms of "discrepancy" or "gap" denoted a constant negative orientation. Therefore, the National Assessment of Educational Progress discussions refer to performance levels in relation to a desirable absolute, and some educators have referred to "level of fulfillment." Coffing and Hutchinson (1974) unveiled a formal needs assessment model that speaks of needs in terms of a desired condition or state (fulfillment) instead of a discrepancy (although their model includes discrepancies also). Lay people do not limit need to a gap or discrepancy; they would include conditions that are currently being met but that could become deficient if the level of support were lowered, such as the need for nutritious food and plenty of exercise. Therefore, it might be questioned why so many educators limit need to a discrepancy or gap.

One of the major experts in evaluation, Scriven, was formerly a proponent of needs assessment being based on the discrepancy definition of need; but he later changed his mind. He declared (1977, p. 25) that because past needs assessment models have been built totally on the discrepancy concept of need, they "are farcical and decisions built on them are built on soluble sand." To replace the discrepancy-only concept, Scriven (1977, p. 25) proposed the following formula as a definition for need:

z needs x = z would (or does) significantly benefit from x *and*

z is now (or would be, without x) in an unsatisfactory condition

If z represents a college student and x represents effective study habits, we might, based on past research, tell students entering our college that they need effective study habits. According to Scriven's definition, we mean students will benefit significantly from effective study habits and further that they will be in an unsatisfactory condition (low grades, academic probation, danger of dismissal) if they do not have or develop effective study habits. Scriven goes on to say that the first clause in his formula is not enough because someone could benefit from a luxury (for example, a million dollars) but not need it. The second clause makes clear that "needs" refers to necessities instead of luxuries. What some would consider luxuries others would consider necessities, but Scriven's point is valid and clear—we are concerned with primary or critical statuses, conditions, and situations, not with superficial or trivial matters.

Coffing and Hutchinson (1974) emphasized that an identified need is composed of both the amount of its fulfillment and the amount of its discrepancy (lack of fulfillment). Building on this idea and Scriven's formulation, Lenning and others (1979, p. 20) proposed the following definition for need: "A NEED is a necessary or desirable condition, state, or situation—whether it be an end result that is actuality (met need) or a discrepancy that should be closed between a current or projected actuality and a necessary or highly desirable end result (unmet need)—as judged by a relevant person or group using multiple objective criteria that have been agreed upon." This definition is a combination of level of necessity and discrepancy. As Burton and Merrill (1977) have suggested, unmet needs can be met by lowering the threshold of necessity, closing up the discrepancy (overcoming the deficiency), or a combination of the two. For example, the need to read well can be met by lowering the score level on a reading proficiency exam that defines the point where proficiency is inadequate, increasing the reading proficiency of students, or a combination of both.

The levels of discrepancy and/or necessity that constitute need and the point at which needs are partially or fully met or unmet depend on the particular situation and context. So does who should make such judgments. For most needs assessment studies, the target groups, the assessor, and those who will use the assessment data should all be involved in making the judgments.

I have already suggested that wants and demands can only be indicators of needs (sometimes they are not even that) and do not constitute the needs. Another problem with the discrepancy concept of need is that it has led many needs assessors to equate needs with wants and demands. However, expressions of want and demand do provide us with very important information that the assessor needs to examine very carefully. Wants are more often than not indications that a real need is present, as judged by outsiders using relevant objective criteria, especially if those wants become expressed in terms of strong and critical demands or expressions of anguish and of grave concern. For example, Taylor, Vineberg, and Gaffard (1974) found that schools with severe problems provided much more reliable needs assessment questionnaire responses than did schools with no serious problems. But an authentic need may not really exist. There have been occasions when some students demanded something merely because other students had it. Similarly, there have been cases where students made demands primarily to attract attention (which suggests an underlying personal need other than the one explicitly stated in the demand) or to keep other students from having it (such as some of the student counterdemonstration marches in the 1960s). Conversely, students may have important needs they are not aware or conscious of, or they may recognize the need but be unwilling to act upon it or express it forcefully. In still other cases, people may know that something is needed but be unable to identify what is wrong.

Not only may wants and demands be indicators of needs, but they also may create needs (just as needs can create other needs). Goodenough (1963, p. 50) illustrated this well and at the same time introduced a different differentiation between wants and needs than proposed here (where wants are equated to end results and needs to instrumentalism): "First distinguish between needs and wants: if people WANT a year-round water supply they may NEED a dam. By wants, then, we refer to desired states of affairs, and by needs we refer to effective means for achieving or maintaining them. Many desires can in fact be perceived as wants or needs depending upon whether the object is perceived as a means to a goal or an end itself."

Another aspect of students' needs or demands for program restructuring should also be discussed—needs placed on students through the needs and demands of employers, industry, and the community. Numerous studies have found that the major reason most students are in college is to get a good job and to attain job security. Thus, colleges and universities need to consider need and demand statements like the following in their program planning: *"Technical Competence versus College Degree.* For the overwhelming majority, it's no contest as to which preparation will command the highest income and the greatest number of jobs to choose from. As Ed Bodine, president of Bodine Corporation, told Forbes at lunch here one day: Finding people who are technically capable gets tougher every day. There seems to be fewer of them and the demand climbs. Meanwhile, college graduates of vague capabilities and high assumptions are a dime a dozen" (Forbes, 1979, p. 32). As another example, a bank president told me several years ago that the most valuable thing colleges and universities could do for him was to teach their students to be flexible so they could readily and effectively adapt to changing circumstances and situations and provide different students with different experiences so his employees could bring markedly varied viewpoints to bear on the bank's decision making and provoke well-rounded and thorough discussion.

Apparent needs and demands of community agencies, institutions, and citizens also can be important for program planning. The community needs citizens with competencies and attitudes conducive to good citizenship, for example, in terms of being an effective and efficient consumer, an informed and perceptive voter, and a good parent. Parsons (1951) formulated a list of nine general but basic community needs. McMahon (1970) provides an extended discussion about local community needs as related to education and points out the community's needs are more than the sum of the learning needs of the people living in it. However, a community can be geographic based—a local community, the state, a region, the nation, or the international community—or interest based—private enterprise communities, association communities such as professions and unions, government communities, and nongovernmental/public service communities (Lenning and others, 1977). Needs and demands arising from any one of these types of communities can legitimately affect program planning; thus, program staff should be on the lookout for and perceptive about demands and other evidence of need concerning all these types of communities. For example, a professional association may specify changes in requirements for joining the association and a state board may issue licensure requirements, and both sets of requirements may affect programming in particular curricular areas.

Another potential source of student needs and demands includes students' families, friends, and peers. Demands or needs of such people could reflect on or influence the demands and needs of the students themselves. And in this day and age, demands and needs implied by the physical environment or ecology can influence student demands and needs greatly.

Differentiating Among Needs

The educational program needs of current students can be differentiated on several different dimensions. Among need schemas that can stimulate thinking about which needs should be considered for assessment, perhaps the earliest is a psychological classification developed by Murray (1938) and his colleagues at Harvard based on intensive interviews with paid Harvard students. Since that time, many *need for achievement* and *need for affiliation* scales have been based on this classification of twenty manifest (leading to overt action) and eight latent (leading to active imagination and fantasy but not to overt action) needs.

Maslow (1970) developed a hierarchical need system where a need at one level presumably cannot be fulfilled until the needs at the level below it are satisfied. His categories of needs, from lowest to highest level, are (1) physiological, (2) safety, (3) belonging and love, (4) esteem, and (5) self-actualization (Maslow, 1970, pp. 35–47). Groves, Kahalas, and Erickson (1975) made Maslow's top level more concrete by dividing it into needs for power and competition, accomplishment, self-insight and self-confidence, service to others, and spiritual needs.

Different types of student needs can also be suggested by developmental tasks that have been noted to be related to maturity and chronological age, where earlier tasks supposedly must be mastered before one can move on to later tasks in the hierarchy. Havighurst (1952) identified ten primary developmental tasks for adolescents, eight for early adulthood, seven for middle age, and six for later maturity. Cronbach (1963) formulated a general list for the early years: affection, adult approval, peer approval, independence, competence, and self-respect.

One can also clarify needs in terms of goals and objectives. Improvement (for example, see Rankin, 1976, or Lenning, 1976) generally focuses on needs in such terms. Beatty (1976) hypothesized a goal-state continuum of needs varying from prescriptive needs (determined by societal norms and standards) to motivational needs (determined by the individual's goals). Lenning (1977a) has compiled numerous classifications of goals that have been developed over the years, some of which are detailed and narrow in focus and some of which are general. For an in-depth discussion of goals and objectives, and their development, see Chapter Nine.

Closely related to goals are outcomes. Educational needs assessment studies during the past decade have generally defined needs entirely in terms of outcomes—presence or absence of the desired outcomes. An especially popular classification of student outcomes is Chickering's (1969) for young adults in college. It consists of seven "vectors" (autonomy, competence, identity, integrity, interpersonal relations, managing emotions, and purpose). A more recent classification of students' college performances was empirically developed for undergraduate students at Yale University (Taber and Hackman, 1976). Table 1 presents a generic (applicable to societal outcomes as well as to individuals) and comprehensive classification of types of outcomes developed at the National Center for Higher Education Management Systems (NCHEMS). For each category, a standard definition and example outcomes are provided.

Needs related to the student environment and to educational process also deserve consideration. Aulepp and Delworth's (1976) ecosystems approach to student development programming (also see Banning and Kaiser, 1974) focuses on these types of need, and Micek and Arney (1974) developed a classification of environmental variables and measures that could conceivably be related to needs.

Another way of viewing needs is in terms of student problems. For example, each of the areas examined by the college student form (traditional aged college students) of the *Mooney Problem Check List* (Mooney and Gordon, 1950) can suggest needs. Pagels (1973), for example, used this instrument in determining specific criteria for a student needs based curriculum. The eleven scales of this inventory are as follows: health and physical development, finances-living conditions-employment, social and recreational activities, social-physical relations, personal-psychological relations, courtship-sex-marriage, home and family, morals and religion, adjustment to school work, the future-vocational and educational, and curriculum and teaching procedures. (An opposite strategy, going from problems to needs, was employed by Campbell and Markle, 1967, who developed procedures for translating needs into problems.) For older students, who are becoming increasingly prevalent in many colleges and universities, there is an "adult" form of the *Mooney Problem Check List.*

Of the several other classifications of need in the literature, one that has potential usefulness in student program modification or development focuses on student discrepancy need types. Bradshaw (1972) outlined the following four discrepancy need types: normative need (absolute standard), felt need (want), expressed need (demand), and comparative need (compared to analogous groups). Burton and Merrill (1977) added a fifth need type—anticipated or projected (future) needs.

Needs Assessment Concepts and Purposes

The following statement by Gill and Fruehling (1979, p. 323) applies to any educational program or service: "Logic requires that needs be identified prior to the design of programs and services to meet those needs. Failure to do so institutionalizes ineffectiveness and legitimizes irrelevance.... All too often . . . the programs are designed to satisfy the program's needs rather than the needs of students." Such identification of needs has generally been referred to as "needs assessment" although other terms, such as "needs analysis" (Coffing and Hutchinson, 1974) and "need diagnosis" (Monette, 1977), have been used. Most

Table 1. Types of Outcomes That Could Be Aimed for in Postsecondary Education

Category Code Number	Entity Being Maintained or Changed	Category Code Number	Entity Being Maintained or Changed
1000	*ECONOMIC OUTCOMES*	2270	Occupational and Employability Skills
1100	Economic Access and Independence Outcomes	2280	Physical and Motor Skills
1110	Economic Access	2290	Other Skill Outcomes
1120	Economic Flexibility, Adaptability, and Security	2300	Morale, Satisfaction, and Affective Characteristics
1130	Income and Standard of Living	2310	Attitudes and Values
1200	Economic Resources and Costs	2320	Beliefs, Commitments, and Philosophy of Life
1210	Economic Costs and Efficiency	2330	Feelings and Emotions
1220	Economic Resources (including employees)	2340	Mores, Customs, and Standards of Conduct
		2350	Other Affective Outcomes
1300	Economic Production	2400	Perceptual Characteristics
1310	Economic Productivity and Production	2410	Perceptual Awareness and Sensitivity
1320	Economic Services Provided	2420	Perception of Self
1400	Other Economic Outcomes	2430	Perception of Others
2000	*HUMAN CHARACTERISTIC OUTCOMES*	2440	Perception of Things
2100	Aspirations	2450	Other Perceptual Outcomes
2110	Desires, Aims, and Goals	2500	Personality and Personal Coping Characteristics
2120	Dislikes, Likes, and Interests	2510	Adventurousness and Initiative
2130	Motivation or Drive Level	2520	Autonomy and Independence
2140	Other Aspirational Outcomes	2530	Dependability and Responsibility
2200	Competence and Skills	2540	Dogmatic/Open-Minded, Authoritarian/Democratic
2210	Academic Skills	2550	Flexibility and Adaptability
2220	Citizenship and Family Membership Skills	2560	Habits
2230	Creativity Skills	2570	Psychological Functioning
2240	Expression and Communication Skills	2580	Tolerance and Persistence
2250	Intellectual Skills	2590	Other Personality and Personal Coping Outcomes
2260	Interpersonal, Leadership, and Organizational Skills		

Table 1. Types of Outcomes that Could be Aimed for in Postsecondary Education

(Continued)

Category Code Number	Entity Being Maintained or Changed	Category Code Number	Entity Being Maintained or Changed
2600	Physical and Physiological Characteristics	3500	Other Knowledge, Technology, and Art Form Outcomes
2610	Physical Fitness and Traits		
2620	Physiological Health	4000	*RESOURCE AND SERVICE PROVISION OUTCOMES*
2630	Other Physical or Physiological Outcomes	4100	Provision of Facilities and Events
2700	Status, Recognition, and Certification	4110	Provision of Facilities
2710	Completion or Achievement Award	4120	Provision or Sponsorship of Events
2720	Credit Recognition	4200	Provision of Direct Services
2730	Image, Reputation, or Status	4210	Teaching
2740	Licensing and Certification	4220	Advisory and Analytic Assistance
2750	Obtaining a Job or Admission to a Follow-up Program	4230	Treatment, Care, and Referral Services
		4240	Provision of Other Services
2760	Power and/or Authority	4300	Other Resource and Service Provision Outcomes
2770	Job, School, or Life Success		
2780	Other Status, Recognition, and Certification Outcomes	5000	*OTHER MAINTENANCE AND CHANGE OUTCOMES*
		5100	Aesthetic-Cultural Activities, Traditions, and Conditions
2800	Social Activities and Roles		
2810	Adjustment to Retirement	5200	Organizational Format, Activity, and Operation
2820	Affiliations		
2830	Avocational and Social Activities and Roles	5300	Other Maintenance and Change
2840	Career and Vocational Activities and Roles		
2850	Citizenship Activities and Roles		
2860	Family Activities and Roles		
2870	Friendships and Relationships		
2880	Other Activity and Role Outcomes		
2900	Other Human Characteristic Outcomes		
3000	*KNOWLEDGE, TECHNOLOGY, AND ART FORM OUTCOMES*		
3100	General Knowledge and Understanding		
3110	Knowledge and Understanding of General Facts and Terminology		

3120	Knowledge and Understanding of General Processes	
3130	Knowledge and Understanding of General Theory	
3140	Other General Knowledge and Understanding	
3200	Specialized Knowledge and Understanding	
3210	Knowledge and Understanding of Specialized Facts and Terminology	
3220	Knowledge and Understanding of Specialized Processes	
3230	Knowledge and Understanding of Specialized Theory	
3240	Other Specialized Knowledge and Understanding	
3300	Research and Scholarship	
3310	Research and Scholarship Knowledge and Understanding	
3320	Research and Scholarship Products	
3400	Art Forms and Works	
3410	Architecture	
3420	Dance	
3430	Debate and Oratory	
3440	Drama	
3450	Literature and Writing	
3460	Music	
3470	Painting, Drawing, and Photography	
3480	Sculpture	
3490	Other Fine Arts	

Source: Type-of-outcome dimension of the NCHEMS Outcomes Structure (Lenning, and others, 1977, p. 27). The structure provides standard definitions and sample measures or indicators for each category, along with procedures for subdividing into additional levels of categories.

needs assessment approaches have focused only on needs as discrepancies, wants and demands as needs, and strictly identification; but in each case more is needed. Coffing and Hutchinson (1974), Lenning and others (1979), and Scriven (1977) point out the importance of focusing on fulfilled as well as unfulfilled needs. The program staff members need to know where the program is meeting needs as well as where it is not meeting needs and how fully different needs are being met. Second, wants and demands constitute the primary data of needs assessment; but they should be supported by other, more objective indications of need before program response is warranted—expressions of want and demand are often not enough (Gill and Fruehling, 1979; Lenning and others, 1979). Furthermore, this multifaceted process must be systematic, even though both formal and informal data can be used.

In addition to identifying needs, the needs assessment process should rank them in terms of seriousness and importance and should promote an understanding of the needs, their interrelationships, and their causal roots (Beatty, 1976; Lenning and others, 1979; Segal and Sell, 1978; Witkin, 1975). Only through understanding the needs and need relationships, why the needs occurred, and why the needs are currently not being met can one determine how best to meet or improve fulfillment of specific needs. In addition, understanding problems the program faces in responding to such needs (such as politics, lack of faculty support, lack of resources, and student realization of the needs lacking) is an important part of needs assessment according to Segal and Sell (1978).

In elementary and secondary education, where formal program needs assessment has been a primary concern for much longer than in higher education (where it has generally been ignored until the last several years), goal setting has often been considered a part of needs assessment (Witkin, 1975). In higher education, however, needs assessment is usually thought of as a separate process that feeds into the goal-setting process. This is the view I favor (see Figure 1). According to the simplified and overly disjointed and linear process outlined graphically in Figure 1, constituent needs are identified and then assessed in terms of priorities, causes, and their makeup. The information and conclusions about needs coming out of this phase are then related to the institutional and program mission and to evaluative data of current program attainment and effectiveness. Based on this integration, broad outcome and process (process to attain the outcomes) goals are developed and priorities are determined; and these in turn are translated or transformed into concrete, specific objectives that can guide action. Before the goals and objectives are applied to the development of plans for program modification or development, program resource acquisition and allocation, program evaluation, and program operation, they are reevaluated in terms of the needs, mission emphases, and current operational effectiveness that were used to develop them. Intended (planned) objectives and best courses of action for meeting them are then determined and implementation activities begun.

As documented by Segal and Sell (1978), needs assessment must be a process rather than a product. Furthermore, needs are continually changing. Thus, they concluded that needs assessment "is not a synonym for survey," as has usually been the case in marketing, "but involves many methods going on constantly and simultaneously" (p. II4). This does not mean it has to be a complex or overly expensive array of activities and process. There are many alternative practices, some much more complex and expensive than others.

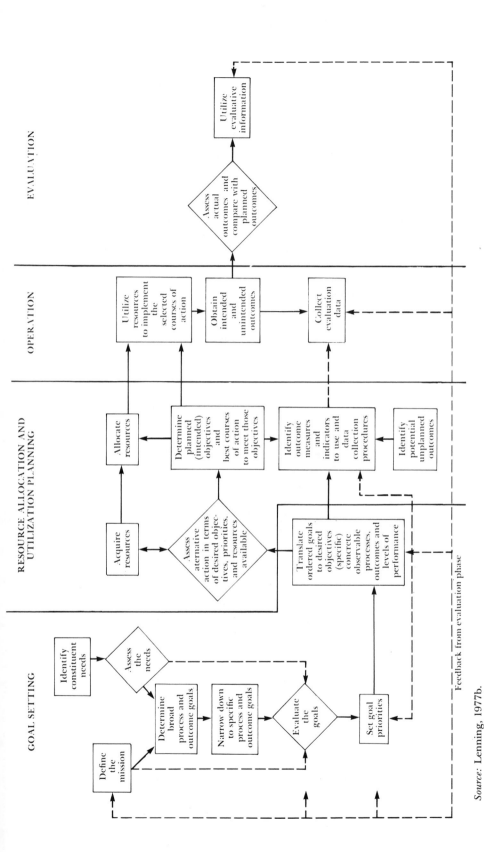

Source: Lenning, 1977b.

Figure 1. A Possible Graphic View of Planning, Management, and Evaluation

Needs assessment as a science is still relatively undeveloped in many areas. These problem areas are outlined in the following two quotes.

> The following shortcomings of needs assessment in practice are generally evident: the concept of need is poorly defined, resulting in misinterpretations and faulty communications about what needs exist; needs assessment is often considered to be a product (for example, an instrument or the report of a survey) rather than an ongoing process; needs assessment efforts are rarely evaluated, either in terms of cost or effectiveness; the objectives and audiences for needs assessment efforts are seldom clearly identified; the focus for collecting and compiling needs information seldom considers the capabilities and constraints of the institution vis-à-vis the needs of learners and communities; needs information, once collected or compiled, usually is not fully analyzed to uncover explanations for and relationships among needs; reports of needs information do not adequately consider the audiences and uses for the information; needs assessment information is not fully considered or used in the decision-making process; and institutions may not have the expertise or technical capability to conduct certain kinds of needs assessment activities [Segal and Sell, 1978, pp. I1–I2].
>
> The field is markedly and sadly lacking in almost any kind of research on the processes of needs assessment. There should be validity and reliability studies of instruments, as well as studies of the effects of different assessment processes and communication strategies on the educational system. Longitudinal studies are needed to trace the impacts of needs assessment on policymaking, curricular change, organizational structure, and student performance. Cost-benefit comparisons of different approaches are needed. . . . Few developers have shown how to relate such qualitative data as values, perceptions, and concerns to such quantitative data as test scores, demographic data, and transiency and absentee rates. Yet until such techniques are widely available, educators will assign priorities and make decisions using one-dimension or oversimplified decision rules [Witkin, 1975, pp. 7–8].

A problem not mentioned in either quote is that when some refer to "needs assessment" (for example, in student affairs), they are talking about assessing individual needs, such as in counseling, course placement, and diagnosis for remediation. Such needs assessment must be distinguished and kept separate from program needs assessment because different procedures and considerations are needed (see Lenning and McAleenan, 1979). Such problem areas commonly hinder program needs assessment from being maximally effective. There are, however, ways to alleviate these problems and allow useful needs assessment to occur.

Planning and Conducting Needs Assessment

As Anderson, Ball, Murphy, and associates (1975, p. 136) have stated, "one man's context evaluation may be another man's needs assessment." We must not let ourselves be bound by terminology; but we should be guided by underlying concepts, purposes, and goals. Furthermore, when one gets down to the concrete process and procedures level, there is significant overlap of content between needs assessment and other types of assessment activities, such as program evaluation. In fact, some program evaluation data can also constitute needs assessment data. However, there are some noteworthy procedural differences, and the target focus is distinctive.

As already noted, needs assessment should be an ongoing process. There should be continuous reassessment (Bowers and associates, 1976). A cyclical process Hecht (1977) tested and found effective for program evaluation makes sense for program needs assessment also, and perhaps these two types of assessment programs can be coordinated on some campuses. One year certain types of needs for particular types of students are examined in depth. The next year other groups and/or needs are examined. This continues each year or on some other schedule, such as every semester or every other semester, until the cycle is completed and a new cycle is ready to begin. In most cases, the new cycle will need to be modified (in many cases, a cycle may also need to be modified while it is occurring) in terms of changes in the institution's mission, clientele, and other areas; changes in the community or society, such as the economic and political situation, employers' personnel demands, societal expectations and values, and what other educational institutions are doing; and changes in the abilities, interests, aspirations and other characteristics of currently enrolled students.

All the while the formal, focused, in-depth needs assessment is taking place, an informal intelligence system also needs to be operating. The needs assessors (who will often include people at both the institutionwide and program levels) should attempt to, in various ways, keep the communication channels open to all areas and levels of the campus community and remain alert for impromptu evidence that needs of a particular group or in a particular area are changing and need in-depth assessment. Being aware of the findings of other types of student assessments and research occurring on campus (such as program evaluation data, student characteristics distributions, grading patterns, student test data, and the like) can also be helpful. Similarly, "antennae" should be kept continually out for indications ("red flags") from the outside community and society at large about changes that could affect student needs. Such informal evidence can be gotten by noticing reports or comments in the media. It can also come from formal or informal conversations with community citizens and leaders, high school counselors and other faculty/staff, additional community agencies, business leaders, advisory committees from the community (which are common to many community colleges in particular), and so forth. Projections and data distributed by government, social researchers, and others can be helpful, too.

Segal and Sell (1978, pp. VII26–VII27) pointed out an additional way of gathering such intelligence information:

> Step one would involve making all personnel, including faculty, library staff, tellers at the finance office, and maintenance workers, aware of a responsibility to notice people's reactions to products, administrative procedures, and services of the institution, and to pass on information about such reactions to those who make decisions. Kotler advocates a training program to achieve this

objective. Such a program would also have the advantage of involving more staff members in institutional development, with a likelihood of improved morale. . . . Within an operating system which encourages the worker to report and take some responsibility for such decisions he/she might feel free to pass on the complaint with possible suggestions for improving the service. The payoff for the individual worker is in receiving fewer complaints and perhaps in recognition for suggested improvements in service. Faculty members are in an outstanding position to receive and pass on information about student needs and to suggest ways of meeting them.

Not only will such secondary and soft data suggest when and where a harder, more focused needs assessment examination is needed—and how previous plans may need to be modified—but they provide supplemental context and need information that can add to the validity of and/or help interpret the needs data collected in the formal, focused assessment being conducted. Such focused data must never be divorced from the "big picture."

The informal intelligence system previously discussed must be well thought out, appropriate to the institutional context, and systematic in its coverage. However, here I shall emphasize developing plans for the formal, focused needs assessment activities. I shall discuss both the preparations for planning an assessment and the planning process itself as well as the actual conduct of the assessment, but in planning terms because good planning must consider implementation in its entirety.

Preparing to Plan a Needs Assessment Study. Needs assessment can be centralized and coordinated by a central office on campus (such as institutional research); it can be largely planned and carried out separately within and by the staff of each program or department; or it can be a combination of central coordination and analysis and largely localized data collection, interpretation, and application. In the first case, economies of scale can occur and institutionwide coverage of programs is assured. Although a central office, usually institutional research or academic planning, is coordinating and carrying out most of the needs assessment activities, program planners and administrators will be using the information for planning and operational decision making, respectively. This means they should be intimately involved in needs assessment planning, deciding what information should be collected and how it should be analyzed and reported. In the second case, activities will be taking place largely within the department or program; but the institutional research office should be proactive in providing technical consultation as needed about useful measures, data collection methodology, analysis, and application to program planning and decision making. Furthermore, all programs will need common data (broken down by program) about the students, the external environment (including campus data), the total institutional situation, and so forth that is already being collected or gathered from other collection sources by the institutional research office or would be best collected or gathered by it.

The most appropriate option among and within any of these three general strategies for needs assessment will necessarily vary from institution to institution, depending on such factors as patterns of staff expertise, political and organizational structures and relationships, and program types and distributions.

Once the project coordinator has thought thoroughly through the options open and potentially feasible (in terms of resources available, purposes, groups, issues, questions, measures and indicators, methodology, and techniques), it is important to get relevant others directly involved in the planning process. A common and desirable approach is to form a planning committee. Included on this committee should be representatives of the program(s) of concern, representatives of other users of the needs assessment results (such as the office of the academic dean and of student affairs), representatives of those from whom data will be gathered (such as students, business and industry, and community agency staff), and a technical consultant (preferably someone from the institution who is knowledgeable rather than an outside consultant). The areas and groups to be represented will depend on the strategy chosen (for example, if it is an institutionwide study coordinated by the director of institutional research, he or she can serve as the technical resource) and the specific situation of the institution and its programs (for example, the internal attitudes and politics and the informal power structure).

It is increasingly being recognized that students must be involved in institutional committees, something often not even considered in the past. Full student involvement (by perhaps a couple of students) in the planning committee deliberations is essential for the success of an effort that is attempting to collect and use information about student program needs. Students clearly have the most to gain or lose from the quality and relevance of the efforts, and they may feel more positive about the study if they are represented on the committee designing it. Furthermore, student members of the committee, if they are chosen carefully, may be able to provide valuable input, effectively communicate the importance of the study to their fellow students, and elicit student support for and cooperation in the data collection from students. It is also a good learning experience for participating students.

It is crucial that much careful thought and consideration go into the choice of specific representatives of the areas and groups selected to be represented. Personalities, motivations, and commitment to the need for this assessment are important, as is the ability to work with others, a high energy level, and being knowledgeable and perceptive about the area or group they represent. It is also important to have respected people involved who can communicate well with and get the attention and support of the persons they represent.

The democratic processes and typical campus channels and lines of authority must not be ignored in the selection process. Thus, the project director should consult with pertinent department and program heads and student leaders. Furthermore, having the formal invitation to the committee come from the institution's chief executive can often provide important motivation for acceptance and demonstrate top administration's support for the needs assessment activities. Finally, the committee should not get too large and cumbersome. The size that will best facilitate involvement, working together, and effective decision making depends on the preferences and style of the leader and other participants. However, most of those experienced in small group process say that more than twelve to fifteen people gets far too unwieldy.

Planning the Assessment Study. Payne (1974) outlined seven steps or stages in assessing cognitive and affective learning that are general and apply to any assessment, including needs assessment: specify detailed goals and objectives of the study, design the assessment system, select measures and data-gathering methods, collect the data, analyze and summarize the data, contrast data and objectives, and feed back the results. Overlapping these but also introducing other actions that are necessary are nine steps specified by Bowers and others (1976) for needs assessment: identifying people and roles, speaking the same language, stating concerns and goals, finding the needs, measuring and rating the needs, setting priorities, determining the feasibility of meeting the needs, planning the program, and continuous reassessment. I consider all these nine steps pertinent for a needs assessment study except the eighth. I do not view planning of the program as part of the needs assessment process but rather as a separate activity for which the outputs of the needs assessment process are valuable inputs. Either way, however, needs and planning are closely related.

The remainder of this section will be ordered according to a combined version of Payne's stages. The steps from Bowers and others will be incorporated as they seem appropriate.

Specifying the Purposes, Goals, and Objectives. Early in planning a needs assessment study, the purposes, goals, and special concerns of the study must be agreed on and specified clearly and succinctly. Examples are suggested by the following questions: What types of needs are of concern and for whom? What data are to be collected and why? How will the assessment data be expected to relate to program goals? How are the assessment data to be applied or used?

Each of these questions relates to the program goals, so identifying and reaching agreement about current and potential program goals is an important part of this process. Although he was talking about institutionwide goals, what Conrad (1974, p. 505) said about goals can be said just as meaningfully for programs: They are the standards against which to judge program success. They provide a source of legitimacy for program activities. They define and order program needs. They define the units of program outcomes. They identify the program's clientele. They define the relationship between the program, the institution of which it is a part, and society.

There is a danger in focusing only on current program goals, and this is the reason I included potential goals (not current goals). If we limit our primary focus to need areas delimited by current program goals, other important needs may have little chance to become known. This is also the reason I include open-ended input about program needs in the procedures to be described. One has to start somewhere, however, and keep the assessment to manageable size; and focusing on current goals and other goals that would seem to have some potential serves this purpose. Of course, as indicated earlier, new goal formulation based on the findings coming out of the needs assessment should also take place, so we are talking about an iterative total process.

Reaching some sort of agreement on program and assessment goals will involve much give-and-take discussion, as will be true of the later phases of planning the assessment study. Thus, specification of terms—a common language—at the onset will be important.

Delineating the Assessment Context. The success of the assessment effort rests on having an integrated, well-thought-out needs assessment strategy and design that effectively relates to the assessment goals and objectives and the situation and environment facing the program(s) and institution. A listing of the factors within the program, institution, or other environments that will assist the assessment effort and of those that will constrain it should be developed. Such factors include faculty, staff, and student attitudes and values (in general and concerning the study); political relationships and pressures; financial, staff, time, and other resources available for the study; the diversity of the currently enrolled students; the programs offered by competing institutions; and the relationship of the program and institution to the outside community. Also a part of the assessment context that should be outlined in writing are specific questions that need to be answered by the assessment in order to assist the program-planning process, the student subpopulations whose needs should be of differential concern in the assessment, and the types of needs of concern for each group.

Next, based on the preceding decisions, decisions should be made and recorded about available measures, indicators, and data sources that may have potential usefulness in the study; the alternative strategies open for consideration regarding analysis and interpretation of data; reporting procedures; and who should have what roles in the assessment. Included for each should be some probable cost figures for the alternatives.

Selecting Indicators, Measures, and Data-Gathering Sources. Selection of indicators, measures, and data collection methods depends on earlier decisions about what needs are of concern, and for whom. (For example, if older learners' needs are of concern, using an instrument not designed for or tested out on that subpopulation of students would be inappropriate.) However, some need areas that should commonly be examined have been proposed. For example, Segal and Sell (1978) suggest needs in terms of program description, purposes, content, methods, financial resources, physical resources, human resources, time resources, information resources, support functions, and outcomes.

Reliability and validity are primary criteria in making the selection. For any met and unmet needs, a number of relevant indicators, measures, and collection methods usually apply, some more reliable and valid than others. Furthermore, validity and reliability can vary for different subpopulations, as already discussed. Because one instrument and method may be weak where others are strong and vice versa, multiple measures and methods should be used whenever feasible. Not only can multiple measures and methods increase validity and reliability of the overall need picture shown, but they facilitate data collection from different student groups. The use of quick and inexpensive data collection methods, such as student self-report (which much research has found to be generally reliable and valid) and data collected for other purposes (secondary data), may provide a valuable supplement to data provided by more expensive and sophisticated data collected with tests and psychometric inventories. Furthermore, sometimes such data can be primary. Baird (1976), for example, has documented the importance of identifying and remedying what he called "brass tacks"—problems, disappointments, dissatisfactions, and complaints reported by students as irritating them. Reported achievements and satisfactions can also be important in identifying needs. A good example of using multiple data sources is the student assessment system developed at Empire State College (Palola and Lehmann, 1976). They supplemented standardized and local test data with student self-report, instructor observations, writing samples, and administrator observation.

Standardized paper-and-pencil instruments have often been used in needs assessments, but too often they do not get at the specific need of concern.

For reviews regarding their validity and reliability, see Buros (1978) and *Educational and Psychological Measurement, NCME Measurement in Education,* and *Measurement and Evaluation in Guidance.* An important fact to keep in mind with respect to reliability is that the instrument will be used to collect data for group rather than individual analysis. Therefore, instrument reliability coefficients as low as .6 may be adequate.

In order to have a paper-and-pencil instrument that measures specifically what is desired, one may have to construct one's own. Lang, Lehmann, and Mehrens (1967) found that revising items developed elsewhere takes less time, effort, and is less costly than developing new ones. However, one must be extremely careful to make certain they are revised appropriately for use in the current program and institution. Potential candidates for revision can be found in studies published or presented at conventions or in informal conversations with staff members of other institutions.

A variety of texts in instrument and item design have been published and can be helpful in developing one's own instruments. Choose carefully to select one most appropriate for the level of staff expertise available and for the purposes and coverage of the assessment to be conducted. For example, most focus on norm-referenced instruments and do not cover (or do not emphasize) criterion-referenced instruments, a form often appropriate for locally developed instruments. Gronlund (1973) provides excellent assistance for developing criterion-referenced instruments.

Usually those doing student need assessments have limited themselves to paper-and-pencil tests, questionnaires, and standard interviews. However, I found almost fifty additional data collection methods in the literature, many of which were reported to be practical, valid, reliable, and cost-effective for particular purposes and contexts (Lenning, 1978). Knapp and Sharon (1975) discuss a number of these nontraditional data collection methods. Webb and others (1966) discuss unobtrusive measures in depth. For example, such things as newspaper help wanted ads and employment agency openings could conceivably indicate personnel needs a program could help meet (Phillips and Tucker, 1975). Thelin (1976) points out that unobtrusive measures must be clustered and tied to a theoretical framework in order to be useful for assessment monitoring.

Concerning secondary data, although no time or money will be spent for their collection, such data can provide misleading indications of need if the secondary user of those data is not completely aware of the purposes for which they were collected, exactly how, when, and under what conditions, and the characteristics of the institution, agency, and/or program and staff for which they were collected. Boyd and Westphall (1972) discuss criteria for deciding when secondary data are appropriate for particular uses in particular situations and places and precautions for avoiding potential pitfalls when using them. Potentially useful secondary data concerning program needs include grouped frequency counts (separately for different target groups of students) from institutional and evaluation study records concerning attendance, complaints, amount of use and ratings of various support services, requests received for assistance of various kinds, interests and aspirations, course placement, job placement, student flow into different programs and courses, transfers to other programs within the institution, transfer to other institutions, dropouts and stopouts, patterns of courses taken by students from other majors and outside of this program by students majoring in it, and so forth. Similarly, pertinent data collected by other community agencies, organizations such as trade associations and policy research centers and by governmental agencies can provide supplemental evidence about program needs. For example, once the 1980 census is completed, much valuable evidence related to program needs will become available. What others have found in similar types of institutions, programs, and locales can also be helpful if care is taken to assess how the situation is different and the same there as compared to the needs assessment context here.

In most need studies, need surveys have been administered solely to the client groups whose needs were being assessed, in this case, enrolled students. The perceived needs as reported by others should also be examined and can provide helpful supplemental evidence of need. Potentially helpful are such groups as faculty, counselors, admissions personnel, community agency personnel (including high school staff), representatives of business and industry, parents and friends of current students, governmental personnel, community leaders, and community citizen subgroups. Concerning the last group mentioned, in one programmatic needs assessment on which I consulted, discussions with college staff revealed the local community contained a large Spanish-speaking population. Yet little prior thought had ever been given to whether such a group had *special* program needs the college could realistically help meet. Undoubtedly, a number of currently enrolled students were from that subpopulation, so this is not a case where only the needs of *prospective students* are of concern.

As is true of self-report, observations and reports by others need to be kept at a specific, concrete level; and clear language must be used in the questioning to minimize subjectivity and maximize reliability and validity. Narratives and portrayals can be useful in this respect and add "life" to the data. It is also good to get expressions of need from individuals with different points of view and assess discrepancy patterns and contexts for reasons those perceptions differ.

It should be apparent by now that there are primary criteria for indicator, measure, and data collection method selection other than just reliability and validity, including appropriateness to the analytical procedures and tests planned, ease of data collection, ease of scoring and tabulation, collection or analysis cost, and whether program planners and administrators will be able to understand readily the implications of such data (see the relationship of the data to their practical concerns).

Focusing specifically on data collection, the following content from a passage in another work by this author should be stressed (Lenning, 1980, p. 241):

> The proper measures and data collection methods are of no avail if one does not plan well and use care in the actual data collection. For example, a poorly worded cover letter sent out with a questionnaire can easily cut the response rate in half or more; so can sending students the questionnaire shortly before mid-term exams. Much time, money, and frustration can be saved if one takes pains to have well-designed interview forms, written instructions to read for test administrators, careful selection of samples, questionnaire items free of bias, well-designed pilot tests to try out procedures ahead of time, procedures for maximizing response rate (such as

showing the need for such data and promising—and giving—respondents feedback about the results), sensible coding and data-formatting rules, careful editing procedures, and so forth.

The importance of watching for evidence of important side needs not suggested by program goals was also mentioned earlier. A strategy to facilitate this is an initial wholistic and "broad-band" focus followed by a more in-depth and detailed "narrow-band" focus. In the broad-band phase, secondary data that are already available and questionnaire or interview data that have a gross level of focus on broad areas in terms of needs (plus broad, open-ended questions regarding needs) are examined to identify important need areas that call for a more detailed focus. Then detailed and in-depth needs data that can support need understanding and setting need priorities (including open-ended data at that level of detail) are collected for those need areas that seemed most important in the broad-band phase.

Analyzing, Interpreting, and Using Data. There are three desired goals in analyzing and interpreting needs sutdy data, as outlined by Beatty (1976, p. 25): identify needs, determine need priorities, and make diagnostic statements and inferences about need causes. All needs studies have attempted to identify needs, and a number of them have also attempted to set need priorities. Few studies have focused on formal attempts to relate causes to needs, however. This is probably one reason many up until now have perceived needs assessment not to impact programs that much. Such information can help one better understand needs, need relationships to one another, and the potential relationship of program aspects to needs. This type of information as an input to program planning can thus assist in generating a list of program planning alternatives.

If the "perceived amount of need" items on a "self-report" or "other report" questionnaire are scaled according to perceived importance, those items having an average score above a certain threshold level (that is logically or definitionally determined) can be considered to indicate needs; the score average rank can suggest need priorities; and score patterns and open-ended comments and clarification can help shed light on why some of the needs are present. This is a procedure Lenning and Cooper (1978) employed in assessing student information needs. If the students, their parents, counselors, and college staff all perceived the need similarly, the need was considered real and important.

Goodenough (1963, pp. 53–59) defined need reality as what an omniscient observer would perceive as the case. He discussed need from four perspectives, where the "client" in the case of this chapter is enrolled students and the "client's agents" could be students, parents, instructors, counselors, or the institutional or program staff. The four perspectives are agent's view with client's goals in mind, agent's view with self's goals in mind, client's view with agent's goals in mind, and client's view with self's goals in mind. Goodenough concluded that if all four perspectives agree a need is present and on what it is, we have much more assurance we are getting at a "real need" than if there is disagreement. Our assurance is increased even more if there is more than one agent-group of relevant, concerned people who have different kinds of perspectives, knowledge, and background experiences.

The questions raised by the planning committee members that need answers for program planning should in large part determine the analyses to be conducted. In addition, the analyses used should be understandable and meaningful to those who will use the information coming out of the analyses. Also, in doing the analyses, care must be taken that different scales are not erroneously equated and that hard and soft data are integrated in a way that does not mislead. For example, changing soft data to numbers can misrepresent the original picture if one is not careful. Subjective analysis ("eyeballing") and logic are often called for in comparing such data. Use of simple tabulations of frequencies and percentages, cross tabulations, matrices (for example, the Induced Course Load Matrix and the Induced Work Load Matrix or programming student distributions by year and student characteristics such as sex, by part-time versus full-time, and by class size) can be useful. Similarly, statistical tests separately on each scale, and across scales that are equivalent in nature, can be helpful in assessing amplitudes, amplitude discrepancies, and amplitude similarities. The use of profile and graphical analyses can highlight such patterns and make them more understandable.

Intercorrelations where there is continuous data or discrete data with a number of points on the scale, and correlations with other student or program factors, can suggest possible reasons for the needs. So can multivariate analyses, such as analysis of variance, analyses of covariance, and discriminant analysis. For student flow data, trend, ratio, or Markov chain analysis can be used.

Witkin (1975) discussed a number of specialized procedures that can be useful in needs data analysis. For ranking needs and identifying critical need areas, these included card sorts, the critical incident technique, Delphi analysis, magnitude estimate scaling, and a paired weighting procedure. She also proposed fault tree analysis (which makes use of an array of possible causative paths that are gradually eliminated from consideration by logical analysis) as a method that can be used to trace cause and effect and help understand the identified needs. Also potentially useful for such purposes are the "checklist" and "modus operandi" methods proposed by Scriven (1973) for use in evaluation. However, such methods and their applications need further development and refinement if needs assessment is to reach its maximum desired potential.

Costs and ease of practice are also considerations in selecting analyses. The least expensive and simplest methods that will give the information and analytical power needed should be chosen over more complex, oversophisticated, and costly methods. In some cases, the most sophisticated and costly method will be needed, however, in order for the needs assessment study to have its desired impact. Common sense related to knowledge about what alternative methods can deliver and what the decision makers need must make the determination.

Once the analyses are completed, interpretations of the results must be made and applied to planning for new programs or revised programs in terms of program goals, priorities, strategies, procedures, policies, publicity, and so forth. (Needs assessment results can also provide information that is useful in justifying the need for an increase in resources.) However, the interpretation is a judgment matter and is not necessarily the same for different people. According to McMahon (1970), this judgment should come out of an agreement between the educator (program planner) and the client (student). Lenning and others (1979) claim the need must be judged by a relevant person or group using multiple, objective criteria that have been agreed on. Perhaps what is most desirable is a judgments team approach, as is often used in evaluation. The planning team, with its representatives of concerned groups, is a logical choice for such a judgments team. Just because an unmet need is judged to be most important to meet does not necessarily mean plans to fulfill that need should have priority over other program plans, although it often will. It may be too costly to try and meet that need; certain people may object to such an effort; or other interfering factors may be noticed.

Once the results, interpretations, and judgments coming from the needs assessment are developed and refined, they need to be fed effectively into the program planning process. The reports can be either written or oral (preferably both) and as brief and to the point as possible. They may be technical or non-technical and involve such communication aids as graphics, scenarios, case examples, or multimedia presentations. Their format and content should be tailored to the characteristics, problems, issues, and information needs pertinent for the decision makers at whom the report is aimed. In many cases, it will be preferable to send different reports to different people. They must be read and be fully meaningful to each person if the needs assessment is to have significant impact on program planning.

Much potentially useful information relating to the assessment of current student needs and demands for program development or restructuring has been presented in this chapter. However, it should be emphasized that the thorough coverage presented here is an ideal. Fiscal resources, time, staff expertise, and political considerations will normally not allow application of all the strategies, procedures, and methods discussed. The reader must pick and choose those concepts and applications that will serve best for his or her particular situation. As was made clear, however, there are a few general principles that should apply for all, such as getting planning involvement and representation from the different data users, client groups, and other concerned groups and areas.

Bibliographical Essay

Those desiring additional, in-depth information on the topic of needs assessment have a number of resources from which to choose. Witkin (1975) provides a thorough review of the literature. Resulting from a project funded by the National Institute of Education, it focuses mostly on program needs assessment in elementary and secondary education; but few needs assessment developments had occurred prior to this time in higher education. It is a well-done review that summarizes and compares the major models developed until that time, and it presents many useful and interesting techniques and methodologies. Included is an extensive discussion of methods for analyzing cause and effect (for example, fault tree analysis).

A provocative think piece about needs assessment is presented by Scriven (1977) in the newsletter of the Evaluation Network, a new membership organization devoted to sharing new developments and happenings throughout the field of evaluation. Scriven raises a number of interesting points in addition to those emphasized in this chapter.

Coffing and Hutchinson (1974) were possibly the first methodologists to question formally the appropriateness of the discrepancy model of needs assessment. They present a viable alternative model, including guidelines and procedures for implementation.

Lenning and others (1979) developed a comprehensive review of the needs assessment literature, and it is that document upon which this chapter is based. There are two parts to the manuscript, one containing chapters that are conceptual in nature and the second providing procedures and guidelines for conducting the various kinds and aspects of needs assessment in postsecondary education. It goes into depth concerning each of the topics introduced here and covers a number of types of needs assessment outside the scope of this chapter. Current plans are to revise and make this manuscript part of a larger document to be published in late 1980 or early 1981. For information, contact Oscar T. Lenning, NCHEMS, P.O. Drawer P, Boulder, Colorado 80302.

Under contract with the College Entrance Examination Board (CEEB) Future Directions for a Learning Society project, Segal and Sell (1978) of the NCHEMS staff developed a preliminary model for a college to use in assessing community educational needs (as embodied especially in the needs of adult learners) called the Needs Assessment Information System. This system was based on a review of the literature and of over a hundred instruments being used in different parts of the country as identified in a survey conducted as part of the project. It is built around three aspects of needs assessment perceived to be most critical to a postsecondary education institution (each of which consists of several major components): learner assessment, community assessment, and provider assessment. Information is provided about a variety of items of information, sources of information, and data collection, analysis, reporting, and use. CEEB has obtained a grant from the Fund for the Improvement of Postsecondary Education to develop and pilot test questionnaires and refine the system and will then presumably publish materials that describe the system and its implementation. For information, contact William Van Dusen, College Entrance Examination Board, P.O. Box 141, Brookdale, California 95007.

References

Anderson, S. B., Ball, S., Murphy, R. T., and Associates. *Encyclopedia of Educational Evaluation: Concepts and Techniques for Evaluating Education and Training Programs.* San Francisco: Jossey-Bass, 1975.

Aulepp, L., and Delworth, U. *Training Manual for an Ecosystem Model: Assisting and Designing Campus Environments.* Boulder, Colo.: Western Interstate Commission on Higher Education, 1976.

Baird, L. L. "Structuring the Environment to Improve Outcomes." In O. T. Lenning (Ed.), *New Directions for Higher Education: Improving Educational Outcomes,* no. 16. San Francisco: Jossey-Bass, 1976.

Banning, H., and Kaiser, L. "An Ecological Perspective and Model for Campus Design." *Personnel and Guidance Journal,* 1974, *52,* 370–375.

Beatty, P. T. "A Process Model for the Development of an Information Base for Community Needs Assessment: A Guide for Practitioners." Paper presented at annual meeting of the Adult Education Research Conference, Toronto, April 1976. (ERIC Document Reproduction Service, ED 128 616.)

Bowers and Associates. *A Guide to Needs Assessment in Community Education.* Washington, D.C.: U.S. Government Printing Office, 1976.

Boyd, H. W., and Westphall, R. *Marketing Research.* (3rd ed.) Homewood, Ill.: Irwin, 1972.

Bradshaw, J. "The Concept of Social Need." *New Society,* 30 March 1972, pp. 640–643.

Buros, O. K. (Ed.) *The Eighth Mental Measurements Yearbook.* Vols. 1 and 2. Highland Park, N.J.: Gryphon Press, 1978.

Burton, J. K., and Merrill, P. F. "Needs Assessment: Goals, Needs, and Priorities." Unpublished paper. Lincoln, Nebr.: University of Mid-America, 1977.

Campbell, V. N., and Markle, D. G. *Identifying and Formulating Educational Problems.* Palo Alto, Calif.: American Institute for Research, 1967. (ERIC Document Reproduction Service, ED 030 985.)

Chickering, A. W. *Education and Identity.* San Francisco: Jossey-Bass, 1969.

Coffing, R T., and Hutchinson, T. E. "Needs Analysis Methodology: A Prescriptive Set of Rules and Procedures for Identifying, Defining, and Measuring Needs." Paper presented at annual convention of the American Educational Research Association, Chicago, April 1974. (ERIC Document Reproduction Service, ED 095 654.)

Conrad, C. "University Goals: An Operative Approach." *Journal of Higher Education,* 1974, *45,* 505–515.

Cronbach, L. J. *Educational Psychology.* (2nd ed.) New York: Harcourt Brace Jovanovich, 1963.

English, F. W., and Kaufman, R. A. *Needs Assessment: A Focus for Curriculum Development.* Washington, D.C.: Association for Supervision and Curriculum Development, 1975. (ERIC Document Reproduction Service, ED 107 619.)

Forbes, M. S. "Fact and Comment." *Forbes,* 1979, *124,* 31–33.

Gill, S. J., and Fruehling, J. A. "Needs Assessment and the Design of Service Delivery Systems." *Journal of College Student Personnel,* 1979, *20,* 322–328.

Goodenough, W. H. "Wants and Needs." In W. H. Goodenough (Ed.), *Cooperation and Change: An Anthropological Approach to Community Development.* New York: Russell Sage Foundation, 1963.

Gronlund, N. E. *Preparing Criterion-Referenced Tests for Classroom Instruction.* New York: Macmillan, 1973.

Groves, D. L., Kahalas, H., and Erickson, D.L. "A Suggested Modification to Maslow's Need Hierarchy." *Social Behavior and Personality,* 1975, *3,* 65–69.

Havighurst, R. J. *Developmental Tasks and Education.* New York: McKay, 1952.

Hecht, A. R. "A Summary of the Moraine Valley Community College Evaluation System." Unpublished paper. Palos Hills, Ill.: Moraine Valley Community College, 1977.

Kaufman, R. A. *Educational System Planning.* Englewood Cliffs, N.J.: Prentice-Hall, 1972.

Kaufman, R. A., Corrigan, R. E., and Johnson, D. W. "Towards Educational Responsiveness to Society's Needs: A Tentative Utility Model." *Journal of Socio-Economic Planning Science,* 1969, *3,* 151–157.

Knapp, J., and Sharon, A. S. *A Compendium of Assessment Techniques.* Princeton, N.J.: Educational Testing Service, 1975.

Lang, A., Lehmann, I. J., and Mehrens, W. A. "Using Item Analysis to Improve Tests." *Journal of Educational Measurement,* 1967, *4,* 65–68.

Lenning, O. T. (Ed.). *New Directions for Higher Education: Improving Educational Outcomes,* no. 16. San Francisco: Jossey-Bass, 1976.

Lenning, O. T. *Previous Attempts to Structure Educational Outcomes and Outcome-Related Concepts: A Compilation and Review of the Literature.* Boulder, Colo.: National Center for Higher Education Management Systems, 1977a.

Lenning, O. T. "Putting Outcomes Measurement into Context: The Outcomes Program at NCHEMS." Paper presented at annual conference of the North Central Region AERA Special Interest Group for Community/Junior College Research, Columbus, Ohio, July 1977b.

Lenning, O. T. "Assessing Student Educational Progress." *ERIC/Higher Education Research Currents,* April 1978. In *AAHE College and University Bulletin, 1978, 30,* 3–6.

Lenning, O. T., and Cooper, E. M. *Guidebook for Colleges and Universities: Presenting Information to Prospective Students.* Boulder, Colo.: National Center for Higher Education Management Systems, 1978.

Lenning, O. T., and McAleenan, A. C. "Needs Assessment in Student Affairs." In G. Kuh (Ed.), *Evaluation in Student Affairs.* Washington, D.C.: American College Personnel Association, 1979.

Lenning, O. T., and others. *A Structure for the Outcomes of Postsecondary Education.* Boulder, Colo.: National Center for Higher Education Management Systems, 1977.

Lenning, O. T. "Assessment and Evaluation." In U. Delworth and G. R. Hanson (Eds.) *Student Services: A Handbook for the Profession.* San Francisco: Jossey-Bass, 1980.

Lenning, O. T., and others. "Identifying and Assessing Needs in Postsecondary Education: A Review and Synthesis of the Literature." Unpublished manuscript. Boulder, Colo.: National Center for Higher Education Management Systems, 1979.

McMahon, E. C. *Needs—of People and Their Communities—and the Adult Educator: A Review of the Literature of Need Determination.* Syracuse, N.Y.: ERIC Clearinghouse on Adult Education, 1970. (ERIC Document Reproduction Service, ED 038 551.)

Maslow, A. H. *Motivation and Personality.* (2nd ed.) New York: Harper & Row, 1970.

Micek, S. S., and Arney, W. R. "Inventory of Institutional Environment Variables and Measures." Unpublished paper. Boulder, Colo.: National Center for Higher Education Management Systems, 1974.

Monette, J. L. "The Concept of Educational Need: An Analysis of Selected Literature." *Adult Education,* 1977, *27,* 116–127.

Mooney, R. L., and Gordon, L. V. *Mooney Problem Check List Manuals.* New York: Psychological Corporation, 1950.

Murray, H. A. "Proposals for a Theory of Personality." In H. A. Murray and others (Eds.), *Explorations in Personality: A Clinical and Experimental Study of Fifty Men of College Age.* New York: Oxford University Press, 1938.

Pagels, C. F. "The Development of a Process for Determining Specific Criteria for a Student Needs Based Curriculum." Unpublished doctoral dissertation, University of Virginia, 1973. *Dissertation Abstracts International,* 1974, *34,* 6368-A.

Palola, E. G., and Lehmann, T. "Student Outcomes and Institutional Decision

Making with PERC." In O. T. Lenning (Ed.), *New Directions for Higher Education: Improving Educational Outcomes,* no. 16. San Francisco: Jossey-Bass, 1976.

Parsons, T. *The Social System.* New York: Free Press, 1951.

Payne, D. A. *The Assessment of Learning: Cognitive and Affective.* Lexington, Mass.: Heath, 1974.

Phillips, H. A., and Tucker, K. "Needs Assessment: Importance in Planning, Present Status, [and] Needs Assessment and Long Range Planning." Paper presented at annual meeting of the Southern Association of Community and Junior Colleges, Atlanta, December 1975. (ERIC Document Reproduction Service, ED 133 012.)

Rankin, G. E. "Developing a Model for Assessment of Student Personnel Outcomes." Paper presented at annual convention of the American Educational Research Association, San Francisco, April 1976.

Scriven, M. "Evaluation Perspectives and Procedures." Draft for a volume in the AERA series on educational evaluation, 1973.

Scriven, M. "Special Feature: Needs Assessment." *Evaluation News,* 1977, *1,* 25–88.

Segal, J. S., and Sell, G. R. "Needs Assessment Information System." Unpublished manuscript. Boulder, Colo.: National Center for Higher Education Management Systems, 1978.

Taber, T. D., and Hackman, J. D. "Dimensions of Undergraduate College Performance." *Journal of Applied Psychology,* 1976, *61,* 546–558.

Taylor, E. N., Vineberg, R., and Gaffard. *Procedures for Surveying School Problems: Some Individual, Group, and System Indicators.* Alexandria, Va.: Human Resources Research Organization, 1974.

Thelin, J. R. "Beyond the Faculty Model: New Strategies for Institutional Evaluation." *College and University,* 1976, *51,* 161–164.

Webb, E. J., and others. *Unobtrusive Measures: Nonreactive Research in the Social Sciences.* Chicago: Rand McNally, 1966.

Witkin, B. R. *An Analysis of Needs Assessment Techniques for Educational Planning at State, Intermediate, and District Levels.* Hayward, Calif.: Office of the Alameda County Superintendent of Schools, 1975. (ERIC Document Reproduction Service, ED 108 370.)

14

Jack Lindquist

Improving the Teaching-Learning Environment

The traditional college environment often made academic learning hard enough: dorm noise, fraternity-sorority rites, athletic games, the strains of late adolescent transitions in self-concept and peer relations, pool and television and pin-ball. Study always has had plenty of competition on most campuses. The contemporary college environment, more common to the sprawling state university or community college than to the private liberal arts college, adds new competition. Commuter traffic, endless parking lots, anonymity in a sea of students, family and job pressures, midlife personal transitions, and worries about being black or brown in a white culture are some of the ingredients in the "new" student's learning environment.

For the teacher, there have always been crowded offices, pressures to publish, administrative red tape and committee tedium, expectations to advise students and teach well without support or reward for either, and worries about personal life and career. Now many professors work amid job cuts, union strikes, increasing teaching loads (still without much payoff for teaching *well*), decreasing public respect, salaries losing ground to inflation, and the same commuting and parking problems students face.

These environmental pressures on college learners and teachers are not likely to go away. Most pundits predict exacerbation of such strains. The ivory tower of quiet contemplation is an unlikely dream. But most teaching-learning environments can, perhaps must, be strengthened. Good teaching and effective learning depend on such improvements. This chapter presents a strategy for strengthening the system of supports students and teachers need in order to succeed at higher learning.

A Five-Factor Strategy

In the Strategies for Change Project and the thousands of planned change studies that preceded it, five factors, ingredients in organizational improvement and renewal, stood out (Lindquist, 1978c). One is a skillful and energetic *force* for learning and teaching (such as a growing leadership group committed to and skillful in facilitating improvement and increasing time, money, and influence devoted to improvement). Second is a *linkage* of learners and teachers to the resources (institutional members and other persons, places, and information) required to carry out their work. Third, the organization and its members must have *openness* to new ways to accomplish learning and teaching goals (such as an increased degree of active seeking, listening, and trying new information and behaviors). *Ownership* of education must be in the hands of those students and faculty engaged in it as well as in the hands of those administrators held responsible and those funders who pay the bills. Those who must support and implement improvements must believe they are the solutions to problems encountered in pursuit of educational goals. Fifth, learners and teachers must receive *rewards* (personal, professional, subgroup, and institutional) for their best efforts.

A quick glance at normal teaching-learning conditions can illustrate the importance—and absence—of these factors. What is the active force encouraging effective teaching and learning in many colleges? There may be a small circle of peers who support one's efforts to learn or teach well, sometimes a dean who cares, if he or she only has the time to do something about it, maybe an adviser or short orientation program that helps a student through the curricular maze, perhaps a tiny faculty development program, or possibly occasional institutional research reports on student demographics. But rarely is there a force for teaching to rival the disciplinary force for research or a force for learning to rival football and "Thank God It's Friday." Industry invests 8 to 12 percent of its operating budget in staff and program improvement, but colleges are doing well to invest 1 percent. The collegiate force for improving learning and teaching, where it exists, usually is an overtime effort whose major product is burnout.

Most professors teach in isolation from one another and from such useful information as data on their students or news of alternative ways to teach. Most students, pulled apart by competition and commuting masses, learn in a similar isolation from one another or from useful information on how they might learn more effectively. The "teaching-learning *community*" is rarely more than a cynic's lament. Both teachers and students are bound by tradition and red tape. Neither is likely even to see, let alone try, alternatives to traditional teaching-learning models, no matter how unproductive the traditional methods may be.

Students enjoy some ownership over their learning by their relative freedom to choose one course of study or another; but rarely do they have much say over the particular learning objectives and approaches to the subjects they pick. Faculty own these. Once a student picks a major, prescription replaces choice. Meanwhile, faculty find that many teaching decisions really are owned by the department, college, or accrediting association. You are free to teach as you please as long as you teach as others please.

As for rewards, the most marvelous student adviser is likely to have a tenure committee that does not even weigh advising except to determine if the teacher was or was not accessible to advisees. Good teaching may count no more than barely adequate teaching. No extra compensation is likely for carrying an extra-heavy advising or teaching load. Even personal thanks from peers and supervisor for a job well done are hard to come by.

The student who is effective at academic performance can garner high grades, scholarships, and a job. But performance rather than learning is being rewarded here. And the student who tries hard, makes progress, but does not match top performers often goes unnoticed. An okay on the margin of a paper, acceptance into a third-choice job, and peer or family comments that "at least he's trying" become the food of self-esteem.

How can these constraints be overcome? And what role can institutional research and planning specialists play in the process? Consider each of these five factors in turn.

Building a Force for Effective Learning and Teaching

Star Wars provided me a name for a simple but powerful notion. Without an active, skillful "Force" for improving learning and teaching, the inertia of the status quo will win the day. To build such a force, start by taking inventory. Most campuses are full of *potential* forces for improvement. There are concerned staff and students, often identified by their volunteering for activities related to teaching improvement or by formal recognition for excellence in teaching or learning. Most faculty and administrative job descriptions include the expectation that some time will be given to curricular and teaching improvement. There is always a curriculum committee around and usually an educational policies council. Offices for professional development exist on most larger campuses. Start by listing those persons, governance bodies, and offices already or potentially committed to the improvement of learning.

There are several ways to mobilize this force. One is the self-study, for accreditation or other purposes. It brings the potential force together to accomplish a short-term task. If its participants find the work enjoyable, if they learn things useful to them, if they accomplish something, and if they strengthen their skills in facilitating institutional self-examination and renewal, a foundation is established. Thus, one objective of self-studies and of institutional research staff active in them should be creation of a skillful force for continued self-study.

Special projects to develop and test new curricula can be approached in similar fashion so that one of their outcomes is a group skilled at designing and implementing curriculum in general. Faculty development activities can also be aimed both at meeting immediate faculty needs and at building a force for improved teaching. For example, Northeastern Illinois University and Los Medanos Community College have "minigrant" programs in faculty development. This small grant strategy is fairly common (Centra, 1976). It usually assists the grantee in solving one particular problem, but it rarely has broader, enduring impact. The force is quickly dissipated. But Northeastern Illinois and Los Medanos ask each grantee, or fellow, to join other fellows in a seminar on the institution's mission and students and on alternative ways to serve diverse learners. A consequence of this seminar is that fellows begin to develop bonds with other faculty who care about learning; they learn about educational challenges beyond their own courses; and they become knowledgeable about alternatives to the status quo. At Northeastern Illinois these fellows become members of an association, so their connection to others concerned with teaching improvement does not end with the minigrant. About 20 percent of the faculty now are members.

Other examples emerge from the Strategies for Change Project (Lindquist, 1978c). At Hartwick College, a voluntary committee on institutional research spent three years meeting one Saturday a month to share studies and plan actions to stimulate college follow-up on teaching-learning problems revealed by those studies. Eventually, a third of the faculty was involved. At the University of South Carolina, a young psychology professor got a few friends together at his house prior to each faculty senate meeting to discuss how they might obtain positive votes on issues affecting undergraduate education. By seeking out opinion leaders as suggested by diffusion research (Rogers and Shoemaker, 1971), they soon had a large, potent group that managed to get student-oriented faculty into the chairs of nearly every senate committee. Along the way, both groups grew in interpersonal support for one another and in the knowledge and skills needed to lead teaching improvement efforts.

Not since the late 1960s have we had strong student forces for teaching improvement; but such a force can be rebuilt. Students can be involved in faculty governance and trained for the role so they can be informed and skilled participants. Students can be included in ad hoc teams or teaching improvement workshops. Students in freshman seminars can be developed into a support group for one another's learning. Professors can be assisted in generating such peer support systems in larger classes. In residence halls, care can be taken to involve students in building a learning community. It is surprising that such efforts to build a student force for learning are so limited, fragmented, or relegated to student services staff (who are usually good at it and care about it but who are separated from the academic side of things).

Linking Campus Members to Print, People, and Programs

One reason American academic disciplines are front-runners is they have sophisticated networks connecting members to each other (the "invisible college" phenomenon) and to the latest information in the field. Data from Exhibit 1 indicate that a sizable percentage of university faculty seem well linked by journals, conferences, and personal interaction with people in their field.

Exhibit 1 offers evidence of much weaker connection between college staffs and the journals, conferences, and conversations that might make them

Exhibit 1. Linkage to Disciplinary versus Teaching-Learning Information

Disciplinary Linkage			*Teaching-Learning Linkage*		
To how many academic or professional journals do you subscribe?			To how many journals do you subscribe that deal primarily with teaching methods, aids, improving teaching or higher education in general?		
	Large School	Small School			
3 or more (%)*	81.1	60.4		Large School	Small School
How many regional or national conventions of your discipline have you attended in the past two years?			3 or more (%)	16.1	14.0
	Large School	Small School	How many regional or national conventions devoted to issues of teaching, learning or higher education have you attended in the past two years?		
2 or more (%)*	69.3	52.6		Large School	Small School
How often do you read academic or professional journals in or related to your field of competence?			2 or more (%)	33.3	28.1
	Large School	Small School	How often do you read academic or professional journals dealing with teaching, learning, or higher education?		
Regularly (%)*	86.2	68.4		Large School	Small School
I am in communication with people in my academic specialty in other institutions.			Regularly (%)	32.8	27.6
	Large School	Small School	I am in communication with colleagues in other institutions about new teaching methods, techniques and aids.		
Frequently (%)*	62.3	50.4		Large School	Small School
I talk with people at my institution about developments, techniques, findings and theories in my own discipline.			Frequently (%)	31.6	28.3
	Large School	Small School	I talk with people at my institution about new teaching methods, techniques, aids and theories.		
Frequently (%)*	71.2	55.7		Large School	Small School
			Frequently (%)	53.5	50.4

*Differences are significant at the .05 level, symmetric test.
Large School, N = 230
Small School, N = 255
Source: Lindquist, 1978c; based on "Professional Development Questionnaire." In W. Bergquist and S. Phillips, *Handbook for Faculty Development.* Vol 2. Washington, D.C.: Council for the Advancement of Small Colleges, 1977, pp. 31-43.

tional studies tell us institutions whose members do not have ready ties to information regarding "performance gaps" and "potential solutions" to those gaps are not likely to have motivation to improve (Zaltman, Duncan, and Holbeck, 1973).

One way the teaching-learning linkage can be strengthened is to create an *informed* and *interacting* force and connect its members to local studies of learners and teachers, of learning and teaching, and of the outcomes for both learners and teachers. Connect them to relevant theory. Introduce them to innovative practices in other departments or other institutions by holding local retreats and by sending them not just to disciplinary conferences but to teaching-learning workshops and to other campuses.

An example is my Institute for Academic Improvement, but it could be Jerry Gaff's General Education Models Project or a dozen others. Within the institute, faculty-administrative-student teams from thirteen colleges and universities engage in a project called Higher Learning for Diverse Adults or HiLDA. Initially, each team examines its adult learners and its institution's effectiveness in serving them. Teams are encouraged to involve other campus members in these studies so many may learn. Teams are assisted in conducting their own diagnoses to strengthen local skill in doing such work. Then, in multiinstitutional workshops and seminars, team members are introduced to adult learning theory, to diverse ways to teach diverse adults, and to colleagues struggling with similar problems on other campuses. They in effect become cosmopolitans about the field of adult learning and in turn put on local workshops to share all this information with colleagues. A crucial function of these local and national workshops is to break into the inertia of crowded schedules, provide time together and new information, without which linkage is unlikely.

In all this linking, a key role is that of the "reticulist" or networker, essentially, the agriculture extension agent of teaching and learning (Sarason and Lorentz, 1979). This person devotes much time just to linking person to person, person to print, and person to program. In the case of HiLDA, each team has a resource person, one of whose functions is to link members to needed information on teaching-learning theory and practice. Another function is to help them learn to be reticulists for their colleagues. Although HiLDA is an interinstitutional project, there is no reason the model will not work as an intrainstitutional project, say, with a number of departmental teams assisted in their own teaching improvement but brought together by institutionwide workshops and seminars.

There are several promising approaches to student linkage for learning. The freshman seminar or senior capstone course brings students together as a support and sharing group regarding their learning. A campus ombudsman, not just to resolve regulatory squabbles but to link students to learning resources, becomes the student's reticulist. Mentors play that role in individualized education, as do brokers in student brokering services. Advisers could play such a role if trained and supported for doing it. Linkage sounds as easy as saying, "Why not get together with so-and-so?"; but it is a far more complicated task of getting to know one's "client," getting to know a wide range of resources, and becoming highly skillful at actually getting one's client and so-and-so together at the right time in the right way.

Peer teaching is another excellent way to link students to one another for learning. Research on peer teaching supports its effectiveness (McNall, 1975). Residential colleges or intensive, short-term residences (as in weekend colleges) also provide settings and opportunities to create strong student-to-student and student-to-professor links (Gaff and others, 1970). Learning resource center staffs, if active reticulists, can connect students not only to print and technological resources in the resource center but to community tutors, to field study sites, to community educational programs, and to public television. Student services staffs can connect students to cultural and recreational opportunities on campus and off, to family and employer, and to community services and churches.

In all these instances, three points become clear. First, colleges must support active, not reactive, networkers. Second, networkers must range far beyond traditional connections (usually student to library, course, and campus events) if the full range of learning resources is to be tapped. Third, linkage is at base interpersonal, a human bond. Because of their own expertise, planners and institutional research specialists can aid the creation and constant renewal of human support systems among students, among staff, between the two, and between both and the wider community of helpful people, print, and practices.

Opening the Environment

Havelock and his associates found *active* openness, a reaching out to new views, new information, and new practices, a vital factor in successful planned change (Havelock and others, 1971). Unfortunately, our positions as professors and administrators press us to act the knower, not the seeker. "I don't know" is an answer the espoused expert has trouble saying. But open inquiry is a very respectable academic norm and one that should characterize the teaching-learning environment. One way to accomplish this is well grounded in developmental learning theory (Dewey, 1938): Encourage active inquiry and problem solving as a major learning mode. Science laboratories, classroom task groups, field study, exams that ask students to go find the answer or to solve problems, class discussions that stress open listening by teacher and student, and advising systems that ask students to explore and formulate their own degree programs are a few of the ways active inquiry can supplement or replace passive absorption of didacticism as "higher" learning. Approaches to teaching and curriculum improvement that involve faculty as active problem solvers, not passive recipients of a small committee's thinking or of some faculty development expert's advice, encourage openness. Such approaches are, not surprisingly, found most useful by those who engage in faculty and curriculum development (Lindquist, 1978a).

Persuasion research tells us that openness is much aided if it is interpersonal and informal over enough time to move beyond wariness (Rosnow and Robinson, 1967). We practice lectures, senate "discussions" among seventy orators, presidential addresses, and one-hour committee or class sessions. Such forms of communication can work—but rarely do. Some colleges therefore encourage "buzz groups" and other ways to break lecture or senate discussions down to size. They use all-day committee meetings once a month and find far more work gets done than in four weekly meetings. Those who teach in weekend college or other short, intensive residency formats similarly find that much more active interaction can be fostered when people are together over several days than when they meet in short sessions over several weeks. Faculty and student retreats create the same sense of close and open community when done well.

Communication research also tells us observability and trialability enhance openness: "I'll believe it when it works for me " (Lindquist, 1980). Classroom demonstrations and simulations are designed to address these factors. The workshop on, say, contract learning in which participants see real contracts in their field and actually develop learning contracts with one another is more likely to create openness to that innovation than one relying on lectures and discussions. The site visit or faculty exchange on the teacher side and the field study or internship on the student side represent seeing and doing as routes to openness.

There are other factors likely to increase chances that faculty members and students will become open to teaching and learning. Messages, whether teachers' to students or committees' to senates, need to be couched in terms *compatible* with the concerns and norms of the particular student or faculty audience.

Faculty members are no different from students in expecting that what is proposed to them relates to their interests and is presented in a language and style with which they feel comfortable.

Complexity and *divisibility* are important factors. Frustrating as it may be to a curriculum committee that has developed a comprehensive general education model or a professor who wishes to teach an elaborate conceptual model, confusion, anxiety, and resistance are common reactions to highly complex messages. The task is not just to put one's message in clear, easy to understand terms; it is also to introduce one notion at a time (a familiar teaching strategy) in an easy to accept sequence. Try learning contracts for just one assignment for a few students this term. Next term, try it with all students for the term project. Third term, try it for the whole course.

Another route to openness relates to linkage: *relative advantages.* Whether the issue is something you want students to learn or something you want colleagues to adopt, spell out how your idea will be advantageous to your audience's concerns for security, status, esteem, and higher needs. Keep in mind that there is no good reason to expect your colleagues to be any more enthusiastic than your students or to exert serious effort to learn some new thing only because it is abstractly "good" for them.

Openness, however, is not just a strategy; it is an attitude and skill. A good place to start it is among your improvement force, perhaps by listening exercises ("I think you said"), role playing in which you step into the shoes of someone you find it hard to be open toward, or creative problem-solving exercises in which you must say what is helpful to you in the last person's remarks before you make that telling transition, "that's all very well, *but.* . . ."

Pilot projects are good strategies to obtain approval of new teaching-learning approaches, for authorities only need to sanction a small, short-term deviation from the status quo. Then they will, by seeing and doing the pilot, be able to judge its worth for continuation or large-scale implementation. Rarely, however, is a pilot really open. Rather, its implementors are so busy making it work, while others are equally busy doing other things, that it functions in isolation. The few implementors get to see it and do it; and if the innovation is a good one, they get hooked. But unless they systematically lure others over to watch the pilot or try a small part of it, chances are the pilot will remain a small program at best and be cut when funds become scarce. But there are antidotes. Set up an advisory committee of opinion leaders among your larger audience. Invite key persons to watch or participate in small ways. Hold workshops in which pilot program teachers and learners share their experiences. Circuit ride to share the program with key faculty or administration and to seek their advice. Conduct careful evaluations designed and analyzed with expert evaluators from your audience, and share those data interpersonally. In all these interactions, practice openness. Move toward criticisms and explore with critics ways to make the pilot more effective. There is no better place to start openness than with yourself.

Strengthening Ownership Among Learners and Teachers

Just as the force merges into linkage and linkage merges into openness, so openness merges into ownership. By opening the committee or pilot to outside people, ownership of the work of such groups also broadens. Others begin to say,

"That is *our* solution to *our* concerns in pursuit of *our* goals." The need for own-ership of whatever is developed in college learning and teaching is understand-able. People are rarely as committed to someone else's solutions to their prob-lems as to their own; someone else rarely is as sensitive to and knowledgeable about a particular person's situation as is that person. The bureaucratic norm, however, is that "higher" people are the primary owners of decisions affecting "lower" people. Democratic norms hold the opposite assumption, and collegial norms say the experts should decide for the rest of us. So deans decide profes-sors' fates and professors decide students' fates, or unions decide, or the faculty senate decides. In such instances, only one of the groups involved really owns the decision.

A fourth norm says *we* should decide, together. We call it "collaboration." We espouse it but rarely practice it, for it is very difficult. It must bring together the bureaucratic norm (those with formal authority decide), the democratic norm (those affected decide), and the collegial norm (those most expert decide). Yet it is the most powerful norm because it includes ownership among the three parties generally needed to carry out effective teaching and learning: the au-thorities, the experts, and those who do the work (the teachers and learners).

The key to strengthening collaborative ownership is working *with* (Lindquist, 1978b). In developing a new curricular proposal or long-range plan, a committee needs to work with the faculty, administration, and students whose understanding and commitment will be needed to implement the plan. In de-veloping a course, a faculty member needs to work with students. "Working with" is not a synonym for "abdicating to." Someone must take the lead, the initiative, if anything is to happen. Rather, it means concerns and ideas of au-thorities, experts, and those potentially affected are sought and used by those who take the initiative in improving teaching and learning. It means professors do not design courses and teach them whether or not they fit the students. It means committees do not develop proposals in isolation and then present them. It means institutional researchers ask their audience what should be studied and how and then do the analysis with, not for, that audience in the action-research way (Buhl and Lindquist, 1979). It means the force is well tempered by linkage and openness.

Vital to broad ownership of teaching-learning goals, needs, and solutions can be a collaborative self-study process. Through periodical surveys and inter-views, students, faculty, staff, and administration are asked what they hope to accomplish in learning and teaching. These people then are brought together to analyze data and identify common goals. Similar inquiry and collaborative analysis concern how well we are doing in meeting common goals, how well pro-fessors are teaching or advising, students are studying or behaving in and out of class, staff and administrators are contributing to learning and teaching, and these processes are working in pursuit of what goals for whom.

Typical institutional research into such questions is not collaborative at all. The researchers or a few higher ups decide what to ask, how to ask it, and what the resulting data say. Then they report *their* findings, not ours. The upshot is that we are uninterested or distrustful. These are not our kind of evidence about our concerns. Our thinking did not go into the analysis. And besides, those in-stitutional researchers are probably under the president's thumb.

Many planning models similarly are made "on high," though decision makers, like institutional researchers, gather our "input" into their thinking and deciding. Unless institutional researchers and planners learn how to do their important work with resident authorities, experts, and affected students as well as staff, their work just is not going to be important. It will be one-way communication to deaf ears.

Two examples illustrate ownership strategies. One is the work of a small, ad hoc team at a large university. The team wanted to get university members to examine systematically their goals for undergraduate education and then to work on areas needing emphasis. Team members used the Institutional Goals Inventory (IGI), for its items seemed relevant and it asks respondents to indicate what *is* and what *should be* the emphasis on each goal. To get the university faculty interested, the team turned to the members of the academic planning committee, composed of professors elected by faculty and administrators appointed by, and including, the president. They asked this committee to complete the IGI. They then scored the responses and shared them with the committee. Committee members got excited about the quick focus and insight this exercise provided. The team then asked the planning committee if it would sponsor the faculty senate's completing the instrument. Once the senate went through the exercise and found it useful, it was asked to sponsor the whole faculty's completing the IGI.

Eventually, thirteen hundred faculty members completed the instrument. Then the team coordinated, and the planning committee led, two eight-hour workshops (Friday afternoon and Saturday morning) during which participants (everyone invited, key people urged to come) studied the results in small, peer-assisted groups. Each group identified a few teaching-learning problems, which were then quickly synthesized into four categories. Participants were asked to volunteer whatever time they could spare (even one hour) to follow up on improvement issues of concern to them. The planning committee then encouraged and facilitated initiatives to resolve these problems wherever they arose in the university. In short, participant ownership was the first principle throughout this process.

An illustration of learner ownership is the individualized degree program and learning contract. In such programs, faculty and administration set general areas of study and minimal achievement standards. The particulars of student learning programs are then negotiated with the students themselves so that what is studied and how it is studied represent student learning goals and styles. Because teachers are directly engaged in working out each student's program and because of faculty and administrative review of these programs, faculty ownership is also quite high. The unique feature, however, is that students are directly involved in shaping their own education. At first, unused to such responsibility, some students wish faculty would just tell them what to do and how to do it. Thoughtful orientation and advising, however, can lead to genuine student excitement. The professional growth contract also permits professors and deans to have this same shared ownership over their own goals and practices.

Rewarding Teaching and Learning

The first four ingredients in a lively teaching-learning environment, if done well, bear their own rewards. The force for improvement should be rewarding in that it can support risk takers and can actually provide a sense of achievement in an organization that is not either teaching or learning centered. If members of the force can say the group is enjoyable, feel esteemed and supported by the group in their teaching or learning efforts, and feel the group is getting someplace, then teaching and learning is being rewarded. Linkage in turn has within it such rewards as learning helpful things about teaching and learning as well as the enjoyment of going to conferences and making presentations, visiting other campuses, attending a well-designed workshop, meeting and being a stimulating consultant, or discovering that someone in another department is willing to share an innovative teaching strategy or would like to learn one. Openness has its rewards in terms of coming to discover and appreciate things you had not recognized and in terms of others' coming to appreciate you, be "you" teacher or student. And ownership carries with it the reward of doing things meaningful to yourself.

But there can also be extrinsic rewards for teaching and learning; and one kind costs no money: recognition. The professor or student who works hard and/or well can be congratulated in private and in public. A pat on the back, a note saying, "I really appreciated and admired . . ." and an awards banquet have their place in college if done with warmth and a light touch (a ponderous awards dinner is no reward).

Another low-cost form of recognition is more readily transferred to one's vita: publication or conference presentation. The number of journals and conferences devoted to college teaching and learning is growing. These provide opportunities for faculty members to strengthen the list of publications and presentations upon which so many promotion committees base their decisions. An equivalent on the student side of the ledger is to grant academic credit for contributions to local teaching improvement projects as well as for performance in class.

At higher financial cost is aid in placement. Many colleges have effective systems for placing students in jobs or higher degree programs, but few have such systems for faculty. As personnel reduction becomes necessary with the enrollment declines of the 1980s, such "career transition" programs will become crucial to the maintenance of a healthy teaching-learning environment. Professors will need to know that if they run out of students, the institution will aid them in retooling to teach other subjects or to obtain attractive positions outside the institution (and, often, outside higher education).

Fundamental to extrinsic rewards for teaching is an evaluation system that sets meaningful criteria for teaching effectiveness, gathers reliable and valid data, and renders fair judgments, all in the eyes of both evaluators *and* persons evaluated. Efforts to create such systems are underway in many colleges (O'Connell, 1977). Their success will do much to make college teaching not an unrewarded burden but a fully rewarding profession.

Institutional Example

Can these five ingredients merge to create a positive environment for teaching and learning? I think so. Each college will find its own specific formula, but one example will illustrate that such an environment is not impossible. Consider Austin College, a liberal arts college in Sherman, Texas. Throughout the 1970s, its administration, faculty, and students were engaged in wholistic institutional renewal (Reddick, 1979). They did not set out to build a teaching-learning environment using the five factors I have discussed, but they did come to embrace most of them.

A first principle of Austin's renewal process was that the first focus of change must be on students and learning (ownership). The college's individual development programs make the student the principal architect of his or her academic program, with faculty members serving as "mentors" rather than directors. "Personal interaction [linkage] and mutual respect [openness] are keys that make the system work" (Reddick, 1979, p. 18). The program itself was developed by a slowly swelling faculty-administration-student force that matured into a governing council that now collaborates in setting campus policies.

This growing force, well-linked to one another and to helpful information, was greatly aided by intensive summer resource laboratories attended by both students and faculty. Linkage and openness were strengthened by a steady stream of external consultants and forays to conferences, workshops, and other colleges. Even courses changed to emphasize the *interaction* Austin members were coming to see as critical both to student and to institutional development.

Rewards certainly have come from succeeding, from the learning and enjoyment of the struggle (when pain and frustration abated), and from seeing students come to grips with their new responsibilities. But the college also attended to formal rewards by instituting a career development program in which each faculty member negotiates a development plan with the dean and is supported by study leaves, conference or workshop funds, opportunities to experiment in an innovative January term, or other appropriate resources. Systematic formative and summative evaluations are used to guide and judge faculty achievement, and the emphasis on the summative side is on contributions to student learning and college development.

Although Austin undoubtedly has its share of continuing problems, it illustrates how paying attention to the ingredients that go into an environment supportive of learning and teaching might lead to a college that puts learning first and rewards effective teaching.

The Challenge to Institutional Researchers and Planners

From the institutional research or planning office, improving the teaching-learning environment may seem an unlikely goal. We are not teachers or learners. We usually work for executive administrators, who are somewhat removed from professors and students. We might conduct a survey of collegiate environment or include the topic in a planning document, but that's about it. Or is it? Institutional researchers and planners are, along with faculty development coordinators and very few others, the improvement staff of most universities. If they do not facilitate improvement of the teaching-learning environment, no one will. But how can they accomplish this? Here are a few tips gleaned from planned change research, from practitioners I have watched, and from my own brief tenure as a policy analyst and planner.

1. Set learning about learning and teaching as a principal institutional research and planning goal. Your job is to encourage and facilitate a learning community, not to make reports and plans.
2. Train yourself and your staff or committee in the "people process" of *action* research and *participative* planning, for it is not you but your audience that

needs to do the inquiring and planning. Train especially in organization development, which stresses not only this human interaction process but regards a more open, collaborative, energetic, and rewarding environment as its goal.

3. Broaden your definition of "client" to include not just executives but faculty members and students. Contract with executives so they agree in advance that you are working "for" teachers and learners as well as for them. Without such client definition and executive agreements, your own access and credibility with your full audience may be seriously impaired.

4. Build and maintain personal connection with key "gatekeepers" (for example, line administrators and governance committee chairs) and "opinion leaders" (for example, the persons to whom physicists or humanities students turn for good advice on teaching-learning issues). Sociometric techniques and just "hanging around" enable you to create this important list quickly.

5. Find, or create, some occasion to initiate a fledgling force for improved learning and teaching. A workshop on the subject, an accreditation self-study, a long-range planning subcommittee on the topic, and a special project team on teaching improvement or "the adult learner" can be the start. The purpose here is to find a few folks in the environment who are willing to direct some efforts toward working with their peers to improve things. The more gatekeepers and opinion leaders in the group, the better; but there is no need to involve them directly until they show interest. A politically representative group is usually a force for frustration, not improvement.

6. Conduct institutional research and planning with and through these influential and/or interested faculty, students, staff, and administrators. Ask them what to study, and ask them to ask their friends. Invite them to help administer research and planning instruments so these things do not come down the always suspect bureaucratic line. Invite them to analyze the data with you and to share it with their peers. Draw from them the improvement priorities surfaced by the instruments and this "feedback," then invite them to get busy on those priorities.

7. One key to this process is your skillful facilitation, which models the environmental factors you seek to create. Ask a colleague or outside consultant to provide "formative" evaluation so you can improve your ability to practice what you seek to create: an open, learning community.

8. Remember learning styles. Humanities and arts professors are often unimpressed by social science data but appreciate case histories, student quotations, or insights of respected colleagues. Most people will have learned about teaching and learning primarily by doing it and watching it, not by reading about it; this "experiential" learning should be appreciated and tapped.

9. Remember that formal, one-way communications (such as lectures or reports) are accepted and used mainly by people who already are disposed to agree with their message. If you want your clients to go beyond their prior conclusions, design two-way interactions that are as close as possible to one-to-one conversation.

10. Be variously persistent. One study and one plan is not going to do much to improve a learning environment. Encourage and facilitate various inquiry and planning activities by yourselves but also by students as class projects,

faculty as professional research and service, and voluntary as well as formally recognized groups. Worry less about correctness than about energy,
less about policing than about active learning. Trust the conservatism of the
system and your own facilitating skill to thwart half-baked research and
half-brained plans. At the same time, line up a pool of expert resource persons among the faculty who will then work with those who take the initiative.

The bottom line in these tips is also their greatest problem. The organization of colleges contradicts the goal of an effective learning community about
teaching and learning. College members are separated into contending camps,
not integrated into a mutually supportive community. Institutional research and
planning is traditionally top-down and closely monitored, not openly involving
and supportive of improvement initiatives outside "proper" channels. Researchers and planners are trained and socialized to research and plan themselves according to established protocols, not to facilitate the research and planning of students and faculty according to their best way to learn.

Where these more facilitative, open, and involving strategies have been
used, however, what seems to happen is not the diminution of established norms
and structures but the addition of an informal learning network that enables the
established order to come to life. It may take an act of courage for institutional
researchers and planners to take up this challenge in some highly traditional
institutions but building a strong teaching-learning environment seems well
worth the risk.

Bibliographical Essay

The following works provide solid social science bases for creating a lively
college environment. Two synthesize vast areas of research regarding what it
takes to introduce innovations into social systems: Havelock and others (1971)
and Rogers and Shoemaker (1971). Zaltman, Duncan, and Holbeck (1973) synthesize research on the organizational context for innovation. Lindquist (1978c)
summarizes planned change and collegiate organization research, provides several case studies of attempts to strengthen college teaching and learning environments, and synthesizes the "adaptive development" strategy for change.
Chickering, Halliburton, Bergquist, and Lindquist (1978) take this model and
describe a step-by-step process for implementing it. Lindquist (1978a) applies
this developmental strategy to building a key resource for a strong teaching-
learning environment, a faculty development program. All three books are
available from the Council for the Advancement of Small Colleges, One Dupont
Circle, Washington, D.C. 20036.

It helps to see in detail a college's wholistic effort over several years to
create a vital collegiate environment for learning and teaching. Here I recommend two books on the Austin College experience: Austin College (1977) and
Reddick (1979), both available from Austin College, Sherman, Texas.

References

Austin College. *Changing Tasks and Roles in Higher Education: A Total Institutional
    Project at Austin College.* Sherman, Tex.: Austin College, 1977.

Buhl, L., and Lindquist, J. "Innovation Through Action Research." In Kellogg (Ed.), *Use of Innovations Handbook.* Ann Arbor: University of Michigan Center for the Study of Higher Education, 1979.

Centra, J. *Faculty Development Practices in U.S. Colleges and Universities.* Princeton, N.J.: Educational Testing Service, 1976.

Chickering, A., Halliburton, D., Bergquist, W., and Lindquist, J. *Developing the College Curriculum.* Washington, D.C.: Council for the Advancement of Small Colleges, 1978.

Dewey, J. *Experience and Education.* New York: Macmillan, 1938.

Gaff, J., and others. *The Cluster College.* San Francisco: Jossey-Bass, 1970.

Havelock, R., and others. *Planning for Innovation through the Utilization of Scientific Knowledge.* Ann Arbor, Mich.: Institute for Social Research, 1971.

Lindquist, J. (Ed.). *Designing Teaching Improvement Programs.* Washington, D.C.: Council for the Advancement of Small Colleges, 1978a.

Lindquist, J. "Implementation." In Chickering, A., Halliburton, D., Bergquist, W., and Lindquist, J., *Developing the College Curriculum.* Washington, D.C.: Council for the Advancement of Small Colleges, 1978b.

Lindquist, J. *Strategies for Change.* Washington, D.C.: Council for the Advancement of Small Colleges, 1978c.

Lindquist, J. (Ed.). *Increasing the Impact.* Battle Creek, Mich.: W. K. Kellogg Foundation, 1980.

McNall, S. "Peer Teaching: A Description and Evaluation." *Teaching Sociology,* 1975, *2,* 133–146.

O'Connell, W. (Ed.). *Faculty Evaluation for Improved Learning.* Atlanta: Southern Regional Education Board, 1977.

Reddick, D. *Wholeness and Renewal in Education: A Learning Experience at Austin College.* Sherman, Tex.: Austin College, 1979.

Rogers, E., and Shoemaker, F. F. *Communication of Innovations.* New York: Free Press, 1971.

Rosnow, R., and Robinson, E. *Experiments in Persuasion.* New York: Academic Press, 1967.

Sarason, S., and Lorentz, E. *The Challenge of the Resource Exchange Network: From Concept to Action.* San Francisco: Jossey-Bass, 1979.

Zaltman, G., Duncan, R., and Holbeck, J. *Innovations and Organizations.* New York: Wiley, 1973.

15

Richard B. Heydinger

Planning Academic Programs

This chapter rests on three premises:

1. Planning is the process of making today decisions that will influence academic programs tomorrow.
2. Academic programs are the instructional offerings of a department, college, or university and do not include other programs such as student services, research, fiscal development, or capital construction.
3. There is no single best method for planning academic programs. Instead, there is a variety of "styles," all of which may prove useful to the institutional researcher or administrator.

It can be argued that the planning of academic programs has been going on for centuries. One of the earliest educational planning documents is Plato's *Republic,* which debated, among many pedagogical issues, the place of fiction in

Note: The author gratefully acknowledges the contribution of Ocheng Jany, the typing of Roxanne Walt, and the suggestions of Carl Adams, Carol Boyer, Mary Corcoran, Mitchell Pearlstein, Steven Schomberg, and James Werntz.

the education of the young and whether music, gymnastics, and military exercises should be taught equally to women and to men. It can also be persuasively
argued that across the centuries academic programs have been planned
effectively—witness the continual growth and evolution of the world's educational systems. But in the past decade, planning per se has become a topic of much
discussion in postsecondary education. New approaches to planning have been
advocated and certain planning styles have become popular. Unfortunately, as
this occurs, older planning styles are often ignored and not recognized as effective alternatives.

This chapter does not prescribe a particular approach to planning an
academic program. Instead, it describes a taxonomy of thirteen different planning styles, compares these styles across a set of common dimensions, and suggests
improvements in program planning in light of the constraints currently facing
postsecondary education. The taxonomy is designed as a diagnostic tool with
which academic administrators and institutional researchers can locate the
planning style in use at their institutions and contrast it with other possible
styles—a comparison that may suggest changes to make the planning process
more consistent with the nature of the institution and the decisions to be made.

Styles of Academic Program Planning

I have derived the thirteen styles of program planning listed here partially
from the literature on planning noted in the references and partially from my
and my colleagues' experience and ideas. I use the term "style" deliberately to
connote the inexact nature of academic program planning, in contrast to "methodology," "system," or "model," all of which imply a structured series of events
that typically does not characterize the process.

- knowledge development
- entrepreneurial
- administrative
- curriculum committee
- governing/coordinating board
- formal democratic
- problem focused
- needs assessment
- program data
- program review
- program development fund
- incremental budgeting
- economic incentives

The thirteen styles are not conceptually uniform, in that the first six focus
more on the individual or group that makes a planning decision and the others
highlight the information around which the decision is framed. Nor does the
taxonomy imply that any style exists to the exclusion of the others or is incompatible with them. In reality, planning the academic programs of an institution requires a variety of approaches or styles. Certainly, the clear distinctions implied
by the delineation of these thirteen approaches are blurred in the real world.

The breadth of this taxonomy is intended to convey that although there are effective and ineffective ways to plan, there is no single best method for all situations. Most likely, the healthiest institutions will be those that use a variety of approaches for planning academic programs.

Knowledge Development. In this first style, planning occurs ex post facto with plans for instructional programs being built after new knowledge has been developed through research. For example, during the 1940s and 1950s, many science and engineering faculty were conducting research on the digital computer. As more became known about the design of digital circuitry and computation, a new academic discipline, computer science, emerged. At first a single course was offered; then a full major was proposed; finally, a new academic department was formed—but not through a carefully formulated set of plans. Instead, the development of new knowledge was recognized and then these resources were used to expand the instructional program of colleges and universities. Over the centuries, knowledge development has been the most widely used academic planning style, and it still plays a major role in planning research universities.

Entrepreneurial. This second style is a hands-off, laissez-faire approach that relies on individual faculty members to propose program developments. There are no planning constraints, no timetables, and no requests for plans. Proposals for new or existing programs are dealt with whenever they are submitted, and curriculum development relies exclusively on the motivation of departmental faculty to refine their existing programs and develop new ones. Competing ideas for the development of programs are decided on in the free marketplace of ideas. The entrepreneurial department will most likely develop, and those satisfied with the status quo will most likely not engage in any formal planning process. Like the knowledge development style, the entrepreneurial approach leaves faculty members to their own devices, free of bureaucratic deadlines or forced planning activities.

Administrative. This third style is most often used in smaller, more centralized institutions, such as liberal arts colleges or community colleges. A dean or president may seize upon an idea and then work with appropriate faculty to develop and implement it. Thus, in marked contrast to the knowledge development or entrepreneurial styles, the initiative for academic planning rests with the administration rather than the faculty.

Curriculum Committee. This fourth style is one of the most prevalent in academic planning. Typically, this committee is organized at the department or college level and is composed of faculty, students, and perhaps administrators. A curriculum committee can consider either the development of existing programs or the initiation of planned ones with equal credibility aand facility. This group can also sit as a program review board for all academic programs and use these reviews for formative improvement of the existing programs or for summative planning decisions on resource allocation. This planning style need not operate on a regular calendar or cycle. If the group reviews program proposals, it can either set deadlines or await the natural course of events; or it can set its calendar to conform to the operational cycles of the institution. Committee members are usually knowledgeable about the overall direction of the institution—its constraints, problems, and opportunities. With this understanding, decisions on academic programs can be made in a context consistent with institutional mission and direction.

Overall, the curriculum committee style has many attractive characteristics. It focuses responsibility for planning in a small group. This group can have broad representation and, if properly managed, can build commitment to the planning process and its decisions—a participatory style that is consistent with the norms of academic governance prevalent in most institutions. However, if the curriculum committee is viewed as an omnipotent and omniscient planning group, its decisions will have no more credibility than administrative fiats.

Governing/Coordinating Board. This fifth style is the newest of those on the list and focuses on the approval of new programs by dictating the procedures and the criteria for their approval, most often by imposing an additional extra-institutional level of bureaucracy onto existing institutional planning procedures. In some cases, however, the coordinating board is the only group initiating academic program planning, which means program initiative rests with the state. In these cases, data-based techniques and political pressures become the main sources of program initiative, and faculty participation is most likely low. Decisions on programs often reflect the political environment and the utilitarian needs of the state, which may or may not be congruent with institutional mission as perceived by the faculty and administration.

This planning style requires a sizable staff at the state level with the technical expertise to collect, collate, and analyze the information necessary to make the required judgments. Up to now, most of its influence has been felt in terms of accountability and *institutional* planning, but coordinating boards are being used increasingly in program approval, program review, and program discontinuance—each an important facet of academic program planning.

In theory, this planning style is appealing. It can add coherence and coordination to the higher education programs within a state, and it may be the only style available for coordinating the programs within a state to avoid unnecessary redundancy. Yet it has the potential for ignoring the unique characteristics of higher education and instead viewing it as another state agency. If this style is to be effective, both state and institutional constituencies must be involved. When the expertise and perspective of each group is valued, this planning style has some noteworthy characteristics. Certainly this style will be increasingly visible in the years ahead.

Formal Democratic. This sixth style involves each department drafting on a periodic basis (for example, every year or every three years) a plan that presents its intentions for its academic programs. All departments participate, just as they do in the annual budgeting cycle. Plans are reviewed by succeedingly higher levels of administration until they are finally coordinated into an institutionwide academic program plan. These reviews may be conducted by a college office, a curriculum committee, or the central administration. This style is "democratic" because all departments engage in the planning process. The style is termed "formal" because the process follows a prescribed calendar and because there is usually a common format for all plans.

The formal democratic style of planning is characterized by a broad base of faculty participation. Planning is initiated at the grass roots, and each faculty member has an opportunity to propose ideas. Because this planning style is decentralized, each department and college may handle the planning process in a style congruent with its governance norms. Leadership responsibility for inaugurating this style and prescribing the calendar of events rests with the administration. Thus, the administration is responsible for the process but the academic departments and the faculty are responsible for the content of that process.

This style of academic program planning has a number of noteworthy characteristics. First, the planning process begins at the most fundamental level of the organization—the faculty member. Second, all departments are required to become involved in planning. Thus, the planning is not conducted by some independent group but by the day-to-day academic decision makers. Third, the style is cyclic. Program planning is not conducted only "when needed." It is recognized as an essential ongoing ingredient of vitality.

As with the previous five planning styles, the formal democratic style is defined by the constituency responsible for initiating or maintaining the process. The following styles focus instead on the planning methodology used—on how academic planning is done rather than *who* is responsible for it.

Problem Focused. This seventh style, like the entrepreneurial, may be described as laissez-faire. Planning is done on an "as needed" basis—whenever problems or opportunities arise. For example, the BS in accounting may be criticized by the community of professional accountants because the curriculum is out of date and the instruction style is poor. This public outcry may result in an examination of the academic program and the creation of a five-year program plan. In this planning style, "the squeaky wheel gets the oil."

In the problem focused style, the initiative for new programs is diffuse. Any constituency may initiate the planning process by making its ideas or demands known. The potential for faculty involvement is high; yet because the process is idiosyncratic to each situation, faculty involvement will not be predetermined. No particular group has responsibility for overseeing the process or ensuring it works effectively. Decision making will most likely reflect the style of the administration, although it too may vary, depending on the nature of the issue raised.

Needs Assessment. This eighth style relies exclusively on students, alumni, or potential employers for ideas on program development. Using surveys, interviews, or unobtrusive measures, the institution collects information from these constituencies regarding the educational needs of college students. (As Lenning shows in Chapter Thirteen, "need" can be defined in a variety of ways.) This information is analyzed and used to review existing programs or plan new ones. Typically, an office of institutional research or a unit with social science research skills will be responsible for conducting needs assessment surveys. Faculty may be involved in interpreting these data and in charting new programs to be developed.

The needs assessment style is becoming increasingly popular as a planning tool, particularly in community colleges. However, it cannot stand by itself as a viable planning style. It can provide essential data for academic program planning, but it must be joined with some other planning style to result in an effective program planning process. (For a detailed treatment of needs assessment as it relates to academic planning, see Chapter Thirteen.)

Program Data. This ninth style collects comprehensive and longitudinal data on each academic program. Typically, this takes the form of a departmental data sheet (Dressel, 1976), which is updated annually and contains basic operating information such as number of majors, student credit hours produced, full-time-equivalent (FTE) faculty, sponsored research funds, operating budget, and number of students graduated. This information is usually maintained by a college or university office of institutional research. An ongoing system of collecting program data can require sizable institutional resources to maintain, and a significant portion of the total effort an office of institutional research expends is often devoted to maintaining this data base.

Leadership responsibility for this planning style rests with the administration and its staff. Faculty involvement in the data collection should be minimal, yet faculty can be deeply involved in analyzing the statistics and monitoring trends. The program data style obviously focuses exclusively on existing programs and has little, if anything, to say about new programs. Because comparable data are collected on all programs, this planning style will provoke debate on the merits of one program vis-à-vis another (Zemsky, Porter, and Oedel, 1978).

Although simply collecting program data on a regular basis does not constitute program planning, this should not overshadow the importance of this activity as an integral ingredient of planning academic programs. Operational data on the status of each program is necessary as background for sound planning decisions. Moreover, if institutions worked solely to improve this style, other existing planning styles would improve as a by-product.

Program Review. This tenth style is a retrospective examination of the quality of existing programs. Typically, a group of faculty qualified to judge the program will be invited to assess the program's overall strengths and weaknesses. The review committee report can be used in a variety of ways. Departmental faculty may set about to correct the weaknesses cited. The administration may use the program review to check its judgments on which programs are weak and which are strong. This planning style has recently received considerable attention as administrators and state agencies have sought mechanisms to ensure educational quality and methods to reduce the number of existing programs.

Because program review is an assessment process, there is no guarantee that this planning style will lead to decisions about academic programs. Citing strengths and weaknesses or recommending program changes does not automatically precipitate decisions on program development. For program review to be an effective planning style, review results must be integrated with decision making. (For more on this approach, see Chapter Twenty-Two.)

Program Development Fund. This eleventh approach awards grants for worthy ideas and for the development of existing programs. A fund of venture capital, set aside by the institution, is allocated on the basis of program proposals, similar to a private foundation or federal agency.

In this planning style, the initiative for program development rests with the departments, which must develop ideas and submit proposals. The potential for broad faculty participation in this planning style is high, yet, like the entrepreneurial style, the innovative and aggressive faculty members are the most likely to participate. Leadership responsibility for this process rests with the administration, which must determine how the venture capital will be generated, whether commitments made to programs will be recurring or one-time, and how the program funding decisions will be made. For maximum effectiveness, this planning style should be executed on a regular calendar, perhaps the same as the institution's budget cycle. Overall, the program development fund is implemented to foster the growth of new programs. It is similar to the entrepreneurial style in that the ideas flow from the faculty; yet, in contrast, this style is a formal process of proposal and approval.

Incremental Budgeting. This twelfth style uses the annual budgeting process as the tool for planning academic programs. Through the budgeting process, decisions are made on which programs will be developed and which will be cut back. Instead of an independent planning style linked to resource allocation decisions, the determination of the budget is the sole planning tool.

With resources growing ever tighter, many institutions have initiated a budgetary process of "retrenchment and reallocation." Monies are taken away (retrenched) from academic programs to create a fund that is divided (reallocated) among deserving programs. There is a variety of methods for retrenching programs, for example, across-the-board percentage cuts, return of retired faculty line positions to central administration, and selective retrenchment based on predetermined institutional criteria. Reallocation decisions can be made any number of ways that incorporate faculty decision-making bodies and the program development fund described previously.

In this planning style, there is an opportunity for high faculty involvement because each program must plan on which items it will retrench. Initiative for program development also rests with the faculty, which must propose ideas for reallocation. Yet because this style is largely a budgetary planning device, leadership rests with the administration. It is difficult to predict the effect retrenchment and reallocation will have on new or existing programs. Although only existing programs can be retrenched, both new and existing programs can compete for reallocation funds. Whether the status quo is favored in reallocation or whether new programs receive the funds will depend on the style of the administration and the mood of the institution. However, one should never underestimate institutional momentum for preserving the status quo.

Overall, a formal retrenchment process offers a cyclic opportunity to refine and redirect the institution's programs in keeping with the desired institutional mission. This planning style can be a formal and legitimate process for "pruning" academic programs. With dwindling financial resources in real dollars, this incremental planning style may be viewed as equitable, with all academic programs contributing to the retrenchment process and each department having an opportunity to compete for reallocation funds.

Economic Incentives. This thirteenth and last style views a college or university as an economic organization that will respond to financial incentives such as reducing costs and maximizing outputs. For example, the budget of academic programs might be determined by means "of a fixed annual amount per unit of 'output,' where output is the sum of students in the first three years of the program plus the number of current graduates" (Hoenack and others, 1974, p. 270). Formulas such as these reward academic programs that move in desired institutional directions or accomplish desired economic outcomes (for example, minimizing the cost of instruction). Although excellent publications on this planning style exist (Cyert, 1978; Hoenack, 1977; Zemsky, Porter, and Oedel, 1978), it is difficult to characterize this approach succinctly, for it encompasses a wide variety of management techniques designed primarily in terms of their economic consequences. Various formats of this style have been referred to as "every tub on its own bottom," "decentralized planning," and "incentive planning." Because the operating constraints placed on public institutions prevent them from experimenting with many aspects of this planning style, the experience with economic incentives is centered largely in private institutions.

Faculty participation can be high as each program moves to maximize its "return from the system." The framework is designed by the administrator, yet the leadership for actual program planning rests with the faculty. Decisions in this planning style are almost exclusively financial in nature, yet the equations used to make these judgments can be based on well-grounded educational policy.

Overall, this planning style is based on the same set of assumptions that underlies economics, that of rational man. Although experience with this planning style is limited, its possibilities are intriguing. The system is designed by the administration, but it then gives faculty members and departments free rein to plan in whatever way they find most effective.

Comparison of Planning Styles

With this description of the thirteen styles as background, it is useful to compare all thirteen in terms of several general characteristics.

Source of Ideas for Program Plans. A critical factor in any planning style is the source of ideas for program development. In other words, "Whose needs will be articulated by the planning process?" Ideas for program plans may come from a variety of constituencies, including students, legislators, faculty, and prospective employers. Overall, it is the planning style that determines whose needs will dominate the process. For example, the administrative initiative style reflects the needs of the administration, whereas the entrepreneurial, knowledge development, and curriculum committee approaches reflect the ideas of the faculty. A needs assessment style collates the ideas of students, alumni, or prospective employers, depending on the methodology utilized. The problem focused approach reflects the needs of the faculty, the students, or the public, depending on who articulates the problem. Incremental budgeting and economic incentives typically reflect the program ideas of both administration and faculty. Exclusive reliance on the governing/coordinating board style could result in only the needs of the public or the politicians being represented.

As institutions review or select their planning styles, it is important to be aware of whose needs and ideas are being injected into the planning process. For example, planning for a new institute of public policy studies founded as a memorial to a deceased United States president will provoke ideas from a much different set of constituencies than the expansion of an existing program in high-energy physics. Recognition of these differences will result in the use of a planning style consistent with the type of program being planned. Also, because it is the faculty that must ultimately teach the courses and because nearly all academic planning decisions affect the courses offered, faculty ideas must be tapped for all types of academic planning. If faculty input is not sought, at best the faculty will be unenthusiastically teaching courses that were someone else's idea.

Breadth of Faculty Participation. Planning styles can also be contrasted by the breadth of faculty participation. The entrepreneurial style, although relying on faculty as the source of program ideas, will most likely result in only a small percentage of faculty participating in the planning process. And only those departments that assume the initiative will participate in this laissez-faire approach to planning. Because the formal democratic style requires that *all* departments periodically review their ideas for the future, this style results in broad faculty participation. The program development fund does not ensure broad faculty participation, but its announced process and formal review of proposals can result in a highly credible, highly visible program planning style. The styles of program data, administrative initiative, governing board, and needs assessment do not require faculty participation; and special effort must be taken if it is to be built in. In program review and incremental budgeting, the level of faculty participation will vary, depending on the characteristics of the particular process.

Broad faculty participation itself will not guarantee an effective academic planning process, but the opportunity for broad faculty input is essential if the planning style is to be credible. Although the entrepreneurial and the problem focused styles originate with faculty initiative, the resulting decisions may lack credibility because they are regarded as ad hoc and responding to the initiatives of a single department. If credibility with the faculty is an important by-product of a planning style, then the opportunity for all faculty to participate is essential.

Source of Leadership. Leadership within a planning style is an important characteristic, for it marks the party responsible for initiating a planning cycle and ensuring that a particular style functions effectively. Most planning styles (for example, program data, incremental budgeting, and economic incentives) are established and guided by the administration. Yet the entrepreneurial, knowledge development, and curriculum committee styles look to the faculty for leadership. External constituencies such as legislators or concerned citizens sometimes assume leadership when planning relies on the problem focused style. In contrasting leadership characteristics, the key distinction centers on the centralization-decentralization of the planning process. If the institution decides coordinated, institutionwide academic planning is needed, an administratively led, centralized style is dictated. If a decentralized, laissez-faire approach is desired, styles characterized by faculty or community leadership are appropriate. If the administration is to assume the leadership, an individual or office must be given this responsibility. Similarly, if individual faculty members are expected to lead the process, they must be informed of this expectation.

Required Staffing. Staffing is related to leadership. Certain styles (needs assessment, program data, incremental budgeting, and formal democratic) can require a sizable staff possessing technical expertise. For example, experience with social science techniques is required for a needs assessment and competence in institutional research and data base design is necessary to support a program data style. In the curriculum committee, program development fund, and program review styles, faculty members contribute their time and act as staff. In each style, the required level of technical expertise and necessary staff time must be carefully weighed; for without the necessary support, any style will fail regardless of its other characteristics.

Cycle of Events. Some of these styles assume a cyclic process of program planning. For example, incremental budgeting and program data are executed each academic year. Other styles (program review, formal democratic, and program development fund) are built on a formal calendar that is announced in advance; however, these planning approaches may be utilized as the need arises and need not occur each academic year. Styles such as the problem focused, knowledge development, and entrepreneurial purposely exist independent of bureaucratic cycles. In this way, the institution can respond to the creative cycles of its faculty, and program decisions are made whenever ideas are formulated and brought forward.

The timing or cycle of the planning style may seem to be a bureaucratic triviality. However, the choice of styles will testify to the administration's operational philosophy. Stated in extreme terms, a regular planning process implies a college or university is a complex organization requiring sound, modern-day management principles. A planning style that is divorced from the regularized functioning of bureaucracies is built on the belief that a college or university is a community of independent scholars and researchers whose creativity cannot or should not be tied to a regular calendar.

Congruence with Institutional Mission. Planning styles may also be contrasted by the likelihood that the emergent plans or ideas will be congruent with an articulated institutional mission. For example, certain planning styles (administrative initiative and governing board) have a high likelihood of developing and approving programmatic ideas congruent with the institution's public goals. Because some of the other planning styles (for example, entrepreneurial and program development fund) are decentralized, the likelihood is much less that the ideas brought forward will be consistent with the publicized mission of the institution.

Admittedly, this characteristic is imprecise, for it begs the question of whose institutional mission and how this mission gets articulated. Yet it is important for an institution to be cognizant of the outcomes likely to emerge from a planning process. It can be most frustrating if the institution has articulated a particular mission yet the proposals repeatedly put forth through the planning process are inconsistent with this institutional position.

New versus Existing Program Development. These thirteen styles also differ markedly in their responsiveness to new programs and to existing programs. Some of the planning styles, by virtue of their characteristics, favor the development of existing programs; other styles are designed primarily to foster new programs. For example, planning styles that require *broad* faculty participation will most likely favor existing programs and result in proposals for only minor program changes. In the formal democratic style, it is not surprising that as each department reviews its programs, the status quo will emerge as the most widely supported alternative. It is rare for a large percentage of any population to want to alter radically its current environment. The majority opts for significant changes only when the situation is dire. Other comprehensive planning styles (for example, program review, program data, and incremental budgeting) also favor existing programs. In marked contrast, the program development fund, knowledge development, and entrepreneurial styles foster the growth of new programs, for they look to the individual faculty innovator to come forward with ideas. Most important, this occurs without a simultaneous, comprehensive review of existing programs in which new ideas must be traded off against current programs. Yet the momentum of existing programs is forceful, and new ideas will emerge only if they are tolerated by the environment and nurtured by the planning style.

Assumed Environmental Dynamics. The dynamics of the environment may also be related to the choice of a planning style. Today, most institutions are witnessing a declining base of financial resources and a projected decrease in enrollment. Of these thirteen planning styles, it can be argued that some are more appropriate than others for this contracting environment. For example, the fiscally conservative incremental budgeting process, when augmented with a retrenchment and reallocation procedure, is frequently being used in this contracting environment. The styles of program review, program data, and the governing board are also most likely to be used during periods of diminishing resources. The entrepreneurial, problem focused, and program development fund styles are advocated during periods of growth. Because these planning styles result in decisions on a case-by-case basis, they are vulnerable to the criticism of not being evenhanded. And with today's tight budgets, either rightly or wrongly, many administrators have adopted a strategy of evenhandedness in an attempt to promote institutional tranquility.

This characterization is not to imply that selected styles are the *best* to use in each environment. Although difficult, perhaps the best planning strategy is to adopt a growth style in a declining environment. For example, setting aside venture capital each year for a program development fund is more critical in a contracting environment than in one with plentiful resources. This strategy may be more effective in creating institutional esprit than repeatedly executing a series of program reviews for the purposes of eliminating weak programs. During periods of expansion, program review procedures or the reallocation of resources will not only be palatable, but it is possible that more effective decisions can be made than during periods of decline. People will be more willing to examine critically their course offerings if they know there is a possibility of receiving funds for program innovations. Thus, the adoption of a planning style might be viewed as a countervailing force used to offset the dynamics of the environment.

Program Level. Finally, it is necessary to define the level of academic program that is the focus of the planning process. As defined earlier, a program could be a single course, a collection of courses making up a degree program, or all instructional offerings of an institution. Some of the planning styles are more appropriate for one program level than another. For example, the knowledge development and entrepreneurial styles are candidates for planning single courses or even degree programs. Yet it is impossible to imagine these styles being used effectively to plan all instructional programs of an institution on a regular cycle. Program review and the program development fund approaches deal with selected programs or courses. Incremental budgeting, formal democratic, and the economic incentive styles are intended to address simultaneously all facets of the institution's instructional program. When critiquing an existing planning style or proposing a new one, it is important to look at the level of program that is the focus.

In addition to the characteristics associated with each planning style, there is a series of factors that must be taken into account when assessing planning approaches. These institutional and programmatic traits exist independent of the planning style, yet the style must complement them if it is to be effective.

Institutional Mission. Users of this taxonomy must take into account the mission or purpose of their institution. Research universities, community colleges, and liberal arts colleges each have different missions. For example, a major purpose of research universities is to expand the existing body of knowledge and to draw on this new knowledge for graduate and undergraduate instruction. Thus, the knowledge development planning style is congruent with the institution's mission; however, if an institution does not envision research as one of its major activities, this style would not be a wise choice. Most community colleges have an expressed mission of responding to the educational needs of the local community. With this as a major tenet of institutional philosophy, a community-based needs assessment style is a viable alternative for community colleges.

Constituency Involvement. It is also important to expect that different constituencies will become involved in the decisions for planning different programs. Constituencies outside the institution are most likely to become involved in decisions on professional programs and applied subject areas. However, further development of the program in classical languages or addition of a new doctoral program in the history of science and technology will probably stimulate little interest unless the program is seen as an unnecessary expenditure of public funds or as running counter to the public interest.

Distinctions can also be made between the decisions on new programs and the decisions on existing programs. For example, any change in the number of programs offered will involve many more constituencies than decisions to develop existing programs. Inaugurating a program may require approval of the state's higher education board. Terminating a program will evoke responses from all the affected constituencies, including faculty, students, and the public; but a decision to expand significantly a particular program may attract little public attention. The irony is that those academic planning decisions that have the most far-reaching effect often go unnoticed while seemingly lesser decisions result in cries of outrage.

The possible combinations of constituencies that would become involved in program planning are too numerous to catalogue. It is most important to recognize that the mix of constituencies suggesting ideas and influencing the planning decisions will vary from case to case. The context of each decision will determine which constituency emerges into a position of leadership. This changing mix of influence is a critical operational characteristic of any planning style.

Decision-Making Style. The style of decision making used by an institution is a critical factor to take into account when selecting or assessing planning styles. The spectrum of alternatives is laid out by Schmidtlein (1974), who discusses two contrasting paradigmatic forms of decision making that have emerged in higher education: the incremental/remedial (I/R) and the comprehensive/prescriptive (C/P). The I/R approach has its roots in the philosophy of the free marketplace and the political process. It is built on the assumption that decision making is a form of bargaining and that conflict is inevitable. The C/P paradigm is a management science approach to decision making that relies on formal planning mechanisms and the tools of the operations researcher. This approach assumes goals and priorities can be ranked, outputs can be quantified, and measurement of goal achievement will lead to understanding and consensus.

It is not my intent to debate these two paradigms or even to portray the alternatives that might exist between these two extremes. Instead, administrators thinking through planning and decision-making styles should be aware of the alternatives. They should examine their current institutional climate and see which style is most congruent with existing norms and which is most desirable. Most of the styles mentioned previously could be adapted to either paradigm, yet each will function differently under these distinct decision-making approaches.

Location of Decision-Making Authority. Finally, characterization of planning styles should heed who makes the decisions on academic program plans: the faculty, the administration, the board of trustees, or the state coordinating board. Undoubtedly, this will vary according to the level of program or perhaps whether it is a decision on a new or existing program. In reviewing this facet of the planning process, it is important to distinguish the person who has the final authority from the one who effectively makes the decision among competing alternatives. Final authority typically rests with the governing board that holds ultimate responsibility for the well-being of the institution. Yet the individual or group that selects the alternatives to recommend to the board may possess the *effective* decision-making power. In any planning style, the placement of this authority must be carefully weighed. "Who" decides will determine the academic values that enter into the decision and which factors are taken into account. The decisions on academic programs should be congruent with the other governance norms of the institution.

This inventory of planning styles and their characteristics is intended to convey the variety of ways academic programs are planned. Line administrators and institutional researchers should examine the planning style currently being used at their institution to determine if it is meeting their needs. If improvements are desired, a decision should be made on which planning style(s) would be appropriate. The criteria for making this decision will be complex. Factors such as governance style, staff availability, faculty acceptance of various styles, and available financial resources will be some of the determinants in mapping out a strategy. If institutional practice dictates a high level of faculty consultation in academic program planning, the formal democratic style or perhaps the entrepreneurial will be most congruent. If the institution has few data collection capabilities, then designing a system for program data or needs assessment may be difficult without hiring additional staff. If the administration feels the need to have a cyclic planning process with a predictable calendar of events, the styles of knowledge development, entrepreneurial, and problem focused are not appropriate. Most likely, *no single planning style will fit an institution.* A comprehensive academic planning process at most institutions should have elements of problem focused planning, needs assessment, program data, program review, the program development fund, incremental budgeting, and economic incentives. Many of the styles complement each other, and they should be selected with this in mind.

Academic program planning is not a science or a series of well-defined methodologies. The effective planner will appreciate the idiosyncrasies and nuances of each environment and each moment in time—different styles are appropriate at different moments in an institution's history. The effective administrator will modify the approach to suit this unique point in an institution's evolution. This taxonomy offers a diagnostic tool for characterizing the current environment and suggests new vistas.

Improving Existing Planning

The remainder of this chapter focuses on improving existing planning styles in light of the contemporary environment for postsecondary education. These concluding sections examine the growing interest in academic program planning and provide suggestions for improving existing planning styles.

The current emphasis on planning—whether it be all-institutional, fiscal, or exclusively academic planning—seeks to alter five facets of decision making. In a rapidly changing environment with a contracting resource base, postsecondary education is being asked to make its planning decisions (1) more comprehensive, (2) more systematic, (3) more public, (4) more regular, and (5) more expansive.

More Comprehensive. In a contracting environment, difficult choices must be made among competing alternatives. It is argued that only with a simultaneous examination of all possible choices can the most effective decisions be made. During periods of growth, it seems less necessary to contrast program alternatives one against the other.

More Systematic. In a society continually expanding its technological capabilities, there is mounting pressure to make decisions in a more systematic manner. It is expected that quantitative indicators will be collected to inform decision makers about competing alternatives. It often is assumed that goals can be assigned priority and productivity measured. Because difficult choices must be made, administrators increasingly rely on quantitative indicators they can defend publicly. Whether such methodologies are used to rationalize a subjective judgment or are actually employed to make an "objective" decision is always open to question. Nevertheless, the expectation is that with improved planning, decisions will be made more systematically.

More Public. With growing distrust of organizational leaders and the need to cut back on program size, there is mounting pressure to make decision-making processes more public. Faculty members demand that criteria for retrenchment and reallocation decisions be debated publicly before the actual process of pruning begins. Data privacy laws, while protecting the individual, may classify institutional planning documents as public information. Thus, not only faculty and students but any concerned citizen may review planning materials. It is not unusual for decision-making meetings to be declared open by statute, through political pressure, or simply based on an institutional desire to be more open. Architects of planning processes have also come to recognize the increased credibility that results from "opening up" the process. Thus, most newer planning styles have become more public.

More Regular. To complement the need to be more comprehensive and systematic, planning styles are increasingly designed around a fixed schedule of events. The formal planning process is repeated annually or biennially, for without this, it is difficult to ensure its comprehensiveness or to justify that it is regular. A planning calendar, like budgeting, recognizes the importance of the activity and does not allow the institution to ignore the regular need to plan. In a rapidly changing environment with a complex set of interdependencies, it is necessary frequently to "take stock" and reassess the status and development of the institution's academic programs.

More Expansive. Newer academic planning styles are also attempting to extend the span of years considered in decisions. Instead of examining a proposed program in the context of today's environment only, there is a felt need to look into the future—perhaps across a number of different environments—to assess the desirability of inaugurating a program. In order to be more systematic and comprehensive, it is necessary to consider events across an expanded period of time. The countervailing force, however, is the ever more rapidly changing environment, which makes it difficult to gaze into an increasingly fragile crystal ball. Recognition of these contradictory phenomena reinforces the need to become more systematic, more comprehensive, and more regular in planning styles.

In response to these pressures, many institutions are moving away from reliance on the individually initiated or faculty-based planning styles (that is, knowledge development, entrepreneurial, and problem focused) and toward administratively led, comprehensive planning styles. Regular, all-encompassing planning of academic programs is recognized as essential in an environment in which resources grow tighter and each decision more difficult.

As institutions seek to change their existing planning styles, there are certain principles to heed. Many of these prescriptive principles have been cited by other authors; a few come from my observation and experience. They can be used to guide the design of an improved planning style or to investigate why an ineffective one is so.

First, creating and maintaining an environment conducive to planning is the responsibility of academic administration. For effective planning to occur, there must be an environment that encourages careful consideration of decisions and their impact on the future. If a regular cycle of academic planning activities is desired, the administration must inaugurate this process and nurture its development. Even if the institution utilizes one of the "free market" approaches to planning, such as the knowledge development or entrepreneurial style, academic administration must ensure that faculty members are encouraged to pursue fresh research ideas and given the impetus to develop new ideas for new instructional programs. The importance faculty members attach to academic program planning will be determined by academic administrators' attitudes and actions and the institutional planning environment. If the administration publicly articulates its planning style and then reinforces its importance through administrative decisions, an environment conducive to effective program planning will result. This responsibility rests exclusively with the administration, and it should examine its actions to assess its level of support for the existing planning style.

Second, an effective academic program planning style requires a high level of faculty involvement. It is impossible to imagine a process for planning instructional programs that does not involve the faculty who will teach and administer the academic program. In planning a program, disciplinary experts will have insights that are not obvious to administrators. Faculty members can build plans on the fundamentals of a discipline while recognizing its subtle distinctions and nuances. The governance norms of higher education also require that faculty be involved in reviewing program proposals. For example, it is impossible to envision an institution that does not have elements of a curriculum committee planning style. Instructional plans have a far greater chance of succeeding if faculty members have developed the plans and thus are committed to them. Without this involvement, planning decisions will be viewed as being passed on ex cathedra and there will be little chance of accomplishment.

Third, academic program planning must be viewed as a process and not simply a product (Mims, 1979). Too often the documents, "the plans," are viewed as the chief results of planning. Although an important aspect of many planning styles, documents are out of date almost immediately. In a dynamic environment, their shelf life is very short. It is the *process* of producing the document that is important, for it is through this series of activities that alternatives are debated, decisions are made, and commitment for the plan is built.

Although it is possible to distinguish long-range planning decisions from daily operational decisions, it is important to recognize their interaction. Once a long-range plan is agreed upon, planning has still *not* been completed. Potentially, each subsequent decision either reinforces or contradicts that plan; and with the ebb and flow of daily events, the environment will change. Ideally, administrators will consider each decision in light of its academic planning implications and the changing environment. If planning is viewed as current decisions that shape the future, academic program planning is seen as an ongoing process.

Fourth, an institution's planning style(s) must be consistent with the organizational structure. Planning, whether it be academic, fiscal, or master, is the primary responsibility of decision makers. It is *not* a staff function. Thus, for a planning style to be maximally effective, it must be laid out in a format consistent with the existing organizational structure of the institution (Haas, 1976). If the planning style runs counter to the usual flow of decisions and responsibility, the results of program planning are likely to be ignored. The greater the degree of integration between the planning style and the administrative structure of the college or university, the greater the likelihood that the decisions of academic program planning will influence other decisions.

Fifth, an improved planning style will require a process strong enough to overcome individual and organizational habits. Most likely the status quo decision-making and planning style is embedded in organizational habit. To alter this will require a process and a set of institutional supports that can break tradition. For example, if the current style is entrepreneurial or problem focused, academic planning will be a series of individually negotiated decisions. Changing to a comprehensive planning style that simultaneously weighs an institutionwide set of alternatives is a major transition. Potentially, the institutional power structure will be altered and a new set of relationships will be established. To prevent an easy retreat to the status quo, the planning process must overcome old habits and reinforce the new, desired behaviors.

This aspect of academic program planning cannot be overemphasized. To some faculty members and administrators, the introduction of a new planning style may seem tantamount to requesting that they change their personalities. The rational, objective, computerlike evaluation of alternatives can be viewed as antihuman. Shuck (1977, pp. 600–601) alluded to this problem: "human nature tends to reflect and communicate specieswide thought influences that override conscious, rational decision making. Part of that species heritage is a devotion to a linear consensus—a linked cause-and-effect cosmogony plus an overload of what we may call accident." If comprehensive academic program planning requires a new form of institutional decision making, then the planning process must be strong enough to overcome our ingrained habits, many of which could be ascribed to human nature, not simply organizational style.

Sixth, academic program planning must be linked to resource allocation. Ideally, budgeting decisions should reflect the priorities and values agreed upon through academic program planning. In this way, budgeting follows the decisions that come out of the academic planning process. If planning decisions are never translated into budgetary realities, the planning style will quickly be recognized as vacuous. Yet at the same time, academic program planning cannot be inextricably tied to resource allocation. Budgeting is a technical process with precise operational deadlines that must at times view the institution in minute detail. These demanding characteristics will inundate planning if the budgeting and planning processes are brought together. Program planning stands back from this perspective and views the institution or a particular program in a broad context. Planning should always look beyond the annual or biennial budget for longer-term implications and ideas. Thus, there is a delicate balance that requires a linkage yet a modicum of independence between planning and budgeting.

Seventh, decisions should reflect the program plan. To whatever extent possible, all decisions ought to reflect priorities established by the academic planning process. Department chairpersons, deans, or central administrators should assess each of their operational decisions for consistency with the institution's planning priorities. Even though many decisions require quick action, administrators should be cognizant of how their decisions will move toward realization of the institution's desired instructional programs. This is not a formal process but more nearly a state of mind. The administrator who effectively builds on planning will have internalized the planning process and its outcomes to such an extent that with each decision she or he will mentally evaluate the approaching decision in light of the academic plan.

Eighth, good ideas must be rewarded in a timely manner. Any planning style, if it is to maintain its credibility, must reward good ideas by allocating resources for development of these programs. Even though the total resource base might be shrinking in real dollars, methods must be found for rewarding those program plans that are consistent with the desired thrust of the institution. If the best ideas are continually shunted aside, participants in any planning style will become weary and ignore the need for planning. Such rewards must be timely and ought not to be delayed any longer than necessary. The shorter the loop between submission of a program proposal and a decision on the idea, the higher will be the regard for the planning style. If it is decided to implement a program two years hence, communicating this decision in a timely manner is also an important aspect of the planning style.

Ninth, all planning styles must possess an "error-embracing" attitude. No planning style will result in making the wisest choices all the time. As Michael (1973, p. 131) points out, "Instead of avoiding exposure to and acknowledgment of error, it is necessary to expect it, to seek out its manifestations, and to use information derived from the failure as the basis for learning through further societal experiment. More bluntly, [it] makes it necessary for individuals and organizations to embrace error." Although this concept has been easy to accept in the planning of technological or mechanistic systems, it has not been accepted in design of social programs. One would think higher education institutions that pride themselves on the development of knowledge through experimentation and the learnings garnered from failure would accept an error-embracing attitude. To improve academic planning, colleges and universities must continually reassess their planning styles and learn from failures. Repeated cycles should lead to improvement, but only if we are willing to embrace our failures and not scuttle the entire operation as a result. A curious, probing attitude is required, not a judgmental and impatient one.

Last, the institution must have the capability to respond to unforeseen opportunities. Regardless of the planning style(s) utilized, an institution must not be so rigid in its adherence to decisions made through the planning process that it does not take advantage of unforeseen opportunities. The traditional example is the wealthy graduate who unexpectedly leaves a large sum of money for the institution to establish and maintain an academic program. The institutional planning style must encompass the mechanism for responding to such initiatives in a timely manner. However, these decisions should be made in light of the academic program plans and reviewed for their complementarity. At no time should the planning style and its resultant decisions be ignored. In the past, opportunistic planning was the only style institutions adopted.

Initiating Improvements in Academic Planning

The previous sections of this chapter presented a framework for diagnosing planning styles and the operational characteristics of an effective, comprehensive, academic planning process. This section looks further into these operational characteristics by addressing the question, "How do I begin?" Whether introducing an entirely new planning style or improving an existing one, the decision about when to begin and how to initiate the improved planning style can immobilize even the most fearless of administrators. Comprehensive academic planning is usually a new way of operating. It requires commitments and creates risks for the leaders of programs, colleges, or institutions. Depending on the level of the program-planning effort, the department chairperson, the dean, or the president must visibly support the planning style. As a result, these leaders stake their credibility on an untried process; the potential gains might be high, but potential losses are commensurate. Often the decision is to postpone the introduction of a new academic planning style, in some cases repeatedly.

Any kind of planning, whether it be for a single course or all college offerings, is an onerous chore. It requires grappling with nebulous and unpredictable issues. It is an open-ended mental exercise with ill-defined standards for judging its effectiveness. It requires making decisions we would rather avoid. Thus, initiating and sustaining academic planning requires adroit leadership. The leaders must be willing to make decisions, take risks, and carefully monitor the process to ensure it is accomplishing the desired ends.

A change in academic planning styles will be accomplished most easily when the institution has a widely felt need to do something (Mims, 1979). Faculty members must recognize the need to alter the existing planning style. Support from other constituencies is also useful. For example, when the University of Minnesota initiated a comprehensive planning process in 1979, each major constituency that influenced policy recognized the need for this change. The legislature, the board of regents, the president, vice-presidents, and the faculty had each criticized the existing planning style. Although there were many different ideas for the design of this process, all constituencies coalesced around the need to initiate a comprehensive planning process. It may be said that the environment was ready for a change in planning styles. And in retrospect, this felt need was one of the most important factors in convincing the large organization to venture into the uncharted waters of a new planning style.

In order to initiate or change, you must start somewhere. Although this may sound rather obvious, when you are immersed in negotiating changes to the planning system, it is easy to delay initiation until every detail has been addressed and every decision is made. This natural tendency must be overcome; if it is not, the planning process will never begin. Rarely is there an ideal time for making a transition to a new planning style. The learning accumulated from executing the process will outweigh the benefits gained from addressing further design details. Generally, I believe two iterations of a "good" planning cycle (within the same time period) will result in more institutional learning and progress than one cycle of an "excellent" process in which every detail is addressed and every piece of documentation carefully prepared. Initiating a new planning style must be viewed as an evolutionary process in which the institution learns from its experiences.

In no case should this point be construed as an argument for haphazard design of a planning style. The design effort will require major time commitments of staff, administrators, and faculty. Careful analysis of the institution's environment must be conducted. Documents that explain the changes in planning styles and clearly communicate each constituency's responsibilities and expectations must be prepared. This recommendation advocates no more than the necessity of beginning and not unduly postponing it. The decision on when to begin requires keen judgment and adroit leadership.

Initiating an improved style also requires a decision on *where* to begin the process. In other words, a decision must be made on which level of the organization to initiate a comprehensive planning style. It can begin at the department, college, or all-university level. The debate on this issue usually divides into two sides. One advocates that a comprehensive planning style must begin with the central administration proposing its academic plans; in turn, the departments and colleges will formulate their program plans within these constraints. The other approach advocates academic programs be initiated at the department level, without the encumbrances of centrally imposed constraints. Critics of the latter approach contend this process produces unrealistic requests; critics of the former argue that some of the best ideas for program plans will be thwarted if they do not meet the guidelines proposed by the administration.

Each institution must decide which approach is best given its governance norms, present environment, and history of planning styles. If faculty members view the central administration skeptically, perhaps it will be an indication of commitment to the new planning style if the administration first prepares its institutionwide academic plan for critique. This approach overcomes the oft-heard criticism that the academic departments are requested to plan but the administration itself rarely engages in the exercise. However, in reality, most administrators will find it extremely difficult to propose constraints and decisions on academic programs—even if very general—without first receiving suggestions from the faculty. A compromise alternative is to prepare a detailed set of planning assumptions each department or college can use in initiating its planning process. This provides central direction and demonstrates central commitment to the new planning style without compromising the need for academic program planning to begin at the faculty level.

A decision regarding the scope of the initial planning effort is also required. For example, the University of Michigan and the University of Minnesota initiated new planning styles by requesting *all academic* units to participate and on the same calendar. This initiation strategy treats all units equally; however, it makes it difficult to modify the style if it is shown to have obvious flaws. A phased approach in which one unit acts as a pilot test allows all participants to review and improve upon the planning style. This strategy need not delay the completion of the first planning cycle, for with limited staff time, the administrators have no choice but to work on collegiate plans sequentially. Thus, a phased approach may permit improvements to the style in the midst of a first iteration while not meaningfully affecting the work flow of those responsible for reviewing plans and discussing them with the units.

Initiating a planning effort is not an easy task. It requires forceful action and a willingness to assume risks. Most important, as Mims (1979) points out, implementation does not flow automatically from the process design. Initiating a new style is not for the faint of heart or those who feel comfortable only with carefully defined research problems or tables of statistics. Initiating a new style requires self-confidence, a desire and appreciation for change, and bravado.

This chapter began with a simple definition of planning, stating all decisions that affect the future are in essence planning activities. In this way, it is difficult to distinguish planning from other activities, yet this is exactly the theme of this chapter. Academic program planning occurs every day throughout a college or university. It occurs in the office of every faculty member as he or she makes decisions about course content. It occurs in departmental meetings as faculty members decide on teaching assignments for next year. It occurs in the academic affairs office when the vice-president, provost, or dean decides which programs will receive discretionary funds. And it occurs when a state coordinating board reviews all nursing programs in the state. In any one college or university, academic program planning takes place in a variety of styles with a variety of constituencies involved (Norris, 1979).

This chapter attempts to make this point by presenting a taxonomy of the many styles used to plan and sustain academic programs. The taxonomy was designed as a diagnostic tool to aid institutional researchers and academic administrators in reviewing their current planning styles and to suggest alternatives for consideration (Poulton, 1979). As discussed, each style has a unique combination of characteristics that can be used to gauge the effectiveness of a particular style in your institution.

Whereas the first portion of the chapter is descriptive, the latter portion shifts its focus and is more prescriptive. The pressure to move toward well-defined academic planning systems is recognized by the necessity to be more systematic, more comprehensive, more regular, more public, and more expansive. When this occurs at an institution, the definition of planning has narrowed to include only the formal, systematic, comprehensive process that rationally charts the institution's future. The influences to move in this direction are both overt and subtle. This chapter recognizes this trend and presents some operational guidelines for designing and implementing a comprehensive planning style. Often the most difficult aspect of this process is deciding when and where to initiate a change in planning style. This chapter briefly presents some suggestions that encourage the administrator to recognize there is no perfect time to change planning styles. There is only a series of alternatives, each of which has drawbacks and all of which have elements of risk.

Comprehensive academic program planning is a continually evolving process, one through which institutions will learn from their experiences. Thus, it is important to initiate the process and then improve it on each iteration. At the same time, we must not lose sight of the fact that each institution currently has some type of planning style. Courses are offered and curricula change. An effective change agent will first assess the existing styles for their inherent strengths and weaknesses. Effective styles must be recognized and nurtured. Proposing new styles or modifications will require a sensitivity to the particular institution, its many constituencies, and to this particular moment in its history.

Bibliographical Essay

The term *academic program planning* has been used in the higher education literature to refer to a number of distinct planning activities. In some writings, it refers to all planning conducted by the institution. Because colleges and universities are academic institutions, their planning is termed academic planning. A more precise terminology for this concept is institutional planning. In other publications, discussion is focused on the skills and background required for a liberal education. This literature focuses on the student as the unit of analysis and debates liberal education requirements. Another portion of the publications on academic program planning inventory the variety of pedagogical techniques available to change agents who would like to breathe new life into a staid course format. Other articles and books discuss the governance of the academic department and the forces that can lead to curricular change. These latter writings could be included within the definition of academic program planning used in this chapter. However, many of them are more accurately characterized as part of the writing on instructional or faculty development.

A lucid overview dealing with many different facets of planning is Michael, 1973. Although his book is not written specifically for a postsecondary education audience, Michael's notions of organizational learning and error embracing provide a much needed perspective to the administrator or institutional researcher responsible for implementing a new planning process. To give perspective to the topic, Shuck (1977) has written a witty, literary essay that both criticizes and supports planning activities. His provocative article is most useful as a discussion piece for a group of faculty and administrators working together on planning. People's preferences for planning styles can be quickly separated when they react to Schmidtlein's (1974) insightful analysis of the two decision-making styles that have emerged in higher education. The tension implied in this article will undoubtedly emerge in any institution that attempts to introduce a comprehensive planning style.

One of the most difficult yet fundamental aspects of academic planning is setting academic priorities and weighing them against "academic values." In a practical yet conceptually rigorous approach, Shirley and Volkwein (1978) describe their method for arriving at a set of academic program priorities. I have found their framework most useful on a number of occasions. Fuller (1976) reiterates the importance of academic values.

For readers seeking a how-to-do-it methodology book for academic planning, there are at least three good references. Kieft (1978) describes the experiences of four institutions and their attempts to inaugurate new planning processes. A companion monograph (Kieft, Armijo, and Bucklew, 1978) builds on these and lays out a model academic planning process. Parekh (1975) offers even more detail by providing forms and suggested procedures. Finally, an excellent publication that combines a thorough conceptual framework with specific recommendations and forms is Sturner (1974). This fifty-page monograph is a good reference work for all institutional researchers.

One of the major points of departure from the comprehensive approach to planning is the decentralized approach I labeled economic incentives in this chapter. A practical overview of the real-world implications of moving to this planning style is provided by Zemsky, Porter, and Oedel (1978) as they describe their experiences at the University of Pennsylvania. Hoenack and others (1974) and Hoenack (1977) lay out suggested approaches for using economic incentives at the college or department level. These articles are complex, rigorous discussions of the topic. They are well organized and must be read by anyone seriously interested in this approach. In a provocative article, Cyert (1978) speaks to many issues related to economic incentives but in nontechnical terms.

Readers looking for procedural guidance are advised to consult Michael (1973) for a general perspective and Haas (1976), Mims (1979), and Norris (1979) for more specific suggestions.

References

Cyert, R. M. "The Management of Universities of Constant or Decreasing Size." *Public Administration Review,* 1978, *38,* 344–349.

Dressel, P., and Simon, L. A. K. (Eds.). *New Directions for Institutional Research: Allocating Resources Among Departments,* no. 11. San Francisco: Jossey-Bass, 1976.

Fuller, B. "A Framework for Academic Planning." *Journal of Higher Education,* 1976, *47,* 65–77.

Haas, R. M. "Integrating Academic, Fiscal, and Facilities Planning." *Planning for Higher Education,* 1976, *5,* 2–5.

Hoenack, S. A. "Direct and Incentive Planning within a University." *Socio-Economic Planning Science,* 1977, *11,* 191–204.

Hoenack, S., and others. "University Planning, Decentralization, and Resource Allocation." *Socio-Economic Planning Science,* 1974, *8,* 257–272.

Kieft, R. N. *Academic Planning: Four Institutional Case Studies.* Boulder, Colo.: National Center for Higher Education Management Systems, 1978.

Kieft, R. N., Armijo, F., and Bucklew, N. S. *A Handbook for Institutional Academic and Program Planning: From Idea to Implementation.* Boulder, Colo.: National Center for Higher Education Management Systems, 1978.

Michael, D. N. *On Learning to Plan—and Planning to Learn: The Social Psychology of Changing Toward Future-Responsive Societal Learning.* San Francisco: Jossey-Bass, 1973.

Mims, R. S. "Facilitating Pervasive Planning: Multi-Level Institutional Planning."

Paper presented at Association for Institutional Research Forum, San Diego, Calif., 1979.

Norris, D. M. "Matching Planning Activities to the Needs of the Organization." Paper presented at Society for College and University Planning, Kansas City, July 1979.

Parekh, S. B. *Long-Range Planning.* New Rochelle, N.Y.: Change Magazine Press, 1975.

Poulton, N. L. "Decisions that Guide Change: Planning for Maximum Impact (The Nature of the Problem)." Paper presented at Society for College and University Planning, Kansas City, July 1979.

Schmidtlein, F. A. "Decision Process Paradigms in Education." *Educational Researcher,* 1974, *13* (5), 4–11.

Shirley, R. C., and Volkwein, J. F. "Establishing Academic Program Priorities." *Journal of Higher Education,* 1978, *49,* 472–488.

Shuck, E. C. "The New Planning and an Old Pragmatism." *Journal of Higher Education,* 1977, *48,* 594–602.

Sturner, W. F. *Action Planning on the Campus.* Washington, D.C.: American Association of State Colleges and Universities, 1974.

Zemsky, R., Porter, R., and Oedel, L. P. "Decentralized Planning: To Share Responsibility." *Educational Record,* 1978, *59,* 229–253.

16

Robert A. Wallhaus

Analyzing Academic Program Resource Requirements

Very seldom does an analysis of the type and extent of resources required to conduct academic programs deal simultaneously with the many facets of this complex problem. For example, chairpersons must carefully maintain the right combination of research skills and the disciplinary expertise of the departmental faculty, and must accomplish these trade-offs within budgetary constraints imposed at some higher level within the institution. But they ordinarily will accept these imposed constraints as given, at least for purposes of analysis. A legislative appropriations committee, however, is usually not concerned with resource mix issues at the faculty level but does attempt to provide different levels of dollar support for academic priorities that will have the greatest societal or economic payoff.

In part, the emphasis given to different aspects of the resource requirements question is a matter of perspective. Different levels within higher education tend to address different dimensions of the problem. At the same time, more attention is given to certain resource requirement issues than others because they are more tractable. For example, a state agency staff will often examine resource mix and efficiency questions (such as analyzing faculty work load data) as a surrogate for analyzing more relevant outcome and value questions because the latter involve far more complex analytical concepts.

Thus, the methodologies and tools available to analyze the resource requirements of academic programs have evolved in piecemeal fashion. This is not a troublesome situation in itself because the decision-making and planning processes involving academic programs continually unfold over time, thus precluding any notion of one-shot, grand-scale solutions. What is worrisome, however, is that analysts and institutional researchers can easily lose sight of what piece of the problem they are working on. Without a knowledge of the overall context, including the interrelationships between the totality of subcomponents, it is unlikely that any analytical insights gained through piecemeal efforts can be applied effectively in real-world processes of academic program planning and development.

Therefore, this chapter provides a broad conceptual overview of the resource requirements problem, discusses separately its various components, relates state-of-the-art methodologies for analyzing the resource requirements of academic programs to these various components and examines these analytical techniques in terms of their applicability and further development in the years ahead.

A Generalized Model of Program Resource Requirements

The allocation and use of resources that will produce the optimal results from an academic program can be determined, at least theoretically, if not practically, by solving a mathematical model of the following general form:

Find a set of values, $O_i (i=1, \ldots, n)$, which denotes the outcomes of academic programs, so as to:

maximize $f(O_i)$	(The objective function)	(1)
Subject to:		
$O_i = g(R_j), j=1, \ldots, m$	(the production functions)	(2)
$h(R_j) \leq b$	(the resource constraints)	(3)
$R_j^{(t+1)} = k(R_j^t)$	(the flow equations)	(4)

Equation 1, normally referred to as the objective function, calls for the maximization of a mathematical relationship among the programmatic outcomes. This relationship would, for example, assign relative values to each of the outcomes and may well be nonlinear. Equations 2, 3, and 4, normally called the constraints, express a set of relationships that spell out how the outcomes are produced, the limitations upon resources (that is, the amounts of each resource that are, or can be made, available), and how resources and activities relate to each other over time.

For example, the objective function (equation 1) could express the sum of the number of degrees awarded in each field of study weighted by the long-term future earnings anticipated by a holder of that particular degree. This expression would be an outcome proxy for the total market value of degrees awarded by the institution, and the objective would be to maximize this outcome. Equations 2 would specify the number of credit hours by level of instruction in each discipline that are necessary to serve student majors in each field of study. In addition, equations 2 would express the resources required to produce credit hours in each discipline. This relationship between resources and credit hours could be disaggregated by resource type (that is, faculty by rank, teaching assistants, computer support costs, and so on) or it could be based on unit costs by level of instruction. Equations 2 spell out how resources are utilized to produce degrees. Equation 3 would reflect the budgets or amounts of each resource type that could be made available to each academic unit (discipline). Since resources are limited, these equations would restrict the number of credit hours that could be offered at each level within each discipline and, therefore, the number of degrees that could be produced within each field of study. Obviously, it would be instructive to experiment with different resource allocations to determine the effect on numbers of degrees of each type that could be awarded, and hence the consequences in terms of maximizing the objective function. Equation 4 would be formulated if the model were to consider a multi-year planning horizon. Little can be done to maximize outcomes if one must take current students in a discipline as a given for all future periods. Therefore, equation 4 would specify the number of student majors being admitted, progressing to higher student levels, transferring to other fields of study, dropping out, and graduating. While it is not difficult to quarrel with this formulation on any number of grounds (for example, misrepresenting the outcomes of higher education through an over-simplification of the objective function, the lack of historical data to describe accurately student flow and resource requirements relationships, the inadequate definition of the production processes of higher education as reflected in credit hour measures), the formulation does illustrate how models of academic processes can be developed and linked to resource requirements.

No algorithm is available that will solve every specific formulation of the generalized model. However, theorems that describe optimal solutions (called the Kuhn-Tucker conditions) have been proved and considerable progress has been made in developing solution techniques for various special cases of this generalized model, particularly for those formulations where all mathematical relationships can be expressed in terms of linear equations (that is, the Linear Programming Model). For a more complete explanation of these concepts and mathematical formulations, the reader is referred to textbooks in operations research and management science (such as Hillier and Lieberman, 1976, chaps. 2 and 18).

This generalized formulation has provided a point of departure for examining the salient features of decision-making and planning processes in higher education. For example, it has been utilized by Turksen and Holzman (1970) to develop a series of dynamic models for academic resource planning; by Hopkins, Larreche, and Massy (1977) in a study of the preferences of university administrators subject to constraints on budget balance; and by Weathersby (1975) as a "general decision paradigm," which is used to illustrate different conceptualizations of how decisions are made in an institutional setting.

However, mathematical programming models are not frequently found in either the literature or the application of analytical approaches to planning and resource allocation in higher education, for reasons that will be made obvious in the remainder of this chapter. A few authors, such as Walters, Mangold, and Haran (1976), Schroeder (1974), and Wallhaus (1971) have formulated goal-programming models that are special cases of the generalized model defined by equations 1, 2, 3, and 4. These formulations can be solved utilizing existing linear programming algorithms. But even these "solvable" models have not gained widespread acceptance in college and university planning and management processes.

Nevertheless, any approach to analyzing the resource requirements of academic programs can be viewed either as a specialized formulation of equations 1, 2, 3, and 4 or as a subcomponent of this more-generalized model. Thus, the various dimensions of this topic are explored from that point of departure.

Analyzing the Objectives and Outcomes of Academic Programs

The first fundamental component of the generalized model to be discussed is the "objective function" (sometimes referred to as the "preference function"). This is expressed in equation 1 as a mathematical relationship among the outcomes of academic programs. An analysis of resource requirements is obviously predicated upon some notion of what results and benefits are desired, but very seldom is the relationship between outcomes and resources made explicit. Often an analytical approach focuses on alternative applications of resources, with the impact on kinds and levels of outcomes left unspecified. Or an independent analysis of goals and outcomes is accomplished, the implicit assumption being that the proper amount and mix of resources can be made available and appropriately allocated. But very rarely are both perspectives embodied in a unified analytical approach.

Defining Outcomes. A number of problems must be addressed if outcome considerations are to be incorporated into an analysis of academic programs. The first and most obvious is the problem of *outcome definition*. In a comprehensive review of the literature, Lenning (1977) reported over eighty different attempts to define and classify educational outcomes. Most of these definitional efforts successively disaggregate broad categories such as "student growth and development" or the "extension and preservation of knowledge" to create hierarchical outcome definitions. The resulting taxonomies not only show the relationships between different kinds of outcomes but also provide options for analyzing outcomes at an appropriate level of detail. Although there will undoubtedly be future attempts to clarify outcome definitions and to create more-comprehensive classifications, the existing "menus" represent considerable progress over the past ten to fifteen years in the development of meaningful definitions of the outcomes of academic programs.

Measuring Outcomes. The second problem centers on *measuring the outcomes* of academic programs. Again, this topic has been the object of a considerable body of literature. A remarkably comprehensive documentation of what is known (and not known) about the consequences and benefits of higher education is provided by Bowen (1977). As Clark Kerr (Bowen, 1977, p. xii) states in the foreword to this book: "The range of relevant studies is enormous—from the outpouring of writing pro and con on human capital theory, to the analyses of how students' attitudes change from freshman to senior year, to surveys of how alumni view their colleges, to arguments back and forth about the measurability of the social benefits of higher education." It is striking how broad a waterfront is covered by attempts to gain insights into the outcomes of higher education. As might be expected, these studies normally focus on a particular kind of outcome or benefit, thus giving rise to widely different methodological approaches for measuring outcomes ranging across psychometrics, social returns, distributional effects, nonpecuniary benefits, and human capital theory. A further complication in measurement arises because the outcomes of one productive process (for example, the knowledge acquired through an academic program) may eventually become input into future productive processes (for example, wise investment decisions). Thus, the analyst is confronted with the problem of choosing an appropriate time horizon for gathering data. If outcomes are measured directly following the delivery of an educational program, some very important results and benefits may be discounted by design. If outcomes are measured after long periods of time, the effects of other learning and social experiences will intervene; and the lack of currency of the information collected could erode its relevance.

Of course, many of the outcomes of higher education that have been defined cannot be measured. Continued progress will undoubtedly be made on this front as well, but it will never be possible to measure quantitatively all the outcomes that have been ascribed to higher education. Nevertheless, it will be increasingly important in the years ahead to incorporate outcome considerations into analyses of academic programs and to provide outcome information to a variety of constituents. In accepting this challenge, we would do well to recognize that quantitative data are not necessarily the only communication or analysis media. Future efforts to capitalize on available qualitative information as a basis for analysis, drawing, for example, upon utility-ordering concepts, could result in large dividends. A number of useful suggestions for tackling the thorny problems associated with outcome measurement and analysis have been provided by Hanushek (1975).

Dealing with Multiple Outcomes. A third consideration in analyzing objectives of academic programs is related to the multidimensional nature of programmatic outcomes, commonly called *the joint product problem.* The formulation of the objective function in equation 1 recognizes the fact that an academic program usually results in multiple outcomes. An example of a joint product situation in higher education is the teaching round in a university hospital, an activity with two products: clinical education and patient service. The difficulty in dealing with joint production is that resources cannot be divided among the various outcomes, a fact not recognized by the state of the art in higher education costing methods. It is impossible to untangle the complex web of interrelationships between resources and outcomes, even though precise accounting methods are used to assign resources to individual outcomes. Nor is this accomplished through more recent efforts to isolate fixed and variable costs. The generalized model described in the preceding section demonstrates that it is not important, conceptually, to delineate separate resource and outcome relationships. Future efforts to analyze resource requirements based on these concepts will probably yield greater payoffs than those directed at further refinements of existing costing technologies.

Assigning Value to Outcomes. A fourth problem centers on *defining the preference relationship between outcomes* expressed in equation 1. Some outcomes of academic programs are clearly more valuable than others, hence the mathematical relationship $f(O_i)$ expresses a "value weighing" among the various outcomes. That is, the objective function assigns values to each outcome and thereby spells out the overall value (of the academic program in this case) for any combination and level of outcomes produced. Therefore, the optimal solution will be that set of outcomes that maximizes the objective function.

Although the concept of an objective function provides a sound theoretical basis for analyzing academic programs, a variety of difficulties are encountered in attempts to implement this concept. For example, the question of whose values are to be utilized is raised. Certainly, many people involved in higher education—students, faculty, legislators, administrators, and parents—place different degrees of importance on different academic outcomes. Further, these preferences change over time as well as with prevailing economic and social conditions. This creates what might be called the "political climate" surrounding the analysis of academic programs. Although the design of a global preference function that captures the myriad value judgments associated with higher education is unthinkable in a strictly mathematical sense, the analyst who ignores the existence of different value judgments will find frustration in understanding why certain analytical results are deemed counterproductive or irrelevant. The concept of a preference function, while mathematically intractable, is essential to good pragmatic analysis. The importance of gaining information about the utility of different academic outcomes for individuals in different roles related to higher education has led to a number of studies such as Romney's (1977) investigation of the goals of faculty, administrators, and trustees in forty-five colleges and universities and Uhl's (1971) use of the Delphi survey methodology to derive pooled judgments concerning the importance of different academic goals. Another example of work in this area is the procedure developed by Geoffrion, Dyer, and Feinberg (1972), which constructs a decision maker's preference function by querying value trade-offs across a set of feasible outcomes of academic programs.

In summary, an analysis of the resource requirements of academic programs must take into account the desired outcomes and the values different decision makers will attribute to these outcomes. It is unrealistic to expect the problems associated with definition and measurement, the multidimensional nature of production processes in higher education, and the determination of value relationships between these outcomes can be overcome in a formalized mathematical design; but it is nevertheless important not to ignore these dimensions. At the same time, there are limitations on the outcomes that can be produced. For example, there are constraints on the levels and kinds of resources that can be made available, and these will restrict the mix and amount of outcomes that can be attained. In addition educational philosophies, instructional technologies, and incentives superimpose conditions that affect academic outcomes. Such conditions, more narrowly referred to as "constraints," are reflected in equations 2, 3, and 4 of the generalized model. As I shall show in the remaining sections of this chapter, these conditions encompass a variety of concepts, including production functions, resource constraints, and flow equations. Each formulation provides an important perspective on analyzing the resource requirements of academic programs, and each concept has been the subject of independent analytical studies in higher education.

The Relationship Between Resources and Outcomes

To the extent that the relationship between outcomes and resources can be defined, it is possible to examine the critical question of what combination and application of resources yields the desired mix and level of outcomes. Studies of the linkage between outcomes and resources have their genesis in the economic theory of the firm, which provides the basic conceptual framework for the analysis of productivity in an industrial setting. At least in principle, this microeconomic theory is applicable to higher education—that is, colleges and universities acquire certain resources, utilize them in various academic programs (that is, production processes), and thereby produce outcomes valued by individuals and society. Benson, Ritzen, and Blumenthal (1974) provide an overview of these basic theories translated into a higher education context. These authors, as well as others, discuss the higher education analogs of industrial concepts of production efficiency and resource allocation and use.

The fundamental building block for analyzing productivity is the concept of a production function, which is expressed mathematically in equation 2 as

$$O_i = g(R_j) \quad j = 1, 2 \ldots m$$

That is, $g(R_j)$ spells out how m resources are applied to produce a level of outcome, O_i. As might be expected, most of the work related to production function analysis assumes a linear or fixed ratio relationship between outcomes and resources, although microeconomic studies have employed more complex nonlinear forms, such as the Cobb-Douglas model. Although the student-faculty ratios or unit costs that provide the grist for many of the studies related to resource allocation in higher education are not normally viewed as production functions, they do characterize the general concept. That is, the average student-faculty ratio, calculated across different disciplines or institutions, carries the implicit assumption that there is a fixed relationship between resources (that is, full-time-equivalent [FTE] faculty) and an outcome proxy (that is, student credit hours). The analogy holds for unit costs and many other forms of ratio analyses. The pitfalls in this common form of analysis in higher education are discussed in Wallhaus (1975) from a productivity perspective.

The simulation models developed in the late 1960s and early 1970s, such as RRPM (Resource Requirements Prediction Model), CAMPUS (Comprehensive Analytical Models for Planning in University/College Systems), HELP/Plantran (Higher Education Long-Range Planning/Planning Translator), and SEARCH (System for Evaluating Alternative Resource Commitments in Higher Education), can be thought of as a series of disaggregated linear production functions calculated sequentially in a large-scale computerized model. These analytical tools facilitate an examination of "what if" questions. For example, "What additional faculty would be required if the production functions incorporating class size were modified to reflect smaller sections?" "What are the resource ramifications if computer science courses are substituted for social science courses in certain curricula?" A survey of the experiences of almost four hundred institutions employing these kinds of analytical models is reported by Plourde (1976); Dresch (1975) provides a critique of the applicability of large-scale planning models in higher education.

Linear production function analyses, ranging from ratios that express a fixed relationship between an outcome measure and a resource measure to more-complex models that simultaneously incorporate many production relationships, are useful tools that have captured the attention of the majority of analytical efforts in higher education. But these forms of analyses do not recognize explicitly the concept of the preference function discussed in the preceding section. Rather, these analysis forms focus on what has been referred to as "allocative efficiency" (that is, given a fixed amount of dollars, can output be improved by changing the input mix—by allocating resources differently?) or "resource use efficiency" (that is, can output be increased by employing a better technology or by using available resources more efficiently?) Many institutions and entire state systems conduct detailed cost studies in order to gain insights into questions of allocative efficiency and resource use efficiency. A study of cost analysis in higher education carried out by the Department of Management Science at the University of Minnesota under the sponsorship of the American Council on Education (Adams, Schroeder, Hankins, and Kingston, 1978) provides a comprehensive review of costing literature and different costing methodologies. A focus on cost studies is not surprising in view of the previously mentioned difficulties in constructing preference functions. And indeed, determining the best allocation and use of resources is critically important. The search for the "efficient frontier of production possibilities," that is, the combination of resources and technologies that will result in the highest possible level of outcomes, has appropriately captured a lion's share of attention. It is interesting, however, to note that the efficient frontier is often defined as the *average* across all production possibilities. That is, the results of cost studies are usually interpreted in terms of being "overfunded" or "underfunded" relative to the average unit cost, which is usually disaggregated by discipline and/or level of instruction. This same assumption is, of course, implicit in formula approaches to budget allocations. Carlson (1975) and Gray (1979) have advanced the state of the art in this area by developing algorithms for locating the efficient frontier of production possibilities and by extending the scope of analysis to encompass more-complex multidimensional relationships.

As might be expected, production functions are usually narrowly conceived to incorporate only resources that can be purchased in the marketplace, such as staff, equipment, and materials, and to reflect only technologies, such as teaching methods and philosophies, telecommunications, or computer-based education systems. However, organizational processes and incentive systems have an equally important impact on the outcomes of academic programs. Kirschling and Staaf (1975) discuss how individual choices and behavior affect productivity in higher education, and Hoenack (1976) explores how positive (and negative) incentives can be created through different planning and resource allocation processes. As institutions face issues of "cutback management" in the 1980s, a host of administrative and behavioral considerations ranging across faculty morale, internal pricing, leadership styles, and staff development will become increasingly critical in attempts to improve the quality and effectiveness of academic programs.

Resource Constraints

An analysis of the resource requirements of academic programs must recognize limitations on what resources can be made available. Theoretically, such constraints can be incorporated in equations 3 of the generalized model. However, different decision makers and different organizational levels may both establish resource constraints for some academic units as well as face resource restrictions imposed by others. For example, the problem of analyzing resource requirements for academic programs confronting a departmental chairperson may consist of negotiations with a college dean to preserve a faculty line that has become available through retirement and then determining in consultation with departmental faculty what academic background and research interest will be sought in recruiting a replacement. An institutional budget officer may encounter constraints on total faculty and staff positions specified in an appropriations bill or restrictions on salary increases resulting from presidential wage guidelines. A hierarchy of constraints always exists and must be taken into account in analyzing the resource requirements of academic programs. This vertical hierarchy of resource constraints produces a series of interconnected models, one embedded in the other. The linkage between these hierarchical models often takes the form of resource constraints. Aside from the difficulty of defining these interconnected resource relationships, it is often difficult to determine the degree of flexibility allowed. For example, "budget numbers" may be passed from one organizational level to another, but there is usually some room for negotiation because each level has an incentive to bank some "flexibility money" in order to respond to emergencies or the pressures of internal politics.

At the same time, there are "horizontal" resource relationships that must be considered, the classical example being the service load academic programs impose across academic departments. The Induced Course Load Matrix (ICLM) (see Suslow, 1976) is an analytical tool that can be used to analyze the student credit hour load imposed by academic majors (for example, mechanical engineering majors) on other academic departments (for example, mathematics, physics, and other engineering departments). The ICLM can provide insights relative to the resource ramifications of shifts in student majors as well as curricular changes in an academic program.

Although the definition of what constitutes a resource is usually glossed over lightly, this question can be more complex than it first appears. For example, there is general agreement that faculty and staff, equipment, and materials (that is, the tangibles that can be easily associated with dollars through a conversion factor called price) are resources; but what about relatively less tangible factors such as reputation, borrowing power, and credibility? These intangibles can be quite important and, when overlooked, can result in answers that are deemed unacceptable, particularly in a broader policy context or in long-term planning considerations.

Flow Relationships

Resources available in one time period bear a relationship to those available in future time periods. For example, most members of the faculty during one academic period will still be employed several years hence. Similarly, endowments that earn money in one fiscal year, if properly managed, can reap dividends for many future years. Reputation, by definition, is developed over time and is important in terms of future payoffs, such as attracting students and research grants.

These relationships that occur over time are not limited to resource considerations. For example, there is an obvious connection between the characteristics of students enrolled during one semester and those enrolled during the next semester. It is possible to accommodate those time dependent relationships in the generalized mathematical model by expressing the objective function (that is, equation 1) in terms of outcome variables defined for each successive period being analyzed and by incorporating a series of flow equations to express time dependent relationships between variables in the constraints (that is, equation 4). This, of course, adds another dimension of complexity to the model and further exacerbates definitional and computational difficulties. Nevertheless, it is not possible to ignore these time dependent relationships. In fact, these relationships have been given considerable attention in the higher education planning literature, primarily in connection with student, faculty, and budgetary flow models.

Lovell (1971) compiled a comprehensive review of the methodologies for analyzing student flow. But very little has been accomplished to advance the state of the art since. The basic construct of student flow models is a relationship of the form:

$$s(t+1)_i = s(t)_j \, p_{ji} + n(t)_i - e(t)_i \qquad (5)$$

That is, the number of students in state i in the next time period, $t+1$ (where i could represent student level and field of study or any other combination of meaningful definitions of student characteristics or status), is equal to the number of students in states j during the preceding time period, t, that transfer into state i plus the number of new students, $n(t)_i$, entering state i during the intervening time period (that is, new admissions or transfer students) minus the number of students leaving state i, $e(t)_i$, during the intervening time period (that is, graduates or dropouts). The critical element of the model is p_{ji} (often called the transitional probability matrix), which represents the proportion of students in state j that will move to state i during a fixed interval of time (that is, a semester or academic year). The number of students in each state at each time period is calculated through successive matrix multiplications or, equivalently, as a fixed interval simulation. Alternatively, student flows can be examined through cohort analyses, that is, by following specifically defined groups of students through various states over time.

It is somewhat surprising that student flow models have not found wider applicability, given the impact that shifts in student interests have on resource requirements. The reasons may well lie in the lack of relevance attached to common definitions of student states, the difficulty in estimating key components of the model, specifically, the p_{ji}s, and the computational burdens imposed by the scale of these models if they are defined at a discerning level of disaggregation. In addition, state-of-the-art formulations often beg the question by assuming the transitional probabilities are stable over time because if this is true, the student flow model will yield few new insights beyond those available by examining historical student distributions. It is reasonable to think these problems can be overcome; if they can, a renewed interest in student flow analysis will result.

Faculty flow models are similar in structure and concept to student flow models. Again, the objective is to trace faculty movements across various states that might be defined as age, rank, salary level, sex, race, and tenure status. Policies relative to retirement, tenure, replacement, and promotion coupled with environmental factors such as mortality and quit rates are incorporated into the model, usually based on historical proportions. The utility of the model lies in varying policy variables, such as promotion rates, to examine their impact on the composition of the faculty at some future date. Most faculty flow models have been formulated as a Markov process (see Hopkins, 1974) based on a transitional probability matrix such as the p_{ji} of the student flow model. This formulation requires a specific definition of the expected proportions of feasible faculty movements between each pair of meaningful faculty states. These fundamental concepts have been utilized by Gray (1980) in a fixed-time-interval simulation to evaluate the effects of various personnel policies on future faculty characteristics.

Managing the faculty resource is of central importance in academic planning. In the years ahead, the issues of retirement, the aging of college and university faculties, affirmative action, and maintaining academic vitality in the face of fiscal inflexibilities will be increasingly critical. Faculty flow models provide a means of studying these issues and can be expected to play an important role in academic program planning.

Another area in which time dependent relationships should be analyzed is the linkage between sources and uses of dollars. Stanford University has examined the long-run implications of differential income and expense growth rates based on a series of difference equations that reflect growth in expenditures, tuition, and endowment (discussed in Chapter Thirty-One of this book and in Massy, 1976). This model has been used to examine the long-term dynamics of budget balance (and instabilities) and to determine how various factors such as the endowment payout rate will affect budget equilibrium in future time periods. What is striking about the application of this model is how apparently conservative financing decisions can result in budget disequilibrium over the long run. It may well be that many institutions faced with enrollment losses or setbacks in expected revenues are attempting short-term corrections such as drawing heavily upon their endowments and are unaware of the disastrous long-term consequences.

Finally, a discussion of time dependent relationships raises the issue of uncertainty. Most analytical efforts to examine the resource requirements of academic programs are based on an assumption of stability, that is, the preponderance of reported models is deterministic. However, this assumption should be made with considerable trepidation because all future events are probabilistic. The only questions are how well they can be predicted or to what extent they will replicate history. Although stochastic models are nothing new as far as the literature of operations research and management science is concerned, such models are several orders of magnitude more complex. Nevertheless, blithely making deterministic assumptions without careful consideration of their potential invalidity welcomes misleading results.

Conclusion

The purpose of analysis is to gain insights and not necessarily to resolve cosmic questions. For this reason, analyses of isolated and perhaps even peripheral aspects of a problem may well be made simply by learning more about the complexity of the problem; and thus, in the future, analytical models may be even more narrowly focused than they have been in the past. But having a solid conceptual understanding of the several dimensions of the problem, such as that proposed in this chapter, will be increasingly important in order to avoid misinterpreting the results of these separate and isolated analytical approaches.

Bibliographical Essay

This chapter has covered concepts and analytical approaches that are relevant to the problem of analyzing the resource requirements of academic programs from a particular perspective—that of examining the various components of a generalized mathematical programming model. Other authors have covered an equally broad spectrum of analytical approaches. To gain additional perspectives, the reader should consider the review of quantitative approaches in higher education provided by Lawrence and Service (1977), Schroeder's and Adams' (1976) assessment of management science applications in higher education, Mason (1976), which examines the use of computerized models, and Kirschling's (1976) assessment of the pros and cons of analytical models. Weathersby and Weinstein (1970) delineated the salient features of analytical models and used them to classify models applicable to higher education that had been developed to that point. The list of models examined is not up to date, but the classification scheme employed is a unique and relevant perspective.

I have not mentioned market analyses, evaluation methodologies, personnel studies, and a host of other topics covered in depth in other chapters of this handbook, even though these issues can be important in analyzing academic programs. To obtain a flavor for the breadth of academic planning, the reader should peruse Halstead's (1979) bibliographic handbook on this topic.

References

Adams, C. R., Schroeder, R. G., Hankins, R. L., and Kingston, G. W. *A Study of Cost Analysis in Higher Education.* Vols. 1–4. Washington, D.C.: American Council on Education, 1978.

Benson, C. S., Ritzen, J., and Blumenthal, I. "Recent Perspectives in the Economics of Education." *Social Science Quarterly,* 1974, *55* (2), 244–261.

Bowen, H. R. *Investment in Learning: The Individual and Social Value of American Higher Education.* San Francisco: Jossey-Bass, 1977.

Carlson, D. "Examining Efficient Joint Production Processes." In R. A. Wallhaus (Ed.), *New Directions for Institutional Research: Measuring and Increasing Academic Productivity,* no. 8. San Francisco: Jossey-Bass, 1975.

Dresch, S. P. "A Critique of Planning Models for Postsecondary Education: Current Feasibility, Potential Relevance, and a Prospectus for Future Research." *Journal of Higher Education,* 1975, *46* (1), 245–286.

Geoffrion, A. M., Dyer, J. S., and Feinberg, A. "An Interactive Approach for

Multi-Criterion Optimization with an Application to the Operation of an Academic Department." *Management Science,* 1972, *19* (4), 357–368.

Gray, P. "A Faculty Model for Policy Planning." *TIMS-ORSA Interfaces,* 1980, *10* (1), 91–103.

Gray, R. *A Convex Hull Approach to the Analysis of Social Productivity.* Boulder, Colo.: National Center for Higher Education Management Systems, 1979.

Halstead, D. K. (Ed.). *Higher Education Planning: A Bibliographic Handbook.* Washington, D.C.: National Institute for Higher Education, 1979.

Hanushek, E. "Learning by Observing the Performance of Schools." In R. A. Wallhaus (Ed.), *New Directions for Institutional Research: Measuring and Increasing Academic Productivity,* no. 8. San Francisco: Jossey-Bass, 1975.

Hillier, F. S., and Lieberman, G. J. *Operations Research.* (2nd ed.) San Francisco: Holden-Day, 1976.

Hoenack, S. A. "Direct and Incentive Planning Within a University." *Socio-Economic Planning Sciences,* 1976, *11,* 191–204.

Hopkins, D. S. P. "Faculty Early Retirement Programs." *Operations Research,* 1974, *22,* 445–467.

Hopkins, D. S. P., Larreche, J., and Massy, W. F. "Constrained Optimization of a University Administrator's Preference Function." *Management Science,* 1977, *24* (4), 365–377.

Kirschling, W. R. "Models: Caveats, Reflections, and Suggestions." In T. R. Mason (Ed.), *New Directions for Institutional Research: Assessing Computer-Based Systems Models,* no. 9. San Francisco: Jossey-Bass, 1976.

Kirschling, W. R., and Staaf, R. "Efficiency and Productivity: A Behavioral View." In R. A. Wallhaus (Ed.), *New Directions for Institutional Research: Measuring and Increasing Academic Productivity,* no. 8. San Francisco: Jossey-Bass, 1975.

Lawrence, G. B., and Service, A. L. *Quantitative Approaches to Higher Education Management.* ERIC/Higher Education Research Report No. 4. Washington, D.C.: American Association for Higher Education, 1977.

Lenning, O. T. *Previous Attempts to Structure Educational Outcomes and Outcome Related Concepts: A Compilation and Review of the Literature.* Boulder, Colo.: National Center for Higher Education Management Systems, 1977.

Lovell, C. C. *Student Flow Models: A Review and Conceptualization.* Boulder, Colo.: National Center for Higher Education Management Systems, 1971.

Mason, T. R. (Ed.) *New Directions for Institutional Research: Assessing Computer-Based Systems Models,* no. 9. San Francisco: Jossey-Bass, 1976.

Massy, W. F. "A Dynamic Equilibrium Model for University Budget Planning." *Management Science,* 1976, *23* (3), 248–256.

Plourde, P. J. *Experience with Analytical Models in Higher Education Management.* Amherst: Center for Educational Management Systems, University of Massachusetts, June 1976.

Romney, L. C. *Measures of Institutional Goal Achievement.* Boulder, Colo.: National Center for Higher Education Management Systems, 1977.

Schroeder, R. G. "Resource Planning in University Management by Goal Programming." *Operations Research,* 1974, *22,* 700–710.

Schroeder, R. G., and Adams, C. R. "The Effective Use of Management Science in University Administration." *Review of Educational Research,* 1976, *46,* 117–131.

Suslow, S. "Induced Course Load Matrix: Conception and Use." In T. R. Mason

(Ed.), *New Directions for Institutional Research: Assessing Computer-Based Systems Models,* no. 9. San Francisco: Jossey-Bass, 1976.

Turksen, I. B., and Holzman, A. G. "Short Range Planning for Educational Management." Paper presented at 38th meeting of the Operations Research Society of America, October 1970.

Uhl, N. P. *Identifying Institutional Goals: Encouraging Conversions of Opinion through the DELPHI Technique.* Durham, N.C.: National Laboratory for Higher Education, 1971.

Wallhaus, R. A. *A Resource Allocation and Planning Model in Higher Education.* Boulder, Colo.: National Center for Higher Education Management Systems, 1971.

Wallhaus, R. A. "The Many Dimensions of Productivity." In R. A. Wallhaus (Ed.), *New Directions for Institutional Research: Measuring and Increasing Academic Productivity,* no. 8. San Francisco: Jossey-Bass, 1975.

Walters, A., Mangold, J., and Haran, E. G. P. "A Comprehensive Model for Long-Range Academic Strategies." *Management Science,* 1976, *22* (7), 727–738.

Weathersby, G. B. "Decision Paradigms and Models for Higher Education." Paper presented at 48th national meeting of The Institute for Management Sciences and the Operations Research Society of America, November 1975.

Weathersby, G. B., and Weinstein, M. C. *A Structural Comparison of Analytical Models for University Planning.* Ford Foundation Program for Research in University Administration, Paper P-11. Berkeley: University of California, August 1970.

17

Melvin D. Orwig
J. Kent Caruthers

Selecting Budget Strategies and Priorities

All institutions make decisions in their budgetary processes that affect the future direction of the institution. Some do this more consciously and systematically than others, but all do it. There is, therefore, a necessary and inevitable interrelationship between the planning and budgeting processes. In this chapter, we explore that relationship through a focus on budgeting in higher education.

Though budgeting is frequently regarded as a dull and tedious exercise, it is one of the most dynamic functions of management. As Wildavsky (1974, p. xxiii) observed, "one is likely to think of budgeting as an arid subject, the province of stodgy clerks and dull statisticians. Nothing could be more mistaken. Human nature is never more evident than when men are struggling to gain a larger share of funds or to apportion what they have among myriad claimants."

The essential purposes of budgeting are to distribute resources, translate plans into action, and foster accountability. In its most basic conception, the budget is an instrument that enables the allocation of resources from one organizational unit to another, whether it be from a department to a faculty member, from an institution to a department, or from a funder to the institution. In allocating these resources, however, explicit choices are made from among alternative ways in which they might be used.

The budget is also the formal mechanism through which plans become undertakings. Not all agree, however, that the planning and budgeting function should be completely integrated. Planning tends to go forward without the specific resource or time constraints that apply in a budget process. But the desire to integrate better the planning and budgeting functions provided the primary rationale for the development of the planning, programming, and budgeting system (PPBS) and continues to be an important dimension in more modern budgeting techniques. Whether planning and budgeting are carried out by entirely different staff or are totally integrated, organizational plans eventually must be translated into some formal budget request if they are to become operational activities. This essential relationship between planning and budgeting cannot be ignored.

The third general purpose of the budget, at all organizational levels, is to serve as an instrument for achieving both internal and external accountability. Internally, budgets provide a mechanism for expenditure and management control of operational activities. Externally, the budget helps to communicate to constituencies the activities that will be supported by allocations and their expected results. To the extent that the results are or are not achieved, the organization's credibility is enhanced or reduced.

Budgeting, therefore, should not be regarded as a routine exercise. The budget—its development, communication, and execution—lies at the heart of the management process and affects, directly or indirectly, most management decisions. In this chapter, we thus explore the relationship of planning and budgeting, identify the forces and factors shaping current approaches to budgeting in postsecondary education, review different budgeting approaches, and describe a typical budget process.

Though we attempt to differentiate between the budgetary process at private and public institutions, we emphasize the budgetary process in the public sector. We devote relatively little attention to federal concerns, revenue forecasting, capital budgeting, or budgeting for support services or restricted funds.

Relationship of Planning and Budgeting

Planning and budgeting are very different activities. They differ in their basic orientation; planning is principally concerned with desired outputs and budgeting focuses on needed inputs. Schick (1971) observed that planning and budgeting frequently require different perspectives: one is forward looking and opportunistic; the other is conservative and control oriented. Similarly, Mosher (1954, p. 48) noted, "budgeting and planning are apposite, if not opposite. In extreme form, the one means saving; the other, spending." Schmidtlein and Glenny (1977, p. 227) found "the long-term coherent program objectives of the planners conflict with the short-term constraints and political demands placed on budgeters. In this conflict planners are accused of utopianism and budgeters with making decisions that lack coherence and consistency."

Despite these differences in perspective, there generally is an expressed need to integrate planning and budgeting more closely. Nearly everyone has some horror story where effective integration was not achieved. Unless the role of planning is understood in relation to the budget process, it frequently is ignored and has little impact on budget decisions.

Planning without Budget Restraints. Planning, when constrained by dollar limits too early in the decision-making process, tends to become a rather lifeless exercise. The plans lack imagination and managers begin to lose a "can do" attitude. Little incentive for innovation exists, and major breakthroughs do not occur. What could have been rewarding long-term investments are never attempted. Given the tendency for such human behavior and reaction, program planning should not be constrained too early by specific dollar amounts because good ideas occasionally can attract previously unknown resources (Resource Center for Planned Change, 1978).

This is not to say, however, that any significant amount of planning should occur without at least some vague notion of resource limitations. Not many unendowed, small, private liberal arts colleges, for instance, can plan productively for the development of a resource center or a medical school. Yet there are certain types of planning activities that require only a modest restraint from the budgeting perspective. For instance, planning that involves evaluating a potential shift in an institution's mission, role, and scope may be profitable when the institution is willing to change those variables under its control (such as its curriculum or staff assignments) sufficiently to allow it to enter new markets. Aquinas College expanded its curriculum to attract adult learners and discovered that the necessary financial base followed (Hruby, 1973). Many community colleges regularly conduct community needs assessment surveys to determine what opportunities exist for further service long before they worry about the sources of the necessary funds. And through research and development proposals, universities attract resources to conduct activities that cannot be supported through their existing financial bases.

The key to planning without a budget restraint is to retain at least some grasp of reality. Planning without some budget reference should never move beyond the generation of ideas to the evaluation of alternatives. And certainly, implementation of a plan without adequate financial information should not be considered.

Budget-Based Planning—Priority Setting. For planning to make a difference in the long-term growth and direction of an institution, it eventually must consider the realities of the budgeting process. Financial commitments must be met, so the budget will be prepared by a certain date regardless of whether the plan is ready. Despite the demonstration of need, only so many dollars will be available for expenditure. A budget can be developed either with or without reliance on planning; but if the budget is to be a tool for institutional development, it should be based on planning decisions.

Rarely has one heard of an instance where the sum of the justified program needs did not far exceed the available resources. When these demonstrated needs exceed the supply of funds, priorities must be established—the most difficult budgeting task at any organizational level. As Wildavsky (1974) observes, this characteristic of budgeting makes it more than a fiscal exercise. Through setting priorities, the budget planner may modify the impacts of the institution and alter basic institutional purposes. From a political perspective, one is tempted to avoid priority setting and instead just scale down the request to match the dollars available through across-the-board cuts that affect each unit equally. In this way, each unit is treated the same and differentials do not have to be justified. Use of this procedure, however, often also causes expectations and performance to be scaled down to a greater degree than the budget allocation; and accountability is lost for the effective use of resources—particularly when institutional priorities and needs are changing. Several of the more recently developed budget planning methodologies, such as the planning, program, budgeting system (PPBS) and zero-based budgeting (ZBB), have been designed expressly to deal with the need to establish priorities.

Even though priority setting is common to budgeting at all organizational levels, its particular form varies. For the most part, priority setting by the chairperson of an academic department is a relatively intuitive process. Though tradeoffs may be considered in setting individual salaries, in deciding to hire a new professor instead of several teaching assistants or additional support personnel, and in authorizing faculty travel rather than purchasing supplies, the relatively small operating scale of most departments makes technical analysis to support priority setting largely unnecessary. Instead, the chairperson relies on firsthand observation, judgment, and occasionally on political pressures from powerful faculty members.

The nature of priority choices changes and is more likely to involve the institutional research office at higher organizational levels. Programmatic priorities are considered when a dean of arts and sciences decides whether the overall reputation of the college would be enhanced more by increasing the allocation to the chemistry rather than the history department or by spending more for research laboratory facilities instead of audiovisual teaching aids. Priority setting and resource allocation for a college dean still remain somewhat informal, especially in those colleges that are small enough for the dean to be acquainted with each faculty member's needs. Thus, the role of technical analysis is small, and the opportunity for political influence is high.

At such institutionwide levels as the academic vice-president and president, priority setting begins to become much more formalized. Often these individuals make allocations to college deans for subsequent reallocation. Unless there is a highly developed budget control system, institutionwide officials often do not know which, from among the broad list of priority needs at lower organizational levels, will be supported by their allocation. Given these circumstances, they tend to rely more on technical analysis—often provided by or derived from work done in the institutional research office—when assessing needs and less on firsthand observations. Nonetheless, political negotiation remains an important factor.

At the system and state level in the public sector, setting budget priorities becomes rather abstract, especially in those states where budget formulas or guidelines are employed. Budgeting decisions frequently do not focus on discrete needs but rather on some abstraction, such as a needed adjustment to work load formulas, which is usually developed through the institutional research function in individual institutions. In those places where formula budgeting or guidelines are not used, decisions may rely less on technical analysis in favor of political responsiveness.

Perspectives on the roles of technical analysis and political negotiation in priority setting differ even more between those in staff and those in line capacities. The junior budget officer approaches budgeting as a series of needed technical adjustments in the institution's accounts either to compensate for mandatory social security and utility rate increases or to implement policy decisions made by others. The institutional researcher finds priority setting and budgeting a fruitful area for analysis and develops information on unit costs, average salaries, and work load. The senior executive, however, views budgeting as an annual opportunity to establish institutional priorities and relies on the institutional research and budgeting staffs for technical information to use in political negotiations.

There probably has always been a need to integrate planning and budgeting. In earlier days, when even the largest colleges and universities were relatively small, such integration could occur largely through the intuition of the institution's senior officers and did not need to be formalized. Then, as institutions began to grow and enjoy a period of strong public support, mistakes in budget allocations could be concealed and remedied by financial growth in subsequent years. But with the changing conditions now upon us, the need to integrate planning and budgeting becomes more deeply felt. No longer can budgetary growth be counted upon to conceal errors or accommodate political concerns. A department chairperson cannot depend on the budget residual to be sufficient for other operating costs after meeting salary demands. At the state level, the comfortable practice of relying on rather crude formulas or work load measures is now being questioned. Higher education is entering a period where the expenditure of every dollar needs to be planned.

Major Issues in Budgeting

The complex and difficult nature of budgeting is characterized by Wildavsky (1974, p. xxiii) as follows: "Budgeting deals with the purposes of men. How can they be moved to cooperate? How can their conflicts be resolved? . . . Serving diverse purposes, a budget can be many things: a political act, a plan of work, a prediction, a source of enlightenment, a means of obfuscation, a mechanism of control, an escape from restrictions, a means to action, a brake on progress, even a prayer that the powers that be will deal gently with the best aspirations of fallible men." Given the diverse and far-reaching purposes served by budgeting, it should not be surprising that many issues, many points of contention, surround budgeting in postsecondary education. Though the issues are interrelated in their effects, we have organized them, for purposes of discussion, into three categories: technical analysis versus political negotiation, participation in budgeting, and information required.

Technical Analysis versus Political Negotiation. Few would argue that budgeting is simply a technical exercise carried out in a routinized system. Nonetheless, there is considerable intellectual disagreement about the role of quantitative analysis and systems in budgeting (Glenny and others, 1975; Schick, 1971; Schmidtlein and Glenny, 1977; Schultze, 1968; Wildavsky, 1974). The roots of this debate can be traced to a central problem in welfare economics regarding the optimal distribution of resources between the government and the private sector. Though there are many technical and philosophical facets to this debate, welfare economics, according to Dahl and Lindblom (1953), is inevitably premised and dependent upon a political mechanism that enables social values to be identified and expressed in public policy and to be served through public programs.

Wildavsky is perhaps the most frequently cited proponent of the need for political negotiation in budgeting processes. Developing the case for political rationality, Wildavsky (1974, p. 191) quotes the philosopher Paul Diesing: "the political problem is always basic and prior to all the others. . . . This means that any suggested course of action must be evaluated first by its effects on the political structure. A course of action which corrects economic or social deficiencies but increases political difficulties must be rejected, while an action which contributes to political improvement is desirable even if it is not entirely sound from an economic or social standpoint."

Wildavsky argues strongly against the particular form of budgeting represented by PPBS and is concerned about the drive to increase technical efficiency in budgeting practices. But the main thrust of his discourse is to promote budgeting processes that allow for political negotiation. Though not opposed to studies based on efficiency criteria, Wildavsky is concerned that this single value might triumph over other values.

Schultze is a more open advocate of the need for technical analysis in budgeting, though he recognizes the importance of political negotiation. Through the political process, he observes, human values are interjected into decisions: "In a democracy, the political tools of decision making—bargaining, advocacy, negotiation, and compromise—are the means by which workable agreements are made amid conflicts about values and interests" (1968, p. vii). But analysis is equally important. "Analysis," Schultze maintains, "can help focus debate upon matters about which judgments are necessary. It can suggest superior alternatives, eliminating or at least minimizing, the number of inferior solutions. Thus by sharpening the debate, systematic analysis can enormously improve it" (1968, p. 75).

Clearly, both politics and quantitative analysis have important roles in budgeting. Political negotiation provides a mechanism through which social and human values can be reflected in budgetary decisions. Quantitative analysis helps to refine options and explore the consequences of alternatives and thereby helps to inform negotiations.

As Dahl and Lindblom (1953, p. 129) point out, "not all of everyone's goals can be satisfied in economic life. Economizing, therefore, requires a process for determining whose goals shall have priority and to what extent." In practice, these processes are a combination of political negotiation and technical analysis. Though the literature is replete with arguments for and against both, their separation is artificial and misleading.

Technical analysis in budgeting is not a substitute for politics. It will not, nor should it, seek to eliminate politics from planning and budgeting. Provided they are not viewed and used as ends in themselves, we regard technical approaches to budgeting as necessary adjuncts to decision making in an increasingly complex environment. We also anticipate an increasing role for institutional research in providing analytical support to the budget process.

Participation. American higher education is an enterprise conducted by individuals exhibiting more differences and interests than they share and serving diverse and often conflicting purposes. The goals of a university are, according to Balderston (1974), general and shrouded in vagueness. "By common consent, there are several goals, but there is not consensus among those concerned with universities about the relative importance of the goals, the interdependencies among them, or ways of measuring attainment of them" (p. 9).

Though not all agree this diffuseness regarding institutional goals is either desirable or necessary, Balderston has captured the current state of participatory decision making in universities and other senior educational institutions. Faculty, students, and administrators are affected by, and therefore desire to participate in, the development of the institutional budget. Externally, the interests of the alumni, the community, and, if it is a publicly funded institution, state agencies and legislators along with federal administrators must also be considered in the development of a budget. As Balderson (1974, p. 2) points out, "the university has become a mixture of institution, enterprise, and agency. This is partly because it has assembled a large and confusing range of activities and operations, but partly also because the major parties at interest want to view it in different ways: the faculty and students, as an institution; the trustees and some administrators, as an enterprise; and the governmental sponsors, as an agency. Conflicts of purpose, law, motivation, and style flow from these different views."

Balancing the diverse interests of these participants in postsecondary education and satisfying their claims for participation is a major challenge in the development of budgets. The problem is further exacerbated by two opposing tendencies, noted by Schick (1971, p. 185), that are part of the budgetary process. "Budgeting is . . . at once a highly fragmented and a highly interdependent process. Fragmentation comes from the dispersion of political power, the tradition of building budget requests from the bottom up, and the heterogeneous roles and interests of budget officers, operating officials, elected executives, and legislators. Interdependence is an inherent characteristic of all budgeting, deriving from the scarcity of resources and the necessity to secure the cooperation of many parties in the making of expenditure policy." Budgeting is a process that must achieve some cohesion and focus from the diverse interests represented by the many participants in the higher education enterprise.

Various budgeting approaches have been developed to try to counter the fragmentation inherent in postsecondary education and to achieve greater commonality of purpose and thrust through the budgeting process. With these new budgeting approaches, however, emerge concerns about centralization of authority. It is an unavoidable fact of budgeting that there are seldom enough resources to do everything. Some requests will be supported and some will not. When budget decisions are made, either implicitly or explicitly, authority is exercised. Whether those decisions are made at the appropriate level and whether the authority is exercised by the right actors are points of major contention.

In considering the requests of an individual institution, should a state agency, the legislature, or the institution decide whether a particular program should be initiated or whether funds should be expended on specific activities? Should the legislature provide a lump sum of resources and allow the institution, through its own processes, to determine how it will be used? The same questions can be asked of institutionwide administrators in relation to the operation of individual colleges and of college deans with regard to the operation of specific instructional programs, research activities, or departmental activities.

An important concern expressed in the reports of the comprehensive examination of state budgeting conducted by the Center for Research and Development in Higher Education at the University of California, Berkeley was the growing staff dominance in state budget making, the increasing redundancy of effort among state agencies in reviewing institutional budgets, a corresponding increase in the burdens imposed on institutions, and the erosion of institutional decision-making authority (Glenny, 1976; Schmidtlein and Glenny, 1977). Similarly, the Carnegie Foundation for the Advancement of Teaching (1976, p. 11) expressed regret regarding "the overall tendency toward centralization of authority over higher education—from the campus to the multicampus system, and from governing boards to state mechanisms."

The environmental stress (in the form of collective bargaining agreements, declining enrollment, increased pressure on the availability of public resources, and others) higher education will face in future years is likely to focus greater attention on the budgetary process in institutions and result in increased centralization of authority. The issue of centralization is likely to remain a point of contention in budgeting as long as choices must be made and decisions rendered. Though most participants in a budgetary process would subscribe to a principle that would enhance the operational flexibility of those responsible for carrying out activities, this inclination is counterbalanced by the desire to contain this flexibility within some limits of acceptable performance. Thus, the two ends of the continuum—the desirability of flexibility and the necessity for accountability—interact at various levels of the postsecondary education budgetary process in such a way that issues related to centralization of authority are not likely to diminish.

Information Required. One of the costs of budgeting is the technical information used in the particular budgeting approach. Information costs are determined by the kinds of computer systems needed to provide the required information as well as the personnel costs of generating, formatting, checking, transmitting, and analyzing the information.

Therefore, a range of issues related to the information used in budgeting is considered in the literature. At the most basic level are questions about the quantity of information required to support different approaches. At a more technical level are important questions about the measurement and use of such concepts as costs, outcomes (benefits), and performance. It is common for the institutional research office to be drawn into each of these issues.

Several efforts have been undertaken over the years to achieve better consistency in the information used in postsecondary education. In recent years, the National Center for Higher Education Management Systems has developed information procedures that are widely used by institutions and state agencies, and the National Center for Education Statistics has published several manuals to support the annual Higher Education General Information Survey. Because of these developmental efforts, it has been possible to improve the consistency of budgeting information. This has not, however, always decreased information burdens in budgeting. Different budgeting approaches require different kinds and amounts of information about different subject matter and at varying levels of detail. In addition, increased data burdens for budgeting frequently occur when changes are made to the budgeting system or approach. Because it is important, for comparative and analytical purposes, to use standardized data definitions and collection procedures, a change in budgeting procedures can impact data procedures embedded in automated informational systems. The consequence may be extensive reprogramming costs or increased personnel costs if the information must be assembled by hand.

The nature of the budgeting approach, the need for standard data definitions and procedures, and changes in budget formats can all lead to increased information costs. Nonetheless, the Carnegie Foundation for the Advancement of Teaching (1976, p. 12) favors "basing budget actions on the best information, the best analyses, and the best judgment of highly qualified persons."

The amount of information needed for budgeting is not the only concern, however. Many questions are raised about the nature of information that is used as well (Caruthers and Orwig, 1979). Information in two areas is particularly at issue: What are the costs of postsecondary education, and how are they measured and used? What are the outcomes of postsecondary education, and how is performance measured?

Even though cost analysis has been used in higher education throughout the twentieth century, the technique has not progressed beyond the average-cost method. "It is only in the last year or two," Hughes and Topping (1977, p. 17) note, "that decision makers in higher education have seriously begun to examine alternatives to average historical unit costs." They go on to point out that although "historically derived cost data can and often do serve all four management functions—planning, budgeting, controlling, and evaluating—other costing approaches, namely the variable costing approach, would be more appropriate for the planning and budgeting functions" (p. 17).

Another problem with the use of cost information in budgeting is that it begins to lose programmatic and decision relevance when aggregated. Budgets are seldom able to include all detailed operational plans and their directly associated real costs. Real costs, according to Schmidtlein and Glenny (1977, p. 249), "are difficult and expensive to determine. The complexities of separating marginal costs from average costs and allocating the costs of activities that have joint products result in the use of conventions to simplify budget estimating. These conventions make it difficult to trace a clear, simple link to costs."

The use of outcomes information to measure performance is equally complex. Many of the outcomes that result from an educational experience do not become manifest until several years after the individual leaves the educational program. Further, higher educational institutions are, according to Balderston (1974, p. 3) "more attuned to their processes and their mechanisms than they are to their consequences. . . . Even the moral commitments of universities are largely to process and mechanism and not to consequences or to agreed goals . . . as to philosophical ends, universities are designed to house enduring disagreements without breaking apart."

As interest heightens in measuring the outcomes and performance of higher education, it is important to recognize the latency of many of the individual outcomes of higher education. To do otherwise could lead to a trade school orientation with institutions evaluated exclusively on the initial job placement of their graduates. Similarly, it is the attention to institutional academic decision processes that enables higher education institutions to house the intellectual diversity and ferment that make them the valued social resource they are. Unfortunately, existing measurement instruments do not enable us to incorporate or even accommodate latent outcomes or institutional process dimensions in existing budgeting systems. It follows, therefore, that the use of performance measures in higher education budgeting requires considerable conceptual as well as technical advances.

The Budget Process

As we observed earlier, the budget serves several purposes. On the one hand, it is used to establish the need for and the desirability of proposed activities—whether it be at the department, college, institutional, or state level. On the other hand, the budget distributes available resources to support authorized purposes and activities during a given budgetary period.

Several roles are necessary in the budget process: advocates, cutters, analysts, decision makers, providers, and expenders. These roles are not mutually exclusive and they are not necessarily on the same continuum. The same individual, as a function of one position, can be both an advocate and a cutter, an analyst and a decision maker, a provider and an expender. In fact, the chief executive officer of an institution may play all these roles during different phases of the budget process.

The more visible players who act out these various roles are faculty, department chairpersons, deans, vice-presidents, chief executive officers, state postsecondary education officials, the governor, and state legislators. Less visible, though increasingly important, are institutional analysts, state agency staffs, and executive and legislative agency staffs involved in both the technical analysis and political negotiations surrounding the budget process.

An even less visible player is the student. Students, by choosing to enroll in a specific institution or a particular program within an institution, impact postsecondary education budgets. Students continue to exercise choices and impact institutional budgets. As a consequence, the choices of students as represented in tuition income must necessarily be reflected in the budget process.

Budget Request Cycle. The budget is used both to request funds and to allocate available funds among competing alternatives. Although many allocation decisions are implicitly made in the process of requesting funds, for purposes of this discussion, we consider the request cycle to culminate in the appropriation of funds by the legislature and the allocation cycle to proceed thereafter. It follows, therefore, that we are concerned primarily with the public sector in postsecondary education.

This distinction between the request and the allocation cycle may be a source of confusion to those more accustomed to budgeting in private institutions. Although many of the procedures used may be similar (for example, the use of budget protocols or guidelines developed by the central administration, the involvement of budgetary committees, and the casting of the budget in the context of overall institutional goals and plans), the separation of budgeting into two cycles is less common in the private sector. In private institutions, the budget planning process tends to be more revenue driven, with requests and allocations handled simultaneously and the distinction between the two much less visible.

Most of the literature focuses on the budget request cycle. This is understandable because, particularly in public institutions, most of the debate, analysis, and decisions occur in the request cycle. Campus or state agency budget hearings rarely are reconvened to determine the allocation of appropriated funds. This is partially a timing issue. In many states, the appropriation may not be finalized until after the fiscal year begins. As a consequence, allocation must occur rapidly to prevent disruption of the academic cycle. In addition, the intense effort put into the request cycle also tends to mitigate the need for prolonged deliberations in the allocation cycle.

In its simplest form, a budget consists of an expenditure and revenue plan that will support the overall educational objectives and plan of the institution. This description, however, conceals the many aspects and subprocesses involved in the development of an institutional budget. Robins (1973, p. 18) points out that the "process by which a budget document is created is cyclical in nature. It has no beginning or end. It is continuous and overlapping." He describes three phases to the preparation of an institutional budget. In the ongoing, long-range planning phase, which is not time bound, the institution is concerned with developing or reassessing institutional goals and the demographics and environmental factors affecting the institution (such as faculty loads, tenure policies, the composition of the student body, the condition of the library and its services, the status of the physical plant, the overall financial situation of the institution related to its tuition charges, and its investment program). One of the final steps in the long-range planning process is the projection of enrollment for the budget year in question.

The institution is then ready to move to the second phase, which is concerned with program planning. Normally, this phase begins about eighteen months before the expected effective date of the budget. It focuses on assessing and planning academic programs, planning support programs, estimating revenue, and revising plans based on revenue estimates.

The final phase of the budget process concerns document preparation and usually begins nine to twelve months prior to the effective date of the budget. It is in this phase that the formal request budget is developed. Many of the major decisions have already been made in earlier phases and are issued as guidelines for the development of the formal request budget. Nevertheless, contention and negotiation continue throughout the preparation of the final request budget.

This description of the budget process shows the institution is simultaneously engaged in different phases of preparation for different budget years. Long-range planning is being carried out for one year and the institution is completing the final document for the most immediate budget year at the same time. This leads to confusion on the part of participants and also has created some confusion in the literature. Is budgeting, for example, top down or bottom up? Although arguments are made on both sides of this issue, if one accepts our description of the budget cycle, budgeting is both top down and bottom up. As a result of the long-range planning phase and, to a limited extent, the program-planning phase, budget guidelines are developed by central administration. These guidelines establish basic budget constraints and provide the planning information on which the departments develop their budget requests. The guidelines serve to mold the budget as it is developed. Typically, the budget request proceeds from the bottom up, based on basic constraints, priorities, and planning assumptions (budget protocols) passed down by the central administration.

Several issues related to timing also cause confusion and problems in the budget cycle. Turrisi (1979, pp. 1–2) points to a dilemma in Florida that is typical of institutions on an annual budget cycle in other states. The operational unit of the academic area, Turrisi notes, is the department. The need to know about available resources is greatest at this level. Yet "department chairpersons are the last to know the resources they will have for the new budget year, which is usually one-fourth over by the time the budgets are announced." And frequently, important allocation decisions are made in August, when the operating managers (department chairpersons) are out. This situation, which is a consequence of the lengthy budget process and the fact that higher education in most states is the last appropriation item handled, induces frustration and uncertainty at all institutional levels.

One wonders why higher education is one of the last appropriation items dealt with at the state level. State governments, like the federal government, have increasingly assumed budgetary obligations of an entitlement nature, which means the basis for funding many programs is defined in the statutes and the level of resources provided to state-supported programs is directly related to the volume anticipated for each. In most states, for example, funding for elementary and secondary education is heavily influenced by tax equalization formulas written into statutes. Similarly, appropriations for welfare, transportation, and highways are largely determined by requirements to match federal grants, by statute-based funding formulas, or restricted tax revenue (such as a gasoline tax). Mental health programs, prisons, and debt maintenance also are continuing obligations that usually take priority. The net result is that higher education, whose funding basis typically is not defined statutorily, remains one of the largest budget items in most states and is treated on a discretionary basis. Indeed, higher education is one of the few remaining major programs over which the state has discretionary power. Thus, appropriations for higher education are determined in part on the basis of the need described in the budget request and in part on the basis of what resources are available after other state program commitments have been met. This phenomenon becomes increasingly important, and potentially forbidding, in the context of the enrollment problems and the severe revenue constraints expected to confront higher education in the next few years.

The development of a budget in higher education is therefore a lengthy process. It is complicated by uncertainty, overlapping activities, and, in spite of the length of the process, difficult timing problems. It is continuous, with no apparent beginning and an imperceptible end. Nevertheless, the budget process endures, and it is the process by which postsecondary education obtains the resources to enable it to endure.

Budget Request Strategies. Several strategies for enhancing budgetary performance in the request cycle are possible. At the departmental level, Turrisi (1979) maintains it is important for departments to justify their budget requests on the basis of college goals; farther up the line, the college should try to relate its goals to overall long-range institutional objectives and goals. This should be done, Turrisi advises, not only in the context of the budget request but throughout the year as well. Effective communication between department heads and deans regarding needs and plans is likely to minimize confusion and misunderstandings at budget time.

Similarly, effective analysis can strengthen budgetary outcomes. Setting aside, for the moment, consideration of whether effective analysis provides insight and facilitates decision making, the mere existence of analytical backup lends credence to the budget request. The existence of analytical backup gives an impression of effective management and induces confidence among reviewing agencies and appropriation committees that the budget request is justified. Thus, in this instance, form transcends substance.

Anton (1975, pp. 208–209) suggests four rules for preparing and submitting budgets: "(1) Avoid requests for sums smaller than the current appropriation. (2) Put as much as possible of the new request (particularly items with top priority) into the basic budget. (3) Increases that are desired should be made to appear small and should grow out of existing operations (the appearance of fundamental change should be avoided). (4) Give the Budgetary Commission something to cut."

Wildavsky (1974) cautions that if an agency develops a pattern of submitting requests in excess of what it actually receives, the budget bureau and the appropriations committee tend to counteract by taking large amounts off the top before examining the budget in detail.

Research by LeLoup and Moreland (1978) on budgetary success in federal agencies does not support Wildavsky's advice, however. Assertive agencies—those that ask for substantial increases in their budgets—experienced larger cuts in the request (partially because their request was so great) but also received larger increments in the eventual appropriation than those agencies that made more modest requests. Assertive agencies are those that can generate public support or that have effective advocacy relationships in the executive or legislative branches. The key to budget growth, according to these authors, is acquiring political support (inside and outside of government) to justify a large increase. "Do not come in too high" is poor advice for an agency wishing to receive more money; "coming in as high as can be justified" would appear to be a better strategy.

The budget request cycle extends over a long period and involves many different participants and complex strategic considerations. Though there are no easy formulas for more successful participation in this cycle, the best defense is an effective offense. To the extent that a departmental chairperson is able to articulate department objectives, to explain how these objectives relate to the overall goals and directions of the institution, and to document the service provided by the department to the other departments in the institution, the budget request cycle is likely to be less uncertain, less forbidding, and more rewarding. In spite of Anton's rules, a budget developed in this manner is likely to be more defensible and more successful than one that relies on the expectation of increments from funders. Such a strategy is not easy to implement, of course. It presumes faculty, through their departments, will subscribe to institutional goals and these goals coincide with environmental realities and are consistent with the needs of the institution's service area. But unless the institution has developed a power base that can overcome analytically based processes, a well-reasoned and effectively documented budget justification is likely to be the best insurance for success in the budget request cycle. An effective institutional research program can, therefore, contribute to improved budget success for an institution by providing analytical backup to the budget justification.

Budget Allocation Cycle. Once the appropriations bill is passed, the allocation process moves fairly rapidly. Though the governor's office is the formal executor of legislative appropriations, in most states, the governor's executive budget office plays a relatively small role in this stage of the allocation process. If legislative appropriations are to be allocated to institutions through a state agency or a system office, some kind of formula allocation, based on work load estimates, is often used.

The nature of the formula and its foundations have normally been worked out in the request cycle. As a consequence, relatively little time is spent during the allocation cycle on reconsideration of the elements of the formula. Seldom, though, is there just a simple application of the formula to determine specific appropriations for institutions. Activities mandated by the legislature frequently are included as "riders" to the appropriations bill and they must be considered. In addition, specific programmatic needs of institutions not sufficiently accommodated in the formula must be reviewed and considered with respect to their combined impact on and interaction with the formula allocations. If the allocations are from the state postsecondary education agency to system offices, relatively more emphasis is placed on the use of the formulas to determine the system allocation, on the assumption that the system offices will, in developing individual institutional allocations, undertake to accommodate specific institutional needs and requirements.

Once the institution receives notification of its funding level, allocations must be made to colleges and departments and to other service functions within the institution. Turrisi (1979) describes the process in Florida—one also used in other states. Mandated types of expenditures are funded first. These include such things as liability insurance and workman's compensation, constantly increasing utility payments, and salary commitments for ongoing personnel. Reserve levels may also be established to provide contingency against enrollment fluctuations that would cause tuition and fee revenue to be less than that estimated in the budget.

The remainder is usually distributed to vice-presidents or college deans, depending upon the organization of the institution, and often with the participation of a budget committee. From that point, resources are provided to the departments and service programs in line with an assessment of programmatic need, enrollment factors, and special requests for new programmatic activities or by using an incremental approach based on last year's budget.

By the time the budget targets are finally provided to the individual departments, the fiscal year has probably already begun and the beginning of the academic year is just around the corner. The result is a time frame totally out of step with the decisions the chairperson must make to manage the department. It is not possible to wait until August to find out about the allocation of a new position and still obtain someone to fill it by the beginning of the academic year. Similarly, graduate student positions must be filled before final appropriation figures are obtained. Thus, vice-presidents, deans, and department chairpersons frequently will take the risk that somehow the funds will be provided for these positions.

These timing problems produce frustration, confusion, and uncertainty and necessitate a certain amount of risk taking on the part of academic administrators. Add to this the inevitable conflict in the budget process, and it is easy to understand the tension that is part of budgeting in postsecondary education.

Major Approaches to Budgeting

Although there is a nearly infinite number of approaches to budgeting in higher education, most can be summarized in discussing five general methods. These are incremental budgeting, formula budgeting, the planning, programming, budgeting system (PPBS), zero-based budgeting (ZBB), and performance budgeting. Perfect distinctions cannot be made among these five approaches because they are similar in many ways. Each attempts to make budgeting a rational process, yet each offers its own definition of rationality. In practice, many hybrid methods are found. For instance, more than one state has legislated PPBS yet relies on approaches similar to what we characterize as formula budgeting. Formulas themselves usually are adjusted in an incremental fashion. Nonetheless, it is useful to consider the major approaches to college budgeting in their generic form.

Incremental Budgeting. The term *incremental budgeting* has been applied to a standard budgeting approach that has been used for a number of years. Despite the growth implications of its name, it can be used in either an incremental or a decremental fashion. Budget increments result in each of the other approaches to budgeting that we discuss, but our references to incremental budgeting are restricted to a particular type of budget planning.

In the highest form of incremental budgeting, each line item in a budget is evaluated for its relative need for an increment. Depending on the substance of the evaluation, there may be an extremely high degree of coordination between planning and budgeting. Most often, however, incremental budgeting refers to an approach where each line item receives a uniform percentage adjustment rather than an individually determined increment. Indeed, the desire to depart from "5-percent budgeting" provided the impetus for most of the budget innovations in the past several decades.

Implicit assumptions in the incremental budgeting approach are that the relative needs and priorities among organizational entities remain unchanged from one budget period to the next and that each line item merely needs its proportionate share of any inflationary allowance. When exceptional needs surface, proponents of incremental budgeting argue it is more efficient to deal with just the exceptions and their new budgetary needs rather than redistribute resources among organizational entities in any wide-scale manner (Wildavsky, 1975). A real danger remains, however, that not all exceptions will be identified and that the institution is merely following a "squeaky wheel gets the grease" budgeting approach.

The degree of integration between planning and incremental budgeting depends on the level of detail at which decisions are made. When the relative priority of each line item is substantively evaluated, the degree of integration is high. All too often, however, the link to planning is minimal. Where incremental budgeting is likely to remain the dominant budgeting approach, the planner's efforts should focus on developing more systematic means of identifying those programs whose relative priorities and resource needs are changing at much faster rates than those of the typical program.

The amount of information required to support an incremental budgeting process is directly related to the degree to which an attempt is made to integrate planning and budgeting. In its crudest form, the budget planner merely needs to know the current budget base of each organizational unit and the percentage increase available to the overall institution. In its more developed stage, information is required to determine separately needed adjustments for various objects of expenditures, for instance, fringe benefits, telephone services, and travel. Where increments are made to implement individual programmatic decisions, a significant amount of information may be required.

Those institutions now successfully using incremental budgeting are likely to find they will need to develop their systems further in the years ahead or change to a completely different approach. The need for change will be felt slowly at first because an incremental budget is perhaps the most politically viable approach as conditions stabilize or only begin to deteriorate. But as the projected demographic trends for the 1980s begin to impact the basic character of the institution, major reallocations among programs will need to occur. At first, these may be accommodated through identifying only the more exceptional needs; but as the number of exceptions increases, incremental budgeting may prove as burdensome as any of the other budgeting techniques.

Formula Budgeting. Although a topic of considerable interest to campus budget planners, formula budgeting most frequently is employed in system- or state-level settings. Formula budgeting has been defined several ways, but Miller's (1964, p. 6) description is most frequently used: "an objective procedure for estimating the future budgetary requirements . . . by manipulating data about the future programs and by utilizing relationships between programs and cost."

The reason many other definitions have been offered is that there are many types of budget formulas. The two most general types are the base-plus-percentage method and the functional approach (Miller, 1964). In the former, the direct instructional expenditures of an institution are determined first, using work load criteria, and defined as the base; then all other expenditures are dealt with as percentages of that base. For instance, library expenditures may represent a 5-percent add-on to the instructional base. Under the functional formula budgeting approach, a separate algorithm exists for each function. The instruction formula may be based on the number of student credit hours, the library formula on the number and level of degree programs offered, and the plant operations and maintenance formula on net assignable square feet. The key to formula budgeting is that resources are allocated according to criteria that have been deliberately established for this purpose.

Formula budgeting is related to planning in at least two ways. First, the formula itself expresses a planned relationship between dollar requirements and various parameters believed to be important programmatically. In this way, Holmer and Bloomfield (1976) note, planned differences in institutional mission can be reinforced in the formula. Also, formulas usually are employed with projected, rather than actual, data. For instance, the number of student credit hours is projected for use in the formula budgeting process. Whenever changing priorities alter the previously planned relationship among the factors, the formula can be modified to reflect the changes.

The information required to administer a formula budgeting process is inherent to the particular formula. If the formula is driven by desired student/teacher ratios, one needs to know the number of students and the desired work load standards. In some cases, the work load standard component itself must be computed annually, such as in those formulas that rely on the previous year's cost data. In those situations, one needs to calculate the cost data, compute the inflationary adjustment available, and project the new student base. In most cases, formula budgeting requires little information beyond that already available in an institutional research office.

Formula budgeting has come under increasing criticism in recent years and there are many calls for its abandonment during the 1980s. The basic problem underlying these pleas is that most formula budgets are based in some manner on average cost concepts. Because institutions feel they will not be able to reduce their costs at the same rate as their enrollments may decline, they foresee that strict adherence to the current formulas will bring financial distress. These pleas do not indicate, however, that formulas will be abandoned. Many state legislators argue that if the institutions were willing to use an average cost formula during a period of growth, they should be able to live with it during different circumstances. A more promising development is the growing interest in developing new types of formulas—relying on fixed and variable cost concepts—that will relate activity levels and resource requirements more closely.

Planning, Programming, Budgeting Systems. The development of PPBS nearly two decades ago corresponded with the growing desire to integrate planning with governmental budgeting. After numerous nationwide executive and legislative attempts to implement program budgeting, the term no longer has a standard definition. Most descriptions, however, emphasize that PPBS represents a conscious attempt to link planning and budgeting. As Kenworthy (1973, p. 19) states, "program budgeting is a managerial technique designed to merge the planning process with the allocation of funds by making it impossible to allocate funds without planning."

Compared with other budgeting practices, PPBS pays greater attention to developing and implementing a plan in making budget choices, has a multiyear rather than a single-year time horizon, analyzes alternatives systematically, and relies on cost-benefit ratios to establish priorities and guide budget choices. The typical PPBS approach involves several sequential steps. In the planning phase, long-range institutional objectives are identified and selected and various courses of action are considered in terms of their relative costs and benefits. The programming phase requires decisions on specific courses of action to implement planning decisions. Budgeting entails the translation of planning and programming decisions into specific financial plans (U.S. General Accounting Office, 1968).

The link between planning and budgeting in PPBS is obvious. Planning is one of several sequential steps in the budgeting process. Because PPBS embodies a systems approach, whenever a budget difficulty arises that prevents implementation of a previously developed plan, the process recycles to develop a new plan rather than seeking only a budgetary solution. Although PPBS practice usually fails to match its theoretical design, this approach does tend to place a greater reliance on planning than do other budgeting techniques.

One of the key difficulties in successfully implementing the PPBS process has been the information required. The problem encompasses not only the large volume of data necessary but also includes the requirement to collect information that is not readily available. Part of the data volume aspect of the problem derives from the multiyear perspective of PPBS. Typically, five or six years of data are collected instead of only one or two, as is common in more traditional budgeting approaches. Also, the more formalized consideration of alternatives requires additional data collection for each decision point. A more substantive problem, however, is that information required for PPBS implementation requires overcoming several conceptual obstacles, particularly in calculating cost-benefit ratios. The development of accurate cost information is difficult enough; the problems in measuring benefits are nearly insurmountable. The pages of PPBS history are filled with examples of attempts to manipulate benefit estimates to justify a political decision. These data problems remain the biggest hurdle to more widespread and successful PPBS implementation.

Although PPBS was developed during a time of seemingly limitless growth and resources, the concept is suited for the period of stabilization and possible decline facing higher education during the 1980s. Considerable planning will be required to respond to the budgetary pressures now envisioned. The importance of current demographic trends provides a need for multiyear planning. Many alternative approaches to achieving the organization's goals must be considered.

Zero-Based Budgeting. ZBB is now reaching the end of the first decade of its current existence (the term was used to describe a different process in the U.S. Department of Agriculture during the 1960s). Though in many ways similar in concept and approach to PPBS and following in the rationalist line of thinking, ZBB employs a microeconomic rather than a macroeconomic approach. Pyhrr (1973, p. 153) makes such a distinction to stress that ZBB is designed to transform objectives into an efficient operating plan instead of being concerned with broad policy decisions. In its pure form, ZBB embodies a relatively simple concept: It demands a total rejustification of every activity from base zero instead of considering only incremental change. In practice, however, ZBB more accurately can be characterized as "80-percent base budgeting." Seldom do budget planners assume an activity can be entirely eliminated but rather that only a few programmatic changes are possible in any budget-planning period.

ZBB relies heavily on the development and ranking of decision packages. Each decision package attempts to describe a discrete activity in a manner sufficient for management to evaluate its relative priority and needs in comparison with other opportunities. Decision packages typically describe the purposes of the activity, provide performance measures, and list cost information. Frequently, the decision package will offer several alternatives. Management establishes the budget by ranking the decision packages in terms of marginal cost utility. An advantage of ZBB is its flexibility, that is, decision packages can be designed to fit the needs or purposes of a specific agency rather than requiring all agencies to fit into the same program structure. Thus, one structure can be used for higher education and a different one for other state agencies.

As can be seen from the description of the decision package, budget making with ZBB involves planning for each discrete activity. ZBB does not necessarily embody, however, a broad planning context. Thus, the planning tends to be more tactical or operational than strategic or long range.

The degree of information required in zero-based budgeting depends on how decision packages are defined within the particular local system. Where decision packages have one-to-one correspondence with budgeting units, the information required probably is not greater than that used in a well-developed incremental budgeting system. When several decision packages are required per organizational entity, the information requirements increase proportionally. The volume of information necessary also depends upon the alternatives offered in each decision package.

Zero-based budgeting was designed for a period like the one many colleges and universities now face. Theoretically, ZBB makes no assumptions about growth or even the continued existence of each operating entity. Certainly, assumptions of this type will be necessary if current demographic and economic projections materialize.

Perhaps even more important for state-level higher education budgeting, ZBB and similar approaches are likely to see increased use during the coming decade. This derives not only from the economic circumstances and taxpayer revolts facing many states, but the sheer political appeal of the term *zero-based budgeting*. These factors, when combined with the recent federal interest in ZBB, suggest considerable growth in public sector ZBB usage in the coming years.

Performance Budgeting. Performance budgeting is even less well defined than the previous four approaches. One approach to budgeting, termed performance budgeting, preceded PPBS in the 1950s. That approach was concerned primarily with quantitative work load measures. In more recent years, the term has again come into use to categorize a variety of goal-driven budgeting procedures.

Peterson, Erwin, and Wilson (1977, p. 2) have defined performance budgeting as "*a budgetary process* that attempts to allocate resources on the basis of anticipated or past results." The performance budgeting structure focuses on activities that produce results for which related resources can be identified. The "results" emphasis in the definition reflects the basic difference between the old and new concepts of performance. Attention is now being directed to qualitative and impact-oriented results rather than quantitative work load.

As contrasted to PPBS and ZBB, the recent origins of performance budgeting interest are not easily traced. Performance budgeting seems to have grown from a combination of an interest in accountability, a need to accommodate nontraditional programs, and a continuing interest in emphasizing quality rather than quantity. Perhaps more generally, there has been a growing interest in rewarding initiative and excellence in governmental budgeting and in diminishing the attitude that every organization has a basic entitlement of public funds.

Performance budgeting has a significant relationship with planning, albeit indirectly. On the surface, performance budgeting appears more concerned with evaluating past performance than assessing planned activities. Because performance is assessed against previously developed goals and objectives, however, a need for strong planning arises over the longer term. Its systematic consideration of the programmatic aspects of the operation rather than just financial manipulations indicates its strong planning link.

Performance budgeting presents a number of informational challenges. Both the standard amount of financial data and a considerable amount of results or outcomes information are required. This latter category requires detail on both planned and realized performance. The major information-related challenge in performance budgeting, however, is linking performance to funding. One needs to know, for instance, if an additional faculty member in the history department will increase future graduates' appreciation of their culture or if another student affairs counselor might reduce the incidence of alcoholism on campus. Although performance budgeting does not require significantly greater amounts of information than other recent budget reforms, the emphasis on results or outcomes presents major conceptual problems.

The same factors that gave performance budgeting a rebirth in recent years (accountability and newly developed nontraditional programs) are likely to continue to be important during the 1980s. To the extent that budget policymakers perceive there is an oversupply of educational opportunity with respect to need, performance will certainly be one criterion for determining where cutbacks may be made. Because other factors also must be considered, however, performance budgeting itself may not present an adequate budgeting methodology. Rather, performance budgeting advances are more likely to be incorporated in the formula budgeting, PPBS, or ZBB approaches already in use.

The evolution of these five budget-planning approaches over the past several decades can be characterized by an increasing tendency to link planning and budgeting. We have gone from incremental budgeting, where little attention was typically paid to planning, through formula budgeting, which specified planned relationships, and then on to PPBS, which made it impossible to allocate funds without planning. ZBB and performance budgeting have continued this trend toward greater reliance on planning. As the role of planning has increased in budgeting, so have the information requirements. In fact, the information provided to support the budgeting process has grown so rapidly that it is sometimes more burdensome than informative. Budgeting developments in the 1980s probably will attempt to minimize the information necessary while retaining much of the planning focus.

Conclusion

No single approach to budgeting can be expected to resolve the complexity and conflict inherent in the forces acting on higher education and the larger society. Enhanced analytical support for decision making will probably be increasingly required as the budget is used more frequently to address value-laden problems. And so the debate surrounding the political and technical dimensions of budgeting, though frequently artificial and clothed in hyperbole, is not likely to diminish.

Perhaps the most pervasive of the forces we believe will affect budgeting in postsecondary education is the predicted enrollment decline. Because an enrollment decline probably will mean budget decreases (at least when expressed in constant dollars), how might the budget planner respond? The most commonly predicted reaction is resource reallocation. Yet American colleges for the most part have not yet had to make the difficult reallocation decisions that will be necessary if the projected enrollment reductions materialize. Some techniques, therefore, that integrate planning and budgeting in a comprehensive sense, such as PPBS or ZBB, most likely will emerge because many institutions will be forced to change substantially their institutional plans in such financial situations. And as planning and budgeting are increasingly integrated, the institutional research function is likely to become more prominent and more decision oriented. Organizationally, one might also expect present trends to continue, with the institutional research function increasingly affiliated with, perhaps formally a part of, the institutional planning and budgeting office.

Not everything will be different, however. The traditional role of institutional research in collecting and developing analytical information will endure. Thus, cost studies, student follow-ups, work load studies, and the like will be continued. In addition, the institutional research function will still include the maintenance of basic data for planning and external reporting.

But new kinds of analytical roles will also emerge. Wallhaus (1979) suggests that the role of the profession should be determined by the challenges to our schools. The institutional researcher will work more closely with both academic and financial planning staffs. As institutions increasingly need to find ways to reallocate resources, the institutional research function will likely focus on providing analytical support to program evaluation. This will occur in several ways: assessing the enrollment/market potential of existing and proposed new programs, developing ways to evaluate the comparative contribution of different programs to institutional goals, and assessing the revenue and programmatic implications of possible new directions for the institution. To support financial planning, the institutional research function will be concerned with examining the price-demand relationships of different tuition structures, analyzing the marginal cost and revenue consequences of programmatic alternatives, and supporting long-range financial planning through analysis of funding sources and the budget implications of different staffing patterns. In many ways, by focusing on issues related to development of the institution, the institutional research function can provide the critical linkage that will facilitate the effective integration of planning and budgeting in an institution. Accomplishing this purpose, however, will require an expanded vision of the potential role of institutional research and an increased appreciation of budgeting as a process through which fundamental institutional decisions are made and future directions established.

Bibliographical Essay

There are several sources in the literature that can provide the interested reader with considerably more depth on various issues related to budgeting. Caruthers and Orwig (1979) review the literature related to budgeting in higher education, focusing on prevailing issues in and examining different approaches to budgeting. Wildavsky (1974) provides perhaps the best examination of the political nature of budgeting, and Schultze (1968) discusses how technical analysis can support political negotiation in the budget process.

Glenny (1976) and Schmidtlein and Glenny (1977) both discuss various aspects of the higher education budgeting process from a state perspective. Robins (1973) and Turrisi (1979) discuss aspects of the institutional budgetary process, and the National Association of College and University Business Officers (1974) discuss the relationship of budgetary accounting to the budget process.

Several sources examine different approaches to budgeting. Schick (1971) discusses the origins of performance budgeting and examines the introduction of PPBS in state budgeting. Peterson, Erwin, and Wilson (1977) explore later developments in performance budgeting. Balderston and Weathersby (1972) also examine the principles of program budgeting, and Merewitz and Sosnick (1971) provide a critical analysis of the same subject. Formula budgeting is

examined by Meisinger (1976) and Miller (1964); and Boutwell (1973) explores
the difficulty of using formulas in a time of stable or decreasing enrollments. For
an examination of the development and principles of zero-based budgeting,
Pyhrr (1973) is the best source. Finally, Wildavsky (1975) provides one of the
most interesting comparative analyses of budgeting at various levels of government in different countries with an excellent analysis of different principles of
budgeting.

References

Anton, T. J. "Agency Budget Roles." In R. T. Golembiewsky and J. Rabin (Eds.),
    Public Budgeting and Finance. Itasca, Ill.: Peacock, 1975.

Balderston, F. E. *Managing Today's University.* San Francisco: Jossey-Bass, 1974.

Balderston, F. E.. and Weathersby, G. B. "PPBS in Higher Education Planning
    and Management." Part 2: "The University of California Experience." *Higher
    Education,* 1972, *1,* 299–319.

Boutwell, W. K. "Formula Budgeting on the Down Side." In G. Kaludis (Ed.),
    New Directions for Higher Education: Strategies for Budgeting, no. 2. San Fran-
    cisco: Jossey-Bass, 1973.

Carnegie Foundation for the Advancement of Teaching. *The States and Higher
    Education: A Proud Past and a Vital Future.* San Francisco: Jossey-Bass, 1976.

Caruthers, J. K., and Orwig, M. D. *Budgeting in Higher Education.* ERIC/Higher
    Education Research Report 3. Washington, D.C.: American Association for
    Higher Education, 1979.

Dahl, R. A., and Lindblom, C. E. *Politics, Economics, and Welfare.* New York:
    Harper & Row, 1953.

Glenny, L. A. *State Budgeting for Higher Education: Interagency Conflict and Consen-
    sus.* Berkeley: Center for Research and Development in Higher Education,
    University of California, 1976.

Glenny, L. A., and others. *State Budgeting for Higher Education: Data Digest.* Berke-
    ley: Center for Research and Development in Higher Education, University
    of California, 1975.

Holmer, F., and Bloomfield, S. D. "A Resource/Acquisition Model for a State
    System of Higher Education." *Planning for Higher Education,* October 1976, *5.*

Hruby, N. J. *A Survival Kit for Invisible Colleges.* Washington, D.C.: Academy for
    Educational Development, 1973.

Hughes, K. S., and Topping, J. R. "Using Cost Information and Analysis in
    Managing Institutional Affairs." *NACUBO Business Officer,* 1977, *11,* 15–17.

Kenworthy, W. "A Program Budgeting Strategy for a Small College." In G.
    Kaludis (Ed.), *New Directions for Higher Education: Strategies for Budgeting,* no. 2.
    San Francisco: Jossey-Bass, 1973.

LeLoup, L. T., and Moreland, W. B. "Agency Strategies and Executive Review:
    The Hidden Politics of Budgeting." *Public Administration Review,* 1978, *38,*
    232–239.

Meisinger, R. J., Jr. *State Budgeting for Higher Education: The Uses of Formulas.*
    Berkeley: Center for Research and Development in Higher Education, Uni-
    versity of California, 1976.

Merewitz, L., and Sosnick, S. H. *The Budget's New Clothes.* Chicago: Rand Mc-
    Nally, 1971.

Miller, J. L., Jr. "An Introduction to Budgetary Analysis." In *Introductory Papers on Institutional Research*. Atlanta, Ga.: Southern Regional Education Board, 1964.

Mosher, F. C. *Program Budgeting: Theory and Practice*. Chicago: Public Administration Service, 1954.

National Association of College and University Business Officers. *College and University Business Administration*. (3rd ed.) Washington, D.C.: National Association of College and University Business Officers, 1974.

Peterson, M. W., Erwin, M., and Wilson, R. "State-Level Performance Budgeting." In J. K. Folger (Ed.), *New Directions for Institutional Research: Increasing the Public Accountability of Higher Education,* no. 16. San Francisco: Jossey-Bass, 1977.

Pyhrr, P. A. *Zero Base Budgeting*. New York: Wiley, 1973.

Resource Center for Planned Change. *A Futures Creating Paradigm: A Guide to Long-Range Planning from the Future for the Future*. Washington, D.C.: American Association for State Colleges and Universities, 1978.

Robins, G. B. *Understanding the College Budget*. Athens, Ga.: Institute of Higher Education, 1973.

Schick, A. "The Road to PPB: The States of Budget Reform." *Public Administration Review,* 1966, *26,* 243–258.

Schick, A. *Budget Innovation in the States*. Washington, D.C.: Brookings Institution, 1971.

Schmidtlein, F. A., and Glenny, L. A. *State Budgeting for Higher Education: The Political Economy of the Process*. Berkeley: Center for Research and Development in Higher Education, University of California, 1977.

Schultze, C. L. *The Politics and Economics of Public Spending*. Washington, D.C.: Brookings Institution, 1968.

Turrisi, I. "Obtaining Departmental Resources Through Planning, Analysis, and Persuasion." In *Workshop Manual*. Tallahassee: Institute for Departmental Leadership, Florida State University, 1979.

U.S. General Accounting Office. *Planning-Programming-Budgeting and Systems Analysis Glossary*. Washington, D.C.: Government Printing Office, 1968.

Wallhaus, R. A. "Institutional Research in the Eighties." Presidential address to nineteenth annual forum of the Association for Institutional Research. San Diego, Calif., May 15, 1979.

Wildavsky, A. *The Politics of the Budgetary Process*. (2nd ed.) Boston: Little, Brown, 1974.

Wildavsky, A. *Budgeting, A Comparative Theory of Budgetary Processes*. Boston: Little, Brown, 1975.

18

Meredith A. Gonyea

Determining Academic Staff Needs, Allocation, and Utilization

Imagine a scene in which a microbiology professor is on his way to address a seminar on the application of his research to the health care delivery system. An administrator stops him and asks, "How much time was involved in preparing for this presentation?" The professor pauses a moment and then responds, "All my life!" In a way the professor is absolutely correct; yet his answer may not be very helpful to an administrator faced with determining academic staff needs, allocation, and utilization. Why? Is the administrator asking the wrong question? Is the professor giving an inappropriate answer? I think not. Most likely, neither person has a clear perception of the problem the administrator's question addresses and neither realizes the role each is playing at the time the question is posed.

The purpose of the seminar is to transmit knowledge, with the hope that the professor's activity will stimulate development of new knowledge and better health care. Thus, the university's missions of teaching, research, and public service are clearly being served by this activity. And not only are the undergraduate and graduate instructional programs affected; it is likely that the professional development of the other faculty members present is enhanced. It would be a relatively easy task to count the number and type of people present at the seminar and the amount of time they spend in the session. It is not, however, an easy task to calculate the time the professor spent preparing for this activity or to assign his time and that of the seminar participants to the missions of teaching, research, or public service or to specific instructional programs within the teaching mission. At this point, the professor may ask why anyone would want to measure these activities with such precision. The most probable response of the administrator would be accountability. Supporters of the institution want to know that academic resources are devoted effectively to academic missions; the administrator is responsible for assuring them of the effective use of resources; and who would know better than the professor about his use of his time?

In an environment of limited resources, the question facing the administrator is the maximum benefit that can be obtained for the minimum cost. This question not only requires a specific answer; it is compounded by the necessity to select among benefits regardless of cost when support is scarce. From the professor's viewpoint, the problem is confusing. He is faced with responsibilities to his students, his peers, his institution, and his discipline, not to mention himself. His task is not easy, and the tools available to measure his activities are limited at best. For example, the institution will most likely record his formally scheduled teaching activities but not his supervision of dissertation research because present faculty record systems are designed to assign credit for student certification and not to account for faculty activity utilization. Similarly, his institution may have a faculty effort report system, but if it involves assigning percentages of effort to particular programs or activities, he may be faced with the problem of reporting his allocation of time on his subjective impression without any clearly defined criteria for doing so. In performing such an activity allocation, he may even ask himself, "How do percentages of where I distributed my time this last year relate to my university service or effectiveness, let alone to what I should do in the future? Why not simply return the form with the answer, 'I spend 100 percent of my time in the service of this institution!' "

Problems from the Past

Why are the tools for measuring faculty activity, utilization, and need so imprecise? There are several reasons, among them: (1) The true nature of faculty activities has not been clearly defined; (2) the complex interaction of their multiple activities has not been described; (3) the reluctance of some faculty to identify in detail what they do and why has inhibited comprehensive studies; and (4) the need to develop precise methods has not existed until recently.

In a situation where the need to know was low and the complexity of interaction among faculty activities has been high, it is not surprising that research has been limited. Generally, accounting for instructional activities after the fact has been the major need and methods such as those described by Yuker (1974) have done that job.

The administrator's primary objective was to determine academic staff needs—that is, the faculty required by the institution. Given a certain number of existing faculty, she or he was also charged with determining their appropriate allocation to teaching units and determining if they were being utilized properly. In order to carry out these three functions, the administrator may have had some explicit or implicit criteria to follow, such as (1) the minimum staff needed to sustain accreditation, (2) efficient allocation of units to minimize overlap, and (3) maximum utilization with contract guidelines. With such objectives and criteria, the administrator then sought methods of measurement. Institutional records provided data on the number of faculty, their allocation to teaching units, and the financial commitments related to them; and student scheduling systems could provide information on faculty course assignments by unit. Very rarely, however, would these data contain information on faculty allocation of time or effort to instructional programs and missions. Self-reports on faculty effort may have been gathered, but their validity seemed questionable, even though they were probably the best measure available.

In reviewing faculty activities, the administrator was primarily seeking a mechanism to allocate faculty and, thereby, financial resources to institutional centers responsible for supplying services in order to justify their continued financial support to funding sources. In reflecting on his task, the administrator might question whether the existing data overestimated or underestimated needs, represented historical or planned allocations and represented effective and/or efficient utilization.

It is little wonder that both professors and administrators have ended up with more questions than they started out with. Even institutional supporters could afford the luxury of a system of accountability with wide variations. In a growth environment, the "needs" question could be "How many more?" The "allocation" question could be "Who presents the best case?" The "utilization" question could be "Can we account for efforts?" The existing methods of allocation on the basis of faculty time determination were adequate and acceptable to all parties.

Today, the problem of determining faculty resource needs, allocation, and utilization has intensified. More institutional research is required on the activities of faculty and their relations to missions and instructional programs. Such research in the 1970s focused on accounting for existing resources in a steady state. It emphasized the description of existing faculty flow activities at departmental levels. The major source of data for this type of analysis was institutional records from the personnel and financial management systems. And allocation of time to programs continued to be calculated on the basis of faculty effort reports. What is the present state of research on faculty resource requirements? Let me rephrase this question into a three-part query: What do we know about (1) existing faculty resource allocation, (2) existing faculty utilization, and (3) future faculty requirements?

Existing Faculty Resource Allocation. Techniques are now available for measuring existing faculty resources in terms of headcount by demographic data to allow an analysis of the faculty flow through the system so that determinations of flexibility may be identified. These methods can identify where faculty are and how long they are likely to be there. They do not, however, determine the need for them to be anywhere.

The major use of faculty flow analyses is providing central administrators with information on the financial resources committed to faculty support due to past decisions on promotion and tenure. This type of information helps identify where faculty resources are allocated and may become available, but it does not help with academic staff needs assessment or evaluation of use.

Existing Faculty Utilization. Faculty utilization is measured by faculty activity analysis reports which are assumed to identify how faculty time is utilized. But the problems of data imprecision still persist. More refined methods of faculty activity analysis that are also linked to course scheduling information systems are available now (Romney and Manning, 1974). These improvements have two advantages: They allow for more extensive analysis, and they make it easier to check the accuracy of basic data.

Faculty activity analysis, whether done by hours per time unit or by percentage of effort, usually identifies six basic activities: (1) direct contact teaching, (2) preparation and evaluation, (3) research, (4) public service, (5) administration, and (6) professional development.

Of these six activities, direct contact teaching is the most reliable measure and the easiest to check for accuracy. With the linkage of faculty analysis and research proposal analysis, more detailed information is becoming available on the research activity and its relationship to direct contact teaching. Public service and its subset, patient care, are a major factor in the analysis of health professions education faculty. With regard to preparation and evaluation, administration, and professional development, the key is understanding their essential nature and their relative relationship to the other major activities. It should be noted that regardless of the reporting method, the basic relationships between these activities remain.

We still do not have a clear perception of the relationship between what faculty say they do, what they actually do, and what administrators perceive they are supposed to do. A major part of this problem is that there are few explicit statements of these relationships in detail before, during, or after the resource utilization.

Future Faculty Requirements. Identifying future faculty requirements is *the* problem of the present. Allocating and utilizing them efficiently and effectively are problems of the future. In the past as well as in the present, faculty activity determination was in the hands of faculty members; and by and large, they accepted and carried out their responsibility effectively. The responsibility was primarily self-oriented, with administration functioning principally to coordinate. Present circumstances demand faculty requirements be determined by responsible academic policymakers who can implement their strategies and evaluate their effectiveness as well. The problem for professors is efficiently playing their allocated activity role to meet the needs of the institution's missions. One such role may be that of assisting the policymakers in identifying future faculty requirements. The problem for administrators is effective management of scarce resources. The piece-by-piece analysis and problem resolution method presently used by management is not going to work effectively in the future because there is very little margin for error. As the saying goes, there is *no* slack in the system.

If the trend is from a growth to a steady to a declining state, the future will require a new outlook because past methods may very well not apply. Planning is the key word and alternative futures analysis is a method. Large institutions have more overall resources to reallocate than smaller ones; but when it comes to faculty resources, the problems are the same. The interrelationships of faculty activities and their discipline orientation are the same for any type of institution.

If institutions are going to respond effectively, they must *recognize the need* to plan and *support the research* necessary to provide the information for planning. It is imperative to recognize the limitations of past and present activities and develop approaches for determining futures. There must be, however, a defined goal *to plan and to develop planning information,* otherwise no effective results will occur.

Steps in Determining Future Faculty Requirements

The first step is to determine current faculty requirements for instructional programs. That *does not* mean asking "How many faculty do we now have?" It *does* mean asking (1) what instructional programs or curriculums are provided, (2) how many students are in these programs, (3) what is the *demand* for faculty time by teaching unit, and (4) what is the *supply* of faculty time by type within each teaching unit. These four questions relate to program planning and should be closely linked to the budgeting process by asking such questions as "What is the faculty cost?" and "What are the other costs, both direct and indirect, related to faculty?" Much of the data to answer these questions is now available within institutions of higher education. Often, however, it exists in segregated pieces in separate organizational units. The development of planning information requires a solution to this organizational problem.

This first step in determining future faculty requirements recognizes the primary mission of an educational institution as that of instruction, with research and public service secondary. The focus is on programs and the units with teaching responsibility for them. Student enrollment is also an essential factor. Curriculum structure and the number of students affect the *demand* for faculty teaching time. The teaching unit designation allows for anlaysis of constraints such as "critical discipline mass" in evaluating alternatives. The *demand* for faculty teaching time is matched with the current *supply* by teaching unit. This matching results in the development of a faculty activity profile by type indicating the average teaching load of a faculty member in the teaching unit. When this faculty requirement data is linked with the financial data, the cost of the program benefits is identified. The objective of this procedure is to determine the faculty requirements by program. The emphasis is focused on faculty discipline teaching as organized in programs. This approach is what is called a "faculty-driven" model as compared with a "student-driven" enrollment-in-course model. The approach recognizes the faculty resource as the *supply-demand* critical point.

As current faculty requirements are being calculated, the institutional research staff can undertake research on the development of comparison standards. This will provide administrators with guidelines for alternative solutions.

This type of analysis is recommended for any level of an academic institution but has major benefit when applied at the level of aggregation from which the decision-making process is taking place or higher. In other words, a top-down analysis is suggested.

The second step in this process is to identify the major constraints on the system, such as limited financial resources, collective bargaining agreements, and student enrollment. Limited financial resources will constrain the funding available for faculty and may necessitate consideration of alternative types of faculty. A collective bargaining agreement, however, may limit the faculty availability to teaching, thereby compounding a financial constraint. Declining student enrollment is a major concern of the 1980s. A key question becomes that of the level to which enrollment can be allowed to fall in a program before consideration must be given to eliminating the program. The emphasis is again on programs and faculty activities related to them.

The third step is to develop alternative futures based on the educational process structure and identified constraints. In this manner, one can plan a path for the future. The role of institutional research in this process is to develop the information and the techniques for collecting data and to develop surrogate methods for analysis when actual data is unavailable.

The fourth step is for the administrators to make decisions and to evaluate them. This is easy to say but very hard to do. Departments with different goals and objectives may have different staffing patterns. With limited resources, some will have to be taken from one and given to another. One of the major concerns here is timing, but the alternative futures analysis can identify the rapidity with which resources can be reallocated.

Up to this point, I have emphasized instructional program planning and direct contact teaching activities, while recognizing the necessity of supporting faculty activities. This focus is appropriate for institutions with a primary mission of instruction, such as community colleges and liberal arts colleges. But instruction is only one part of the responsibilities of research universities, particularly those with academic health centers. In these environments, the academic needs of all of the institution's missions must be determined, their allocation of resources checked, and their utilization evaluated. When discussing missions planning, particular consideration must be given to faculty research and public service activities. Traditionally, these missions have been dealt with separately from instruction, primarily because their source of funding was separate. This is especially the case with "sponsored" research funded on "soft" money. If we consider the concept of research time from the point of view of the faculty member, he or she may consider it as serving the teaching mission of the institution by transmitting knowledge to doctoral candidate research assistants, contributing to its research mission by developing new knowledge, and contributing to its public service mission by providing sources for applications research. All these statements may or may not be true, but until more research is done in describing and assigning these activities to functions, we cannot say one way or the other. This, however, only "begs the question" and does not help us solve our problem, namely, the determination of faculty resource requirements. It does, however, clarify the problem. Faculty members utilize their time in multiple missions and multiple programs within missions. So if academic administrators are going to determine academic staff needs, this should be done within the context of the determination of missions and goals as well as programs because changes in one will ultimately affect faculty resource requirements in the other.

The alternative futures method is appropriate; the scope is simply broader. The procedure should include the following steps: (1) description of current mission and program *demand* for faculty time, and *supply* of faculty (leading to the determination of *what is* the case), (2) definition of constraints affecting *demand* and *supply* (helping define what might be the case), (3) definition of alternate *demand* and *supply* relationships (focusing on faculty time, the need for it, its allocation to teaching, research, or public service missions and to instructional programs at the undergraduate or graduate levels, and its utilization in carrying out these functions), and finally, (4) a decision on the direction to take.

An Approach to a Solution

Time is a fundamental resource. Its cost in relation to its benefits in terms of amount, allocation, and use is a major concern of institutions. In academic institutions, faculty time is a precious resource. Faculty members, as the providers of this resource, have a major interest in how much of their time is distributed among their many activities. Administrators, as the managers of all the institution's resources, including finances, facilities, and information, have a major interest in how much time is needed to provide what services. Faculty and administrative viewpoints of the problem are clearly different, but the problem is the same. Any solution to it must encompass the views of both parties or it will fail to satisfy a major interest area. If the whole problem is kept in perspective, various parts may be solved using a basic approach but varying the role of the interested parties.

The four steps are (1) description of current resource requirements, (2) definition of constraints, (3) description of alternative futures, and (4) choice of future direction.

The three roles of participants in the process are those of (1) resource requirement describer, (2) constraints definer, and (3) decision maker.

In assessing academic needs, allocation, and utilization, let us start with the problem of faculty *utilization* and with how individual faculty members spend their time.

Utilization. This problem involves predominantly a single faculty member and the department chairperson, with the faculty member serving primarily as the resource requirement describer and the chairperson as the constraint definer. On the basis of their information, alternative futures are developed and, collectively by negotiation, a decision on future direction can be made. Written documents in the form of performance contracts (before-the-fact information) and faculty activity analysis reports (after-the-fact information) may serve as the means of evaluating the utilization of time and its assignment to programs and missions.

Allocation. Faculty allocation problems usually exist at two levels of organization: (1) allocation to departments by central administration and (2) assignment by department chairperson to individual faculty members. In this setting, the department chairperson functions in all three roles—resource requirement describer, constraints definer, and decision maker. The chairperson's ability to function appropriately will depend on his or her knowledge of the process step and role at that step point. In this type of situation, the department chairperson should be the describer of the *collective* faculty requirements for time for the discipline, while the mission and program constraints should be described by the central administration.

Department chairpersons *should be* aware of the time resources of the collective faculty. If they are not, the institutional research staff should assist in describing current resources and requirements and communicating that information to the central administration, which may also need information on its role at this step in the process. Constraints definition may be provided both by the chairperson and the administration. Future direction may in large part be affected by the constraints from both levels. With this analytical approach, both levels of management are aware of the decision process, the information used to make the decision, and the decision makers. This is not to say all decisions will be equitable. They will in all probability not be. As the saying goes, you win some; you lose some. But in this case, you should know why.

Needs. Academic staff needs assessment is an institutional-level problem that predominantly involves decisions on missions and goals and on programs within those goals to determine *all* faculty resource requirements for time. Existing master plans usually talk in global terms. The simple fact is that very specific information is now needed not only to account for past activities and justify present activities but also to negotiate for future activity support. The central administration is the resource requirements describer for the financial supporters of the institution, who in many cases are the constraint definers and ultimately the decision makers. If central administration wishes to participate in the decision-making process, it should have alternative futures solutions available based on detailed *aggregated* information that considers the constraints. In this type of situation, negotiations for future direction may proceed in a more productive manner for all parties concerned.

In summary, faculty time is *the* key resource of academic institutions. Past processes and techniques for measuring their time are inadequate. Faculty members, individually and collectively, need to work closely with administrators more clearly to identify their activities and their *relationship* to the programs, goals, and missions of the institution. No "form" is ever going to accomplish this task. The process is a negotiated one based on clear definitions of the problem to be solved, the criteria to be used in solving the problem, and the participation of all interested parties. If this is not the case, valuable "time" for the development and transmission of knowledge *will be utilized* but for naught—and that time includes administrator resources as well as faculty.

Bibliographical Essay

A starting point in reviewing the problems and procedures associated with faculty activity analysis is Harold E. Yuker's "Faculty Workload: Facts, Myths and Commentary" (1974). Though Yuker points out that very few advances have been made since the turn of the century in our understanding of academic staff resources, his book presents an overview of the concepts involved in the measurement of faculty work load as a basis for determining academic efficiency by which to set academic policies. Its bibliography references the major documents that support the material presented. As its title indicates, it presents the facts and the myths and provides constructive suggestions for future research on the topic. Those suggestions are very pertinent today and will continue to be so through the 1980s. This sixty-two-page report is recommended as required reading for new administrators in any level of decision making in higher education.

Having read Yuker and deciding you want more detailed information, I suggest the NCHEMS reports on faculty activity analysis, particularly Leonard Romney's and Charles Manning's (1974) "Interpretation and Uses of Data" before any procedures manuals are reviewed. The reason is to be able to recognize the potentials for misuse and the high sensitivity of faculty to *any* use of such data.

The article by John C. Koehler and Robert L. Slighton (1973) illustrates the complexity of analyzing faculty activities. This article reviews methods to deal with the "joint product" problem and indicates their use in the academic health center decision-making environment. Comments on the usefulness of these methods in policy planning are also presented. The references provide entry to the classic research on the use of faculty effort analysis as a basis for cost allocation for medical education, where academic staff needs, allocation, and utilization are probably the most complex in higher education (not to mention the most expensive). A fourth reference, which attempts to build on previous research: *Analyzing and Constructing Cost* (1978), which I edited. It defines problems, gives solutions (with extensive references), and presents ideas for future directions with a major focus on faculty resource requirements.

References

Gonyea, M. A. (Ed.). *New Directions for Institutional Research: Analyzing and Constructing Cost,* no. 17. San Francisco: Jossey-Bass, 1978.

Koehler, J. C., and Slighton, R. L. "Activity Analysis and Cost Analysis in Medical Schools." *Journal of Medical Education,* 1973, *48,* 531–550.

Romney, L. C., and Manning, C. W. "Faculty Activity Analysis: Interpretation and Uses of Data." Technical Report 54. Boulder, Colo.: National Center for Higher Education Management Systems, 1974.

Yuker, H. E. "Faculty Workload: Facts, Myths, and Commentary." ERIC Higher Education Research Report No. 6. Washington, D.C.: American Association for Higher Education, 1974.

19

John E. Corbally
Kristin Holmberg-Wright

Identifying Administrative Staff Needs

This chapter speaks to the topic of how administrators, in concert with other members of the institutional community, approach the allocation of resources for administration. It describes how institutional purposes shape administrative staffing needs, various kinds of administrative positions and administrative structure, ways of measuring administrative costs and administrative effectiveness, and administrative staff development. In each of these areas, it provides a way of looking at specific institutional problems and possibilities rather than a model for use in each specific situation.

Planning, Institutional Research, and Administrative Staff Needs

In most colleges and universities, institutional research and planning specialists provide a major portion of the responsibilities described in this chapter regarding the determination of administrative staff needs and the allocation and utilization of resources to meet those needs. Several specific comments about this role of planners and of institutional researchers can serve as a summary for the chapter.

Purpose Determination. Plans are made to achieve purposes, and institutional data are gathered to assist in evaluating the degree to which purposes are met. In the development of institutional plans, some seemingly mundane but nonetheless important purposes should be on the planning agenda that often are not. Planners often fail to include sufficient emphasis upon planning as an institutional purpose. The need to conform to laws and government rules and regulations is rarely recognized as a task of the institution. The maintenance of facilities—or, more broadly stated, the creation and maintenance of an academic environment—is an institutional purpose that needs to be recognized by planners and by those who study institutions. If such institutional purposes are a key in determining administrative staff needs, then planners must maintain a broad and comprehensive view of purposes so that staff needs are fully described.

Descriptive Terms. Plans and institutional data often create institutional dichotomies and confusion. Too few institutional researchers maintain clear understandings of either the purposes or the actual magnitude of administrative costs. Administrative costs often are aggregated from what is left after commonly accepted academic costs are allocated. Little attention in higher education has been given to the actual costs (or savings) of technological developments, most of which occur in areas assigned to "administrative costs." Planners and institutional researchers need to press questions related to productivity, to efficiency, and to labor-technology offsets even though such questions are often not deemed appropriate for institutions of higher learning. Planning and research are designed to clarify matters and to reveal complexities and thus to avoid simplistic responses to questions. Certainly, this clarification is needed in the analysis of administrative costs and of administrative staffing patterns.

Evaluation. Planners and institutional researchers play major roles in assisting institutions to evaluate their activities. In the area of administrative staff needs, evaluation is particularly important but has lacked sophistication. The enunciation of purposes to be met by administrative staff, of the ways such purposes are essential to the attainment of overall purposes, and of ways to measure the degree to which both special and general purposes are met are important tasks that will remain either undone or incompletely done unless planners and institutional researchers accept responsibility for them. Evaluation and the development of new plans based upon evaluation are important tasks in every area of concern, but they have special importance in administrative staffing.

Purposes of Administration

Administration in its best form is leadership. Thus, an administrator can be defined as one who has been selected by a group or selected for a group to be responsible for helping the group move from wherever it is to wherever it should be. Today's complexities of life do not permit that simple definition to suffice for institutional administration. Thus, in today's colleges and universities, there are *general administrators,* who are assigned overall leadership roles; *academic administrators,* with specific assignments for one or more academic units within an institution; and *support service administrators* and other personnel often included within the phrase "the administration," who are responsible for necessary activities ranging from food service to computer service. In addition, in the higher education establishment, one also finds coordinating administrators working for state coordinating boards; liaison personnel working for state and federal agencies, governors, or members of Congress; and a host of others who either define themselves or are defined by others as administrators.

One can speak of administrators in terms of function (for example, "leadership") or in terms of accounting clarifications (such as "administration, general, all units, or all funds"). One can speak of "the administration" as if that term encompasses all nonfaculty personnel or only an evil or benign president. This chapter is concerned with the allocation of resources for administration, so to some extent, the accounting definition might be expected to prevail; but when one is determining need, it is often better to concentrate upon function and let the accountants categorize the resulting dollar decisions.

It is also necessary to recognize that functions today are both generated from within an institution and imposed upon institutions. The chapters in Part One spoke of the impact of various agencies upon institutional planning and research. These external groups have had major impact upon administrative staffing requirements. Divisions of and administrative officers for occupational health and safety, equal employment, educational opportunity, energy conservation, pollution control, or research time and effort reporting are examples of requirements imposed by such agencies. In many cases, the functions—or at least some portion of them—exist without external pressure; but special external requirements make it necessary to elevate the functions to special levels not required by internal needs. The purposes of administration clearly cannot be achieved without some form of subdivision.

General administration is the provision of leadership in assisting a group to define and achieve both institutional and individual purposes. As an institution develops plans based upon stated institutional purposes, its members look to general administrators, such as its president or executive vice-president, to provide leadership in proposing, achieving, and evaluating those plans and to provide an environment and a reward system that permits them to meet their individual purposes and plans while contributing to the attainment of institutional plans. A general administrator assists a group in defining problems, developing and assessing alternative solutions to problems, selecting and pursuing one alternate solution from among several possibilities, and assessing the degree to which perceived solutions have been actual solutions. Depending upon the quality of the group and upon the complexity of the problems or purposes facing it, the leader may be primarily a facilitator and stimulator, as in most institutions of higher education, or the primary source of creative ideas.

Academic administration is a major task in a college or university. Academic administrators include department heads, deans of schools or colleges, and vice-presidents for academic affairs. General administrators are concerned with all aspects of a unit, from its teaching and learning programs to providing heat and light in the facilities where teaching and learning take place; academic administrators, usually through a combination of delegation from a general administrator and of expressed desires of the members of the group as recorded in institutional statutes, bylaws, or regulations, are responsible for a slightly narrower range of responsibilities related to the academic programs and plans of an institution. The administrative or leadership techniques involved in academic administration vary not at all from those involved in general administration. Many general administrators in a college or university (presidents, for example) describe themselves as "academic administrators," probably in an effort to ensure respectability and to acknowledge the central core of their work.

Another group of administrators, those in support service administration, deal with the range of services that support attainment of the central academic purposes of the institution. In many cases, administrators in these support divisions are specialists, often specially licensed. They range from hospital administrators to food service directors. Some support service administrators, such as admissions and records officers and the director of the physical plant, are common to almost every college or university; others depend upon the nature of the institution. A commuter campus without residence halls but with a large student union facility requires different student service administrators than a residential campus. Administrators in support divisions receive their responsibilities and assignments through delegation from general administrators. Although the role and authority of academic administrators are often the subject of many institutional rules or statutes developed by or in concert with faculty members, the role and authority of support service administrators are usually determined by general administrators.

Among these three kinds of administration—general, academic, and support—many areas overlap; and the effort to classify an administrator in one of these groups is not worth long argument. The librarian, for example, is often considered to direct a support service and yet can easily lay claim to an academic administration role. The dean of a comprehensive college of liberal arts and sciences in a large university is clearly an academic administrator and yet may have responsibilities greater and broader than those of many college presidents. This difficulty in classifying administrators is why data concerning administrative costs are difficult to compare from institution to institution and why planning models often fit only one set of institutions. It is important to understand for a given institution what is meant by general, academic, and support service administration, in order to help clarify planning and the evaluation of administration and of administrative costs. But the classification of administrators is not an exact science.

Administrative Organization

If administration is leadership and if it involves assisting groups to meet institutional and individual purposes, there must be structures that place administrators, groups, and institutional units in appropriate configurations. The structure of institutions has become increasingly complex, making it more difficult than ever to describe typical administrative organizations. It is equally difficult to provide a universal list of institutional purposes administrative leadership will work toward at every college or university in the nation. Those purposes are essential elements of the institutional plans discussed in Parts Three and Four and to be discussed in Part Seven of this volume. A university with one set of purposes will require a group of people led by one or more administrators in the area of public service and extension activities. A small liberal arts college may have no purposes that require such people or such leadership. The determination of an administrative organization for a specific institution grows from the purposes of that institution. Thus, this chapter discusses administrative staffing from a consideration of the factors involved in making staffing decisions rather than with the intent of providing universal formulas or models for staffing decisions.

It is important, then, to restress that the need for administrative staff grows from the known purposes to be met by the institution—including, in today's world, a whole new set of purposes related to adherence to local, state, and federal laws, rules, and regulations. Few master plans state that among the institution's essential purposes are the conduct of its affairs in such a way as to conform to all appropriate acts of state legislatures and of the Congress; to conform to all appropriate regulations and rules of local, state, and federal agencies; to defend the institution in local, state, and federal courts; and to respond accurately and punctually to requests for data and for general information from governmental and private groups of all kinds. Unfortunately, these purposes must be added to the more traditional purposes of the conduct of programs of teaching, research, and service to foster the transmission, creation, and utilization of knowledge. In many cases, the costs of meeting the former purposes have outstripped the costs of meeting the latter. Thus, the discussion of administrative organization can only indicate the factors to be considered. Perhaps the best way to approach this task is to follow a synthesizing rather than an analyzing approach.

Single-Campus Institution. The basic form of academic structure is the college or university (made up of two or more colleges) located on a single campus and governed by a board of trustees responsible for that campus only. This structure usually provides for one general administrator (president), several staff administrators assisting the president (such as an executive assistant, counsel, and public relations officer), one or more vice-presidents (at least one for academic administration and one or more for support services), college and department academic officers (deans and chairpersons), and directors of support units.

The purposes to be met by administrators within the organization must govern decisions about numbers of, levels of, and interrelationships among administrators. A single-college, single-campus institution with one residence hall will need fewer administrators than will a large university; but in each case, it is likely that the purposes to be achieved will be similar. Decisions about administrative structure should grow first from an understanding of the purposes of the structure.

It is clear that a set of considerations related to resources will influence the degree to which the organization asks single administrators to meet multiple purposes. It is ironic that a large, well-financed university will have no difficulty creating a fund-raising (or development) unit but a small and needy college must ask people to add fund raising to already full schedules. Actually, the needs of the small college may dictate more administrative emphasis upon and a greater allocation of dollars and people to fund raising than would seem proper. It is a rare institution that can staff to meet administrative needs to an extent that there are not multiple purposes assigned to each administrator. It is important to ensure that the real assignments and responsibilities of specific administrators and administrative positions are known and understood rather than to assume titles or organization charts reveal this information.

Within the single-campus institution, the general administrators will be required to meet complex purposes coming from both inside and outside the institution. One factor that has led to the creation of multicampus colleges and universities and to the creation of multiperson "offices of the president" in single-campus institutions is the increasing scope of the environment in which general administrators must work. As one contemplates administrative staff needs within an institution, the realities of the amount of work a single human being can manage require more attention than has been the case. Many administrative staffing patterns do not reflect the expanding arena outside the campus in which the administrative role must be played. This lack of attention leads to inefficiencies and lower quality in administrative performance and high turnover. Assigning too few administrative staff to meet institutional needs is "penny wise and pound foolish."

Although there has been increasing consolidation of institutions into multicampus systems in recent years, the single-campus institution with a single governing board is still the predominant form of organization in terms of number of institutions. In terms of numbers of students served by type of institution, more students find themselves in multicampus systems than in single-campus colleges and universities.

Multicampus System. The exact definition of a "multicampus system" is hard to develop. For the purpose of this discussion, we define it as a grouping of campuses each of which is headed by a designated campus chief executive officer (usually either a chancellor or a president) in which the entire group is headed by a chief executive officer and governed by a single governing board. Examples of such systems are the University of California, the State University of New York, and the University of Illinois.

If a multicampus system is a public college or university system (such systems are rare in the private sector of higher education) and contains every public institution of higher education in the state, that system also represents "statewide governance." The University of Wisconsin and University of Utah systems are examples of statewide governance. If the multicampus system is not all inclusive of the public sector of higher education in a state, statewide governance does not exist and one or more systems or systems and campuses or campuses are probably subject to coordination by a statewide coordinating agency as well as to governance by individual governing boards. Illinois provides an example of this form of organization. Four governing boards govern four multicampus systems of senior universities that include thirteen campuses. In addition, an Illinois Community College Board has certain governing responsibilities for the community colleges in Illinois—each of which is also in a community college district governed by a local board of trustees. These five systems plus private higher education in Illinois are subject to certain limited powers of a statewide coordinating board, the Illinois Board of Higher Education.

The four multicampus senior university systems in Illinois exhibit two distinct forms of administrative organization, each of which leads to different staffing patterns. The University of Illinois (UI) and Southern Illinois University (SIU) are single-university systems. In each, a system executive officer (called the president at UI and the chancellor at SIU) reports directly to the governing board and is responsible for the administration of the entire university. The other two senior university systems are organized as federations of separate universities. The systemwide officer (an executive director) and the campus chief executive officers report directly to the governing board.

Obviously, the requirements for systemwide administration as well as for campus administration will vary, depending upon which of these two forms of governance is followed. In the so-called hierocratic or single-university, multicampus system, many of the support services are provided through system rather than through campus offices. In either form of organization, academic decision making and leadership remain largely decentralized to the campus, college, and department levels, subject only to certain minimum policy requirements established for the system.

Once again, however, administrative staffing needs will depend upon the institutional purposes to be served by a system level of administration. To some extent, a system group deals much more with external agencies and concerns than will a campus group. The University of Illinois (1972, pp. 1–2) developed the following list of functions to establish the purposes to be met by the system level:

> 1. The enunciation of the mission of the University of Illinois; the development of long-range, comprehensive plans for the attainment of that mission; and the development of a plan of evaluation on a regular basis of the success of the university in meeting that mission.
> 2. The attainment of the resources necessary to permit the support of plans and the development of facilities to meet the mission of the university.
> 3. The allocation of resources, as available, to the campuses and to other units of the university within the requirements and the priorities of the long-range comprehensive plan for the attainment of the mission of the university.
> 4. The development of relationships both within Illinois and in the nation and world to ensure that the University of Illinois plays its appropriate role as a member of the larger education community.
> 5. The coordination of the operation of the various components of the university to ensure that the university functions as an organic university rather than as an aggregation of unrelated campuses and capitalizes upon the advantages of its resources as a system.
> 6. The administration of universitywide educational programs. Examples include the Institute of Government and Public

Affairs, the Survey Research Laboratory, and the Division of University Extension.

7. The operation of various specific tasks, which should function at a university level either for efficiency or to ensure the consistency necessary to permit the university and its governing board to meet their responsibilities.

8. The development of information programs to attempt to secure full understanding of and support for the mission and activities of the University of Illinois.

A list of purposes or functions such as this one is an appropriate framework for determining staffing needs and staffing assignments.

Statewide Coordination. For a variety of reasons discussed in Chapter Five, state agencies to coordinate various institutions of postsecondary education have been established in almost every state unless that state has a system of statewide governance. In general, the coordinating agencies have assignments in planning, in reviewing the academic programs of institutions within the state, and in providing governors and/or legislators with recommendations and advice about fiscal matters as they affect postsecondary education. These agencies usually are charged with planning responsibilities affecting both the public and private sectors of postsecondary education and, increasingly, affecting proprietary schools. In most states, the coordinating agency has more authority vis-à-vis the public sector than with either the private or proprietary sectors.

The determination of staffing needs in these agencies also has an impact upon staffing needs in the institutions. It is an unfortunate fact that the creation of one position to seek information requires the creation of many more positions to provide information. Much of the so-called proliferation of administration in higher education is a direct result of that fact, as the age of "accountability" has led to overlapping agencies and individuals seeking data from institutions. Staffing needs—indeed, the basic need for agencies—at a statewide coordinating level require careful analysis of real and necessary purposes to be served by that level because of the great leverage effect of the creation of each such position or agency.

Regardless of the organizational form of higher education in a state, the total system of higher education exists to serve what should be known purposes. Each different form of organization is created because of a set of conditions and because of traditions and of history unique to that organization. The purposes to be served, however, are similar from state to state and from institution to institution. The staffing of each form of organization and of the various agencies or units included within a total organization depends upon the purposes to be served. It is the purposes to be served rather than the shape of the organizational chart or the shape of someone else's organizational chart that determines staffing needs.

Administrative Style

One's personal style does not change the purposes of an institution. It may be a factor in one's effectiveness in either changing or reinforcing institutional purposes, but institutional purposes are the basic determinants of staffing needs. But how one works does influence both the number and the kinds of staff people who may be needed to meet institutional purposes. The president of a single-campus university who tends to devote major attention to external groups (legislators, alumni, or opinion leaders) will need different staffing patterns in his or her office and in the offices of other administrators than will a president who devotes major attention to internal academic and budgetary concerns. University administrators come to a new position and are given a set of existing administrative positions and people. Changes to reflect one's style need to come through normal turnover, through gradual readjustment of assignments and emphasis, and through some adjustments of one's own style.

There are also certain givens within a college or university that influence the degree to which one can permit style to govern staffing patterns. A president in a senior university may decide that a vice-president for public information is not necessary and may divide the assignments of such an office among several offices and people; similar freedom does not exist with regard to the position of vice-president for academic affairs. The latter position is so traditional, is so much the faculty's representative in higher administration that a proposal to abolish it would appear to be a blow against that faculty. This appearance is an example of the "mystique factors" that must be considered in staffing and that in some cases will override changes that might be made because of style.

Style will determine administrative assignments in other ways. Some administrators prefer clear-cut, specific, nonoverlapping position descriptions in which one person and one person only is responsible for an area of concern. Others prefer less-specific assignments in which some overlap is encouraged. As long as style does not interfere with the attainment of purpose or lead to wasted resources, it can, does, and should have some impact upon staffing. And although there are obvious limits, it cannot be said that one style is good and another is bad. Each person making staffing decisions is unique, and an organization will always reflect the humanness of those who people it at any given time.

Administrative Costs

All organizational decisions are made after some consideration of probable costs. Decisions within institutions of higher education—institutions of limited financial resources—must include particularly careful consideration of cost. Any decision involves two major cost factors: costs associated with choosing and implementing alternative A or B or C and costs associated with the failure to choose and implement alternative A or B or C. The costs of doing something are more easily identified and quantified than the costs of not doing something, but the net cost of doing anything must be the difference between the cost of doing and the cost of not doing that thing.

Few people who look at administrative costs consider the costs of not supporting administrative activities or the costs of supporting administrative activities insufficiently and receiving poor-quality administrative service. Just as it is dangerous to "save" money by not maintaining physical facilities, so is it dangerous to eliminate administrative "overhead." There is a set of functions that must be performed in a college or university in order to permit the functions of teaching, research, and service to be performed. A reasonable level of resources must be devoted to the performance of those functions, and that level can be determined only as one is aware of the functions to be met.

Data. The University of Illinois (1978, pp. 3–4) provides insight into the problems of generating and using cost data related to administrative costs.

> Detailed comparisons of administrative costs among systems of higher education are always dangerous, because of the absence of precisely comparable data. In Illinois, there are differences in size, scope and mission, and organization of the four systems of public universities. Some functions carried out at the general university level at the University of Illinois, for example, are performed at the campus level at other institutions. Thus, no attempt has been made in this study to isolate specific administrative functions and compare them across campuses or even among systems.
>
> On the other hand, when individual administrative functions are accumulated on the basis of standard guidelines for each system, general trends are revealed which may be used to compare the relative efficiency with which each system provides for its administration. For this study, the category of "Institutional Support" used by the Illinois Board of Higher Education to record expenditures for administrative functions was selected as the one which offered the highest degree of comparability for systems in Illinois. Operation and maintenance costs were not included in the IBHE figures in order to focus most directly on administrative expenditures.
>
> The comparisons reveal that the University of Illinois provides a smaller portion of its total budget for administrative costs than do the other systems of senior institutions. This result may be attributed to two interrelated factors:
>
> 1. The overall size of the University of Illinois, which allows for economies of scale not possible in smaller institutions; and
> 2. The organization and operation of the university following the "organic whole" concept, which enhances the sharing of resources among the campuses to a greater extent than is likely to exist among independent campuses.

This quotation supports the ideas that administrative form and cost follow institutional function and purpose and that organizational factors such as size influence costs.

If one assumes administrative costs in Illinois are somewhat typical, current studies suggest such costs as a percentage of total institutional expenses have declined slightly over the past five years and they ranged from about 5 percent to about 9 percent of institutional expenses in fiscal year 1979. Even this general kind of statement, however, is more inexact than it appears. It includes a host of classification decisions that, it is hoped, balance themselves but that may, in fact, lead to either an understatement or an overstatement of administrative costs. Department chairpersons, for example, are "out"; deans and their entire offices are "in"; library administration is "out"; relations with high schools are "in"; and so on through literally dozens of decisions. One institution operates a hospital; others do not. One institution operates a laboratory school; others do not. Administrative cost data comparisons may not be considered a comparison "of apples and oranges," but they certainly represent comparisons among widely different varieties of either apples or oranges. Each institution will be differently organized with different headings for various offices. Generation of cost data that are really useful clearly requires great staff attention in and of itself.

Evaluation. If the generation of meaningful data related to administrative costs is difficult and if the ability to use such data in comparison studies is even more difficult, is any purpose served in generating the data? The response depends upon the form in which the data are gathered and displayed. It is important to be aware of what it costs to meet some purpose or to perform some function. Unfortunately, the classification systems—primarily standard accounting systems—used to organize cost data do not speak to real functions. They ignore the real costs of faculty time devoted to assist in meeting administrative functions; they arbitrarily include or exclude costs on the basis of position titles with little regard for function; and they aggregate costs in ways that blur the functions through which costs were incurred.

If cost data are to be useful—other than merely serving to meet some legal reporting requirement or to provide general year-to-year trend data that reveal results but not causes—the institution must go beyond simplistic definitions of administration and of administrative staff and organize data around functions. Because various costs are associated with more than one function, it is necessary, if one is to attempt to use cost data, to create small cost data units that can be put together in appropriate ways to provide information about the total costs of various functions. The creation of data systems to provide meaningful cost analyses is difficult, but institutions now must provide so much data in so many different configurations to so many agencies that the addition of one more configuration to be of real value to the institution could be considered a minor addition to an already large data-reporting requirement. Only as one analyzes costs as they relate to real functions can one begin to determine the degree to which one's staffing decisions appear to be efficient. To this analysis must be added the evaluation of how functions or purposes are being served so one can determine both the efficiency and the effectiveness of administrative staffing patterns.

Administrative Staff Development

When one has developed a clear sense of the purposes to be met by an administrative staff, an organizational pattern in which the staff will be arranged to meet those purposes, and a budget plan to support the staffing of that pattern, the next tasks are to find, recruit, and retain people to fill the positions. In addition, one needs to have a plan through which one can analyze both the pattern and the staffing of that pattern to ensure that what is appropriate today is still appropriate tomorrow.

Preparing and Selecting Administrators. The need for special kinds of expertise has long been recognized as people are sought to staff administrative positions in the support service areas (business and finance, computer services, auditing, admissions and records, and so forth), but the concept of "amateur administrators" for both general and academic positions has been prevalent. It is still generally true that one who aspires to a university presidency or academic vice-presidency is probably well advised to keep that aspiration a secret. However, a review of the criteria statements recently prepared and published to guide searches for general and academic administrative staff does indicate an increasing recognition of the need for high-level administrative and management skills in those who lead institutions of higher education.

No pattern that can be viewed as the ideal or model pattern for the preparation of general and academic administrative staff has yet emerged. It is clear that those who would undertake to lead faculty should have faculty experience, so most general and academic administrators have completed undergraduate, graduate, and/or professional degrees in fields other than management or administration and have taught or done research as faculty members. Preparation for administrative duties has, then, been on a sort of "catch-as-catch-can" basis along with "sink-or-swim" administrative assignments. Probably no profession—if college and university administration can be viewed as a profession—is filled with as many self-taught professionals. Probably no profession is filled with as many individuals who deny they really want to practice their profession.

It is increasingly apparent that some increased amounts of preparation and of professionalism are necessary in the general and academic administration of higher education. This effort is not designed to create a "managerial class" so feared by faculty members but rather to prepare faculty members and others to meet the real and complex demands placed upon general and academic administrators by the environment in which administration is now practiced.

Programs similar to executive development programs in business and in other areas of public administration, short courses both to provide refreshers to restore old skills and information and to provide information about necessary new skills and knowledge, and sabbatical leave programs in which administration is viewed as the discipline under study are needed to contribute to the preparation and development of administrators. Graduate-level programs in the field of higher education need to be redesigned to involve literally an entire campus rather than merely one or two traditional areas of concern.

Increasingly, the process of staffing—the search process—should recognize that the choice to enter general or academic administration will need to be made by younger faculty members, who therefore will not accrue the usual pattern of professorial accomplishments but will instead accrue both professional and administrative records. Indeed, some attention should be given to career paths within an institution with the purpose of finding ways to promote people from one level of responsibility to another without the constant costs in time and in dollars of de novo search processes. Because of the lotterylike nature of search processes, it is difficult to advise a young man or woman interested in administration on what steps should lead to administrative responsibilities. Thus, higher education loses potential administrators to other fields where career paths are understood and accomplishment and quality are more likely to lead to promotions and increased responsibilities.

The preparation of administrators for higher education and the selection of individuals for specific administrative positions are critical elements in a staffing plan. Unfortunately, as the demands for and upon administrators in higher education increase, neither preparation programs nor selection processes seem equal to those demands.

Reviewing Administrative Assignments. Colleges and universities are growing, living entities whose purposes change and whose environments shift. Although these changes are evolutionary rather than revolutionary, significant changes do take place over relatively short periods of time. Thus, specific administrative positions and the descriptions of responsibilities assigned to them require regular review. One problem associated with the lengthy tenure of a single individual in a key administrative position is the danger that position requirements will change and the individual's abilities will not. Another problem in higher education is a reluctance to develop personnel programs that include efforts to retrain and redirect competent people whose positions are eliminated. The so-called "tenure problem" exists in part because of a view in higher education that professors' skills can be used only in one narrow set of ways. Ironically, these same professors attempt to prepare graduates who possess flexibility and who can adjust to a changing society.

A regular review pattern in which administrative assignments are analyzed to ensure they speak to current purposes and take account of current states of the art as well as states of the institution should be established. The adjustment of individual assignments should be seen as a regular rather than an extraordinary event. Assignment changes should reflect changes in conditions in the institution and in the individual administrators. Some assignment shifts can keep individuals alive and growing and have therapeutic value for both the individual and the institution. One cannot breathe a sigh of relief after developing a pattern of administrative staffing; one can only pause, knowing that any pattern is subject to change and requires evaluation.

The difference may be subtle, but there is a difference between the evaluation of an administrative staffing pattern and administrative assignments and the evaluation of a given individual's performance in a specific administrative position. Chapter Twenty-Four discusses the purposes of and processes for the latter type of evaluation. This chapter has dealt in a number of ways with the former type. Both are important elements of an overall plan for administrator evaluation in a college or university.

Types of Administrative Assignments. As one attempts to maintain a current administrative structure, one deals with two sets of terms that are supposed to aid in defining administrative roles. First, one speaks of "generalists" and of "specialists." This chapter has already mentioned three areas of administrative concern—general, academic, and support service. Each area will include positions in which one is responsible for the overall management of a unit and others in which individuals are responsible for specialized tasks within a unit. The differences between a "generalist" and a "specialist" in administration are primarily differences of degree of involvement. The president, for example, needs to know enough about computers to have realistic expectations of them and to avoid being frightened or fooled by them. He or she does not have to program them, to troubleshoot them, or even to know all the model numbers and component names that identify them. The director of computer services must have much more specialized knowledge about computers and about the people who operate them. But neither the president nor the director is an operator of computers—both in their own ways are responsible for the operation. Even the specialist is an administrator of a special service, not a crafts person providing that service.

The other terms are "line" and "staff." In a pure structure, the line administrators are in the direct flow of authority and responsibility and staff administrators are responsible for providing services that assist the exercise of line authority and the meeting of line responsibilities. As administration has become recognized as a team function, the line and staff dividing line has grown less distinct. In most universities, individuals will serve both roles interchangeably. The "staff person" (a public information officer, for example) will usually have administrative responsibility for a unit or units performing staff functions. The "line officer" in one area (chief financial officer, for example) will provide staff assistance to another. The words of a staff officer, such as an executive assistant to a president, often carry "line weight," particularly if experience shows his or her words reflect the line officer's plans (or, occasionally, vice versa).

The development and assessment of administrative staffing patterns and assignments are not helped greatly by the concepts "generalist-specialist" or "line-staff." What is essential is that the purposes to be served by a staffing pattern are understood and that the responsibilities within a pattern are clear.

Administration and Institutional Purpose. The attainment of the purposes of a devoted to learning and to human development, staff development is a legitimate institutional purpose. Too often, the institution consumes its human resources while preparing people for service outside the institution and does little or nothing to restore its internal resources. As an institution attempts to keep its administrative staffing patterns current and productive in meeting institutional purposes, the nurture of that staff should be included among the purposes to be met. In the private, profit sector of the economy, staff development is an important activity and is recognized as a cost of doing business. These activities lead to expenses that can be written off against taxes. In the nonprofit sector, tax advantages are not applicable and appropriations on behalf of staff development are either nonexistent or negligible. More attention than has usually been the case needs to be given to staff development of a college or university, and part of a staffing pattern should be devoted to the attainment of that institutional purpose.

Administration and Institutional Purpose. The attainment of the purposes of a college or university requires people with a wide range of skills. Every staff member should be in place because of contributions he or she can and does make to the attainment of institutional purposes. There is an unfortunate tendency in discussing college or university staffing to ignore a whole host of people, from cooks to electricians, who are critical to institutional life, and to create a false dichotomy when discussing the two "nonignored" groups—faculty and administrators. It is almost as if these two groups existed to meet their own group purposes rather than to meet institutional purposes and as if these separate group purposes were in total and direct conflict. Particularly in times of financial pressures, accusations between the groups flow freely. Faculty is said to be wasting money and the administration is said to be hiding money.

Those who have spent a number of years as members first of one of these groups and then of the other view these kinds of discussions with some alarm. One solution is to ensure that the total institutional staffing pattern is viewed in the context of the attainment of institutional purposes. There should not be an administrative staffing pattern imposed upon a faculty staffing pattern—both of which exist in some undefined relationship with a support service staffing pattern. This kind of arrangement leads easily to a "them and us" concept of the institution rather than a "we" concept. Although total harmony and understanding will not be achieved in any known arrangement of human beings, institutional staffing must work toward creating common purposes and common understandings rather than divisiveness.

Finally, it is important to remember that in many ways, colleges and universities and their administrators are shaped by the times rather than shaping their times. It is not sheer coincidence that university presidents who served during the 1950s and 1960s are almost universally characterized as "builders." Neither is it coincidence that university presidents in the 1980s will be consumed by fiscal management concerns and will, to an increasing extent, be described as "managers." As one grapples with difficult and important institutional problems, perspective upon one's place in history is an important attribute to possess.

Bibliographical Essay

Several volumes speak to the definition of administration. Baldridge (1971) describes administration as a process; Kerr (1972) uses a series of descriptive terms in his depiction; Eble (1978) sees administration as a service; and Burns (1962) views the purpose of administration to facilitate the objectives for which the college or university exists. Though there may be differences in the written definitions of administration, all authors agree administration in its best form is leadership. Henderson (1970, chap. 19) discusses the perceptions of leadership in higher education administration.

Historically, the administrator was the president. To meet the multitudinous demands of today, administrative "teams" have been developed, with each member specializing and delegating responsibilities under the president's leadership in the areas of management, planning, external relations and development, and academic administration (Harvard University Committee on Governance, 1971). The roles and functions of academic administrators, those persons with a slightly narrower range of responsibilities related to academic programs and plans of the institution, are comprehensively outlined by Burns (1962) and to a lesser degree by Corson (1975). Another group of professionals obtaining power includes the specialists or "technocrats," as defined by Baldridge, Curtis, Ecker, and Riley (1978).

An analysis of administrative organization and purposes in the United States shows the bewildering diversity of institutional patterns. The Carnegie Commission on Higher Education (1973) constructed a twelve-category typology of higher education institutions based on the clustering of similar institutional characteristics. The Carnegie typology and the eight-category typology introduced by the Stanford Project on Academic Governance (Baldridge, Curtis, Ecker, and Riley, 1978) cover the range of American higher education institutions from the elite multicampus systems with doctoral programs to the small, specialized proprietary schools.

Balderston (1974) explains the single-campus institution; the multicampus system is included in works by Lee and Bowen (1971, 1975), Epstein (1974), and Balderston (1974). Statewide coordination of higher education is presented in volumes by Feinstein (1971); Palola, Lehmann, and Blischke (1970); Glenny and Dalglish (1973); Hook, Kurtz, and Todorovich (1978), and Halstead (1974).

The manner in which an institution is governed is reflected primarily by the style of leadership the president and other key administrators provide. Though no works have dealt completely with administrative styles and behaviors, Feltner (1975), Mortimer (1978), and Demerath, Stephens, and Taylor (1967) have discussed the effects of differing administrator styles. Corson (1975) holds leadership styles vary among individuals, largely in the degree to which the leader chooses (and is able) to concentrate authority in his or her own hands or to delegate authority among those he or she leads. Baldridge, Curtis, Ecker, and Riley (1978) found the diversity that permeates higher education produces significantly different management styles and decision-making patterns; Cohen and March (1974) found that presidential behavior was influenced by the images presidents hold of their office.

Cost analysis, combined with attention to authority and organization structure design, may facilitate increasingly efficient management. Balderston (1974) offers a rationale for cost analysis. Yet the O'Neill (1971) study was able to make only rough adjustments for the use of higher education resources to produce outputs other than instruction. This entanglement of input usage is a characteristic problem in cost analysis. Thus, one must question the interpretation of many of the cost analysis studies.

In addressing this problem, the National Center for Higher Education Management Systems developed a resource requirement prediction model (National Center for Higher Education Management Systems, 1973a, 1973b) used at various universities. One of the purposes of the model is to have common classification schemes and data definitions that enable institutions to generate cost figures and share them in meaningful ways.

The realization of the need to improve the preparation and training of higher education administrators has been cited in literature for many years by people such as Bolman (1964), Fisher (1978), Henderson (1970), Knapp (1969), and Schultz (1968). Many authors are now addressing the area of preparation of administrators (see Cleveland, 1977; Dressel and Mayhew, 1974; Feltner, 1975; and Higher Education Management Institute, 1977). Schultz (1968) determines that there are three methods of preparation for higher education administrators: formal study, in-service education, or informal study.

Epstein (1974) believes the cessation of growth in higher education calls for more flexibility in making readjustments in past patterns of operation. Lahti (1973a) suggests administrators conduct position evaluations. Position evaluations of jobs are made on the worth of the position as opposed to the person's worth.

Baldridge, Curtis, Ecker, and Riley (1978) recommend that long-range institutional plans provide administrator development programs. On-the-job experiences need to be combined with professional development activities that are designed to meet specific needs of the individual administrators (see Eble,

1978; Gaff, Festa, and Gaff, 1978; Galloway and Fisher, 1977; Knapp, 1969; Lahti, 1973b; and Shtogren, 1978). Administrative development programs may include in-service or management workshops, informal professional reading, postgraduate course work, institution-sponsored seminars or internships, and release time for study and travel to other campuses. Richardson (1975) and Lindquist (1978) stress that the essential relationship is between growth and development of the individual and that of the organization itself.

Any one of these references should be consulted for a more comprehensive bibliography on the specific topic of interest.

References

Balderston, F. E. *Managing Today's University.* San Francisco: Jossey-Bass, 1974.

Baldridge, J. V. (Ed.). *Academic Governance.* Berkeley, Calif.: McCutchan, 1971.

Baldridge, J. V., Curtis, D. V., Ecker, G., and Riley, G. L. *Policy Making and Effective Leadership: A National Study of Academic Management.* San Francisco: Jossey-Bass, 1978.

Bolman, F. D. "Can We Prepare Better College and University Administrators?" In *Current Issues in Higher Education: 1964.* Washington, D.C.: Association for Higher Education, 1964.

Burns, G. P. *Administrators in Higher Education: Their Functions and Coordination.* New York: Harper & Row, 1962.

Carnegie Commission on Higher Education. *A Classification of Institutions of Higher Education.* New York: McGraw-Hill, 1973.

Cleveland, H. *The Education of Administrators for Higher Education.* Urbana-Champaign: University of Illinois Press, 1977.

Cohen, M. D., and March, J. G. *Leadership and Ambiguity: The American College President.* New York: McGraw-Hill, 1974.

Corson, J. J. *The Governance of Colleges and Universities: Modernizing Structures and Processes.* New York: McGraw-Hill, 1975.

Demerath, W. J., Stephens, R. W., and Taylor, R. R. *Power, Presidents, and Professors.* New York: Basic Books, 1967.

Dressel, P. L., and Mayhew, L. B. *Higher Education as a Field of Study: The Emergence of a Profession.* San Francisco: Jossey-Bass, 1974.

Eble, K. E. *The Art of Administration: A Guide for Academic Administrators.* San Francisco: Jossey-Bass, 1978.

Epstein, L. D. *Governing the University: The Campus and the Public Interest.* San Francisco: Jossey-Bass, 1974.

Feinstein, O. *Higher Education in the United States.* Lexington, Mass.: Heath, 1971.

Feltner, B. D. "Training Programs for College Administrators: Impact on Governance." *Educational Record*, 1975, *56*, 156–159.

Fisher, C. F. "The Evaluation and Development of College and University Administrators." In J. A. Shtogren (Ed.), *Administrative Development in Higher Edu-*

cation. Vol. 1: *The State of the Art.* Richmond, Va.: Higher Education Leadership and Management, 1978.

Gaff, S. S., Festa, C., and Gaff, J. G. *Professional Development: A Guide to Resources.* New York: Change Magazine Press, 1978.

Galloway, S. W., and Fisher, C. F. (Eds.). *A Guide to Professional Development, Development Opportunities for College and University Administrators.* Washington, D.C.: American Council on Education, 1977.

Glenny, L. A., and Dalglish, T. K. *Public Universities, State Agencies, and the Law: Constitutional Autonomy in Decline.* Berkeley: Center for Research and Development in Higher Education, University of California, 1973.

Halstead, D. K. *Statewide Planning in Higher Education.* Washington, D.C.: U. S. Government Printing Office, 1974.

Harvard University Committee on Governance. *The Organization and Functions of the Governing Boards and the President's Office: Discussion Memorandum.* Cambridge, Mass.: Harvard University, 1971.

Henderson, A. D. *The Innovative Spirit.* San Francisco: Jossey-Bass, 1970.

Higher Education Management Institute (HEMI). "Management Development and Training Program for Colleges and Universities." Bulletin 2, May 1977.

Hook, S., Kurtz, P., and Todorovich, M. *The University and the State: What Role for Government in Higher Education.* New York: Prometheus Books, 1978.

Kerr, C. *The Administration of Higher Education in an Era of Change and Conflict.* Urbana-Champaign: University of Illinois Press, 1972.

Knapp, D. C. "Management: Intruder in the Academic Dust." *Educational Record,* 1969, *49,* 55–59.

Lahti, R. E. *Innovative College Management: Implementing Proven Organizational Practice.* San Francisco: Jossey-Bass, 1973a.

Lahti, R. E. "15 Ways to Increase Staff Productivity." *College and University Business,* 1973b, *54,* 37.

Lee, E. C., and Bowen, F. M. *The Multicampus University.* New York: McGraw-Hill, 1971.

Lee, E. C., and Bowen, F. M. *Managing Multicampus Systems: Effective Administration in an Unsteady State.* San Francisco: Jossey-Bass, 1975.

Lindquist, J. *Strategies for Change.* Berkeley, Calif.: Pacific Sounding Press, 1978.

Mortimer, K. P., and McConnell, T. R. *Sharing Authority Effectively: Participation, Interaction, and Discretion.* San Francisco: Jossey-Bass, 1978.

National Center for Higher Education Management Systems (NCHEMS). *Introduction to the Resource Requirements Prediction Model 1.6.* Technical Report 34A. Boulder, Colo.: National Center for Higher Education Management Systems, 1973a.

National Center for Higher Education Management Systems (NCHEMS). *Resource Requirement Prediction Model 1.6 Reports.* Technical Report 34B. Boulder, Colo.: National Center for Higher Education Management Systems, 1973b.

O'Neill, J. *Resource Use in Higher Education: Trends in Outputs and Inputs, 1930–1967.* Berkeley, Calif.: Carnegie Commission on Higher Education, 1971.

Palola, E. G., Lehmann, T., and Blischke, W. R. *Higher Education by Design: The Sociology of Planning.* Berkeley: Center for Research and Development in Higher Education, University of California, 1970.

Richardson, R. C. "Staff Development: A Conceptual Framework." *Journal of Higher Education,* 1975, *46,* 303–311.

Schultz, R. E. "The Preparation of College and University Administrators." *Phi Delta Kappan,* 1968, *49* (7), 390–394.

Shtogren, J. A. (Ed.). *Administrative Development in Higher Education.* Vol. 1: *The State of the Art.* Richmond, Va.: Higher Education Leadership and Management, 1978.

University of Illinois. *Faculty Letter,* May 10, 1972, No. 230, pp. 1–2.

University of Illinois. Office of Resource Planning, March 1978, pp. 3–4.

20

Jon H. Regnier

Improving the Utilization of Capital Facilities

Since the late 1950s and early 1960s, the percentage of capital costs in the annual budget expenditures of many institutions that were then rapidly expanding has dropped from an approximate 50-percent split with operating costs to less than 10 percent. Despite this decline, capital expenditures remain an important concern of institutional research and planning. The rapid growth of past decades, when the physical master plan was the only published planning document, has been succeeded by a period of reorganization and change without the growth component to cover planning mistakes. Presidents, boards of trustees, and development officers can no longer welcome any facility proposed by wealthy donors, new program interests, legislation, or even student demand without carefully evaluating the total operating cost impact on the institution. Declining enrollment, enrollment shifts within the campus and between campuses, and increased competition for operating funds will result in demands for capital expenditure deferrals and create deferred maintenance backlogs.

And we are now faced with a very real possibility that operating costs for "surplus" or "low-use" facilities, particularly because of high energy costs, may indeed bankrupt the institution.

To avoid these physical plant and capital expenditure problems will require an integrated institutional planning team as a staff arm for institutional decision making. Facilities planners and capital budget analysts must become part of this planning team along with academic, fiscal, and institutional research personnel; and this team must have direct access to, or support of, the chief operating officer of the institution. Administrators and governing boards can no longer afford to address the component problems of facility, personnel, and equipment utilization and operation expenditures in an isolated analysis that maximizes initial dollar expenditures only in these component parts. Utilization of the total dollars available to the institution through changes in utilization rates of all these component parts will become a key issue of overall study. For example, higher facility utilization rates to avoid additional capital expenditures might result in overall increases in total institutional costs because of less-efficient use of teaching personnel, lack of consideration for the value of students' time, or increased energy costs.

This planning team should develop data necessary to judge the various possible alternatives in facilities utilization and capital expenditure. Using both qualitative and quantitative measures and involving the total institutional community in the evaluation of the physical plant and its utilization can result in no-cost scheduling changes, low-cost improvements, and conservation practices that not only reduce costs but retain and even enhance enrollment.

The Facilities Inventory

To determine capital needs accurately, some form of facility inventory is required. Most campuses have at least a handwritten set of records they would call their facilities inventory. It usually contains square footage, or at least a count of the number of student stations assigned to each discipline, with at least some notes about the quality of each facility. Many institutions have now computerized their inventories to comply with federal reporting requirements; but this process has often resulted in the loss of the qualitative information in favor of quantitative measurement.

The most elusive element in the process of developing and maintaining an adequate facilities inventory is the measurement of quality. The qualitative ranking of physical facilities may be a new experience for those accustomed to measuring assignable square feet (ASF) per full-time-equivalent (FTE) student, ASF per student station, hours per week, or percentage of station occupancy; and yet it will become a major challenge of the 1980s. It will be increasingly important to develop ratings and gather statistics to help choose the order of renovations and provide comparative data to explain poor utilization in some older or even poorly designed new facilities.

The increased emphasis on health and safety features of the institutional environment and the recognition of employees' ability to "bargain" or "grieve" about the condition of the workplace will accentuate this need for qualitative evaluation of the physical plant. It will require integrating the environmental health and safety office as a part of the evaluation team and possibly using the health and safety officer's list of code violations and potential hazards as the major priority ingredient in the evaluation. Beyond the health and safety officer's critique, probably the best approach is the use of simple rating charts of "good," "fair," and "poor" or identifying the top and bottom 10 percent of facilities in terms of condition, along with noting the age of the facility and the date of the last major renovation. An actual room-by-room facility visit by the planning team in the annual program and facility review process, coupled with discussions with the facility users, such as departmental leaders, and analysis of enrollments in courses offered in the facility can become the basis for this qualitative evaluation. The many qualitative factors of room configuration, ventilation systems, windows, lighting, access to support facilities, condition of furniture, and special equipment such as student lockers as well as specific discipline-related facility requirements can be discussed in detail and noted by the planning team. Photographs can be taken for later use when requesting specific capital funds for renovation.

On the basis of this qualitative inventory, a good preventive maintenance program can be scheduled, including interior painting and replacement of light fixtures, floor tile, venetian blinds, or other elements. Moreover, using this inventory to assess the impact of the environmental setting on the learning process can lead to integrating renovation with the other instructional program improvements of the institution. The ability to improve the physical environment through cosmetic changes at minimal cost is enormous, and faculty and student expertise can be captured to encourage study and implementation of environmental changes related to color, light levels, conditioned air requirements, and instructional fixture improvements. Many times a small investment in student wages, faculty research, or independent study time will yield great benefits. New interior colors can be integrated into the normal painting schedule without increased costs. Fine arts students can offer their alma mater a legacy of murals and sculpture to enhance the environment. Architecture student design projects can help expedite the planning and funding of capital improvements. And engineering and industrial education students can be involved in minor remodeling design and even construction.

By a cooperative approach to the facilities inventory such as this, facilities planning and capital expenditures come to be accepted as equitable and understood by the entire institutional community.

Quantitative Analysis

As institutions move away from physical master planning and capital budget planning in isolation from other institutional research and planning, the goal in setting building square footage standards and calculating facility utilization rates must shift from that of reducing capital expenditures to one of becoming accurate cost measurement tools for evaluating total institutional expenditure requirements.

Comparable quantitative information on facilities and facility utilization is increasingly available from U.S. Office of Education surveys and those of other organizations, such as the Society for College and University Planning (SCUP). Institutional planners and administrators can use these data in assessing the supply and use of facilities on their own campus.

Assignable Square Feet. A 1976 SCUP survey found that 60 percent of the reporting institutions had less than 100 ASF per FTE. The range of ASF per FTE is shown in Table 1 and approximates that in federal higher education facilities manuals and the Western Interstate Commission for Higher Education's *Inventory of Physical Facilities in Institutions of Higher Education.* An earlier survey (California Coordinating Council for Higher Education, 1971, Appendix Table 4) illustrates this range of assignable space for selected institutions, as shown in Table 2.

Space Standards. Acceptable measurement criteria for determining how existing facilities are utilized are also necessary. Most large institutions and systems of higher education maintain extensive facility utilization comparisons. These gained their impetus under federal construction and equipment grant programs. If utilization data have not been kept, they can easily·be developed by calculating the enrollment for all classes, using a specified number of ASF per each lecture and laboratory station as a standard.

Table 1. Percentage of Institutions by Range of Assignable Square Feet of Space Per Full-Time-Equivalent Student, 1976

ASF/FTE	Percent of Institutions
0–50	11
51–75	25
76–85	6
86–100	20
101–125	13
126–150	15
151–175	0
176–225	6
226–275	0
275+	4

Table 2. Assignable Square Feet Per Full-Time-Equivalent Student at Selected Institutions, 1971

Institution	ASF/FTE
Brooklyn College, CUNY	61.3
California Community Colleges	71.0
California State University and Colleges	64.2
City College of New York, CUNY	84.1
Oregon State University	160.9
Southern Illinois University	157.8
Stanford University	262.4
State University of New York at Albany	136.6
University of California	169.8
University of Illinois (Urbana)	180.6
University of Michigan	227.0
University of Southern California	140.4
University of Washington	144.7
University of Wisconsin (Madison)	165.3

The 1976 SCUP survey indicated that fifteen assignable square feet of space per lecture station is the majority standard among responding institutions, as Table 3 shows, although there was a cluster at twenty ASF per station and some institutions reported using a sliding scale based upon room size. The actual experience of the institutions showed a much broader range.

According to the survey respondents, laboratory square footage standards for individual disciplines are utilized in California, Colorado, Illinois, Oregon, South Carolina, and Washington. California has the highest facility utilization standards of any state, and Table 4 lists its laboratory student station standards for various subjects (Matsler, 1966, pp. 8, 17).

One way to determine whether use of a specified facility by a particular class is appropriate is to compare the class size with the average for the room and with its standard student station capacity. Significant shifts that are not discovered unless this course-by-course comparison is done often occur in a discipline's course enrollments. For example: Many of the social science classes that used to be taught in classrooms designed to hold forty to fifty are still using the same set of classroom facilities assigned ten years ago and the course enrollment levels may now be only twenty-five to thirty. Because calling that poor room utilization to someone's attention would also point out the poor utilization of personnel, disciplines are reluctant to recognize the problem. At the same time this drop is occurring, business class enrollment, which may have been twenty-five to thirty in the past, particularly in specific accounting classes, may, because of enrollment pressure in that discipline, result in thirty-sized classrooms being utilized by forty to fifty students. The overall institutional average, of course, would remain the same; but the frustration level on the part of students and faculty in the over-crowded classrooms would be enormous. This suggests that room-by-room analysis may result in reassignment of rooms that, although not improving the overall utilization rate, would significantly improve the morale of the students and faculty and aid in enrollment retention. Much of these data can be developed from hand-kept records, particularly if one is in a small institution. The larger the institution, the easier it is to computerize the data and program the computer to perform the analysis. One must be sure it does not take two programmers, six months, and $10,000 worth of computer time to perform what a good staff analyst could do in three months by hand.

Utilization Standards. Among the states that have developed utilization standards for public colleges and universities, California has perhaps the longest

Table 3. Assignable Square Feet of Space Per Student Station for Lectures, 1976

Number of ASF	Percent of Institutions Reporting Standard	Percent of Institutions Reporting Actual Experience
12	0	4
13	0	12
14	3	19
15	64	30
16	18	19
17	3	4
18	3	0
19	0	4
20	9	8

Table 4. Assignable Square Feet of Space Per Student Station for Laboratory Classes, California Public Segments of Higher Education

Subject Field	ASF Per Student Station	Subject Field	ASF Per Student Station
Life sciences		Home economics	
Agriculture		Lower division	60
Lower division	60	Upper division	60
Upper division	60	Journalism	
Biological sciences		Lower division	60
Lower division	55	Upper division	60
Upper division	60	Health sciences	
MPE sciences		Lower division	—
Physical sciences		Upper division	50
Lower division	60	Community college	
Upper division	70	Classifications	
Mathematical sciences		Agriculture	150
Lower division	30	Business	30
Upper division	30	Home economics	60
Engineering sciences		Applied graphic arts	80
Lower division	90	Health services	50
Upper division	110	Public personnel serv.	50
Social sciences		Aero. technology	175
Psychology		Air conditioning	130
Lower division	40	Building trades	175
Upper division	60	Ceramic technology	40
All other social sciences		Chem. technology	70
Lower division	30	Drafting technology	60
Upper division	30	Electrical technology	70
Humanities		Electromechanical	100
Art		Electronic technology	60
Lower division	65	Engin. Gen.	90
Upper division	65	Engineering technology	70
Other humanities		Industrial technology	75
Lower division	40	Mechanical—Auto.	200
Upper division	40	Metallurgical techn.	65
Professions		Metal trades	130
(U.C. & C.S.U.C.)		Textile technology	120
Business administration		Welding	90
Lower division	30	Other trade technology	75
Upper division	30		
Education			
Lower division	—		
Upper division	40		

and most extensive experience. Facilities for higher education in California were initially planned for the traditional 8 A.M. to 5 P.M. enrollment; and in 1948, the Strayer Report (Deutsch, Douglass, and Strayer, 1948, p. 65) recommended twenty-nine hours per week as an acceptable standard utilization rate for class-rooms and class laboratories. In 1955, McConnell, Holy, and Semans recommended lecture classroom utilization standards at thirty-six hours per week with a 67 percent room capacity and laboratory utilization standards of twenty-four hours per week with 80 percent of the seats filled. In 1960, the *Master Plan for Higher Education in California* (p. 96) recommended that the classroom utilization rate be reduced to thirty hours per week with a 60 percent seat occupancy rate and that the laboratory rate be reduced to twenty hours per week while retaining the 80-percent occupancy rate. By 1967 (Matsler, 1966), the lecture classroom utilization rate was increased to thirty-four hours per week at 66 percent station occupancy; lower-division laboratories were to be used twenty-five hours per week with an 85 percent station occupancy rate; and upper-division laboratories retained the previous standard of twenty hours at 80 percent occupancy. By 1970, the California legislature recommended that classrooms be utilized fifty-three hours per week by extending daytime programming into the evening hours; and in 1973, the legislative analyst recommended increasing the laboratory utilization standard by 10 percent.

These increases in facility utilization standards may have been valid when the demand for access to higher education exceeded the physical plant capacity during daytime hours, but the fifty-three-hour standard for classroom utilization per week has proven to be unattainable despite scheduling required courses in late afternoons and evening, computer-assisted registration and scheduling, and continued enrollment increases. Afternoon classes never were popular, and institutions' ability to force afternoon schedules is less successful than it was a decade ago. Students are no longer willing to take any course, at any time, from any instructor just to get through their program. The shift from restricting student admission to recruiting student enrollment has created a student clientele that is becoming highly selective of courses, course offering times, and faculty.

As Table 5 shows, eight other states that have adopted utilization standards have specified lower and more realistic classroom standards than California (California Coordinating Council for Higher Education, 1971).

Table 5. Space Utilization Standards of Nine States for Classrooms and Class Laboratories

State	Classrooms				Class Laboratories[a]		
	Hours Per Week Room Expected To Be Used[b]	Expected Percent of Student Station Occupancy	Weekly Student Station Hours Expected To Be Used	Assignable Square Feet Per Student Station	Hours Per Week Laboratory Expected To Be Used	Expected Percent of Student Station Occupancy	Weekly Student Station Hours Expected To Be Used
California	53	66	35.0	15	25[c] 20[d]	85[c] 80[d]	21.3[c] 16.0[d]
Colorado	28	60	16.8	15	24	80	19.2
Florida	36	60	21.6	15	25	80	20.0
Illinois	30	60	18.0	15	20	80	16.0
Michigan	30	60	18.0	15	20	80	16.0
Minnesota	30	60	18.0	15	20	80	16.0
Oregon	33	60	19.8	15	20	80	16.0
Washington	30	60	18.0	15	20	80	16.0
Wisconsin	30	67	20.1	16.5	24	80	19.2

[a]Based upon a 45-hour week, 8 A.M.–5 P.M. Monday through Friday.
[b]Based upon a 45-hour week, 8 A.M.–5 P.M. Monday through Friday, except for California, which is based upon a 70-hour week, 8 A.M.–10 P.M. Monday through Friday.
[c]Lower division.
[d]Upper division.

Table 6 shows the standards and actual experience of institutions responding to the 1976 SCUP survey, first for lecture classrooms and then for laboratories. This survey found that public four-year urban commuter colleges tend to have particularly high utilization rates resulting from demand exceeding the capacity of frequently old facilities. Rural four-year public institutions with unique programs of good reputation also showed high utilization rates and low square footage per student. In contrast, traditional liberal arts colleges averaged considerably lower utilization rates and a concomitant large square footage per student.

I recommend that lecture classroom facilities under one hundred twenty-five seats in size should be scheduled forty-five hours per week with an average of 75 percent of the seats filled when scheduled. This percentage of student station occupancy encourages remodeling to make the facilities support the program. Lecture facilities over one hundred twenty-five seats in size should meet an average of one half this proposed standard.

For laboratories, I recommend physical science and engineering facilities be scheduled for use twenty-four hours per week on a disciplinewide average. This average enables the disciplines to have specialized low-use facilities offset by high-use, general-purpose laboratories rather than meeting a course-by-course standard. Disciplines that should follow a twenty-seven-hour standard include

Table 6. Space Utilization Standards and Actual Experience of Institutions for Lecture Classrooms and Class Laboratories

			Lecture Classrooms		
Weekly Room Hours Range	*Standard* *Weekly Room Hours*	*Actual* *Weekly Room Hours*	*Station Percent Occupancy Range*	*Station Utilization Standard Percent* *Occupancy*	*Station Utilization Actual Percent* *Occupancy*
20–24	0%	13%	45–49	0	7
25–29	0	20	50–54	0	7
30–34	55	33	55–59	1	15
35–39	7	7	60–64	53	33
40–44	0	15	65–69	26	21
45–49	25	7	70–74	13	11
50–54	12	3	75–79	5	6
55–59	1	2	80–84	2	0
			Class Laboratories		
Weekly Room Hours Range	*Standard* *Weekly Room Hours*	*Actual* *Weekly Room Hours*	*Station Percent Occupancy Range*	*Station Utilization Standard Percent* *Occupancy*	*Station Utilization Actual Percent* *Occupancy*
20–24	58%	70%	40–59	0	17
25–29	25	20	60–64	0	8
30–34	17	10	65–69	0	8
			70–74	0	17
			75–79	0	0
			80–84	70	17
			85–89	20	17
			90–100	10	16

agriculture and natural resources, architecture and environmental design, communications, health professions, home economics, industrial arts and technology, military science, performing arts, physical education, and psychology. Those that can follow a thirty-hour standard include art, area studies, business and management, computer and information science, education, foreign languages, interdisciplinary programs, law, letters, library science, mathematics, public affairs, and social science. Laboratory utilization standards should vary by level of instruction as well. Lower-division laboratories should average 95 percent of their stations filled when scheduled; upper-division and graduate laboratories should average 90 percent. This percentage of occupancy rate would encourage facility remodeling to meet specific laboratory program needs and better utilize these high-cost facilities.

The weekly time frame available for scheduling should be restricted only by personnel, energy, and other cost factors. A six-day schedule covering twenty-four hours per day would seem to have merit, particularly for urban and residential institutions, and might tend toward a staggered four-day week for employee schedules and a two-day-week class schedule for students, as well as increased extracurricular activity schedules involving the total community with repeat offerings all six days of the week at appropriate times.

These suggested standards may provide a guide for determining appropriate utilization rates and occupancy percentages, but they are useful only for overall measurement. They should not be used on a room-by-room basis. For example, though a specific discipline's total facilities may equate the average utilization rates, one specialized laboratory or classroom, because of its support equipment, its environment, or other reason, may be used only twice a week. To compensate for this supposedly low utilization, a general-purpose room could be highly utilized compared to the standard, so the total space assigned to that discipline would essentially meet the overall standard rate of utilization or average square foot per student or average student station per full-time-equivalent student. The minute one forgets that standards are averages, to be considered on a campuswide or disciplinewide basis, the potential for the capital analysis to skew the academic program requirements is enormous.

Factors Affecting Utilization Rates and Costs

The accurate assessment of capital needs depends on interpreting data on utilization rates in the light of factors that affect utilization and capital costs. For instance, large lecture facilities tend to be the least utilized of any classroom space by traditional standards; but if total costs are considered, including those of the teaching faculty, these large lecture halls may still be cost-effective even with "low" utilization. They are also usually the easiest to shut down during nonuse periods to reduce their energy consumption. Other factors important to consider include weekly scheduling practices, daily schedules, and rising energy costs.

Weekly Schedules. In the future, new scheduling procedures that emphasize intensive modes of teaching throughout the day as well as evenings and weekends, faculty traveling to off-campus sites rather than students coming to the institution, and one- and two-day block schedules will alternate with traditional Monday-Wednesday-Friday, Tuesday-Thursday, Saturday scheduling practices.

Alternatives to the traditional Monday-Wednesday-Friday, Tuesday-

Thursday, Saturday (one hour per day) or Monday-Wednesday-Friday alternating with Tuesday-Thursday (one and a half hours per day) schedules are now being tested. Three-hour block schedules one day a week in the afternoon similar to the evening program schedules, which are typically one three-hour block or two evenings of hour-and-a-half blocks, are one promising alternative. There appears to be a move toward four-day-week schedules, which seem to be predominantly two days a week of one and one half hours per day schedule to replace the three-day-a-week, one-hour block for the predominantly lecture mode of instruction. The two-day-a-week schedule fits the traditional laboratory offerings component of the scheduling process. Thorough market research should be performed in this area by each institution in its analysis related to enrollment retention and enrollment attraction. There are many individual discipline differences in instructional methods that may result in alternative scheduling plans by the different disciplines at the same institution. The interface of a student schedule then becomes a key element.

If innovative scheduling practices enable students to reduce their commuting time to campus by one day per week, the potential for individual savings is enormous. This possible savings would also be available for employees. Changes from traditional scheduling could reduce the demand for additional classrooms and laboratories because of the traditional peak demands that occur between 9 A.M. and 2 P.M. It would at least reduce the overcrowded conditions occurring between these hours and tend to improve the occupancy rates of facilities in what were formerly less desirable hours, particularly Friday afternoons.

Daily Schedules. As noted earlier, afternoon classes traditionally do not achieve the percentage occupancy rate of morning courses. For example, at the institutions within the California State Universities and Colleges system, the station occupancy rate between 2 P.M. and 6 P.M. is only 60 percent, compared to 80 percent between 7 A.M. and 2 P.M. This 2 P.M. to 6 P.M. time period would thus seem to be particularly appropriate for student and faculty government activities, student athletic activities, guest speakers, colloquiums, and faculty departmental activities and office hours for counseling students and grading papers. These activities can also serve as an excellent integrator of daytime and evening students and faculty members. Teaching costs increase substantially in the afternoon and evening hours because of small class size during these hours, and reducing the scheduling choices available to students during the morning or even computer-assisted scheduling does not seem to reduce this problem. As one respondent to the SCUP survey noted, "students are no longer willing to put up with crowded classrooms, inconvenient hours, or poor quality instruction." And another averred, "There is no hurry in gaining a degree, so postponing a class until it is available at the appropriate time from the chosen instructor in a setting conducive to learning is the predominant option elected by students."

Energy Costs. Energy costs are rapidly becoming a major factor in the annual operating budget. Within the California State Universities and Colleges system, these costs rose from approximately 1 percent of the budget in 1972 to 4 percent of the budget in 1978, even with major conservation efforts. It will become necessary for planners to look at the potential for reducing this impact on institutional operating budgets, and facility utilization practices appear to have the most potential for effecting overall energy savings.

For example, the Southern California Edison Company has received approval from the California Public Utilities Commission for a three-level rate: "off-peak demand" from 10 P.M. until 8 A.M. Monday through Friday and all day Saturday and Sunday at the lowest rate; "mid-peak demand" from 8 A.M. until afternoon (specific hours dependent on season) at medium rate; and "on-peak demand" in the afternoon and evening hours at the highest rate. At California State University, Long Beach, peak demand currently occurs at approximately 2 P.M. until 6 P.M. The university is thus subject to the highest rates for its peak usage at hours when classes have their smallest class size. Its present scheduling practices are being reexamined, as a result, in hope of reducing these costs.

Energy conservation beyond rescheduling will require extensive information and education campaigns among students, faculty, and staff; but their grass-roots involvement can pay enormous dividends in operating costs. Student-developed graphics and news articles can increase energy awareness throughout the total institutional community and spark a full-fledged change in institutional behavior toward conservation.

Making Capital Decisions

Having conducted both qualitative and quantitative studies, compared utilization data with appropriate data and standards at other institutions, improved existing facilities through renovation, and increased utilization wherever possible and at the same time reduced operating costs, an institution can weigh alternative capital development decisions.

From integrated cost studies and planning analyses, we may not only change our pattern of facility utilization but provide a more appropriate program and schedule for attracting and maintaining student enrollment. Enrollment declines may lead to the consolidation of programs, allowing portions of the plant to be used for other purposes and even leased out to generate operating budget revenues, possibly as community centers, senior citizen housing, research and development office complexes, or even campus-type shopping centers. (See Educational Facilities Laboratories, 1978, for examples of new uses for surplus school facilities at the kindergarten through twelfth-grade level.) If the choice confronting an institution is between more space or more operating funds, most departments will participate in increased utilization and consolidation of facilities rather than face added costs.

The careful evaluation of alternatives by the integrated planning team, with the goal of maximizing the use of the total resources available to the institution—physical, human, and financial—may lead to minimal fund requests for capital improvements; but these requests will result in funding ahead of those that reflect only limited standard cost and utilization comparisons of physical facilities. Private donors, boards of trustees, legislators, governors, and other sources of capital funds all favor thorough alternatives analysis and comprehensive master planning. From this analysis and planning, alternative capital development scenarios can be prepared to take advantage of funding that may come from other than anticipated sources. For example, if an interested donor or new federal program offers to provide capital funding for new nursing department facilities, the existing facilities occupied by the department can be considered for minor conversion to accommodate another department's capital facility requirements, rather than using these funds to add to the existing facility.

The common mistake in capital decisions is to skew the institution's academic program by accepting capital funding *because* of its availability. Having the institution's facilities needs documented on the basis of integrated planning and having as many different scenarios as possible prepared for possible construction and renovation will assure that program priorities are achieved by means of campus facilities rather than being determined by them.

Bibliographical Essay

The joint publications of the Educational Facilities Laboratories and the Society for College and University Planning titled *Planning for Higher Education* are the best current literature on the integrated planning process and in specific capital development and facility utilization study areas. Some recent examples are Douglass and Williams, 1975; Haas, 1976; Loomis and Skeen, 1977; and Agro, 1978.

University Space Planning by Bareither and Schillinger (1968) is an excellent book, considered by many to be the "granddaddy" or "benchmark" in the area of predicting space needs based on specific discipline utilization practices.

The Western Interstate Commission for Higher Education (WICHE) in cooperation with the American Association of Collegiate Registrars and Admissions Officers (AACRAO) has published a series of manuals under the title *Higher Education Facilities Planning and Management Manuals* (Dahnke, Jones, Mason, and Romney, 1971). This series is an authoritative source in support of general or specialized facility requirements. The first provides an overview of the philosophy and assumptions and introduces the facilities planning cycle integrated with comprehensive planning. The second manual contains a full discussion of classrooms and class laboratories, detailing evaluation methods, projections of square footage needs for new and existing institutions, and utilization rates and their limitations. The third manual is devoted to office and research facilities. This area will become more important as working conditions become a bargainable issue in the collective bargaining process. The fourth covers academic support facilities; libraries; audiovisual, radio, and television facilities; museum, gallery, and other exhibition facilities; and data-processing and computer facilities. Large amounts of space are involved in this essential area. The new generation of hardware in the computer field and the assumptions on centralized large versus dispersed minicomputers is a new area requiring additional study that is not covered. The fifth manual contains a general discussion of spacious support facilities: physical education and athletics; residence hall and dining facilities; and student health, physical plant, and special-use facilities. The sixth discusses program planning and analysis as the basis for institutional and systemwide facilities planning. This is a key concept and should be read after the first manual. The seventh manual is a reference guide containing the table of contents of all the manuals, glossary of terms, and an index.

The California Higher Education Facilities Planning Guide (University of California System, 1970) is a good, comprehensive, general-purpose facilities planning document. It combines the major elements existing in the planning guides of the three public segments of higher education in California. The main body of material is from the University of California documentation.

The California Coordinating Council for Higher Education Inventory and Utilization Study for Public Higher Education (1971) is an excellent data source on each of the public institutions in the state of California. It is a good document to compare utilization experience between types of campuses. Comparisons between campuses with similar academic program emphases provide meaning for aggregates of campuswide square footage, square footage per student station, and square footage per discipline.

Actions, Objectives, and Concerns—Human Parameters for Architectural Design by Deasy and Bolling (California State College, Los Angeles-Foundation, 1969) provides an excellent analysis of the effect of architecture on the human experience using the large urban California State College at Los Angeles campus as a study base. It has informative data on how and where students spend their time on the campus. It includes program design criteria for a projected student union and does an excellent job of determining the priority needs of students, faculty, and staff.

A comprehensive analysis of community involvement in determining the appropriate use for surplus school space is provided in the Educational Facilities Laboratories (1978) six-booklet series on community school centers. Titles of the booklets are *A Concerned Citizen's Guide to Community School Centers, Planning Community School Centers, Managing Community School Centers, Facility Issues in Community School Centers, Using Surplus School Space for Community School Centers,* and *A Resource Book on Community School Centers.* These booklets provide specific, detailed examples on alternative uses of school space. Architectural sketches and studies are included.

Guidelines for Site Selection, Long-Range Facilities Master Planning, and Facilities Program Planning (Colorado Commission on Higher Education, 1973) is a good working document the state of Colorado uses for its higher education segments to cover the total capital development process. It contains specific building square footage by types and addresses the component parts for developing a long-range facility master plan.

References

Agro, D. "Space Management for Medical Education." *Planning for Higher Education,* 1978, 7 (2), 13–18.

Bareither, H. D., and Schillinger, J. L. *University Space Planning.* Urbana: University of Illinois Press, 1968.

California Coordinating Council for Higher Education. *Inventory and Utilization Study for Public Higher Education,* Report 71-2. Sacramento: California Coordinating Council for Higher Education, 1971.

Colorado Commission on Higher Education. *Guidelines for Site Selection, Long-Range Facilities Master Planning, and Facilities Program Planning.* Denver: Colorado Commission on Higher Education, 1973.

Dahnke, H. L., Jones, D. P., Mason, T. R., and Romney, L. C. *Higher Education Facilities Planning and Management Manuals.* Boulder, Colo.: Western Interstate Commission for Higher Education, 1971.

Deasy and Bolling, A.I.A., Architects. *Actions, Objectives, and Concerns—Human Parameters for Architectural Design.* California State College, Los Angeles-Foundation, 1969.

Deutsch, E., Douglass, A., and Strayer, D. *A Report of a Survey of the Needs of California in Higher Education.* Berkeley: University of California Press, 1948.

Douglass, R., and Williams, P. C. "Cooperative Planning at the Oklahoma Health Center." *Planning for Higher Education,* 1975, *4* (4), 1–5.

Educational Facilities Laboratories. *Community School Centers.* New York: Educational Facilities Laboratories, 1978.

Haas, R. M. "Integrating Academic, Fiscal, and Facilities Planning." *Planning for Higher Education,* 1976, *5* (5).

Loomis, W., and Skeen, O. "Evaluating the Adequacy of Campus Physical Facilities." *Planning for Higher Education,* 1977, *6* (3).

McConnell, T. R., Holy, T. C., and Semans, H. H. *A Restudy of the Needs of California in Higher Education.* Sacramento: California State Department of Education, 1955.

A Master Plan for Higher Education in California, 1960–1975. Sacramento: California State Department of Higher Education, 1960.

Matsler, G. *Space and Utilization Standards, California Public Higher Education: A Report to the Coordinating Council for Higher Education.* Sacramento: Coordinating Council for Higher Education, 1966.

University of California. *California Higher Education Facilities Planning Guide.* Berkeley: University of California, 1970.

21

Richard I. Miller

Appraising
Institutional
Performance

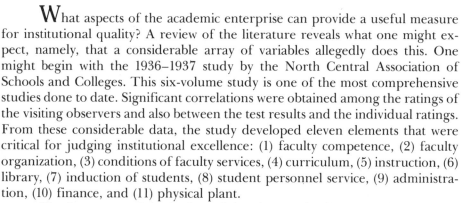

What aspects of the academic enterprise can provide a useful measure for institutional quality? A review of the literature reveals what one might expect, namely, that a considerable array of variables allegedly does this. One might begin with the 1936–1937 study by the North Central Association of Schools and Colleges. This six-volume study is one of the most comprehensive studies done to date. Significant correlations were obtained among the ratings of the visiting observers and also between the test results and the individual ratings. From these considerable data, the study developed eleven elements that were critical for judging institutional excellence: (1) faculty competence, (2) faculty organization, (3) conditions of faculty services, (4) curriculum, (5) instruction, (6) library, (7) induction of students, (8) student personnel service, (9) administration, (10) finance, and (11) physical plant.

The best composite criterion of the eleven criteria was used as the best determinant of institutional excellence; it was called criterion XIII. Faculty organization correlated most highly with criterion XIII (r = .67), yet faculty competence had the lowest correlation (r = .45), although it is still positive. Instruction (r = .65) and the curriculum (r = .64) rated high. The relatively low ratings given to administration (r = .60) and finance (r = .47) probably reflected another era when institutions were much smaller and less complex and therefore easier to manage. Yet data for the North Central study were collected during the Great Depression, when many schools were encountering severe fiscal difficulties. One would think the crisis times of the thirties would have given administrators and financing greater importance.

The Middle States Association of Colleges and Schools, Commission on Higher Education (1978b, p. 3), has developed the following useful statement on characteristics of excellence in higher education. The qualities and characteristics that distinguish superior educational institutions depend somewhat on the type of institution; but according to the commission, they have important common denominators *irrespective of particular settings*. The commission identifies these common elements:

- clearly stated purposes and objectives appropriate to the institution's resources and the needs of its constituents
- persistent concern as to the relation between objectives and outcomes
- curricula that provide, emphasize, or rest upon general or liberal education
- programs and courses that develop abilities to form independent judgment, to weigh values, to understand fundamental theory, and, where appropriate, are attuned to professional or occupational requirements
- an atmosphere conducive to continuing and broadening each student's education beyond the minimum point necessary to obtain credit, certificates, or degrees
- counseling sensitive to the educational, personal, and career aspirations of students
- clear definitions of administrative and academic responsibilities
- emphasis on continuous intellectual and professional staff development, within a secure framework of academic freedom
- a board of trustees actively fulfilling its responsibilities of policy and resource development
- effective ongoing institutional self-study and planning procedures
- physical facilities and learning resources proportional to the requirements and nature of the educational program
- stability of resources to maintain the quality of instruction and assure its continuity

Factors Used in Institutional Evaluation

This section considers the seven elements often involved in institutional evaluation, whether it be impressionistic or systematic. These are student outcomes, administrative leadership, constituent perceptions, community impact, fiscal indicators, state-level boards, and federal agencies.

Student Outcomes. Much discussion and literature in recent years has focused on student outcomes; in other words, what does the undergraduate student take from the college after four years of study? Some earlier, simplistic approaches have given way to more sophisticated approaches. The "value-added" dimension has become commonplace in the outcomes discussions. However, Verry and Davies (1976, p. 12) point out that the value-added approach "becomes difficult—certainly at the aggregate or sectional level of this study—because the fragmentation and specialization of the university curriculum makes it extremely difficult to devise tests of the 'end product' that are comparable either across subjects in a given university or across universities in a given subject." Yet the value-added dimension can be very useful if developed carefully.

The current extensive revisionary effort directed toward general education is recognition that student outcomes need to include greater attention to the broad aesthetic and cultural aspects as well as preparation for one's lifework.

Student outcomes are measured in a number of ways, including tests for professional certification or licensure. A wide array of these tests can be found in Buros's *Mental Measurements Yearbooks;* and the seventh edition lists standardized instruments for the following fields: accounting, biology, business, business education, chemistry, computer programming, dentistry, economics, education, engineering, English, fine arts, foreign languages, geology, health and physical education, history, home economics, industrial arts, law, mathematics, medicine, nursing, philosophy, political science, psychology, physics, reading, religious education, selling, skill trades, sociology, speech and hearing, supervision, and transportation.

The American College Testing Program is developing the *College Outcome Measures Project* (COMP) for assessing general education knowledge and skills. The purpose of COMP is to design, develop, validate, and implement assessment instruments and procedures to measure and evaluate the knowledge and skills that undergraduate students are expected to acquire as a result of general or liberal education programs and that are important to effective functioning in adult society. The project focuses on communicating, solving problems, clarifying values, functioning within social institutions, using science and technology, and using the arts. The three assessment instruments developed in the project are a measurement battery, an objective test, and an activity inventory.

A new service, Student Outcomes Information Services (SOIS), is sponsored jointly by the National Center for Higher Education Management Systems and the College Board. The system is designed to assist in evaluating the effectiveness of an institution's student services and facilities, to assess student needs, and to measure the impact of programs on student goals and aspirations. And a study of student outcomes by Bowen (1977) provides an outstanding summary of what is known about the literature on this subject.

Bowen (1979, pp. 22–26) has suggested the following seven basic principles that should be followed in the identification and evaluation of outcomes:

1. The study of outcomes should avoid the common confusion of inputs and outputs. . . . The only valid tests of outcomes are *What happens in the development of persons? How do persons change and grow as a result of their college experiences?*

2. Assessment should be linked to all the major goals of education, and not con-

fined just to aspects of human development that can be easily measured or that are related to economic success.

3. Educational outcomes should relate to the development of whole persons. . . . One must ask, not what was the average gain in verbal skills of a college's entire student body, but rather what happened in the total personality and in the life experience of individual students as a result of their college careers when these students are seen as whole human beings.

4. Outcomes assessment should be based upon the study of alumni as well as of students.

5. Outcomes assessment should be concerned with change in students as a result of their college experiences, not merely with their absolute level of performance during and after college.

6. The evaluation scheme must be practicable, not too time-consuming or expensive. It should concentrate on major goals of students and alumni and not try to cover the entire universe.

7. Outcomes assessment should develop from the bottom up within individual colleges and universities rather than be imposed from the top down by federal or state government or by national accrediting bodies.

Chambers (1979, p. 31) has written that outcome measures that can be reasonably used for evaluating educational quality should meet two tests: "First, each outcome should represent something that is teachable; that is, it is generally accepted that the particular educational objective adopted can be achieved through an instructional or didactic process. . . . Second, each outcome should measure something judged relevant to the graduate's functioning throughout adult life."

The use of outcome measures can be helpful; and a number of questions should be considered when deciding upon such a study: (1) What are the purposes of the undertaking? For example, is the study designed to change the academic and/or student program, to learn more about the student body, or to change the nature of the student body mix? (2) What are the estimated direct and indirect costs? (3) Who will interpret the data? The biases and skills of the analysts and interpreters will significantly determine the directions and content of the report. For example, will the conclusions reflect a strict or liberal interpretation of the data?

Administrative Leadership. The management of higher education is receiving renewed attention as the "management of decline" becomes the normal way of life. Generally speaking, nonprofit institutions, including colleges and universities, have not been administered efficiently and effectively. To borrow from Drucker, efficiency is doing things right and effectiveness is doing the right things. Higher education is one of the very few major enterprises where top-level management positions often are obtained as a result of talents and selection processes that have little to do with responsibilities and nature of the actual position. It is no wonder that Cohen and March (1974, pp. 2–3) concluded, "Decision making in the university seems to result extensively from a process that decouples problems and choices and makes the president's role more commonly sporadic and symbolic than significant." Yet research by Hodgkinson (1974, p. 19) on successful federal Title III programs concluded, "Campus leadership potential appears the most important single characteristic in distinguishing the successful Title III programs from the less successful ones." We have very little higher educational research evidence that causally relates academic leadership with institutional quality.

Administrative evaluation needs to be an integral part of institutional evaluation, and it should have the same two overriding purposes advocated for faculty evaluation: improving professional performance and judging professional competence. I suggest the following guidelines for developing procedures for administrative evaluation: (1) The system should be rooted in the traditions, purposes, and objectives of each institution. (2) The overall purpose of the evaluative procedure should be to improve the quality of administration and its basic approach should be positive. The procedure should be built on the view that each administrator possesses different administrative abilities and skills, and no one individual should be expected to have peerless performance in all areas. (3) Performance should be evaluated against expectations, which requires that job descriptions exist, are current, and are reasonably specific. Job descriptions that are more than two or three years old usually need revision. (4) Evaluation procedures should employ both objective and subjective measures. (5) Evaluations should be sought from those in a position to make valid judgments, with immediate superiors having the major responsibility in each case. (6) Evaluation should take place in cooperation with the individual being evaluated. (7) Confidentiality should be maintained throughout the process of evaluating, and distribution of results should be clearly understood and controlled.

Constituent Perceptions. Constituents include parents, trustees, alumni, various communities (local, state, national), and key business and industrial figures. Institutional evaluations by individuals or groups take place more often than we realize. When trustees vote on priority matters, when parents and their offspring choose colleges, when grants are awarded, when the media report, when alumni contribute—at these times and many others, colleges and universities are evaluated.

A common approach to obtaining constituent evaluations is surveys and interviews. The Ohio Board of Regents (1978, p. 10) conducted an opinion poll of Ohio citizens and found "Ohioans interviewed think that higher education is doing a good job. Women interviewed tend to think more highly of Ohio's job than do men (72 percent of women think Ohio is doing an 'excellent' or 'good' job; 63 percent of the men feel this way)." A considerable number of occupational prestige studies have been conducted since 1925. One longitudinal study was conducted by the National Opinion Research Center (NORC) in 1947 and replicated in 1963 by Hodge, Siegel, and Rossi (1964). The 1947 ratings found the category of "college professor" rated ninth, and the 1963 study correlated, $r = .99$, with the earlier one. Hodge, Siegel, and Rossi (1964, pp. 322–334), studying various occupational ratings since 1925, concluded, "There have been no substantial changes in occupational prestige in the United States since 1925."

Community Impact. What difference does the college make on its surrounding community? External relations vary considerably among different colleges and universities; but to most institutions, at least a few of these relations are crucial. The influence of a college on its primary community can be measured. One approach to assessing this impact has been developed by the National Center for Higher Education Management Systems (NCHEMS). The best-known model was developed for the American Council by Caffrey and Isaacs

(1971); and a lesser-known but operationally useful system was developed in 1970 by the State University of New York and has been used almost every year since. Perhaps the most complete recent study of overall community impact was done by the University of Wisconsin system (1975a, p. viii; 1975b) in response to Governor Lucey's request for "a plan for phasing out, phasing down, or consolidating institutions and programs." As a result of excellent staff work, no institutions were closed down.

Three questions may be useful in appraising the extent of community impact: (1) Is the external program consistent with the institutional goals and objectives statement? If not, what is out of step? (2) Where are the institution's strengths in public service? (3) What are the advantages and disadvantages of making a greater commitment to public service?

Fiscal Indicators. In his survey of major issues of concern to state higher education agencies, Millard (1976, p. 59) found that appropriations and funding were at the top of the list, and the Paltridge and others (1973, pp. 31–32) study of board of trustee actions by subject area indicates that over 50 percent of their actions directly relate to fiscal matters. Fiscal indicators will continue as a crucial element in the eighties, and more sophisticated models will be developed for ascertaining fiscal impact.

The use of fiscal indicators as a measure of accountability is not questioned; the misuse or overuse of such indicators is. Members of governing boards are often successful businesspersons accustomed to using a "bottom line" criterion for measuring success. It is a mistake, however, to consider financial health as synonymous with academic excellence because a well-managed and efficient college is not necessarily a place where excellence in learning and teaching is evident also.

State-Level Boards. The influence and power of state-level boards has increased significantly in recent years as fiscal constraints have required institutional desires and needs be ranked by priority, as legislative pressures and the large number of bills introduced move legislators toward dealing with few constituencies, and as pressures continue for greater accountability of public funds.

State-level staffs are becoming increasingly interested in institutional evaluation, as indicated by the Fund for Improvement of Postsecondary Education (FIPSE)-sponsored self-assessment study by the New York State Education Department; and the size of staffs for state-level program evaluation has increased significantly in recent years as review procedures have become more rigorous. Also, most states have computerized data systems to assist in managing their accountability procedures.

State-level boards are probably entering a period of less staff growth and greater stability. From 1970 to about 1978, these staffs in many states were inexperienced and mobile, thus leaving their staff work and institutional liaison open to legitimate criticisms by the institutions. Staff stability and competence are increasing, but so are the pressures for greater accountability and evaluation. Now that state-level operations have become more stabilized, institutional representatives have become more adept at spotting weaknesses in state-level work. For example, institutions are raising many questions about simplistic, state-developed budget formulas and about undifferentiated application of formulas to differing institutions.

Institutional representatives need to be aware of the balancing act between required and reasonable state-level accountability and evaluation efforts and those that go beyond what is required and reasonable and what is desirable in terms of optimal institutional autonomy and flexibility.

Federal Agencies. The role and scope of the federal government in institutional evaluation has become the subject of controversy in recent years, and this pattern can be expected to continue. The federal government has the right, indeed, the responsibility, to expect public funds to be managed properly and to be audited on a regular basis. The "leave-it-on-the-stump" approach to funding and philanthropy belongs to another era. Yet in carrying out its public safeguard function, the federal government has ensnarled colleges and universities in much red tape and paperwork that require inordinate amounts of time, money, and energy; discourage local initiative; encourage institutions to develop self-protective, benevolent ways to avoid restrictions that border on illegality but are accepted within the institution as necessary in order to cope; and accentuate the "we-they" mentality. Van Alstyne and Coldren (1976) document costs of implementing federally mandated social programs. Grant (1977) provides an excellent discussion and data on the larger issues; and *Saturday Review* (1979) provides an industrial perspective on federal regulations.

The activities of the U.S. Office of Education's (USOE) accreditation and institutional eligibility staff impact most directly on institutional evaluation; and this agency's increased activities have been of concern to some higher education officials, particularly to the Council on Postsecondary Accreditation (COPA), which represents the interests of the regional accrediting associations.

The 1980s will likely see further efforts toward increased federal accountability, and this activity is supported by the higher education community in areas such as loan defaults. However, further federal inroads into institutional programs, academic freedom, and additional red tape need to be examined critically and opposed vigorously.

Approaches to Evaluating Institutional Quality

What Kipling once wrote—"There are nine and sixty ways of constructing tribal lays, and-every-single-one-of-them-is-right"—points up the importance of developing approaches to institutional evaluation that are tailored to specific institutions. Not all of them may be "right" in terms of conceptual design, institutional climate, and personnel involved; but the particularizing process must be given careful attention in the earliest deliberations. And this process does not rule out making use of information from national surveys and comparative data.

Two general types of evaluations can be identified. One cluster of evaluations is less than institutionwide in scope, usually focusing on a department, college, or programs. Various graduate school ratings, which have taken place beginning with R. Hughes in 1924, are interesting and useful in providing a national perspective on perceived quality, although one should not place too much weight on specific ratings. And the ratings include only certain types of institutions.

The area of institutionwide evaluation has received considerably less attention than the programmatic area, although interest in overall institutional quality is increasing significantly. This section discusses five approaches to institutional evaluation: educational auditing, external consultant reports, self-studies for accreditation, self-studies for other purposes, and state and federal reviews.

Educational Auditing. The Securities and Exchange Commission was established in 1934 in response to serious questions about the conduct and disclosure of business operations. In 1917, the American Institute of Accountants had published a list of standards for the preparation of audits. Although the form and nature of the audits vary, the following eight basic postulates were developed by the American Accounting Association (Mautz and Sharaf, 1961, p. 42):

1. Financial statements and financial data are verifiable.
2. There is no necessary conflict of interest between the auditor and the management of the enterprise under audit.
3. The financial statements and other information submitted for verification are free from collusive and other unusual irregularities.
4. The existence of a satisfactory system of internal control eliminates the probability of irregularities.
5. Consistent application of generally accepted principles of accounting results in the fair presentation of financial position and the results of operations.
6. In the absence of clear evidence to the contrary, what has held true in the past for the enterprise under examination will hold true in the future.
7. When examining financial data for the purpose thereon, the auditor acts exclusively in the capacity of an auditor.
8. The professional status of the independent auditor imposes commensurate professional obligations.

As pointed out by Harcleroad and Dickey (1975, p. 15): "With some slight modification and changes in terminology, these same postulates might very well be applied to the process of institutional auditing and accrediting. The verifiability of data, determination of adequate sampling, and probability theory would be characteristic of both business and educational institutions."

Of the various differences that exist between the business and educational audits, perhaps the most important one relates to scope. The fiscal audit is only a part of the educational audit, but it is *the* significant aspect for business. Some individuals, particularly those with business backgrounds, may relate institutional health almost exclusively to fiscal health. Such close equating should be avoided by institutions of higher education because of fundamental differences in purposes and funding procedures.

Harcleroad (1976, p. 18) writes that educational accreditation can profit in a number of ways from some of the experiences of the auditing profession:

(1) There might be improvement in the total process if more of the work were to be carried on by full-time professionals, without losing the value of having many of the participants serving on a part-time basis as at present. (2) There is a need for a research staff, similar to that of the Financial Accounting Standard Board, to be working on basic principles of assessment and procedures to be followed. (3) Some form of continuity is needed for the institution

involved and the main members of the team that will work with it as a representative of the accreditation body. (4) The standards of the regional associations and the specialized associations, and their respective commissions, should be similar enough to discount claims that great differences invalidate the entire process. The business auditing system, even with all its current problems and its many auditing firms, has sufficient comparability in its standards and their application to be quite credible, most of the time.

Private managerial firms are becoming interested in the audit approach to higher education; and the first report by Newman (1971, p. 70) spoke of the creation of "new regional examining universities." In considering the need for evaluating higher education, Bowen (1974, pp. 1–21) wrote that one of the needs of higher education is to find a means of evaluation that is genuinely disinterested and yet takes account of the many intangible elements. Perhaps a new profession of independent judges of productivity and performance should be created to evaluate institutions as well as higher education as a whole.

External Consultant Studies. A number of institutions of higher education as well as state systems have chosen to use external consultants for departmental and institutional studies. The New York Board of Regents study of doctoral program quality, the Illinois Board of Higher Education's Commission of Scholars, and the Louisiana Board of Regents Doctoral Program study all relied upon external consultants as a primary data source. The University of Chicago, for example, makes extensive use of recognized scholars from similar universities in analyzing its various programs. Their reports are printed in an official publication of the university called *The University of Chicago Record.*

The use of external reviewers/consultants carries the primary advantages of expertise and impartiality. One disadvantage is characterized in the "Report of the Visiting Committee to Evaluate the Department of Anatomy" (1975, p. 109) of the University of Chicago: "None of us is confident that a single experience, however concentrated, can reveal all the details of a complete system, nor that our responses are the most appropriate ones possible." The use of the phrase "the most appropriate ones" implies another possible disadvantage: institutional repercussions from ill-advised remarks, statements, or conclusions. The reviewers leave on the afternoon airplane, but those remaining must live with the report. The reviewers can create more problems than they solve if their report opens old wounds, makes strong recommendations on extremely sensitive matters that are not subject to solution at the time, or discusses the wrong problems and issues.

O'Connell and Meeth (1978, p. 41) discuss the following advantages and disadvantages for internal and external evaluators: The external evaluator has the advantages of being competent in program evaluation techniques, having no vested interest in the program, and removing the evaluation burden from the existing staff. Disadvantages are that he or she may take longer to understand the program and the evaluation requirements, lacks working relationship with program staff and institutional personnel, and may be regarded with suspicion by program staff. Advantages of the internal evaluator are that he or she is familiar with the program and staff, understands channels of communication within the institution and its larger community, is familiar with program details, and may be able to integrate the evaluation into the life of the program. Disadvantages of the internal evaluator are that he or she may not have the skills required for the evaluation, may have a vested interest in the program, and may be overburdened with other duties.

Based upon a report by Pottinger (1975), I devised the following questions to assist in choosing and using consultants:

1. How do you decide that a reviewer/consultant is needed?
   a. What is the nature of help needed?
   b. Is the circumstance specific enough to articulate clearly what is needed in the way of outside assistance? Some possible motivations include sorting out ambiguous problems, instilling motivation, gaining fresh perspectives, and recommending decisions that internal personnel prefer not to make.
2. How do you choose the proper consultant?
   a. Does the consultant have expertise in your specific area of need?
   b. Several questions might be asked of others who have used the consultant:
      (1) Did the consultant help you further articulate your circumstance without prematurely anticipating a solution?
      (2) Did the consultant help identify resources and approaches within your situation that assisted after departure?
      (3) Did you feel more capable of dealing with the problem after the consultant left?
      (4) Knowing what you know now, would you hire the same consultant if you had it to do over again?
3. How do you most effectively use consultation?
   a. Make one person clearly responsible and accountable for the consultant's work.
   b. Take ample time to define the problem clearly.
   c. Explore expectations again about what can and cannot be done. Have a written record.
   d. Use the consultant's time effectively. This requires carefully developed visitation schedules.
   e. Have a clear understanding of what evaluations and reports are expected or required from the consultant and within what time frame.

Self-Studies for Accreditation. Self-study for regional accreditation has been in existence throughout the twentieth century, and it takes place through the six regional accrediting associations. The Council on Postsecondary Accreditation (1976a, p. 3) gives these historical and current goals of accreditation:

- foster excellence in postsecondary education through the development of criteria and guidelines for assessing educational effectiveness
- encourage improvement through continuous self-study and planning
- assure the educational community, the general public, and other agencies or organizations that an institution or program has both clearly defined and appropriate objectives, maintains conditions

under which their achievement can reasonably be expected, appears in fact to be accomplishing them substantially, and can be
expected to continue to do so

- provide counsel and assistance to established and developing institutions and programs
- encourage the diversity of American postsecondary education,
and allow institutions to achieve their particular objectives and
goals
- endeavor to protect institutions against encroachments that
might jeopardize their educational effectiveness or academic
freedom

The New England Association of Schools and Colleges, Commission on Institutions of Higher Education (1973, p. 1) wrote that the purpose of evaluation is
twofold: "First, the institution is encouraged to analyze and appraise its own
functions, its educational effectiveness, its strengths and weaknesses, in order to
improve the quality of its performance. Second, the results of this analysis, together with the report of an evaluation committee, will be considered by the
commission in deciding whether or not to recommend an institution's application for membership." And the statement by the Middle States Association of
Colleges and Schools, Commission on Higher Education (1978a, p. 3) contends,
"Middle States accreditation involves a long-range process designed to help an
institution analyze its functions, appraise its educational effectiveness, and discover means by which its work can be strengthened. Institutional improvement is
the objective, and the accrediting process should facilitate the attainment of that
goal rather than make accreditation an end in itself."

The accreditation approach has come under increasing attack in recent
years, including the following criticisms: (1) Accreditation has not been able to
define "quality of education" except in terms of specific criteria (Ph.D.s for the
faculty or numbers of books in the library); and the validity of these criteria
never has been demonstrated. (2) Accreditation has not focused on "educational
outcomes." Thorough longitudinal studies would show little or no relationship
between accreditation standards and subsequent success (however defined and
measured) of the graduates of accredited institutions and programs. (3) Accreditation depends upon a "peer evaluation" system that by its very nature is guaranteed to be suspect. (Just as in a murder trial, where the prosecutor can find an
expert psychiatrist who will declare the defendant sane and the defense attorney
can find one who says the defendant is insane, so becoming accredited is assisted
by getting the right committee.) (4) Accreditation, utilizing the norm of established institutions and programs, tends to discourage innovation and experimentation. (5) Accreditation has moved so far toward the concept of evaluating an
institution or program in terms of its own statement of scope and purposes that
meaningful comparisons cannot be made. If a school for thieves states its objectives accordingly and accomplishes them, accreditation would have to say "well
done." (6) As accreditation becomes more tied to the determination of eligibility
for federal funds, it becomes less of a voluntary process and may have lost significant control of its own destiny. (7) Accreditation is used by some special-interest
groups not so much for legitimate public purposes but as a mechanism for
achieving or protecting private benefits.

Pfnister (1971) wrote that regional accrediting associations face four decisions: Can they now return to assessing the overall quality of an institution? Will increased pressure for accountability have an impact on their criteria? Can they assist more directly in the improvement of institutions' educational programs? Can accrediting agencies move more toward general accrediting functions and away from geographical boundaries?

The criticisms are answerable in a number of ways. One response by Dickey (1970) contended that accrediting institutions have often been instrumental for the maintenance of high educational standards; they have protected society from inadequately prepared professional and technical practitioners; they have aided licensing authorities and facilitated the transfer of students; they have been helpful to students and parents seeking to identify sound institutions; they have aided institutions in withstanding improper political or other noneducational pressures; and they have stimulated broad considerations of educational problems and issues of more than local concern.

The federal government is a factor in the future of regional accrediting associations. USOE officials are using accreditation as the principal criterion for determining student aid eligibility. Congress first decided to use accrediting associations as "reliable authority as to quality of training" in determining eligibility for federal funds. The USOE established an accreditation and institutional eligibility staff and an advisory committee to assist the commissioner in recognizing accredited institutions. Two other USOE developments are outlined in Council on Postsecondary Accreditation (1976b, p. 8): "USOE began to press the accrediting associations to change or modify certain practices in order to accommodate better the eligibility process. . . . [And] . . . the USOE . . . has attempted to require that the accrediting associations take on a role that would go beyond that of evaluating educational quality. . . . It is possible that, if this road were to be followed far enough, nongovernmental accrediting associations could become quasi-governmental and eventually governmental arms."

Vigorous activity by federal officials in this arena has made some officials of regional accrediting associations quite nervous. Others are also apprehensive about further efforts by federal officials to use established accrediting procedures to develop stricter accreditation procedures.

Some critics of regional accreditation have pointed out that 90 percent of postsecondary collegiate-type of institutions are accredited and that the reasons for most of the remaining 10 percent not being accredited are unrelated to poor quality; therefore, few or very minimal qualitative bases exist. This view oversimplifies the benefits that can accrue to an institution through self-study, which can result from preparation of the accreditation report and through professional activities with the regional accrediting associations. Also, those who know the accrediting process realize the campus visitation team reports generally do not rubber stamp the institution's self-study and sometimes raise substantial questions that require additional data and further discussion.

The "bottom line" question is, "Do regional accrediting associations perform sufficiently valuable services to warrant their continued existence?" The United States is almost unique in having a nationwide network of voluntary regional accrediting agencies.

In visiting offices of the regional accrediting associations, one is impressed with the high productivity achieved by relatively small professional staffs. The small central staff has required extensive use of professional personnel in the region. The visiting teams are an integral part of the accrediting process; and, as one would suspect, their effectiveness may vary considerably. But the visitations do assist team members in knowing and understanding well another college or university, and this knowledge very likely improves their general professional effectiveness at their base institution. Both friends and foes have overlooked this benefit.

The size of accrediting agency staffs alone precludes the "probity" role and the establishment of much more stringent evaluation standards for institutions. Increasing probity and standards likely will flow from those who distribute fiscal resources and who have the mandated authority.

Regional accrediting agencies can continue to have a valuable catalytic role if they do not take on those powers and authority that probity and standards require. Serving the future needs and directions for higher education will require accrediting agencies to stress educational improvement through innovation, clearinghouse functions, consultative roles, interinstitutional cooperation, and more detailed procedures for institutional self-study. These are crucial roles for the future of postsecondary education, and regional associations can continue to make significant contributions to them.

Self-Studies for Other Purposes. Hundreds of institutional self-studies unrelated to accreditation have been initiated in recent years, and dozens are underway at any one time. The national trend is toward institutional evaluation with greater rigor and frequency. Institutional self-study can be an important means for self-improvement. The regeneration of the University of Kentucky in the mid-1960s, sparked by a dynamic and experienced new president, came from an extensive self-study, which then became the basis for a comprehensive master plan. Mayhew and Ford (1971, p. 125) mention that "Stanford University shifted its character from that of a strong regional university appealing to bright, wealthy, underachieving students to a university of international stature primarily as a result of the findings of a self-study. Stephens College undertook a self-study when its administration believed that the time had come to minimize the traditions of an earlier era. That self-study was used to loosen the soil of academia so that a new president could have a reasonable chance of exercising academic leadership."

The results of self-studies, however, have not been evaluated to any noticeable extent. An exception is the study undertaken by Ladd (1970), which included self-studies done at the University of California, Berkeley; University of New Hampshire; University of Toronto; Swarthmore College; Wesleyan University; Michigan State University; Duke University; Brown University; Stanford University; and two partial cases: Columbia College and the University of California, Los Angeles. The author reached several conclusions based upon firsthand study of these eleven case studies as well as upon analysis of other self-studies:

> Unhappily, the results of these studies seem to lend support—at least in a negative way—to the efficacy of pressure politics as a way of bringing about change. There is little indication in any of the experiences to support the idea that the study-and-

report technique is an effective way of gaining acceptance of the *need* for change or creating enthusiasm for involvement in developing new policies. Where the study-and-report processes were intended primarily to challenge the *status quo,* they largely failed to do so. When the essential objective was to develop the details of a change in the *status quo* after the community had already accepted the need for some change, the study-and-report processes were much more effective . . . or where pressures for change from outside the faculties were much in evidence [pp. 197–198, 200].

The cases indicate in both positive and negative ways that strong, skillful leadership is virtually mandatory for the success of any serious effort at educational reform. . . . A primary task of academic leadership is to try to counter the pressures favoring the *status quo* by creating or maintaining an atmosphere of receptivity to change [pp. 205–206].

On the whole the educational policy changes proposed vary considerably in their venturesomeness, and they often seem to speak indirectly—if at all—to the deep malaise that presently affects so much of American higher education. Nevertheless, if the proposals were to be adopted by the institutions concerned, truly consequential changes would be made in the educational policies of those institutions. Generally speaking, the cases demonstrate that the proposals developed in the studies became less venturesome or simply disappeared as they passed through the various centers of decision making except where some form of countervailing power was present [p. 9].

The self-studies chosen by Ladd were undertaken between 1966 and 1969, or during the student unrest days. One suspects some studies were undertaken to alleviate the tense and policitized campus climate at the time. Dressel's (1976, p. 409) words may be relevant: "When the only goal of self-study is the alleviation of pressure, the preservation of accreditation, or the attainment of a foundation grant, success or failure in attaining the goals often ends the self-study." One can surmise that results of self-studies conducted under these circumstances would be minimal, yet Ladd's conclusions bear careful study.

Research studies have compared studies made of outside, monitored internal, and strictly internal evaluation reports. According to Chambers (1979, p. 32), "these findings show that internal evaluation is as reliable and accurate a method of depicting the current situation as the other two. This does much to dispel the criticism that the self-study—on its face—is self-serving, biased, and unreliable."

Self-assessment procedures for institutions of higher education also have been developed outside of academe. The American College Testing (ACT) Program (1970) initiated the Institutional Self-Study Service (ISS) to assist a college or university to evaluate the effectiveness of its programs and services. The ACT program was designed to "enable an institution to see itself through the eyes of its students; aid in the quantitative appraisal of college student development; and enable the institution to observe and explore longitudinal trends in student development and opinions on campus" (p. 1). Aspects of student services covered in the survey are faculty advising, counseling, financial needs, extracurricular advising, orientation, housing selections, housing advising, health, and remedial. The ISS survey asks students to indicate the degree of importance they attach to academic vocations and social and nonconventional goods. Instruction, school policies, and physical facilities also receive student evaluation.

The ISS places the student as primary evaluator; and few will disagree with having a significant student input in an institutional self-study, provided students answer questions within their scope of knowledge and experience. The quality of the faculty, academic and institutional leadership, and fiscal management are some essential components in any comprehensive self-study students cannot evaluate effectively. Their opinions may be useful, but data on several key variables in institutional self-study need to be gathered from other constituencies.

Manning (1976), working with the Research and Development Center for Teacher Education at the University of Texas, has developed a troubleshooting checklist (TSC) for higher educational settings to assist those concerned with change in their assessment of organizational variables predictive of an institution's potential for successfully adopting innovations. The TSC consists of one hundred Likert-type items grouped in five categories: organizational change, organizational staff, communications, innovative experience, and student characteristics. The diagnostic and predictive instrument is designed to aid users in estimating the effects of particular variables on the adoption/diffusion process. That is, the TSC provides users with a means of systematically organizing descriptive information in a predictive way. The validity of the TSC remains to be determined, although data on reliability are positive.

The following ten general areas and forty-five evaluative statements form the framework for my system of institutional evaluation (Miller, 1979):

- goals and objectives
  1. The goals statement serves as an effective guide for the present and future.
  2. Objectives reinforce goals.
  3. The institution has adequate planning capabilities.
  4. Institutional admissions policies and procedures are consistent with institutional goals and objectives.
  5. The institution's goals and objectives help it maintain a reasonable identity within a statewide system of institutions.
- student learning
  6. Students give a good rating to their advising and counseling system.
  7. Retention rates are reasonable.
  8. An array of individualized and compensatory learning resources is available.
  9. The student affairs administration is effective.
  10. Satisfactory progress toward learning goals is evident.
- faculty performance
  11. Current policies and procedures for evaluating individual faculty members are satisfactory.
  12. Current instructional improvement/faculty development programs serve their purpose.
  13. Faculty personnel policies and procedures are considered satisfactory.
  14. Faculty salary scales and fringe benefits are competitive.
  15. The overall quality of the faculty's performance is optimal.

- academic programs
16. The institution has effective policies and procedures for developing new programs.
17. The institution has effective policies and procedures for the review and evaluation of existing programs.
18. The general education component is an intellectually stimulating and integral part of the curriculum.
19. The quality and size of the graduate program are consistent with institutional goals and objectives.
20. The library or learning resources center provides good service to the academic community.
- institutional support services
21. The physical plant and facilities are adequate for the size of the student body and for the nature of the academic program.
22. The institution has a relevant and current long-range plan for developing and maintaining its physical plant.
23. Salaries and other benefits for support personnel are sufficient to attract and retain competent individuals.
24. Systematic procedures are used for evaluating the performance of support personnel.
- administrative leadership
25. The administration gives adequate attention to planning.
26. The chief campus administrator and his or her team have effective working relationships with other campus administrators.
27. Institutional governance policies and procedures allow for effective institutional management.
28. The policies and procedures established for administrative evaluation and for professional development are satisfactory.
29. The institution has an effective affirmative action program.
- financial management
30. The tuition and fee structure is compatible with the institution's needs and with the students' capacity to pay.
31. The institution has an efficient management system for accounting and financial reporting.
32. Costs and expenditures are comparable with benchmark institutions.
33. The investment portfolio is well managed.
34. The institution has an effective system for demonstrating its accountability.
- governing board
35. The policies and procedures for conducting board affairs are satisfactory.
36. Trustees understand the differences between policy formulation and policy implementation and apply this knowledge.
37. The governing board works effectively with external constituencies.
38. The board contributes positively to improving the institution.
- external relations
39. The institution's activities contribute to the quality of life in its primary service area.
40. The institution has effective relationships with the state higher education (coordinating or governing) office.
41. The institution has an effective relationship with the federal government.

42. The institution is able to secure acceptable levels of funding from private sources and foundations.
• institutional self-improvement
43. The institution seeks improvement through innovation and experimentation.
44. Campus groups have positive attitudes toward self-improvement.
45. The institution has established procedures for evaluating its own effectiveness.

State and Federal Reviews. The general expansion of state and federal governments in higher education can be documented, but the more specific state and federal roles in institutional evaluation have not been as widely considered.

State educational agencies have moved aggressively in the area of program evaluation since about 1972, largely in an effort to stem the tide of new graduate programs being developed without careful consideration of fiscal requirements or long-range institutional goals. Perhaps the most extensive effort has been the doctoral review project undertaken by the New York Board of Regents, assisted by outside funding. Initiated in 1975, this program utilized out-of-state scholars carefully selected jointly by board of regents staff members and the institution being reviewed. The program has reviewed all doctoral English and chemistry programs in the state of New York. The Illinois Board of Higher Education developed a commission of scholars, a group of five distinguished educators and scholars, to review selected doctoral programs and to make their recommendations to the board's academic staff. The Board of Regents for the State of Louisiana initiated in 1975 a review of all doctoral programs in the state. The study plan used out-of-state consultants selected on the basis of national eminence, representation from public and private schools, and representation from varied geographic areas. Their recommendations in latter 1976 called for elimination of several programs and consolidation of others.

Two state agencies for higher education have undertaken studies of educational quality and self-study. The purpose of the performance funding project undertaken by the Tennessee Higher Education Commission was to explore the feasibility of allocating some portion of state funds on a performance criterion. Each of the eleven campus-based pilot projects contracted to produce a set of institutionwide instructional goals, a set of corresponding performance indicators, and a report on how these goals and indicators were developed. A major assumption of the project is that state funding will continue to be primarily on an enrollment basis but that a complementary feature might be built into the formula to promote instructional effectiveness. Supported by national foundations, the pilot project selected two doctoral universities, six regional universities, and three community colleges. Final plans call for development of a model framework presenting a composite of quality indicators developed by the eleven campuses. The framework is based on types of institutions and programs, types of students served, and types of institutional goals. This framework is designed to highlight the importance of indicators of instructional effectiveness being developed locally and to provide background data for addressing the question of funding institutions for performance on those indicators.

The New York State Education Department (1979), assisted by a federal grant, established a project on self-assessment of colleges and universities. The project's goals are recognizing the need for self-assessment, developing assessment techniques, training faculty and staff as evaluators, and using the findings for decision making and action. The nine projects at public and private colleges and universities focus on career preparation, curricular ingredients for success, faculty evaluation, curricular design for industrial careers, professional preparation, student achievement, contract learning for graduate students, program effectiveness, quality of achievement, evaluation for quality, the part-time student, planning, faculty as evaluators, review of staff evaluating systems, and assessment of administration. The expertise developed in self-assessment through this project should encourage more frequent self-assessment as well as allow for more effective self-assessments and follow-ups.

State-level auditing of higher education activities is becoming more prevalent. In order to forestall auditing from outside the system, the state university system of Florida has developed an office of internal management auditing and its director reports directly to the chancellor of the state university system. The office has a full-time auditor on each campus who reports directly to the system director of internal management auditing. The auditing thus far is confined to fiscal affairs. This approach is preferable—at least to educators—over increased activity on the part of regular state auditors toward broadening this responsibility to include performance review of institutions of higher education.

The Auditor General (1976, p. 6) for the state of Illinois issued an audit guide for Illinois state agencies that includes the state colleges and universities. These guidelines contain a program audit that is a postaudit that "seeks to determine according to established or designated program objectives, responsibilities, or duties, including statutes and regulations, program performance criteria, or program evaluation standards: (1) whether the objectives and intended benefits are being achieved, and whether efficiently and effectively; (2) whether the program is being performed or administered as authorized or required by law; and (3) whether the program duplicates, overlaps, or conflicts with another state program."

The auditors approach higher education like any other service, and this is proper because education should be able to stand systematic and thorough fiscal scrutiny; but institutions of higher education also are different from those related to other state agencies. It is these differences that allow colleges and universities to make their vital contributions to society—some of which are experimental, trial-and-error, and therefore not particularly cost-effective. A balance needs to be maintained between systematic costing, individualistic learning, and experimental research.

The federal government has taken an increasingly active role in appraising, or asking others to appraise, the quality of institutions of higher education. The Council on Postsecondary Accreditation (1976b, pp. 7–8) points out that since 1968, the USOE has "aggressively answered" in its own ways the question: "Should accreditation be used for determining eligibility for federal funds? If so, what procedural pattern should be employed?" The accrediting associations, with some reluctance and occasional misgivings, have generally gone along with the government's approach. These actions by the USOE can be identified: (1) The Congress decided to make use of accrediting associations as "reliable authority as to quality of training" in the process of determining eligibility for federal funds. (2) The USOE created an accreditation and institutional eligibility staff and an advisory committee to assist the commissioner of education in "recognizing" accrediting associations for this purpose. (3) The USOE has pressed the accrediting associations to change or modify certain practices in order to accommodate better the eligibility process. (4) The USOE has sought to move the accrediting associations to take on a role beyond their traditional functions; namely, the USOE has proposed they serve as "reliable authority as to the quality of education or training and the *probity of institutions and programs.*" This latter function would put accrediting associations much more in the monitoring business than has been the case.

The federal government has been active in a number of other ways that can indirectly or otherwise influence the quality of institutions of higher education. Examples are federal funds and various grant and loan programs and civil rights and affirmative action procedures and mandates. As the federal government continues or expands its activities in higher education, it will continue to be concerned about institutional quality. Because it appropriates billions of dollars of public funds for higher education, this concern is proper and should be expected. Concern, however, is different from control or excessive influence. Institutional- and state-level educational officials are willing to work cooperatively with the federal government in achieving mutually desirable goals of better quality control through cooperation and coordination.

General Guidelines for Institutional Evaluation

The following six guidelines may be helpful in tailoring an evaluation plan to a specific institution or system. First, vigorous and sensitive administrative leadership, which includes providing initial impetus for the appraisal, keeping a leadership role in terms of the group directing the efforts, and moving recommendations into action, is crucial to effective institutional appraisal. Dynamic administrative leadership need not be confused with the Machiavellian approach, although there may be a grain of it in effective administrative leadership. Good administration includes developing broad support, hard work, perspective, and empathy; and it includes healthy respect and understanding of the two primary campus constituencies—students and faculty members.

Second, an overall evaluation plan should be developed and communicated. Members of the academic community should have ample opportunity to know an evaluation effort is underway; certain individuals have some designated responsibilities; mandates and/or charges exist for the effort; some reporting dates are scheduled; open hearings are planned; and recommendations are anticipated.

Several characteristics of institutional evaluation have been developed. The Northwest Association of Schools and Colleges, Commission on Colleges (1975, p. 6) determined the self-study process is flexible and permits different approaches; is attuned to current institutional priorities; utilizes recent institutional research or studies; involves as many people as possible; has enough breadth and depth to review accountability; focuses study on results of the educational program; uses information and results to improve the document; yields a concise, readable, useful document; and fosters ongoing self-study and planning.

The New York State Education Department (1979) project on self-assessment for colleges and universities has been described earlier. Based upon the project's experience, I have developed the following steps in self-assessment:

1. A clear definition of the goals of the assessment, as distinct from the goals of the specific area being assessed, should be made. The main focus of assessment should be on evaluation of educational quality as measured by goal-oriented outcomes.
2. All persons who are affected and interested in the programs under review should be continually made aware of and often involved in the assessment process. Responsibility for setting priorities, designing the assessment, collecting and analyzing data, and evaluating and using them should be assigned to appropriately skilled persons.
3. A determination of how well the goals of the specific area assessed are being met should be made. The appropriate instruments and techniques must be selected and administered to the constituencies involved (for example, administrators, faculty, students, graduates, employers, and outside groups).
4. The process of collecting data should be established in such a way that it can continue beyond the first self-assessment as a routine function of the master planning and decision-making process.
5. Analysis of data, reporting of findings, and recommendations for action should be carefully monitored by the person(s) responsible for the self-assessment. Periodic follow-up of recommendations is essential to determine if any *actual* results have occurred.
6. Essential to effective self-assessment is the periodic evaluation of the system itself. The system should be cost-effective in both dollars and human time spent to provide vital information for decision making.

Third, the process of institutional appraisal is at least as important as the product (outcomes). The way activities are conducted—the process—is very important to its eventual success or failure. Included in process are careful attention to composition of the working group, systematic study design, and openness in the group's deliberations, with adequate opportunities for discussion with various constituencies. It is better to touch bases than mend fences, yet not every decision should be put to a faculty and/or student vote. Just as excessive controls and secrecy about the project can diminish credibility and ultimate acceptance, so excessive participation and openness can grind the effort to a halt through frustration and excessive slowness. Some evaluation committees start with "givens" over which they had no control, such as reducing the number of academic personnel. The most sensitive and fairest procedure in such circumstances will not blunt the human problems caused by such decisions.

Fourth, institutional evaluation should use objective data where available and purposeful but make no apologies for using subjective data. Or, it is better to be generally right than precisely wrong. Objective data is important, yet considerable variation exists in the availability and quality of such evidence. The absence of objective data should stimulate those responsible for institutional evaluation to devise their own survey instruments, guidelines, and checklists or to use systematically treated judgment as bases for decision making. The lack of "hard" data should not deter careful and systematic decision making about important institutional matters. Solid bases for decision making can be developed by using whatever hard data are available along with experience, judgment, and common sense. Important institutional decisions often are made on much less.

Fifth, institutional studies should be action oriented, with plans for moving reports to action. "Filed and forgotten" should not be ascribed to any institutional evaluation, considering the investment of thousands of hours and dollars and the importance of keeping the institution abreast or ahead of its problems. But the history of institutional studies does not provide cause for exuberance about effective implementation of recommendations. Today, however, there are a number of excellent case studies of institutional evaluations that are action oriented because the times demand more rigorous approaches to implementing recommendations.

The administrative charge to the institutional evaluation committee should make clear that its work plan is geared toward recommendations for action. This position from the outset will remind those involved in the project, and others, that their efforts are less likely to be filed and forgotten.

Sixth, a plan for evaluating the evaluation should be included. Most evaluation reports make little or no provision for evaluation of their effectiveness. Such evaluations of evaluations are useful as testimony to the importance of evaluation in future improvement, for providing systematic checkpoints on progress, and for providing a procedure for orderly modifications based upon subsequent findings.

Institutional Evaluation in the Context of Institutional Planning

Institutional evaluation should be integrally related to institutional planning, and the office of institutional research needs to be closely related to the effort. The initiative for institutional evaluation, however, should come from the chief administrative official, who would probably delegate the more immediate leadership to someone like the vice-president for academic affairs.

The relationships described in the previous paragraph are simple enough and seem to be clear, yet many colleges and universities do little to develop them. For example, the Carnegie Commission survey on institutional research (Bogard, 1972, p. 20) found that institutional research "was difficult to locate within the organization, it was hard to identify specifically; and its exact role or function in the administration was not easily determined. The typical administrator in the sample survey perceived himself as competent and as possessing highly adequate information for the decisions he made." This quotation illustrates the problems that might arise with respect to use of important base data and data collection capabilities of the office of institutional research.

Institutional evaluation should always be considered in the context of other planning and evaluation that may be planned or underway at the institution. The compartmentalized nature of many campuses encourages poor communication about such efforts, and departments and colleges may respond to requests for data that are not coordinated through a single office. The office for institutional planning is the logical locus for coordinating such efforts.

A series of questions, such as these raised by Dressel (1976, pp. 412–414), should be considered before undertaking any sizable evaluation:

1. Is the problem one requiring restudy of goals of operating policies, or is it primarily a failure in supervision, management,

      or administrative performance? . . . A self-study usually avoids pinpointing individual weaknesses and is not likely to correct problems created by poor administration.

2. Is the problem one that should be considered and resolved through existing committees or other agencies?
3. Is the problem of sufficient significance that resources can be allocated to support in-depth study over a period of weeks or months?
4. Are the incentives or pressures that appear to require the . . . study of sufficient gravity to cause general acceptance of the need for the study, willingness to contribute to it, and readiness to attend to the results?
5. Are administrative officers willing to make available to a . . . study group all the information required to fully understand a problem and the implications of various solutions?

Other questions may be raised also, such as the following:

1. Is the campus political climate receptive to such a study?
2. Is the *timing* of the study right? The answer lies in previous and current campus activities and in the campus climate.
3. Does the campus have sufficient expertise to conduct the study if that alternative is chosen, or can funds be found if outside expertise is preferred?

      Various dimensions of evaluation, such as faculty, student, program, administration, and accrediting reports, may be more or less continuous, depending upon the institution. Some individual, probably at the assistant vice-president level, should have overall responsibility for these efforts. The coordination within the institution of all types of evaluation over a multiyear period is essential to optimize coordination, reduce confusion, and minimize costs.

Conclusion

      This chapter has covered some aspects of institutional appraisal. Its tone and spirit are reflected in statements by Cartter and by Riesman: "Diversity can be a costly luxury if it is accompanied by ignorance. Our present system works fairly well because most students, parents, and prospective employers *know* that a bachelor's degree from Harvard, Stanford, Swarthmore, or Reed is ordinarily a better indication of quality and accomplishment than a bachelor's degree from Melrose A & M or Siwash College. Even if no formal studies were ever undertaken, there is always a grapevine at work to supply impressionistic evaluations. However, evaluation by rumor and word of mouth is far from satisfactory, particularly in advanced training for scholarship and professions" (Cartter, 1966, p. 3).

      Stating the case for studies of quality education at the undergraduate level, Riesman (1958, p. 5) has argued, "the quality of a school changes faster than its clientele recognizes; and colleges that have developed a novel and more demanding program cannot get the students to match it, while other institutions that have decayed cannot keep away students who should no longer go there. While autos carry their advertising, so to speak, on their body shells, which speak as loudly as print or TV commercials, colleges can change inside their shells with hardly anyone's noticing. And the result can be tragic, not only for misled students, but for imaginative faculty and administrators who may not live long enough to be rewarded by the appearance of good students attracted by those changes."

Evidence from an array of sources in this chapter should provide substantial impediments to those who want to oversimplify the appraisal of institutional quality, using one or two elements. Yet those who refuse to say that some indicators are more important than others are in danger of suffering the fate of being ignored by those who are being pressured toward answers or who are looking for simple answers to complex problems. There is a middle ground somewhere in between that will not satisfy either extreme yet just might be workable.

Bibliographical Essay

In addition to citations in the chapter, several works deserve special attention for those starting institutional evaluations. The New York State Department of Education's *Handbook for Self-Assessment* (1979) provides useful guidelines, some models of self-assessment, and articles on this topic. The Council on Postsecondary Accreditation (1975) is the most comprehensive and current compilation on evaluation instruments. Chambers (1979) contains papers by Alexander W. Astin, Howard R. Bowen, and Charles M. Chambers. Burns (1978) directed a study entitled *Evaluation of Institutions of Postsecondary Accreditation: Assessment in Terms of Outcomes Through Institutional Self-Study*. Andrews's (1978) four-volume report will also be helpful for this area.

Each of the six accrediting associations has abundant materials on self-study and evaluation. Middle States Association of Colleges and Schools, Commission on Higher Education (1978b), will be of particular interest.

Several parts of Dressel (1976) will be useful, and I would rate the chapter on institutional self-study as the best thirty-two-page discussion in print. Balderston (1974) includes a useful checklist for academic quality assessment and program evaluation. And I would like to think Miller (1979) would be useful.

References

American College Testing Program. *The Institutional Self-Study Service.* Iowa City, Iowa: American College Testing Program, 1970.

Andrews, G. J. *Assessing Nontraditional Education.* 4 vols. Washington, D.C.: Council on Postsecondary Accreditation, 1978.

Auditor General. "Audit Guide for Performing Compliance Audits of Illinois State Agencies." Springfield: Office of the Auditor General, State of Illinois, 1976.

Balderston, F. E. *Managing Today's University.* San Francisco: Jossey-Bass, 1974.

Bogard, L. "Management in Institutions of Higher Education." In A. M. Mood and others (Eds.), *Papers on Efficiency in the Management of Higher Education.* Berkeley, Calif.: Carnegie Commission on Higher Education, 1972.

Bowen, H. R. "The Products of Higher Education." In H. R. Bowen (Ed.), *New*

Directions for Institutional Research: Evaluating Institutions for Accountability, no. 1. San Francisco: Jossey-Bass, 1974.

Bowen, H. R. *Investment in Learning: The Individual and Social Value of American Higher Education.* San Francisco: Jossey-Bass, 1977.

Bowen, H. R. "Goals, Outcomes, and Academic Evaluation." In *Evaluating Educational Quality: A Conference Summary.* Washington, D.C.: Council on Postsecondary Accreditation, 1979.

Burns, N. *Evaluation of Institutions of Postsecondary Accreditation: Assessment in Terms of Outcomes Through Institutional Self-Study.* Washington, D.C.: Council on Postsecondary Accreditation, 1978.

Caffrey, J., and Isaacs, H. *Estimating the Impact of a College or University on the Local Economy.* Washington, D.C.: American Council on Education, 1971.

Cartter, A. M. *An Assessment of Quality in Graduate Education.* Washington, D.C.: American Council on Education, 1966.

Chambers, C. M. "What Have We Learned?" In *Evaluating Educational Quality: A Conference Summary.* Washington, D.C.: Council on Postsecondary Accreditation, 1979.

Cohen, M. D., and March, J. G. *Leadership and Ambiguity: The American College President.* New York: McGraw-Hill, 1974.

Council on Postsecondary Accreditation. *Evaluation of Institutions of Postsecondary Education: An Annotated List of Instruments.* Washington, D.C.: Council on Postsecondary Accreditation, 1975.

Council on Postsecondary Accreditation. *The Balance Wheel for Accreditation.* Washington, D.C.: Council on Postsecondary Accreditation, 1976a.

Council on Postsecondary Accreditation. *Major Issues in Accreditation.* The President's Annual Report, 1975–76. Washington, D.C.: Council on Postsecondary Accreditation, 1976b.

Dickey, F. G. "The 1970s: Time for Assessment in Accreditation." Annual Report of the Executive Director. Washington, D.C.: National Commission on Accreditation, 1970.

Dressel, P. L. *Handbook of Academic Evaluation: Assessing Institutional Effectiveness, Student Progress, and Professional Performance for Decision Making in Higher Education.* San Francisco: Jossey-Bass, 1976.

Grant, A. T. *The Impact of Federal Policies on Higher Education Institutions.* Tucson: College of Education, Higher Education Program, University of Arizona, 1977.

Harcleroad, F. F. *Educational Auditing and Accountability.* Washington, D.C.: Council on Postsecondary Accreditation, 1976.

Harcleroad, F. F., and Dickey, F. G. *Educational Auditing and Voluntary Institutional Accrediting.* ERIC/Higher Education Research Report, No. 1. Washington, D.C.: American Association for Higher Education, 1975.

Hodge, R. W., Siegel, P. M., and Rossi, R. H. "Occupational Prestige in the United States." *American Journal of Sociology,* 1964, *70,* 286–302.

Hodgkinson, H. L. *How Much Change for a Dollar? A Look at Title III.* ERIC/Higher Education Research Report, No. 3. Washington, D.C.: American Association for Higher Education, 1974.

Ladd, D. R. *Change in Educational Policy: Self-Studies in Selected Colleges and Universities.* New York: McGraw-Hill, 1970.

Manning, B. A. *The "Trouble Shooting" Checklist for Higher Educational Settings.*

Austin, Tex.: Research and Development Center for Teacher Education, 1976.

Mautz, R. K., and Sharaf, H. A. *The Philosophy of Auditing.* Chicago: American Accounting Association, 1961.

Mayhew, L. B., and Ford, P. J. *Changing the Curriculum.* San Francisco: Jossey-Bass, 1971.

Middle States Association of Colleges and Schools, Commission on Higher Education. *Policies and Procedures.* Philadelphia: Commission on Higher Education, 1978a.

Middle States Association of Colleges and Schools, Commission on Higher Education. *Characteristics of Excellence in Higher Education.* Philadelphia: Commission on Higher Education, 1978b.

Millard, R. M. *State Boards of Higher Education.* ERIC/Higher Education Research Report, No. 4. Washington, D.C.: American Association for Higher Education, 1976.

Miller, R. I. *The Assessment of College Performance: A Handbook of Techniques and Measures for Institutional Self-Evaluation.* San Francisco: Jossey-Bass, 1979.

National Opinion Research Center. "Jobs and Occupations." *Opinion News,* September 1, 1947, pp. 3–13.

New England Association of Schools and Colleges, Commission on Institutions of Higher Education. *Evaluation Procedures.* Burlington, Mass.: New England Association of Schools and Colleges, 1973.

Newman, F. *Report on Higher Education.* Washington, D.C.: U.S. Department of Health, Education and Welfare, 1971.

New York State Department of Education. *A Handbook for Self-Assessment: Self-Assessment for Colleges and Universities.* Albany: New York State Department of Education, 1979.

Northwest Association of Schools and Colleges, Commission on Colleges. *Accreditation Procedural Guide.* Seattle: Northwest Association of Schools and Colleges, 1975.

O'Connell, W., Jr., and Meeth, L. R. *Evaluating Teaching Improvement Programs.* New Rochelle, N.Y.: National Teaching Program, 1978.

Ohio Board of Regents. "Public Opinion Polling and Higher Education Programs." Staff Report. Columbus: Ohio Board of Regents, 1978.

Paltridge, J. G., and others. *Boards of Trustees: Their Decision Patterns.* Berkeley, Calif.: Center for Research and Development in Higher Education, 1973.

Pfnister, A. O. "Regional Accrediting Agencies at the Crossroads." *Journal of Higher Education,* 1971, *42,* 558–573.

Pottinger, P. E. "Some Comments on the Effective Use of Consultant and External Advisors." Paper presented at project directors' meeting of the Fund for the Improvement of Postsecondary Education. Boston: Institute for Competence Assessment, Division of McBer and Company, 1975.

"Report of the Visiting Committee to Evaluate the Department of Anatomy." *University of Chicago Record,* 1975, *3,* 109.

Riesman, D. *Constraint and Variety in American Education.* New York: Doubleday, 1958.

Saturday Review. "A Special Section: Overregulation?" *Saturday Review,* 1979, *6,* 24–41.

University of Wisconsin System. *President's Report in Response to the Governor's Re-*

quest: On Reducing the Scope of the University of Wisconsin System. Madison: University of Wisconsin System, 1975a.

University of Wisconsin System. *Report of the System Advisory Planning Task Force.* Book 1. Madison: University of Wisconsin System, 1975b.

Van Alstyne, C., and Coldren, S. L. *The Costs of Implementing Federally Mandated Social Programs at Colleges and Universities.* Washington, D.C.: American Council on Education, 1976.

Verry, D., and Davies, B. *University Costs and Outputs.* New York: Elsevier, 1976.

22

Eugene Craven

Evaluating Program
Performance

The basic challenge to academic institutions during the 1980s will be maintaining the quality of instructional programs while controlling and perhaps even reducing costs. Attendant to this dilemma is a series of problematic questions: How should declining resources be distributed to the instructional units within an institution—should all units share proportionally in cutbacks or should resource reductions be made selectively and, if so, on what basis? Regardless of program enrollment, what fixed resources must be available if a program is to be offered and its quality maintained? How can programs continue to be responsive to the needs of students, society, and scholarship? How can access for a broad socioeconomic range of students be maintained despite pressures to raise tuition and fees? And how can the intellectual vitality of the faculty be maintained when faculty are threatened with the prospect of layoffs?

The success with which institutions cope with these problems will depend, in large measure, upon the effectiveness of their academic program evaluation processes. Evaluation contributes to the ability to make sound judgments among alternatives; institutional ability to adapt to the changing conditions of the 1980s will depend upon the scope and quality of those judgments. Thus, the need for academic program evaluation is clear.

This chapter provides a conceptual framework for understanding evaluation and its relationship to academic programs and decision-making processes, examines a variety of approaches to evaluation drawn from different fields of inquiry, outlines general guidelines for conducting academic program evaluations in higher education, identifies some agenda items for further development of program evaluation capabilities, and discusses certain implications of evaluation for institutional research.

The Concept of Evaluation

Evaluation is not new in higher education: It is implicit in the development of new knowledge and in the creative reinterpretation of existing knowledge. In this sense, it has been a part of higher education since its beginnings. In the literature on evaluation, however, one finds comparatively little about program evaluation in higher education; and often what has been written is fugitive, existing as unpublished manuscripts. Outside the field of higher education, however, there is a burgeoning literature on evaluation, a literature written largely by and for professional evaluators. In reviewing this literature, one quickly realizes there is not yet a common philosophy, focus, or terminology of evaluation or agreement about how to conduct an evaluation. A sampling of the literature defining evaluation illustrates this point.

Stufflebeam and others (1971) note three definitions of evaluation have gained some acceptance over the past sixty years, each having certain advantages and disadvantages. One, developed during the 1920s and 1930s, equates evaluation with measurement. This view limits evaluation to an examination of those program variables for which science has developed measurement instruments and obscures the basic fact that value judgments necessarily are involved in evaluation. A second definition depicts the process of evaluation as determining the congruence between program performance and objectives. One of the difficulties this definition poses is the task of developing a sufficiently operational set of objectives by which to test for congruence. Also, in practice, this definition tends to lead people to think of evaluation as a terminal process conducted at the conclusion of a program, thereby missing the opportunity for program improvements during design and implementation. A third definition of evaluation equates evaluation with professional judgment, raising questions about the reliability and objectivity of such evaluations.

After reviewing these limitations, Stufflebeam and others (1971, p. 40) define evaluation as "the process of delineating, obtaining, and providing useful information for judging decision alternatives." This definition, however, does not indicate the nature of the decision alternatives that accompany program evaluation. Another definition, offered by Suchman (1967, p. 7), states evaluation is "the social process of making judgments of worth." And Dressel (1976, p. 1) writes, "evaluation is both a judgment on the worth or impact of a program, procedure, or individual, and the process whereby that judgment is made." Although these definitions provide insights into the general nature of program evaluation, they do not convey an operational understanding of it.

Despite this lack of agreement, there are similar elements in many of the definitions and, in recent years, there has been a strong movement to relate evaluation to decision making. With these observations in mind, I propose the following definition: Program evaluation is the process of specifying, defining, collecting, analyzing, and interpreting information about designated aspects of a given program and using that information to arrive at value judgments among decision alternatives regarding the installation, continuation, modification, or termination of a program. In this chapter, the term *program* refers to academic instructional activities, including degree programs and nondegree instruction, offered by institutional units such as departments or divisions.

The actual effectiveness of program evaluations obviously can vary in terms of decision-making results. Consequently, an effective evaluation will be regarded as one in which (1) evaluation results are useful in arriving at judgments about decision alternatives for a given program, (2) the wisdom or quality of those decisions is better than had the evaluative information not been available in making those judgments, and (3) the decision alternatives selected are implemented.

In general terms, academic programs can be viewed as having inputs, such as students, faculty, support staff, physical facilities, equipment, and finances, and outputs and outcomes. Outputs can encompass such measures as student credits taught or the number of degrees granted; outcomes are the longer-term effects of more immediate outputs and can include such results as the impact of the program on the value formation, earning power, or civic participation of graduates.

The actual conduct of academic programs is accomplished through a series of decision-making processes: The programs must be planned; resources must be anticipated, acquired, and allocated to organizational units responsible for them; and the programs must then be implemented. Typically, many people view evaluation as the assessment activity that occurs at the end of these decision-making steps. However, Scriven (1967) has distinguished "formative" from "summative" evaluation, with formative evaluation undertaken during the development and implementation of a program, and summative evaluation conducted after the program has been in operation for a period of time. The purpose of formative evaluation is to guide and assist program development and improvement; that of summative evaluation is to determine the overall worth of a program and to assist in making decisions concerning its continuation, modification, or termination. Thus, evaluation is not a linear activity at the end of the implementation process; rather, it is dialectical, interacting throughout the process.

Two other terms that describe specific applications of summative evaluation should be noted. "Program review," as the term is used in this chapter, connotes an "early warning" system of summative evaluation, using selected quantitative indicators by which the general performance or health of a program can be monitored periodically. Depending upon the indicators, a more extensive and thorough summative evaluation may be required. Also, "program auditing" is an evaluation of the program evaluation process itself.

The actual process of evaluation is divided into two broad phases: a design phase and an implementation phase. In order to make an informed judgment between or among several decision alternatives, certain evaluative information is needed. The design phase identifies this information and defines the analytical methods necessary to generate the data. In the implementation phase, the execution of the design plan occurs in almost the reverse order of their consideration in the design phase: Data are collected and analyzed; the resulting information is interpreted and reported; and judgments are made concerning appropriate decision alternatives. These judgments, when implemented, can lead to changes in the program, in other institutional processes, or in the program evaluation process itself. At a later time, the impact of these judgments can be assessed and the evaluation process itself can be evaluated.

Approaches to Evaluation

There have been three arenas in which approaches to evaluation developed during the 1960s and 1970s continue to have an impact on program evaluation in higher education: school and social action programs, government and industry, and higher education itself. In this section, the major approaches to evaluation in these three areas are outlined and their strengths and limitations are assessed. The term "approaches to evaluation" is used in preference to the term evaluation "models" because most of the applications do not meet the conceptual requirements of a true model.

School and Social Action Programs. The outcry of public concern following the launching of Sputnik in 1957 initiated rapid growth in evaluation; and this growth was reinforced and greatly extended in the early 1960s by the civil rights movement and the massive federal projects that followed in its wake to increase minority student access to education, fight poverty, reduce crime, control disease, and rebuild cities. With the tremendous increase in funding for these projects came the call for accountability. Thus, the Elementary and Secondary Education Act of 1965 became milestone legislation by requiring that every project funded under it be evaluated to continue receiving federal funds.

Significant differences among the approaches to educational and social program evaluation can be summarized according to their focus. For example, some focus primarily upon inputs to programs; others concentrate on program outputs or objectives; others attempt to assess program processes; and still others endeavor to examine the entire range of program inputs, processes, outcomes, and goals. I discuss each approach briefly.

One of the first approaches to evaluation was to equate the excellence of a program with the perceived quality of its *inputs*. This approach is still popular because certain program inputs are tangible and can easily be described. Consequently, academic programs in higher education sometimes are judged by such measures as the academic achievement levels of their entering students, the academic accomplishments and reputation of the participating faculty members, the adequacy of the program-related special equipment and physical facilities, and the level of the program funding. Although it is important in program evaluation to know the state of program inputs, an evaluation based solely upon an assessment of inputs will reveal nothing about the eventual outcomes of the program or about program processes. Input evaluation will not provide answers to such questions as "What changes occurred as a result of this program?" or "Could the program results have been obtained more efficiently?" Only a limited range of decision-making needs can be supported by input evaluation.

A second category of approaches to program evaluation arose in reaction to the deficiencies of program input evaluation. This category of program evaluation focuses upon program *outputs* and *objectives*. The early work of Ralph Tyler in the 1930s and 1940s led to the development of a number of goal attainment models. Using such goal-based approaches, evaluators attempt to discover the extent to which intended program goals or objectives have been achieved. For example, a foreign language program in higher education might have an objective of developing native speaking fluency in all baccalaureate graduates. The extent to which this objective has been attained can be measured by various tests of speaking performance.

This category of evaluation approaches is not without limitations, one being that program objectives must be clearly stated and specific so the degree of goal attainment can be measured. A second is the narrow focus of the approach. Using the example of a foreign language program, this evaluation approach could answer such questions as "How many students were able to achieve native or near-native speaking fluency in this program?" But it could not respond to such questions as "What changes in the instructional method might produce better results?" A third shortcoming is that program goals or objectives often are accepted as given and are not subject to their own evaluation.

In response to the third shortcoming, Scriven (1967) has urged that the quality of program objectives be established through assessment at the outset of an evaluation. In this approach, information is identified and gathered only on program outputs or outcomes, whether intended or not, and then the importance of such outcomes is evaluated. Evaluators do not use knowledge of the stated program goals or objectives. Goal-free evaluation is not intended to replace goal-based evaluation, but to complement it. Taken together, the two approaches provide a more complete and valid understanding of program outputs and objectives.

The limitations of the goal attainment approaches to evaluation, coupled with the difficulties with experimental designs often used in goal attainment approaches and the deficiencies of evaluations based almost exclusively on quantitative analysis, stimulated an interest in *process-oriented approaches.* Four examples of this general type are the Countenance Model, responsive evaluation, transactional evaluation, and illuminative evaluation.

Developed by Stake (1972), the Countenance Model consists of two matrices (program description and judgment). Each matrix is divided into three rows, one for antecedent information, another for transaction information, and a third for outcome information. Antecedents are defined as conditions existing prior to program implementation that could affect program outcomes. Transactions are the processes of the program. Outcomes are broadly defined, covering the full range of program consequences. In the descriptive matrix, information is gathered on the intents and the observations of program antecedents, transactions, and outcomes. Similarly, in the judgment matrix, information concerning the standards and the judgments made with respect to the antecedents, transactions, and program outcomes is recorded. In addition, program rationale is recorded, including the underlying philosophy and basic purpose of the program. This establishes a basis for evaluating program intents in the descriptive matrix. The evaluation process in this Countenance Model consists of checking for congruencies between intents and observations and examining the information for contingencies between program outcomes, transactions, and antecedents.

Stake (1975) has also developed an approach to program evaluation called responsive evaluation. Based primarily upon observation and reaction, responsive evaluation focuses more directly on program activities than on program intents, responds to program participant requirements or expectations for information, and refers to the different value perspectives of the various individuals or groups related to the program in reporting program success or failure. This description clearly conveys an operational sense of responsive evaluation: "To do a responsive evaluation, the evaluator, of course, does many things. He makes a plan of observations and negotiations. He arranges for various persons to observe the program. With their help he prepares for brief narratives, portrayals, produces displays, graphs, and so forth. He finds out what is of value to his audiences. He gathers expressions of worth from various individuals whose points of view differ. . . . He gets program personnel to react to the accuracy of his portrayals. He gets authority figures to react to the importance of various findings. He does much of this informally, iterating and keeping a record of action and reactions" (Stake, 1975, p. 11). Responsive evaluation is decidedly subjective; but Stake believes it can raise important, though sometimes embarrassing, questions about an academic program.

Another approach to program evaluation is transactional evaluation (Rippey, 1973), which is used to study social systems undergoing planned program change. This approach is helpful in learning how to overcome resistance to the planned program changes. As such, it is best used as part of a good plan for formative evaluation for identifying and overcoming system barriers to planned program changes. Transactional evaluation has two main phases: uncovering sources of conflict among program participants and developing and implementing an evaluation plan to address the mutual concerns identified in the first phase. A questionnaire that includes items developed by all involved in the programmatic change is used to identify areas of conflict. Transactional evaluation is most effective when used on a new, small-scale program under the most favorable conditions for success that can be arranged or when the new program is experimental and has an evaluation scheme that requires both protagonists and antagonists to set up criteria for evaluating the planned and unintended program outcomes.

A final approach is Parlett and Hamilton's Illuminative Evaluation Model (1977). Illuminative evaluation employs a case study approach to examine what is happening in a given program and why. This approach makes extensive use of observation and interviews; it places less emphasis on needs analysis and quantitative assessment methodologies. This model has been used to evaluate programs at several colleges and universities in recent years.

Like the approaches discussed in the input and output evaluation categories, the evaluation approaches that focus on program processes are limited in application and usefulness by the restricted scope of their inquiry. Several rely heavily on observation and interview techniques, thereby raising questions about their objectivity and reliability.

In an effort to respond to a greater range of decision-making needs with respect to program evaluation, several more *comprehensive approaches* have been developed. Two examples of these are the CIPP Model and holistic evaluation. The CIPP (Context-Input-Process-Product) Model, developed by Stufflebeam and others (1971), postulates four decision settings based upon the magnitude of the program changes expected from decisions and the amount of relevant information and expertise needed to make those decisions. The four decision settings are metamorphic, homeostatic, incremental, and neomobilistic.

A metamorphic decision setting would be directed toward large-scale program changes requiring complete information and expertise. Because this requirement cannot actually be met, it is regarded only as a theoretical possibility. The objective of a homeostatic decision setting is to restore a program to its intended plan of operation, to keep it "in balance." This decision setting usually involves small changes based upon a large fund of available program information and expertise. The objective of an incremental decision setting is to seek continued program improvements. Usually, the expected changes are small and little information or expertise is available. It is essentially trial-and-error decision making. In a neomobilistic decision setting, broad program changes are sought but little information or expertise is available to guide the decision making. The significance of these four decision settings is that no single approach to evaluation can suffice. Each decision setting requires a different evaluation approach.

Four types of decisions are associated with the model: planning, structuring, implementary, and recycling. Planning decisions specify program objectives and determine the setting in which program decisions are to be made. The remaining three types of decisions can occur in any of the decision settings. Structuring decisions design the means to achieve planned program objectives. Implementing decisions control day-to-day program operations. Recycling decisions judge program attainments in light of program objectives and, if necessary, lead to adjustments in program activities.

For each of the four decision types, there is a corresponding type of evaluation from which the model derives its name. First, there is context evaluation, the purpose of which is to define program environment boundaries and to identify program needs, opportunities, problems, and evaluation objectives. A second type of evaluation is input evaluation. Its purpose is to provide information for determining how resources can be used to meet program objectives. The result of input evaluation is a cost-benefit analysis of various procedural designs. A third type of evaluation is process evaluation, in which a record of the program implementation or process is kept and operational difficulties are identified and addressed while the program is in operation. The fourth type of evaluation is product evaluation, and its purpose is to assess program accomplishments in light of stated program objectives.

These four types of evaluation need not be undertaken separately. For example, context evaluation provides the objectives by which the outputs are judged in product evaluation. Similarly, input evaluation established the criteria for assessing the program process in process evaluation. Taken together, the information from these various types of evaluation provides a stronger rationale than that from any one type alone in judging whether a program ought to be continued, modified, or terminated. For example, the findings of product evaluation are more fully understood by interpreting them in the light of other context, input, and process evaluation information. Though the CIPP Model is widely known, its complexity and obscure terminology may limit its use.

Two other models that share certain similarities to the CIPP Model and also represent significant approaches to program evaluation are the Discrepancy Model (Provus, 1971) and the CSE Model, developed by the UCLA Center for the Study of Evaluation.

Holistic evaluation is a hybrid of outcome-only and process-only evaluation approaches (Nyre, 1977). It requires that (1) specific program objectives be developed, (2) critical issues associated with the program be identified, (3) the attainment of the program objectives be measured objectively, (4) the information needs of various constituent groups be identified and responded to, and (5) program process information be obtained in case study style by means of interviews, perceptions, or observations. Consequently, the holistic approach to program evaluation considers program process and product, program goals, and participant attitudes and incorporates both objective data and perceptual reports in the program analysis.

The *adversarial approach,* still being developed, is based on the processes of legal inquiry and the assumption that "truth emerges when opposing forces submit their evidence to cross-examination directly before the eyes of judge and juries" (Stake, 1975, p. 7). Two evaluation teams or individuals independently assess a given program. One prepares a summary of the most positive claims that might reasonably be made about the program; the other prepares a summary of the most damaging charges that reasonably might be made. The evaluators then are given an opportunity for follow-up statements to respond to each other's program assessments. The resolution of the claims and counterclaims then is left to a third-party evaluation committee. There are several potentially serious defects to the adversarial approach. First, program evaluation outcomes appear to depend too much on the forensic skills of the advocate and adversary evaluators and upon the perceptiveness and fairness of the "judge" or third-party evaluation committee. Second, there is no court of appeals to which rulings can be submitted for reconsideration. Third, decisions concerning academic programs are often complex and not amenable to a simple "yes" or "no" resolution (Popham and Carlson, 1977).

Government and Industry. A second grouping of approaches to program evaluation is taken from the fields of government and industry. Four approaches from these fields that have had some impact on institutions of higher education are PPBS (planning, programming, and budgeting system), ZBB (zero-based budgeting), and MBO (management by objectives).

The purpose of *PPBS* is to improve planning and management decisions by allocating resources to those program alternatives that promise to attain program objectives consistent with established program or institutional goals in an effective and efficient manner. PPBS consists of four phases: planning, programming, budgeting, and evaluation. In the planning phase, program needs are identified and ranked, and then program goals and objectives are set to meet those needs. In the programming phase, alternative program plans that will contribute to the accomplishment of the program objectives are specified. In the budgeting phase, a financial plan is prepared for each of the program alternatives. In the evaluation phase, certain program alternatives are selected for implementation; and, at a later time, the outputs and processes of those program alternatives are evaluated with respect to the stated program goals and objectives for effectiveness and for efficient use of budgeted resources (Hartley, 1968).

There are several operational difficulties associated with the use of PPBS in higher education. First, there is the long-standing difficulty of identifying and measuring the outputs of higher education, especially those that pertain to the quality of education. Second, there is the operational problem of joint products, in which a given activity leads to several different results or in which different activities, such as research and instruction, combine to produce a shared outcome. Third, the precise nature of the production functions in higher education is not known. Consequently, there are no generally accepted algorithms for determining the resource requirements for a specified unit of output (Farmer, 1970).

ZBB is a more recent product of tight budgets and disillusionment about the effectiveness of government programs. ZBB originally meant an institution's entire budget was to be rejustified by a bottom-to-top review every funding period rather than submitting an incremental request for funding. ZBB requires two distinctive techniques. First, alternative courses of program action, tied to different funding levels, are related to an assessment of costs and benefits in a series of "decision packages." Second, the institution ranks the decision packages in order of priority. Ideally, the decision packages are to be prepared for the lowest level or smallest unit within an institution for which a budget request can be formulated. Obviously, this approach leads to a very large number of decision packages. In practice, ZBB in its pure form causes excessive budgetary and political upheaval, often does not provide budget makers with the necessary tools to make proper decisions, and does not recognize the necessity for a certain degree of program continuity over time. As a result, ZBB has evolved into a procedure for conducting marginal analysis by focusing on a restricted number of decision packages of program alternatives above and below the existing base budget level. Thus, ZBB is being adapted for potential use in decremental, as well as incremental, budgeting (Schick, 1977).

In the *MBO* approach, each level of administration is responsible for developing objectives compatible with the goals of the larger organization as stated by the chief administrative officer. Subordinates also are involved in the process by which the program goals and objectives are specified and the criteria for judging performance are developed. After the objectives have been established, the priorities and required resources for accomplishing them are determined. After program implementation, overall goal achievement can be assessed and each person's performance can be evaluated and rewarded on the basis of how well program objectives were attained. The major accomplishments of MBO are seen as "(1) providing common purposes and goals for the entire institution; (2) forcing top administration constantly to define and review goals and priorities and relate resources and individual assignments to these goals; (3) indicating specific tasks for each person, providing for accountability and relating individual efforts to the total task; (4) assuring that institutional goals are known and understood and that they continually provide direction for each individual" (Dressel, 1976, p. 100). Whereas the goal-setting aspects of MBO originally were seen as a means to improve program performance, it has generally been acknowledged that this feature has contributed to increased staff morale due to interaction and unity of program purpose. Accordingly, the emphasis of MBO has shifted from formative to summative evaluation. Although some proponents have touted the efficacy of MBO, empirical research results have been less clear in attesting to its success (Dressel, 1976).

Higher Education. Indigenous approaches to program evaluation have been developing in higher education during the past twenty or thirty years not only because of external pressures for accountability but also internal pressures for resource reallocation and the need to maintain and improve program quality. In general, these approaches are comprehensive because they seek to respond to a wide range of decision-making issues within institutions. Further, because these approaches address similar issues and share similar purposes, they share a conceptually common core despite institutional variations in substance and procedure.

Typically, the core of these approaches first involves the designation of an individual or group as the responsible agent for administering the evaluation. This may be a faculty committee appointed by the faculty governing body or an academic administrative officer such as the academic vice-president. If the evaluation of graduate and undergraduate programs is to be handled separately, graduate program evaluations may be administered by the dean of graduate studies.

The second step typically is a program self-study. This step is initiated by the individual or group responsible for the evaluation sending a set of evaluation guidelines to the program unit and requesting that the faculty and a sample of current students and, perhaps, recent alumni participate in the self-study. The guidelines usually indicate the purpose of the evaluation, the general protocol to be followed, and the program areas for which information is to be collected and evaluated. The guidelines also may contain standardized data forms that are to be used by the unit in data collection and analysis. More often, however, they provide an outline of information areas to be explored or program questions to be answered, recognizing that a set format may not be responsive to important differences among programs or to the professional preferences of faculty members participating in the self-study. A profile of the academic program, prepared from a central data source and containing basic information about the program, may be provided to the unit; and a series of questionnaires may be supplied to be answered by the program faculty, student majors, and a sample of recent graduates.

A list of the major dimensions of the program with which the self-study often deals is as follows:

1. *context:* the historical, organizational, and academic setting or context of the academic program
2. *need:* the demonstrated need for the academic program, as indicated by societal needs, student demands, or requirements of scholarships
3. *program:* the nature of the academic program, including information on admissions and degree requirements, the actual and intended average length of time to degree completion, feedback mechanisms on student progress, available subfields in the program, and recent external ratings of program quality
4. *curriculum:* the scope and adequacy of the curriculum and the relationship of course offerings to the requirements of other degree programs
5. *students:* the nature of student enrollments, including such information as recent student application and acceptance rates, the number and quality of entering student majors, the average annual attrition rate, the number of degrees completed in recent years, the recent employment experience of graduates, future potential student markets, and a forecast of future student demand
6. *faculty and staff:* the nature of faculty and staff resources, including such information as a profile of all program faculty and staff, estimates of faculty quality and potential for growth in scholarship, faculty development and renewal plans, tenure densities, promotion and tenure criteria and proce-

dures, anticipated faculty and staff turnovers, potential new appointment opportunities, faculty salary policies and practices, work load patterns, staff evaluation mechanisms, and judgments of faculty and staff morale

7. *finances:* the sources, amounts, and adequacy of current and projected finances, indicating projected budgeted requirements, the possibility of funding new program growth through a base reallocation of resources, and the adequacy of student financial aid

8. *facilities and capital equipment:* the current adequacy and projected needs of program facilities and capital equipment

9. *academic support services:* the adequacy and effectiveness of academic support services, such as library and media resources and student academic advisory and career counseling services

10. *recommendations:* a summary of the self-study recommendations for program changes and improvements

If a data profile is furnished to the unit, it may only require validation before being used in the evaluation; but for specific program areas, additional data may need to be collected and analyzed by the faculty members of the unit. If surveys are requested, the unit distributes the questionnaires to the appropriate respondents and tabulates the results. Once the self-study has been completed, a written summary of findings, including program recommendations, supporting data tables, and survey results, is prepared by the program unit and transmitted by its chairperson or head to the individual or group administering the evaluation.

After the self-study report has been reviewed by this individual or group, one of two things can occur. If it is decided that the academic program is in good health and can be continued without change or with only minor modifications, the evaluation process concludes with the implementation of the final program recommendations. If, however, the self-study indicates the need for further evaluation, then an evaluation team may be appointed to assess independently the program.

This evaluation team is most often composed of faculty members from outside the academic program under review, either from related departments within the institution or from other institutions. But sometimes a faculty member and a student representative are included on the team in order to provide an "inside" perspective of the program; or two teams are appointed: an internal one and an external one. In such circumstances, each team conducts its evaluations independently and submits separate reports on its findings and recommendations. Whether one or two teams are used often depends upon the nature of the program evaluation and the available funds.

Regardless of the option selected, the team receives evaluation guidelines and copies of the unit's self-study report. After reviewing this report, the team conducts an on-site evaluation, interviewing program faculty and students and observing program processes and facilities. The team also may request that additional quantitative information be prepared by the unit or by the central data source for its further consideration. At the conclusion of its study, the team prepares a summary of its findings and recommendations and forwards it to the individual or group administering the evaluation for review.

Next, the program unit may itself review and comment on the report. The individual or group administering the evaluation and members of the team may confer with key program representatives about the team's findings and recommendations. This review mechanism enables the team to explain its findings and provides the program faculty the opportunity to correct any errors of fact or to clarify any errors of misinterpretation. Further, this practice offers the courtesy of first review to those most directly concerned with the team report. The chairperson or program head then prepares a written response to the team report and sends it to the administrator of the program evaluation, who forwards it along with the team report to the appropriate academic administrative officer for final review and action according to the institution's established protocol. Finally, the individual or group administering the program evaluation may prepare a public release to the campus community describing the findings, recommendations, and actions taken with respect to the completed program evaluation.

There are several problems institutions must resolve with respect to this typical approach to academic program evaluation. The first concerns the intended focus of the evaluation effort. Is an academic department or a degree program, or both, to be the object of the program evaluation? Some institutions evaluate degree programs as such; others evaluate the activities of academic departments because departments represent the basic repository for program resources; and still others believe degree programs and their sponsoring departments must be evaluated simultaneously. Given the necessary interdependencies of academic programs and departments and the nature of the issues with which institutions are confronted, this third approach, simultaneous evaluation, is recommended.

A second problem concerns the level of the academic program to be evaluated. Should undergraduate and graduate programs in a given field of study be evaluated separately or jointly? There may be special instances when separate evaluation studies are to be preferred, but in general, it is recommended that, due to their interdependence, undergraduate and graduate degree programs be evaluated jointly.

A third problem is determining what considerations should guide a decision to evaluate an academic program. Generally, program evaluations are triggered by an established review cycle, the results of a preliminary quantitative review that indicate a possible need for further evaluation, the departure or retirement of key faculty members in the program, a pending site visit by an accrediting agency, special planning studies initiated by the institution or mandated by an external agency, or recommendations from a task force on curriculum changes. It is urged, as a matter of good academic practice, that a self-study of each academic program be conducted every five or six years. Depending upon the results of the self-study, a program may receive a comprehensive evaluation by an independent evaluation team. Thus, in any given year, only a limited number of academic programs would be undergoing a comprehensive evaluation. In the interim years, between self-studies, each academic program can be monitored by appropriate, quantitative review mechanisms; and if circumstances warrant, an academic program can be selected for further evaluation study.

A fourth problem is posed by the different levels of program review that become focused upon an institution. How can the evaluation purposes and requirements of state agencies, multicampus system offices, accreditation agencies, and the various levels within an institution be articulated and coordinated? Wherever possible, an effort should be made to join the evaluation requests and requirements of multiple users into a single, coordinated evaluation study. This would enable a saving of human and financial resources.

Conducting an Evaluation

No single approach to program evaluation is best for all decision-making purposes. Selection of an approach is influenced by such factors as the traditions and values of the institution and the availability of resources and personnel skilled in the desired evaluation methods. In this section, I propose a series of questions that can contribute to the design and implementation of an effective evaluation approach.

Defining Issues, Participants, Purposes, and Processes. The first task in designing program evaluation is to clarify issues, identify participants, and define the purposes and processes of the proposed evaluation. Eight questions are pertinent to this task. First, what is at issue and why? Evaluation begins with a recognition that there are decision-making issues that define a need for evaluation. Issues play a major role in defining the ultimate nature of an evaluation and serve as the context for eventual program judgments. Consequently, it is important that the issues be clarified at the outset so it is clearly known why an academic program is to be evaluated.

The second question is who are the participants to this issue. It is educationally and politically important that all individuals or groups with a legitimate stake in the outcome of any evaluation judgments be identified and considered for inclusion in the evaluation study. The views of those who are involved in the academic program are essential to a proper understanding of the program. In instances where evaluators are not politically sensitive to the participant question, the acceptability, if not the credibility, of the evaluation study has been placed in jeopardy before the study is even implemented.

Third, what are the objectives of the evaluation? The specific objectives of the evaluation can now be defined, based upon the expectations, values, and interests of the participants in the evaluation process. The evaluation objectives should be stated clearly so all parties share an understanding of the study's purposes. If there are apparent and extreme differences in value/interest orientations and resultant decision-making expectations, an effort should be made to accommodate them at this point in the design phase or they could undermine the effectiveness of the evaluation. In this regard, however, it should be noted that no evaluation can be totally comprehensive. Thus, it is an inherent potential difficulty of all evaluation studies that all participants' decision-making needs and preferences cannot be met equally well.

A fourth question concerns the decision-making alternatives. The next step is to identify the anticipated range of decision-making alternatives relative to the evaluation objectives and to specify the questions for which answers will provide a basis for judging among the alternatives.

Fifth, what evaluation information is needed? The evaluation study questions indicate the information that will be needed to enable participants to make judgments among decision alternatives. It is important that the precise nature of the evaluation information be defined so participants can be certain proper information has been stipulated in response to the evaluation questions and so subsequent specification of data elements needed to generate this information can be completed accurately. Also, if any of the evaluation information is to be displayed in certain formats, those formats should be designed. Such information considerations can have implications for the decision-making process as well as for subsequent information analysis and data-handling procedures.

The sixth question is by what process the judgments will be made. This step makes explicit the process by which evaluation findings, interpretations, and recommendations will be used to assist in making judgments among the decision alternatives. The participants to be involved in the review and recommendation steps of the decision making should be identified; the protocol to be followed in that process should be outlined; and the individuals or groups who will assume the responsibility and authority for making the final determinations regarding program evaluation results should be specified. Finally, the evaluation protocol should be compatible with an institution's traditions of shared governance.

The seventh question concerns the organizational policies, priorities, or assumptions that apply in the decision-making process. Those relevant to the evaluation process and the specific program decision alternatives that are likely to be under consideration should be stated. Explicit recognition of these factors in the evaluation decision process is necessary to ensure the effectiveness of the program evaluation.

Eighth, what constraints might operate in the evaluation process? A number of constraints can shape the nature of the evaluation design and even determine whether an evaluation study can be conducted at all. Typical constraints are time, finances, and human resources. For example, a case study approach might not be possible if an evaluation judgment of a program must be made in a short period of time. Because of a tight budget, an institution might decide to forgo the use of external consultants in evaluating a program even though an external evaluation would be highly desirable. Or an evaluation approach requiring the use of multivariate analytical techniques might be set aside and another approach adopted simply because the staff is not well versed in that methodology.

Designing Information Analysis and Data Collection. The second design task is to establish the information and analytical requirements, to specify the appropriate data collection instruments and procedures, and to determine the data storage and retrieval mechanisms. The following eight questions indicate the steps in this task.

First, what data are required? Knowing the information needed to respond to the evaluation questions and to assist in judging among decision alternatives, one can specify the data elements required to generate that information. It is imperative that each data element be clearly defined in order to avoid miscommunication and to ensure that, in fact, the right information will be provided. This implies that a narrative description be developed for each data element and that the population to which the data element applies be clearly indicated. For example, the ostensibly straightforward term of faculty can be defined in several different ways with potentially significant implications for related analysis. Faculty can be defined with various ranks included, by different fund and activity accounts, and by ten- or twelve-month pay bases. Further, faculty counts could be enumerated by headcount or full-time equivalents. In the case of derived data elements, the specific algorithms by which other data elements are combined to produce the derived element must be delineated as part of the definition. For example, the cost per credit of instruction is a derived element that is subject to varying formulations. Hence, the specific algorithms must be made explicit. It is these kinds of definitional distinctions that, though seemingly minor, can greatly affect the validity and utility of the resulting evaluative information.

Second, what analytical methodologies are needed? The next step is to specify those analytical methodologies needed to convert the data elements into the required evaluation information. The methodologies may vary in complexity, depending upon the specified information outputs. In this regard, there is nothing inherently superior about evaluations that employ sophisticated analytical techniques; the important criterion is whether the analytical methodologies and the resulting information meet the requirements of the evaluation questions and objectives in a valid, reliable, and objective manner. Further, as a basic guideline, it is preferable to keep the analytical requirements within a moderate range of complexity in order to facilitate participant understanding and communication of the evaluation findings.

Third, what are the sources of the data? Having defined the data required by the evaluation, the next consideration is to identify appropriate sources, which are likely to be multiple and may include institutional records, faculty, students, administrators, graduates, or some other external source. Data sources, in conjunction with possible data collection methods, must be assessed for their probable impact on the validity, reliability, and objectivity of the data. If there are several sources from which certain of the data can be obtained, such concerns as the ease and cost of collection and the timing of data availability can be determining factors in selecting sources.

The fourth question is whether the required data are to be collected regularly or only once. In certain instances, the data required for the evaluation are routinely collected and are readily available. In many cases, however, at least a portion of the data must be collected on a special-request basis. Because ad hoc data requests can quickly become a burden to institutional participants and resources, the periodicity of the data need should be examined. If the data will be needed regularly, it might be advisable to consider a data collection mechanism that will serve the institution not only for the given evaluation study but also regularly for other purposes in the future.

Fifth, how will the data be collected, by whom, and when? This step focuses upon instrumentation and data collection procedures. The specific design of the instruments and procedures by which the data are to be collected is influenced by such interacting considerations as the nature and sources of the required data and the investigatory framework, which, in turn, depend upon the evaluation objectives and the type of judgments to be made. The particular approach selected may feature an experimental or quasi-experimental design or rely upon correlational methods, surveys, systematic judgments from experts in the program area, clinical or case studies, or informal observation and testimony (Anderson and Ball, 1978). Dressel (1976, p. 131) has noted, however, that "evaluation in the higher education context does not often lend itself to elaborate experimental projects and designs. Projects to be evaluated are ongoing and are seldom subject to the variable manipulation and controls required for comparative analysis using the sophisticated technique of statistical analysis."

The sixth question is must the data be coded. If any of the data being collected for the program evaluation are to be submitted for computer data processing, it is likely that certain of the data will require coding. Thus, coding forms, code translation tables, and coding guidelines must be prepared so the raw data can be transcribed properly. Further, arrangements must be made for the coding service.

Seventh, if they are to be processed by computer, how are the data to be entered into the system, stored, retrieved, and edited? There are several possible modes of data entry into a computer-based system. The most common mode is card input, which requires the coded data forms be keypunched and then read by the computer. An increasingly used alternative is direct data entry by means of a terminal device, such as a CRT (cathode ray tube) or a teleprinter. A far less frequent mode of data entry is mark-sense forms. Next, the data storage medium must be selected. Data can be stored on computer cards, magnetic tape, computer disk, or drum. Such factors as the size of the data base, frequency of use, and type of analysis to be done should be considered in selecting the most appropriate storage medium. The procedures for retrieving the data also must be defined. Of special importance is the accuracy of the data, which must be ascertained by editing procedures. Those who will be conducting the data analysis portion of the evaluation, in conjunction with computer programmer analysts, should define the data-editing criteria and standards.

The eighth question concerns the policies that will control data access and confidentiality. Since the adoption of the Buckley Amendment, increased public and legislative concern has been focused on access and confidentiality of personnel data. Consequently, if the program evaluation information contains any data by individual faculty members or students, policies and procedures must be developed and implemented to safeguard the confidentiality of that data from unauthorized access.

Deciding on Interpretation and Reporting. The next task is to establish the protocol by which the program evaluation information is to be interpreted and to determine the mechanism by which findings are to be reported. Two questions are relevant to this task. First, what are the program evaluation criteria? The objective criteria should be stated so that reviewers and interpreters of program evaluation information proceed from a common starting point. Subjective standards based upon participant values and interests also govern the interpretation task, and subjective considerations often take precedence over objective criteria and hard data measurements in evaluation interpretations and judgments. In preparing evaluation reports, the evaluators should strive to make explicit the subjective considerations on which the findings, implications, and recommendations were based.

The second question concerns the type of reports to be prepared, who is to prepare them, for whom, and when. For example, it is often desirable to prepare a summary report of the evaluation findings in addition to a more complete report of the study. In certain instances, institutions of higher education have found a third type of report, a brief release for external audiences, also can be useful. For each type of report envisioned, it is necessary to decide whether to

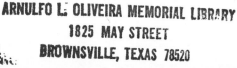

include the evaluation implications and program recommendations. Further, it must be determined to whom the draft reports should be distributed, by whom, and according to what protocol and timetable. These arrangements should include an opportunity for those people whose program was the subject of the evaluation to review and respond to the draft reports. Finally, provisions should be made for incorporating participants' and evaluators' responses into the final drafts. The distribution list for the final reports and the individual or group having the responsibility and authority for release of the final documents must be designated.

Planning an Audit. Good evaluations evaluate the evaluation process itself. This task has been variously referred to as program audit or metaevaluation. Like program evaluation, audit can either be formative or summative. In the design phase, the last step is to evaluate the proposed design and decide whether it is ready for implementation or whether further improvements must be made. This corresponds to performing a formative audit of the evaluation design. In a formative audit, design adequacy is evaluated in light of the considerations already discussed in the design preparation phase. Particular attention should be given not only to the conceptual and technical adequacy of the design but also to those other sociopsychological and political factors that can affect the academic credibility and final acceptability of the proposed evaluation study. In addition, it must be determined whether the proposed evaluation design has an acceptable cost-benefit relationship. In other words, does the anticipated benefit of the program evaluation justify the estimated costs, including nonfiscal costs? If it is decided that an evaluation design is not cost-effective, several options are open. First, the intended scale of the evaluation study could be reduced by narrowing the focus of the design or by evaluating fewer programs. Second, certain of the objectives might be altered so that high-cost related data requirements, collection procedures, or analytical methodologies could be modified or eliminated. It is possible a given design proposal might not meet audit criteria, requiring the design proposal be extensively changed or the evaluation study be forgone at that time. It is important that people who are independent of the evaluation proposal conduct the audit of the evaluation design. Stufflebeam (1974) has developed an audit checklist.

A summative audit can be conducted after a program evaluation has been completed. In this case, the evaluation design and implementation performance are assessed in light of the program evaluation findings and subsequent program decision actions. In short, an audit is intended to determine the effectiveness of the program evaluation process and contribute to its improvement.

Implementing the Design. Once the design proposal has been accepted, the implementation phase can begin. Most of the considerations already discussed in the earlier design phase apply to implementation. The general order of the evaluation tasks in implementation is (1) data collection, editing, and storage; (2) data analysis; (3) evaluation information interpretation; (4) draft report preparation; (5) draft report review and response; (6) final report preparation and distribution; (7) evaluation judgments and decisions; (8) evaluation decision implementation; (9) program evaluation follow-up; and (10) audit.

Once the evaluation has been completed, the question becomes whether it will be judged effective or will accumulate the proverbial dust accorded to many reports. To be effective, evaluation approaches should possess several attributes.

First, the evaluation process must be approved by those directly interested in the program under review. The process must be academically credible and politically acceptable to them. Second, the report of evaluation findings, implications, and recommendations must be relevant to the decision issues that defined the evaluation need in the first place. The evaluation information must be valid, reliable, and timely. The study recommendations must be economically and politically feasible. The report form should promote an easy understanding of the information and facilitate its use in subsequent program decisions. Third, the results must be communicated to those in a position to make decisions regarding the given program. A widely circulated report cannot be ignored as easily as one that has had limited circulation. Finally, an integration of evaluation efforts with program planning and resource allocation activities should be sought through institutional policies and practices. This not only can create the opportunity for an effective evaluation but will likely raise the expectation and the probability of an effective evaluation.

Program Evaluation in Multicampus Systems

The discussion of program evaluation thus far has assumed an institutional perspective. Indeed, institutions should bear the primary responsibility for academic program planning and evaluation. System administrations in multicampus systems also can play a vital role in program evaluation, but the nature of their involvement appropriately is different.

System-Level Evaluation. The boundaries for the participation of system administrations in program evaluation can be illustrated by the following responsibilities, which reflect policies and procedures in the University of Wisconsin system. First, a system administration should develop broad guidelines for the practice of program evaluation. Such guidelines should require that each institution establish its own program evaluation policies and procedures. Second, a system administration then should verify by audit that the institutions have designed and implemented evaluation mechanisms that are effective and consistent with systemwide evaluation guidelines. By exercising these responsibilities, a system administration is contributing indirectly to the quality of its academic programs. Third, in the interests of stewardship, a system administration should review existing academic programs and new program proposals and identify unnecessarily duplicative programs for possible modification or elimination. Also, institutional programs should be reviewed periodically to identify those with excessively and persistently low enrollments. Such programs may require further institutional inquiry. Fourth, a system administration should seek to preserve the differentiation of institutional missions within the multicampus system by ensuring that new program proposals from institutions are within the scope of their respective missions. Fifth, the equitable allocation of resources among institutions also requires that a system administration be responsive to the needs of institutions identified through the evaluation process. Sixth, a system administration should share with the institutions in the responsibility for monitoring and interpreting the general program needs of the state and the system. Also, in those instances when special concerns about selected programs are raised by external agencies, a system administration should be a party to any evaluation effort in response to such concerns. Finally, a system administration should review the results of institutional evaluation studies and prepare a summary report of institutional evaluation efforts and share it with the governing or coordinating board.

These systemwide program evaluation responsibilities can be met in several ways. For example, periodic program reviews, using selected quantitative indicators, can be used to address questions of unnecessarily duplicative programs and programs of excessively and persistently low enrollment within a multicampus system. Special evaluation studies can be conducted in response to program concerns of interinstitutional or systemwide nature. Also, audit studies can be used to improve institutional evaluation practices.

New Program Entitlement. The review and approval of new program requests within a multicampus system can entail yet another type of evaluation. The University of Wisconsin system has a process of evaluating new program plans that is worth noting. Each institution is asked to prepare a preliminary list in priority order of programs being considered for possible introduction over the next four-year period. These lists of program intentions are updated annually and submitted to system administration for review. The institutional lists are reviewed for competitive program intentions among institutions, for program aspirations that do not meet institutional mission requirements, or for other constraints.

If selected program intentions for a given institution are approved by system administration, institutions are given an entitlement to plan those programs in greater detail. Faculty members and administrators then prepare a descriptive plan for those academic programs the institutions wish to implement in the immediate future. The descriptive plans should stop short of requiring an extensive commitment of time and other resources for their preparation. These program plans then are submitted to system administration for review. If approved, the program plans are forwarded to the board of regents for formal action.

Pending approval by the board, the institution is given authority to prepare a detailed implementation plan for each approved new program. The chancellor of the institution then reviews the detailed plans for program implementation and, upon concurrence, each approved new program can be implemented. Further review and approval by system administration is not required unless substantive changes are made in a new program during the preparation of the detailed implementation plan. There is a mandatory, comprehensive evaluation of each new program after it has been in operation for four years.

This approach to the evaluation of new program planning is formative in nature. In addition to improving the balance and quality of academic programs systemwide, the evaluation/entitlement approach significantly reduces the frustrations and cost of extensive program planning and development by institutional faculty and administrators.

Integration of Planning and Evaluation. The task of integrating evaluation processes with academic program planning and resource allocation activities poses a special challenge in multicampus systems. First, a system administration should take the initiative in defining the major principles and assumptions that will guide planning. General statements of mission should be defined for each institution so future program decisions do not lead to a homogenization of institutional purposes and direction. Long-range planning papers should be prepared periodically by system administration in which the major demographic, socioeconomic, and educational trends and issues are identified. Such planning papers can clarify the issues confronting the system and the context within which planning must occur and can establish broad goals toward which the system should direct its planning efforts. Within this framework, each institution should prepare detailed statements of institutional planning principles and assumptions and develop specific statements of planning issues and trends.

Second, each institution should prepare a long-range academic plan covering an eight- to ten-year horizon. Academic program needs and intentions should be identified for the first four or five years, but only general program needs and possible program direction should be indicated in the final four or five years. These plans should be developed within the context of systemwide and institutional statements of planning principles and assumptions and should consider the issues and trends contained in the background planning documents. The details of the academic plans should stem from institutional evaluation activities. These institutional plans should be updated every two years.

Third, the immediate and concrete expression of institutional and system planning intentions is contained in the multicampus system's budget request. The aforementioned system and institutional documents and the results of recent evaluation studies should provide the framework for considering specific program and resource needs.

Fourth, upon receiving funding, a system administration must make equitable resource allocations to the institutions. Resource allocation decisions should be conditioned by evaluations of each institution's academic program plans, needs, and performance. Each institution, in turn, upon receiving a budget allocation, must make internal resource allocation decisions. These decisions should be guided in part by the findings and recommendations of previous evaluation studies.

Two points should be clear from this brief summary. Evaluation is a pervasive and ongoing activity, and it should explicitly support program and resource planning activities at all levels of the higher education enterprise. In a multicampus system, the task of establishing effective planning and evaluation policies and procedures must be a cooperative and complementary effort between a system administration and the institutions.

Achieving Effective Evaluation

The purpose of effective evaluation is the improvement of academic programs. This implies that program evaluation not only will involve the improvement of individual programs but will contribute to decisions of priority setting and resource allocation among programs for the betterment of the institution's total academic mission. In order to progress toward these ends, several difficulties must be overcome. These difficulties constitute agenda items for future research and development in higher education.

A primary difficulty at many institutions still is the lack of articulation between the program evaluation process and program and budget planning. Priority setting and resource allocation among academic programs will be the focus of the critical decisions in the 1980s. For program evaluation to be effective, it must contribute to implemented decisions. There is no universal prescription for the problem. Each institution must work out the specific policies and procedures that will lead to an integration of program/resource planning and program evaluation cycles.

A second major concern centers upon the appropriate conceptual basis for academic program evaluation in higher education. Pace (1972, p. 14) argues, "evaluation, if it follows administrative, management, and efficiency models, can and probably will contribute to the industrialization of higher education—education in which order, duty, responsibility, efficiency, and performance are the dominant values." Certainly, these values are not without merit; however, they become counterproductive when their overemphasis leads to the stifling of academic creativity. Pace (1972, p. 14) suggests "the relevant analogies are biological, ecological, organic, psychological, sociological, and philosophical. A college or university is a habitat, a society, a community, an environment, an ecosystem. It should be judged by the quality of life that it fosters, the opportunities for experience and exploration it provides, the concern for growth, for enrichment, and for culture that it exemplifies. The question is not just 'what does your machine produce?' but also 'how does your garden grow?'"

A third problem is the need for a greater sharing of institutional approaches to academic program evaluation in the higher education community. A number of institutions currently have exemplary approaches to academic program evaluation. The concepts, guidelines, and operating experience that accompany these evaluation approaches should be shared more widely with other institutions. Such exchanges can be undertaken through regional or peer institutional associations. In addition, workshops on academic program evaluation can be sponsored by national associations, such as those offered by the Association for Institutional Research. Also, there is a need for more published accounts of various approaches to evaluation in higher education, outlining the conceptual framework, the procedural aspects, case results, and a critique for each approach.

Closely related is the need for the training of more faculty and administrators in the skills of academic program evaluation. Peer group exchanges, workshops, and publications can assist in meeting this training need. An even more direct means of dealing with the problem might be to establish a curriculum design and evaluation office at an institution or have qualified individuals in certain academic departments or administrative offices, such as institutional research, provide leadership in assisting others in the institution to learn evaluation skills and methodologies. Further, such "internal consultants" could assist in the actual design and, if necessary, the implementation of academic program evaluations.

One of the principles on which this chapter is based is that evaluation will be an effective force for the improvement of academic programs only as long as the incentives for evaluation remain positive. Given the likely issues of the 1980s, program attenuation may become a major theme in many program evaluation considerations. Under such circumstances, it will be difficult to maintain the positive incentives associated with academic program evaluation. Without faculty support and involvement, however, the effectiveness of evaluation efforts would diminish significantly.

Another issue that long has plagued evaluation in higher education is the identification and operational definition of outputs, outcomes, and goals. Bowen (1974, p. 2) has stated succinctly the problem associated with the identification, measurement, and use of outcomes data: "Outcomes are numerous, complexly interrelated, often subtle, sometimes unintended, difficult to identify and substantiate, hard to measure, sometimes negative, and valued differently by different observers. Because of these complications, it is inherently impossible to state precisely, objectively, or quantitatively the contributions of higher education." Yet the need remains. Accountability demands that higher education be able to evaluate its outcomes more fully.

Related to the problem of evaluating outcomes is the general difficulty of gauging long-term program effects (Anderson and Ball, 1978). Often it is difficult to seek follow-up information from graduates over an extended period of time due to their mobility. Another problem is the difficulty of maintaining the privacy and confidentiality of longitudinal records. Also, individuals in groups outside of the institution (such as government agencies or elected officials) sometimes demand to receive evaluation results before an evaluation study can be completed. Thus, there is a need to find more effective and efficient ways of measuring academic program results over extended periods of time. Such follow-up information can provide the dimension that is critically missing from most program evaluations today.

In recent years, institutions of higher education have been attempting to serve new clientele, particularly adult part-time learners, in ways that will facilitate their access to higher education and incorporate more fully into their advanced educational programs the practical learning they have acquired outside of educational institutions. Consequently, many institutions have developed and implemented outreach degree programs, featuring off-campus, frequently self-guided instruction and often including a credit assessment of a student's prior learning and experience. In many instances, these outreach programs are operating on an experimental basis before institutions make a further commitment to their expansion. In almost all cases, there is concern within the academic community regarding the maintenance of standards of quality for such outreach programs. Hence, there is a pressing need to develop appropriate approaches for evaluating the performance of these outreach programs.

Finally, one of the fundamental components in any institution's ability to conduct effective program evaluations on a regular basis is the responsiveness of its management and planning information systems. In the late 1960s and early 1970s, the benefits to be immediately derived from investing in expensive computer-based information systems frequently were oversold. When the glowing promises were not fulfilled, negative reactions to the further development and use of information systems in higher education frequently were encountered. The challenges of the 1980s, however, require that institutions have access to valid, reliable, and objective information on a timely basis and in a form that will facilitate the decision-making process. Computer-based information systems will not guarantee better decisions; but, if used properly, they can contribute to improved decision making. Consequently, institutions not having comprehensive information systems capable of responding effectively to a wide range of decision-making needs should seek to upgrade their information delivery capabilities. But expectations should be realistic, recognizing that such improvements usually require several years of development before their benefits can be realized.

Implications for Institutional Research

The requirements of effective program evaluation raise several implications for institutional research. First, there is the matter of conceptual competence. Institutional researchers should be thoroughly familiar with the conceptual nature and role of program evaluation in higher education. They should become knowledgeable of the wide range of possible approaches to program evaluation and have an understanding of the strengths and limitations of each approach so they can judge which is appropriate for a given situation. Institutional researchers should seek to gain firsthand experience in actually designing and conducting a variety of evaluation approaches.

Second, institutional researchers must be analytically competent. They should have the knowledge and ability to conduct program evaluations in various investigatory frameworks, that is, to conduct sound evaluations using experimental, quasi-experimental, or preexperimental methodologies. They should also be able to develop the proper instrumentation to ensure the collection of valid, reliable, and objective data.

Third, institutional researchers should be technically competent. They should understand computer-based data-processing techniques and be able to interface between evaluation users and data processors concerning the technical requirements of data collection, editing, storage, retrieval, and analytical processing in an evaluation study.

Fourth, institutional researchers should be politically competent. The success or failure of a program evaluation often depends on political considerations rather than analytical or technical factors. Institutional researchers must be sensitive to the expectations and fears of those participating in a program evaluation. Decisions concerning who will be involved, in what manner, and to what degree determine to a considerable extent the eventual credibility and acceptability of program evaluation findings and recommendations.

In a broader context, there must be organizational support for effective program evaluation. Such support begins with a commitment by the top academic administrators and faculty leaders. Institutional policies and procedures should integrate the evaluation activity and results into the decision-making processes for academic program planning and resource allocation. Within this framework, the institutional researchers' role should be made explicit. If the nature of their involvement or the base of their authority is not clear, it is likely their contributions will be limited. The organizational location of the institutional research function and, even more important, the day-to-day working relationships of institutional researchers with academic decision makers will affect the potential role of institutional research in program evaluation and the effectiveness of its contribution to decision-making processes.

Finally, institutional researchers should be prepared to exercise initiative in matters relating to program evaluation. This includes helping others within an institution to recognize the need for program evaluation and its importance; urging that policies and procedures for establishing ongoing program evaluation be established if such mechanisms currently do not exist; and serving as a resource in the actual design and implementation of program evaluation studies. The issues of the 1980s concern the very survival of quality higher education. Seldom has higher education been faced with such important issues. Seldom has institutional research been in a position to contribute so much.

Bibliographical Essay

A good introduction to the general field of evaluation is provided by Anderson and Ball (1978), Rose and Nyre (1977), and Scriven (1967).

Although literature on academic program evaluation in higher education is just in its beginnings, several important works are offered by Barak and Berdahl (1978), Dressel (1976), Folger (1977), and Hodgkinson (1975).

Additional references also can be consulted regarding specific approaches to selected dimensions of program evaluation. For example, Metfessel and Michael (1967) and Glaser (1970) outline some goal-attainment approaches to program evaluation. Among the process-oriented approaches to evaluation, Stake presents the Countenance Model (1972) and discusses responsive evaluation (1975), Rippey (1973) examines transactional evaluation, and Parlett and Dearden (1977) discuss illuminative evaluation. More comprehensive evaluation approaches are provided by Provus (1971) and Stufflebeam and others (1971). Suchman (1967) presents a good introduction to evaluation research, while Pyhrr (1973) provides a thorough discussion of zero-base budgeting and Drucker (1964) presents the principles of management by objectives.

Pace (1972) offers a stimulating essay that questions the effects of efficiency-oriented evaluation models in higher education and suggests other conceptual bases that might be more appropriate.

There are several other general sources that can serve as a continuing source of information on program evaluation. First, the Evaluation Center at Western Michigan University issues the Occasional Paper Series on program evaluation. Second, Jossey-Bass publishes a quarterly sourcebook on evaluation, *New Directions for Program Evaluation*. Also, monographs on program evaluation sometimes can be found in two other Jossey-Bass quarterly series, *New Directions for Institutional Research* and *New Directions for Higher Education*. Third, there is a growing number of periodicals on program evaluation, including *Educational Evaluation and Policy Analysis, Evaluation Comment, Evaluation and Program Planning, Evaluation Review,* and *Evaluation.* The focus of these periodicals is not specifically on evaluation in higher education, but they do provide an interdisciplinary forum for the discussion of evaluation issues, concepts, and methodologies which may have relevance within higher education. Fourth, comprehensive journals, such as the *Journal of Higher Education* and the *Educational Record,* occasionally publish articles on academic program evaluation.

Further assistance can be obtained in the form of institutes, workshops, consulting services, professional advisory networks, annual meetings, annotated bibliographies and other written materials from certain professional organizations and associations. For example, the American Council on Education offers the Higher Education Management Institute; the American Association of State Colleges and Universities sponsors the Resource Center for Planned Change; the National Center for Higher Education Management Systems provides institutional consulting services and a wide range of written materials, including approaches to educational outcomes assessment and a Strategic Planning Model that integrates information on an institution's external environment with its capabilities and purposes; the Association of Institutional Research sponsors regional workshops and sessions at its annual forum on academic program evaluation; and the American Educational Research Association has a special interest group on program evaluation. Also, the ERIC Clearinghouse on Tests, Measurement, and Evaluation and the ERIC Clearinghouse on Higher Education are other continuing sources of monographs and bibliographic resources.

References

Anderson, S. B., and Ball, S. *The Profession and Practice of Program Evaluation.* San Francisco: Jossey-Bass, 1978.

Barak, R. J., and Berdahl, R. O. *State Level Academic Program Review in Higher Education.* Denver, Colo.: Education Commission of the States, 1978.

Bowen, H. R. (Ed.). *New Directions for Institutional Research: Evaluating Institutions for Accountability,* no. 1. San Francisco: Jossey-Bass, 1974.

Dressel, P. L. *Handbook of Academic Evaluation: Assessing Institutional Effectiveness, Student Progress, and Professional Performance for Decision Making in Higher Education.* San Francisco: Jossey-Bass, 1976.

Drucker, P. F. *Managing for Results.* New York: Harper & Row, 1964.

Farmer, J. *Why Planning, Programming, Budgeting Systems for Higher Education?* Boulder, Colo.: Western Interstate Commission for Higher Education, 1970.

Folger, J. K. (Ed.). *New Directions for Institutional Research: Increasing the Public Accountability of Higher Education,* no. 16. San Francisco: Jossey-Bass, 1977.

Glaser, R. "Evaluation of Instruction in Changing Educational Models." In M. C. Wittrock and D. E. Wiley (Eds.), *The Evaluation of Instruction: Issues and Problems.* New York: Holt, Rinehart & Winston, 1970.

Hartley, H. J. *Educational Planning-Programming-Budgeting: A Systems Approach.* Englewood Cliffs, N.J.: Prentice-Hall, 1968.

Hodgkinson, H. L., and others. *Improving and Assessing Performance: Evaluation in Higher Education.* Berkeley: Center for Research and Development in Higher Education, University of California, 1975.

Metfessel, N. S., and Michael, W. B. "A Paradigm Involving Multiple Criterion Measures for the Evaluation of the Effectiveness of School Programs." *Educational and Psychological Measurement,* 1967, *27,* 931-943.

Nyre, G. F. "The Institutional Researcher as Evaluator: Bridging the Gap." Paper presented at seventeenth annual forum, Association for Institutional Research, Montreal, May 1977.

Pace, C. R. "Thoughts on Evaluation in Higher Education." Talk given April 26, 1971, in Iowa City, Iowa, at the invitation of the American College Testing Program and the College of Education, University of Iowa, Iowa City. American College Testing Program, February 1972.

Parlett, M., and Dearden, G. (Eds.). *Introduction to Illuminative Evaluation: Studies in Higher Education.* Berkeley, Calif.: Pacific Soundings Press, 1977.

Parlett, M., and Hamilton, D. "Evaluation as Illumination: A New Approach to the Study of Innovatory Programmes." In D. Hamilton and others (Eds.), *Beyond the Numbers Game.* Berkeley, Calif.: McCutchan, 1977.

Popham, W. J., and Carlson, D. "Deep Dark Deficits of the Adversary Evaluation Model." *Educational Researcher,* 1977, *6,* 3–6.

Provus, M. *Discrepancy Evaluation for Educational Program Improvement and Assessment.* Berkeley, Calif.: McCutchan, 1971.

Pyhrr, P. A. *Zero-Base Budgeting: A Practical Management Tool for Evaluating Expenses.* New York: Wiley, 1973.

Rippey, R. M. (Ed.). *Studies in Transactional Evaluation.* Berkeley, Calif.: McCutchan, 1973.

Rose, C., and Nyre, G. F. *The Practice of Evaluation.* ERIC/TM Report 65. Princeton, N. J.: ERIC Clearinghouse on Tests, Measurement, and Evaluation, 1977.

Schick, A. "Zero-Base Budgeting and Sunset: Redundancy or Symbiosis?" *Bureaucrat,* 1977, *6* (1), 12–31.

Scriven, M. "The Methodology of Evaluation." In R. E. Stake (Ed.), *Perspectives of Curriculum Evaluation.* AREA Monograph Series on Curriculum Evaluation. Chicago: Rand McNally, 1967.

Stake, R. E. "The Countenance of Educational Evaluation." In C. H. Weiss (Ed.), *Evaluating Action Programs: Readings in Social Action and Education.* Boston: Allyn & Bacon, 1972.

Stake, R. E. *Program Evaluation, Particularly Responsive Evaluation.* Paper #5 in Occasional Paper Series. Kalamazoo: Evaluation Center, Western Michigan University, 1975.

Stufflebeam, D. L. *Meta-Evaluation.* Paper #3 in Occasional Paper Series. Kalamazoo: Evaluation Center, Western Michigan University, 1974.

Stufflebeam, D. L., and others. *Educational Evaluation and Decision Making.* Itasca, Ill.: Peacock, 1971.

Suchman, E. A. *Evaluative Research.* New York: Russell Sage Foundation, 1967.

Summary of University of Wisconsin System Academic Program Audit and Review. Academic Informational Series #4. Madison: University of Wisconsin System, Office of Academic Affairs, 1977.

23

Robert T. Blackburn
Colman O'Connell
Glenn Pellino

Evaluating Faculty Performance

The evaluation of faculty performance, an issue of increasing importance during the 1970s, can be expected to attract greater attention during the 1980s. Forces external to higher education are contributing to the urgency with which institutions seek to evaluate faculty performance and thereby assess the heart of their institutional vitality. Besides inflation, reduced resources, and a declining pool of high school graduates, calls for accountability from legislators, taxpayers, parents of undergraduates, and students themselves, recently alerted to their rights as higher education consumers, are forcing administrators to explore ways of measuring faculty work load and assessing faculty performance to justify their requests for appropriations.

Coupled with these outside pressures, legal threats from faculty members have prompted colleges and universities to design and adhere to carefully codified personnel policies and procedures, often including student ratings of faculty performance as well as peer review and administrative review, to protect themselves in court. Increased competition for a decreasing number of faculty positions contributes to this movement, and fear of having too high a percentage of tenured staff members has resulted in higher standards for employment and tenure as well as a search for clearer evidence of both promise and achievement in teaching and research. Finally, institutions are using evaluation to assist faculty members to grow and develop both personally and professionally, in order to counteract the dangers of atrophy or stagnation that could accompany low turnover and the gradual aging of the faculty as a whole.

How can institutions increase their efficiency and effectiveness and meet demands for accountability and productivity without resorting to simplistic, bureaucratic, or mechanistic forms of personnel assessment? To answer this question, this chapter reviews evaluation practices of the recent past and present, examines research findings on faculty performance as they relate to faculty evaluation, calls attention to problems and issues that complicate the evaluation task, advances a case for comprehensive performance reviews, recommends courses of action for implementing such reviews, and closes with references to further reading on the topic.

Evaluation Practices

In view of these current demands for accountability, it should be noted that attention to faculty work load and performance and the evaluation of faculty effort are not altogether new phenomena in higher education. Researchers have long been interested in the problem of faculty work load and activity (Blackburn and Trowbridge, 1973; Bunnell, 1960; Hansen and Sandler, 1967; Koos, 1919; Reeves and Russell, 1929; Richardson, 1967; Russell, 1946; Stecklein, 1961); and much is known about the practices surrounding the evaluation of faculty, including how evaluations are conducted, by whom, and with what evidence.

Generally, faculty assessment occurs as a part of two major processes in higher education: first, those procedures surrounding tenure review and promotion and, second, those activities (undertaken largely by public institutions and often coordinated through offices of institutional research) that codify faculty work as a function of the institution's budgeting and planning processes.

Tenure Review and Promotion. Wilson (1942) articulates the tenure and promotion responsibility of evaluation when he points to the critical problem facing institutions in assigning requisite status on the basis of demonstrated achievement. In studying the practices used by colleges in evaluating faculty for these personnel decisions at the beginning of the 1960s, Gustad (1961) found that primary responsibility for conducting the evaluation rested with the president, the dean, and the department chair; that classroom teaching was the most important factor evaluated, regardless of the type of institution; and that six sources of data were most frequently used for evaluating classroom performance: informal student opinion, formal student opinion through student ratings, classroom visitation, colleagues' opinions, the opinions of chairpersons, and those of deans. In a follow-up study, Gustad (1967) found a decline in the use of systematic student ratings and in classroom visitation, greater use of committee evaluation and informal student opinions, and evaluation conducted primarily by deans and department chairs rather than by presidents.

Similarly, Astin and Lee (1966) found the sources most frequently used to determine teaching effectiveness were evaluations by department chairs and deans. However, their data indicated research and publications, rather than teaching effectiveness, were the primary considerations in these evaluations. More recently, Seldin (1975) found deans placing more emphasis on systematic student ratings and committee evaluation than they had in 1966, but with the department chair's evaluation the most important element in the process. The next year, in a survey for the Southern Regional Education Board, Boyd and Schietinger (1976) indicated responsibility for evaluation still rested with the chair and the chief academic officer, but that doctoral institutions were gathering evaluation data primarily to provide information for administrative decisions pertaining to advancement while two-year colleges were using them more to assist in faculty development activities.

Finally, in one of the most comprehensive studies conducted in this area, Centra (1976, 1979) discovered that systematic evaluation of instruction by students is widely used. This would appear to satisfy both faculty and students who have increasingly favored the use of student ratings as a means of evaluating instruction (Blank, 1978).

In general, administrators appear to be satisfied with current evaluation practices (Boyd and Schietinger, 1976), despite the lack of consensus on what constitutes good teaching (Meeth, 1976); and research continues to support the fact that faculty evaluation is often a very subjective and imprecise process (McKeachie and Lin, 1975). Although administrators may argue that teaching performance is the most important factor in faculty evaluation, faculty perceive the evaluation structure is skewed toward research (Hind, 1971; Luthans, 1967). Faculty opinion on the matter is confirmed to some extent by studies showing that salaries and promotion are determined more by the amount of research done than by teaching awards or student evaluations (Katz, 1973; McKeachie, Salthouse, and Lin, 1978; Siegfried and White, 1973).

Dissatisfaction with the state of the art has led to increasing calls for institutional reappraisals of their evaluation practices. Systematic approaches, responsive to the increasing demands for accountability, have been prepared by Miller (1972, 1974), Genova and others (1976), and the Southern Regional Education Board (1977). Complementing these approaches are the more general conceptual schemes proposed by Smock and Crooks (1973), Dressel (1976), and Glasman (1976). Although each proposal differs from the others in certain respects, several themes are common to all of them: First, all suggest evaluation programs ought to be comprehensive, with clearly articulated and publicly acknowledged purposes and criteria. Second, they agree faculty members should be involved from the outset, not only in determining the purposes of the evaluation program, but in its continued operation. Third, they recommend the evaluation system be flexible, open to data from a variety of sources, and encompass the full range of faculty activities. And fourth, they propose programs provide data both to facilitate faculty development (formative evaluation) and to permit personnel decisions (summative evaluation).

Budgeting and Planning. Paralleling this evaluation of faculty for personnel purposes has been the implementation of increasingly sophisticated mechanisms for gathering faculty work load data for use in unit cost studies, program budgeting, planning, and cost-benefit analyses. Stecklein (1974) traces the use of work load studies through several major periods, concluding changes have been those of intent or purpose rather than those of technique. Early efforts in the 1950s, designed primarily as a means of assuring equity of loads, identifying areas of needed staffing, and justifying budget requests to legislatures, gave way to the generation of data that could readily be converted to dollar amounts as concern for costs increased during the 1960s. More recently, earlier attention to faculty input has begun to be balanced by attention to outcome measures that can identify the kinds of productivity emanating from the allocation of faculty resources, such as course credits per full-time-equivalent (FTE) faculty member, and student credit hours (SCH) per FTE faculty member.

A number of recently developed resource allocation models are in current use and have been described in the literature. They include CAMPUS (Comprehensive Analytical Methods for Planning in University/College Systems) (Judy and Levine, 1965), HELP/PLANTRAN (Higher Education Long-Range/Planning Translation) (McKelvey, 1970), RRPM (Resource Requirements Prediction Model) (Clark and others, 1973), and SEARCH (System for Evaluating Alternative Resource Commitments in Higher Education) (Keane and Daniel, 1970). These resource allocation models are designed to project the effects on resource needs of changes in student enrollment, class size, and other key variables (Lawrence and Service, 1977).

Supplementing these general planning models are a number of management information system models of faculty flow, designed to help administrators calculate the possible future composition of the faculty by rank, age, discipline, salary, and other characteristics in order to help set policy on faculty selection, promotion, tenure, and retirement (Schroeder, 1973).

Research on Faculty Performance

Studies of the extent to which faculty work at their "jobs" consistently report that faculty average more than fifty hours per week on the job (Yuker, 1974). In fact, across all institutional types and from almost every discipline, faculty average above fifty-five hours per week—more than any other professional group that has been studied, including advertising executives and dentists (Gerstl, 1959). A report from the University of California shows that faculty at that institution work an average of sixty-two hours a week (University of California, 1970). Most of these work load reports are from professors' self-estimates, but the hours worked have been corroborated by diaries and by studies involving the interviewing of spouses.

Increasing faculty productivity thus cannot be accomplished by increasing the number of hours most faculty put in on the job. Rather, productivity has to be increased either by reallocating faculty time among their different duties or by restructuring time so faculty effort can be more efficient than it is at present.

With respect to allocation of time, studies show not only how faculty presently spend the time in their different work roles but also how they would prefer to distribute that time were they free to do so (for example, Clark, 1973). These studies show that, in the main, faculty want teaching to remain their first priority and desire little change in the proportion of time they give to this dominant role. But they want to increase the time they can give to creative and scholarly work in contrast to the effort they now give to their service responsibilities, particularly the time spent on committees. We consider research evidence on each of these roles in turn and then institutional and individual characteristics that affect role performance.

Teaching. A spate of empirical investigations of student ratings of class-room teaching over the past dozen years contrast with limited research on other ratings of teaching. Costin, Greenough, and Menges (1971), Kulik and McKeachie (1975), and Feldman (1976a; 1976b) have summarized the research literature on *student ratings* along a number of dimensions; and Felder (1979) has reviewed these summaries. For the most part, the studies show student ratings are statistically highly reliable, correlate modestly with student learning (Centra, 1977), and indicate little faculty change over time (Felder, 1979). They also show that a number of factors thought to bias student ratings have either no effect or at best a slight effect. Such factors as class size, upper- or lower-division course, sex of the instructor, student's expected grade, or required or elective course normally account for less than 5 percent of the predicted variance among student ratings.

The usefulness of student ratings in making critical judgments is, however, limited. Even if everyone agreed they are valid—still a lively point of contention among many academics and administrators—the problem is that, for the most part, students rate faculty very high as teachers. In fact, in a study at the University of Michigan (Ericksen, 1978), over 90 percent of the faculty were rated as very good or outstanding teachers. Hence, such ratings can be used for judging faculty performance among only a small percentage of faculty—those at both extremes. Their practical value in assigning merit increases is severely limited.

Blackburn and Clark (1975) summarize the few studies that report *administrator, peer,* and *self-ratings*. These studies tend to show a high degree of agreement between faculty and students on the evaluation of the teaching role, a statistically significant but somewhat less strong relationship between administrators and faculty and between administrators and students, and a very low relationship between the individual professor and all three constituencies—students, peers, and administrators. Moreover, faculty assess themselves higher than any other group does. A Fund for the Improvement of Postsecondary Education (FIPSE) study (Blackburn, Boberg, O'Connell, and Pellino, 1980) indicates the high value faculty place on their teaching performance and their desire to increase their repertoire of teaching skills. Hence, serious confrontations are inevitable when administrators inform individual professors of their unsatisfactory ratings as teachers.

Scholarship and Research. There have been many studies on scholarly productivity among faculty, but they are limited by the measure of the dependent variable—in almost all cases, the number of articles or books published in some time interval. Almost never is scholarly productivity related to works of art, creative curriculum reform, adoption of new teaching styles, development of new courses, or other activities that might be called "scholarly." Thus, the measures and the correlates of scholarly productivity have the limitation of being ascertained for faculty in research universities, and then almost exclusively for those in arts and sciences departments. One can argue that the personal attributes responsible for scholarship are the same ones necessary for creative teaching and curricular revision, but this has not been documented (Blackburn, 1979). There are, nonetheless, a number of studies on faculty productivity. These have been analyzed by Blackburn, Behymer, and Hall (1978). The findings show, among other factors, the faculty member's institution of advanced training, place of work, age at first publication, and work environment correlate positively with faculty scholarly output.

In addition, interviews on a FIPSE project (Blackburn, Boberg, O'Connell, and Pellino, 1980) uniformly indicate faculty members are anxious about their scholarly role. Faculty from every type of institution—community college, liberal arts college, and university—share this concern. They want to give more time to scholarship and to increase their output. The tension in this role was greater than for any other dimension of faculty life. Faculty, and especially junior faculty, readily discern the conditions for winning tenure and receiving promotion are becoming more and more dependent upon scholarly productivity, regardless of institutional type. However, faculty desire was not just to protect careers, although this was no small matter.

In addition, there seems to have been a universalization of the professional norm of scholarship. Faculty want to engage in scholarly activity in order to prove their membership in the profession. Faculty at two-year colleges are now coming from universities, mostly with a master's degree, but some with a Ph.D. No longer are they being recruited from the high schools. They, too, talked about wanting to publish, to do creative work that leads to visible products, to attend professional meetings, and to have professional (disciplinary) contacts.

As already noted, time allocation is a serious issue. The more one teaches, the less time one has for scholarship, unless one can combine the two activities. Hence, the scholarly role is one that is producing very high tension among academics today. Evaluating its many forms can be expected to be an area of increased activity.

Service. Service has been a catchall phrase to cover the many activities faculty do when they are neither teaching nor engaged in scholarship. These activities can be divided into those done within the institution and those done primarily on the outside. However, even with this simple division, there is overlap and confusion.

When faculty members judge the importance of this activity with respect to their own careers, they express uncertainty. For the most part, they do not believe the service role really matters. They know they are expected to serve on some committees; but how many, how actively, and to what purpose seems uncertain. If there is a consensus, it is that one is expected to give service but doing so probably does not count much in performance evaluations. Not to serve might count against one, but that would be about the extent of the matter.

Nonetheless, some service activities are important to the faculty member and the institution. Two of these are *governance* and *consulting.* (Time spent with students on their personal lives—counseling, student organizations, and the like—is considered part of the teaching rather than the service role.)

Faculty members want to be consulted about matters that affect the academic program and its administration—who sets policy with respect to entrance requirements, curriculum and degree requirements, the selection of colleagues and supervisors, and the like. Although faculty complain about the time they give to committee assignments, they do not want to be left out of those governance activities that affect their work.

Studies on faculty participation in governance (especially with respect to participation on a faculty senate) tend to show that senior academics exercise control (Baldridge, 1971; Mortimer, 1969). There are differences by institutions. Fulton and Trow (1974), for example, found a high interrelationship between the teaching, scholarly, and governance role among faculty in research universities; in regional universities, faculty seem to select one role at the expense of the other two. Baldwin (1979) found liberal arts college faculty members sporadically participate in governance activities in order to provide differentiation and diversion in their careers. Governance, then, becomes an alternative to scholarship and seems to be rewarding for middle-aged faculty in these institutions.

Consulting, especially for pay outside the institution, is a taboo area in higher education. Faculty members know administrators judge consulting schizophrenically. Consulting is good when it brings fame to the institution and when presidents can show their faculty members are of such a caliber that others seek their professional expertise. Consulting is an evil when it takes time from the job the institution is paying the faculty member to perform.

Lanning and Blackburn (1978) have done the only study on faculty consulting for pay. The data, from the 1968 Carnegie survey, show faculty members who consult a moderate amount are also more active in their organization's governance and produce more than those who do not consult at all. These consultants teach just as much as the nonconsultants and enjoy it. However, when consulting reaches a significantly high level—more than 20 percent of the professor's time—a different phenomenon appears. These very active consultants (less than 3 percent of all U.S. academics) do not publish more, talk about moving more (but in fact move less), and are less satisfied with their careers. In essence, this small group is removed from the main body of professors. Although consulting has both institutional and individual benefits, this very small group gives it an unsavory reputation in the minds of many.

Nothing is known about faculty volunteering their expertise to community organizations, such as school boards, health clinics, or ecology centers. Nor is anything known about the amount of time faculty give to their professional organizations, locally and regionally as well as nationally—by reviewing proposals, serving as readers of papers, or attending meetings.

Organizational Factors. As previously indicated, the institution at which a faculty member works is significantly related to his or her satisfaction and performance. Crane (1965) identified this variable, and Long (1978) and Blackburn and Havighurst (1979) confirmed it. Pelz and Andrews (1976) identified a number of organizational variables that affect productivity. For example, both support and challenge are essential: Scientists must be assured of support even when success is not immediate; at the same time, a competitive environment challenges them. Studies show that internal rewards motivate faculty members more than external ones. A healthy work environment, one the organization can provide, makes an appreciable difference and requires special attention.

Effects of Age and Rank. Many persist in believing that rank and tenure are counterproductive to faculty performance. They believe that once security is attained and age increases, faculty members become less productive. For the most part, the data do not support this position. In fact, evidence indicates the opposite is true. Blackburn (1972) has reviewed much of the literature in this field and found no correlations between age and rank and productivity. If anything, the trends are more positive than negative. Centra (1978) has reported some data that show students judge older faculty to be slightly less effective as teachers.

However, other data indicate no correlation between teaching effectiveness and either age or rank.

The nature of faculty productivity will vary as the career advances. For example, short, research-type articles will give way to more synthetic and philosophical pieces. There is some evidence that productivity dips a bit at midpoint and then rises again (Blackburn, Behymer, and Hall, 1978; Pelz and Andrews, 1976). However, productive people remain productive throughout their career and at age sixty-five are producing more than they were at age thirty-five. In fact, the difference between producers and nonproducers increases, not decreases, with the passing of time (Allison and Stewart, 1974).

Intercorrelation of Roles. As indicated, teaching and scholarship and service go hand in hand for some faculty. Their service (consulting, for example) can provide fresh information for their teaching as well as ideas for publications. But some faculty members make fairly clear distinctions between their professional activities. For them, assessing performance in each role is considerably easier. In the main, however, the faculty role is not singular; and its multiplicity produces serious problems for those evaluating performance.

Evaluation Problems and Issues

Of the many evaluation models available for assessing faculty performance—illuminative, discrepancy, adversary, historical, descriptive, case, formative, and summative, to mention those receiving the most attention these days—we consider the last two most appropriate for the task at hand. This is a judgmental statement, but one that can be argued. There is no evidence that the different evaluation models produce the same outcomes when attempting to assess the same performance. In fact, a debate continues about the appropriateness of each model and about its limitations and virtues.

The formative model is appropriate when faculty development is the principal objective. Using this approach, the clients (that is, the faculty) are active participants in the design and ongoing collection of data to be used to judge successful goal attainment. "Growth contracting" is an excellent example of the use of the techniques and strategies of formative evaluation. Management and workers set the goals and agree on what will constitute evidence of accomplishment. These goals are typically negotiated on an annual basis even when they are set for longer intervals of time, like five years. Faculty peers as well as administrators are involved in the process. Growth contracting and faculty development are frequently kept separate from the formal evaluation system of the institution. Hence, formative evaluation models seem most appropriate under circumstances involving faculty development.

Institutions also are faced with making hard decisions that affect individuals. Whether to award individuals tenure, to promote or dismiss them, or to award them merit increases above any across-the-board adjustments are irreversible decisions. They are clearly in the domain of summative evaluation. Criteria are set, judgments of whether an individual has met these criteria are made, and a final decision is reached. There is no escape from the summative model when an institutional decision is made to continue or terminate a faculty member.

At the same time, there are difficulties in separating self-improvement from sanctions. It is no simple matter to isolate extrinsic from intrinsic rewards.

As noted, although faculty are innerdirected people who seek to improve themselves for reasons of their own personal satisfaction, they are not unaware that their performance is going to affect their future life. No other professionals have invested as much time in preparing for a career. They want to remain in it. Measurements of faculty performance make tension inevitable. Wise administrators are sensitive to the high stakes involved and do not label professors schizoid when their behavior appears contradictory at critical career stages.

In this spirit, we discuss some of the unintended consequences of evaluation. First, it seems inevitable that evaluating faculty performance, even when it is formative, but particularly when it is summative, will lead to increased stress that, in turn, will lead to decreased performance. For example, student ratings of teachers will be lower for those suffering high qualitative and quantitative overload if they happen to be somewhat inflexible or likely to get anxious (Clark and Blackburn, 1973). Their overall contribution to the organization will also be perceived to be less effective if they are suffering from stress. Flexible individuals and those who seem not to get anxious under tension-producing conditions will actually show an increased level of performance on both their teaching and their contribution to their college when overload is increased.

Second, an unintended consequence of evaluating human performance has been demonstrated in the business world and can be expected to be true in academe as well. When professional workers are evaluated in a frequent and visible way, they tend to produce less. They become dissatisfied with the work environment and react negatively to the process. They do not see "constructive" evaluation as being personally helpful, even though improvement and growth may be an evaluation program's expressed aim (Meyer, Kay, and French, 1965).

Third, the very act of evaluating professors can create a negative climate. One of the defining ingredients of a professional life is the lack of supervision. Professionals, historically, set their own performance standards. Evaluation, then, is a highly sensitive issue that must be recognized as such by the organization engaging in it.

Fourth, faculty in different disciplines produce different kinds of products, prefer different styles of teaching, and have different service expectations. Variations make it difficult to use the same criteria across an entire institution. For example, people in the hard sciences tend to be involved in research projects that lead to a number of short articles, many of them coauthored. People in the humanities, say, in history, are much more likely to produce a lengthy work—a monograph or a book—and to be the sole author. Establishing equivalencies of products can be an endless activity. Similarly, mathematics teachers value a tightly organized presentation—a proof of a theorem, for example. A professor of literary criticism may proceed in a discussion-type class with a great amount of (apparent) disorder as critiques from various sources are examined, contrasted, and compared. Hence, even an instrument for measuring teaching effectiveness, which frequently inquires about how well the instructor is organized, may be questionable in terms of its appropriateness for faculty in two different disciplines. With respect to service, some faculty in the social sciences are more likely to get involved in the political arena than are those in the sciences, who do not find this role attractive. This points up the difficulty of using the same criteria for different disciplines.

Fifth and finally, most faculty are going to meet even higher objective standards (number of publications, for example.) Faculty are competitive individuals. They believe in meritocratic, universalistic standards (Peterson and others, 1978). Objective data alone will not make easy the critical decision to award or not award tenure to a particular individual. In the final analysis, it is a qualitative judgment. Yet quality is an attribute not completely reducible to behavioral definitions and disagreements on critical decisions will sometimes result. No evaluation strategy can eliminate differences of opinion and it is well to keep this fact in mind when entering a judgmental process.

The Case for Comprehensive Performance Review

Some form of performance assessment is inescapable in the life of faculty members, and constructive assessment can elevate quality. However, in the light of the problems noted previously, one is ineluctably drawn to the conclusion that evaluation in piecemeal fashion may be more detrimental than beneficial. Evaluation neither guided by principles of sound evaluation design nor sensitive to the subtleties and complexities of the professorial role is disruptive and counterproductive to the maintenance of quality academic performance.

In addition, disjointed evaluation activities mask the creative function a comprehensive performance review program can serve. When seen as necessary to a personnel program, systematic and comprehensive performance review can both provide a context and serve as a catalyst for articulating and negotiating the interrelationship of institutional goals with professional aspirations and individuals' goals. This procedure of building and clarifying role expectations is a necessary dimension of the personnel planning process. Attempts at such a clarification, however, ought to be cognizant of the similarity of faculty members' preparation for their work in diverse college environments.

Few would argue against the legitimacy of institutional heterogeneity. No college or university can attempt to do all that needs to be done; each must choose priorities. One institution may work toward solution of societal problems; another may emphasize graduate education; one college may develop a strong multidisciplinary professional program; another may commit itself to a research role. Whatever its priorities, an institution chooses among possible options on the basis of its faculty resources, its available or preferred pool of students, its traditions, its financial limitations, society's pressing problems, or a combination of these.

Despite this accepted heterogeneity in institutional missions, preparation of academics is remarkably homogeneous. Embodying the integrated teaching-research model of the university professor, graduate schools are the prime agents of professionalization and socialization among academics. Therefore, faculty members arrive on the academic scene with a somewhat determined set of professional values related to standards of academic performance, general goals of education, and specific methods of teaching. Conscious attention, therefore, must be paid to the process of integrating faculty into the particular college setting, building on positive professional values, and completing the process of socialization to incorporate the shared norms and goals of the particular college or university within which the faculty member will be working.

Again, we suggest a systematic and comprehensive program of performance review is one strategy for undertaking the process of integration. Evaluation in this instance helps faculty members shape specific performance goals and stimulate alternative strategies (among those available in the specific environment) for satisfying them. In addition, performance review can provide much needed information for incorporating flexibility in the design of work situations by aligning work load more closely with faculty orientations and capabilities so as to nurture and maintain productivity.

Both formative and summative in nature, a system of performance review should capture faculty members' mutual commitment to each other's continued professional development as well as legitimate the symbolic future commitment engendered in the act of awarding tenure.

Several general principles should guide the design and implementation of a comprehensive performance review program. First, certain characteristics of the faculty role and life-style must be understood in order to assess the faculty's capacity to perform in desired ways. Standard shibboleths must give way to an appreciation and sensitivity to the highly complex and integrated nature of the faculty role. Understanding demands not only an acquaintance with the variety of research findings on faculty attitudes, work, and performance but also a thorough knowledge of the statistical, as well as personality, profile of the college faculty. Faculty flow models, mentioned earlier, can be valuable tools for understanding the broad dynamics of a faculty.

Second, the faculty's expected responsibilities must be carefully negotiated. Research on faculty work suggests performance is dictated to a high degree by the complex interaction of a set of internalized standards of professional performance. Faculty members do not automatically respond, with what administrators feel to be appropriate activity, to performance expectations reflected in institutional reward structures. The interactive process of socialization and professionalization must continue in some intentional fashion if individual faculty members' goals and institutional mission are to be mutually supportive. To be truly effective, this negotiation process must begin at the point of faculty selection. Career performance is predictable; career preference must also be ascertained.

Third, standards and criteria developed to evaluate actual faculty performance must reflect sound evaluation procedure. At the same time, they must be flexible enough to respond to individual faculty member differences that are dictated by differences in academic discipline, predilection for work activity, and career stage. Meeting the first of these requirements suggests the specific design should heed what educational evaluators have pointed to as ideal characteristics of evaluation. In general, these have been the following:

- *clarity:* clear understanding of how and why the evaluation is occurring
- *specificity:* comprehensive identification of the sources and kinds of information to be used in the evaluation
- *communicability:* appreciation that the evaluation must be understood by a diversity of audiences
- *efficiency:* lack of redundancy
- *political sensitivity:* cognizance of the political realities of evaluation

Satisfying the second part of the equation, that of evaluating faculty members' performance of their responsibilities, demands evaluations be individual in focus and qualitative in nature. Judgments of faculty performance are judgments of persons; and as such, they must be flexible yet holistic in scope. That is, they must be sensitive to the integrated nature of the faculty role and open to the uniqueness individuals bring to the collective work environment. Efforts to separate activities, to reference them to specific costs and productivity increments, destroy the harmony and balance of academic work. Informed and consensual professional judgment remains the most practical and ultimately desirable way of eliciting a judgment of the "quality" of a faculty member's performance. A wide range of sources of evidence, including student evaluations of teaching, should be gathered; but peers are still in the best position to make global assessments of academic performance.

Fourth, concern for vitality in faculty performance warrants that a performance review system be complemented by programs that support faculty growth and development. Evaluation has made a constructive contribution to higher education; assessing faculty performance needs to have this positive dimension, too.

Suggested Courses of Action

As indicated, the procedure of moving upward from a unit (for example, a department) review to the next larger body (for example, a collegewide promotion committee) and finally to the chief administrative office (for example, dean and an executive committee or academic vice-president and chancellor) is the typical practice in evaluating faculty performance for summative decisions. What data are collected, what constitutes evidence, and how things are weighted vary from institution to institution. Nonetheless, institutions are alike at least to the extent that qualitative judgments ultimately must be made. We do not intend to criticize the traditional evaluation technique here. Instead, we shall describe some less-common practices.

External Reviewers. Some colleges and universities have developed procedures for systematically engaging experts from outside the institution. The faculty member up for promotion not only prepares a portfolio for internal use but also provides names of experts at other colleges who are qualified to judge the quality of his or her work. Most often the judgments will be made on written work, that is, on the quality of scholarship produced; but this technique can also solicit professional judgment on artistic creations or on contributions made in a service capacity, say, as a committee member in a disciplinary society.

Experts in the field whose names the candidate did not advance can also be used. The evaluation committee can ask known national figures to assess the candidate's portfolio and answer the question, "Would you hire this individual as a colleague?" What weight institutions give outside testimony varies. The use of external evaluations has obvious advantages for smaller units, which may not have a sufficient number of colleagues of similar training to make critical judgments. In addition, using outsiders can temper the concerns some have with regard to the use of personal (nonrelevant) rather than professional attributes in the final decision. Use of outsiders also aids the candidate and the institution in maintaining standards vis-à-vis a set of peers. That is, outsiders who transcend the local setting can set performance standards against which the college can assess the quality of its enterprise.

The practice does place a burden on experts in the field. However, the indications are that such a professional request is respected, considered important, and responded to with care and minimum delay. The practice can be likened to the journal review process, in which submitted articles are sent out to faculty experts for critique and recommendation on acceptability. Faculty willingly participate in this process because they value it and care about the treatment of their peers. They want the best persons to be retained and to advance; they want to weed out those who do not credit the profession.

Contract and Performance. Professional growth plans are being tried in a number of institutions. Most often the plan takes on the form of a "contract," a set of accomplishments the faculty member is to achieve in a given time period along with statements regarding what will constitute evidence the goals have been met. The last dimension frequently designates who will decide whether the contract is fulfilled. It is during this stage that performance evaluation enters.

When the contract has as its purpose faculty development, evaluation may be done by a peer. In fact, pairs of faculty members may be formed to critique one another to facilitate growth and development. However, when the contract has summative consequences, that is, will be used in making decisions affecting the faculty member's career, then evaluators will include person(s) in a supervisory role. In these instances, the judgments move into the traditional pattern discussed at the beginning of this section (up through the organization's review process for a summative decision).

It is still a bit early to judge the strengths and weaknesses of professional growth plans. Their attractiveness lies in the fact that the individual and the institution assess needs and contributions together. They may also function as a means of achieving professional and personal development. Concerns about growth plans rest with the possible absence of universal standards and institutional inability to make the tough decision to prune when it "knows" it should.

Systematic Peer Review. Informal peer review—even the use of rating forms—is almost always a part of the typical process described in the opening of this section. Here we describe a more elaborate mechanism in which at least one college engages. This college has an elected faculty committee that is almost continuously involved in evaluating faculty performance. Its activities are not limited to tenure and promotion cases, although it is involved in every one of these decisions as well. It evaluates contracts that faculty members prepare. It deals directly with any faculty member reported (and documented) to be deficient in some aspect of her or his role. Students as well as colleagues can report the underperforming faculty member to the committee. (Student government has a thorough and careful process for investigating individual complaints.) Whether the professor is tenured matters not at all, for the committee is empowered to recommend the dismissal of any faculty member who does not meet minimum standards.

In its capacity of evaluating reported deficient faculty, the committee sees its role as a remedial rather than a completely judgmental one. That is, it views its charge as one of assisting the low-performing faculty member to improve. It works directly with the faculty member, suggests where expert advice can be attained, and the like. It also draws up a contract for a future evaluative review. Hence, the committee is serving both developmental and summative concerns.

Naturally, such a body is powerful. Committee members are chosen from the most highly regarded faculty on campus. Although its success depends upon administrative acceptance of its recommendations, it nevertheless is a peer process and is highly respected by the faculty. Even though it consumes a great number of individual faculty hours, the fact that the process is held in high regard is one indication that it is working well.

Faculty Counseling and Evaluation. Many colleges and, because of their large size, universities have grievance mechanisms for handling complaints on nonpromotion and tenure denial. Some institutions have appointed faculty ombudspersons. These review mechanisms might also be viewed as evaluative. However, most often such cases are on the fringe of formal litigation and deal with the process rather than the substance of evaluation.

Recently, other professional staff who serve in an evaluative role have been added to institutions. They can be faculty development specialists, media experts, or personal counselors. Most often the professor approaches such individuals for assistance—in teaching techniques, course redesign, examination construction, or the like. Professors can also seek advice on possible career changes.

In almost every instance, some kind of assessment takes place. The evaluation can range from informal self-reports to a highly formal, thorough, and systematic performance analysis. A teaching consultant might, for instance, obtain student classroom ratings and videotape a professor before advising a particular program intended to strengthen the faculty member's teaching behavior.

Still, most evaluations in this domain fall in the formative rather than summative classification, with the instructor being responsible for setting and meeting goals. Such evaluations normally are not used in tenure/promotion decisions unless the faculty member voluntarily submits such information.

Program Review. Although the growing activity of program review has purposes other than the evaluation of faculty performance, faculty evaluations almost inevitably enter in. More often than not, however, it is the collective performance of a program's faculty that is measured, not the assessment of individuals. That is, program reviews ask questions about the production of faculty student credit hours, instructional costs as they relate to faculty salaries, faculty-generated outside funding, and scholarly articles published. These are aggregated data and typically are not used by any group in making personnel decisions on individuals.

Obviously, however, information on individuals forms the basis for the collected programmatic review. Furthermore, several data items have relevance for the tenure/promotion evaluation. There is no reason why program review activity could not be linked to other evaluation processes. In addition, program review is becoming a regular rather than an emergency phenomenon in many institutions. Hence, utilizing review opportunities would be a simple way to increase the number of evaluative factors that enter into personnel decisions.

The Institutional Research Office and Faculty Evaluation

The institutional research office in most institutions is already involved in program review and hence is already assessing faculty performance. Unfortunately, program review and program curtailment and/or elimination have an intimate connection in the eyes of many faculty. (This is understandable because many colleges and universities never engaged in systematic review until they were in a difficult situation and were forced to cut back programs.) Consequently, the institutional research image frequently is not a positive one. It is the office that wants forms filled out, that reports on the number of small (never too large) classes, that prints out tenure densities, in short, that reports mostly bad and threatening news as far as faculty members are concerned—and concerned about their jobs and their careers they are.

There is no reason, however, why an institutional research office cannot contribute to the positive aspects of faculty evaluation. As the previous section demonstrated, not only is evaluation of many kinds an integral segment in higher education activities, but assessment can also be a constructive force. The college that prepares for accreditation through a self-study invariably improves itself in its own evaluation process.

So could and should the institutional research office contribute to making faculty performance evaluation a constructive and developmental process. By conducting performance studies, by carrying out research on the interrelatedness of performance variables, by running analyses on variables faculty members hypothesize correlate with performance, by obtaining norms of faculty performance at peer institutions, by a whole host of activities, institutional research offices can help evaluating faculty performance rise above its current negative status and become the respected supporter for enriching the work enviroment and for elevating performance quality.

Bibliographical Essay

Centra (1978, 1979) discusses several types of student ratings: of courses, of curricula, and of teaching performance. He describes the effects of each on faculty performance and vitality. Defending what is now a widespread use of student ratings of instructors, Centra points to the validity of such ratings in that students generally learn more from highly rated instructors. He points out also that such instruments are reliable when a large enough sample of students do the rating. His article seeks answers to three questions: Do ratings improve instruction and therefore help faculty members improve their performances? Are ratings suitable measures of teaching effectiveness to aid in making tenure, promotion, and salary decisions? Can ratings help improve departmental performance? The answers suggest that student ratings, regardless of their limitations, are useful enough to justify their continued use in colleges. Cognizant of their limitations, however, Centra advises their use as only one among "multiple indicators of performance and multiple perspectives on vitality" (p. 46).

Glasman (1976) develops a conceptual framework for an administrative perspective on faculty evaluation. The perspective is grounded in the assumption that the task of "facilitating an increase in instructor's acceptance of having their teaching evaluated has become an important role for university administrators" (p. 309). Glasman's framework uses three domains: an individual need satisfaction domain, an institutional influence-consensus domain, and an evaluation instrument's appropriateness domain. The exploration of each throws light on the realistic possibilities and limitations of administrative review of faculty performance. Advocating a kind of "process" evaluation in evaluating faculty performance, Glasman describes how administrators ought to distinguish those components in the variables of qualification, purpose, and teaching situation that are to be evaluated as the teacher's responsibility and as the institution's.

Pointing to the limitations of scope in both student and administrative evaluation, Batista (1976) advises using various forms of colleague evaluation. He provides a list of ten activities or faculty behaviors he claims can more reliably be validated by colleagues than by either students or administrators. According to Batista, peer evaluation can attach significant importance to the reward structure and thereby encourage good teaching.

Several other authors—Doi (1974), Bess (1977), Lindquist (1978), and Smith (1978)—treat the matter of evaluating faculty performance less directly when they point out relationships between evaluation of faculty motivation, organizational policies, methods of work load assessment, and institutional personnel policies. Bess examines the relationship between important personal and professional needs of faculty members and the processes and contexts of college teaching that might affect their ability to satisfy those needs. He speculates that the ineffability of the goals and effects of teaching, the ambiguities in the social context of teaching, and the difficulties of measuring the success of teaching all serve to block the satisfactions faculty might experience and, consequently, tempt them to turn to other pursuits for rewards. Bess's advice for designing faculty development activities to assist faculty in overcoming obstacles in order to discover profound satisfaction in teaching deserves a trial.

Lindquist (1978) urges abandoning bureaucratic and political ways of forcing or maneuvering faculty to try new modes of instruction that could lead to more effective and efficient learning. Instead, he advocates strategies of social learning and problem solving that appeal to a wider range of human motivation. Lindquist claims these newer approaches could improve both faculty performance and vitality.

Doi's (1974) collection of essays (by Stecklein, Jedamus, Hunther, Mortimer, Lazier, Carter, and Blackburn) is important for its coverage of problems connected with efforts to assess faculty work loads. The authors warn that the very nature of academic work is such that analyzing it destroys its essence. Nonetheless, administrators continue to attempt to measure the amounts of time faculty members devote to various activities. Furthermore, inferences continue to be made concerning faculty performance and vitality from those measurements.

Smith (1978) insists any inquiry about faculty performance or vitality ought to address the process by which faculty members are selected, promoted, and otherwise rewarded. Warning that traditional concepts, governance forms, and personnel policies are currently under attack, Smith proceeds to explore both the values and problems inherent in shared governance, faculty responsibility for personnel policies, tenure, and the merit principle. He concludes, "the good in traditional faculty personnel policies and procedures, where it is found, or where it is genuinely sought, may warrant sustenance *in the public* interest" (p. 15).

References

Allison, P. D., and Stewart, J. A. "Productivity Differences Among Scientists: Evidence for Accumulative Advantage." *American Sociological Review,* 1974, *39,* 596–606.

Astin, A. W., and Lee, C. B. T. "Current Practices in the Evaluation and Training of College Teachers." *The Educational Record*, 1966, *47*, 361–365.

Baldridge, J. V. *Power and Conflict in the University.* New York: Wiley, 1971.

Baldwin, R. G. "The Faculty Career Process—Continuity and Change: A Study of College Professors at Five Stages of the Academic Career." Unpublished doctoral dissertation, Center for the Study of Higher Education, University of Michigan, 1979.

Batista, E. E. "The Place of Colleague Evaluation in the Appraisal of College Teaching: A Review of the Literature." *Research in Higher Education*, 1976, *4*, 257–271.

Bess, J. L. "The Motivation to Teach." *Journal of Higher Education*, 1977, *48*, 243–258.

Blackburn, R. T. *Tenure: Aspects of Job Security on the Changing Campus.* Research Monograph No. 19. Atlanta, Ga.: Southern Regional Education Board, 1972.

Blackburn, R. T. "Academic Careers: Patterns and Possibilities." In R. Edgerton (Ed.), *Current Issues in Higher Education.* Washington, D.C.: American Association for Higher Education, 1979.

Blackburn, R. T., Behymer, C. E., and Hall, D. E. "Research Note: Correlates of Faculty Publications." *Sociology of Education*, 1978, *51*, 131–132.

Blackburn, R. T., Boberg, A., O'Connell, C., and Pellino, G. *Assessing Faculty Development Programs.* Washington, D.C.: Fund for the Improvement of Postsecondary Education, HEW, 1980.

Blackburn, R. T., and Clark, M. J. "An Assessment of Faculty Performance: Some Correlates Between Administrator, Colleague, Student and Self-Ratings." *Sociology of Education*, 1975, *48*, 242–256.

Blackburn, R. T., and Havighurst, R. J. "Career Patterns of Male Academic Social Scientists." *Higher Education*, 1979, *8*, 553–572.

Blackburn, R. T., and Trowbridge, K. W. "Faculty Accountability and Faculty Workload: A Preliminary Cost Analysis of Their Relationship as Revealed by Ph.D. Productivity." *Research in Higher Education*, 1973, *1*, 1–12.

Blank, R. "Faculty Support for Evaluation of Testing." *Journal of Higher Education*, 1978, *49*, 2.

Boyd, J. E., and Schietinger, E. F. *Faculty Evaluation Procedures in Southern Colleges and Universities.* Atlanta, Ga.: Southern Regional Education Board, 1976.

Bunnell, K. *Faculty Workload.* Washington, D.C.: American Council on Education, 1960.

Centra, J. A. *Faculty Development Practices in U.S. Colleges and Universities.* Princeton, N.J.: Educational Testing Service, 1976.

Centra, J. A. "Student Ratings of Instruction and Their Relationship to Student Learning." *American Educational Research Journal*, 1977, *14*, 17–24.

Centra, J. A. "Using Student Assessments to Improve Performance and Vitality." In W. R. Kirschling (Ed.), *New Directions for Institutional Research: Evaluating Faculty Performance and Vitality*, no. 20. San Francisco: Jossey-Bass, 1978.

Centra, J. A. *Determining Faculty Effectiveness: Assessing Teaching, Research, and Service for Personnel Decisions and Improvements.* San Francisco: Jossey-Bass, 1979.

Clark, D. G., and others. *Introduction to the Resource Requirements Prediction Model 1.6.* Technical Report No. 34A. Boulder, Colo.: National Center for Higher Education Management Systems at Western Interstate Commission for Higher Education, 1973.

Clark, M. J. "Organizational Stress and Professional Performance Among Faculty Members at a Small College." Unpublished doctoral dissertation, Center for the Study of Higher Education, University of Michigan, 1973.

Clark, M. J., and Blackburn, R. T. "Faculty Performance Under Stress." In A. L. Sockloff (Ed.), *Faculty Effectiveness as Evaluated by Students.* Philadelphia: Temple University, 1973.

Costin, F., Greenough, W. T., and Menges, R. J. "Student Ratings of College Teaching: Reliability, Validity, and Usefulness." *Review of Educational Research,* 1971, *41,* 511–535.

Crane, D. "Scientists at Major and Minor Universities: A Study of Productivity and Recognition." *American Sociological Review,* 1965, *30,* 699–714.

Doi, J. I. (Ed.). *New Directions for Institutional Research: Assessing Faculty Effort,* no. 2. San Francisco: Jossey-Bass, 1974.

Dressel, P. L. *Handbook of Academic Evaluation: Assessing Institutional Effectiveness, Student Progress, and Professional Performance for Decision Making in Higher Education.* San Francisco: Jossey-Bass, 1976.

Ericksen, S. C. "The Dimensions of Merit." University of Michigan, Ann Arbor: *Memo to the Faculty,* No. 61, December 1978.

Felder, N. L. "A Study of Students: Reactions to Faculty Role Concepts." Unpublished doctoral dissertation, Center for the Study of Higher Education, University of Michigan, 1979.

Feldman, K. A. "Grades and College Students' Evaluations of Their Courses and Teachers." *Research in Higher Education,* 1976a, *4,* 69–111.

Feldman, K. A. "The Superior College Teacher from the Students' View." *Research in Higher Education,* 1976b, *5,* 243–288.

Fulton, O., and Trow, M. "Reasearch Activity in American Higher Education." *Sociology of Education,* 1974, *47,* 29–73.

Genova, W. T., and others. *Mutual Benefit Evaluation of Faculty and Administrators in Higher Education.* Cambridge, Mass.: Ballinger, 1976.

Gerstl, J. "Career Commitment and Style of Life in Three Middle Class Occupations." Unpublished doctoral dissertation, Department of Sociology, University of Minnesota, 1959.

Glasman, N. S. "Evaluation of Instructors in Higher Education, An Administrative Function." *Journal of Higher Education,* 1976, *47,* 309–326.

Gustad, J. W. *Policies and Practices in Faculty Evaluation.* Washington, D.C.: Committee on College Teaching, American Council on Education, 1961.

Gustad, J. W. "Evaluation of Teaching Performance: Issues and Possibilities." In C. B.T. Lee (Ed.), *Improving College Teaching.* Washington, D.C.: American Council on Education, 1967.

Hansen, B. L., and Sandler, S. *Report on a Study of Faculty Activities at the University of Toronto.* Toronto: Office of Institutional Research, University of Toronto, 1967.

Hind, R. R. "An Analysis of Faculty: Professionalism, Evaluation and Authority Structure." In J. V. Baldridge (Ed.), *Academic Governance.* Berkeley, Calif.: McCutchan, 1971.

Judy, R. W., and Levine, J. B. "A New Tool for Educational Administrators." Report to the Commission on the Financing of Higher Education, appointed by the Canadian Universities Foundation. Toronto: University of Toronto Press, 1965.

Katz, D. A. "Faculty Salaries, Promotions, and Productivity at a Large University." *American Economic Review,* June 1973, pp. 469–477.

Keane, G. F., and Daniel, J. N. *System for Exploring Alternative Resource Commitments in Higher Education (SEARCH).* New York: Peat, Marwick, Mitchell, 1970.

Koos, L. V. *The Adjustment of the Teaching Load in a University.* Bureau of Education Bulletin 15. Washington, D.C.: Superintendent of Documents, 1919.

Kulik, J. A., and McKeachie, W. J. "The Evaluation of Teachers in Higher Education." In F. N. Kerlinger (Ed.), *Review of Research in Education.* Itasca, Ill.: Peacock, 1975.

Lanning, A., and Blackburn, R. T. "Faculty Consulting and the Consultant." Paper presented at AERA Annual Meeting, Toronto, April 1978.

Lawrence, G. B., and Service, A. L. *Qualitative Approaches to Higher Education Management: Potential, Limits, and Challenge.* ERIC/Higher Education Research Report No. 4. Washington, D.C.: American Association for Higher Education, 1977.

Lindquist, J. "Social Learning and Problem Solving Strategies for Improving Academic Performance." In W. R. Kirschling (Ed.), *New Directions in Institutional Research: Evaluating Faculty Performance and Vitality,* no. 20. San Francisco: Jossey-Bass, 1978.

Long, J. S. "Productivity and Academic Position in the Scientific Career." *American Sociological Review,* 1978, *43,* 889–908.

Luthans, F. *The Faculty Promotion Process and Analysis of the Management of Large State Universities.* Iowa City: Bureau of Business and Economic Research, College of Business Administration, University of Iowa, 1967.

McKeachie, W. J., and Lin, Y. *Use of Student Ratings in Evaluation of Classroom Teaching.* Final Report. Washington, D.C.: National Institute of Education (DHEW), 1975.

McKeachie, W. J., Salthouse, T. A., and Lin, Y. "An Experimental Investigation of Factors Influencing University Promotion Decisions." *Journal of Higher Education,* 1978, *49,* 177–183.

McKelvey, J. *HELP/PLANTRAN: A Computer Assisted Planning System for Higher Education.* Kansas City, Mo.: Midwest Research Institute, 1970.

Meeth, L. R. "The Stateless Art of Teaching Evaluation." In G. W. Bonham and others (Eds.), *Change Report on Teaching 2.* New Rochelle, N.Y.: Educational Change, 1976.

Meyer, H. H., Kay, E., and French, J. R. P., Jr. "Split Roles in Performance Appraisal." *Harvard Business Review,* 1965, *43,* 123–129.

Miller, R. I. *Evaluating Faculty Performance.* San Francisco: Jossey-Bass, 1972.

Miller, R. I. *Developing Programs for Faculty Evaluation: A Sourcebook for Higher Education.* San Francisco: Jossey-Bass, 1974.

Mortimer, K. P. "Academic Government at Berkeley: The Academic Senate." Unpublished doctoral dissertation, Department of Education, University of California, Berkeley, 1969.

Pelz, D. C., and Andrews, F. M. *Scientists in Organizations.* New York: Wiley, 1976.

Peterson, M. W., and others. *Black Students on White Campuses: The Impacts of Increased Black Enrollments.* Ann Arbor: Institute for Social Research, University of Michigan, 1978.

Reeves, F. W., and Russell, J. D. "Instructional Loads." In F. W. Reeves and J. D. Russell, *College Organization and Administration.* Indianapolis, Ind.: Board of Education, Disciples of Christ, 1929.

Richardson, H. D. "Faculty Workload Study and Analysis." *College and University,* 1967, *43,* 108–114.

Russell, J. D. "Service Loads of Faculty Members." In J. D. Russell (Ed.), *Problems of Faculty Personnel.* Proceedings of the Institute for Administrative Officers of Higher Institutions. Chicago: University of Chicago Press, 1946.

Schroeder, R. G. "A Survey of Management Science in University Operations." *Management Science,* 1973, *19,* 898–906.

Seldin, P. *How Colleges Evaluate Professors.* New York: Blythe-Pennington, 1975.

Siegfried, J. V., and White, K. J. "Teaching and Publishing as Determinants of Academic Salaries." *The Journal of Economic Education,* Spring 1973, pp. 219–230.

Smith, D. K. "Faculty Vitality and the Management of University Personnel Policies." In W. R. Kirschling (Ed.), *New Directions in Institutional Research: Evaluating Faculty Performance and Vitality,* no. 20. San Francisco: Jossey-Bass, 1978.

Smock, H. R., and Crooks, T. J. "A Plan for the Comprehensive Evaluation of College Teaching." *Journal of Higher Education,* 1973, *44,* 577–586.

Southern Regional Education Board. *Faculty Evaluation for Improved Learning.* Atlanta, Ga.: Southern Regional Education Board, 1977.

Stecklein, J. E. *How to Measure Faculty Workload.* Washington, D.C.: American Council on Education, 1961.

Stecklein, J. E. "Approaches to Measuring Workload Over the Past Two Decades." In J. I. Doi (Ed.), *New Directions for Institutional Research: Assessing Faculty Effort,* no. 2. San Francisco: Jossey-Bass, 1974.

University of California. "Faculty Effort and Output Study." Berkeley: Office of the Vice-President, Planning and Analysis, 1970. (Mimeo.)

Wilson, L. *The Academic Man.* London: Oxford University Press, 1942.

Yuker, H. E. *Faculty Workload: Facts, Myths and Commentary.* Research Report No. 6. Washington, D.C.: ERIC Clearinghouse for Higher Education, 1974.

24

Barry Munitz

Examining
Administrative
Performance

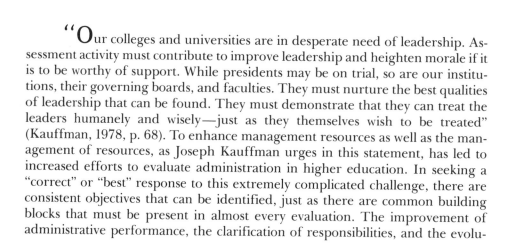

"Our colleges and universities are in desperate need of leadership. Assessment activity must contribute to improve leadership and heighten morale if it is to be worthy of support. While presidents may be on trial, so are our institutions, their governing boards, and faculties. They must nurture the best qualities of leadership that can be found. They must demonstrate that they can treat the leaders humanely and wisely—just as they themselves wish to be treated" (Kauffman, 1978, p. 68). To enhance management resources as well as the management of resources, as Joseph Kauffman urges in this statement, has led to increased efforts to evaluate administration in higher education. In seeking a "correct" or "best" response to this extremely complicated challenge, there are consistent objectives that can be identified, just as there are common building blocks that must be present in almost every evaluation. The improvement of administrative performance, the clarification of responsibilities, and the evolu-

478

tion of a more refined reward system emerge repeatedly as the goals of administrator evaluation. Yet in my experience, no one model is necessarily, or desirably, the best approach for every situation because each process must be fashioned to meet the needs of a particular institution and its administrators. The potential of institutional leadership can be assessed and the quality of its management can be strengthened, but much work remains before most institutions can assume their assessment programs are not only securely in place but adequate in meeting Kauffman's criteria for them.

Administrative Performance and Review

As more and more institutions have established administrative evaluation programs, a debate has ensued regarding their relative impact. The administration of a contemporary university is an increasingly complex assignment, one vulnerable to many conflicting and changing objectives. If they are to improve education while maintaining institutional stability, chief executive officers and their administrative staffs must channel diverse interests toward relatively consistent constructive activities. The task is herculean.

Writing more than fifteen years ago, Clark Kerr (1964, pp. 29-30) described the challenges confronting a university president in terms that have been only magnified by today's conditions:

> The university president in the United States is expected to be a friend of the students, a colleague of the faculty, a good fellow with the alumni, a sound administrator with the trustees, a good speaker with the public, an astute bargainer with the foundations and the federal agencies, a politician with the state legislature, a friend of industry, labor, and agriculture, a persuasive diplomat with donors, a champion of education generally, a supporter of the professions (particularly law and medicine), a spokesman to the press, a scholar in his own right, a public servant at the state and national levels, a devotee of opera and football equally, a decent human being, a good husband and father, an active member of a church. Above all he must enjoy traveling in airplanes, eating his meals in public, and attending public ceremonies. No one can be all of these things. Some succeed at being none.
>
> He should be firm, yet gentle; sensitive to others, insensitive to himself; look to the past and the future, yet be firmly planted in the present; both visionary and sound; affable, yet reflective; know the value of a dollar and realize that ideas cannot be bought; inspiring in his visions yet cautious in what he does; a man of principle yet able to make a deal; a man with broad perspective who will follow the details conscientiously; a good American but ready to criticize the status quo fearlessly; a seeker of truth where the truth may not hurt too much; a source of public policy pronouncements when they do not reflect on his own institution. He should sound like a mouse at home and look like a lion abroad. He is one of the marginal men in a democratic society—of whom there are many others—on the margin of many groups, many ideas, many endeavors, many characteristics. He is a marginal man but at the very center of the total process.

Leaders willing to navigate through those exquisite paradoxes can be attracted to their positions and, once attracted, freed for their essential work only through an environment marked by structured openness and mutual understanding. Yet the criteria for presidential appointment a governing board announces at the beginning of a search may differ from those factors that actually motivate its ultimate choice of candidate and differ even more from the measures it subsequently uses to assess presidential performance. Moreover, each board member has his or her own unique understanding of the institution's mission and the consequent expectations for presidential responsibilities. The longer a chief executive is in office, the fewer board members remain who were serving at the time of his or her selection and who were involved in defining the actual circumstances that conditioned it. Indeed, board members are in an ambiguous position to assess presidential performance because they are being educated by, while simultaneously judging, the one college employee who reports directly to them.

If mutual expectations between president and board are vague or are in conflict, relationships with other constituencies are likely to be expedient at best and chaotic at worst; but if those expectations can be clarified, other relationships are likely to assume their proportionate place. The same may be said for interactions between employer and employee at other levels of the institution. The balance between a president and vice-president, or between a dean or department head, or between an administrative officer and the director of purchasing, cannot be stabilized—much less improved—without willingness of each to confront candidly issues facing his or her component of the institution. Indeed, in many instances, a call for evaluation is nothing more than an urgent plea for an honest look at current working conditions.

Concerns Regarding the Evaluation Process

The dangers of a rapidly imposed or carelessly structured assessment process have been articulated concisely by Kauffman (1978, p. 63): "The announcement of the imposition of an evaluation system is often a symbolic act, calculated to give the appearance of tough management or the assertion of greater control by the governing board. . . . The concern about formal evaluation is that by institutionalizing we may distract and detract from what ought to be done in order to meet the evaluation systems expectations. . . . In the area of higher education, presidential evaluation has been predicated on a governance model that is more myth than reality; on decision making that is more political than rational; and on criteria and objectives that are often in the eye of the beholder rather than observable for objective assessment." These points can be extrapolated meaningfully for administrators at other levels of the institution. Any attempt at assessment that does not recognize the vulnerable position of higher education's managers, or is insensitive to the special circumstances within which they work, will undermine its own objectives. It would be foolhardy to take the sources of such problems lightly. It would be naive to dismiss the critics of formal evaluation programs as people who want to avoid public scrutiny or who would place key administrators in a privileged position isolated from constituency attitudes.

Many administrators remain skeptical about any formal strategy for evaluation. They assert that such a trend not only reflects insensitivity toward their responsibilities but also devaluates the relationship between their position and those directly above or below them. The balance between values received and risks taken in the evaluation process, therefore, remains in serious question. Even the sharpest critics, however, agree that unless the higher education community can direct expectations into channels that reinforce quality performance, constituents throughout that community will inadvertently add to the burden of college executives.

The pressures are greatest closer to the traditional center of the institution—the academic program. Therefore, the evaluation of academic administrators, with meaningful participation from faculty and students, receives the greatest attention. A process based upon the assumption that an educational institution is a community of scholars in which mutual interests imply mutual evaluation must be designed. Administrators and faculty members can understand the legitimacy of concerns about the evaluation process while they simultaneously acknowledge the inevitability of formal review. Any evaluative actions based upon superficial comparisons with the corporate world or ignoring the unique nature of student-faculty relationships at a college or university risk grave injustice to individuals as well as serious damage to the institution.

In an ideal world, self-assessment might be sufficient to identify areas of required emphasis and to provide alternatives for improved performance. But human beings are not given to unbiased self-analysis. Even if they were, the factors that characterize success are so ambiguous that individuals require reasonably objective procedures to gain an enhanced measure of self-direction. For similar reasons, the informal daily review of employee progress by individual employers cannot serve as the sole basis of assessment. Nor in our current educational environment can those indirect judgments take the place of more formal occasions to study the state of college management. Far from being disruptive, more formal procedures can shed light upon issues while generating support among the institution's constituencies. An evaluation program based on the in-service improvement of performance offers an opening for professional development in a field where the opportunities for adequate training remain scarce. A governing board, and its key administrators, can establish conditions so that when new executives are required, or when an individual with some tenure requests the chance to gain additional perspective upon his or her performance, the institution can respond effectively. If remedies for the disintegration of more traditional assessment patterns are available, then formal review of an institution's governance framework must be identified as one of them.

Advantages of Systematic Assessment

The evaluation of institutional leadership is just as vital for the enlightenment of employers—up to and including the governing board—as it is to the enhancement of administrative performance.

To the Governing Board. The review process offers the board a unique opportunity to become active participants in the exploration of management obligations. The disclosure of constraints upon and incentives available to college and university executives sharpens a board's perception of the educational body politic. The crucial challenge to trustees in the 1980s will be providing adequate support for their chief executive officer by strengthening their own relationship to the institution. They can learn to transform potential conflicts, which result from misunderstanding current conditions, into a stronger interaction achieved through mutual understanding. Presidents and board members find it equally difficult to ascertain how well they are functioning in an uncomfortably polite or constantly pressured relationship. A more professional attitude toward the administration of higher education, wherein one acknowledges room to learn even where significant expertise exists already, allows both board members and their employees to improve performance without the implied threat of admitting weakness. Those who possess the power to appoint and to remove presidents must learn to appreciate a variety of academic administrative subtleties. The clearer the expectations of interest groups interacting with the president, the greater the possibility for reducing the gap between those expectations and the actual demands upon that office.

At some of our best colleges and universities, the myth prevails that substantial confidence in the president must be combined with or reflected by a distant, automatically supportive board. Some regents still believe their finest contribution to an institution is to support a president, unequivocally, just as some presidents still insist that an informed board member usually becomes a troublesome one. We work in an environment of financial constraints, tensions in educational assumptions, and pressures of public accountability. Trustees can learn through a more formal evaluation process to comprehend and therefore to protect a president's interests when correct decisions are nonetheless unpopular ones. In such a condition of mutual respect, where institutional problems are dealt with in a relatively calm, public manner, support can be bestowed upon the president without compromising ultimate board responsibility.

To the President. It has been noted that academic leadership responsibilities are considerably more involved than they are perceived by the general public or even can be suggested by a common pattern of assessment criteria. Because too many members of governing boards tend to base their evaluation of executive leadership on unidimensional perceptions of the presidential role, it is essential to establish opportunities for elaboration upon the actual complexity of their position. The difficult position in which an executive can suddenly be placed due to a capricious environment can be transformed into a climate wherein performance goals and trustee attitudes are continuously clarified.

The fundamental credibility of the administrative process itself can be substantially enhanced if the principal administrator of a campus personally demonstrates the ability of his or her institution to address management problems and to accomplish required changes as they become evident. Such credibility also will influence the relationship between a president and a governing board. Given the nature of most searches for chief executive officers, it is difficult for candidates to confront candidly any gap between the board's expressed expectations and his or her own expertise. Someone under consideration may sense that the board's requirements are unrealistic, that they do not actually fit the conditions at that institution, or even that it is unreasonable to expect anyone, upon entering that position, to have the entire range of talents the search committee has stipulated. Yet, it is extremely difficult to confront honestly those areas of "perceived inadequacy." Presidents with a number of years already in office, and confident that their employers wish continued service, usually are far more willing to work with a board in identifying areas where changing priorities require different skills and experience on their staffs.

Such an exchange between the board and the president also can extend the tenure of an individual at a time when presidents are appointed at an earlier age, are serving shorter terms, and therefore are creating crises of transition at many institutions. The evaluation process has been able to prolong productive stay in office by allowing a president and a governing board to refine their priorities and improve their performance in an environment that expects, indeed encourages, changing emphases. There have been special circumstances wherein assessment has enabled the board and a president to reach mutually agreeable conditions for the transition to a new chief executive. At times, it has allowed a president to indicate to the governing board that although its members remain confident in his or her performance, changing working conditions make the position less desirable for this particular individual.

To Other Principal Administrators. An important step toward clarity—and thus toward stronger institutional leadership and operations—is for the governing board, acting in partnership with the president, to adopt a formal assessment process that focuses on the quality of university management. Such a commitment at the highest levels of administration cannot help but influence the interaction throughout other administrative areas. This awareness of assessment issues should not only be evident during a search deliberation but should also be demonstrated at regular intervals during an administrator's tenure. Periodic systematic review can offer a clearer perspective toward the countless challenges confronting major executives, will result in a calmer context for responding to those challenges, and will establish a sounder basis for subsequent searches whenever they are required. Ad hoc or crisis-generated assessment cannot provide these benefits.

Higher education has recognized for some time important distinctions between the administration of academic programs and the management of support areas for those programs. Not only are responsibilities significantly different between those areas, but career patterns for potential administrators in each are fundamentally different. Academic administrators frequently come to the department head or dean position relatively inexperienced in the day-to-day burdens of managing a department or college. They have developed superb skills in teaching, curriculum development, scholarship, and the facilitation of research projects. Nonetheless, once they become academic administrators, they are expected to demonstrate a range of talents they have exercised rarely, if at all, in earlier positions. As constituencies throughout the institution exert pressure for systematic evaluation—in part because their programs and personnel are coming under more intense scrutiny—these academic officers must have the opportunity to sharpen their skills while remaining publicly accountable. Their security and their pleasure in office rest critically upon a sensitive assessment procedure. In fact, the success of their superiors rests just as crucially on a process that attracts rather than deters potential quality administrators.

Just as with the governing board, the evaluation of college administrators is as vital to the education of an *employer* as it is to the strengthening of *employee* performance. The disclosure of leadership strategies available to university executives allows higher-level administrators to learn far more about the actual challenges facing their division while it educates a multitude of publics as to the complexities of the whole institution. Colleges and universities can gather the data required to anticipate changes in values at their institution or within their constituencies. The impact of administrative performance upon institutional effectiveness can be more sensitively assessed. Moreover, the process will help tie administrative implementation more directly to the formulation of organizational policy and thereby close dangerous gaps between college goals and management strategies. A well-formulated evaluation program will create new channels of communication. Where trust exists, it will be strengthened; and where skepticism reigns, the possibility of good faith and mutual assistance can be constructively tested.

An Exploration of Evaluation Objectives

In 1973, leaders of the University of Illinois expressed substantial interest in the values of administrative assessment. The campuses of the university had begun extensive projects of program evaluation; and in an era of increased public scrutiny, it seemed undesirable to hold administrators apart from a general review of institutional progress. As academic vice-president of the system and as someone who was working nationally on issues of chief executive-board assessment, I was asked to serve on a task force to explore the relative merits of an administrative evaluation program. In fact, one question asked in the charge was whether universitywide policies would be helpful or detrimental to the achievement of our objectives.

The report that finally emerged focused upon major substantive issues: Were the benefits theoretically derived from a formal evaluation process sufficient to outweigh the inevitable costs in time and resources? Would first-rate candidates for administrative positions be disenchanted by a systematic evaluation process? Could constituencies be involved in an assessment without risking values of confidentiality and professional development? Based upon lengthy deliberations, the committee concluded that a formal approach would benefit the institution. They recommended the following:

1. The university should adopt the practice of regularly evaluating academic administrators through a formally administered system.
2. This practice should be subsequently codified through appropriate revisions of the university statutes.
3. Overall implementation and coordination of the plan should be the specific responsibility of an appropriate officer at the system level.

The study group determined its focus had to be those administrators directly responsible for academic units or programs. This category was determined to range from department heads through deans and vice-chancellors—those executives whose primary responsibility was the academic well-being of the university. The group also concluded that, although there is a symbiotic relationship between an administrator and the unit administered, it is possible to evaluate each separately while recognizing the closeness of the interaction.

The following values were suggested for a formal administrative assessment program:

1. Improve the performance of an executive and consequently of the unit administered.
2. Make visible to each party concerned the interests and understanding of the others.
3. Improve the credibility of the administrative process.
4. Provide decision makers with the necessary information for rewarding, strengthening, or even changing those administrators who were responsible to them.

On balance, even though the study group recognized the dangerous loss of credibility if an evaluation process was poorly structured, developed excessive expectations, or overwhelmed its participants with time and energy demands, it nonetheless believed benefits derived substantially outweighed potential costs.

At Illinois, a pilot project was established under the direction of a well-known senior member of the faculty who has since assumed the system's academic vice-presidency. The project employed "fact-finding groups" composed primarily of faculty to discover fact and generate opinion for use by subordinate administrators. Numerous elements of group composition and conduct were compared and evaluated during this period of trial implementation of the views expressed by the earlier study group. The university is now attempting to bring that intense experience to bear on administrator evaluations done as part of program reviews and to create there a formative dimension.

Essential Components of an Evaluation Program

Once a governing board or a principal administrator decides to establish an evaluation process, there is a range of options available for structuring it. Those alternatives actually fall along a continuum extending from a relatively simple, closed, employer-focused assessment that concentrates almost exclusively upon an individual under analysis to a comprehensive, public, constituency-involved assessment that explores fundamental governance issues.

At each administrative level, analogous alternatives are available. The unstructured informal process based upon self-directed evaluation remains quite common. A more-structured, documented procedure, with more formal inquiries and evaluators, has been introduced recently at a number of institutions. "Rating scales" are used by supervisors or subordinates to assess individual performance. Categories for evaluation are more frequently discussed at the time of initial appointment, and such an exchange allows for a smoother flowing assessment whenever it is implemented.

Most administrators still prefer the traditional confidential interview with their supervisor. Such a preference is understandable, given the vulnerabilities created by a more-public evaluation and the nebulous state of the assessment art itself. We have learned, however, that considering more extensive sources of information and involving a limited number of relevant constituencies can provide a review that teaches instead of threatens an administrator.

Whatever the format selected for a particular evaluation, there are components of the process that remain critical throughout the spectrum of alternative models. Each institution represents a significantly different educational and political context, and every administrative level requires careful adjustment; but the existence of a common framework allows a college or any unit to develop its own context while learning from others' experience.

In almost every instance, a review should begin with a statement from the administrator being assessed. This document should spell out his or her objectives on assuming office and then analyze progress toward their achievement. Such an analysis provides an opportunity for the administrator to present a personal view of the leadership function, to comment upon his or her own working style, and then to analyze how both of these relate to the perceived needs of the institution or division. It is entirely appropriate that the individual being evaluated serve as the initiator for the process and then remain a pivotal figure as it unfolds.

As an example, when a chief executive officer is under review, the original statement should include the following:

1. expectations and objectives upon assuming office, including comments on the presidential search process
2. assessment of success within the context of those initial objectives
3. adequacy of those first expectations, based upon present knowledge
4. principal issues presently confronting the presidential office
5. a revision of original objectives in response to those issues
6. attitudes toward the nature of academic institutional leadership, based upon past as well as present experience
7. a comparison of present responsibilities and working style with those in earlier executive roles
8. suggestions concerning those "significant others" whose response to the statement would be most helpful if drawn within the evaluation process and concerning the types of response most useful to the president

At other administrative levels, a similar document can be prepared by making those issues more directly relevant to the academic or administrative unit governed. While the statement is being prepared, the evaluator should be establishing a frame of reference. The problems and prospects of the unit under review should be scrutinized prior to determining the specific context. An elaborate self-study is not required. Governing boards, president, or principal administrators can examine major current or potential problems and identify the type of talents required to address them. Many institutions and programs are without such an analysis when the assessment begins. In those cases, the administrators in charge of an evaluation must spend some time discussing the highest-priority items currently confronting any administrator of that particular program.

Criteria. This approach to priorities allows the evaluation of administrative performance to lay a foundation for more effective planning and for the utilization of institutional research as support rather than as a substitute for decision making. However, if such an orientation for planning and institutional research is desired, there must be an effective linkage between the analysis of current priorities and the establishment of criteria for the evaluation. The danger of using any simplified format for criteria is that various levels of administration require different approaches to performance expectations. *Criteria that can be applied to any administrative position inevitably become so general they are virtually empty of useful meaning.* But a unique set of questions cannot be designed for each administrative position without entailing a severe time commitment; indeed, such a design inevitably leads to dubious debates regarding the "ideal" department chairperson or collegiate dean.

Some campus task forces, dismayed by such prospects, have patterned their evaluation recommendations after programs designed at other institutions, thereby extrapolating lessons from other contexts and transforming them for local circumstances. Such exchanges have increased during the past years and in fact lead to chapters such as this one. However, there are general guidelines that can remain under consideration whatever particular position is being reviewed. To remain meaningful, criteria should

1. relate to those high-priority tasks identified at the time of administrative search and appointment
2. reflect any changes since adoption of primary objectives and any new priority goals in the identification of administrative responsibility (This mutual determination of current priorities protects an administrator against the arbitrary application of new criteria while it educates the evaluator regarding any shifts in management objectives.)
3. take account of unpredictable or quickly altered factors (Evaluators must try to be as conscious as possible of their own assumptions or biases in rapidly changing circumstances.)
4. serve as a framework for generating quality-oriented replies (They should be used as a guide for talking about performance and never be applied as a report card that substitutes for judgment.)
5. be refined systematically until the evaluator is relatively certain they are both comprehensive and representative for a particular review (Different constituencies will provide valuable suggestions regarding the ultimate criteria, but the individual in charge must establish those standards that will constitute the evaluative framework.)
6. provide information useful to the ultimate evaluators by asking questions that can be legitimately answered

Information. At the stage of the assessment process when criteria have been refined, the evaluator must begin to gather background materials for informed judgments. Decisions must be made regarding the range and intensity of constituency involvement. Those ultimately responsible for reaching evaluative conclusions must hear responses to their criteria. The tone of an assessment often will be set by the attitude of the questioner, for example, asking whether the program has been improved rather than seeking a list of detailed complaints. Regardless of how limited or how broadly based their request for information is, in almost every instance, survey instruments will turn out to be far less important than sophisticated interview procedures.

Opinion polls and questionnaires that lead to popularity contests or require objective quantification should be avoided whenever possible. Although some types of statistics will be of interest, they will inevitably be less useful than informal, qualitative responses and candid personal impressions. Ultimately, an evaluator will do more listening than measuring. Even at the departmental level, leadership at an academic institution rests more crucially on intangible interpersonal skills than upon quantifiable products. Information must be gathered and judgments made based upon it. However, the ability to ask the right questions and to gauge the qualitative nature of responses must be one of the primary skills required for any coordinator of an administrative assessment.

Finally, a report must be prepared. Although, like the criteria themselves, the format as well as the content will differ substantially, depending upon administrative level and institutional context, there are basic components that indicate the type of information desired. Each institution will have to determine how extensive such a report should be, how widely it will be distributed, and how publicly it will be discussed. Such decisions must be reached before the evaluation begins and will rest crucially upon the principles of confidentiality and academic community assumed to be most vital by the institution's administration.

Evaluation at Public Urban Universities*

In order to test many of the previously discussed assumptions in preparation for this discussion and, more crucially, in order to design an administrative evaluation program for the central campus of the University of Houston, an inquiry was made recently to members of the "Urban 13" regarding their current administrative assessment practices.** We focused almost exclusively upon campus-level offices and described our own efforts to each institution while requesting assistance based upon their review experiences. The request sought perspectives that might prove useful in establishing an equitable system dedicated to the in-service improvement of administrative performance.

The responses were unanimous regarding the need for acceptable procedures to evaluate administrative personnel and stressed the difficulties of establishing such procedures. Moreover, anxiety that in the rush toward action, inadequate attention would be given to the sensitive nature of the process was often expressed. Frequently, respondents emphasized that plans had to be formulated carefully and reviewed extensively in order to avoid destructive misunderstandings. In addition, even those not currently planning such programs agreed that although the risks were great, the benefits would be even greater.

All respondents expressed great interest in the project, although several

*My deep gratitude goes to Chel Lipshultz for assisting with this and other sections.

**The composition of these metropolitan institutions varies least where control is concerned: Only one is independent and private. All others are state, state-related, or state-local campuses. Although student enrollment ranges from a low of 7,700 to a high of 35,600, the geographic location has a narrower spread. Only ten states are involved, most of which are located in the northern sector of the country, a small number in the Midwest, and only one in the sunbelt. Among the members of the Urban 13 are: University of Illinois, Chicago Circle; City College of the City University of New York; University of Missouri, Kansas City; University of Missouri, St. Louis; The Cleveland State University; Wayne State University; University of Cincinnati; Temple University; University of Pittsburgh; University of Massachusetts at Boston.

institutions had no evaluation processes at this time and were contemplating none. One reply described a "well-qualified process for the evaluation of deans and chairpersons that was conducted annually but no process for those at presidents or vice-presidential evaluation." They admitted such a step was under serious consideration. Another respondent stated that the institution had a "scheme" for the evaluation of administrators. It was called a scheme because "it was less than it should be and left a great deal to be desired." That chief executive officer urged that all evaluations start with the definition of an administrator's role based upon an agreement with other constituencies. This carefully articulated definition would serve in turn as a basis for their limited assessment endeavors. They had devised an instrument for collecting data but learned it did not produce the expected results. Interestingly, they were reluctant at this point to devote the additional resources deemed necessary to take that effort any further. Even more interesting, the structured instrument they described as being inadequate for their objectives was being utilized currently at three other institutions.

These three institutions were using that traditional evaluative instrument—a rating scale—as a "feedback or developmental tool." Sample items listed on the scale include knowledge, capacity, dependability, adaptability, interpersonal relationships, resourcefulness, and commitment to professional growth. At some institutions, the scale was modified to assess the quality of relationships between an administrator and his or her supervisors. During the past six months, one institution further extended the rating scale so that it requested the names of individuals with whom an administrator regularly interacted both on the campus and at the system level. This procedure led to an additional dimension involving an unstructured narrative appraisal. This technique asks the evaluator to write a page or so describing the administrator's activities over a specific period of time. Criteria are implied in the essay, although in some instances, they are stipulated in the original request for information.

The administration at another urban institution expressed satisfaction with its "well-worked-out system." In 1976, they had established an ad hoc committee of their faculty senate, which issued a report calling for the implementation of an ongoing administration evaluation program. During the 1976–77 academic year, that report was reviewed by a standing senate committee. Finally, a policy assumption that pertained to the president, the vice-president, the dean, and their supporting staffs emerged:

> In order to assure maximum administrative efficiency, university administrators require information about their performance in order to guide and improve future action. . . . An evaluation and guidance plan for all university administrators above the department chairperson shall be established and implemented.
>
> Their evaluation is based upon the following characteristics:
>
> 1. The objectives of an evaluation program should be clearly stated and known by everyone concerned.
> 2. The policies and procedures of a program should reflect current research on evaluation.
> 3. The criteria by which each person will be evaluated should be known and agreed upon.

4. The policies and procedures should be cooperatively planned and carried out to reflect the involvement of all levels of administration.
5. The evaluative process should give consideration to *the* validity and reliability of administrative objectives. This should concern the degree to which the criteria are related to the needs and conditions and the degree to which several evaluations occur.
6. The evaluation should be developmental and diagnostic rather than judgmental.
7. Self-evaluation should be included in the process.
8. Self-image and self-respect should be maintained and enhanced by the process.
9. The process should provide for clear, personal, and constructive feedback.
10. The program should include in-service training for everyone.
11. The program should be reviewed as a process of learning and developing.

In statements that echo what we have learned from other universities, this institution's specifications insisted that performance evaluation:

1. is the direct responsibility of the administrator's immediate supervisor with the appropriate consultation of peers and affected constituencies at stated intervals
2. for any position, must be based on the particular institutional goals and objectives for the involved unit
3. for any position, must be based on a written position description specifying the objectives and functions of that position
4. must be based on an annualized set of objectives set jointly by the administrator and his or her immediate supervisor within the framework of unit objectives as recommended by the appropriate policy board
5. shall take place annually with consulted input to be included at five-year intervals

Several colleges were implementing evaluation programs for their chief executive officers but had yet to approach administrators at other levels. They suggested that putting such a program in place at the top would provide credibility at other administrative levels while establishing a focused pilot project to test evaluation assumptions. One very large institution prepared assessment guidelines for its chief executive officer to "facilitate the exercise of the board's responsibilities for the evaluation, and assist the chancellor and the president to become more effective as chief executive officers." The evaluations will also serve other functions. They will "provide a mechanism for publicly demonstrating the university concern about the quality of its constituent colleges and its desire for accountability of its chief administrative officers. The evaluations will also allow the university a formal opportunity to clarify its own sense of mission and to communicate that mission more effectively to the colleges and to the community at large."

In summary, our survey uncovered no comprehensive assessment programs consistently applied at the public urban institutions. Although there was considerable interest in the subject, some were watching carefully before they moved into this sensitive area. Others had rather detailed reviews for their chief executives; some had very specific evaluation instruments at the departmental level but nothing at all for the college or the campus. Nevertheless, we detected a consistent sense of urgency based upon a general constituency expectation for administrative accountability. Although several respondents insisted the evaluation reply to calls for accountability was a dangerous fad, almost everyone agreed a review candidly directed toward the improvement of administrative performance could make a substantial contribution to the quality and stability of their institution.

Role of Planning and Institutional Research

I have emphasized that a review process should begin with a statement from the individual being evaluated that describes his or her objectives upon assuming office and then should analyze progress toward their achievement. This initiation allows the evaluatee to set the tone of the review. It also provides an opportunity for that administrator to present a personal view of the management function and to speak candidly about his or her aspirations, needs, and problems. As that statement is being prepared, the employer is establishing the evaluation framework. When both context and initial document are ready, the criteria can be specified and relevant information can be gathered. It is in structuring the process and in collecting the material that leads to informed judgments that an office of planning and institutional research can be most important. Its members can prepare the necessary documentation, design the appropriate evaluation model, and consult with relevant constituencies regarding the type of information desired.

An institutional researcher will have the skills required to collect, study, and interpret data. The planning and research staff can provide information to the governing board and to other administrators implementing an evaluation process. The use of analytical experts is a management strategy that reduces cost, expedites procedures, and supplies understandable information to those who must interpret and depend upon it. Most employees can produce stacks of qualitative data and spew forth mounds of computer-based statistics; but experienced planners and institutional researchers can translate data into usable information. Timely and sophisticated background material cannot replace informed, experienced judgment. It can, however, complement common sense and reduce those extraneous burdens that confuse issues or misuse time required for sophisticated analysis.

An office of planning and institutional research can review factors such as credibility of source and reliability and validity of information. Its staff can transform raw materials into accurate information that is easy to understand. When so much emphasis is placed upon the potential dangers of an unstructured evaluation, the office of institutional planning and research can design mechanisms that provide balance between required insights and privileged attitudes.

During any evaluation, there is a natural inclination toward rumor and anxiety. A premium must be placed on expeditious and sensitively shaped re-

views. The world is increasingly litigious; contracts and formal agreements govern more and more of our activities. A college administrator cannot survive on
rules alone; regulations cannot replace judgments. Administrative evaluation for
our colleges and universities must underplay contract renewal or hire-fire
negotiations. It must emphasize the development of administrative skills. Those
contemplating such programs must constantly reiterate the need for information, caringly delivered so service to the institution can be enhanced. These values are far more likely to be achieved if a limited but talented office of institutional planning and research plays a major role in establishing the assessment
process.

Conclusion

"Above all, the absorption with short-run, specifiable goals may dilute attention to the likely outcome of a long and complex process of leadership-
fellowship interaction. Attention may continue to center in the predictable, visible matters of technique and process and personality rather than in the prospects
and future of fundamental, substantive alterations in people's lives and welfare
and opportunities—of real change. Political leadership, however, can be defined
only in terms of, and to the extent of the realization of, purposeful, substantive
change in the conditions of people's lives. The ultimate test of practical leadership is the realization of intended, real change that meets people's enduring
needs" (Burns, 1978, p. 461). There is a growing trend toward the professionalization of academic administration. That development is based in large measure
upon the desire to allow university leaders to provide "intended, real change that
meets people's enduring needs." Governing boards, chief executive officers, and
faculty-based search committees are all recognizing the requirement for carefully trained and specially talented men and women to administer our nation's
colleges and universities. Yet career ladders for academic leaders are undefined
at best. There is little credible preparation available for these executive-
managerial positions. We must help our administrators do better and work more
happily; but we cannot establish—in the name of professional development—
programs that place them in even more precarious or pressured positions.

The selection and, of equal importance, the retention of quality administrators for higher education are more likely to be achieved successfully when
employers are willing to analyze candidly what they are asking of their administrative employees (both as candidates and as incumbents). An appropriate
assessment program must take into account diverse and shifting factors of responsibility. A systematic evaluation promising in-service improvement of performance can provide a credible mechanism for strengthening administrative
skills. The refinement of criteria, the consultation with relevant constituencies,
and the education of ultimate employers can all help create an environment
far more conducive to courageous and imaginative leadership.

The major issue confronting higher education today is the recruitment of
first-rate people. Professional evaluation programs shaped by caring administrators committed to educational values can reinforce responsible performance.
The danger is that some of our finest people will be driven away by crude assessment devices. A more sophisticated evaluation provides everyone involved
with a finer understanding of the multifaceted forces within which a president

and his or her administrative team must work. No one denies we are responsible to a variety of publics. No one insists we can carry out our administrative responsibilities without ever learning how well we are doing or what might help to make us better. The nature of our professional commitments, and the quality of our contributions to the institutions we serve, will be markedly improved if those around us understand what we do and are taught how to help.

Bibliographical Essay

Although there are an increased number of articles addressed to the general problems of institutional leadership and administrative evaluation, the material available is still painfully sparse. *Developing and Evaluating Administrative Leadership* (Fisher, 1978) offers the best collection of perspectives in one volume, and Fisher has done an excellent job of providing both introduction and conclusion to the articles. He emphasizes that in contrast to the commitment higher education gives to the evaluation and development of its faculty, there has been far less undertaken in the area of assessment regarding the enhancement of professional administrative performance.

My own work has focused upon the assessment of chief executive officers in both educational and corporate settings. With the publication of Jossey-Bass' *Handbook of College and University Trusteeship,* and the Association of Governing Boards' text on presidential evaluation, I have placed in print a concise update of my earlier book.

The best strategy for learning about administrative evaluation further along the hierarchy is to contact institutions directly. The Urban 13 institutions referred to in this article have been experimenting with evaluation strategies for almost a decade. Other major public and private institutions have available documents that describe their efforts and comment upon specific pilot projects. As summary documents, John Nason's two recent texts for the Association of Governing Boards are superb.

Finally, the finest analysts of the educational scene in general, such as Clark Kerr (1964, 1970) and David Riesman, offer within broader surveys of the college and university landscape valuable insights into the selection and retention of administrative personnel.

References

Anderson, G. L. *The Evaluation of Academic Administrators: Principles, Processes, and Outcomes.* University Park: Pennsylvania State University Press, 1975.

Burns, J. M. *Leadership.* New York: Harper & Row, 1978.

Fisher, C. F. "The Evaluation and Development of College and University Administrators." ERIC/Higher Education Research Currents. Washington, D.C.: American Association for Higher Education, 1977. (ERIC ED No. 136 707; ED No. 139 363.)

Fisher, C. F. (Ed.). *New Directions for Higher Education: Developing and Evaluating Administrative Leadership,* no. 22. San Francisco: Jossey-Bass, 1978.

Kauffman, J. F. "Presidential Assessment and Development." In C. F. Fisher (Ed.), *New Directions for Higher Education: Developing and Evaluating Administrative Leadership,* no. 22. San Francisco: Jossey-Bass, 1978.

Kerr, C. *The Uses of the University.* Cambridge, Mass.: Harvard University Press, 1964.

Kerr, C. "Presidential Discontent." In D. C. Nichols (Ed.), *Perspectives on Campus Tensions: Papers Prepared for the Special Committee on Campus Tensions.* Washington, D.C.: American Council on Education, 1970.

Munitz, B. *Leadership in Colleges and Universities: Assessment and Search.* Oakbrook, Ill.: Johnson Associates, Inc., 1977.

Munitz, B. "Strengthening Institutional Leadership." In C. F. Fisher (Ed.), *New Directions for Higher Education: Developing and Evaluating Administrative Leadership,* no. 22. San Francisco: Jossey-Bass, 1978.

Munitz, B. "Renewing Presidential Leadership." In R. T. Ingram (Ed.), *Handbook of College and University Trusteeship.* San Francisco: Jossey-Bass, 1980.

Nason, J. *Presidential Search.* Washington, D.C.: Association of Governing Boards, 1979.

Nason, J. *Presidential Assessment.* Washington, D.C.: Association of Governing Boards, 1980.

Riesman, D. *Constraint and Variety in American Education.* Lincoln: University of Nebraska Press, 1958.

25

John D. Millett

Relating to
Governance and
Leadership

In this chapter, the meaning of the concepts of governance and leadership is of critical importance. Individuals concerned with the operation of colleges and universities hold quite different definitions of these terms and from their different conceptions would draw different conclusions from the chapter without a definition of both words as used here.

Governance

Governance is the act of decision making about institutional purposes (mission), about basic policies, about program objectives, and about resource allocation. There has been a substantial amount of writing about college and university governance since the discussion of this subject was in large part initiated by John J. Corson in 1960. I have reviewed this discussion at some length elsewhere

(1978) and need not repeat it here; but developments in academic governance since 1960 do warrant review here in light of their implications for institutional research and planning.

The formal authority for campus decision making has been vested in boards of trustees, sometimes designated as a board of regents or as a board of directors. As is well known, these boards are almost always made up of members who serve part-time, with a general rather than a professional interest in higher education. The board of trustees of a private college or university is the voice of a public conscience concerned with the performance of the campus; it is also a device of governance interposed between state government on the one hand and campus operations on the other hand.

In general, boards of trustees of private colleges and universities serve a single institution with a single campus location. This observation is simply one way of pointing out that most private colleges and universities have not established branch campuses. The prevailing pattern in publicly sponsored higher education is the multicampus governing board, a board of trustees with the authority of governance over several campuses rather than one. In twenty-one states all senior institutions are governed by a single statewide board of trustees. In another twenty-two states there are two or more multicampus systems of senior colleges and universities. Only in seven states do all senior state universities have a board of trustees with governing authority restricted to a single institution. In this enumeration I omit community colleges, technical institutions, and two-year state university branches.

I believe that the relative merits, or advantages and disadvantages, of the multicampus state university governing board versus the single-campus state university governing board have not had the study or debate the subject deserves. I do not doubt the need for a state board of higher education, but do question whether the state board of higher education must also be a statewide governing board. However, I can appreciate the need or desirability for multicampus governing boards in public higher education.

Let us take for illustration the structure of teachers colleges that developed in so many states. When the great expansion of secondary education took place in America roughly between 1880 and 1920, there was a substantial need for secondary school teachers. And the flowering of primary education in these same years led to efforts to professionalize school teaching. As a result many state boards of education created teachers colleges, or asked state legislatures to authorize teachers colleges, in order to staff the elementary-secondary educational endeavor with professionally educated teachers.

The general disposition of state legislators was to approve the location of teachers colleges at various places throughout a state. In turn, many if not all of these teachers colleges tended to become "general purpose" state colleges and state universities after 1945. Before 1940 in many states these teachers colleges were "governed" by the state board of education. In the years after 1945 the change of purpose within these colleges was signified by removing the authority of governance from the state board of education and by substituting a new multicampus governing board.

The multicampus governing board has certain advantages. It lessens the coordinating burden of a state board of higher education. It is in a position to order the introduction or elimination of various instructional programs in accordance with state needs. It is in a position to require some desirable degree of cooperation or collaboration among state universities and to establish uniformities in the utilization of income on various campuses.

The multicampus governing board also has certain disadvantages. Inherently it cannot give the same attention to the unique characteristics of a particular campus as does the single-campus governing board. The multicampus governing board may develop an extensive and expensive bureaucracy separate from a campus setting. It may delegate considerable management authority to the campus president and give   inadequate consideration in governance matters to faculty and student points of view. It may establish uniform requirements of campus behavior where differences in behavioral patterns might be more appropriate, and may tend to be more responsive to political pressures than the single-campus governing board.

An additional set of advantages and disadvantages may be formulated for the statewide governing board. Such a board may be more successful in developing a planning, coordinating, and budgeting authority than a state board of higher education lacking governance authority. Such a board may better translate political requirements into state university operations than a single-campus governing board. In contrast, a statewide governing board that places its political autonomy ahead of political representation may alienate governors and legislators. And a statewide governing board is in a poor if not impossible position when it comes to developing a concern for the fate of private colleges and universities within the state.

Whatever the merits and deficiencies of the multicampus governing board and the statewide governing board, the fact remains that more state universities are governed by multicampus statewide governing boards than by single-campus governing boards. In consequence, any discussion of the impact of governance upon state universities must necessarily draw a distinction between two kinds of governance structure: a multicampus governing structure and a single-campus governing structure.

There are two other complexities that must be acknowledged in the governance arrangements for public higher education. One is the accommodation of a faculty and of a student role in governance. This complexity is evident in the trend toward increased state government involvement and even decision making about campus problems. This is a matter of external structure and process in higher education governance.

During the late 1960s and early 1970s some governors and legislatures—notably in Florida, North Carolina, Utah, West Virginia, and Wisconsin—declared a preference for the statewide governing board over a state board of higher education with planning and budget authority only. These political leaders saw the statewide governing board as more likely to impose controls and limitations upon state universities and better able to ensure campus (and presidential) response to state directives. The possible deficiencies of the statewide board were overlooked in the expectation of increased political accountability on the part of state higher education.

But even where a statewide governing board was not advocated or installed, state governments proceeded to establish state boards of higher education with authority to plan, coordinate, and develop budgets for public higher education institutions. In either arrangement, state governments insisted upon a new voice in determining the tuition charges to students, in fixing desirable workload standards for faculty members, in deciding the need for new residence halls to house students, in establishing new instructional programs (as in medicine and in law), in fixing minimum and maximum desirable campus enrollment, in approving standards of admission, in reviewing institutional utilization of all income resources, and in maintaining campus law and order.

In other words, campus governance found more and more decision-making authority being moved from the campus to the level of state government. This transfer was probably inevitable given two or three major circumstances: the continued demand of state universities for greater support from the tax resources of the state; the increased importance of all higher education and of public higher education in meeting an expanding enrollment demand; and the popular perception that higher education services (instruction, research, and public service) were instrumental in meeting state goals for economic development and in satisfying the labor market demand for educated talent. There was no way that state universities could receive greatly increased state expenditure support, could satisfy rising expectations of individual benefit to be derived from higher education, and could respond to economic aspirations without becoming more politically involved with state governments. The price of state university affluence and importance within a state was some loss of campus autonomy in planning and in decision making.

A statewide governing board or a state board of higher education may be assigned a role in advising governors and legislators about state needs in higher education service. Neither the statewide governing board nor the state board of higher education can proceed to meet these needs independent of governors and legislatures. Boards of higher education have no authority to levy taxes or to appropriate funds for the support of state universities. Only governors and state legislatures can provide tax resources for state universities, thus the power to support has become increasingly the power to govern.

Moreover, governors and state legislatures have begun more and more to look to their own staffs for advice and assistance on matters of higher education. Increasingly one encounters among governors and legislatures some agreement about the problem areas which they perceive to need some kind of resolution. These problem areas are identified as including: (1) an apparent duplication of state institutions serving the same general area of a state and an apparent duplication of instructional programs throughout the state; (2) an inefficient use of state government funds by public colleges and universities; (3) a deterioration in the quality standards of expected student performance within public colleges and universities; (4) a growing competition among public colleges and universities in offering off-campus instructional programs.

To the extent that these and similar problems appear to be inadequately or only partially addressed by statewide governing boards and by state boards of higher education, governors and legislatures will undertake to find answers for themselves, often with the assistance of executive and legislative staff and occasionally with the advice of consultants. There is no doubt about the fact that the governance of public higher education has tended to become increasingly governance by state government rather than by a governing board.

For the private sector, which enrolls about 22 percent of all students today but spends nearly 33 percent of the expenditures by all colleges and universities, these complexities of governance involving state governors and state legislatures do not exist in quite the same fashion. Yet privately sponsored colleges and universities cannot afford to be indifferent to state government either. Although only one state government (New York) exercises substantial authority over the instructional programs of private colleges and universities, all private institutions have various concerns with state government actions in the field of higher education. These various concerns include: (1) the location of public colleges and universities in such a way as particularly to compete with private institutions; (2) the considerable gap in tuition charges between public and private institutions which may encourage student enrollment in the public sector; (3) the reality or expectation of state government support of financial assistance to students, some of whom are enrolled in private institutions; (4) the reality or expectation of state government subsidy to private institutions, as in medical education programs and, in some instances, other instructional programs; (5) the reality or expectation of state government assistance in borrowing funds for capital construction.

Private colleges and universities cannot plan their own purposes, policies, programs, and financing without careful attention to the possible impact of current or possible state government actions. Private colleges and universities are involved in state politics even as are public colleges and universities. The private sector of higher education is no longer master of its own destiny but must continually be alert to and concerned with state government planning and decision making.

It is scarcely necessary to observe that considerable authority of governance is now being exercised also by the federal government and by federal government agencies. The growth of this authority has been notable ever since the enactment of the National Defense Education Act of 1958. Moreover, this authority of governance tends to be applicable equally to public and private colleges and universities. From federal government interest in the support of research and in the support of student financial access to higher education the federal interest has expanded to include nondiscrimination and affirmative action requirements, retirement and pension arrangements, occupational health and safety, access for the handicapped, and control of environmental pollution. Neither public nor private institutions of higher education are exempt from these federal government restrictions upon institutional governance. And in the instance of private colleges and universities, the National Labor Relations Board has expanded its jurisdiction to include collective bargaining procedures for any and all categories of personnel other than some vaguely defined management group. I believe this is a concept appropriate to business establishments but singularly inappropriate for higher education.

Internal Governance

The 1960s was more than a time of troubles in academic government; it was a decade of experimentation in restructuring the decision-making processes on many campuses. Corson (1960) postulated a concept of "organizational dualism" as characteristic of college and university decision making. He identified this dualism as consisting of faculty decision making and administration decision making. In matters of academic affairs, faculty members, through a general faculty or a representative faculty senate, had considerable if not final authority upon such questions as degree programs, degree requirements, course offerings, faculty personnel actions, admission standards, the academic calendar, and student conduct regulations. But matters of fund raising, public relations, campus planning, enrollment objectives, budgeting, student services, auxiliary enterprises, and academic support tended to be resolved by administrative action or by governing board action upon the recommendation of the president.

This organizational dualism broke down during the 1960s in the face of student disruption and campus conflict, which eventually led to the tragic death of students at Kent State and Jackson State. Many efforts were made in that decade to develop faculty and student participation in the decision-making process; they eventuated in action by the governing board. Without reviewing either the history or the specific composition of the various structures developed in the 1960s, I note that on many campuses, some kind of institutionwide senate or council brought together administrators, professional staff, faculty members, and students in the process of decision making. As a consequence, in planning and in making recommendations to the governing board, presidents generally have had to seek faculty and student advice prior to action by the board.

One of the ironies of our day, however, is the fear of planning within colleges and universities. When campus planning was concerned with enrollment growth, program expansion, increased resources, and new construction, planning was generally accepted by faculty members, students, and staff groups. But today planning is perceived as concerned with reduction of enrollment, retrenchment of programs, reallocation of resources, and restrictions on space. As a consequence, faculty members, students, and staff tend to look upon it as a threat rather than as an opportunity for intelligent choice. Thus, for the most part, the new governance structures of faculty and students have been more accustomed to criticism than to positive action. Should departments in the arts and sciences give greater attention to career objectives in their programs? The immediate response of faculty members has generally been negative, even though enrollments in these programs may be declining. Should instructional resources allocated in the past to teacher education be redistributed to nursing education or instruction in other health professions? Should resources allocated in the past to the humanities and the social and behavioral sciences be shifted to programs in business administration? The immediate response of the threatened disciplines has been to protect their turf at all cost. Similarly, should students at public universities be asked to pay 35 percent of the cost of undergraduate instruction rather than 20 or 25 percent? And should students in private universities be asked to pay increased tuition, part of which would be devoted to financing student aid and part of which would go to financing overhead or even direct cost of faculty research? The immediate student response is likely to be hostile to either proposal. And if the students at the private institution are less vociferous in their response than those at the public campus, the explanation may be lack of information about resource use rather than lack of interest.

The campus governing board tends to act on the basis of presidential recommendation regarding such issues, provided there is some indication of internal consensus about them. The governing board is well aware, however, of the need for some degree of balance between faculty interests, student interests, and institutional necessity. The problem is not what plan may be best for the institution in the long run, but what plan will be least disruptive of campus interests in the short run. Few governing boards have the competence or the inclination to be innovative, to be experimental, to chart new courses. By their very nature, governing boards tend to conserve what is and to seek new paths only when a crisis is clearly at hand.

In addition to this problem of consensus, confusion has reigned over the responsibility of the new representative councils or senates for institutional planning. Despite the need and the wisdom of involving faculty, students, and staff in the consideration of plans, this confusion has resulted because the new governance structures and processes have not been clearly differentiated from management structures and processes.

Planning is a management process. It is necessarily a process that must eventuate in plans being submitted for action by the appropriate governance body: a faculty senate, a student senate, an institutionwide senate under delegation from the governing board, or the governing board itself. But planning must be undertaken in the first instance by managers. For instructional programs, research programs, and public service programs, these program managers are individual faculty members, academic departments and their executive officers, and deans. For student financial aid programs, the program manager may be a college dean or a central, institutionwide student financial aid officer. For academic support programs, the program manager may be either the vice-president for academic affairs or a professional officer reporting to the vice-president. For student services, the program managers are professional officers reporting usually to the vice-president for student affairs. For plant operations, the program manager is usually the superintendent of buildings and groups reporting to a vice-president for administration. For auxiliary enterprises and administrative services, the program managers are professional officers reporting usually to this same vice-president.

In addition to program plans, another set of plans is developed within a college or university. For lack of a better designation, I refer to these plans as "institutionwide" or "foundation" plans. Such plans include enrollment size, organizational structure, personnel management, facilities and campus design, financing and resource allocation (budgeting), management information, and performance evaluation. The program plans of individual program managers must necessarily fit the constraints of institutionwide planning, and this institutionwide planning is the responsibility of the executive officer of the institution.

In sum, managers plan. They plan work objectives because they also have the managerial authority and responsibility to perform the work they are expected to accomplish. They plan because they are work specialists and because they are professionally competent to develop work objectives, the appropriate work technology, and the needed work resources of personnel, equipment, facilities, and support. And they advise the governance process about desirable program objectives and institutional goals, desirable program and institutional policies, and desirable resources.

Thus, in a college or university, faculty members have a dual role: managing programs and participating in governance. I believe faculty members' management role, including that of planning, is even more vital to the effective and efficient performance of a college or university than is their governance role. If planning is a management process that leads to the governance process of decision making, the creative initiative lies with managers who plan; governing boards make final decisions about these plans. Between the planning by managers and the action of governing boards, it is highly desirable to involve faculty representatives and student representatives in discussions and the review of plans as a means of obtaining useful advice, as a means of internal communication, and as a means of achieving faculty and student participation in decision making. In addition, alumni ought to be involved in the planning review as an important constituent group of the academic community; and support staff such as technical, clerical, crafts, trade, and service personnel ought to be involved as well. I suspect collective bargaining by support staff members has been in part a response to a sense of alienation from or noninvolvement in campus planning and decision making. But to expect faculty, students, alumni, or staff in a council or senate to undertake planning is unrealistic. Their role in the internal consultative processes of governance has taken on a new importance in recent years and has a very substantial impact upon planning and upon decision making about plans. But the initiative for planning must come individually from program and institutional leaders.

Leadership

Campus *leadership* involves an external and an internal dimension. Externally, it involves being alert to the expectations of the governing board, of the state coordinating or governing board where such a board exists, of officials of state and federal governments, and of the many civic groups, associations, and bodies comprising the "public" of higher education. This external role involves the president of a public institution in a network of government relationships; the president of a private institution is apt to be involved more extensively in a network of philanthropic, or potentially philanthropic, relationships.

Internally, campus leadership is concerned with providing guidance to and maintaining communication and cooperation among the constituent groups of the institution. On the one hand, the president must remind faculty members, students, support staff, and even alumni of the social expectations brought to bear upon the campus, ranging from regulations for affirmative action, occupational health and safety, environmental protection, and access for the handicapped to demands for greater accountability, cost containment, program review, or increased productivity. On the other hand, the president must encourage constituent groups in their own aspirations for achievement while encouraging appropriate caution in their aspirations for autonomy.

The peculiar organizational circumstances that give campus leadership its particular complexity have been noted by many observers. For example, in an economic analysis of the university, Buchanan and Devletoglou (1970) observed three unique characteristics of the university as an economic enterprise: First, those who consume its product do not purchase it; second, those who produce it do not sell it; and third, those who finance the production process do not control the enterprise. Similarly, Cohen and March (1974) ascribe the ambiguous leadership role of the college president in large measure to the "organized anarchy" of the campus, which they identify as exhibiting three general properties: problematic goals, unclear technology, and fluid participation. Both descriptions suggest not only peculiarities in but limitations to administrative leadership in higher education.

Obviously, college or university leadership means more than the efforts of a single individual as chief executive. Even in the smallest of colleges, the presidency has become institutionalized and established as a collegial endeavor rather than as that of one person. The president is still extremely important as a person, but the presidential role can be performed effectively only if the president has able associates.

These presidential associates are of two principal kinds. Because there is no generally acceptable nomenclature within the descriptions of higher education organizations for these two kinds of positions, I shall designate them "executive assistants" and "managerial associates." The executive assistants are an extension of the president's own personality in the performance of institutionwide specialized efforts, including planning and budgeting, public affairs, personnel management, and legal counsel. The planning and budgeting effort includes institutionwide planning, institutional research, budgeting for current operation, capital planning (including building design), and capital budgeting. The public affairs effort includes community and legislative relations, alumni relations, development, and public information. The personnel management effort includes the design of a universitywide position classification plan and its application, as well as supervision of an affirmative action plan. And legal counsel includes advice about the numerous legal issues of university operations, from collective bargaining to faculty contracts or enforcement of student conduct regulations to the defense of suits claiming individual discrimination based upon sex, race, religion, or national origin.

The managerial associates are responsible for planning and performing separate services or units. They include the vice-presidents for academic affairs, student affairs, administration, and, where there is a medical college as part of the university, health affairs. Each of these vice-presidents supervises a number of important programs, engages in extensive program planning, lays claim to the available resources of the institution (personnel, finances, and facilities), and evaluates program performance.

The program planning of these managerial associates is concerned with the output programs and the support programs that constitute day-to-day campus operations. The program classification structure developed by the National Center for Higher Education Management Systems (NCHEMS) and now in large part incorporated into the chart of accounts recommended by the National Association of College and University Business Officers (NACUBO) provides a program basis for both planning and budgeting at the campus level.

In the first edition of the program classification structure published in 1972, the authors proposed dividing institutional programs into two categories: primary and support. Although this distinction was dropped in the revised program classification structure published in 1978, I think it is both organizationally and financially desirable. Accordingly, I suggest the principal program categories for an institution of higher education be classified as follows:

Output Programs	*Support Programs*
Instruction	Academic Support
Research	Student Services
Public Service	Plant Operations
Student Aid	Institutional Administration
Hospital Operations	Auxiliary Enterprises
Independent Operations	Transfers

These program categories embrace the full array of activities and current operating financial commitments of a college or university as an academic enterprise. Each of these program categories falls within the management oversight of one of the management associates of the president. Within these program categories are to be found the various management components of the campus: within instruction, a college of arts and sciences, a college of business administration, a college of education, a college of engineering, and so forth; within research, the various separately budgeted research centers and projects; within public service, the various activities such as clinics, public broadcasting, agricultural extension, and continuing education; within student aid, the grants to help achieve educational justice and institutional enrollment quality; within hospital operations, the management of a teaching hospital; and within independent operations, the management of separately budgeted research centers and public services operated and financed under contract with state and federal government agencies. Similarly, we might enumerate the various component support programs: libraries as a part of academic support, student aid management as a student service, utility services as a part of plant operation, fiscal service as a part of institutional administration, student residence hall management as a part of auxiliary enterprises, and debt service on academic plant as a mandatory transfer.

All these programs share several characteristics: They are essential to institutional operation; they must be carefully managed; they have specific work objectives; they lay claim to available resources (personnel, finance, and facilities); they plan; and they evaluate their work accomplishment. Program planning is an integral part of program management, and management authority is delegated to program managers as designated throughout the enterprise.

But institutionwide or institutional planning is different from program planning. Institutional planning is concerned not with the program parts but with the institution as a whole. Institutional planning involves the following kinds of planning:

- statement of mission
- enrollment plan
- organizational plan
- personnel plan
- budget plan
- facilities plan
- management information plan
- evaluation plan

These institutional plans are peculiarly the province of institutional leadership. To be sure, program managers contribute to the development of institutional plans, and eventually all program plans must become component parts of institutional plans. But institutional plans are the overarching reality of what the campus is and what the campus may become. Regardless of the ambiguities of authority and responsibility, the campus president is the only officer who can exercise campuswide leadership in planning. The governing board depends on presidential recommendation. The constituent groups and managers internally look to the president to guide their program planning and to develop institutionwide plans. No other officer can perform this leadership role.

Unfortunately, in selecting presidents, governing boards—usually with the advice of faculty, students, and alumni—often select a chief executive officer without any real insight into his or her planning competencies. Some campus presidents possess or develop abilities as planners. When I was president of Miami University from 1953 to 1964, I was grateful indeed, for example, to a predecessor, Raymond M. Hughes, who from 1911 to 1927 had anticipated future growth, bought many acres of land, and developed a master plan for building locations. His planning made our plans executable. Yet other presidents, equally beloved by faculty colleagues, students, and alumni, have not been interested in planning but in survival. They tend to be fearful about planning. They may complain about the constraints imposed by the external environment or by internal expectations, yet they appear to be content to react to circumstances rather than to anticipate and modify them.

The planning effectiveness of a campus depends upon the planning effectiveness of its presidential leadership. There is no escape from this situation. I have known vice-presidents for administration and vice-presidents for academic affairs as well as directors of institutional research and of planning who have sought to fill the planning vacuum of presidential ineptitude. Sometimes these officers' efforts have been helpful to campus effectiveness, but these efforts almost always have fallen short of the accomplishment that might have been achieved by presidential leadership in planning.

If campus planning is to result in plans, it must propose recommendations acceptable to the instrumentalities of campus governance. The role of the president, of the president's executive assistants, and the president's managerial associates may be dominant in the planning process and in the recommendation of plans; but this role is not without its limitations. Presidential leadership requires the mustering of political resources. On a campus, these political resources are not extensive. What persuasion can a president offer to induce a faculty senate to alter the institutional mission, approve new program thrusts, or endorse a reallocation of resources? What persuasion can a president offer in order to mute student opposition to increased charges or make students less vocal in demands for unlimited visitation hours in university residence halls? The president cannot terminate faculty appointments or discipline student dissent. The president can only suggest the direction in which the enlightened self-interest of both faculty members and students may lie.

If the times favor plans for growth, and if growth is generally acceptable to faculty and students, a planning-minded president may be considered highly successful. If the times favor reduction, reallocation, and retrenchment, however, and if the constituent groups of the academic community fear such change, then a planning-oriented president may be considered a threat. In such a case, campus plans for reduction, reallocation, and retrenchment will not be superior in community satisfaction to no plans for such cutbacks—or to externally imposed plans for them.

Presidential leadership during the 1980s will be challenged because plans for retrenchment are yet to be perceived as preferable to no plans. Presidential leadership in planning and the adoption of plans is yet to be demonstrated as certain to avoid the necessity for retrenchment; and yet campus planning will not eventuate in campus plans unless the president is a planner.

Governance, Leadership, and Planning

Planning is a process that cuts across the governance, management, and leadership structures of a campus. A *plan* is a decision of the campus governance structure. Work planning or program planning is an essential element of program management. A plan envisages purposes, program objectives, basic policies, and resource allocation for the institution; and the governance structure must approve the plan for leaders and managers to execute. Leadership is the necessary link between management and governance, between academic community and society.

The planning process, including both program planning and institutional planning, cannot concentrate upon one kind of planning to the exclusion of the other. Both forms of planning are necessary on a campus. Program planning offers details about the current situation in work performance and proposals about how to move from what is done today to what will be needed tomorrow. Institutional planning offers a framework for program planning. It provides an integration of program plans with external realities and an integration of program objectives with the constraints of social expectation and available resources.

Planning is a continuous process because plans must be adjusted to changing circumstances, needs, opportunities, technologies, and economy. Program plans and institutional plans should look ahead at least five years, with tentative projections ten years ahead. As each year of experience is concluded, the plans should look forward for an additional year.

Finally, the planning process is intended to produce plans, not planning papers, not statistical data, not discussions of alternatives, and not speculation about possible futures. The planning process is completed only when it eventuates in a particular choice or a particular set of choices. Planning is often confused with institutional research, and certainly planning requires information and data. Research provides a knowledge base for planning, the knowledge base available from the current state of knowledge. But planning cannot wait for knowledge to catch up with decision needs, for it is the act of making intelligent decisions today based upon today's available knowledge.

These general observations about governance, management, and leadership are intended to provide an organizational context for developing the essential relationship between planning and institutional research. When I first became acquainted with offices of institutional research some thirty years ago, they were involved primarily in preparing analytical studies for presidents and their managerial associates. Data from the registrar's office and the admissions office were analyzed to suggest enrollment trends, student input quality, dropout rates, major fields of student interest, and grade point averages. Data from the budget and accounting offices were analyzed to indicate trends in income sources and expenditure pattern. Often there was no analytical framework for this data analysis; the information about institutional operations was considered inherently useful to presidents, their managerial associates, and governing boards.

On some campuses, offices of institutional research evolved into units of academic support, assisting faculty members in experimentation with the technology of instruction and in the evaluation of student performance, both areas in which the ordinary instructional program for the Ph.D. degree was sadly deficient. In effect, these offices, working in close conjunction with vice-presidents for academic affairs, tended to become faculty resource centers for teaching and learning improvement. In a sense, these offices forecast later formalized efforts at faculty development.

Offices of institutional research, other than those primarily involved in learning research, appear to have been overtaken by two other trends: the growing concern with institutional planning and the development of comprehensive management information systems. To some extent, offices of institutional research have had to make a choice: to become planning offices or to become management information offices. The management information function seems more likely to be compatible with the history of many institutional research offices.

A management information system is indispensable to a formalized planning process. But the two endeavors are different. Management information is concerned with a procedure for bringing together, analyzing, and projecting data about students, staffing, facilities, and finances. Planning is concerned with the impact of the environment (demographic, economic, political, and social) upon the institution and with institutional choices as it confronts the future on mission, programs, enrollment, staffing, facilities, and finances. Management information is essentially analytical. Planning is essentially the determination of a desirable and feasible future.

Organizationally, both management information and planning as units of specialized staff effort and as a process must be closely related to the structure and process of management, governance, and leadership on a campus. Managers provide information about their operations and prepare work plans. Representatives of campus constituencies involved in providing advice to presidents need to be fully acquainted with information analysis and planning concerns. Internal governance bodies need to be asked to give their advice about the institutional future in the light of external circumstances and internal aspirations. The campus president must be prepared both to lead and to follow.

A central office of management information and of planning must be effectively tied to the role and person of the campus president. The president is the internal link between campus management and campus governance. The president needs to have a vision of the future, a realistic appreciation of institutional constraints, and a commitment to institutional effectiveness. Faculty, students, and alumni can assist the president in making critical choices. The president must present the recommended course of action to the governing board and to the external publics of the institution. If the choice proves realizable, both president and institution are fortunate. If the choice fails, both president and institution are in dire trouble. The challenge to institutional research and planning is to achieve the first and to avoid the second fate. It will be a formidable challenge indeed in the 1980s.

Bibliographical Essay

There is a substantial volume of writing on the subject of governance, and a review of this literature would be extensive. This writing has been examined in

Millett, *New Structures of Campus Power* (1978). To the references listed there two other volumes should be added: Mortimer and McConnell, *Sharing Authority Effectively* (1978), and Baldridge, Curtis, Ecker, and Riley, *Policy Making and Effective Leadership* (1978).

The writings about academic leadership are equally voluminous, although much of the literature consists of memoirs of particular college or university presidents and is anecdotal in nature. The book by Burns, *Leadership* (1978), deserves special mention because of its insights and scope. Dealing more specifically with higher education leadership, we should note the following: Heyns, *Leadership of Higher Education* (1977); Millett, *The Multiple Roles of College and University Presidents* (1976); Brown, *Leadership Vitality* (1979); Bennis, *The Unconscious Conspiracy* (1976); Richman and Farmer, *Leadership, Goals, and Power in Higher Education* (1974); Kauffman, *At the Pleasure of the Board* (1980); Walker, *The Effective Administrator* (1979); and the two booklets prepared by Nason for the Association of Governing Boards, *Presidential Search* (1979) and *Presidential Assessment* (1980).

In a special category is the book by Millett, *Management, Governance, and Leadership* (1980), written as a practical guide for college and university administrators.

References

Baldridge, J. V., Curtis, D. V., Ecker, G., and Riley, G. L. *Policy Making and Effective Leadership: A National Study of Academic Management.* San Francisco: Jossey-Bass, 1978.

Bennis, W. *The Unconscious Conspiracy: Why Leaders Can't Read.* New York: AMACOM, 1976.

Brown, D. G. *Leadership Vitality.* Washington, D.C.: American Council on Education, 1979.

Buchanan, J. M., and Devletoglou, N. E. *Academia in Anarchy: An Economic Analysis.* New York: Basic Books, 1970.

Burns, J. M. *Leadership.* New York: Harper & Row, 1978.

Cohen, M. D., and March, J. G. *Leadership and Ambiguity: The American College President.* New York: McGraw-Hill, 1974.

Corson, J. *Governance of Colleges and Universities.* New York: McGraw-Hill, 1960.

Heyns, R. W. (Ed.). *Leadership of Higher Education.* Washington, D.C.: American Council on Education, 1977.

Kauffman, J. F. *At the Pleasure of the Board.* Washington, D.C.: American Council on Education, 1980.

Millett, J. D. *The Multiple Roles of College and University Presidents.* Washington, D.C.: American Council on Education, 1976.

Millett, J. D. *New Structures of Campus Power: Success and Failures of Emerging Forms of Institutional Governance.* San Francisco: Jossey-Bass, 1978.

Millett, J. D. *Management, Governance, and Leadership.* New York: AMACOM, 1980.

Mortimer, K. P., and McConnell, T. R. *Sharing Authority Effectively: Participation, Interaction, and Discretion.* Jossey-Bass, 1978.

Nason, J. W. *Presidential Search: A Guide to the Process of Selecting and Appointing*

College and University Presidents. Washington, D.C.: Association of Governing Boards of Universities and Colleges, 1979.

Nason, J. W. *Presidential Assessment.* Washington, D.C.: Association of Governing Boards of Universities and Colleges, 1980.

Richman, B. M., and Farmer, R. N. *Leadership, Goals, and Power in Higher Education: A Contingency and Open-Systems Approach to Effective Management.* San Francisco: Jossey-Bass, 1974.

Walker, D. E. *The Effective Administrator: A Practical Approach to Problem Solving, Decision Making, and Campus Leadership.* San Francisco: Jossey-Bass, 1979.

26

Bernard S. Sheehan

Developing Effective Information Systems

This chapter views institutional research and institutional planning in light of their information systems and organizational interdependencies. Although institutional research and institutional planning are not identical, they have much in common. Those who undertake institutional research on a campus are often the planners; the two functions can cohabit in one organizational unit; and they are similar in their dependency on and influence of information systems. I posit models of institutional research practice, of planning processes, of evaluation frameworks and of information systems. These models capture the essence of the processes in order to analyze (1) the several processes, that is, institutional research, institutional planning, evaluation, realizing these functions on campus, and finally, their information system interactions, (2) practical issues that may require attention by institutional research and planning specialists.

Note: I gratefully acknowledge Alberta Advanced Education and Manpower support for research leading to development of some of the material presented here. Also, I wish to express my appreciation to my longtime colleague, E. A. Hillman, for his contributions to many aspects of this work.

This approach permits an economical and structured analysis of a topic which is inherently complex. The complexity arises because of the numerous practical aspects and subtle factors impinging upon notions of institutional research, institutional planning, evaluation, organization and information systems. Any model of processes which vary by country, by jurisdiction, by the many categories of institutions, by level within an institution, and over time will, like any average, show only central tendencies, not specific local features and characteristics. Hence, analysis or a deduction made on the basis of interaction among such models is itself a model, that is, an abstraction, hopefully of the essential features but not of specific detail.

Institutional Research

As the study and analysis of the operations, environment, and processes of institutions of higher education for the purpose of supplying information for decisions in higher education, institutional research clearly is not all done by a staff office organized specifically for this purpose. Nonetheless, the purposes of this chapter require that besides agreeing on what institutional research is and how it relates to institutional planning, we have to address the following: (1) What factors influence its internal organization, and how the institutional research office ought to fit into the institution's organizational structure? (2) What are institutional research's information interests, requirements and systems impacts? These questions were the first two addressed in the "AIR Professional File" (Ridge, 1978; Saunders, 1979).

Communication is a major difficulty facing institutional research practitioners (IRP). Although there is need for its own technical language to facilitate communication among experts, communication with nonspecialists is essential and must not be hindered by specialist jargon. In addition, institutional research is essentially interdisciplinary, borrowing expertise, insights, techniques, systems, procedures, and language from many fields as well as organizations other than colleges and universities. Thus, many nonrelevant concepts are borrowed with the language and may be misapplied in higher education. In order to pursue the organizational and information problems posed, two models which are helpful in overcoming inadequacies of the technical language are discussed in this section.

The "three-hat theory" may help capsulize the role of the institutional research practitioner (Sheehan, 1974). This theory suggests that in responding to the need for planning and management information, institutional research analysts must be sufficiently versatile to assume three perspectives: those of (1) *the decision maker,* such as the president, academic senate, or faculty committee, asking for information and proposing to use it for decision making; (2) *the analyst,* wearing his or her own hat and translating the information needed into terms that will admit a solution—that is, taking into account the imprecisions of the question, inadequacies of the data base, limitations of available systems and techniques, time, talent, and other resources for proper analysis; and (3) *the technician,* to whom the practical and systems aspects of gathering information are clear and the meaning of resultant data is unmistakable. The analyst must understand and fully appreciate the technician's role and hence be able to direct the study, analysis, and other activities of the technician so as to be able to judge the worth of the results critically, insightfully, and perceptively. As an adviser and data provider, the analyst must be one with the decision maker to the extent that there is full communication of the question and, subsequently, of alternative solutions or strategies based on a delicate perception of the decision context and paradigm. The effectiveness of the communication between the analyst and the decision maker depends on the confidence they have in each other, including their confidence in their language of communication.

A central area of concern needing agreement between analyst and decision maker on terms and concepts is that of information systems. A facet of campus organization which colors the attitude of analysts towards information systems is the requirement that the office of institutional research and planning work not only with someone else's data, but with data essentially imperfect for most research and planning purposes. Figure 1 presents a hierarchy of information systems, a framework suggested by Sheehan and others (1972) and improved by a number of other authors, including Haight and Romney (1975), Lawrence and Service (1977), and Lasher (1978), to organize the basic ideas and language about information systems that are fundamental to their communication. It categorizes information systems into three levels: (1) operational data systems, (2) management information systems, and (3) planning and management systems.

The essential foundation of the hierarchy at the first level of operating

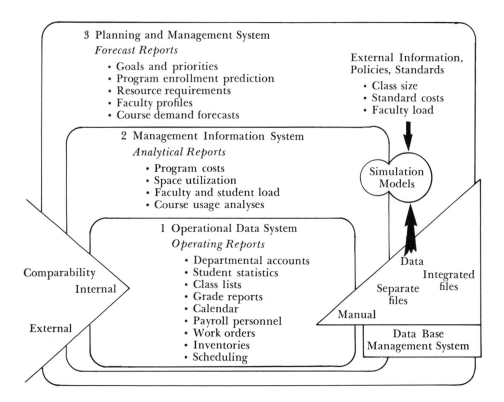

Figure 1. Hierarchy of Information Systems

data is data collected in the regular operation of the institution. Thus, transactions associated with student admissions; course registrations and grades; and daily business in the controller's office, the various student affairs departments, research administration, personnel offices, the several plant and maintenance offices, and the purchasing department together form an important source of information for planning and management. The transformation of these records into management information and its successful use in planning and management processes is the essence of institutional research and planning interest in information systems.

The basic *operational data system,* which deals with these transactions of the institution, includes procedures for collecting, organizing, maintaining, updating, manipulating and retrieving data generated by these transactions. Computers are not essential to this notion of information systems, but the people who gather, interpret, and use its information are critical components of all the systems in the hierarchy. In other words, an information system is more than computer equipment (hardware) and programs (software), and too much emphasis on them may distract one from the information needs of decision makers.

If data in the operational data system are to be useful beyond the operational and control considerations that created them, they must be integrated with data from other transactions. Organizing files in which data may be linked systematically by standard element definitions and in which data are updated on a coordinated schedule makes the resulting integrated files useful at higher levels in the hierarchy. The best practical arrangement is to have the analytical reports characteristic of the second level of the hierarchy, that is, *management information systems* (MIS), produced primarily on the basis of data from the first level. These MIS reports typically require that information from two or more basic files be processed according to an agreed algorithm. An essential aspect of the information to be integrated is that it is comparable to the extent necessary for these calculations. The resultant reports include historical studies of resource use, activity costs, and changing student and course enrollment patterns that provide managers with an improved understanding not readily deduced from basic statistics of institutional transactions.

The highest level in the hierarchy is the *planning and management system* arising from a capacity further to integrate transactional data and external information in support of planning and management decisions. To the extent that comparison with other institutions is important, files must contain information externally comparable. Thus, the compatibility of data through the use of common data codes, definitions, and procedures allows for the integration of information sources within the institution and over time and as appropriate for the use of comparative data from other institutions. Many National Center for Higher Education Management Systems (NCHEMS) products evolved over the last decade are important contributors to the realization of institutional planning and management systems as well as to the technical language previously mentioned.

The hierarchy of information systems expressed in Figure 1 is a simple model of a complex reality. Thus, one would not expect it to be all-encompassing but, rather, selectively relevant. It is not a universal categorization of all information sources and sinks. The information encompassed in any practical computer-based campus system is a minute portion of the information that supports decision making. Nonetheless, the notion of information systems in the hierarchy has people as a component, including the people described by the three-hat theory. Thus, the planning and management system includes knowledge of higher education sufficient to determine the significance of other information and the necessary technical know-how (computers, architecture, accounting, and so on, not ordinarily thought of as data in information systems) to evaluate decision circumstances as well as alternative strategies open to decision makers.

Depending upon the state of evolution of an institution's information systems, institutional research and planning personnel may expend most of their energy attempting the integration of data and information from many uncoordinated sources. Their office may hold the only truly integrated view of information systems on the campus. The uniqueness of this perspective is an important factor to consider in deciding how institutional research and planning should be organized and how it ought to fit into the institution's organizational structure. In this context it will be useful to elaborate the notions of planning, evaluation and information systems.

Planning Processes

The determination of an appropriate plan and accompanying techniques and procedures for its practical realization are circumscribed by possibilities and constraints inherent in planning processes themselves and in the jurisdictional structure of higher education. Some of the factors that influence processes for developing and managing a plan will be discussed because they help identify information system and organizational structure alternatives for institutional research and planning. The components of a planning process, and the scope and operational relevance of a plan, vary according to the intent, commitment, knowledge and influence of those involved in its formulation and implementation (Hillman, 1978). Despite the complexities involved, the fairly simple general planning process illustrated in Figure 2 can serve to identify some key components in the planning process and provide a reference point for illustration of technical and human considerations.

A comprehensive view of planning involves processes of setting or identifying goals; defining specific objectives aimed at the goals; developing, continuing, or altering programs to meet the objectives; monitoring and evaluating the results; and feeding back information for decisions that affect programs, objectives, or goals. The model in Figure 2 represents such a view of planning at the institutional level, and similar processes apply at the academic department and the multicampus system levels. The model illustrates the steps for developing and managing the plan and gives examples of those involved in the process who provide information at each step. Information (the "what") includes the full range of fuel for the process, that is, facts in the narrow sense of statistical data as well as assumptions, strategies, proposals, recommendations, procedures, measurements, judgments, and decisions provided by the hierarchical information system outlined in Figure 1.

The starting point for planning in higher education typically is the need to respond to problems that have resource implications: increases or decreases in student numbers, choosing which programs to preserve and which to discard,

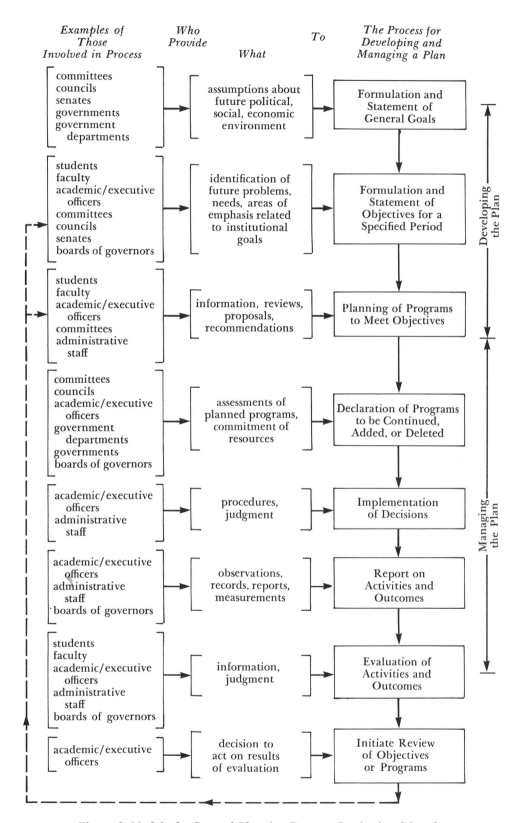

Examples of Those Involved in Process	Who Provide	What	To	The Process for Developing and Managing a Plan

committees
councils
senates
governments
government
   departments
→ assumptions about future political, social, economic environment → **Formulation and Statement of General Goals**

students
faculty
academic/executive
   officers
committees
councils
senates
boards of governors
→ identification of future problems, needs, areas of emphasis related to institutional goals → **Formulation and Statement of Objectives for a Specified Period**

students
faculty
academic/executive
   officers
committees
administrative
   staff
→ information, reviews, proposals, recommendations → **Planning of Programs to Meet Objectives**

committees
councils
academic/executive
   officers
government
   departments
governments
boards of governors
→ assessments of planned programs, commitment of resources → **Declaration of Programs to be Continued, Added, or Deleted**

academic/executive
   officers
administrative
   staff
→ procedures, judgment → **Implementation of Decisions**

academic/executive
   officers
administrative
   staff
boards of governors
→ observations, records, reports, measurements → **Report on Activities and Outcomes**

students
faculty
academic/executive
   officers
administrative
   staff
boards of governors
→ information, judgment → **Evaluation of Activities and Outcomes**

academic/executive
   officers
→ decision to act on results of evaluation → **Initiate Review of Objectives or Programs**

Developing the Plan

Managing the Plan

Figure 2. Model of a General Planning Process (Institutional Level)

responding to public disenchantment and demands for accountability, or following government directives specifying an institutional plan. Thus, although there may be rhetorical support for planning, there may also be latent or psychological resistance to it because of its association with unhappy internal circumstances or outside pressure. Such passive resistance may manifest itself in the neglect of the practical necessities for planning—in particular, the necessary resources and influence to ensure that it is not crippled by weaknesses in information systems.

Goals. In addressing the raison d'être of institutions, terminology such as "goals," "purposes," "objectives," "missions," and "roles" is commonly used, often synonymously. There is a trend in educational planning literature to distinguish between goals, which are viewed as statements of broad, general direction, and objectives, which are statements of specific accomplishments which can be measured or assessed in some way. The New York Regents' (1971) definition has often been used as a source for distinguishing between goals and objectives, and the model makes the same distinctions.

Given that goals reflect policy that is subject to change, and recognizing that multiple goals increase the potential for goal conflicts, it should be no surprise that publicly stated "official" goals differ from "operative" goals, which are reflected in day-to-day decisions and operating policies. Evidence from complex organizations indicates that official goals are purposefully vague, priorities among goals are not declared, and methods of achieving goals are not elaborated (Perrow, 1969). In official plans, there are usually enough goals, sufficiently abstract to cover the interests of groups who have a say in approving the plan. Organizational activities, however, reflect the "operative" goals and may support, impede, or be irrelevant to the achievement of "official" goals. As a starting point for practical institutional planning, therefore, this may mean that the identification and priority among goals can only be inferred from practice.

The situation is further complicated when one considers organizational ramifications. At each level in the organizational structure, there are "operational" goals which, if not in direct conflict, may have quite different priorities (Hoenack, 1979). This fact is evident in financial planning processes when funds allocated at one level in support of particular goals are reallocated at the next level in a way that does not seem aimed at attainment of the articulated goal.

A variation of the problem of operative goals is the perception of what goals "are" versus the opinion of what goals "should be." Results of a survey of universities indicated considerable differences in the ranking of "is" and "should be" goals (Gross, 1968). Institutional planning over a longer term requires recognition and assessment of the extent to which the "should be" goals will affect resource allocation decisions. Where choices exist in the resource allocation process, the goals of those who influence allocation decisions will tend to prevail. Thus, it would seem that the vague and changing nature of goal statements, their determination and their impact are so elusive as to be useless for operative and practical determinants of a plan. Hodgkinson (1972) summed it up: "Goal statements are next to meaningless without specific agreement on how the goals are to be implemented, by whom, what resources are to be used, and how the effort will be evaluated. Note that I did not say measured. Many things can be evaluated even if we cannot affix a number value to them."

Objectives. Objectives are specific statements of interest supporting one or more goals, and requiring for their achievement policies, resources, programs, and activities. Included in this notion of objectives is that progress towards attainment can be evaluated.

It seems obvious that consensus on an objective, at least among those who directly can influence efforts toward the objective, is a necessary condition for its achievement. It is also generally accepted that the objective should be stated unambiguously, with sufficient substance to imply the consequences of its pursuit. Unfortunately, these two conditions are often mutually antagonistic because as objectives become sharpened, the threats to various interest groups increase. Interests of parties who must arrive at consensus on an objective are often achieved through compromise such as by reducing the specificity of the objective or by agreeing not to pursue the objective too vigorously. Hartle (1976) observed that in the public sector, planning and management techniques that depend heavily on the formulation of and agreement on objectives and measurements of their attainment have not achieved the benefits ascribed to them a priori.

Achieving consensus on objectives has become more complex as decision-making environments change. Three eras in higher education are relevant. Formulation of objectives in what Sibley (1976) has described as the "age of authority" was a matter for those who were charged with the responsibility for providing leadership and management. Higher education institutions moved from the "age of authority" when relatively few were involved in *making* the rules, to the "age of participation" in the 1960s when groups and individuals representing students, faculty, support staff, and alumni were made legitimate contributors to processes that *changed* the rules. More recently, decisions in institutions have moved into the "age of litigation" where the *rights* to make the rules are the issue and conflicts on these matters increasingly involve courts, governments, and other bodies outside the institutions.

Planning processes typically involve the establishment of priorities among objectives. The ordering of priorities in educational institutions is usually based, at least in form if not in substance, on academic considerations, and the statement of priorities is a number of items listed in order of importance. In the sphere of policy analysis and evaluation, this type of ordering of priorities was referred to by Braybrooke and Lindblom (1963) as the "naive priorities method." Their discussion on ranking the values of a number of policies is relevant to the model notion of establishing priorities among objectives.

> Merely announcing that one is putting "freedom" ahead of "equality" does not explain in what sense it is being "put ahead" or how far. In general, if the list of priorities runs V_1, V_2, V_3, V_4, V_5, V_6, V_7, V_8, and so on, the list itself gives no indication of which policy to choose when the choice lies between policies offering different combinations of benefits. For example, the list does not indicate whether or not a policy offering V_1, V_5, V_7 is preferable to a policy offering V_2, V_4, V_6. It does not even indicate whether or not a policy that offers more V_1 alone is to be preferred to a policy that offers more V_2 alone. If V_1 is assumed to be preferred, absurd consequences follow: Is any amount of V_1, no matter how small, to be preferred to any amount of V_2, no matter how large?

Objectives may be compatible in relation to a given goal, but in circumstances where resource levels are unknown or are known only for a short term, the selection of priorities among objectives that have long-term implications can be futile. Priorities among objectives can also involve strategic considerations of "which one will fly" at the next higher level in the organizational structure. External social or economic objectives can reflect chances for success that can affect the ordering of institutional priorities. Some would argue that the process of establishing priorities among objectives is so complex that in reality priorities are rarely selected, rather, they are earned.

The previous discussion indicates some of the subtleties that cannot be captured by a simple model of the comprehensive planning process. Another factor is that many higher education decision makers are academics who sit for a short period on planning committees or senior academic administrators who serve short (relative to many planning cycles) terms in office. Hence, the important lessons of history with respect to institutional management, for example, the experience of the institution with various planning modes in response to changing circumstances on campus and public policies, must reside with institutional research and planning professionals or else be lost. Therefore, it is an important organizational consideration to ensure this experience becomes an institutional investment paying dividends over many years.

Programs. The reason for examining alternative programs is, theoretically, to find "the best way." In their review of planning in colleges and universities, Cohen and March (1974) observed that plans in academic departments were either lists for Santa Claus or fantasies in which no one believed. Without clear financial guidelines, program planning tends only to propose additional programs and to seek additional capacity to deliver existing programs. Rarely does it include the elimination of academic programs. Financial constraint encourages serious planning efforts that seek to reduce the number of programs; first in support areas and then gradually in academic departments. Also, when financial assumptions and guidelines are given for a longer term, rather than on an annual basis, the potential for focusing upon a realistic set of alternatives in program planning is considerably increased.

In higher education, the "delivery system" for programs of instruction, research, and public service has not changed dramatically in the recent past. Research program planning in universities is decentralized to the academic departmental level, and research program alternatives are not usually examined at the college, institutional, or system level. Exceptions are research proposals that lead to establishment of research institutes or to acceptance of a research project that will affect directly more than one department. While the purposes, needs, directions, and resources attached to research programs are not usually examined at an institutional level for compatibility with other institutional programs, the manifestation of the programs can be identified—the numbers of graduate students, postdoctoral fellows, and research associates; the quality and size of library collections; the income from research grants; specialized facilities and space; the numbers of books and articles published, and so on. Measures of these kinds are usually part of research program planning, but the relationship between research programs and other programs is not usually spelled out at levels beyond those departments immediately concerned. The availability of this sort of information in a form suitable for analysis is an indication of the potential of an institution's planning and management system.

In contrast to research program planning, programs of instruction are usually planned in considerable detail and examined at several organizational levels. Consistent with specific institutional or system objectives, instructional program proposals can be elaborated with fairly "hard" information on curricula, types of instructional methods desired, numbers of staff and students involved, space and facilities required, through various stages of program phasing over a period of years. Typically, new instructional programs receive the most scrutiny where system planning and coordination is involved, while programs already in place have been regarded as ongoing commitments. Public service programs provided through colleges of continuing education or extension are structured in a manner similar to instructional programs—lectures, seminars, workshops, and so forth—but these programs are not usually subject to planning and coordination at the system level. In part, this may be because the financial commitments involved in most public service programs are short term in contrast to instructional programs culminating in diplomas and degrees, and in part because most of the direct costs for public service programs are recovered by fees.

Alternatives within the instructional program have not been developed and implemented to a great extent. Even though a good deal of thought and experimentation has occurred, the lecture/seminar, tutorial, and laboratory class are typical modes of instruction and current practice in teaching is much the same as it was a decade or two ago. Bowen (1975) illustrates this in Table 1:

Table 1. Old and New Methods in Teaching/Learning

Presentation of information, ideas, works of art, and the like	*Independent study (for resident students as well as non resident or "external" students)*
1. Live lecture	1. Student assignments in classes or groups
2. The printed word, pictures, diagrams, etc.	a. Exercises and short papers
a. Library	b. Term papers
b. Textbooks	c. Oral reports
*c. Paperback books	d. Senior theses, masters theses, and dissertations
d. Other printed materials	e. Laboratory exercises
3. Museums and live performances in the arts	f. Research
4. Mechanical devices	g. Creative art or artistic performances
a. Motion picture	2. Individualized independent study
b. Still projectors with or without sound	3. Programmed independent study (programmed for large numbers but with each student working individually)
c. Recordings	*a. Credit by examination
d. Radio	*b. Contract learning
e. Television	*c. Competency-based instruction
*f. Videotape, cassettes, other audio-visual aids	*d. Self-paced instruction
Presentation of information, ideas, analysis, works of art, and the like, with interaction between teacher and student	*e. Modular instruction
1. Lecture-discussion	*f. External degree
2. Seminar	4. Practical experience relating to fields of study
3. Tutorial	a. Internships, residencies, practice teaching, etc.
*4. Team teaching	b. Cooperative work-study
*5. Peer-group instruction	c. Off-campus study abroad or elsewhere
*6. Computer assisted instruction	d. Travel
7. Teacher aides or assistants	*e. Granting credit for experience

Table 1. Old and New Methods in Teaching/Learning *(Continued)*

Extracurricular environment	*Admissions, evaluation, credentialing*
1. Residential and recreational facilities and programs	*(important for incentives and screening)*
2. Guidance and counseling, and placement	1. Testing
3. Cultural events	a. Test prior to admission
4. Clubs, special interest groups, social activities	b. Tests during or at the end of courses
5. Sports	c. Comprehensive tests during or at the end of programs
6. Other	2. Granting of degrees, certificates, letters of recommendation

*New methods
Source: Bowen, 1975, pp. 6–7.

It is the various quantifications of staff and other resources in relation to the modes of instruction shown in Table 1 that have been accepted as indicative of resource requirements. Thus, it is these elements of the instructional program that have received most attention in planning and information system development. In contrast, there tends to be far less documentation of accepted techniques, criteria, and information on which to base planning for support programs. With a few exceptions, for instance, student financial aid and computer services, planning and coordination of support services at the system level rarely occurs. It can be argued that the extent and level of detail with which instructional program plans are examined for unnecessary duplication and long term implications are excessive when compared to the attention given to support program plans in such areas as counselling services, admissions, and libraries.

Reporting and Evaluation. These components relate to the notion of accountability. The sense in which an institution is called to account for its activities and expenditures is a major factor determining the extent of detail and the scope of the planning process. As such, the specifics of institutional accountability in a jurisdiction will shape institutional research and planning organization and influence the evolution of information systems. The concept of accountability includes responsibility for selecting courses of action that may ensure that desired educational outcomes can be achieved over a period of time within agreed policies and resources. It also implies that there should be credible evidence on the degree to which this is being accomplished. Traditional views of financial accountability focus on whether funds are spent legally, with properly audited statements serving as evidence. More recent perceptions of accountability include whether value was given for funds spent. It is in this latter sense of accountability that it is difficult to agree on and acquire evidence.

Demands for accountability have increased since the 1960s. One response in governments and institutions has been to call for and generate more information, analyses, and evaluations which stand alone or form an integral part of a planning process. The elements of the planning process model clearly relate to views of institutional accountability held by Howard Bowen (1974, pp. 1–2): "The significant steps in attaining true institutional accountability are (1) to define the goals and to order their priorities, (2) to identify and measure the outcomes, (3) to compare the goals and outcomes and then to judge the degree to which the goals are being achieved, and (4) to measure the cost and judge the degree to which it approaches a reasonable minimum. Each step in this process involves extraordinary feats of identification, measurement, and judgment. No one with experience in higher education believes that true institutional accountability can be readily achieved by gathering a few bits of readily available data, feeding the data into a computer, and reading off the answers." Thus, while agreement on a precise specification of ends and the best ways of achieving them is a rare condition in education, accountability cannot be discarded just because objectives and other components of a plan cannot be finely specified. Accountability involves responsibility and trust, and the bearer assumes those burdens when carrying out assignments that can only be stated in general terms. Most would argue that, given reasonable bounds of autonomy, authority, resources, and freedom to exercise professional judgment, educational systems can legitimately be called to account for their activities.

In the model planning process, a report on activities and outcomes relates to that view of accountability which answers the question What are you doing? Responses to the question come in a variety of forms. In addition to financial statements, the institution's annual report has traditionally been used by government departments, commissions, and institutions to convey both general and specific information about the year's achievements and problems. College and university calendars and timetables, newsletters, bulletins, handbooks, press releases, and student newspapers are other common sources of information. The distinction in the model between reporting and evaluating is somewhat artificial, but allows the term *report* to be used as it has been defined earlier, whereas *evaluation* can be directed towards answering questions like, How well? and What is it worth?

A commonly accepted meaning of evaluation has to do with the assessment of performance relative to objectives. This view of evaluation focuses on the identification and measurement of program outcomes and the cost of program activities designed to achieve agreed objectives. Technical capabilities of providing information on what activities and costs are involved in various programs have increased in recent years. Limitations of information systems become most evident when information on products of educational programs is required. There are difficulties of determining, identifying, measuring and analyzing outcomes. A further complication is that educational programs have multiple and joint outcomes—some intended, others occurring as side effects. These latter outcomes should be judged without regard to specific institutional objectives, but on the basis of whether they address concerns or bring benefits in a wider context. Analytical techniques, data bases, and information from longitudinal studies are not available in sufficient quantity to provide the types of "hard" outcomes measurements that are reported in business and industrial sectors.

It is not simply problems of measurement and quantification that thwart efforts in evaluation. Wildavsky (1972) notes that it is the nature of organizations to resist evaluation. Ideally, organizations would be self-evaluating, monitoring their own outcomes to determine whether they were meeting their objectives, and if not, they would set about changing objectives or adjusting programs in order to achieve certified objectives. However, support and enthusiasm for regular and systematic processes of evaluation are difficult to obtain. Organizational structures tend to be stable, and the instinct to preserve existing programs runs counter to processes of continuous evaluation which *imply* change. Further, self-generated change requires that a climate of trust and support, rather than potential penalties, prevails throughout the institution. Individuals and groups will tend to withhold support and information for evaluation if the record of evaluation shows that recommendations lead only to reduction of resources or to reinforcement for some predetermined position.

The preceding is not meant to imply that evaluation does not occur in the planning process, but that its predominant form is often sporadic and decentralized evaluation *in* rather than *of* the institution. Some examples are as follows. Formative evaluations—appraisals made during the operation of a program—are conducted by instructors, peers, department chairmen, students, academic committees, managers, senior institutional officers, and others who can contribute evaluative information to improve continuing programs. Summative evaluations—assessments made at the end of a program or at the end of a particular phase of a program—are conducted with the "users" in mind, and often seek opinions and facts from graduates, alumni associations, employers, other institutions, and other public groups. People evaluations—examinations and reviews that assess the performance and accomplishments of students and staff—are conducted routinely and are important, perhaps sufficient, for that view which holds that the quality of a program and its outcomes is a reflection of the people involved.

While evaluations may fall short of identifying the "value" of outcomes and inputs, and may not occur as a decision-oriented, continuous process, efforts at program evaluation in higher education should not be dismissed lightly. Although, as Wildavsky (1972) points out, the propensity to avoid change in organizations is the antithesis of continuous self-evaluation, there are certain commitments to stability that precipitate rigorous evaluation of programs and desired outcomes. The obligation a college has to maintain an agreed curriculum for students is an example. Some of the consequences of this commitment can be observed in the evaluations that accompany major curricular reviews. Such reviews may be far more rigorous than in other public institutions. The participatory nature of governance usually means that several individuals, committees, faculty councils, and occasionally, senates, boards of trustees, and funding sources, are involved in the critique, approval, or disapproval of the components or the whole of academic programs. Through various stages of program review and approval, evaluative questions are sure to arise, particularly when academic units are competitors for scarce resources. Because curricular changes or new programs will often require commitment of finances, facilities, and other resources for several years, it is not surprising that queries in the review of programs depart from purely academic considerations.

Evaluation often involves assessment of whether outcomes can be increased given a fixed level of resources. There is an underlying element of comparison required in this view of evaluation, namely: how well do programs produce desired outcomes compared to alternatives that are available at similar cost? Outcome measurement difficulties typically force financial evaluation, in terms of efficiency and productivity, to focus on unit costs such as dollars per student credit hour or productivity ratios such as student credit hours per FTE faculty. However, while neither measure can directly reflect the resources and technologies used or the outcomes that are produced, evaluations of this kind invariably accompany annual budgeting, an essential step in the planning process. Budgeting focuses on anticipated income data, expenditures, workloads, and the consequences of alternative budgetary allocations. The common practice of organizationally associating the budget office with campus financial units such as the controller overemphasizes the fiscal and monetary aspects of budgeting. This imperils the natural cyclic flow of the planning process and jeopardizes the influence that the budgeting experience should have in directing the evolution of planning and management information systems.

In recent years much institutional research and planning activity has related to the development of strategies for evaluation of learning, teaching, programs, and personnel, hence it is useful to examine this aspect in the broadest context. Fortunately, Gardner (1977, pp. 586–587) has identified five definitions of evaluation that serve as a basis for his "Five Evaluation Frameworks." These are reproduced as Figure 3. The summary of the frameworks given in this figure is remarkably self-explanatory and is perhaps another example of a response to the need for a technical language. Gardner chooses the following principal dimensions along which the frameworks are arrayed: statement and explanation of the principal focus of the definition; examples of the definition in current practice; basic assumptions and premises; "advance organizers," variables that structure the evaluation (basic value perspective of the approach, nature of typical evaluation designs, typical evaluator roles, nature of typical methodologies, types of communication and feedback); nature of expected outcomes and mode of interpretation; advantages and practical strengths; implementation limitations and theoretical disadvantages.

Often there is a need for background information to provide context to support comparative arguments and to allow evaluators to get their bearings. In this sense, each evaluation approach may use or benefit from information from each system in the hierarchy. Thus, in general, evaluation activities demand evolution of integrated information systems.

The information needed in the decision-oriented paradigm is precisely that suggested by the comprehensive planning process model and that modeled by the hierarchy of information systems. It is significant to note that the framework lists "'rational decision making' not predominant model in most real-life situations" as an implementation limitation and a theoretical disadvantage. The congruence approach is also envisaged in the comprehensive planning process when the emphasis is on results-compared-to-objectives. In brief, therefore, there are no new informational or organizational ramifications. Nonetheless, to the extent that all institutional research and planning is not done in these offices one would not expect all evaluation to be centralized; each school, department, and instructor plans and evaluates. The provision of informational services for these clients may vary depending upon the specific topic. Evaluation as measurement theoretically fits within the institutional research definition and easily relates to planning activities. The examples listed in the frameworks suggest instruments used in institutional research and are part of the management information system described in the hierarchy. Again, given that not all institutional research is done in one office there are many practical reasons why special units on campus could be charged with particular types of evaluation. For example, a unit concerned with measuring the effectiveness of certain teaching methods in the college of medicine may well be a unit reporting to the dean.

The professional judgment approach is a familiar mode of evaluation in higher education. The peculiar focus of the method, the "expert opinion of a

Figure 3. Distinguishing Characteristics of Gardner's Five Evaluation Frameworks

	"Professional Judgment"	"Measurement"
Principal Focus	Expert opinion of qualified professional (s) .	Measurement of results, effects, or performance, using some type of formal instrument (test, questionnaire, and so on) .
Examples	Accreditation teams. Doctoral Committees. Peer review of grant proposals. Referees for selection of manuscripts for publication. Promotion/Tenure decisions.	GRE scores. Faculty activity question- naires. Attitude surveys. Teaching effectiveness questionnaires.
Basic Assumptions	Best evaluation is the expert opinion of a qualified professional. There is a commonly shared value system in the "arena" of the program or thing to be evaluated and/or, A "compromise mechanism" exists for accommodating differences in professional opinion.	Best evaluation is obtained from measurement data. Thing to be evaluated has measurable attributes. Instrument effectively measures attributes selected.
"Advance Organizers"	Values may or may not be explicitly defined. Evaluator expected to be an information collector, syn- thesizer, and judge.	"Norm-referenced," quantita- tive values. Formal setting required for application of the measurement instrument. Instrument must be validated, reliable, and so on. Evaluator must be a measurement expert.
Nature of Outcome/ Interpretation	Educated, personalized opinion (judgment of worth) of a qualified judge or panel of judges. Interpretation in form of a "pronouncement."	Number or set of numbers which can be compared to other numbers or a standardized scale, data, descriptive statistics. Interpretation in reference to norms.
Advantages	Easily implemented. Uses assimilative and in- tegrative capabilities of human intellect. Recognizes outstanding expertise.	Proper validation and con- sistent application results in high comparability and replicability. Data mathematically manipulable. Generalizable results.
Disadvantages	Results criticized as non- replicable, non-comparable, and overly subjective. Generalizability difficult or impossible.	Many variables difficult or impossible to measure. Often inappropriate and/or inflexible — serving available measurement tools instead of the "problem." Measurable attributes often irrelevant.

Source: Gardner, 1977, pp. 586-587.

"Congruence Between Performance and Objectives"	"Decision Oriented"	"Goal-Free/Responsive"
Comparison of performance or product with previously stated standards of performance, goals, or objectives.	"Delineating, obtaining, and providing useful information for judging decision alternatives."	Identification and judgment of actual outcomes (irrespective of goals, standards, and such) and/or the "concerns of constituents."
Teacher certification based on achievement of prescribed competencies. Evaluation of academic departments on the basis of stated goals. Behavioral objectives. Contract learning.	Management Information Systems. NCHEMS Costing and Data Management System. HEPS (Higher Education Planning System).	Evaluation reports of "program side effects." "Holistic" evaluation of educational programs in the arts.
Best evaluation is based on an examination of achievement in light of goals or objectives. Goals or objectives exist and are identifiable. Attributes exist (and can be measured) that indicate relative success in achieving goals.	Best evaluation is one that serves decision makers in specific decision situations. Decision making processes are rational. Different types of decisions require different information. Many decisions are cyclic; systematic processes can be devised to support them.	Best evaluation highlights actual outcomes and/or concerns of constituents and sponsors. The "real" effects of a program or thing can be identified (as can the concerns of affected individuals). The most effective approach is "open minded" and "sensitive."
"Criterion-referenced" (goal oriented) values. Measurement technology commonly used within the context of performance versus goal assessment. Evaluator may be expected to "judge" as well as measure.	"Decision-oriented" values. Information system methodology. Evaluator should be an information system specialist.	"Wider-context" values (selected by evaluator). "Holistic approach" (all contributive elements, and so on considered as they relate to each other). Evaluator must be skilled in human interaction and identification of concerns.
Judgment of worth based on comparisons between performance data and objectives or standards of performance. Interpretation based on relative discrepancy or congruence.	"Continuous," timely, and relevant information for administrators to assist in judging decision alternatives. Interpretation an administrative function; evaluator concerned with extraction and reduction of data.	Descriptive information regarding "actual" outcomes. Interpretation responsive to constituent concerns.
"Goal-orienion" provides objective basis for evaluation. Judgment criteria pre-established by objectives versus performance measures selected. Relevant to current societal concerns.	Increased understanding of decision setting and information requirements. Focus on decision information needs assures relevancy of data. Encourages analysis of all factors affecting important decisions.	Flexible, adaptive approach. Useful in complex, relatively unstructured situations. All outcomes potentially relevant. "People-oriented" — high acceptance potential.
Focus may be too limited — not all worthy goals easily identified. Important side-effects may be overlooked. Tendency toward over-emphasis on end-product evaluation.	"Rational decision making" not predominant model in most real-life situations. In practice, frequent inability to cope with changing decision information needs. Inflexibility of "packaged" systems.	Relatively unstructured approach may be difficult to focus and manage. Results criticized as non-replicable, non-comparable and overly subjective. Questionable credibility if evaluator non-expert in area of thing evaluated.

qualified professional," will not induce much direct development of information systems beyond the general impact of all evaluation on information system evolution because of the scope, comparability, and integratability of the information expected as background. Similarly, shaping of an institution's planning and institutional research structure as a result of this mode of evaluation is likely to be minimal. Likewise, the nature of goal-free/responsive evaluation seems to preclude any a priori estimate of likely impact in information systems or organizational structure. The experience of a specific goal-free/responsive evaluation may lead to both information system evolution and organizational structure change, but the central notion of this paradigm of evaluation inherently does not suggest tendencies that will influence information systems or organizational structures.

The overall organizational question is addressed succinctly (Gardner, 1977, p. 582) when, following a description of the proposed evaluation unit (Guba and Stufflebeam, 1970) within the institution, Gardner opines "In real life, the functions described above are typically carried out by offices of institutional research, MIS development teams, systems analysts and programmers, and research and evaluation units—with varying degrees of coordination depending upon the situations."

Feedback. As the planning model in Figure 2 illustrates, one would expect that results obtained through reports and evaluations are "feedback" to provide information for reconsideration of objectives and programs in a continuous, formalized, cyclical process, which, being flexible and iterative, regularly adjusts the plan to changing circumstances. Reality may be quite different from the model, however: Statements of goals may differ in scope and comprehensiveness; objectives may not be clearly articulated, detailed, or systematically related; and their linkages to operating and capital financing may not be obvious. Even "official" planning documents may be ignored or forgotten as a reference point in arriving at major institutional decisions. However, in spite of the difficulties, various planning processes (Lockwood, 1978) are advocated, attempted, and in some cases continued, in postsecondary education. Important aspects of the "real" situation include the decision paradigm, decision structure and organizational phase which apply. Readers interested in pursuing these important topics as they relate to planning in higher education should see Weathersby (1974) and (1975).

Relations with Computing

Over the past decade, while institutional research and planning has advanced and matured as a field and a profession, another field about the same age, computing science, has also made remarkable if somewhat uneven advances. Its advances in hardware, software, and organization have significant consequences for institutional research and planning.

Hardware. Advances in the microminiaturization of electronic components has greatly influenced computer hardware evolution over the past decade. New characteristics of size and capabilities computers have acquired continue to change the practice of institutional research and planning across all classes of institutions. Those who have used computer-based information systems for many years are getting their continuing work done more cost effectively and are coming to depend even more on the computer. Computer-based information systems are used by more campus units. These units are automating jobs previously done manually or expanding their scope by introducing new services that capitalize on new computer capacities. Also, hardware advances have been instrumental in gradually lessening the importance of the computer technician in the interface between institutional research and planning practitioners and information systems.

A present-day minicomputer standing alone is more powerful and cheaper than earlier medium or even large computers. Hence, it is easy to be convinced not only that combinations of minicomputers, large computers, and various communications equipment offer significant increase in computing capacity but also that the flexibility of systems architecture offers considerably more options to institutional research and planning and also to the institution regarding how computing services will be acquired and managed. The decreasing cost of computer hardware seems to have begun an irreversible trend toward distributed systems. Distributed systems will require changes in technical systems and procedures as well as in institutional policies and attitudes toward almost all aspects of computers. Hence, the change in institutional organizational structures and the change in locus of decision making and influence that attend the new flexibility foretell a set of predictable problems.

One impact of distributed systems is to move computing activity from the computer center to the user departments. Besides computer terminals, departments may have small miniprocessors that converse with the central computer and access institutional data bases. The user's access to a computer terminal raises a number of alternative modes of service. Traditionally, institutional research and planning applications were delivered to the computer center for batch processing according to some priority algorithm and the adequacy of the service was gauged, in part, on the basis of turnaround time necessary to get the runs back. Distributed systems offer the possibility of various types of direct interaction with the computer depending upon the capabilities of the terminal and computer system itself. A straightforward and convenient use of the terminal is for remote job entry. This use of teleprocessing saves the research and planning staff tracing back and forth to the computer center for those jobs that can be handled in this on-line mode. Of course, the terminal may allow data bases to be updated or accessed and computer operations and calculations to be monitored and adjusted as they occur, in real time. In this latter mode, it might appear to the terminal operator as if the full computer system is at his or her personal command.

Even though hardware and software advances are introducing the day of "personal computing," important issues remain with which the research and planning office and other users of distributed systems will need to grapple. These arise primarily because the office of institutional research and planning uses someone else's data. Thus, the terminal may provide the possibility for both updating and reading data bases, but such capability requires that the fundamental conflict between accessibility and security be addressed. The registrar is typically charged with maintaining institutional student records and protecting the individual's privacy; hence, other users' ability to write on and read from files must be controlled. However, the control should be exercised so that institutional planning and management are not crippled. One way appropriate trade-offs can be achieved is by the appointment of a data base manager or director of information systems who accepts responsibility for accessibility and security. The data base approach has data elements linked so that retrieval can be done practically and according to a logical structure (Hussain, 1978). It also has a certain systems overhead associated with it. The systems complexity that follows from the data base approach can lead to increased lead time of systems development and even to a shortening of the time between acquisitions of additional capacity to handle systems overhead.

The decentralization of computing heralded by distributed systems will involve many user departments in decisions on items such as common data element definitions, standards for documentation, system planning, design, maintenance control and operations. This will generally raise the level of literacy about computers. The accessibility to computerized data bases through agreed institutional procedures and policies encourages the view of information as an institutional resource and the computer system as a utility. Both trends are healthy and will tend to free the office of research and planning from some of the more routine data acquisition and manipulation tasks that siphon resources from productive analysis and the anticipation of planning and management problems.

Software. The scope of researchers' and planners' dependency on computers is illustrated by Figure 4, adopted by Thomas (1979) from Hamblen and others (1980). Thomas notes that nonproprietary software development in the past few years has been encouraged by technological developments in general support of software and in computer hardware, including standardized higher-level languages (primarily COBOL), sophisticated programming and analytical techniques (structured programming and "HIPO"—Hierarchical Input Process Output), data base technology, on-line processing capabilities, network and distributed processing, minicomputers and microcomputers, and lower cost and increased performance of general computer hardware.

Most administrative computer software held by colleges and universities is nonproprietary, so it is available through formal and informal exchange mechanisms. The professional association for development, use, and management of information systems in higher education is the College and University Systems Exchange (CAUSE), which maintains an exchange library of nonproprietary software contributed by member institutions. Because it is generally agreed that software development for the past decade has not advanced at the same pace as hardware, institutions must maximize the return on their investment in systems development. Ryland (1979) suggests that as more institutions use proprietary software, institutional researchers and planners ought to be involved in the process of evaluating and acquiring the software. Table 2 summarizes Ryland's description of the appropriate institutional research and planning involvement.

Computer System Organization. One of the continuing and perplexing problems in computing systems organization is whether on a campus there ought to be a single computer center or one for administrative computing and another for academic computing, or even several centers for special needs such as medicine. The essential differences in the style of operation of an academic computer center, which resembles a utility responding to many different needs of many users, and of the administrative computer center, characterized by rigid

Table 2. Institutional Research and Planning (IRP) Assistance in Selection of Proprietary Software

Types of Proprietary Software	IRP Involvement in Evaluation
General systems software	IRP should rely on the professional judgment of the computer systems staff.
Generalized data base/data communications software	IRP needs and priorities should be communicated to the systems staff, entrusting them with the choices on the basis of complete information from potential users. IRP is the most likely user of the more sophisticated capabilities of data base systems.
Retrieval systems, both interactive and batch	IRP as a major user should play an active role in evaluating alternative packages.
Applications-oriented and analytical software, including statistical problem-solving packages	Where there are several users, cooperative evaluation is indicated. However, some packages will be used almost exclusively by IRP and will require some tailoring to meet specific institutional needs. Hence, significant IRP input to selection decisions is necessary.

production schedules and critical deadlines servicing a few regular clients, can lead to a lack of harmony as one attempts to accommodate both functions and philosophies in the one office. Yet current practice does not suggest that the argument for one center is overwhelming. The individual circumstance on each campus has to be judged against the background of the potential for conflict and this weighed against the potential advantages. The staffing problems of university computing centers are well known and are becoming even more acute. This is especially troublesome to researchers and planners because, although recent advances in computer hardware have reduced their dependency on computer technicians, they still depend on consultations with experienced applications programmers who have broad backgrounds, experience with the institution's information systems, and problem-solving aptitudes. These specialists can help institutional research and planning maximize the utility of information systems for increasingly complex applications. Fortunately, the significant hardware advances allow one to trade off certain inefficient uses of the hardware against development time of more elegant solutions.

The special interdependency of institutional research and planning and computer-based systems demands that a special relationship evolve between the respective staffs. As in the purchase of proprietary software, researchers and planners bring an important and often unique perspective to institutional computer system discussions and decisions. Mann (1979, pp. 73–74) summarizes the role of the institutional researcher in the development and use of administrative information systems in higher education as follows:

> 1. Institutional researchers are perhaps more familiar with more different data in the institution than any other users of the data-processing facility. From their perspective, they can offer advice and direction to data processing and to the user/owners of the data as to their most efficient organization, use, and processing. They should sit on advisory committees for the administrative data-processing center because of this perspective.
> 2. Their analytical background and experience with various

Figure 4. Administrative Applications of Computers in U.S. Higher Education for 1976–1977

Planning, Management and Institutional Research

Budget Forecasting	Budget Preparation
Budget Analysis	Budget Position Control
Institutional Cost Studies	Faculty Salary Analysis
Support Staff Salary Analysis	Faculty Activity Analysis
Support Staff Activity Analysis	Resource Requirements Modeling
Student Flow Modeling	Long Range Planning
Enrollment Forecasting	HEGIS Reporting
Data Element Dictionary	Institutional Coding Structure

Financial Management Applications

General Fund Ledger	General Fund Expenditures
Departmental Expenditures	General Accounts Receivable
Students Accounts Receivable	Accounts Payable
Payroll	Employee Benefit Accounting
Retirement System Accounting	Bank Account Reconciliation
Cash Flow Projection	Investment Records
Investment Evaluation	Grant and Contract Administration
Research Project Accounting	Research Proposal Monitoring
Financial Aid Accounting	Tuition and Fee Accounting
Residence Hall Accounting	Stores Accounting
Telephone Accounting	

General Administrative Service Applications

Facilities Inventory (space)	Facilities Utilization Analysis
Classroom Utilization Analysis	Personnel Records
Personnel Evaluation	Personnel Placement
HEW Compliance Reporting	Staff Ethnic Group Reporting
Civil Service Position Records	

Auxiliary Service Applications

Faculty/Staff Directory	Faculty Club Billing
Residence Hall Assignment	Student Directory Preparation
Student Housing Reports	Food Service Menu and Inventory
Bookstore Inventory and Operations	

Logistics and Related Services

Purchase Order Follow-up	Purchasing Information System
Vendor Information System	Stores Inventory
Office Machine Repair Control	Equipment Inventory
Automobile Registration	Parking Lot Space Assignment
Traffic Violation Records	Crime Reporting
Car Pool Matching	Motor Pool Records

functions of the university make them ideal persons to be involved in the process of systems development. With a data-processing auditor from the business office, the institutional researcher can ensure that integrity is built into the application system, can see that management information needs of the institution are addressed,

Physical Plant Operations

Physical Plant Accounting
Building Maintenance Costs
Key Inventory

Physical Plant Job Scheduling
Equipment Preventative Maintenance

Admissions and Records Applications

Undergraduate Admissions Processing
High School Testing Records
Schedule of Classes Preparation
Tuition and Fee Assessment
Class Rosters
Course Add/Drop Processing
Enrollment Statistics
Term Grade Reporting
Student Transcript Records
Correspondence Course Records

Graduate Admissions Processing
Course Catalog Records
Student Class Scheduling
Student Registration Processing
Term Student Records and Reports
Enrollment Reporting
Student Ethnic Group Reporting
Honors Program Records
Degree Requirements Evaluation

Financial Aid Administration

Financial Aid Evaluation
Student Employment Records

Financial Awards
Work Student Records

Library Applications

Acquisitions
Card and Material Preparation and
 Control
Serials Holdings
Fugitive Material Indexing

Cataloging
Circulation Control
Bibliographical Search Service
Educational Media Services

Other Administrative Applications

Alumni Records
Test Scoring and Analysis
Teacher Evaluation
Fraternity/Sorority Rush Record
Student Psychological Testing

Foundation and Gift Records
Curriculum Planning
Teacher Placement
Student Counseling Records
Athletic Event Ticket System

Source: Thomas, 1979, pp. 55-56.

and can help interpret to the novice user the implications of data processor proposals.

3. Institutional researchers can also play a role as the front end analyst in developing certain user application systems. By training and experience, they are often capable of analyzing procedural as well as informational problems of users. In some cases, the institutional research office is asked to act as the bridge in defining the user needs to the staff, which may not have the capability or the resources to define them.

4. Institutional researchers should build a special relationship with the administrative data-processing department because their use of information varies considerably from that of the average user. In order to ensure that data are available on a nonscheduled, ad hoc basis, they must establish a close relationship

with the administrative data-processing department. Most institutional research offices have developed their own programming and analytical capabilities within their staffs. Within reasonable limits, the prudent data-processing office will not oppose this.

    5. Institutional researchers, through their unique familiarity with much of the data in the institution's data bases and files, can play a central role as managers or coordinators of the university data with the data-base administrator, the data-processing department, and (if one exists) the data administration committee representing the campus. The institutional research office can significantly shape the standards for data currency, specifying user update and access guidelines, the design of data bases with appropriate users and data-processing staff, the management reporting requirements from operational application systems, and other tasks important to the data-processing organization and the university as a whole.

Organizational Issues

    There is an endless mosaic of alternative internal organizational arrangements for institutional research and planning units and for their organizational relationship with other components of the institution because, in a sense, the organizational chart is a mapping of the program classification structure (PCS). The nearly infinite variety of organizational arrangements which seems to exist suggests that probably the most practical approach to understanding organizational questions is to read many examples of specific arrangements, their strengths, and their limitations in the contexts within which they have evolved. The chapters of this volume afford a rich source of experience and pertinent analysis. However, there is a paucity of general information and overviews of current practice around the world. Organizational questions, beyond those of the one-room schoolhouse, are difficult to frame and hence it is not easy to construct a suitable instrument with which broad and general surveys can be conducted on topics as penetrating and subtle as organizational and informational impacts. It has been possible to survey a reasonably select group of institutions with the intent of exchange of information among individuals who are reasonably familiar with the contexts of each other's offices. A recent example of this is Baudin (1977), who has surveyed institutional research colleagues in the Southern University Group of Twenty-Five. There was a limited number of other studies over the last decade which gathered statistical profiles of practitioners and offices and the topics studied and made valuable analyses that are useful in gaining insight into the profession over that period. This includes Tincher (1970), Tetlow (1973), and Morstain and Smart (1974), all of whom used the membership of the Association for Institutional Research (AIR) as the group surveyed. Nadeau (1975) sampled the AIR membership as well as numerous other French and English speaking institutions and associations in Canada, the United States, Australia and New Zealand, and western Europe.

    It is evident that there are numerous institutional characteristics and circumstances that are not so much determinants of the organizational structure as they are influences on institutional structures. A typical list includes the size of an institution, whether it is a university or a college and what type of institution within those broad categories, whether it is public or private, its history or tradition and, of course, similar characteristics of the national and state postsecondary educational systems in which the institution is embedded. None of these factors alone or even together are infallible predictors of structures. The preferences and intuition of a strong campus personality now or in the recent past are among the numerous intangibles that undoubtedly influence organizational structure. The idiosyncratic nature of organizational structures on specific campuses and the apparent lack of an overall theoretical base for the existing structure suggests part of the reason for the difficulty in constructing a suitable survey instrument.

The organizational chart seen as a mapping of PCS contains the germ of an important concept. The programs, activities, resources, technologies, and policies of institutions of higher education as summarized, classified, and systematized by PCS (Gulko, 1972) provide one of the few examples of such order, consistency, and precise language that we have in analysis of higher education management. Hence, the image serves as a point of departure for a more theoretical discussion of organizational structures. It seems to be an often played game to change the organizational structure in response to institutional problems, whether internally or externally inflicted, in hope that the unpleasant symptoms arising from mismatches of processes will go away for a suitable period of time. The method of choosing senior administrative officers and the length of their terms may encourage this practice and help define the "suitable" period. I would not move outside the scope of this chapter to pursue this topic except to emphasize that the notion of the spectrum of alternative structures all mapping adequately the more or less invariable PCS is an important one, helpful in keeping organizational concerns in perspective. It should focus attention on the importance of evaluating structures also from the point of view of whether they encourage the practical workings of essential planning processes.

One of the important organizational structure questions is the relationship of the research and planning office to other units. There is a natural tendency for all units that have campuswide functions to recognize the advantages of reporting to the president or executive head of the institution or its local branch. In the case of research and planning, the argument is that the product is most effective when it is prepared from the broadest institutional perspective. An office that reports to the vice-president (Finance) may have a tendency to be more concerned with budgeting than with, say, academic planning. To carry this example one step further, the lack of emphasis on academic planning may follow from the de facto exclusion of the office from academic planning related matters by the vice-president (Academic) who does not involve the research and planning office because it is convenient to have some office reporting to him do analysis in support of academic planning. What is lost is the integration and cross-fertilization at the analytical staff level that could enrich academic planning with financial realism, and budgeting with an academic planning perspective. Thus, a principal reason for reporting to the president is to give the office natural clients at senior levels in each segment of the institution and, hence, to expose office development to their synergetic influences. Another reason, and one which may not be universally accepted, is that the research and planning office ought to have a certain independence from the administration. Reports and documents emanating from the office should be seen as neutral or unbiased, the results of research. These two reasons suggest that the ideal circumstance is one in which institutional research and planning reports administratively to the president and is responsible professionally through the president to the institutional community. The office is a unit with long-term staff responsibilities. Organizational structures ought to allow for separation of staff work and the general perception of those in the institution about the direction of institutional planning, administration, and management.

The two principles of independence and integration have consequences for the qualifications and mode of operation of institutional research and planning staff. Integration implies that the staff work as a team on most major projects with each analyst bringing his or her experience and expertise to bear on the definition, resolution of the problem, and the presentation of the report. It further implies that analysts are capable of serving as consultants to senior officials. In the example mentioned earlier, a fertile situation would have one planner sitting in on academic planning committee meetings and another analyst as a resource person to the university budget committee.

For purposes of this discussion, we are not addressing a number of practical questions that, of course, limit the capacity of any office or unit. We are focusing here on a few general points that have their manifestation on any campus in many forms. For example, in a small office the director may sit on both the academic planning and the budget committees. Before leaving the question of the quality of the staff and their ability to integrate information gained through their collective experiences, the point should be made that if the institutional research and planning service is to be maximally useful to senior decision makers, it must be the product of a competent professional (Cope, 1979) whom decision makers can respect. Finally, independence implies considerable responsibility. This trust is kept if the office is able to anticipate, and hence prepare for, major demands for institutional research and planning services and to use effectively the lead time, whether to prepare answers for straightforward questions or to have in place complex systems and trained personnel required to generate the required service or information when necessary. The extent to which the research and planning office is able to anticipate is clearly a function of the level and experience of the staff.

The decentralized organizational structure of most institutions and the typically participatory style of decision making make it important that the role of the professional analyst be well understood. Institutional research and planning are support functions. Analysts are not charged with making planning and management decisions but with supplying information including strategy and alternatives. Staff owe professional integrity to the process. However, as an employee of the organization, practitioners have a vested interest in decisions which influence their workplace, yet the decision maker has the right to expect professional disinterest in the provision of institutional research and planning services. Thus, while planning may be seen as a high level line function, the professional who supports this function plays a staff role.

Whatever the organizational realization of the office, it is evident that not all campus institutional research and planning activities are done within its confines. Still, it is best for the office of institutional research and planning to adopt a formal operating relationship with its clients. The reason this office must remain on a proper operating basis with the rest of the institution is to avoid being drawn into day-to-day crises and, hence, distracted from those planning and management analysis tasks for which it has unique responsibility. Thus, the balance sought is one that while ensuring office independence from special interests and the objectivity of its recommendations and protecting it from excessive ad hoc requests to assist with short-range operating problems, does not render analysts ineffective because they are too remote from ongoing institutional operations. The balance will be struck judiciously and continuously adjusted by a perceptive office to meet the practical situation that exists on campus at any given time.

Bibliographical Essay

Examining New Trends in Administrative Computing (Staman, 1979), a sourcebook written by professionals with direct knowledge and experience in running computer services and information systems, presents the role computing plays in institutional research as well as the implications of advances in computing for organizational structures. It has a readable introduction to computer technology that addresses current issues in computer systems (for example, size, cost, ease of use, expandability, and availability) and indicates the reason delivery systems for computing power have become increasingly integrated networks of balanced resources that include hardware, software, and telecommunications. There is a good summary treatment of institutional research and planning's use of proprietary and nonproprietary software as well as a practical, insightful review of the people problem in higher education computing. The volume is a good review for the advanced person, a good introduction for the beginner, and a good source of further information.

Appraising Information Needs of Decision Makers (Adams, 1977) is based on the widely held premise that the overall record of information systems development in support of decision processes in higher education is not good. Written by a group of contributors who have extensive experience in higher education administration, the criticism is constructive and provides a checklist of ideas for those who will be considering information needs in the future. Several important notions are developed, including the importance of asking the right question; weaknesses of total information systems approaches; misunderstandings of the nature and use of information in organizational settings; new approaches of assessing outcomes, especially those related to the whole student; and the conflict between systematic management and traditional academic values.

Applying Analytic Methods to Planning and Management (Hopkins and Schroeder, 1977) is concerned with the practical use of operations research in institutions of higher education and is written especially for institutional researchers. There are six papers dealing with the following subjects: faculty resource planning, student enrollment forecasting, financial modeling, departmental faculty scheduling, cost analysis, and management system design. This is an excellent compendium that illustrates analytical approaches used by institutional researchers and planners.

Assessing Computer-Based Systems Models (Mason, 1976) is an important collection of papers on the theory, experience on two continents, and evaluation of computer models as tools for planning, management, and policymaking in postsecondary education. It is both comprehensive and concise in reviewing practical models and in pointing out how researchers and planners can benefit from the mature use of computer tools.

References

Adams, C. R. (Ed.). *New Directions for Institutional Research: Appraising Information Needs of Decision Makers,* no. 15. San Francisco: Jossey-Bass, 1977.

Baudin, J. "A Profile of the Operations and Organizational Structure of Institutional Research Offices Belonging to the Southern University Group of Twenty-Five." Baton Rouge: Louisiana State University, 1977.

Bowen, H. R. "The Products of Higher Education." In H. R. Bowen (Ed.), *New Directions for Institutional Research: Evaluating Institutions for Accountability,* no. 1. San Francisco: Jossey-Bass, 1974.

Bowen, H. R. "Teaching and Learning: 2000 A.D." In C. T. Stewart and T. R. Harvey (Eds.), *New Directions for Higher Education: Strategies for Significant Survival,* no. 12. San Francisco: Jossey-Bass, 1975.

Braybrooke, D., and Lindblom, C. E. *A Strategy of Decision.* Toronto, Ontario: Collier-Macmillan Canada, 1963.

Cohen, M. D., and March, J. G. *Leadership and Ambiguity: The American College President.* New York: McGraw-Hill, 1974.

Cope, R. G. (Ed.). *New Directions for Institutional Research: Professional Development for Institutional Research,* no. 23. San Francisco: Jossey-Bass, 1979.

Gardner, D. E. "Five Evaluation Frameworks: Implications for Decision Making in Higher Education." *Journal of Higher Education,* 1977, *48.*

Gross, E. "Universities as Organizations: A Study of Goals." *American Sociological Review,* 1968, *33,* 418–544.

Guba, E. G., and Stufflebeam, D. L. "Strategies for the Institutionalization of the CIPP Evaluation Model." Paper presented at eleventh annual PDK Symposium on Educational Research. Ohio State University, June 24, 1970.

Gulko, W. W. *Program Classification Structure.* Technical Report 27. Boulder, Colo.: National Center for Higher Education Management Systems at Western Interstate Commission for Higher Education, 1972.

Haight, M., and Romney, L. C. *NCHEMS Overview: A Training Document.* Boulder, Colo.: National Center for Higher Education Management Systems at Western Interstate Commission for Higher Education, 1975.

Hamblen, J. F., and others. *Fourth Inventory of Computers in Higher Education: An Interpretive Report.* Princeton, N.J.: *EDUCOM,* 1980.

Hartle, D. G. "Techniques and Processes of Administration." *Canadian Public Administration,* 1976, *19* (1).

Hillman, E. A. "Information Strategies for an Institutional Planning Process." Paper presented at eighteenth annual forum of The Association for Institutional Research. Houston, May 24, 1978. (ERIC ED 161 368; HE 010 599.)

Hodgkinson, H. L. "Goal Setting and Evaluation." In *Planning and Management Practices in Higher Education: Promise or Dilemma?* Report No. 26. Denver, Colorado: Education Commission of the States, 1972.

Hoenack, S. A. "Direct and Incentive Planning Within a University." In *Socio-Economic Planning, Science.* Vol. 2. Oxford, England: Permagon Press, 1979.

Hopkins, D. S. P., and Schroeder, R. G. (Eds.). *New Directions for Institutional Research: Applying Analytic Methods to Planning and Management,* no. 13. San Francisco: Jossey-Bass, 1977.

Hussain, K. M. "Planning Data Systems for Higher Education." *International Journal of Institutional Management in Higher Education,* 1978, *2* (2), 193–206.

Lasher, W. F. "The Comprehensive Institutional Planning Process and the Role of Information in It." *Planning for Higher Education,* 1978, *6* (4).

Lawrence, G. B., and Service, A. L. *Quantitative Approaches to Higher Education Management.* Higher Education Research Report No. 4. Washington, D.C.: ERIC, 1977.

Lockwood, G. "Planning." *International Journal of Institutional Management in Higher Education,* 1978, *2* (2), 121–139.

Mann, R. I. "The People Problem." In E. M. Staman (Ed.), *New Directions for Institutional Research: Examining New Trends in Administrative Computing,* no. 22. San Francisco: Jossey-Bass, 1979.

Mason, T. R. (Ed.). *New Directions for Institutional Research: Assessing Computer-Based System Models,* no. 9. San Francisco: Jossey-Bass, 1976.

Morstain, B., and Smart, J. "Institutional Research in Higher Education: Different Problems, Different Priorities?" In *Public Policy: Issues and Analyses: Proceedings of the 14th Annual Forum, The Association for Institutional Research.* Tallahassee, Fla.: Association for Institutional Research, 1974.

Nadeau, G. G. "Institutional Research Data for 'What' Decisions? Results of a Survey of Institutional Research Practices in Canada, United States, Western Europe, and Australia." In *Information for Decisions in Postsecondary Education: Proceedings of the 15th Annual Forum, The Association for Institutional Research.* Tallahassee, Fla.: Association for Institutional Research, 1975.

Perrow, C. "Analysis of Goals in Complex Organizations." In *Readings on Modern Organizations.* Englewood Cliffs, N.J.: Prentice-Hall, 1969.

Regents of the University of the State of New York. *Education Beyond High School.* Albany: New York State Education Department, 1971.

Ridge, J. W. "Organizing for Institutional Research." In *The AIR Professional File,* no. 1. Tallahassee, Fla.: Association for Institutional Research, 1978.

Ryland, J. N. "Proprietary Software and the Institutional Researcher." In E. M. Staman (Ed.), *New Directions for Institutional Research: Examining New Trends in Administrative Computing,* no. 22. San Francisco: Jossey-Bass, 1979.

Saunders, L. E. "Dealing with Information Systems: The Institutional Researcher's Problems and Prospects." In *The AIR Professional File,* no. 2. Tallahassee, Fla.: Association for Institutional Research, 1979.

Sheehan, B. S. "The Question of a Synthesis in Higher Education Management." In *Innovative Systems: Solution or Illusion? Proceedings of College and University Systems Exchange 1974 CAUSE National Conference.* Boulder, Colo.: College and University Systems Exchange, 1974.

Sheehan, B. S., and others. *Western Canadian Universities Task Force on Information Needs and Systems,* Report No. 1. Calgary, Alberta: University of Calgary, 1972.

Sibley, W. M. "Modes of University Government." *Canadian Journal of Higher Education,* 1976, *6* (1), 19–27.

Staman, E. M. (Ed.). *New Directions for Institutional Research: Examining New Trends in Administrative Computing,* no. 22. San Francisco: Jossey-Bass, 1979.

Tetlow, W. L., Jr. "Institutional Research: The Emergence of a Staff Function in Higher Education." Unpublished doctoral dissertation, Cornell University, 1973.

Thomas, C. R. "Nonproprietary Software as an Institutional Resource." In E. M. Staman (Ed.), *New Directions for Institutional Research: Examining New Trends in Administrative Computing,* no. 22. San Francisco: Jossey-Bass, 1979.

Tincher, W. A. *Summary of a Study of the Members of the Association for Institutional Research.* Auburn, Ala.: Auburn University, 1970.

Weathersby, G. "Inquiring Systems for Higher Education: A Perspective Based on Theories of Development of Organizations, Individuals and Decision Structures." In *Innovative Systems: Solution or Illusion? Proceedings of College and University Systems Exchange 1974 CAUSE National Conference.* Boulder, Colo.: College and University Systems Exchange, 1974.

Weathersby, G. "Decision Paradigms and Models for Higher Education." Presented at forty-eighth national meeting of the Institute for Management Sciences and the Operations Research Society of America, November 17, 1975.

Wildavsky, A. "The Self Evaluating Organization." *Public Administration Review,* 1972, *32* (5), 509–520.

27

Raymond M. Haas

Winning Acceptance for Institutional Research and Planning

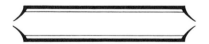

Perhaps the major problem in developing an effective planning and institutional research capability and structure for college or university decision making is the difficulty of getting the necessary structures and processes implemented or operational. The intent of this chapter is to analyze this problem and present a strategy or strategies for developing and organizing the planning and institutional research process.

A Conceptual Framework: Diffusion Theory in Developing and Organizing a Planning and Institutional Research Process

The problems involved in initiating a planning and institutional research process are not very different from problems that arise in the introduction of any new idea or new approach in any context. As a result, the body of knowledge on the adoption and diffusion of ideas and inventions can provide the conceptual context within which the following suggestions are based (see Rogers, 1973; Rogers and Shoemaker, 1971).

A first and elemental lesson from research on innovation is that new products that require dramatically different patterns of user behavior do not have a high probability of being adopted by the consumer. Therefore, in every way possible, a fledgling institutional research and planning function should be incorporated into the established processes of the institution. If, as has often been said, every institution has always engaged in planning and self-evaluation, then, in a very real sense, the formal establishment of a planning and institutional research process should represent merely the enhancement of ongoing functions. However, more often than not, planning and institutional research functions are set up separate from ongoing management processes, bypassing existing activities and structures rather than enhancing them.

The formation of a "new" office of planning and institutional research or a special task force on planning may guarantee that they will find it difficult to survive. Because administrators cannot abdicate their responsibility for planning, they cannot assign this function to a separate committee of specialists or representatives of administration, faculty, and student body. Rather, the planning system should enhance the process of administrator, faculty, and student consultation—a process that has strong roots in academia. In essence, a formal planning system is, more than anything else, an elaborate communications system for complex organizations, and in that light, it should be structured to make ongoing systems more effective. Similarly, because all administrators engage in institutional research, a new process for such activity has the highest chance of success if it becomes, at least initially, an extension of the current work of the administrators. This principle holds no matter what the size of the institution.

In most cases, the planning function can be a major role of the assistant to the president. In small institutions, this role may be performed by a member of the faculty on a part-time basis, in which case the role of the faculty may be far more direct than consultative. But the overriding principle is that established processes and offices be used.

Offices of institutional research often evolve out of presidential or vice-presidential fact-finding units that aid in policy analysis or from academic research bureaus or assistant dean's offices that become stretched to their limit by the need to complete forms for transmittal of data to governing boards or government agencies. In either case, the process of institutional research should remain close to established administrative offices. Ultimately, the planning and institutional research functions must cross the administrative route along which policy questions pass on their way to resolution. Unless they do, they have little chance of affecting resource allocation decisions.

The second principle for achieving acceptance of a new idea is that those who will use it or will be charged with its implementation must participate in its development. This principle certainly holds for those developing the planning and institutional research function. Participation can be most effective when it is structured or at least well defined in advance. Few persons can say with assurance, "I participated," unless their participation is defined in terms of activities that can be monitored. These activities will vary from institution to institution and between administrators within an institution. Exhibit 1 illustrates participation in planning and in institutional research as might be developed by the faculty, staff, and student body of a large university and stated in the form of a plan of work for a council on planning:

Exhibit 1. Plan of Work for Council on Planning

1. Prepare a suggested statement of planning assumptions, including an enrollment forecast, for the planning period.
2. Coordinate the review and revision of the statements of objectives for each college, school, and major nonacademic area.
3. Review proposals submitted by deans and directors and recommend a schedule of capital improvement projects for the planning period.
4. Review and suggest needed modifications to the space allocation plan for all buildings, schools, colleges, and nonacademic areas.
5. Review the contents of the most recent edition of the institution's statistical report and recommend items that could be added, deleted, or presented in a different way.
6. Recommend the development of formal statements of planning assumptions for the individual units that have newly formed planning councils. Recommend means for involving all unit planning councils in more activities performed by the council on planning on an institutionwide basis.
7. Continue the practice of meeting with the planning bodies representing the city and county.
8. Develop a proposed program evaluation process for the institution using the groundwork established in the current budgeting and planning activities of the institution, including especially the material and procedures developed as part of the accreditation self-study and the policy statements of the board of trustees on this topic.

Just as participation in developing the planning and institutional research process is important for its acceptance, so it is important that the newly established processes provide immediate and palpable assistance to staff outside the central administration. This assistance need not be in the form of increased resources. For example, department heads may count a new system valuable if it helps them have a common perception of the future of the institution, saves time spent in administrative activities, improves communication, assures equitable consideration of program proposals, increases direct and timely feedback to proposals, or assures that academic priorities are established solely by academic officers. But no invention can find acceptance solely on the basis of alleged or rumored benefits. Data files and management information systems can help furnish evidence of actual benefits, but the majority of the benefits derived from planning and institutional research are not dependent on the quality of the data systems available to them but stem from a mind set. They manifest a commitment to a way of doing things and that way has benefits that come independently from how well the effort is carried out. Moreover, institutions at this stage should avoid falling prey to proposals for complete data systems. It is most unlikely that an institution new to planning or institutional research would have in-house the level of abstract thought and operational skills required to operate a comprehensive system of data collection and analysis. And, no mention has even been made of available computer hardware. In summary, the planning and institutional research process must be supported by appropriate data files and a management information system. However, that which is appropriate need not be very sophisticated and may not be too accurately identifiable until some progress has been made in specifying the functions of planning and institutional research. Further, these functions have benefit if they only improve the qualitative judgments that always have to be made regardless of the availability of data systems.

A fourth principle is the difference between an invention and an innovation, in that an innovation is an invention that has been assimilated into the institutional or social fabric. In the life of an institution, planning and institutional research will vacillate between the invention stage and the innovation stage. Unlike a budget, planning and institutional research typically have no formal lives of their own. As a result, the managers of these functions must constantly instruct participants in them regarding how they fit in the scheme of things. The stage must be set for planning and institutional research over and over again, for example, by including in every set of operating instructions a note about the overall procedural context in which the function is being performed. This is not because the value of planning and institutional research is neither self-evident nor easily demonstrable but, rather, because of the overwhelming inertia against planning as a process and against formal analysis as a basis for decision making. Some managers may look for the "burning decks" on which to make decisions of great consequence when there obviously is no time for calm, rational analysis carried out as part of an orderly planning process. However, among airline pilots, sports stars, and administrators, it is well known that long hours of practice in a controlled process is the sole approach to sound performance when an urgent situation arises.

Finally, as in aiding the diffusion of ideas of any type, the strategy for developing and organizing a process of planning and institutional research should unfold in a gradual and orderly manner within the context of a flexible plan for bringing the process to full acceptance. Planning and institutional research cannot emerge full-blown within a single year; thus, various activities should be introduced according to an annual schedule for bringing the process to maturity. In keeping within this proposed framework for successful innovation, the institutional research process should begin by assuming responsibility for gathering and reporting data requested by outside agencies. By proceeding in this way, the institutional research function can be woven into the fabric of the institution. It becomes important to its daily operation. Moreover, some of the data provided to external agencies, if properly assembled and analyzed, can be highly valuable to persons within the institution. Therefore, a good second step in the development of an institutional research function is the regular publication of a statistical profile of the institution, perhaps using only data extracted from reports to external agencies.

In describing any object, person, or institution, the narrator chooses certain salient characteristics or facets as parts of a framework for a complete description. The use of a framework becomes especially important if more than one institution is to be described for the sake of comparison or if descriptions are to be made at various intervals of time. If planning is to be effective, it must be done regularly and persistently; so it is useful to develop an institutional taxonomy for planning. Ideally, this taxonomy should reflect the data elements in the data base for the institution. For an institution new to institutional research and planning, the following six elements may suffice:

- the scope of the mission
- programs
- student body
- faculty and staff
- financial resources
- facilities and equipment

On a practical basis, these facets of the institution can serve as a table of contents for an annual statistical report or profile of the institution's past.

Admittedly, the six facets are all endogenous to the institution. Some institutions may also wish to report on external variables that affect them. A useful but elementary taxonomy for that purpose may include:

- legal environment
- political environment
- economic environment
- state of benchmark institutions
- social and cultural environment
- supply and demand for faculty and staff
- supply and demand for students

After developing these reports on a regular basis, an office of institutional research can progress reasonably to the preparation of annual forecasts of them. The goal, of course, is to include in the statistical profile and forecast all data used regularly in the decision-making activities of the institution. Many institutional research offices begin as described, but few consciously develop their activities as part of an overall plan whereby institutional administration and faculty are being brought to a commonly held level of awareness of the past from which they potentially can cast a commonly held design for the future.

Having refined and routinized the preparation of historic profiles and forecasts of the future and having settled in for the task of preparing all reports to outside agencies, the institutional research function typically reaches a plateau in its development. The next level of functional sophistication may be reached with the establishment of a planning function. A formal planning effort provides the context within which institutional research can come of age in the sense of being used in its most mature manner as an adjunct to the decision-making and resource allocation functions. Like the institutional research function, the planning function should be planned to come to fruition gradually, gathering momentum until it is capable of achieving a life of its own and, if possible, being divorced from the particular level of support accorded it by any particular person in the succession of institutional presidents.

Organizing for Research and Planning

Among the questions of policy and philosophy that arise in the development of the research and planning process is that of who should be responsible for planning. The answer is simply that every manager is responsible for planning and none can delegate that responsibility without losing his or her effectiveness. As a result, when an institution establishes a planning office, care must be taken in assigning its charge. This charge must not create the illusion that the planning office will plan and managers therefore need not do so. Rather, the role of the planning office is to develop a planning process within which each manager carries out his or her planning activities.

Ideally, the role of a planning office should be to develop a planning process, to provide planning aids or tools for managers (in cooperation with institutional research), and to monitor the execution of the planning process on behalf of the overall institution (see Haas, 1976). Because planning should be the responsibility of each manager, the staff required to start a planning function is not large (typically, one professional person and some clerical help).

Just as there must be a long-range plan for the planning and institutional research process, there must be a short-range plan as well. Plans produced through an orderly process will probably be better than those that are not. It follows that both the planning and institutional research process should be scheduled for the year. Although the schedule can be flexible and certainly must be subject to revision, it can provide the orderly approach that puts a premium on rational decision making and, by not being random in nature, allows administrators to schedule their work, leaving more time for their responsibilities as academic leaders.

An initial step in developing a planning schedule can logically be the documentation of all present activities related to planning. With no change in present practice, the planning staff can schedule all planning activities for the following year, noting especially any discontinuities in the process. Another early step in the evolution of a planning process involves scheduling the output from the institutional research function so it reaches participants in the planning process in a timely manner.

Some institutions use the program evaluation review technique (PERT) and/or the critical path method (CPM) in developing their schedules. No matter how elementary or sophisticated, the schedule also serves a role in the strategy for developing an institutional research and planning process. For instance, scheduling invariably helps identify missing steps and demonstrate that the president is serious about planning and institutional research. A schedule also helps in achieving integrated planning, if only because its use will help the various parts of the institution complete their planning activities at roughly the same time. Exhibit 2 illustrates a schedule for planning and the typical activities in a planning process. The institutional research deadlines are both inferred and explicitly stated throughout.

Unlike the planning function, institutional research is not an easily decentralized task. The need for a central office is strong and the use of one promises some benefit. This point is related to the idea advanced earlier regarding the importance of a perception of institutional past and future commonly held by all the administrators so an institutional sense of direction can be achieved. In that

Exhibit 2. Schedule of Activities Associated with the Development of the Annual Plan and Operating Budget for 1980–81

Date	Activity
Jan. 1979	Prepare schedule of activities associated with the development of the annual plan and operating budget for 1980–81.
July 1979	Council on planning completes the statements of institutional objectives, planning assumptions, and the enrollment forecast for the period 1980–1990.
	Institutional research office completes preparation of planning data for each college and school.
	President's office approves and distributes the statements of objectives, planning assumptions, and the enrollment forecast for the period 1980–1990.
	Planning office proposes resource allocation guidelines for 1980–81.
	Planning office prepares and distributes procedural instructions for developing the 1980–81 annual plan and operating budget.
Aug. 1979	Deans prepare the annual report for their college or school and submit it to the president's office.
	Using the planning materials and format provided them, deans prepare a draft of their annual plan and operating budget request and rank proposals for resource allocation and resource reallocation in priority order. Deans review draft of their annual report, annual plan, and operating budget request with faculty.
Sep. 1979	Deans present annual report for 1979–80 and operating budget request for 1980–81 to president's office.
	President's office holds planning conference with each dean.
Oct. 1979	Using the statements of objectives and planning assumptions as decision criteria, president's office establishes universitywide priorities from among the plans and budget requests submitted.
	President's office tests budgetary implications of its planning decisions and evaluates alternative resource allocation schemes.
Nov. 1979	President makes decisions necessary to formulate a proposed annual plan and operating budget request for 1980–81 for the institution.
Dec. 1979	Submit annual plan and operating budget request for 1980–81 to the board of trustees.
Jan. 1980	Board of trustees makes decisions regarding the annual plan and operating budget for 1980–81.
	President briefs deans on proposed annual plan and budget so revisions may be started based on this feedback.
May 1980	President and board of trustees reassess the annual plan and its attendant resource allocation decisions in light of any new developments. Any changes are communicated to the deans.
June 1980	Prepare operating budget for 1980–81.
July 1980	Institution begins implementation of annual plan and operating budget for 1980–81.

Note: For a more detailed presentation on planning schedules as used at the author's institution, see Kieft, R. N. *Academic Planning: Four Institutional Case Studies.* Boulder, Colo.: National Center for Higher Education Management Systems, 1978, pp. 5–63.

regard, a centralized institutional research function assures more uniformity of data, standards of measurement, and quality of analysis in the planning and evaluation functions all administrators must perform.

Institutional research offices need not become overly expensive and institutionally domineering. For instance, it makes good sense to keep research separate from record keeping and place the responsibility for data collection and data file maintenance on the administrative offices that have the greatest need for the data and are in most direct contact with its source. For instance, the registrar should be responsible for student records and for reports required from those records. The role of institutional research in this regard is to expedite report preparation by administrative offices so they are ready in a timely manner and to coordinate the collation of data as produced by several offices to assure the consistency and relevancy of summary reports. The persistent tension this particular separation of assignments produces revolves around the fact that the administrative offices typically have needs different from the institutional research office in terms of the timeliness, accuracy, and format of the data files.

Beyond routine reports, the more substantive work of the institutional research function lies in either policy analysis or "pure" educational research. As mentioned earlier, this part of the assignment is a natural outgrowth of the establishment of a formal planning process. As in many areas of organizational behavior, the creative part of the assignment is the feature that makes the routine work bearable. If properly managed, there is little doubt that the work can be cost-effective.

For most institutions, a policy decision is made to orient the work of the institutional research office toward managerial needs rather than toward a form of scholarly research that competes with the work of faculty members employed in the particular academic disciplines involved. To obtain effective policy analysis, it becomes necessary to provide the persons working in institutional research with an appropriate perspective on institutional operation. For this reason, it is important that institutional research personnel attend the policy and decision-making meetings of the president's cabinet, if only as "back-benchers." In listening to the deliberations on institutional policy, directors of institutional research can identify some of the data gaps their offices might fill. Indeed, only this perspective will allow institutional planners to develop processes for future-oriented decision making with which the leaders of the institution might feel comfortable.

Placement of the Functions

The need for access to policy deliberations leads naturally to a consideration of the appropriate place for the planning function and the institutional research function in the overall organizational structure. The need for a "view from the top" must be tempered by the need for the president to have a manageable span of control. If it is inconvenient for the president or a presidential assistant to monitor directly the functions of planning or institutional research, the choice among vice-presidents should be based upon the primary function of the institution involved and the level of team relationship existing at that level. If the vice-presidents work as a team, it seems desirable to have the institutional research function and the planning function report to the office of the vice-president for administration or its equivalent. In that way, the administrative functions of managing a planning process and providing data for decision making can be provided as a service to the academic affairs function, leaving administrators in that area more time to devote to academic and institutional leadership. However, if the vice-presidents do not work well as a team, the planning function and the institutional research function should appropriately serve academic affairs.

Some institutions merge the functions of planning and institutional research into one office. Under this approach, the development of planning data and other aids for administrators receives the major attention of the institutional research personnel along with detailed analyses of proposed plans. As an aside, it may be more consistent with administrative theory and practice to merge the functions of planning and budgeting wherein the managerial rather than accounting aspects of the latter assume full stature and to merge the functions of institutional research and internal audit wherein the evaluative rather than compliance aspects of auditing achieve full stature. Of course, in smaller, less complex institutions, it is acceptable to merge the institutional research and planning functions in one office (and perhaps in one person), if only because the work to be done may not require the efforts of more than a single professional.

Because the choice of organizational structure is hypothesized to depend on the level of administrative teamwork that exists, it is important to realize the countereffect of sound planning processes on teamwork. Generally, the result of planning in an institution of higher education is that the many parts of a characteristically unwieldy organization move in the same direction at roughly the same rate of speed. This is done not so much by plotting a course as by providing a common understanding of the institution's past and present for its constituents and administrators and by keeping its collective eyes on its objectives. Achieving the objectives is served by planning in the same way follow-through aids a golfer or tennis player in hitting a ball to the target selected. Accuracy becomes less a matter of force and aim than of concentration and maintaining a sense of direction. In this respect, planning (especially in a large organization) is, more than anything else, an effective communications process with the potential consequence of driving an institutionwide perspective far down inside the organizational structure. The result is not only potentially greater teamwork among the various administrators but a concomitantly higher probability for the more consistent application of available resources to the highest priority concerns of the institution. This line of reasoning, when carried to its logical and perhaps more easily obtainable conclusion, would suggest that effective planning permits more regular and less severe pruning of institutional activities, which in the end fosters institutional health and goal-directed growth.

Irrespective of the place of institutional research and planning in the overall organizational structure, adequate provision must be made for the participatory nature of governance in the academic community. Collegiality, after all, should be central to anyone's idea of a university. As a result, the question of the role of the faculty, staff, and student body in planning and institutional research is begged. From a practical point of view, every service unit in a college or university should consider having an advisory committee made up of users of its services. However, the broader question concerns the role of the faculty, staff, and students not in shaping administrative processes but rather in shaping the substance. What role should the members of the body politic have in shaping the future of a college or university?

In the philosophy of college and university planning described earlier in this chapter, one of the key determinants of institutional destiny is its statement of objectives. Again, this is so because it is principally by keeping its collective eyes on its objectives that an intrinsically and desirably unwieldy organization like a college or university moves toward goal attainment. However, statements of objectives ultimately must be used not only as direction finders but also as decision criteria for resource allocation. It is only in this latter use that planning becomes more than an institutional aside. To be explicit, the extent to which it contributes to the attainment of institutional objectives is the only defensible basis for arguing the merits of any proposal for funding a particular program or mix of programs. As a result, while management theory would hold that administrators are responsible for planning, it follows in a collegial environment such as a college or university, plans prepared by administrators should embody the perspective of the faculty, staff, and student body, especially regarding institutional objectives.

In developing and organizing a planning and institutional research process, most institutions provide a faculty, staff, and student perspective to the determination of their future by constituting a planning committee made up of representatives of each constituency. Certain principles govern the creation of planning committees. As with planning offices, the charge to a planning committee cannot be "to plan." That function is reserved to the managers. To do otherwise would cause the administrator to abdicate his or her responsibility for planning and cause the committee's planning to be ineffectual, if only because it was being carried on outside the usual administrative and decision-making processes. The resultant role of a planning committee is to see that the plans developed by the administration are prepared with a clear bias and deference to its membership's perspective. In a practical sense, under this approach, the faculty, staff, and students shape the institution's future by playing a major role in determining the decision criteria (objectives and planning assumptions) on the basis of which administrators make plans and allocate resources. Out of concern for there being checks and balances, the system described requires resource allocation decision criteria (objectives and planning assumptions) be published for all involved to know and resource allocation decisions (in priority order) also be published so participants in the planning process may determine whether resources were allocated in accordance with the published criteria.

There are other principles that should be followed in assuring participatory governance encompasses participatory planning as well:

1. The constituent groups should select their representatives in a manner they choose. As an alternate, some administrators choose persons they feel are leaders or are especially well qualified members of their groups. However, given the "check and balance" role of planning, this approach may undercut the planning committee's credibility.
2. The work of planning committees should be very well planned. Participation in planning is an amorphous and vague assignment at best. In addition, given the long-term results that accrue to planning activities, it is common for planning committees to suffer from a feeling of lack of accomplishment. The preparation of a plan of work on an annual basis allows for a mutual understanding of a fairly precise definition of what it means to participate in the planning process. It also forestalls some of the frustration involved in waiting for long-term benefits to materialize because committee members acting according to a plan can better see their efforts take effect.
3. In larger institutions, there is a need to replicate at the level of a college, school, or department the participatory planning occurring on an institutionwide level. By using plans of work complementary to those used by

the institutional planning committee, the college or departmental committees can aid deans or chairpersons in the same way as the president is aided by the parent committee.
4. The members of the planning committees must be kept well informed regarding their institution and higher education generally. A possible standard for members of the institutional planning committee is that they be briefed to the level of a dean.

Because of the importance of a planning committee to participatory planning, the head of the planning office and therefore the chief staff member to the planning committee should be someone with credibility, through credentials and experience, among the constituent groups. A member of the faculty with a penchant for decision processes and diligent staff work is ideal. Faculty status also is desirable for the leader of the institutional research function. In this latter case, it is important to have someone with an academic perspective because of the need to see that the data on academic affairs are properly understood in their many nuances so they are not improperly presented as a basis for decision making regarding resource allocation.

Intrainstitutional Effects

The establishment of a process for planning and institutional research will have certain predictable effects on the institution that, because they can be far-reaching, deserve consideration when these processes are themselves still in the planning stage. For instance, a more analytical and planned approach to decision making typically reduces the effectiveness of persuasion and the hidden agenda as managerial tactics. Admittedly, this result will vary among institutions, but it will occur. That is not to say that politics do not have a part in planning and institutional research. Nor can one say there will be any major reduction in the use of qualitative data in making some types of decisions. However, it is likely that political decisions and value judgments will be brought more sharply into focus when they are introduced within the context of a process of planning and institutional research. In addition, just as a capitalistic economic system tends to reward capitalistic behavior, so a planning system tends to reward those who think ahead and institutional research tends to reward those who employ an analytical approach to decision making.

Every planning and institutional research process ever established contains the seeds for potential self-destruction because the orderliness of the processes and the discipline they require seem to create the expectation of growth and prosperity. A good planning and institutional research process may only serve to aid the institution in managing an unavoidable period of decline.

Some of the results of introducing planning and institutional research will depend upon the institution's past experience with those activities. For instance, the history of institutional persistence with planning is not very good. Therefore, when a planning process is reintroduced after a period of discontinuity, there is some level of doubt that the current attempt will survive. As a result, some persons may understandably refrain from full participation. This problem can be solved only by a new level of demonstrated persistence. Indeed, it may take an administration as many as three consecutive years of annual planning to demonstrate it is serious about using planning in the decision-making process. This acceptance period can be shortened by the administration's unflinching allegiance to the planning process and by the use of every means possible to identify the procedural context of even seemingly isolated incidents in it. Regular training programs help in this regard and help the trainer gain new insights into the process.

Institutional research may be less affected by the persistence phenomenon, perhaps because it seems to be more uniformly accepted as a necessary part of institutional administration. This may be solely because institutional research units produce physically observable reports that line officers then need not prepare. As compared to planning, therefore, the value of institutional research is more self-evident. The institutional research function has shown itself to be far more durable than the planning function at most institutions of higher education; and as a result, its role is better defined and there is a stronger professional society and sense of identity for its practitioners.

The Effect of Extra-Institutional Factors

Factors and organizations external to the college or university affect the development of a planning and institutional research function within the institution. They include the federal government; statewide boards charged with regulation or coordination; accrediting agencies; state legislatures and/or principal donors; constituent groups served by the institution; competing institutions; social and political attitudes toward higher education; and economic conditions. Aside from recognized shifts in the locus of decision making in public higher education from individual institutions to central boards, the principal recent effect of external agencies has been a potential compromising of the internal relevancy of the institution's data bases and reporting mechanisms. As a result, in developing a process for planning and a process for institutional research, adequate provision must be made for the data requirements and reporting deadlines of the external agencies without sacrificing the needs of the institution itself. Work being done nationally in developing data element dictionaries may help solve this problem.

Statewide coordinating and regulatory boards have had an impact on planning for public higher education principally because the emphasis on planning has gradually been shifting from the individual institutions to the state system. As long as resources are to be allocated at the broader level, it is only natural that this trend will continue. However, a result will be the need for more rather than less sophistication in planning at the level of the individual institution. This fact is caused by the greater level of coordination of effort required in the execution of any multitiered plan and by the increased level of sophistication in fiscal management caused by the allocation of resources across another layer of subaccounts. While there is no apparent move toward direct federal coordination of higher education institutions as there is at the state level, there are substantial federal reporting requirements in support of federal regulations and policies. These regulations and policies must be considered in the development of institutional plans and their reporting requirements have the potential for monopolizing all of the budgeted effort of an office of institutional research.

In recent years accrediting agencies have given special recognition to the need for continuous planning and evaluation. Instead of insisting on the standard institutional self-evaluation, some accrediting agencies have permitted colleges and universities to submit a description of their in-house system of planning and evaluation as a means of demonstrating their ability to evaluate themselves. Indeed, it seems ironic that some institutions have been conducting self-studies in the absence of an explicit institutional plan. The old saw, "If you don't know where you are going, any road will take you there," suggests that it is impossible to measure progress in the absence of a plan. Any institution considering the establishment of a function of planning and/or institutional research might explore the possibility of tying it to a forthcoming institutional accreditation. As in the politics of national governance, the presence of an outside force may prove to be the catalyst required for the acceptance of innovation and change.

Federal regulations, state legislatures, boards of trustees, and principal donors may all provide an impetus for planning and institutional research, as noted in Part One of this book; but this pressure may be too sporadic to have lasting effect. Again, this latter statement is true simply because planning must be continuous to be effective. As might be expected, institutions that have developed and sustained useful processes for planning and institutional research have found it beneficial to make their legislatures, trustees, and donors aware of their efforts because the knowledge of such work tends to promote confidence in the accountability of the administration.

More than anything else, deteriorating economic conditions tend to be the single most influential external incentive for expanding the planning and institutional research process. This is so much the case that there may be a general subliminal association among persons in higher education between bad times and the need to plan. Actually, bad times may be the worst times in which to start planning because there is too much impatience for results and too little experience with the selective use of resource reallocation to let the new processes be effective. In addition, there is little receptivity to new modes of operation when everyone knows the intent is to reduce effort rather than to reallocate or expand it. Finally, an institution must invest money to earn money from planning and analysis, and it is precisely when times are hard that long-term investment capital is most difficult to find.

In summary, the best time to begin institutional research and planning is the present. Indeed, for most institutions, it is less a question of starting out fresh than of beginning again or, even more likely, of formalizing and enhancing what is being done presently on an informal or modest basis.

Conclusion

The problems involved in implementing a process of planning and a process of institutional research are not very different from those involved in earning acceptance for a new idea in any context. There is a body of knowledge on the diffusion of ideas which can provide a useful conceptual framework within which to proceed. The new processes should themselves be well planned and should employ established administrative procedures for their operation. There should be extensive participation in the development of the new systems especially by those who will be using their results. Also every available opportunity

should be taken to reinforce the acceptance of change by using a regular program of instruction for users of the systems. Finally, while the new processes
should be useful to the central administration, care should be taken to see that
planning and institutional research provide immediate and appreciable assistance to deans and department chairpersons.

Certain questions of policy and philosophy arise in the development of a
planning process and a process for institutional research. As in the development
procedure for any administrative system, these questions concern: the appropriate locus of responsibility; the roles of various participants; the desirable administrative structure; and the most appropriate stance in questions involving
values. Just as the judgments regarding policy and philosophy will affect the
final shape of the planning and institutional research process, so, too, the new
processes will have an impact on the organization. The probable principal impact
will come in the form of a reduction in the effect of persuasion as a force in
decision making. Of course, no college or university develops new administrative
systems in a vacuum. External agencies and other forces impinge on the systems'
development process and on the operation of systems once they are installed.
These external agencies include statewide boards, all levels of government,
accrediting agencies, constituent groups, major donors, and competing institutions. One of the main effects caused by these agencies on institutional research has been a compromising of the internal relevancy of data bases and reporting mechanisms. As regards planning, the influence of external forces has
led to a greater centralization of resource allocation decisions and a concomitant need for processes that can serve several levels of program aggregation
simultaneously.

Bibliographical Essay

In *Academic Planning: Four Institutional Case Studies,* Kieft (1978) reports in
detail on the planning processes used in four types and sizes of institutions. The
material is especially useful for persons and institutions just developing a planning and institutional research function because it includes statements from the
institutions regarding the impetus and motivations for academic planning. The
book also includes a large variety of forms, schedules, and illustrations that could
profitably be adapted to any institution.

Kieft, Armijo, and Bucklew (1978) provides a three-step approach to developing a planning process in a college or university. The work also is useful to
persons starting an institutional research function because, in a chapter on the
context of planning, the authors describe the institutionwide information studies
needed to support the planning process. The authors also suggest various forms
and schedules.

In this chapter, I hypothesized that the introduction of a formal planning
process, a function of institutional research, presents many of the same problems
involved in introducing a new managerial approach or new idea to any organization. There is a body of knowledge on the diffusion of innovations that can be
very helpful to the executive charged with establishing new administrative practices. Rogers and Shoemaker (1971) have been widely quoted on the topic.

Various publications of the Society for College and University Planning
(SCUP) and the Association for Institutional Research (AIR) should be useful to

the person introducing a formal planning process or a function of institutional research. Each organization publishes the proceedings of its annual meetings. The SCUP publishes a journal titled *Planning for Higher Education*. The AIR sponsors a journal titled *Research in Higher Education* and a quarterly sourcebook titled *New Directions for Institutional Research*. Both organizations also sponsor seminars for persons new to their fields. Lyons (1976) provides the newly appointed institutional research officer a descriptive compendium of available resources.

Perhaps the greatest benefit to be derived from attending the annual meetings of SCUP and AIR is the opportunity to converse with persons who are or have been struggling with the same types of problems. The papers presented tend to deal with those problems. Bluhm (1971) is of use to persons developing a process of institutional research. Case studies on new efforts also occupy a part of the agendas for both organizations (see Freeman and Yeager, 1976).

Some more or less packaged and complete systems of institutional planning are available from various vendors. Because they are viewed as being the analytical base for the planning function, these systems, at least inferentially, offer suggestions for establishing a process of institutional research. Each packaged system has some merit, but none has universal applicability across the broad scope of existing institutions of higher education. Therefore, those wanting to adopt a packaged system should pursue references carefully in order to achieve the best fit possible between system and institution and to determine if the best fit possible is satisfactory.

Finally, two bibliographies are noteworthy for their comprehensive coverage of topics related to planning and institutional research. Halstead (1979) and Staman (1978) should be especially useful to persons attempting to initiate a new process in either field.

References

Bluhm, H. P. "The Place of Institutional Research in the Organizational Structure: Publications and Reports." In C. T. Stewart (Ed.), *Institutional Research and Institutional Policy Formulation*. Claremont, Calif.: Association for Institutional Research, 1971.

Freeman, J. E., and Yeager, J. L. "The Design and Implementation of a Comprehensive Planning and Resource Management System: A Case Study." Paper presented at eleventh annual meeting of the Society for College and University Planning, July 1976.

Haas, R. M. "Integrating Academic, Fiscal, and Facilities Planning." *Planning for Higher Education*, 1976, 5 (5), 2–5.

Halstead, D. K. (Ed.). *Higher Education Planning, A Bibliographic Handbook*. Washington, D.C.: U.S. Government Printing Office, 1979.

Kieft, R. N. *Academic Planning: Four Institutional Case Studies*. Boulder, Colo.: National Center for Higher Education Management Systems, 1978.

Kieft, R. N., Armijo, F., and Bucklew, N. S. *A Handbook for Institutional Academic and Program Planning: From Idea to Implementation*. Boulder, Colo.: National Center for Higher Education Management Systems, 1978.

Lyons, J. M. *Memorandum to a Newcomer to the Field of Institutional Research*. Tallahassee, Fla.: Association for Institutional Research, 1976.

Rogers, E. M. "Social Structure and Social Change." In G. Zaltman (Ed.), *Processes and Phenomena of Social Change*. New York: Wiley, 1973.

Rogers, E. M., and Shoemaker, F. F. *Communication of Innovations*. (2nd ed.) New York: Free Press, 1971.

Staman, E. M. *A Catalogue on Planning in Higher Education—Organizations, Periodicals, Bibliography*. Halifax, Canada: Society for College and University Planning, 1978.

28

Dorothy M. Knoell

Planning in Community Colleges

Community colleges were the last segment of public higher education to be developed, largely in response to the nation's commitment after World War II to the provision of two years of low-cost education beyond high school for all who were interested and would benefit from it. In many states, community colleges were established as an extension of the common school system, with local funding from property taxes, governance by locally elected boards, and responsive to community needs and values. When these conditions prevailed, community colleges were not in direct competition with four-year institutions for state funds for operations. They often enjoyed a considerable amount of freedom to plan and then develop, with a minimum amount of interference from state agencies and governing boards. Until the early 1970s, planning for continuing growth was the dominant mode in the community colleges. Growth was expected to result from the addition of programs and services for new constituencies, for example, the handicapped and older adults, as well as the expansion of physical facilities in previously underserved areas.

Unlike planning in four-year colleges and universities, community college planning has been anchored in the assumption that there were no real limits on the kinds of students they should serve or the programs they might develop as long as they did not move into upper-division and graduate courses. As a result, community colleges have planned not only for the recent high school graduates seeking preparation for employment or transfer into a baccalaureate program but also for older adults and lifelong learners at one end of the age scale and for preschool children and their parents, high school dropouts, and accelerated students at the other. Looked at another way, community colleges have planned not only for the middle-class, white majority in all age groups but also for minorities by virtue of their racial/ethnic identification, family income and socioeconomic status, physical and other disabilities, readiness for college, and overall ability to profit from traditional programs. Thus, the community colleges have been less constrained than the four-year institutions in their planning by traditional notions about "higher" education and the selection of students to pursue it. Instead, they have been responsive to the needs of new constituencies for opportunities for education beyond high school and of the more traditional students for new kinds of programs and services during a time when higher education has lost credibility as a guarantor of good jobs and a high standard of living.

Changing Conditions in the Eighties

As community colleges plan for the 1980s, they share many of the constraints facing other segments of higher education—the decrease in the number of eighteen- to twenty-four-year-olds; declining interest among young people in seeking college degrees, particularly in fields not related directly to employment; a lack of public confidence in education at all levels; and rising costs related to inflation, accompanied by limitations on state funding. The special constraints facing community colleges include, first, increased competition for students on the part of both public and independent colleges and universities. This new competition is a natural concomitant of there being fewer young people to compete for, but with vastly increased financial aid available to low-income students who would not attend community college in the absence of such aid. Special outreach and recruitment activities undertaken by four-year institutions under their new student affirmative action programs have also increased the competition for students from racial/ethnic minority and other disadvantaged groups. Furthermore, community college domination of remedial or developmental education at the postsecondary level is ending as other types of collegiate institutions conclude that large numbers of their students cannot read, write, and compute at a level judged to be appropriate for college work and start new remediation programs. Finally, institutions granting the baccalaureate degree are now attempting to respond to their students' increased interest in career preparation and, in so doing, are entering into competition with community colleges in some occupational areas in which the associate degree has been regarded as appropriate preparation.

A second constraint somewhat unique to community colleges is the absence of consensus concerning priorities among the various constituencies the community colleges serve, or among the programs and services appropriate to different groups. While denying that they are or should be "all things to all people," community colleges have added constituencies during the recent era of rapid growth without taking time to address questions of priorities for an era of limited resources. Failure in past planning to deal adequately with issues related to program and service duplication is a third problem that may impede present planning. Duplication in this instance may involve adult schools and regional occupational centers administered by other public educational agencies, proprietary schools offering occupational training at the postsecondary level, and other community colleges that offer the same high-cost programs. Fourth, the past inattention to criteria and standards for defining what is "education" versus "experience" or "activity," or "credit" versus "noncredit," may also limit the freedom of community colleges to plan in an era of limited funding. Enrollment-driven funding mechanisms have given some colleges an incentive to "enroll" participants in programs with limited educational outcomes, for example, handicapped adults in sheltered workshops and patients in convalescent homes, in order to obtain funding for such programs. Finally, the traditional community college commitment to provide low-cost education to the residents of the areas they serve may be a constraint in future planning if, as expected, states' willingness or ability to provide funds in lieu of tuition and fees is less than in the past. A big question in planning for the 1980s will be how much rather than whether to charge students for various programs and services. However, as student charges are increased, the community colleges must expect increased competition from four-year institutions in attracting students who formerly chose the community colleges for economic reasons.

The outlook for planning for the 1980s is not entirely a compounding of enrollment and fiscal constraints. Goals for student affirmative action are unlikely to be achieved by the end of the present decade, even under the condition of full funding for student financial aid. Although women are no longer a minority group at the undergraduate level, other groups for whom affirmative action plans and goals have been developed are moving rather slowly toward equal participation in higher education with the present majority. To the racial/ethnic minorities and low-income groups that were the target of special planning activities in the mid 1970s have been added the handicapped and older adults, variously defined. The latter group is of particular concern in planning for the 1980s because of the currently high level of interest on the part of community colleges and others in serving lifelong learners, reentering students, seekers of second careers, workers in need of upgrading or retraining, those about to be retired, those in retirement, and most others over the age of sixty. Planning to equalize opportunity for the handicapped, that is, students with various types of disabilities, has of course been given high priority following federal and state mandates; but limitations on special funding will make it necessary for planning to continue into the 1980s in order to achieve affirmative action goals.

A final note of optimism for the 1980s may be found in the improved opportunities becoming available for mediated instruction at relatively low cost via radio, television, telephone, recordings, and combinations thereof. There is little doubt that community colleges thus far have underutilized the electronic media as a means of extending regular instruction beyond the classroom. Faculty attitudes, student preferences, and costs are among the major deterrents to the use of mediated instruction in higher education. Expectations about expanded use of the electronic media in the 1980s are tempered by the prospect of underutilized faculty and lecture halls resulting from the projected decline in the enrollment of traditional students. At the same time, two contrary conditions are developing that may necessitate greater use of mediated instruction. The first is the growing need to conserve energy, from the standpoint of both cost and fuel availability. Thus, community colleges may find they can no longer plan for large numbers of part-time students to drive long distances to the campus, particularly for the kind of instruction that can be delivered by other means. The second condition is the increasing press for opportunities for lifelong learning for constituencies that cannot afford to pay the cost of in-class, on-campus instruction but do not qualify for student aid. Mediated and other nontraditional instruction modes may be the most feasible means of providing such programs if, as expected, the 1980s are a time of limited support for postsecondary education from public funds.

Alternative Planning Environments

Several alternative planning environments may be described for community colleges in the 1980s, all within the framework of constraints that have been set forth. The alternatives may be characterized as expansion, steady state, curtailment, and consolidation.

Expansion, albeit with fiscal constraints, is still possible in areas that were underserved in the 1970s because of geography, population shifts, mission or goal changes, or simply the delayed development of the community college. The goal of locating a community college campus within commuting distance of most residents has become virtually impossible to achieve in most states because of rising construction costs and logistical problems of serving sparsely populated areas. Still, some states and community college districts are now completing the implementation of long-range master plans for physical facilities and programs to provide opportunities for students not adequately served in the past. Expansion in the 1980s may well take place at off-campus centers designed for a student body more likely to be older, enrolled part-time, and intending to be at the college for more limited objectives than past generations of students. Other expansion may take place in response to new needs that arise as large housing developments are built in areas that produced few community college students in the past. Locally organized community colleges have a rather unique planning problem arising from differences in population projections for the 1980s, that is, some will experience growth in potential enrollment as a result of population shifts while most will have a decline because of an earlier decline in the birth rate; and a few will project no change. The problem is whether to expand facilities and staff in districts with enrollment projections that will exceed capacity or to change district boundaries, regulations, or both to encourage students to migrate to districts with unused capacity. Expansion may also take place in the 1980s as a result of a new or increased commitment to serve particular constituencies, for example, high school dropouts or adults defined as senior citizens; but fiscal constraints make it unlikely that students from new constituencies will exceed the number that would simply replace the declining traditional student population, at least in terms of full-time-equivalent students.

Community colleges were probably best prepared to plan for the steady state enrollment alternative that had been anticipated before the present decline in enrollment occurred. Steady state might be achieved in a time of significantly fewer college-age youth by increasing the college-going rate of this group, attracting students from new constituencies, or both. The replacement approach to achieve steady state enrollments may be laborious because three or four students from new constituencies may need to be enrolled to replace one student from the traditionally younger, full-time, college-going group. This will be true to the extent that older students with objectives other than degrees and certificates are more likely to enroll for only one or two courses per term and to drop out at the end of the term or enroll irregularly. Another alternative to replacing traditional students involves attempts to increase the persistence of students already enrolled. High attrition rates for community college students have been defended in the past on the grounds that many (perhaps most) students enrolled with limited objectives that could be achieved during one or two semesters of course work. Examples included students preparing for jobs that did not require an associate degree, making up deficiencies before transfer to a four-year institution, and pursuing a personal objective or an avocational interest through credit courses. Two distinct types of students to whom efforts to increase persistence might be directed are recent high school graduates who drop out as a result of lack of interest or a feeling of inadequacy to do college work and lifelong learners whose objectives do not require continuous enrollment in some sequence of courses over a period of time. Encouraging persistence among students in the latter group may, however, require the community colleges to confront the policy issue of whether some limit should be placed on the amount of credit students should be allowed to accumulate in a community college once they exceed an amount equivalent to an associate degree.

Most community colleges may expect to plan in an environment of curtailed enrollment, programs, and resources or retrenchment. Even in the absence of a decline in enrollment, there is a reasonable probability of a decline in the past level of support for community colleges from state and local tax funds. The ability of the college to make up such a loss of revenue from increased tuition and other charges is questionable because increases tend to produce a decline in enrollment. Curtailment in any aspect of planning tends to have a spiraling effect. For example, a decline in enrollment results in a reduction in the operating budget, requiring some reduction in programs and course offerings, that usually produces a further decline in enrollment and related cancellation of courses or sections of courses because of low enrollments. The most difficult aspect of planning for curtailment involves the full-time faculty in colleges with tenure, collective bargaining, or both. The right of faculty members with tenure to continuing employment tends to limit the degrees of freedom in planning for retrenchment. In other words, decisions about courses to be dropped or programs to be curtailed are to a considerable extent contingent on the specialties of faculty members who can be laid off. The extent to which tenured faculty in fields to be curtailed can be reassigned to teach courses that are to be retained is one indicator of success in planning, if there is congruence of student interests and decisions about courses to be retained. Planning for curtailment is obviously more difficult than planning for steady state or expansion, in that mistakes about what to retain and curtail are costly and likely to require still further curtailment in response to unanticipated enrollment declines.

Consolidation in times of steady state or declining enrollments is a more positive approach to planning than curtailment of programs and services. Consolidation may take place within both a college or district and a larger geographic region probably served by several types of postsecondary institutions, including community colleges under other governing boards. Within colleges, it is usually possible to combine certain options within majors, majors within departments or divisions, and related courses offered by different departments, with the objective of making better use of faculty and facilities. In multicampus districts, some occupational programs normally offered on more than one campus may be consolidated on one campus, particularly sophomore-level courses in which enrollments may be small. An example of a program that might be consolidated on a single campus is nursing, whose high cost is beginning to outweigh factors of student demand and personnel needs. A program that might be consolidated at the sophomore level is auto mechanics, from which many students drop out after the first year in order to take jobs for which they qualify after a few courses. Still other students enroll in elementary courses in auto mechanics while pursuing other majors in order to acquire skills they can use in repairing their own vehicles. Other examples of such programs can be found on most community college campuses. The relatively few students seeking a degree or advanced work might be brought together on one campus for the sophomore year to ensure sufficient enrollment to justify offering advanced courses.

Examples of options within majors, or majors within departments, may also be drawn from occupational education. They might include options within a secretarial science major, specialties in agriculture offered by a small college, options in fine and applied arts, and various majors in business administration and management. As community college enrollments increased, options within majors tended to proliferate, often in the absence of enough depth in the area to justify its identification as an option or major, at least for purposes of employment. Similarly, there has been an unnecessary proliferation of courses during the era of rapid growth in enrollments, with different departments offering similar courses taught by their own faculty, for their own students. Examples may be found in the fields of mathematics, writing, and the basic sciences, for example, separate courses taught for science majors, nurses, other health technicians, and home economics/nutrition majors.

Consolidation within the regions in which community colleges are located requires a new level of cooperative planning and coordination. Community colleges organized by district or attendance area may find new incentives for sharing students and other resources with nearby colleges in different districts. Boundaries for districts and attendance areas are often arbitrary, and there have been financial disincentives to the free flow of students in the past. Although resistance to free flow may be very strong on the part of some colleges as prospects grow for a decline in enrollment, there are equally strong reasons to reduce the duplication of high-cost programs with low enrollments by allowing students to leave the district to pursue such majors. If enrollments of traditional students decrease as expected in the 1980s, or if funding is much more limited than in the past, community colleges may wish to seek cooperation with other types of postsecondary institutions offering roughly similar occupational programs. In some states, statutes are already in place to allow community colleges to contract with private postsecondary institutions—often called proprietary schools—to provide certain occupational programs for their students. Of more recent origin are indications of the possibility of community colleges entering into articulation agreements with private postsecondary schools to allow their students to transfer with past work credited toward an associate degree. In this new cooperative arrangement, community colleges might well offer general education and other courses to broaden the perspective of students whose postsecondary work has been primarily occupational in nature while allowing more of their own students to obtain some types of occupational programs in other institutions. Consolidation of some programs with other public postsecondary institutions should be of at least equal interest to community colleges. These might include adult schools administered by public school districts and regional or area occupational centers and programs under other jurisdictions. Although such programs are generally regarded as postsecondary rather than collegiate and are offered without credit, there is little excuse in a time of fiscal and enrollment constraints for not coordinating occupational education with other types of postsecondary institutions in a way that should enhance opportunities for students to get the training they want and to progress up the occupational/educational ladder to associate degrees and beyond.

Still other types of regional program consolidation that might involve community colleges and four-year institutions are possible. One such possibility would entail remedial or developmental programs in the basic skills—writing, reading, and mathematics—for which nearby colleges and universities might send their students to community colleges. Until recently, the community colleges dominated the field of remedial/developmental education, offering instruction to both traditional students with deficiencies from high school and the racial/ethnic minorities who enrolled with various disadvantages resulting from their prior education and environment. As the 1970s came to an end, most postsecondary institutions, including the major universities with selective admissions policies, realized they had to provide or require remediation of basic skills for nearly a majority of their entering students. It is no longer realistic to require students needing remediation to attend community colleges if they meet other standards for regular admission to four-year institutions as freshmen. However, in areas with community colleges nearby, four-year institutions may find it desirable to send such students to community colleges for remedial/developmental programs under contract or other arrangements for student exchanges. Such an arrangement assumes that community colleges have gained expertise through experience in this area of instruction and that students can benefit from enrolling in other types of courses offered by the four-year institutions while pursuing remediation. Four-year colleges and universities might in turn assist community colleges by allowing the latters' students to enroll in some courses the community colleges may no longer be able to offer as a result of declining enrollments and related budgetary support. Foreign languages are one example of courses that might be shared by two- and four-year institutions, particularly when community college students need them in their transfer programs.

Along different lines, community colleges and four-year institutions may need to consolidate outreach, recruitment, and other types of preadmission programs and services in response to decreasing operations funds. As numbers of young people of college-going age decline, institutional reactions are to increase outreach and recruitment efforts in competition with other institutions rather than to cooperate. However, state and other funding agencies seem unlikely to provide increased support for competitive efforts of public colleges and universities to recruit a declining number of potential college students. Instead, cooperative programs, often regional in nature, may be developed in which staff and other resources will be pooled so as to ensure the largest numbers of potential college students are reached. Community colleges have a double role in such cooperative programs, as recruiters of first-time students and as senders of transfer students to four-year institutions. Regional cooperative programs involving different types of institutions may provide information and advice to prospective students about alternative postsecondary educational opportunities, requirements, costs, success rates, experience in placing graduates in jobs in various fields, and other institutional characteristics. The recently funded federal program for planning educational information centers offers one possibility for cooperative, statewide information services. Other federal programs have provided funding for regional and community educational and career advisement centers, for example, the Fund for the Improvement of Postsecondary Education, the Vocational Education Act, and Title I of the Higher Education Act (Community Services and Continuing Education). Community colleges may also find advantages in working cooperatively with other colleges and universities to plan student affirmative action programs designed to increase opportunities for racial/ethnic minorities and other groups underrepresented in higher education.

Planning Tools and Aids

Six essential tools or aids in institutional research related to planning are campus, systemwide, and state-level data bases; census data; enrollment projections; needs analysis; community and regional or service area analysis; and trend analysis. The institutional research office will generate some campus and community data for data base development; will obtain other types of information from various public agencies and private organizations; and should analyze college, community, and regional data so as to be able to relate the results to economic, population, personnel, and other analyses of trends and projections performed by experts outside the community colleges.

Enrollment Projections. During the past era of rapid growth in the community colleges, planning was for the most part driven by enrollment projections, which in turn drove budgets. Projections of increased enrollments led to the planning of new campuses and facilities, in which new and expanded curricula were to be offered by faculty added to serve the expected enrollment increase, all of which were contingent upon increased funding for construction and operations. As enrollments stop growing and projections foretell fewer students, many community colleges find themselves unable to plan for the future because they have neglected to develop other tools and aids essential in an era when growth does not occur simply as a function of projections based on past enrollment experience. Several types of enrollment projections appear to be important for community college planning, although they may no longer drive the budget process. District and campus projections—expectations—need to be made for use in negotiations with state-level planners and budget makers, within a framework of statewide enrollment projections for community colleges and other types of postsecondary educational institutions. Past projections tended to be simplistic and overdependent on enrollment experience. However, they were relatively reliable and effective in making it possible for community colleges to obtain the funding needed to add facilities, faculty, and programs. The projections often ignored both demographic changes and college plans to serve new constituencies, as well as some events external to education. Enrollment projections appear to have been much more useful in times of growth than in retrenchment because planning for growth cannot simply be reversed when enrollments decline. Therefore, community college enrollment projections will continue to be important as a guide in planning but are no longer the single most important element. Projections obtained as an extrapolation of past experience may be replaced by enrollment planning techniques, that is, the careful estimation of the effects of changes planned by community colleges in both constituencies to be served and programs offered, and in both development and retrenchment.

Refinements are needed in the definition and calculation of participation rates for the various age groups served by community colleges, which will reflect more accurately changes in demographic characteristics, level of prior educational attainment, and objectives of the increasingly heterogeneous community college student body. Some planners, having found that the percentage of enrolled persons in the age groups had declined, have now concluded that the participation rates have declined for certain age groups in the community colleges and have projected future enrollments accordingly. The conclusion tends to ignore differences between enrollment and continuation (or retention) rates for students with different types of objectives. Furthermore, gross participation rates are often based on full-time student enrollments and may be in error when there has been simply a decline in the average credit load. Lower participation rates may also reflect higher attrition before the degree, certificate, or transfer or a larger percentage of students achieving their objectives after one or two terms. When enrollments are rising, refinements in participation rates may be less important than when enrollments are declining, when critical decisions have to be made about terminating programs and services or devising strategies for increasing participation rates.

Data Base Refinement. Community colleges have often developed data bases simply to satisfy federal and state reporting requirements rather than as an aid in long-range planning. This limitation was often compounded by a lack of concern about accuracy in reporting because colleges suffered few or no penalties as a result of poor reporting. Now, as they move from an era of rapid growth to one of sudden decline, colleges have little historical data of value in analyzing changes in student characteristics, enrollment patterns, abilities, interests, and goals. The institutional research office may have no direct responsibility for developing data bases for the college, but its staff needs to be involved in specifying the kinds of data to be obtained and defining the variables for use in planning. A comprehensive student data base has highest priority in most models for community college planning because colleges' primary mission is instruction. In addition to enrollment data needed for federal reporting, student files should contain information about prior educational experience and attainment, eligibility for financial aid and other special programs, goals and objectives (in a way that reflects changes from term to term), choices of courses and programs, and performance. Data bases are often deficient with respect to information about students enrolled in noncredit courses and community services programs, although such students have become more important to colleges as numbers of traditional students in credit courses decline. Other data bases that need to be developed at the campus level for planning involve faculty and staff, courses and programs, degrees and certificates, facilities, and financial information.

Institutional research staff needs to have access to additional data bases for planning, most of which will not be maintained at the campus level. Those most likely to be readily available are statewide and national enrollment files for community colleges and other systems of higher education or tapes incorporating data provided in the federal Higher Education General Information Survey and to various state-level offices and agencies. State and regional data bases containing a variety of occupational information are very important aids in community college planning, although less well developed in most states than enrollment files. Community colleges are sometimes excluded from participation in the development of occupational information systems, with their interests represented by vocational education staff from the elementary/secondary school sector. In any case, community colleges need to be able to have access to and, where possible, influence the development of employment-related data bases in order to make decisions about adding, dropping, and maintaining courses and programs that prepare students for employment. The externally developed occupational information data base should yield information about projections of personnel needs and the supply of trained workers to fill them, training opportunities, locations of anticipated personnel shortages and overages, and prevailing wages and benefits. At the campus level, community colleges may interject information about enrollments, program completion, and placement rates in the various occupational curricula during the planning process. Past efforts to develop occupational information systems have been incomplete in that educators did not provide data on numbers of students being trained for particular types of employment. Past communication problems between educators and personnel planners have been further complicated by the very large, federally funded Comprehensive Employment Training Act programs, many of which are in fields for which community colleges also train workers. Finding the proper balance between student demand and personnel needs and between local and regional or overall state needs for trained workers is difficult for community college planners at a time of declining enrollments and funding. Therefore, refinements in the state occupational information system are regarded as essential to community colleges faced with decisions about changes in curricular offerings related to employment.

Census Data. Federal census data, supplemented by more frequent, selective census taking by state government, constitute still another important aid for community college planners. Information available on tapes for census tracts can be aggregated for zip code or other geographical regions in the college service area and used in lieu of extensive data collection by the college. Zip codes in addresses in the student data base may be used in enrollment analyses designed to find neighborhoods underrepresented in the student body and with census data to describe neighborhood groups with respect to socioeconomic status, educational attainment, age, racial/ethnic distribution, type of employment, and other variables important to planners. Population research units in many state governments conduct a partial census several times during the period between the federal census taking at ten-year intervals to document changes in the size and composition of the population for which the state must plan. Some community colleges find it possible to have certain needs for population data included in the state census, on either a one-time or recurring basis. Thus, the federal and state census yields data tapes that should be useful to community colleges in assessing the extent to which they are accommodating various constituencies in their service area.

Community and Regional Service Analysis. Community college planning for the 1980s also involves the use of community and regional data that go beyond demographic information for the service area. In addition to information about personnel projections, community college planners need to be aware of economic forecasts; business, industry, and government plans for expansion or curtailment in the college service area; proposals for phasing out military installations with large civilian payrolls; real estate developments that would greatly increase the number of potential students seeking college programs and services; planning to improve transportation—both roads and regional/rapid transit; and other noneducational developments that may have an impact on community college enrollments. Such developments may also have implications for community college facilities planning, for example, the vacating of buildings that might serve as off-campus centers. Community colleges are believed to be an asset in attracting business and industry with needs for trained personnel and with employees wanting opportunity for postsecondary education for themselves and their families. However, new aids to planning in concert with the community at large are needed to replace those of the past era of enrollment growth that occurred largely in the absence of anticipatory planning by the community colleges. In other words, community college planning in response to changes in enrollment projections appears to be inadequate for the 1980s if the colleges are to continue to be dynamic institutions offering community-based education.

Needs Analysis. Needs analysis is an important tool available to community colleges with projections of declining enrollments but good prospects of funding for programs and services to meet newly identified needs. Community colleges vary widely from state to state and within states in the nature and percentage of the adult population they enroll, that is, high school graduates and others beyond compulsory school age. Some portion of the variation is attributable to differences in community college mission and the availability of alternative opportunities for postsecondary education. However, another important source of variance is related to the quality of various needs analysis conducted by community colleges. In its simplest form, needs analysis is little more than a survey of attitudes and opinions about the college, including some attempt to find out how much the community knows about the institution. This type of needs analysis may be useful as a public relations device for increasing community awareness of the college and changing negative attitudes or erroneous information. However, the exercise is unlikely to identify unmet needs or increase the enrollment of underrepresented community groups. Another approach to needs analysis involves enrolled or about-to-be-enrolled students, who are surveyed to obtain information about their felt need for educational or career counseling, remedial programs, financial aid, tutoring, child care services, and a variety of less commonly offered support services the college might offer. An increase in this type of needs analysis is likely to occur as community colleges attempt to increase both enrollment and retention rates of students already disposed to enroll in college. In a more classic approach to needs analysis, community colleges devise strategies for identifying the unmet needs of various groups in their service area for opportunity for postsecondary education, limited only by the statutorily defined mission and functions of the colleges. A relatively small, stratified sample of residents may be selected for interviewing, from census tracts with large numbers of adults whose needs are not likely to be met by four-year institutions, that is, with low socioeconomic status, little prior history of college enrollment, limited command of English, and a high incidence of single-parent families. An additional type of needs analysis may be undertaken in states where lifelong education is clearly a function of the community colleges, irrespective of the level of prior educational attainment of the adults to be served. Community colleges may compete for such students with university extension and other types of institutions offering continuing education programs while taking responsibility for the survey of unmet needs for further educational opportunity.

Trend Analysis. Finally, trend analysis has been somewhat neglected by community colleges that planned primarily in response to enrollment projections. For purposes of planning, trend analysis should be concerned with changes in both the enrolled student body and the community from which most students are recruited. Among enrolled students, there needs to be monitoring and analysis of changes in characteristics and enrollment patterns. Among the student characteristics to be analyzed are trends in distributions by age, sex, racial/ethnic composition, socioeconomic status, place of residence (or high school of record), placement test scores, and other measures of prior educational attainment. Analysis of trends in enrollment patterns should address changes in average credit load, enrollment in day versus evening classes, withdrawal rates from courses, persistence from term to term, choice of occupational versus general educational or transfer courses, and other variables related to student objectives. At least of equal importance in community college planning is the analysis of demographic trends in the college service area and the state in general. Among the most important trends to be analyzed are changes in birth and mortality rates, racial/ethnic composition, rates of high school completion, types and rates of employment, and size and age distribution of the population. Colleges that perform trend analysis on a continuing basis may be able to anticipate likely changes in enrollment and then take corrective measures to prevent the projected decline. Measures designed to combat the projected decline might include offering English as a second language, increasing student financial aid, providing child care services, increasing evening courses, and emphasizing employment preparation.

Planning Models

Four Stages of Planning. Most community colleges and their related districts go through at least four stages of planning, some of which may be repeated several times. By the early 1980s, most colleges will have completed the initial, master planning stage, which begins when a new college or district is established. Master plans are often developed for a period of from ten to twenty years and must be updated periodically to reflect changes in the economy, laws and regulations affecting community colleges, the population to be served, and society at large, as well as to correct mistakes in the original plan. This updating constitutes a second stage. The third stage involves planning beyond the master plan; the fourth arises from a need to plan for redirection, retrenchment, or both.

Planning in community colleges, more than in other systems of higher education, is viewed as an ongoing, dynamic process that is never completed, although the nature of the planning changes as the college or district matures. Planning beyond the master plan, when buildings and major programs are in place, is difficult because of the likelihood of little further growth in the student population or the resources that enrollment growth produces. This stage of community college planning resembles the kind of planning undertaken in anticipation of steady state enrollments. In planning beyond the master plan, however, steady state is the result of the college(s) reaching the enrollment ceiling designated in the master plan rather than an enrollment projection of steady state. Once enrollment ceilings are reached in particular campuses or districts, planning efforts are reoriented toward finding ways to keep the fully developed campuses from becoming stagnant with respect to program development, staffing, and instructional technology and acquire sites for new campuses or centers to accommodate future enrollment above the planned ceilings. Planning beyond the master plan will probably necessitate some reallocation of programs and services among the campuses and centers rather than the simple addition or replication of courses and curricula. In making decisions about the relocation of programs, student preferences and convenience will need to be weighed against organizational efficiency and, in some cases, the rights of tenured faculty to employment on a particular campus.

Problems of declining enrollments and reduced funding will probably force most community colleges into planning for retrenchment or redirection rather than further expansion in the early 1980s. Retrenchment and redirection are not regarded as the same process but as two types of planning arising from different philosophies. Retrenchment requires redirection in course offerings, programs, faculty, staff, and services in response to declining enrollments and resources. Reductions may be made in the number of sections and the times courses are offered, hours during which campus facilities are open, options within curricula, counseling and other support services, availability of campus facilities to community groups, maintenance and janitorial services, and numbers of students served when there is decreased funding for reasons other than enrollment projections. These reductions may be accompanied by increases in class size, faculty and counselor load, or both where collective bargaining does not preclude such changes.

Redirection involves determination of priorities among student constituencies, functions and programs, community and student services, athletic programs, on going versus innovative programs, and recruitment versus retention of students. Setting priorities among student constituencies may be difficult because decisions are often more closely related to values than to enrollment projections. If all potential students cannot be served equally well, should the community college give priority to the young versus the elderly, for whom there was little opportunity for postsecondary education during their tax-paying years; to those prepared for and motivated to attend college versus the disadvantaged, whose prior education and experience did not prepare them for college; to full-time students in degree and transfer programs who are likely to persist or part-time, older students with other, more limited objectives; to students in high-cost occupational programs or those who enroll in less-expensive transfer courses, which tenured faculty are available to teach? Should community colleges conduct needs analysis in their service area to find residents' needs they are not yet meeting or limit priorities to meeting the needs of enrolled students? Quantitative values cannot be ignored in making decisions about redirection of community colleges' efforts because funding and enrollment levels are highly correlated. A mediating factor in setting priorities among student constituencies is the willingness of the legislature and local voters to provide funds to subsidize various types of programs, for example, avocational courses and remedial programs in the basic skills. Retrenchment may be a safer planning mode than redirection, which requires community colleges to make choices and set priorities among constituencies, programs, and services. Institutional research is, of course, essential to both planning models, in estimating costs, impacts, and long-term outcomes with respect to enrollments and revenue.

Participation Patterns. Another approach to describing community college planning models involves the various types of participants in the process rather than stages. More than other types of colleges and universities, the community colleges are likely to invite representatives of a variety of community groups to participate in planning, during both the master planning and subsequent stages. However, in its simplest form, community college planning may involve only the planning/institutional research officer, staff in the fiscal office, and president (or other chief executive). This minimum participation or administrative or staff team model of planning is largely enrollment driven. The college is given a projection of full-time-equivalent student enrollment that is apportioned among departments and divisions for use in planning courses and employing faculty, taking into account both past enrollment and departmental budget requests. The enrollment projection is also used by the planning team to analyze the capacities of existing facilities to accommodate any expected growth in enrollment and to initiate plans for new buildings, where needed. Such planning tends to be characteristic of institutions that are part of a strong state system of community colleges, with statewide formulas and regulations for faculty and other staffing, class size, facilities utilization, and budgeting in general. Planning driven by the budgetary or resource allocation process may also involve only this same small team of administrators, with little participation by others on the campus or in the community. In this situation, the budget allocation approved for the college determines the full-time-equivalent enrollment, which is then distributed among departments and divisions for use in planning offerings and faculty utilization. In the first instance, the college is usually assured of adequate funding for as much enrollment as it projects and then generates. In the latter, the college is in effect limited with respect to the amount of additional enrollment that will be funded, especially during periods of fiscal conservatism. The most important aid to planning in this mode is, of course, the college data base, with files for enrollments over a ten-year period, courses, majors, faculty load and assignment, facilities, and financial information.

The local governing board is involved with the administrative or staff group at the second level of participation in planning, a broadened executive team model. Board/staff planning is most likely to occur when the college develops its first master plan, before there are significant numbers of faculty and students, and again in times of retrenchment or redirection. At one or both of these stages, the board is called upon to decide among options and alternatives concerning college size, sites, program emphasis, staff organization, and other matters where data are helpful but do not lead to routine decision making. Staff can assemble community, regional, and statewide information, together with college data after it begins operations, for use in evaluating the alternatives available to the board. The board's philosophy, goals, and priorities provide the framework for organizing the analysis of data to be used in such evaluations. In planning for redirection or retrenchment, the alternatives among which the board will have to choose are likely to be weighed in terms of cost versus access, affirmative action, retention, and outputs for the various student constituencies served by the college. The alternatives might, in the early 1980s, relate to decisions about the operation of off-campus centers, special support programs for disadvantaged students, community services, and, perhaps, staffing for institutional research and planning. Under almost any circumstances, the governing board is an important participant in planning, on whom responsibility rests for making choices and decisions in areas where data are at best helpful.

The faculty is the next group to be added to the other limited participants in the planning process, once the college has begun operations, forming a college planning group. The assumption is made that the long-range master plan for the college or the district has been developed before most of the faculty has been employed and that faculty participation is appropriate as the master plan is updated and in subsequent stages of planning. The community college faculty role in planning is somewhat different from that of faculties in other institutions of higher education because the community college is to a considerable extent a creation of the constituencies it serves. Thus, the faculty is only one of several participant groups in making decisions about who is to be admitted to the college, what kinds of programs are to be offered, what services are needed, and where all of this is to take place. An alternative view is that the community college faculty role in planning should be similar to that of faculties in colleges and universities that are selective with respect to the students they admit, where responsibility for planning and decision making in most academic matters is delegated to the faculty. Where this occurs, the governing board reviews the results of faculty planning but restricts its own involvement in planning to nonacademic matters relating to funding, facilities, and more general policies affecting the institution. Where the faculty is one of a number of participating groups in planning, it may be represented by either the academic senate or a similar faculty organization or individuals selected by the president or some other appointing authority for the planning process. The faculty role in planning is especially important in the early 1980s as community colleges confront problems arising from projections of a decline in enrollments, compounded by evidence that students are poorly prepared to undertake college-level courses and programs. Faculty participants in planning are likely to request analyses of student data different from those performed for governing boards and administrators involved in planning. The latter groups may give priority to questions of cost and cost effectiveness, access, and enrollment trends; but faculty concerns in planning are more closely related to questions of student preparation for college, academic standards, and the quality of instruction by nontraditional means, for example, instructional television and work experience programs. Thus, the faculty adds an important dimension to planning at a time when both enrollments and standards for preparation for college may be declining.

The next groups to be involved in community college planning as it adopts an expanded college planning team are professional staff who may not be regarded as faculty, for example, counselors and librarians; students; and support staff from areas such as buildings and grounds, fiscal affairs, and public information. As in the case of faculty, these groups are more likely to participate in updating and planning beyond the master plan than in its initial development, particularly in times of retrenchment or redirection. Together with the governing board and the faculty, they constitute a kind of community-related planning group with interests and affiliations that extend far beyond their campus roles. Community college students are a particularly important group to be involved in campuswide planning for various reasons. First, the student body has been changing during the past decade in ways that make it a more accurate reflection of community characteristics and values. The student body on most campuses is no longer composed primarily of recent high school graduates enrolled full-time in day classes, pursuing degree and transfer programs. Instead, it resembles somewhat a cross section of the community with respect to age, employment, racial/ethnic background, educational attainment, and other demographic variables. Students are also important as participants in planning insofar as they and their successors are the major benefactors of good planning. Little justification is needed for involving other types of professional staff in collegewide planning, particularly representatives of groups with responsibility for some aspect of student welfare. These should include but not be limited to counselors and other student personnel workers, librarians and other learning resource center personnel, and staff in admissions and records. Finally, representatives of classified personnel in other service areas should be included in campuswide planning, particularly when redirection or retrenchment is called for. Examples of areas that might be represented are the custodial, buildings, and grounds staff; secretarial and other clerical employees; computer center personnel; business office employees; and the campus police. With the exception of student personnel, staffs providing support services are frequently omitted from the planning process. Such staff may not be organized into a group or groups like a faculty senate or student government association, from which representation can be obtained for participation in collegewide or districtwide planning. Collective bargaining units, where they exist, are probably not a very satisfactory means of obtaining such representation. In any case, planning under the constrained conditions projected for the 1980s may require input be obtained from all levels and types of college staff, including those who may have little interest in decision making related to educational programs.

The highest level of participatory planning involves the community or larger area served by the community college or district in a community planning team with varying patterns. One possible model involves selection of a special community advisory committee on planning, with college staff serving primarily as a resource to the committee rather than in a leadership role. A second model provides for community representatives to be appointed to a college- or districtwide committee on planning, with the college supplying both leadership and staff resources. In still another model, the community may be represented on a number of task forces appointed to make recommendations about particular problems, for example, child care programs or sites for off-campus instruction. The task forces might be responsible to a broadly representative coordinating committee on planning that could be limited to college personnel, including board members, or include task force chairpersons who are community representatives. The college administration needs to be sensitive to the possibly bifurcated role of the locally elected governing board for the college or district in broadly participatory planning. The board is in a sense representative of the community, having been elected by it. At the same time, it serves as a kind of advocate for the colleges and the district while representing community interests. Thus, the board role needs to be clearly delineated vis-à-vis the administration and the community in any planning model that involves community representatives who are not board members. One approach to such delineation involves board appointment of the community representatives to task forces or the advisory committee on planning from nominations, applications, or some systematic inquiry leading to identification of community persons who could play certain roles in the planning process. The resultant groups would report to the college or district administration, however, and through it to the governing board. The desirability of having board members participate in the planning process, as well as act on the results of planning, sometimes makes it difficult to maintain clear lines of authority for planning. Community participants in planning should, as a group, be representative of the community with respect to racial/ethnic backgrounds, income levels, types and levels of employment, educational attainment, geography, and age distribution. A community profile may be developed for use in the selection of participants in planning to ensure as much representation as possible of constituencies the college might serve. The special needs of the handicapped, non-English-speaking residents, the unemployed, business and industry, labor unions, and the military (if present in the community) all need to be taken into account in selecting community participants in the planning process.

Finally, educators from other types and levels of institutions must be involved in some significant way in community college planning. Input is needed from representatives of elementary and secondary schools and nearby public colleges and universities that compete with community colleges for students and to which community college students may transfer. Liaison with both private postsecondary institutions offering vocational training and independent colleges and universities should also be sought because of the importance of their updated plans for both program and enrollment changes to long-term community college planning. Colleges and universities outside the service area to which reasonably large numbers of community college students transfer also need to be consulted as planning proceeds, again with the purpose of keeping informed about their plans for changes that would be expected to have an impact on the community colleges. Institutions in the local service area or region are regarded as having a different, more important role to play in community college planning than others to which students may transfer. The community college may find it useful to establish as part of the planning structure an interinstitutional advisory committee whose major function would be to facilitate information exchange and resource sharing. The committee might also play a role in the voluntary coordination of program planning in the region, that is, the addition, deletion, or other modification of courses of study, including the locations in which they are offered. Although campus and community representatives may sometimes serve on a single, broadly based planning committee, it appears that the interinstitutional advisory committee should be established as a separate entity that may continue to function after the completion of a particular stage of community college planning.

Consultants under contract may also perform a variety of functions related to community college planning. At the extreme, consultants may take full responsibility for developing a master plan or updating it, with little participation by the board or college staff between the negotiation of the contract and receipt of the plan or an update. Once the college or district has been in operation for some time, outside consultants will probably be used to perform more limited or specialized functions, if at all. Such roles include evaluation of the implementation of prior plans; conduct of studies needed for planning, particularly in the community; leadership of groups involved in planning activities; coordination of planning activities; and service as resource staff to planning groups. Consultants in these roles do not produce plans for the college or district; they assist planners and planning groups in developing plans. Evaluation may involve an assessment of the extent to which master plan goals have been achieved or of the cost effectiveness of certain programs when choices had to be made among several options. Examples of studies contractors might perform are community needs analysis, trends in employment requiring postsecondary education, and opinion polls. Leadership roles in which contractors might be engaged range from organizing and convening various committees and task forces appointed by the college to assist in planning to leading the groups through a series of structured planning activities to achieve specified outcomes. Coordination implies a less-active role in working with planning groups, for example, summarizing, integrating, and feeding back the results of planning by diverse groups for further refinement, toward the goal of achieving some level of consensus about future directions for the college to take. Finally, consultants may be under contract to be available to planning groups as resource staff, bringing expertise and experience to bear as needed. Thus, contractors not employed to produce plans and updates may be used in roles complementary to or supportive of regular staff in planning and institutional research. As community colleges and districts complete implementation of their initial master plans and move to a new type of planning, which will probably be either maintenance, retrenchment, or redirection, contractors' roles are likely to shift accordingly, from plan producers to consultants and information providers for other planning.

The previous discussion of planning models was based for the most part on an assumption that community colleges are governed by local boards, administered under state laws and regulations that allow considerable local autonomy and serve constituencies from a designated geographical area or region. No distinction has been made between single- and multiple-college or campus districts, although the organization of planning by the latter is more complex because of the additional layers of staff usually employed at the district or central office level. Community colleges governed by and administered through a strong state-level board have considerably fewer degrees of freedom in planning than those to which authority has been delegated to plan and make decisions about educational programs, services, and facilities within broad state guidelines. Community colleges without a significant amount of local autonomy may find that some planning models for public four-year colleges are more appropriate to their needs than those described, particularly in states where two-year colleges have certain statewide responsibilities for programs. However, as their name implies, community colleges in their purest form have prescribed service areas that may in fact provide much of their financial support through local taxation, are governed by locally elected boards, and are responsive in planning to the needs and characteristics of the local population.

Case Studies

Three case studies illustrating different phases of planning are presented. They are based on the current planning activities of three community colleges or districts but elaborated upon in order to show how institutional research might be helpful in each situation. The three phases of planning the case studies illustrate are planning beyond the implementation of the original master plan, planning under conditions of retrenchment, and updating of the master plan where redirection is called for. The three were chosen under the assumption that few community colleges will be developing or simply updating master plans for the 1980s because of projections of declining enrollments or, at best, steady state. The case studies involve planning by a multicollege district, a college in an urban community college district, and a community college in a suburban area that constitutes a single-college district. All are in states that grant a considerable amount of autonomy to colleges and districts for decision making about educational matters under growing fiscal constraints.

District A: Planning Beyond the Master Plan. The first case study is for community college district A, established by the voters of the county it encompasses about twenty years ago. When the district began development of its first long-range master plan, it had one college fully operational and a second under construction. At the present time, with its major master plan and subsequent updates implemented for the most part, the district has an enrollment of more than forty thousand students in credit courses at three comprehensive college campuses and a large number of off-campus centers of varying size and function. District A has now begun planning again in a mode best described as planning beyond the master plan in that the physical development of the campuses has been completed and the projection of future enrollments is for slow growth under severe fiscal constraints. There were few constraints on enrollment growth and program development while the first master plan was being implemented. The district was given whatever resources it needed to meet the needs of the students it could attract and enroll. However, as the buildings on the last campus to be developed neared completion, the era of unrestricted enrollment growth ended. Planning for the future, beyond the district master plan, assumes a modest enrollment growth that is related to a projected increase in the number of people residing in the district and an intent to serve more adequately the needs of the growing racial/ethnic minority groups in the district (for the most part, black and Hispanic).

Having decided to plan beyond the master plan for a modest expansion of enrollments rather than retrenchment or redirection, the district chose a participatory planning model that involved the appointment of a joint college/community steering committee and the use of contractors to conduct certain research projects and to serve as a resource to the committee. Planning was in a sense to be open-ended in that it had as a major objective the identification of educational needs the colleges had not yet fully met, barriers to enrollment, and community groups underrepresented in the student body. A professional polling organization was engaged to survey the community served by the college district with respect to information about the colleges and the district, including their admission requirements, costs to the student, and location; opinions about program and instruction quality, availability, attractiveness of the campuses, and college and district expenditures; experience in enrolling in courses and programs or participating in other college activities; interest in enrolling in courses and programs; barriers to and anticipated problems in enrolling at some future time; and general expectations about college functions. Information about the respondents was also obtained, including age, sex, income level, employment, racial/ethnic identification, handicaps, prior educational attainment, and place of residence. This was related to the other categories of responses. The cross tabulation of information was designed to reveal underserved community areas with educational needs the colleges might meet and community subpopulation attitudes and information about the colleges. The latter is useful as the colleges attempt to combat negative attitudes and opinions and correct errors in facts.

The community college district has also produced a compendium of statistical information about the colleges from its computerized data bases for use as a reference work by the planning committee. The publication contains extensive information and analysis of enrollment trends and projections, choices of major, student persistence and performance, outcomes, class size and faculty work load, facilities utilization, and costs and expenditures. Historical data, current information, and projections were included when available. The institutional research and information systems staffs collaborated in producing the publication for the district, with guidance from the planning staff about what would be useful. Another institutional research staff project involved goal-setting activities, using the Delphi technique. Staff worked with the districtwide planning committee, the governing board, the faculty, student organizations, and other college groups to establish and assign priorities to goals for planning. The Delphi technique is designed to produce consensus by means of an interactive process that normally involves only one group of participants. The involvement of several groups working simultaneously but independently to develop planning goals made the Delphi technique more complex than in the use of a single group. In order to reduce the total number of groups with whom the goal-setting process would be used, staff worked with a combined group of faculty, staff, students, and other personnel on each of the three college campuses, in addition to the governing board and the steering committee. The outputs of the various groups were integrated for submission to the college/community steering committee for further iteration of the goals.

The institutional research office undertook several special studies in support of the planning activities to supplement analyses of data appearing in the statistical compendium. Among the special studies were a follow-up of former students, with particular attention to those who completed occupational programs or transferred to four-year institutions, to assess the extent to which they were placed successfully after leaving the college; interviews with currently enrolled, part-time students whose objectives are other than an associate degree, a certificate, or transfer into a baccalaureate degree program, to learn about their expectations concerning future enrollment at the college in relation to their past attainment in postsecondary education; and a survey of graduates and others who had completed college programs five and ten years earlier, among those still residing in the colleges' service area who could be located, to learn about their needs for continuing education the colleges might meet, together with the needs of others in their households. The special studies dealt largely with students (current, former, and potential) because the overall planning effort was oriented toward improving the colleges' effectiveness in meeting the needs of their changing constituencies.

Planning beyond the master plan in district A is expected to yield a blueprint for meeting the changing educational needs of the adult residents of the district in the 1980s. It should prove useful to the governing board and the administration in setting policies and making decisions about the year-to-year operations of the colleges and centers.

District B: Planning for Retrenchment. Community college B is the largest of eight located in a densely populated metropolitan area with a total enrollment of about twelve thousand students for credit and an additional enrollment of eighty-five hundred students in noncredit programs. Governance of college B and its sister institutions might be viewed as a shared responsibility of the district and the state boards, with local autonomy severely constrained by the fiscal problems of the city that provided a significant portion of the colleges' operating budget. College B was the first community college to be established in the city, shortly after World War II, and was developed without the kind of master planning urban areas undertook during the era of rapid community college expansion in all parts of the country. The college has been engaged in two successive phases of planning during the past ten years, the first of which was a kind of redirection and the second of which was retrenchment. Redirection occurred as a result of a new commitment by the city and the state to both open admissions and student affirmative action. Retrenchment was forced upon the college a few years ago when student charges were increased significantly to replace revenues from other sources and enrollments declined. The moral commitment to open access and opportunity remained strong, but resources to provide special programs and services to assist disadvantaged students were limited. The major goal in planning for retrenchment was to find ways to cut programs, services, activities, staff, and related budget items in a short period of time for planning and with the least possible damage to the integrity of the institution.

Having to plan for retrenchment with little lead time minimized opportunities for participatory planning and maximized the need for institutional research and information for use in decision making. Community participation was not considered seriously as an option in planning for retrenchment, and participation by most college groups was limited to consultation as planning proceeded and tentative decisions were reached. The planning team assembled by the president was comprised of college administrators from the areas of general and academic administration, business affairs, and student personnel, assisted by staff in planning, institutional research, and information systems. The team identified three major areas in which institutional research was judged to be needed for effective planning for retrenchment: enrollment projections under varying conditions, course and program audits, and faculty work load analysis. The team recognized that decisions about reductions would have to be made in many areas where institutional research had little or no relevance, for example, budgets for equipment and supplies, maintenance of buildings and grounds, and travel. Furthermore, participants agreed on the need to limit the amount and scope of the studies to be done in order to have the results available for planning as soon as possible while keeping costs to a minimum.

The estimation of enrollments for the following year and over the next five-year period was the first research project undertaken. Enrollment trends and status quo projections were available as a base from which to make a series of revised estimates using differing assumptions. The status quo projections had been based on an assumption of no change in tuition or other student costs, requirements for admission, or major program offerings. However, a significant tuition increase had been imposed with little lead time before taking effect, and the revenue from tuition would be used to replace a certain portion of the college's income previously appropriated by the state. The status quo enrollment projections were thus regarded as "best case," with little expectation they could be achieved. "Worst case" and other projections were then estimated, using varying sets of assumptions about the impact of the increased tuition charges. Because students had little time to adjust to the increased tuition, the assumption was made that the immediate impact on enrollments would be significantly greater than the long-term impact. Research involved estimating the family income of potential and currently enrolled students, in relation to their probable eligibility for student financial aid; the ability and willingness of families to increase their contribution to the student budgets; and the availability of additional resources for self-help programs (loans, work-study, and other funds exclusive of grants). Other variables that had to be taken into account in making assumptions underlying enrollment estimates included level of student (first-time freshman, continuing or returning student, sophomore), time of day enrolled (day, late afternoon, or evening), and student objectives. The analysis of courses and programs was designed to yield information to be used in assessing the impact of reducing or eliminating certain courses, majors, options within majors, sections within courses, or requirements. The data used in the analysis included, for each of the courses or programs audited, student enrollments, rates of persistence and completion, uses of courses to meet various college and transfer requirements, placement rates of graduates, and student preferences with respect to times courses are offered. Decisions about curtailing or eliminating courses and programs will, of course, affect the enrollment estimates that were made under differing assumptions about ability and willingness to pay the increased tuition. Rather complex simulation models were developed to test the added effects of reducing course and program offerings at different times of day or eliminating them entirely. Finally, the planning team had available from institutional research the results of an analysis of faculty work load for use in making decisions about consolidating course sections and program options, assigning faculty to teach at different times, and employing part-time instructors outside the tenure track. The major data elements were weekly student contact hours, full-time-equivalent students, and class size for part-time and full-time faculty members teaching in the various departments and majors at different times of day.

The end products of the planning for retrenchment by community college B were enrollment and budget projections for the following year, with a series of related decisions about program and course offerings, course scheduling, class size, and faculty assignment. In addition, "best case," "worst case," and intermediate-level enrollment projections were made for the five-year period following the increase in tuition, with plans for modifying them on the basis of enrollment experience during the first year of the increase.

District C: Planning for Redirection. The third case study involves community college C, which chose the option of planning for redirection, instead of retrenchment, when a decline in enrollment brought about fiscal problems. The college is a single-campus operation in an upper-middle-class suburban area, with a local governing board. Its master plan is complete in the sense that all its facilities are in place and its educational offerings are fully developed. No further growth is expected in the community because there is no room for additional housing. The college was relatively satisfied with its record of enrolling about 35 percent of the recent graduates of local high schools and about 10 percent of all adult residents at least eighteen years of age. However, about three years ago enrollments began to fall short of projections, and last year showed a decline over the previous year in the total number of students enrolled, none of which had been anticipated.

The first step the college took to combat the deteriorating enrollment pattern was to ask the institutional research office to design and carry out a statistical analysis of the changes in enrollment patterns and student characteristics that had occurred over a five-year period. The analysis paid particular attention to changes in the composition of the student body, for example, percentages of first-time, continuing, and reentering students; age, sex, and racial/ethnic composition; educational goals and objectives; graduation and transfer rates; average student credit load (or other measure for noncredit programs); and times of day when different types of students enrolled. In addition, a one-time analysis was made of the high school and geographic origins of currently enrolled students. This entailed the computation of a college-going rate for each high school in the college service area, for first-time students under twenty years of age, and a tabulation of the total numbers of students residing in census tracts and zip code areas served by the college. State and national census data were then used to develop profiles of the residents of areas from which the college was drawing comparatively few students in various age categories. The profiles included information about racial/ethnic groups in the census tracts or neighborhoods, levels of prior educational attainment, types of employment by heads of household, percentages of families below the poverty level, size of family, and other demographic information that would be useful to the college in planning and outreach activities.

The analysis of changes in enrollment patterns and community characteristics led to a tentative conclusion that college enrollments would continue to decline if steps were not taken to redirect some college efforts toward serving groups underrepresented in the student body in the past. A community-based task force was then appointed, with membership drawn largely from the neighborhoods from which few students were enrolled. At orientation sessions led by college staff, the task force was informed about the college mission, functions, offerings, and commitment to serving all residents of the community without regard to age, sex, socioeconomic status, or prior educational attainment; selected findings from the community demographic analysis showing groups the college was not yet serving; and the intent of the college to redirect some of its efforts and resources so as to reach a larger percentage of adult community residents. The task force was charged with proposing new directions the college might take to increase its effectiveness in meeting the postsecondary education needs of all parts of the community. Examples of such directions included offering some courses off campus in neighborhood facilities, providing educational and career advisement services to adults who may not be students at the college, expanding child care services, and permitting limited registration of new students under a waiver of admission requirements, for example, placement testing. At the same time, the college decided to look for ways to increase the retention rate of students already enrolling at the college and to improve its outreach to local high schools. Some redirection of effort was implied because the college had not regarded high student attrition as a problem in the past.

Planning in this instance involved establishing a college task force with student, faculty, and student personnel staff to make recommendations to the administration concerning ways to improve retention. The outcomes of participatory planning for and by community college C were a number of sets of recommendations concerning new directions that might be taken to improve service to the community, increase student retention, and, as a consequence, ensure at least steady state enrollments.

Prospects and Proposals

Four stages of community college planning have been identified, together with several levels of participation by various campus and community groups. Few master plans for new community colleges or districts will be developed in the 1980s because some system of public two-year colleges will have been established in most states by then and little growth in enrollment, which would necessitate the planning of additional colleges, is expected. Most master plans and their updates will have been fully implemented by the early 1980s in terms of the development of both physical facilities and program offerings. Until recently, planners had anticipated an era of steady state enrollments in which college planning would be for the primary purposes of maintaining quality and providing some opportunity for dynamic change with no increase in resources. It now appears that steady state planning will be replaced almost immediately by planning for retrenchment or redirection. The combination of a decline in enrollment before it was projected and more severe fiscal constraints than expected has produced a new context for planning to which community colleges are not yet accustomed.

If fiscal constraints are sufficiently severe, a community college may have no real options for planning; retrenchment is the sole option. Participatory planning involving either the community or the campus at large is seldom practical for various reasons, although widespread consultation with groups that would be affected by retrenchment is strongly recommended. Planning for retrenchment is a kind of high-risk activity because of the rapidity with which it must usually be done and the likely cost of mistakes resulting in lower enrollments and thus less income than planned. Planning for retrenchment is best done by a small team of college or districtwide administrators, supported by staff in institutional research, information systems, and planning. A student/enrollment data base with information extending over a period of at least five years is a primary resource for such planning, coupled with comprehensive data relating to income, costs, and expenditures for the same period. Good data are needed for both the analysis of experience and the simulation of the impact of alternative decisions about retrenchment.

Planning for redirection appears to be the most positive mode available to community colleges for the 1980s and the most likely to maintain them as dynamic, responsive institutions. Redirection implies some enrollment and fiscal constraints that limit the degree of freedom available to the college for planning, as opposed to the kind of open-ended funding for expansion that characterized much planning in the past, or a reduction in enrollment and income, which some colleges must now plan for. Planning for redirection also implies some freedom to reorder priorities and goals, shift resources, change emphases, and take other actions that do not require the additional expenditure of public funds and should not result in a loss of enrollment. Participants from both the community at large and the college as a kind of community need to be involved in an advisory capacity in planning for retrenchment. Staff in institutional research and information systems serve as a major resource for the advisory group in providing statistical information, leading it in the Delphi or other consensus-producing process, directing student or community needs analyses, and performing studies needed by the planning advisory group in evaluating alternative directions the college might take with respect to outreach to prospective student constituencies, curricular emphasis, sites for off-campus instruction, and other aspects of the college mission and functions. The product of participatory planning for redirection is most likely to be the recommendation of a blueprint for future college development, to be adopted and then used by the governing board in making policies and decisions about the use of resources. Institutional research and information systems are an integral part of any planning endeavor; but their contribution becomes ever more significant as community colleges move beyond simple expansion to accommodate increasing enrollments in accordance with their master plans into an era of redirection or retrenchment in which there is a high price for poor decisions.

Bibliographical Essay

Planning Colleges for the Community (Knoell and McIntyre, 1974) was written when community colleges were in an expansionary phase as an aid in carrying out the unfunded mandate of the federal Higher Education Act Amendments of 1972 to plan at the state, regional, and local levels for comprehensive postsecondary education for all citizens. The 1970s were a time of dramatic change in the community colleges, as well as rapid growth, as their already diverse student body became much more heterogeneous. The young, full-time, middle-class students pursuing degree and transfer programs became a minority among the community college students, with the majority now including racial/ethnic minorities who are variously disadvantaged, students beyond the usual age for college enrollment, the handicapped, and, most of all, local residents who enroll part-time, irregularly, and with more limited objectives. (See also Knoell, 1973, 1976.) The need for a new kind of community college planning was identified. It was to be a continuous process bringing together academic, facilities, and fiscal planning on a particular campus or in a district. Like the master plan approach, which is based on enrollment projections, the new enrollment planning proposal assumed almost limitless growth as the community colleges reached out to serve all groups in their communities.

Coping With Reduced Resources (Alfred, 1978) addresses the community college planning problems for the 1980s, that is, enrollment contraction, budget reductions, surplus faculty and staff, and the high cost of educating students who are ill prepared for college. Among these many problems, the issue of funding sources and levels for community colleges in the 1980s is undoubtedly the most critical. If adequate funding can be obtained from public sources, with only modest student charges imposed, community colleges can continue to plan to meet the changing needs and characteristics of their communities. *More Money for More Opportunity* (Wattenbarger and Cage, 1974) recognized the need for more sophisticated techniques for community college planning and budgeting, the use of which might reassure the tax-paying public that subsidizing community college education is a cost-effective use of public funds. The authors also addressed the issue of increased state-level planning and financial support versus continued local autonomy and lessening local support. Garms (1977) also deals with issues of economic equity in a way that is useful to planners.

Gleazer (1974) advocated a strategy for coping with constrained resources that was adopted by the American Association of Community and Junior Colleges. It might serve well as a theme for planning for redirection. Gleazer and the association regard community colleges as instruments for the development of both individuals and communities, offering community-based, performance-oriented education.

References

Alfred, R. L. (Ed.). *New Directions for Community Colleges: Coping With Reduced Resources,* no. 22. San Francisco: Jossey-Bass, 1978.

Garms, W. I. *Financing Community Colleges.* New York: Teachers College Press, 1977.

Gleazer, E. J., Jr. "Beyond the Open Door: The Open College." *Community and Junior College Journal,* 1974, *45,* 6–12.

Knoell, D. M. (Ed.). *New Directions for Community Colleges: Understanding Diverse Students,* no. 3. San Francisco: Jossey-Bass, 1973.

Knoell, D. M. *Through the Open Door: A Study of Patterns of Enrollment and Performance in California's Community Colleges.* Sacramento: California Postsecondary Education Commission, 1976.

Knoell, D. M., and McIntyre, C. *Planning Colleges for the Community.* San Francisco: Jossey-Bass, 1974.

Wattenbarger, J. L., and Cage, B. N. *More Money for More Opportunity: Financial Support of Community College Systems.* San Francisco: Jossey-Bass, 1974.

29

J. Victor Baldridge
Michael L. Tierney

Techniques for Small Colleges

In most ways, planning in small colleges is similar to the process in large institutions; among the sometimes subtle differences, there are fewer people involved in the process, fewer layers of organizational hierarchy, fewer outside interest groups clamoring for influence, and often a greater sense of shared responsibility among institutional members. Such sharing does not always exist—small colleges have their share of tight-fisted, domineering presidents and strong boards of trustees—but on the whole, planning in small colleges is basically a simple and less-complicated version of all other planning processes.

For a variety of reasons, small college planning has taken a critical turn in the last few years. In the 1970s, private liberal arts colleges were particularly hard hit by the "new depression" in higher education, to use Cheit's (1973) phrase. Dozens of them closed their doors and many that remained open were plagued by financial problems, declining enrollments, and intense competition from less-expensive public colleges (see Bowen and Minter, 1976). In the midst of these crises, many colleges tried to improve their management. Like most other institutions, they began to experiment with computerized management information systems (MIS), Delphi techniques, management by objectives (MBO), and other management improvement strategies. Some of these programs were specifically designed to overcome financial problems; others were used to improve planning, staffing, and curriculum development.

In some cases, the institutions developed computerized data banks for MIS to analyze carefully the relations between cost and educational programs, to forecast the impact of various management decisions, and to simulate the outcomes through computer models (Mann and others, 1975). Their degree of sophistication varied substantially. Some had virtually no data base and started from scratch. At the other extreme, several had maintained sophisticated data banks for years. Their goal was to develop computer simulation models that would allow them to predict future trends or show future impacts of current decisions.

Still other institutions turned to management by objectives systems. These were quite different strategies, based primarily on *planning* activities rather than data collection (Odiorne, 1965). All institutions that used MBO approaches also incorporated data banks into their planning; but the primary focus was on improved use of the data in planning, in contrast to the gathering and computerization of data. A number of institutions tried, with some success, to combine the MBO and MIS approaches.

In this chapter, we will focus on the MBO and MIS techniques for small college planning. We will begin by briefly describing the two techniques and will continue by looking at some research on the use of the techniques in forty-nine colleges; we will conclude by making some observations about positive and negative impacts of MIS and MBO processes.

Management Information Systems

There has been a phenomenal growth in the number of institutions using computer-based information systems to support various administrative functions. One survey of forty-eight large institutions indicated administrative computing expenditures increased at an average annual rate of 33.4 percent between 1963 and 1968 and averaged 2.3 percent of an institution's total operating budget (Mann and others, 1975). A 1970 survey of 1,873 colleges and universities indicated that only 13 percent have some type of information system (Bogard, 1972). In 1978, we estimated about 50 percent of the institutions had some type of computer-based information system, although they varied substantially in their sophistication. Such information systems are more likely to be used in large public institutions, although many small private colleges are trying to start programs.

Simple Data Banks. The overwhelming majority of the so-called "management information systems" are really nothing more than simple data banks. Colleges have always gathered and compiled statistics about students, finances, faculty, alumni, and dozens of other items. In the early years, someone in the dean's office probably kept most records with a few sheets of paper in a notebook. As time passed and institutions became more complex, the data-gathering and statistical activities grew. The admissions office often kept one set of records, the financial office, another, and the academic dean, still another.

For the vast majority of colleges and universities, a discussion of an MIS would almost exclusively mean a discussion of the simple data banks compiled by the institutional research office. Using computers to compile these statistics has given the operation an aura of science and precision, but the logic behind a fancy institutional research office and the early pencil records is fundamentally the same. We call these simple management information systems *data bank networks*. They collect and store data and retrieve information for periodic reports. They may have many different data files on students, courses, personnel, financial accounts, and classroom space. The focus is on collecting data and producing simple reports, with little stress on using the data in the management process or on predicting. Consequently, these simple systems have limited applications for analyzing the data collected.

Today a number of commercially developed data management systems cover a broad spectrum. They are able to integrate data from, say, student records and faculty records, financial aid information, and admissions records; and this ability is a significant advantage. Examples of these more integrated data management systems are IBM's Information Management System (IMS), Informatic's Mark IV, and CINCOM System's TOTAL. These are all general application data management systems, not limited to one area.

Advanced Management Information Systems. Advanced systems always incorporate simple data banks, but they add a major component: software to simulate the behavior of the institution by data manipulation. This simulation capability allows decision makers to ask "what if" questions. For instance, it is possible to predict with fair accuracy the cost implications of increases in the student-faculty ratio or to compare the cost implications of two different methods of changing the ratio.

Plourde (1976) reported that nearly 400 colleges or universities use some type of simulation model in planning. However, we are skeptical of those numbers because only one hundred eighty-six institutions gave Plourde information. And about half of these gave incomplete information, and only a few said the models were used frequently. In spite of the question about their use, these models deserve careful analysis because many people have high expectations for their future usefulness.

The most common type of advanced information system is designed to improve the allocation of resources. The basic purpose is to predict the cost implications of changes in various institutional policies. Although there are important differences between specific models, most resource allocation models share a common logic (see Hussain and Freytag, 1973).

First, these instructional cost models are all student driven. The basic input is an estimate of the total number of students who will enroll in each academic department. These enrollment forecasts must consider such factors as the number of students who continue at the college, the number who transfer from other institutions, and the number of first-time students. These forecasts are affected by changes in the unemployment rate, student dropout rates, and other factors.

Once the total anticipated work load has been calculated for the various departments, it is possible to estimate the costs of operating each department. Departmental costs are a function of institutional policies concerning the structure of the academic program (that is, the distribution of lecture and laboratory courses), average class size (for both lecture and laboratory sections), number of courses a faculty member is expected to teach, amount of a faculty member's work load credited to laboratory as opposed to lecture courses, rank distribution of faculty in each department, and faculty salary schedule. In addition, these instructional cost models can allocate the costs associated with nonfaculty expenses, such as nonacademic personnel, departmental supplies, and equipment. By manipulating these policy variables, the resource allocation model can assess the cost implications of managerial changes. For example, an advanced MIS network could predict the cost of changing faculty work load or average faculty compensation.

There are management information systems besides those that help make decisions about budgets and money. These include student flow models, faculty flow models, and space utilization models. *Student flow models* are concerned with three fundamental processes: prediction of student enrollments, student progress within the institution, and the student enrollment status at the end of each academic term. In each case, the task is to predict trends based on past experience and an assessment of changing conditions. *Faculty flow models* assist administrators in determining the composition of faculty by rank, age, discipline, and salary (see Gray, 1976; Schroeder, 1972; Weathersby and Weinstein, 1970). Simulations help provide information to answer policy questions: the rate of faculty promotion, the proportion of tenured faculty, or the impact of institutional retirement practices. *Space utilization models* help allocate physical space optimally.

Management by Objectives Systems

Drucker (1954) probably introduced the term "management by objectives"; but the best-known discussion of the technique may be Odiorne's (1965). Many different activities occur under the general rubric of MBO; there are almost as many versions of it as there are people who talk about the issue. However, Odiorne's discussion is probably the most widely accepted version. He considers MBO basically a planning process in which goals are set, tasks are assigned to people throughout the organization, and evaluations are made in light of goal achievement. Setting goals and assigning tasks were key managerial functions long before the MBO process was conceived, but MBO proponents argue it offers a more structured and systematic method for planning and appraising performance. In effect, MBO is a systematic and careful procedure for activities managers have always performed in looser form.

Odiorne (1965, pp. 70–73) outlined the basic steps for establishing a management by objectives system:

1. Identify the common goals of the whole organizational unit for the coming period. This is based on your desired goals for the whole organization, which are stated in terms of measures of organizational performance you intend to apply at the end of the period. . . .
2. Clarify your working organization chart. Sketch the actual organization of the group under your supervision, showing titles, duties, relationships, and impending changes. . . .
3. Set objectives for the next budget year with each man individually. Here's how you go about this:
   a. Ask the subordinate to make notes on what objectives he has in mind for next year. . . .

     b. Before the meeting, list some objectives you would like to see him include for the next year and have them ready.

     c. In your personal conference, review the man's own objectives in detail; then offer your own suggestions or changes.

     d. Have two copies of the final draft of his objectives typed; give him one and keep one yourself.

     e. Working from the final agreement, ask him what *you* can do to help him accomplish his targets. Note his suggestions, keep them with your copy, and include them in your objectives, if pertinent.

4. During the year, check each subordinate's goals as promised milestones are reached:

     a. Is he meeting his target? . . .

     b. Are you delivering on your part in helping him? . . .

     c. Use the jointly agreed-upon goals as a tool for coaching, developing, and improving each man's performance on a continuous basis. Reinforce good results by feedback of *success* when you see it. . . .

5. Near the end of the budget year, ask each subordinate to prepare a brief "statement of performance against budget" using his copy of his performance budget as a guide. . . .

6. Set a date to go over this report in detail. Search for causes of variances.

7. At this meeting, also, you can cover other things that may be on his mind. If he's so disposed, you might discuss such matters as relationships on the job, opportunity, job-related personal problems, and so on. . . .

8. Set the stage for establishing the subordinate's performance budget for the coming year.

     Here, of course, the manager finds himself back at step 1 of the goal-setting stage, but better equipped by reason of his experience to set more realistic goals for the next budget period.

From this discussion, it is clear the MBO process has some critical elements. First, it is an important planning procedure by which organizational goals and objectives are set on an annual basis. Second, Odiorne frequently mentions the importance of linking the planning and budgeting cycles so budgets are clearly understood as instruments for achieving organizational goals. Third, the MBO process allows the assignment of tasks and responsibilities to people in the organization. Fourth, the procedure provides for systematic evaluation of people's performance. A worker's achievements can be compared with the original objectives to identify areas for improvement. The MBO procedure has frequently been attempted in business organizations. In addition, several colleges and universities have tried to implement MBO procedures, with mixed results.

The heart of the MBO program is a planning and budgeting process that is repeated each year. We shall review a typical small college cycle consisting of five steps. The first is *goal and objective setting for the institution and administrative components.* Each August the executive staff and the president participate in a retreat at which institutional goals are reviewed and evaluated. A similar process occurs for each administrative group. Goals and objectives are compared with actual performance, on the basis of which institutional goals are revised or modified and new ones are set for each group. Each executive identifies the expectations she or he has for other administrative groups. All objectives are discussed, modified if necessary, and agreed on before the retreat is over. Preliminary overall budget guidelines for the upcoming fiscal year are also set at this time.

The second step is *objective setting for program units.* The members of the executive staff and program directors meet jointly to discuss and review institutional goals and establish priorities for the college and its various components and programs. Program directors, in turn, begin to work with their staffs to develop objectives and plan for the present and following years. Program directors also prepare cost estimates to accompany the plan and objectives. A deliberate effort is made not to use budgeted or audited expenditures from previous years as a decision-making basis.

Third is the *budget review,* which involves joint meetings of all executive administrators and program directors to review all programs, their objectives, plans, and budgets. The executive staff outlines the overall financial position of the college—fixed costs, likely revenues, and general budget parameters. Meetings follow during which considerable discussion and negotiation—"give and take"—occur. At the conclusion of this process, a completed budget emerges.

The fourth step is *evaluation.* At the beginning of each calendar year, all program directors review the individual objectives and actual performances of all faculty and staff reporting to them. This review is followed by a conference with the executives in which the performance evaluation is reviewed and salary, retention, promotion, and reassignment recommendations are agreed on. The president uses the same procedure to evaluate the executives. Using performance evaluations and the corresponding recommendations, the president makes all final decisions on retention, promotion, and salary. These decisions are then incorporated into the final budget draft and submitted to the trustees.

Fifth and last comes *planning.* Early in the summer following the performance evaluations, the executives and program directors evaluate their total operation to determine whether their goals and objectives have been met. At that time, they identify future goals and establish priorities. This information is forwarded to the central administration as a basis for the retreat that will occur later in the summer. Thus, the whole cycle begins again.

MIS and MBO Research

To promote wider use of MIS and MBO strategies in liberal arts colleges, the Exxon Education Foundation embarked in 1973 on a program of grants called the Resource Allocation Management Program (RAMP). The program was limited to private liberal arts colleges, which were challenged to submit proposals to introduce modern management practices to their campuses. Approximately two hundred institutions applied for funds under RAMP, and forty-nine were eventually awarded grants. In 1974, the Exxon foundation asked the Higher Education Research Institute (HERI) in Los Angeles to study RAMP's impact on the institutions to determine if and how college planning and financial stability were affected by changes in management techniques. The evaluation concentrated on the behavioral consequences for administrators, faculty, staff, and students, using interviews, questionnaires, document analyses, and on-site case studies to gather information (see Baldridge and Tierney, 1979).

Using these multiple sources of data, our staff members, who were highly knowledgeable about the institutions, rated the thirty-four colleges that provided adequate data independently in terms of their type of project (MIS, MBO, or combination) and its success (more successful, less successful). We finally concluded that all thirty-four could be placed into one of five categories: (1) "Too Early to Tell," institutions who received grants so late that judgment was premature; (2) "Least Successful," institutions whose projects had essentially failed and been disbanded; (3) successful "Data-Bank MIS," simple computerized data banks with minimal sophistication; (4) successful "Advanced MIS," systems that not only had data banks but added sophisticated capacities to project trends and simulate the impact of decisions; and (5) successful "Combined MIS/MBO," projects that added an MBO planning component to a basic MIS program.

The Exxon foundation had spent millions of dollars on RAMP. What had it bought with the money? Our overall impression is that some real improvement in some colleges' management resulted from Exxon's investment. Of the thirty-four we evaluated, eight had projects that were too new to be judged (first category). Nine had projects that, in our opinion, were outright failures: Usually, the project did not even exist at the end of the grant period, thus providing valuable insights about how *not* to implement management innovations. The other seventeen of the thirty-four—exactly half—were relatively successful. College planning practices improved, budgetary procedures were streamlined, and administrators rated the projects a success.

Administrators' responses to one of our surveys are shown in Table 1. The first three questions are general ratings of project success. As can be seen, the "Combined MIS/MBO" projects had the highest percentage of administrators reporting that the project was successful (44 percent).

An interesting phenomenon emerged from the first three questions: Almost nobody was willing to say a project was disappointing. The administrators at 9 percent of those colleges where we felt the projects were quite *unsuccessful* thought the project was very successful, and only 18 percent of them were disappointed. The answers to question 4 were also striking: Naturally, the more suc-

Table 1. Percentage of Administrators Agreeing with Questions in Different Categories of Colleges

	Category of College				
	Least Successful	Too Early to Tell	Data Bank MIS	Advanced MIS	Combined MIS/MBO
1. Project was very successful	9	22	26	36	44
2. Project was moderately successful	46	55	32	41	46
3. Project was disappointing	18	0	16	0	0
4. Costs of the project were reasonable for the benefits received	23	29	31	43	51
5. Project has become an integral part of the college management process	18	27	31	57	72

cessful a project, the more often administrators thought its costs were reasonable. But for the colleges with the least successful projects, fully 23 percent of the administrators felt the cost was justified. Among the institutions with successful projects, the costs of the combined MIS/MBO projects most often seemed justified.

Finally, in question 5, when we asked "Has this project become an integral part of the college management process?", there were enormous differences in the responses. Seventy-two percent of the combined MIS/MBO project administrators thought the activity was an integral part of the college management. By contrast, only 18 percent of the administrators in the institutions with the least successful projects agreed.

Was a 50-percent success rate a reasonable expectation? Was half the money wasted? Was Exxon wise to use its money on these programs? These questions are, of course, matters of judgment and emotion rather than fact. In our opinion, a success rate of 50 percent in a complex program such as this is a highly respectable outcome. We have been studying innovation and change processes in colleges and universities for years and have argued (Baldridge and Deal, 1974) that the overwhelming majority of new innovations in colleges and universities—as in most other organizations—fails completely. The reasons are numerous: inadequate technology, funding, and staffing; resistance by entrenched groups; and a host of other factors. To have a 50-percent success rate, then, seems reasonably good in comparison to other attempts at educational innovation.

Data Base Improvements

Most projects tried to improve the data base for decision making. The more successful ones seemed to translate those initial good intentions into reality; their data bases did improve significantly.

Increased Data Quality. In Table 2, questions 1, 2, and 3 concern improvements in the data base. Several patterns emerged. First, the institutions that combined a data base with a "simulation" capacity or an MBO program (that is, "Advanced MIS" or "Combined MBO/MIS") showed significantly greater improvement than the other institutions. In a few cases, there were dramatically high levels of improvement.

Second, data about students and their enrollment patterns improved much more than any other data. This result is consistent with the intention of most data systems because they are "student driven" (the whole system is based on enrollment patterns).

Third, the institutions with "Data Bank MIS" had an unusual split in their results. They showed strong improvements in their student data (65 percent) but relatively weak improvements in their faculty data (22 percent) and financial data (36 percent). In these institutions, the real focus seemed to be on improving the student data. As simple systems add the ability to simulate and model decisions, they also probably improve the data on faculty and finances. The student data are the base; more-sophisticated systems gradually add frosting on the cake.

Increased Problem-Solving Speed. In institutions where the MIS has been able to develop a solid data base and the software to process it, decisions are often made much more quickly. The dean of instruction at a small New England

**Table 2. Percentage of Administrators Agreeing with Questions
in Different Categories of Colleges**

	Category of College				
	Least Successful	Too Early to Tell	Data Bank MIS	Advanced MIS	Combined MIS/MBO
1. Overall improvement in student data	41	58	65	66	81
2. Overall improvement in faculty data	25	48	22	50	62
3. Overall improvement in financial data	33	52	36	53	62
4. Institutional forecasts and long-range planning improved	42	35	63	67	85
5. Overall improvement in setting objectives	38	54	52	49	80
6. Overall improvement in implementing goal attainment	33	36	39	40	83
7. Overall improvement in assessing goal attainment	26	32	45	44	70
8. Overall improvement in curriculum planning	29	32	40	45	50
9. Overall improvement in allocating faculty positions	28	28	21	43	56
10. Budgetary and faculty allocation decisions are more centralized	22	5	20	17	14
11. Budgetary and faculty allocation decisions decentralized to department chairs	4	5	9	29	44
12. Overall improvement in budget process	33	47	32	61	80

college said, "I really don't feel like our new MIS told us anything we didn't already know. Every college is probably like ours. There is somebody stationed somewhere in the bowels of the organization that keeps up with the statistics. Every college has its old Ms. Jones or old Mr. Smith, who has been around for years, collects up all the data, and every so often makes a report. So in one sense we've had the data for as long as I can remember. But with the new MIS system, we can get the data *faster,* we can get *more* data when we need it. We can cover a *broader spectrum* of issues in the same amount of time. We always had the potential to get the data eventually; but now we can get it when we need it. I think that's the real breakthrough. The improvement is a timing question."

This dean's comments were supported by most people in institutions with successful projects. However, there was some tendency in the opposite direction. In some institutions where the projects got stalled, a major complaint concerned timing. In MIS programs, the data were not always available when the decision makers needed them; in an MBO process, the planning cycle did not often mesh with the budgeting process.

Another problem that plagued both the successful and the unsuccessful institutions was the "junk" issue. Some projects furnished entirely too much unfocused data, tons of junk with no point of concentration. Sometimes it actually took the administrators longer to sort through the printout and make decisions. This complaint arose many times. The decision process can actually be slowed down by data if they are not focused and condensed.

The timing has to be delicately balanced. On the one hand, computers can provide more information more quickly. If that information is focused, condensed, and directed toward concrete decisions, it can speed up the decision-making process. On the other hand, some systems deliver reams of printout with little focus and a high degree of "noise." This deluge is likely to slow down the process while the decision makers plow through the pages. The administrators have to stop and translate the raw data into "information" they can use. Timing, then, is a delicate matter and can easily tip decision making in either direction.

Facilitated "Hot-Spot Analysis." The president of a small religious college in the South framed this issue: "Having these data allows me to do overall planning better. But one of the features I like best is that it also allows me to move in the other direction—to focus very narrowly on the 'hot spots.' By 'hot-spot analysis' I mean I can see small problems in the data that are sure to grow bigger. By isolating some of these hot spots, I can usually catch some problems before they go too far. Of course, if I had known the right question, I would have been able to get this information without the MIS system. But that's just the point—the system sometimes spotlights issues that I never would have dreamed to ask about. When these hot spots jump up, they almost call attention to themselves. In my opinion, this is one of the most valuable aspects of our data system."

That interview came early in our research. Subsequently, when we were interviewing in other colleges, we asked people if they had similar experiences. Most people could immediately identify with the notion of hot-spot analysis. In fact, they usually had an illustration of a problem that jumped out of the data at their college. For example, at Furman University, South Carolina, one data system put the spotlight on extreme fluctuations in gift income. So Furman decided to skip one year of gift income and bank it, then budget the next year on the past year's gift income. Although anyone could have suggested this strategy before the college had the data system, having the data pinpointed the problem. Once it was recognized, the strategy was undertaken. At West Virginia Wesleyan College, the hot-spot analysis focused on recruiting patterns. The new data system showed that much effort was going into recruiting programs for students in extremely expensive fields. Armed with this information, Wesleyan began a concentrated recruiting effort in other subject areas. Using this strategy, which had evolved partly from a hot-spot analysis of the data, Wesleyan was able to reverse its enrollment pattern dramatically.

Time and again during our interviews, people pointed out examples where the data had highlighted previously neglected issues. It was not that the data were unavailable; it was simply that they had not become salient in anybody's mind. They had never "jumped out," so no one had paid attention to them. Although MIS systems are most likely to cause spotlighting, during the process of planning in an MBO project, the same focused attention sometimes occurs.

Planning Process Improvements

Question 4 in Table 2 shows the percentage of administrators who felt long-range planning had been improved as a result of the Exxon project. There are some strong conclusions from the data. First, the category of institutions with a "Combined MIS/MBO" program had a high level of people who felt improvement—85 percent. The MBO programs were intended to improve the planning process. If the administrators were responding accurately to this question, that intention was certainly translated into reality. Large numbers of faculty members and administrators worked together to produce departmental plans and institutional guidelines.

The second obvious result from question 4 is that the two types of MIS also significantly improved planning, although not as much as the "Combined MIS/MBO" projects. Approximately two-thirds of the administrators in the "Data Bank MIS" and the "Advanced MIS" colleges felt institutional forecasts and long-range planning had improved. This percentage stands in sharp contrast to the institutions that were "Least Successful" and "Too Early to Tell." In those institutions, only about a third of the people felt there had been improvement.

There was an increase in the general sophistication about problems. We noted one advantage of a good data system is its ability to spotlight problems, to do a hot-spot analysis. At the other extreme, however, the successful systems also seemed to build a generalized sophistication about problems. In our interviews, faculty members often commented that they now understood the administration's problems better than they ever had before. They did not necessarily agree with the administration, but they understood more of the implications of the empirical data. They often argued over those data, pointed out how "biased" they were, or challenged the assumptions behind them. Nevertheless, even in rejecting unfavorable data, faculty members were educated to the problems administrators faced.

For example, we heard faculty members say they really understood for the first time how expensive some departments were compared to others or how students were distributed within departments. Most important, many faculty members commented that for the first time they understood the interdependency among departments. The English department, for example, was teaching a large number of business school students; without them, many English professors would be unemployed.

The planning cycles in an MBO project also fostered this general sophistication about institutional problems. The planning within each department promoted discussions about departmental goals and objectives that might never have occurred otherwise. As those discussions moved forward, the general awareness about departmental problems increased. The same thing happened as those departmental plans were passed to higher levels. Then department heads had to discuss their plans in conjunction with other department heads and deans. This sharing of perspectives helped educate everyone to the interdependencies among departments. The special problems and unique concerns of different departments were shared.

Planning became a focused, systematic, collegewide process. Most of the individuals interviewed indicated there was a greater institutional focus on planning since the projects had been initiated. As one respondent said, "The MBO program helped us avoid the 'drift' we were experiencing before." The planning process, as developed in most institutions, was more comprehensive and participatory than the procedures used before RAMP began. The entire planning cycle usually took a year. Each cycle involved goal setting, budget making, and evaluating. Collegewide participation was often effective in creating a willingness to plan and to assume responsibility for the plan. Participation also facilitated a common understanding of institutional purpose, budgetary constraints, and future projections.

Budgeting sometimes improved. Previously, the president and business manager had made all budget allocations. In some institutions, most notably Arkansas College, budget making has become central to the planning process. Like planning, budget making can be highly participatory. For example, at Arkansas College, over 75 percent of the persons interviewed indicated the process was more decentralized; 90 percent felt the process was equitable and the persons involved possessed an adequate understanding of the issues; 100 percent indicated there was an overall improvement in the total budgeting process. The results from interviews at a variety of other campuses also verified that when individuals have control in setting budgets and concomitant responsibility for spending, there is more concern with budget outcomes and costs.

Goals became clearer, more timely, and quantifiable. Most respondents at our MBO institutions indicated there had been significant improvement in the quality of goals submitted. The assessment of the previous year's goals and establishment of new goals became intimately linked to planning and evaluation. When program goals and objectives became the basis for evaluating performance, the specificity of the goals and objectives improved.

Delegation of authority and decision making increased. Most program directors indicated the project had helped the president relinquish some control by delegating more authority and responsibility to the executive staff and program directors. Interviews and questionnaire data indicated a substantial increase in decentralization in most MBO institutions. Perceptions of faculty participation and support were high. Managerial activities were no longer confined to the top administrators.

The legitimacy of decisions increased. Extensive participation in planning, budgeting, evaluating, and decision making created a political environment that encouraged openness, trust, and compromise. As the participants shared more in the decision making, their willingness to abide by decisions increased. Participants almost always expressed a positive attitude toward the process. Most also indicated that, where consensus was lacking, there was still an understanding of the issue and an acceptance of the decision. In short, communication and morale increased on most campuses, and confidence in the leadership and administration of the colleges increased.

Managerial skills became more sophisticated. Managerial participation and increased responsibility augmented the capabilities of second- and third-level managers. Administrative participation in a variety of seminars and workshops also increased managerial competence.

Data became an adjunct to decision making. It soon became obvious that accurate and useful data were essential to planning. Interviews with top-level administrators indicated financial and student data were the most useful. Due to the small size of the colleges, there was little need for highly detailed faculty data and sophisticated enrollment data like the Induced Course Load Matrix.

Formalized plans ensured that planning occurs. The MBO projects provided the basic framework for planning on several campuses. The projects facilitated staff involvement in planning, which ultimately was the key to securing a commitment to the plan. It also stimulated faculty and staff consciousness about planning: the need to plan and the potential benefits that could be derived. The process itself, rather than the actual plan that emerged, became the critical element in the success of the effort. The Arkansas College president summed it up in an interview: "Our MBO plan (SCAMP) is no better than a thousand other plans might have been; it only ensured that *planning actually happened*. It wouldn't have made much difference what plan was used, as long as the planning actually got done."

MBO programs offered unique strengths for planning. We have been talking until now about MIS and MBO systems together. Both types of projects had favorable impacts on the data base and on the planning process. However, it is important to note that the MBO projects seemed to have a uniquely strong impact on the planning process. There were no "pure" types of MBO projects. Everyone also had a strong data base and was coupled with an MIS system. In a sense, then, these projects used a basic MIS system *plus* an MBO effort.

When the MIS and the MBO were combined, the improvement of planning seemed dramatic. Examine Table 2. On several questions, the "Combined MIS/MBO" group is significantly higher than any other type of project—usually twice as high. Eighty percent of the administrators in those institutions with combined projects felt there was an improvement in setting objectives (question 5); 83 percent saw an improvement in implementing objectives (question 6); and 70 percent saw an improvement in assessing goal attainment (question 7). We mentioned earlier that 85 percent of the administrators in institutions with "Combined MIS/MBO" projects saw improvements in the long-range planning process (question 4). It is obvious the "Combined MIS/MBO" programs concentrated on the planning process, and they had substantial success.

The research indicates one of the most useful managerial innovations is a strong data-based MIS system linked to a vigorous MBO program. This is a sharp change from our initial opinions. When we began this study, some staff members were frankly doubtful about the impacts of the MBO projects. At the end of the study, however, we were highly impressed with their value. MBO projects were particularly useful in improving the planning processes; and when linked to an MIS program, they also captured most of its positive effects. In fact, we were somewhat surprised that the "Combined MIS/MBO" systems were able to do *both* tasks fairly well. They improved planning (the major thrust of the MBO strategy) while simultaneously improving the data base (the major thrust of the MIS programs). It is surprising how often the "Combined MIS/MBO" institutions had the highest improvement on almost every question (see Table 2).

General Guidelines

The nature of the management project will largely determine whether it does the job. In the Exxon RAMP program, many different types of projects were selected. Some were sophisticated computer-based management programs; others stressed setting institutional planning and objectives. Although the projects were varied, there are some rules that apply to almost all of them.

Make sure the project fits the institution's needs. One major problem in initiating a project is that consultants sometimes try to sell their bag of tricks without serious assessment of the institution's needs. This was particularly true for the institutions that adopted MIS. The consultants pushed prepackaged computer programs that were supposed to do the job. In many cases, however, the prepackaged programs did not meet the college's needs. They were usually developed at large institutions, with thousands of students and faculty and complex administrative arrangements. When these small colleges bought the prepackaged programs with their Exxon grants, they quickly found that systems designed for large institutions were not easily adapted.

The lesson is simple: An institution should buy an MIS appropriate to its specific needs. This rule also applies to the other types of management innovations, such as MBO. However, the most complaints were voiced about the software packages of the MIS, not about the planning and workshop activities of the MBO systems. It is particularly important to realize that programs developed for large institutions require substantial modification if they are to be useful in a small institution.

Crash programs of data building do not work. In almost all the projects funded by RAMP, there was some data-gathering component. Even where MBO programs were started, they were usually supplemented with data gathering. We found great variations among the institutions. Somewhat over half appeared to have adequate data bases. The rest, however, found their data were either nonexistent or in such poor condition that they had to be substantially revised.

Crash programs to improve the data base are rarely effective. Instead, the most successful programs build their data gradually over a long period. Of course, this is rather discouraging news for an institution that does not already have a good data base. Nevertheless, institutions should be skeptical of mounting an MIS without first giving careful attention to the data base underlying it. In many cases, the administrators felt a computerized capacity for processing the data was a problem. But it appeared to us that the underlying process of gathering quality data in the first place was often the faulty link. In short, a strong infrastructure of high-quality data must be built before anyone attempts to superimpose a sophisticated processing system.

"Information glut" can be deadly. A little sign sat on the desk of a president we interviewed: "KISS." When we asked its meaning, "Keep It Simple, Stupid!" was the answer. This advice is well taken for everyone who launches these projects. We found that where projects failed, the universal complaint was they had "gotten out of control"; complexity had mushroomed. In every project, there was a fatal tendency toward information glut. A new project director invariably wants the project to have high visibility among the faculty and administrators. As a consequence, there is an extensive buildup of newsletters, memos, directions for activity, and planning documents.

With MIS, there is a particular tendency toward information glut. We frequently saw frustrated administrators sitting behind piles of computer paper, afraid to ignore the sacred tablets, insecure about reading the foreign language, and frightened to perform the logical—but sacrilegious—act of throwing it away. They simply did not know how to deal with the information overload. The wise director of a management information system quickly learns that too much information is as bad as not enough. The rule is clear: Information must be condensed and focused to be useful.

The data must be timely. One frequent complaint about the Exxon projects was that the critical data from the MIS came *after* the decisions were made. And in some MBO programs, the planning cycles and the workshops that were supposed to produce plans did not match the budget cycle's timing. The planning was sometimes done after the budget process had occurred. These seem like absolutely ridiculous cases of mistiming. We could not imagine any sensible administration running an elaborate planning process that did not match the budget timing. And the production of MIS reports after the decisions were made seemed equally wasteful.

There are many explanations for mistiming. Usually, it means the left hand does not know what the right hand is doing. For example, the MIS might be so isolated organizationally that the program director does not know when people need the information. Or an MBO planning project may be run by a person who has little input into the budgeting process. To paint a more sinister portrait, we are sure some administrators deliberately cause mistiming so the planning cannot affect budgets—which the administrator wants to control. Under those circumstances, it is no surprise that the planning and the budgeting processes do not go forward together.

The simple conclusion is data production in an MIS or the planning cycle in an MBO program must carefully match the decision-making and budgeting cycles. That this obvious point is overlooked repeatedly is due to lack of coordination, incompetence, and political expedience. Nevertheless, anyone running a project should pay careful attention to timing and coordination.

Finally, accurate, focused, and timely data is expensive. Hopkins (1971) indicates the price of implementing a cost simulation model is approximately $75,000, a large portion of which is consumed by the gathering of data that meet specific requirements. Further, an adequate data base is subject to Gresham's Law: Routine data maintenance tends to foreclose opportunities to extend and refine the basic data base. Yet these costs must be borne because an adequate data base is the sine qua non of a cost simulation model.

Finally, *project directors and administrators must cooperate to ask the right questions.* A critical element in implementing a computer-based model concerns the expertise to operate such models. Such expertise may be present on campus or it may be a service provided from external consultants. Plourde (1976) reports that the presence of in-house technical expertise was considered to be among the top factors in successfully implementing a cost simulation model. However, in-house expertise is not without its problems. As the academic dean of a southern college said, "We worked hard to develop a first-class data base and an excellent software system. But in spite of that, in the early stages we had a hell of a problem getting the appropriate information. After a while we realized the difficulty: the project director was giving us answers to questions we weren't asking! And, more often than not, when we asked a question, he did not furnish appropriate data. He had his own idea of what we needed and was giving us tons of information about it. But we usually wanted something else. Wow, the amount of miscommunication over this problem was unbelievable. Finally, the president called the committee together, and for about six weeks we thrashed through the kinds of information we needed and wanted. We insisted that the *amount* be reduced and the *focus* be on things we really needed. After that the situation got dramatically better."

It is almost impossible to specify exactly how a communication linkage should be built. In some cases, the project directors should be aggressive in helping administrators and faculty understand the planning process and the use of data. In other cases, administrators will have to reach out, insisting that the project directors concentrate on real problems rather than spinning out endless reports with no focus. The exact style is open to question, but it is clear that two-way communication must be established.

Purchasing this expertise from an outside consultant is subject to these same communication problems. Organizational consultants tend to bring specific biases and procedures to bear on those problems (Baldridge, 1971). As a result, consultants tend to claim their models are able to do more than they can, create an appearance of certainty, and be too technique oriented (Kirschling, 1976). However, consultants can be invaluable in reprogramming their software to meet the needs of the institution and in training on-site personnel in the use of these models. This latter aspect is particularly important in ensuring the institutionalization of such models once they are implemented and consultant services are terminated.

Pitfalls

There are three common pitfalls of which users should be aware. First, always be skeptical and alert about data quality; they are often wrong in spite of their surface precision. Second, the use of statistics and data is a highly political enterprise, in spite of its seemingly "scientific" nature. Third, there is a seductive temptation to count as important only those things that are concrete, measurable, and can be neatly tabulated, even if they are trivial.

Data Quality. The data from an MIS often seem completely scientific. The columns of numbers and pages of printout almost assume a reality of their own. Rather than mere facts *about* the real world, they begin to look like they *are* the real world. There is a seductive quality to this numbers game. No matter how scientific these numbers look, however, there is an amazing amount of sloppiness behind every printout. The data must be collected by forms filled out by students, faculty, secretaries, clerks, administrators, and janitors. Many data are missing or incorrect. People often make errors when the different sources of information are merged. It is not at all unusual for batches of data simply to get lost in the process. The list of accidents that threaten data quality could be extended indefinitely. This does not mean MIS networks are any more prone to mistakes than other human inventions, but neither does it mean these systems are any less prone to sloppiness.

There is no need for overanxiety about data quality. Becoming paranoid would be just as false as being overconfident. Nevertheless, any intelligent user of an MIS must constantly raise questions about the quality of the data. Are they accurate? Are they comprehensive? Is all the material there? Have major pieces of information been lost? Is everyone who contributes to the data base using the same definitions? Can the data be tracked to their source if necessary? Data quality simply cannot be assumed; there must be unending vigilance to make sure they are clean, accurate, and comprehensive.

Politics of Numbers. Deliberate misuses of data are also possible. The data that look so scientific are often rife with political manipulations. In our interviews with Exxon representatives and campus administrators, we came across literally scores of cases where people had learned to play the "numbers game." An example best illustrates this point.

Let us examine the affirmative action program of a college in the Southwest. The community where this college is located has three major racial groups: white, Mexican-American, and black. In preparing the affirmative action plan to meet federal guidelines, the college used data from its MIS. The guidelines said the college must try to employ the "same percentage of each racial group as exists in the community."

The numbers game was played with the concept of "community." It was important to know how the different racial groups were distributed in the local area. The locale immediately around the college was predominantly white; the city where the college was located had a large number of blacks; and the surrounding five-county area was heavily Mexican-American. The task of the MIS seemed simple: to supply the "equal percentage" that matched the college work force with the local community. A computer printout that showed the number of each racial group each department should hire was produced.

Then the controversy erupted. What was the "community" on which this printout was based? People who wanted to keep the college employees limited to whites insisted the college community was the area within a mile or so around the campus. Black civic groups, however, insisted the appropriate reference community was the city—but not the county. Mexican-American civic groups demanded the community be the five-county area around the institution. And one top administrator, who wanted to keep things essentially the same, grandly declared the college's community was the entire United States and the college already met the principle of equality for that reference group.

The director of the MIS program, who had rather naively produced a document based on the idea that the city was the appropriate reference group, ran into an immediate hailstorm of criticism from everybody except the black groups, which were pleased at the choice. The numbers looked concrete and scientific, but the source of those numbers became a hot political potato.

There are many examples of the numbers game. There is the college president who deliberately clouds the distinction between "full-time-equivalent students" and "student head count" to make people believe his college is bigger. An institutional research director once "lost" over five hundred class drop cards just as the state auditors were taking the attendance census. These cases of blatant misrepresentation are fairly rare; but the more subtle types of change, manipulation, and distortion go on all the time. Charts, for example, can be prepared so that small changes look enormous—a ploy known to every muckraking journalist in the world. "Statistics never lie, but statisticians certainly do." This warning applies with a vengeance to the political manipulations surrounding an MIS.

Tyranny of the Concrete. Unfortunately, the availability of computerized data systems helps promote the notion that things are important if they can be measured, counted, and reduced to computer printout. We feel very strongly that adequate data and a good MIS are utterly invaluable aids to decision making, but data systems and their output have sharp limits to what they can do.

At the spring 1977 Montreal meeting of the Association for Institutional

Research, we gave a conference session on our research. We reported the various trends we saw developing and the various promises and problems involved in the system. We had just completed a round of hundreds of intensive interviews on the campuses. In addition, we had just completed a huge computer analysis of questionnaires from the various administrators. We tried to blend the results from our interviews and questionnaire studies, as we have done in this chapter. After the conference session, the president of a college came up to talk about the issues. In discussing the matter, we told him about a particular problem that had emerged from our interviews. Finally, he turned away and said in a rather disgusted voice, "Don't give me all those opinions—I want the *hard facts* that came from your computer analysis."

In short, he was playing the "tyranny of the concrete" game. Somehow the opinions of administrators expressed in short-answer questionnaires and reduced to numbers were more real to him than the same opinions expressed in intensive interviews where we could probe in depth. To our minds, we had learned at least as much about the process from the interviews as from the "hard data." But to this man's mind, the only reality was the one that could be expressed in numbers. The same subtle threat exists whenever an MIS is used.

There are, of course, dangers on both sides of the issue. Decisions made without adequate data are often faulty; and decisions made solely on concrete data, with little attention to subjective and judgmental factors, often have an unreal air about them. People who attack the use of data in decision making are often simply ignorant about the process. But people who virtually worship at the altar of data can be just as far off the mark.

Linking Planning and Budgets

One final issue loomed large for these colleges. We are convinced project impacts could have been increased substantially if the planning process and the budgeting process were more closely linked. We have seen that projects combining MIS and MBO systems seem to have the most positive impacts. We think a threefold combination would have been even better: a strong data base, a solid planning program under an MBO project, and a budgeting cycle that linked both.

A few projects were related to the budgeting process. In nearly all cases, the data collected for an MIS were used in the budgeting process. There were many positive impacts on the budgeting process: Priorities were clearer; the "hot-spot analysis" helped highlight problems in the budget; the interdependency between departments was clearer; and budget decisions affecting one department were expanded to consider other departments. So in some ways, the MIS projects did tie the planning process to the budgeting process by providing a data base on which to make decisions.

By contrast, in only a few cases was the MBO program directly linked to the budgeting process. In one case, Arkansas College, many people felt there had been an improvement in both the planning and the budgeting processes. Plans cannot be made in a vacuum. To plan with one hand and budget with the other is to invite gross inefficiency. Most important, people want to believe their plans are somehow going to influence budgeting decisions. They become disillusioned when there is no such influence. In our interviews, a number of department chairpersons felt they had participated in a make-believe planning process that was never linked with budgeting. A link between planning and budgeting is critical for efficient planning; it is also essential for the planners' morale.

This does not mean "wish lists" constructed during planning must dictate the budget. In fact, the real world of the budget must be considered at every point. We believe the process actually works in the other direction. When budget realities are known, they can have a sobering effect on planners. Consequently, people are more likely to abandon their wish lists and design realistic, cost-conscious plans.

Earlier we said coupling a strong MBO program with an MIS program was one of our most important recommendations. A second is that the planning process must be linked with the budgeting process. Without that linkage, the planning process is nothing more than a sham in which people spend time and energy but become extremely disillusioned. Budgets are only useful when they implement serious plans. The planning process is only sensible when it can be linked to real-world budgets.

This can be a threatening enterprise for administrators who have traditionally held the reins over the budget. It is one thing to let faculty members and department heads go off and plan—"to play games in the sand box," as one president cynically noted. It is quite another thing to involve the faculty, department heads, and deans in a serious planning exercise that has real-life financial consequences. This probably means conflict will also increase. Planning in a vacuum usually does not cause conflict; make-believe play rarely does. But when the planning is connected with the budget, the conflict level will surely rise.

Thus, administrators can be threatened by a double-edged sword: a need to share power and an increase in conflict. Nevertheless, in the real world of management and administration, shared power and conflict over resources have to be handled rather than hidden. Linking the planning process, the data-gathering process, and the budgeting system is absolutely essential.

Bibliographical Essay

Until recently, much of the literature on Management Information Systems remained fugitive, buried in the operations manuals of individual institutions and consulting firms. The most extensive public literature of MIS was produced by the National Center for Higher Education Management Systems (NCHEMS) in Boulder, Colorado. Minter and Lawrence produced one of the best collections, entitled *Management Information Systems: Their Development and Use in the Administration of Higher Education*. This edited volume contains a variety of articles on information and planning. NCHEMS publications are among the best sources (see Clark and others, 1973; Brady and others, 1975; and Mann and others, 1975). Other good references on MIS are Hopkins (1971), Hussain and Freytag (1973), Kirschling (1976), and Mason (1975).

Turning to the "Management by Objectives" approach, Drucker's *The Practice of Management* (1954) is the classic discussion. However, probably the best-known discussion of the technique is Odiorne's book, *Management by Objectives* (1965). Baldridge and Tierney (1979) give a brief, to-the-point review of basic MBO principles.

In *New Approaches to Management* (1979), Baldridge and Tierney give descriptions of both MIS and MBO systems as planning tools. In addition, they do a systematic evaluation of the impact of these planning processes in forty-nine liberal arts colleges. This book is a good starting point for anyone interested in using MIS or MBO processes in small colleges.

References

Balderston, F. E. *Managing Today's University*. San Francisco: Jossey-Bass, 1974.

Baldridge, J. V. *Power and Conflict in the University*. New York: Wiley, 1971.

Baldridge, J. V., and Deal, T. *Managing Change in Academic Organizations*. Berkeley, Calif.: McCutchan, 1974.

Baldridge, J. V., and Tierney, M. L. *New Approaches to Management: Creating Practical Systems of Management Information and Management by Objectives*. San Francisco: Jossey-Bass, 1979.

Bogard, L. *Management in Institutions of Higher Education*. Papers on Efficiency in the Management of Higher Education (Technical Report). Berkeley, Calif.: Carnegie Commission on Higher Education, 1972.

Bowen, H. R., and Minter, W. J. *Private Higher Education: Second Annual Report*. Washington, D.C.: Association of American Colleges, 1976.

Brady, R. W., and others. *Administrative Data Processing: The Case for Executive Management Involvement*. Boulder, Colo.: National Center for Higher Education Management Systems, Western Interstate Commission for Higher Education, 1975.

Cheit, E. F. *The New Depression in Higher Education—Two Years Later*. New York: McGraw-Hill, 1973.

Clark, D. G., and others. *Introduction to the Resource Requirements Prediction Model 1.6*. Boulder, Colo.: National Center for Higher Education Management Systems, Western Interstate Commission for Higher Education, 1973.

Cohen, M. D., and March, J. G. *Leadership and Ambiguity*. New York: McGraw-Hill, 1974.

Drucker, P. *The Practice of Management*. New York: Doubleday, 1954.

Gray, P. *Faculty Planning Models: The Use of Faculty Simulation Models*. Paper presented at "Academic Planning for the Eighties and Nineties." Los Angeles: Office of Institutional Studies, University of Southern California, 1976.

Hopkins, D. S. P. "On the Use of Large-Scale Simulation Models for University Planning." *Review of Educational Research*, 1971, *41* (5), 467–478.

Hussain, K. M., and Freytag, H. L. *Resource, Costing, and Planning Models in Higher Education*. Munich: Verlag Dokumentation, 1973.

Kirschling, W. R. "Models: Caveat, Reflections, and Suggestions." In T. R. Mason (Ed.), *New Directions for Institutional Research: Assessing Computer-Based Systems Models*, no. 9. San Francisco: Jossey-Bass, 1976.

Mann, R. L., and others. *An Overview of Two Recent Surveys of Administrative Computer Operations in Higher Education*. Boulder, Colo.: National Center for Higher Education Management Systems, Western Interstate Commission for Higher Education, 1975.

Mason, R. D. "Basic Concepts for Designing Management Information Systems." In A. Rappaport (Ed.), *Information for Decision Making: Quantitative and Behavioral Dimensions*. (2nd ed.) Englewood Cliffs, N.J.: Prentice-Hall, 1975.

Minter, W. J., and Lawrence, B. (Eds.). *Management Information Systems: Their Development and Use in the Administration of Higher Education.* Boulder, Colo.: Western Interstate Commission for Higher Education, 1969.

Odiorne, G. S. *Management by Objectives.* New York: Pitman, 1965.

Plourde, P. J. "Institutional Use of Models: Hope or Continued Frustration?" In T. R. Mason (Ed.), *New Directions for Institutional Research: Assessing Computer-Based System Models,* no. 9. San Francisco: Jossey-Bass, 1976.

Schroeder, R. G. "A Survey of Operations Analysis in Higher Education." Paper presented at 41st national meeting of the Operations Research Society of America, Minneapolis, April 26–28, 1972.

Weathersby, G. B., and Weinstein, M. C. *A Structural Comparison of Analytical Models for University Planning.* Berkeley, Calif.: Ford Foundation Program for Research in University Administration, 1970.

30

Foster S. Buchtel

Approaches of Medium-Sized Universities

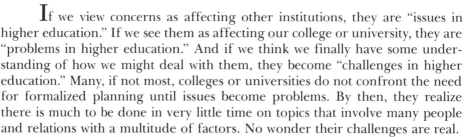

If we view concerns as affecting other institutions, they are "issues in higher education." If we see them as affecting our college or university, they are "problems in higher education." And if we think we finally have some understanding of how we might deal with them, they become "challenges in higher education." Many, if not most, colleges or universities do not confront the need for formalized planning until issues become problems. By then, they realize there is much to be done in very little time on topics that involve many people and relations with a multitude of factors. No wonder their challenges are real.

In the contradictory democracy we refer to as collegial governance, planning creates threats, value attacks, factions, and territoriality even when introduced under the most pleasant and stable conditions. (See, for example, Salloway and Tack, 1978.) When introduced under the siege of declining enrollments, resources, and public confidence, planning can easily become the symbol of an

602

aggressive governance system, threatening the final vestiges of collegiality and academic progress.

This chapter describes how three universities—the University of Akron, Wichita State University, and Furman University—introduced a planning process into their ongoing activities. Two of the universities, Akron and Wichita, are state assisted; Furman is private. Each was at a different stage of readiness when it undertook to formalize its planning process; and each, after diagnosing its situation, developed and implemented a plan for change distinctive to its own conditions. But a basic similarity among the three schools was an unstated, underlying philosophy that powered the process—that planning was not an end in itself but rather a vehicle for the prudent integration of appropriate and ongoing change into the academic and administrative processes. In a general sense, they viewed planning as bringing the future into the present so they could start to do something about it "today." In each case, planning involved recognizing issues as potential or real problems and turning them into challenges.

Planning Process: A Linear Definition for a Non-Linear Process

Earlier, we shared a general definition of planning. The working or operative definition of planning that appeared to be consistent for the three universities that will serve as our model is best described as that critical part of the university governance process that attempts to predetermine a course of action through a systematic consideration of goals and objectives, identification of programs, calculations and allocation of resources, identification of priorities and alternatives, and program evaluation (Ohio Board of Regents, 1973). Although accurate, this working definition omits the humanity of the planning process introduced by the three universities, each of which realized the importance of the human element in the change process and of involving the variety of campus constituencies in the planning process. A superimposition of the human-action model of a planning concept (see, for example, Ozbekhan, 1969; Michael, 1976) on the above definition would allow for the integration of the human elements through their identification of and working with values, objectives, and goals; their defining—or at least seeking—of purpose; and their seeking of norms. This would put the necessary meat on the otherwise dry bones and make the definition both more palatable and more descriptive of that which was introduced at the three universities.

Two other points need to be made about the definition before we move on to the descriptions and the analyses. First, we are describing a planning process and not a plan. Second, the planning process at these universities is described in this chapter in a logical, sequential manner, but it must be admitted that the process is seldom linear in its application: The logic or orderliness lies in the description of the system model (Haas, 1976). Suffice it to say that universities rarely initiate a planning process by starting with a systematic consideration of goals and objectives and then proceed neatly and in sequence through the steps of identifying programs and priorities, analyzing required and available resources, selecting among alternatives, allocating resources, and evaluating the results. Nor should they, for to do so would be to ignore local organizational dynamics and readiness and doom the effort. However, because the planning process is an iterative system, wherever it is entered, all these components have to be experienced if the process is to be successful. The point of entry and the order of the steps are best determined by the readiness, needs, and idiosyncrasies of the institution.

The University of Akron: A Network Approach to Planned Change

To the outsider, it would appear the University of Akron's entry into the planning process was at the goals and objectives step with the campuswide development and publication of two statements, "The Urban Mission of the University of Akron" and "Goals and Purposes of the University of Akron" in 1975. Both the development and content of these statements were consistent with the University of Akron's pride in its heritage as a small, private liberal arts college that had developed over a period of 104 years to a state university with twenty-three thousand credit and five thousand noncredit students, nine degree-granting colleges, thirteen doctoral programs, two professional schools (law and nursing), and a branch campus. In addition, it had a consortium partnership in a medical school with two other universities and additional consortium arrangements in public television, a joint Ph.D. program in sociology, and a cooperative master's program in nursing. Located in the heavy population and industrial area of northeastern Ohio, the University of Akron has a predominantly commuter student body. It enjoys the autonomy afforded by its own separate board of trustees, a sound fiscal base, and a healthy enrollment growth that is expected to level off.

Although developing the two statements was the first visible step taken, this was not the first step. The rest of the process was not followed in a sequential order, and all the elements of the process are not yet in operation.

An earlier step was taken in 1974 when the president of the university provided in his annual all-faculty address a broad outline of an institutional change plan via the planning process (Guzzetta, 1974). In general, this presentation signaled the human-oriented, organizational development approach that would be taken in the development of a planning process at the University of Akron. There was no measurable, defined goal or goals offered, only an implicit agreement on a general concept of the mission and goals for a starting point and the promise that a more defined set of goals and objectives would be developed through mutual cooperation and understanding. At the same time, the presentation outlined the intended elements of the planning process to be introduced regrouped under the three words that were the title of the talk, "Continuity, Change, and Challenge." These elements were essentially the same as those noted earlier—systematic consideration of goals and objectives, identification of programs, calculations and allocations of resources, identification of priorities and alternatives, and program evaluation. What followed, over the next three years, was the conscious evolution of a "network of change," using existing academic and administrative units of the university wherever possible and identifying new elements that would have to be created, all moving deliberately—and, at times, awkwardly—toward a combined planning and change process.

Chronologically, following the development and publication of the statements of mission and goals and purposes a year after the president's talk, a program for the development of team leadership at an urban university was designed and implemented with the support of a major grant from the W. K. Kellogg Foundation. This program combined training in interpersonal/intergroup dynamics, university organizations, and environmental influences (for example, national issues) on education with participant activities on task forces and interdisciplinary/interdepartmental internships to establish faculty/ administration team leadership development potential. The program was designed and conducted so that the mission and goals and purposes statements were an obbligato throughout the classes and task forces, reinforcing the unifying theme of the urban mission.

One hundred and seven faculty members and administrators were involved in four classes of twenty-five to thirty participants over a two-year period. Each class included a three-day retreat and eight weekly one-day class sessions and represented a heterogeneous mix, both horizontal (disciplinary) and vertical (status), of faculty and administrators. During the class sessions, in addition to experiential and involved learning activities designed around university experiences, the participants identified tasks they felt needed to be accomplished to move the University of Akron toward meeting the mission and goals and purposes statements. These class-identified tasks became the basis for presidential task forces allowing the participants to put into practice skills they had learned. Additional opportunities to convert learning into constructive practice were provided by internships. Upon completing the classes, participants were invited to apply for involvement in self-designed problem-solving or need-meeting activities that cut across departmental and disciplinary lines and related to the university's urban mission. Examples of the focuses of the resulting seventeen task forces and eight internships include a performance evaluation and reward system; greater interaction with the local community and northeastern Ohio; establishing an active faculty club (including the acquisition of the building to house the club); interdisciplinary activities; integration of experiential learning into the university curriculum; new approaches to lifelong education; establishing an exchange network with area secondary schools; use of retirees as resource persons; risk management in higher education; faculty improvement in the classroom; a referral and support system for handicapped students; development of a team leadership training program for students; identification, evaluation, and coordination of management information data available to academic deans and department heads; continuing education for professionals; stimulating and coordinating off-campus teaching activities; and creating a council of organizations, institutions, and agencies engaged in continuing education activities in the area.

An on-campus ripple effect was further facilitated by "miniteam leadership classes," which were requested by university departments. Departments and groups requesting and receiving these two- to three-day workshops included university relations and development, division of student services, community and technical college, university library, university nursery school, Commission on Institutional Planning and Development, Department of Speech Pathology and Audiology, registrar's office, computer center, and the academic department heads group. In all, the program reached approximately four hundred members of the university's faculty and staff (The University of Akron, 1978).

Thus, the University of Akron Kellogg-sponsored program developed a resource pool of faculty and administrators prepared to exercise their responsibilities in the change process and laid the groundwork for a constructive campus temperament for involvement in the planning process.

Shortly after the team leadership development program was launched at the University of Akron, the Commission on Institutional Planning and Development was established to serve as a coordinator and a catalyst for developing a planning process and the accompanying network of change. The commission is chaired by the president and has its membership drawn from faculty, administration, students, and the community.

The planning and change process at the University of Akron is still evolving. The Commission on Institutional Planning and Development is coming to grips with its identity and is ready to move into a more assertive role in the process; commission task forces are building on the foundations laid by the original Kellogg task forces in areas of student recruiting and retention studies, outreach programs, and performance evaluation and reward systems; the recently established Institute for Futures Studies and Research has tested its wings, gained confidence from the results of a Delphi survey aimed at identifying activities and priorities, and is ready to take a position of strength in the network; the office of team leadership development is continuing its training and facilitating role through a continuation of on-campus workshops and is facilitating community involvement through combined campus/community workshops and a second Kellogg-sponsored two-year team leadership program to extend the original concept to a model of a university/community team leadership network; and a special study group is starting to bring together the wide array of campus data and information systems into a consolidated management or planning information system. The scattered pieces are starting to resemble a process. However, even after the process is completed and functioning, it is intended to maintain it as an evolutionary system because it has to keep pace with the university's mission and function, which is, or should be, also evolutionary.

Wichita State University: A Top-Down Approach to Planned Change

In many respects, the history and development of Wichita State University and the University of Akron parallel each other. Both started as private liberal arts colleges and developed into comprehensive universities with a sense of oneness with their urban environments. Today, Wichita State University has fifteen thousand students and offers degree programs in six colleges, ranging from the associate degree level through two doctoral degrees. Most of the students reside in the Wichita metropolitan area, which has a population of a third of a million people. These students are often older than traditional college age, working, and usually do not enroll in a full load of courses. As a result, Wichita State programs are especially responsive to the needs of the community and surrounding region. The city of Wichita is the population center of a basically agricultural area, providing the university with a strong commitment of responding to the needs of an urban environment and a mixed urban/rural student body. Significant enrollment gains in the 1960s were not yet matched by commensurate increases in physical resources when enrollment fluctuations started in the mid 1970s. However, the university's academic programs have continued to mature and respond to the changing needs of the predominantly nontraditional student body. Policy and budget for Wichita State University is set by a statewide board of regents.

The current, formalized planning process at Wichita State University grew out of the Leadership and Management Development Project. This program, also sponsored by the W. K. Kellogg Foundation, was concerned basically with anticipating, planning, and managing a changing future. The two basic goals of the project were to improve the university's abilities to anticipate, plan, manage, and implement change to meet steady-state conditions or new opportunities and respond to the needs for nontraditional approaches in higher education while preserving the values and strengths of the traditional approaches.

The following five objectives were identified to achieve the two goals (Ahlberg and Christenson, 1977, p. 2):

1. developing leadership abilities and techniques appropriate to steady-state management, including the ability to anticipate change and function as a change agent, to be responsive and flexible, to clarify values and priorities, to use sophisticated tools of analysis, and to function as a member of a team
2. implementing a new, more effective institutional planning and research system that will enable the institution to create and retrieve data for making management decisions, analyze institutional needs and model alternative futures, and foster a data-supported realism that will reduce the margin for error
3. strengthening internal and external communications to create an environment in which change of all kinds is articulated and discussed internally and a base of confidence is maintained among people within the organization
4. optimizing individual faculty effectiveness through implementation of continuing evaluation and career redevelopment and assisting faculty to meet the newer needs of the nontraditional approaches to educational program and services
5. organizing and implementing an administrative internship and development program that will involve people at all levels in changing basic processes, qualify them to assume a broader role within the university, and generate new sources of leadership in the steady-state future

The project was divided into two phases. Phase I involved a ten-person project leadership team consisting of the university's top-level administrators and faculty members and a member of the Kansas Board of Regents. Its objectives were development of the long-range planning skills of the leadership team, reassessment of the university's goals and objectives, and planning of four programs to be undertaken during phase II.

During phase I, project goals and methodology were clarified without attempting to propose solutions. This "clarify and not propose" approach was considered critical for the success of phase I and conducive to innovation and creativity. The project leadership team was also able to take advantage of the results of four surveys that had just been completed in preparation for a North Central Accreditation visit: the student outcomes questionnaire, the student perceptions questionnaire, the faculty perceptions questionnaire, and the institutional goals inventory. In addition, the team invited the North Central task force chairpersons and the dean's council to participate in identifying major issues, problems, and opportunities that confronted Wichita State University; appointed four task forces of three to four persons each to assist in the planning of the four programs to be undertaken during phase II; and established two joint Kellogg project/council of deans task forces to assist in enrollment projections and student market analysis.

By the time the twelve months of phase I were completed, the Kellogg project leadership team (or its representatives) had held three team retreats, reviewed and analyzed material and data from their own resources and from other universities, consulted with outside resource persons, attended a workshop on small-group procedures, visited fourteen universities, participated in eleven conferences, received seven resource persons on campus, and conducted a systematic search of more than one hundred forty books and special reports to glean approaches and practices of other universities that might be applicable to the needs and aspirations of Wichita State University.

The first twelve months were busy and fruitful, establishing both a direction and a momentum for phase II. Some of the tangible results of phase I included a working draft of a statement of mission and strategies for the future, the active involvement of thirty members of the campus community, the establishment of a project/planning support staff, and the design of the four programs of activity to be undertaken during phase II.

The intangible benefit from phase I was the raising of the level of awareness on the part of many concerning the need for and means of preparing strategies for planning and change. For example, in the process of drafting the mission and strategies statement, new or reawakened realizations occurred concerning the distinctive nature of Wichita State University, its strengths, its problems, and its future. The concept of the university as a comprehensive state university with an urban mission was analyzed and better understood. Changes occurring nationally in higher education and their implications for and potential impact on Wichita State University were identified. And Wichita State University's opportunities, strengths, constraints, and areas of concern had been realistically assessed (Ahlberg and Christenson, 1977). By the end of the twelve months of phase I, Wichita State University had reinforced its self-identity through reflection and enlarged its awareness through self-examination.

The four programs of activity designed for phase II were planning and information systems, communications, faculty development, and administrative development. They were organized and conducted under four task forces:

- *The planning and information systems task force* consisted of two new committees, the committee on program planning and the committee on program review and evaluation, which operated independently as "sub–task forces." These committees developed a process for program planning and a process for program review and evaluation, concentrating initially on academic programs, by identifying the present methods used at Wichita State University, identifying and analyzing approaches used at other universities, and developing a process for initial implementation.

    Although the committees were unable to meet their goals in the refinement of the university's information system in the time available, they still intend to refine the university's six major data bases to the level where data elements will be in computer form and it will be possible to move from one data bank to another with a minimum of effort. In addition, some areas of institutional research needs were identified, as well as needs for a central depository of institutional studies and an ongoing "fact book" of systematically collected data.

- *The communications task force* employed the International Communication Association (ICA) to conduct an internal communication audit. A communication audit advisory committee was formed to design and oversee the audit, serve as liaison with the ICA, receive the report from the ICA, and suggest ways to implement the findings. In addition, the task force conducted surveys of students, community leaders and alumni, and media representatives to determine the image these groups had of the university and the effectiveness of its publications and other media.
- *The faculty development and evaluation task force,* working with four committees, designed a faculty development program to identify and better serve the development needs of the faculty. The four committees were in the areas of instructional development, scholarly and creative activities, service activities, and professional and personal development. This task force identified existing faculty development and evaluation activities at Wichita State University, reviewed the approaches taken by other universities, developed an assessment of faculty development needs at the university, identified the priorities and activities for its program, analyzed how resources currently devoted to faculty development were being used, and recommended the resources needed and methods of organizing and administering the program.
- *The administrative development task force* implemented an internship program, designed a program for continuing administrative development, and recommended a process for evaluating administrators. The administrative internship program involved five faculty during the 1977–78 academic year and was coordinated by a seven-person internship advisory committee. Procedures were developed for recruiting and selecting interns, designing each intern's program, identifying and making arrangements with mentors, and evaluating interns.

To design a program for continuing development of administrators, a series of workshops was conducted. Planning committees designed and conducted workshops for department chairpersons, graduate coordinators, assistant and associate deans, and the central administration. A combined workshop for all these groups was conducted to help design an ongoing administrative development program. In addition, a workshop was conducted for staff members not classified as administrators or faculty.

The complex interplay of task forces and committees involving close to a hundred and fifty members of the campus community is the hallmark of Wichita State University's approach to the development of a planning process. The successful results—still ongoing—are an ironic testimony to the planning skills of a group of people who felt they needed to develop planning skills. The approach did result in the development of a team that can maintain leadership in planning, a model of wide-ranging campus involvement in the process, improved perception among a sizable group of faculty and administrators of higher educational issues, and a futures planning orientation and approach to major issues. More specifically, some of the tangible results included a professional development office that works with both administration and faculty, an ongoing process for program planning, an ongoing process for program review and evaluation, and resource packets describing the project and its outcomes.

Neither program thus far discussed originated or was coordinated in a formally identified planning office, although both were intended to deal with planned change. I believe this common characteristic is an example of an approach responding to the special temperament of the institution and its readiness for change. The third institution to be described, Furman University, is distinguished from the first two in that its program for planned change was originated in and facilitated and maintained by an office designated as a planning and institutional research office.

Furman University: A Decentralized Approach to Planned Change

Furman University is a coeducational, primarily residential, liberal arts college located in Greenville, South Carolina. Its aim is to be a community of scholars that introduces students to the methods and concepts of liberal learning and prepares them for the lifelong process of becoming educated. Founded in 1826 by the South Carolina Baptist Convention, the university enrolls approximately twenty-two hundred undergraduates and has a full-time faculty of one hundred forty-five. In addition to the undergraduate curriculum, there are small graduate programs in education, business administration, and chemistry. Admission standards are selective. Approximately 45 percent of the graduates go directly to graduate or professional schools.

Early in 1971, Furman's leaders became concerned about the growing potential of conflict between the need for maintaining high-quality academic programs versus limited, and perhaps even shrinking, resources and about management problems growing out of this conflict and aggravated by external influences. Out of this concern came the conviction that only a comprehensive approach to management planning could have any positive influence on these conditions and needs. Therefore, with financial support from the Ford Foundation and the Exxon Education Foundation, Furman began a comprehensive program to revitalize its management planning processes and to develop a management planning model. Early in the development stage, its leaders identified twelve factors critical to effective institutional planning (Winstead, 1975, 1976):

1. Make certain there is general agreement regarding management style, organizational relationships, and information requirements.
2. Clarify basic policies and establish general guidelines.
3. Take appropriate steps to avoid rumors, minimize surprise, and gain acceptance and support for the planning efforts.
4. Create a planning environment and provide a practical planning process before asking people to engage in planning activities.
5. Make certain the planning process is designed to meet the needs and requirements of the institution and not just a copy of someone else's process. (Do not reinvent the wheel, but do not accept blindly either.)
6. Provide enough flexibility to meet changing conditions and enough adaptability to be able to cope with all of the types of planning that need to be done.

7. Provide and keep in focus adequate decision-making information at the times and places where it is needed.
8. Be certain that the planning process makes it possible to revise agreement as well as to reach agreement.
9. Be certain to identify and monitor all important developments that will have a major impact on future performance or results.
10. Continually identify and evaluate the institution's capabilities and opportunities as well as the strengths and weaknesses.
11. Keep the planning process simple and minimize paperwork.
12. Provide staff support for planning. Do not let staff people do the planning, but conserve the time of key people in the institution as much as possible.

These twelve factors became the "conscience" of the planning process as it developed.

A twenty-four-member committee on institutional planning chaired by the president was created and charged with overall program direction. Membership on the committee included the top administration, deans, faculty members, students, an alumnus, and a trustee. Concurrently, an external group—a management task force—was appointed by the university's advisory council and charged with providing advice and counsel. The administrative and committee structure had been established; now it was time to get to the job at hand.

The project included three sequential phases. During phase I, the committee on institutional planning explored the use of a planning model developed by Planning Dynamics, Inc. (PDI); conducted a preliminary analysis of Furman University concerning readiness for the program; and oriented key participants to make certain that the nature, scope, and purpose of the project were understood. The committee decided to use the PDI model as the nucleus of its own planning and management model, as it enhanced participation and flexibility through the use of a planning book technique as an organizing mechanism to help collect, process, distribute, and revise essential information for decision making. Once this decision was made, and the in-depth orientation meetings and discussions with faculty, administrators, students, and staff were completed to the satisfaction of the committee, it was felt they were ready to move into phase II.

During phase II, a hypothetical management planning model was designed for Furman, a prototype planning system developed, and a workshop conducted for key administrators and faculty to demonstrate the applicability of the tentative model. When these activities were completed, the committee on institutional planning again reviewed the campus readiness for the project and decided to move into phase III. At this time, the need for an office of institutional planning and research was recognized; and a planning specialist was appointed as the coordinator of institutional planning and research and a member of the committee.

Phase III consists of nine activities. The first is *goal clarification.* Using a preliminary version of the institutional goals inventory developed by the Educational Testing Service, Furman established a background for the development of goals both for the university as a whole and for each of the organizational units during the summer and fall of 1972.

Second is *management by objectives*. Using the goals as a foundation, each organizational unit was asked to derive measurable objectives and test a management by objectives approach to administration. Earlier, a workshop had been held for selected budget unit heads to help them in analyzing their goals, specifying measurable objectives, and reaching agreement with members of their staff in the assignment of responsibilities. Objectives for each organizational unit were reviewed by appropriate higher echelons of the organization for consistency with the other university objectives before they were authorized. Then responsibility for each objective was assigned to appropriate persons and the available resources made known to them. During the designated period of time, the persons would be given wide latitude in choice of methods but would also provide frequent updates using milestone reporting techniques. At the end of the fiscal year, the actual results were jointly reviewed against the agreed-upon goals and objectives. It was at this point that the evaluation influenced the reward system.

The third activity is *strengths, weaknesses, opportunities, threats (SWOTs) analysis*. To be practical, management by objectives must relate to the assignment of priorities, particularly when resources are limited. Therefore, before an objective would be authorized, it was also weighed against the following criteria:

1. Is it suitable to one of Furman's goals?
2. Is it feasible?
3. Is Furman willing and able to pay the cost?
4. Is it worth the cost?
5. Is it achievable?
6. Is it measurable?
7. Can it be changed if necessary?
8. Is there firm determination to succeed?

To assist in making these judgments, each functional unit conducted a SWOTs analysis in the form of an annual report. Next, the individual SWOTs were consolidated into a universitywide analysis. The SWOTs analysis thus provided a framework, along with institutional goals and available resources, for weighing the proposed objectives against the needs of the individual unit as well as the university as a whole.

Fourth, a *planning book* system served as the principal organizing vehicle for the entire project, providing for the integration of purpose, goals, objectives, management by objectives, basic data, and other elements of systematic planning into the university's ongoing administrative processes. The system included a loose-leaf notebook with color-coded pages keyed for distribution on a need-to-know basis. Each page could be updated individually. The planning book contents were organized around data categories needed to provide information for decision making based on a normal trip analogy (see Exhibit 1). To keep them from being discouraging in their bulk and unmanageable in their data, each book contained only the information its holder would need for his or her area of responsibility. The exception, of course, was material applicable on a universitywide basis, which was included in every book.

Fifth is a *policies and procedures system*. Special task forces were appointed to recommend universitywide policies supportive of the management planning effort in the five areas of governance, organizational relationships, growth, institu-

Exhibit 1. The Trip Analogy and Sections of the Planning Book

Trip Analogy Questions	Planning Book Sections
A. Where are we?	1. Statement of purpose or mission
	2. Analysis of environment and competition
	3. Assessment of capabilities and opportunities
B. Where do we want to go?	4. Assumptions
	5. Goals and objectives
C. How do we want to go?	6. Policies and procedures
	7. Programs and projects
D. When do we want to go?	8. Priorities and schedules
E. Who is going with us?	9. Human resources and staffing of programs or projects
F. What will it cost?	10. Financial and physical resource projections
G. How do we know when we get there?	11. Appraisal or evaluation data
	12. Miscellaneous

tional identity, and policies. Also, the faculty status committee was asked to revise the *Faculty Handbook* consistent with the new format and the vice-president for business affairs was asked to oversee the conversion of the *Business Office Procedures Manual* to the new system. All policies and procedures were then maintained in loose-leaf binders of color-coded pages with specific file numbers, and distribution was limited to a need-to-know basis.

The sixth activity was development of *computer-based information systems*. At the time Furman decided to plan purposefully for planning, there already existed on campus a computer-based generalized information retrieval system and a computerized general ledger system that could be keyed to both a line-item budget and a program budget. Believing a computer-based simulation model was important to the planning process, members of the planning staff examined several before determining that two were applicable to their needs: the original HELP version of HELP/PLANTRAN to simulate revenue and resource allocation functions and the NCHEMS/RRPM 1.6 model to answer questions concerning the effects of curriculum changes, decreases or increases in students in the various major fields, and the effects of these changes on all the academic departments within the institution.

Seventh, *institutional research* activities were conducted continuously to address special problems and to provide administrators and faculty with alternatives for decision making. Two types of institutional research documents were used for distribution: a planning report series dealing with topics of general interest and with universitywide applicability and a planning memo series responding to specific requests by administrators or faculty members.

The eighth activity was formation of a *priorities task force*. The management planning techniques and devices described thus far assisted greatly in goals clarification, improved communications, management by objectives, more objective research, and other components of systematic institutional planning. Yet the problem of how to decide among worthwhile activities across major units of the university as well as within major units persisted. Thus, the priorities task force was created as a subcommittee of the committee on institutional planning and included the four vice-presidents, the academic dean, four faculty members, the athletic director, and the president of the Association of Furman Students, with the business manager and treasurer and the coordinator of institutional planning and research serving as resource persons. The task force was charged with examining all aspects of Furman's operations and making recommendations to the president as to the expenditures making the greatest contributions toward achieving Furman's primary goals and appropriate ways of balancing expenditures with income. The task force, which meets almost weekly, takes a universitywide view and looks especially at budget allocations across the major units of the university.

Ninth is *advice and timing*. The advisory and training activities were interspersed consciously and continuously through the planning process; for example, in addition to providing general guidance, the committee on institutional planning provided the means for assimilating the work in management planning into the regular university operating procedures; the management task force of the advisory council, along with general advice and counsel, produced specific reports suggesting ways of improving institutional effectiveness and efficiency and was especially helpful in assisting staff members to assess the environment and develop reliable assumptions for planning purposes; workshops were held for all university administrators to discuss the conceptual base for the project and the implementation techniques; and the president continued his practice of holding three-day administrative council retreats off campus each summer to discuss in depth the major issues facing the university and to finalize the universitywide SWOTs analysis (Winstead, 1975, 1976).

By 1975, based on external and internal evaluations as well as experience, Furman was satisfied that a planning system was underway that was effective primarily within the administrative area. It was, however, lacking in both full faculty and student involvement and directly observable benefits to the classroom. Therefore, a program was developed to extend the benefits of the management planning process to the entire faculty, with the ultimate target being the classroom (Hipps and Winstead, 1978). Funded by the W. K. Kellogg Foundation, this program became a phase IV in the development of the Furman Planning and Institutional Renewal Program. Again, a committee, the faculty steering committee, was appointed. This time, however, the committee was elected through the normal procedures for electing faculty committees to assure a sense of faculty ownership. The steering committee developed policies and procedures for the project that had four major components: faculty proposals for planning activities (individual, departmental or divisional level, and institutional level), special colloquiums, planning orientation sessions, and special training in planning.

The three-year program was divided into six six-month periods with three to seven faculty proposals for planning activities supported during each six-month period. The major guidelines for evaluating the proposals were that activities proposed had to be for planning in some area of curriculum and instruction and the planning would result in a direct improvement of students' educational experiences. The main linkage between the individual planning grant program and the planning process described earlier was the requirement that each faculty proposal include a statement relating the proposed activity to the SWOTs analysis of a department and/or the university. Individual planning activities were assumed to involve primarily the interests and works of the individual faculty member—revising a course, adapting a new teaching technique, creating a new one, and so forth. Departmental, divisional, and institutional planning activities, although proposed and conducted by an individual faculty member, concerned the work of the total unit. In all, thirty-one individual planning activities proposals were funded over the three years, with all including—among other needs—provision for travel by the individual faculty members to seminars, workshops, and sites of programs similar to those proposed to learn firsthand the necessary knowledge for the specific instructional change desired.

The intent of the departmental-, divisional-, and institutional-level planning activities of Furman's Faculty Development in Academic Planning Project was to encourage and enable the faculty members to engage in planning projects that went beyond their own classroom setting. The twenty-eight projects funded in this category during the three-year period included eighteen departmental, four divisional, and six institutional programs.

For each of the three years of the program, two to four special colloquiums were organized around a predetermined theme for the year, with the intent of presenting new thoughts and academic activities to the Furman faculty. This, in turn, was intended to stimulate thought and generate new ideas for possible new programmatic efforts on campus. The theme for the first year, "The Purpose and Scope of a Liberal Arts College like Furman," was supported by four special colloquiums conducted by off-campus scholars and practitioners on the future of liberal arts colleges, the role of policy study in a liberal arts college, evaluating teaching and teacher effectiveness, and (in a combination colloquium) general education—philosophy, requirements, and recent trends and issues—and a competency-based program. The second- and third-year themes were alternative instructional strategies and the role of values in higher education (Hipps and Winstead, 1978).

The Furman approach to planning began with the more formalized, technical approach, with the surface agenda being a plan for planning. Nonetheless, care was taken to involve the critical campus constituencies and eventually to fold in the human-action emphasis. It was essentially, as were the Akron and Wichita approaches, a program for constructively involving people in the planning and change process and attempting to institutionalize the process.

Shortfalls of the Programs

This description of the three programs has thus far glossed over the problems and deficits they encountered and that warrant attention even though there were at least sufficient positive points for each program to offset the negative.

The external evaluators for the University of Akron Kellogg-sponsored Team Leadership Development Program observed that the task force projects had not made substantial contributions to university functioning "to date" and were seen by many as addressing unmanageable or unimportant problems in the university. Further, they noted many saw intern projects as duplicative of regular university job assignments and team leadership concepts taught in the workshops were not yet fully implemented by the university administrators (Lippitt and Aurelio, 1978). The training consultant also observed several "latent possibilities" (a thoughtful euphemism for "shortcomings" but intended to imply more). For example, he noted that the team leadership development portion of the process was labeled a "program," which meant to many a definite beginning and end. This, of course, ran contrary to the desire for an ongoing sense of process. He also noted the lack of a formalized organizational diagnosis as part of the human development strategy and the need to focus on targeted, homogeneous work groups in the future (DeShon, 1977). The first and third concerns are being addressed, and the response to the second concern is being developed. Relating the team leadership portion of the planning and change process to the overall process, the project director comments that, if it were to be done over again, the Commission on Institutional Planning and Development would have been established prior to the Team Leadership Development Program and made its advisory council, thus establishing immediate and appropriate change control relationships. Second, the issues dealt with by the task forces and internships would have been developed in close cooperation with the commission. That is, there would have been broader, representative involvement in the identification of issues and a more sensitive recognition of relating task force and intern activities to existing university vehicles (The University of Akron, 1978).

Wichita State University noted a serious concern at the close of the first year of its program (and at the close of the project) that the project was too ambitious in terms of the time needed to initiate major new programs and the project's resources. The time required of team and task force members was significant in itself. However, when added to regular, ongoing duties, it became burdensome almost to the point of collapse. The ambitiousness of the project also contributed, in some cases, to unrealistic expectations of what it could accomplish (Ahlberg and Christenson, 1977).

Both a primary evaluation consultant and a visiting team reviewed Furman University's program at the close of phase III (but prior to the initiation of phase IV). Their comments, although positive for the most part, included the following constructive critiques (Winstead, 1975, p. 2):

1. Although an excellent job has been done of identifying and discussing important developments that will have a major impact on future performance or results, the data have not been distributed to key personnel in a dynamically quantified manner with historical approach, current status, and future projections so that they could detect deviation and take appropriate action.
2. Although a superior job of goal clarification has been accomplished, not enough time and effort has been spent supporting assumptions and objectives and clarifying the difference between an "objective" (a result or end) and a "project" (an activity or means).
3. Although much necessary information has been gathered and distributed, the planning program would be more effective if paperwork were reduced and greater emphasis placed on determining information requirements and seeing to it that the proper information is kept in focus at the times and places

where plans and recommendations are proposed, authorized, and revised.

4. Most planning has been on an annual basis or ten-year financial projection; to achieve desirable long-term growth, a better range time frame would be three to five years.

5. Planning appears to be essentially an activity for administrators, department chairpersons, and committee members; the faculty should be involved.

6. Follow-through is needed in academic areas.

7. No network or vehicle has been established by students to gather recommendations or to disseminate information back to their fellow students.

8. Objectives are too broad and heavily oriented to activities rather than results.

9. Few academic departments have made notable progress in formulating their objectives; academic departments should be encouraged and helped to utilize management by objectives (MBO).

10. The annual budget is approved before all objectives and plans have been developed; this places the budget at the wrong end of the objective-setting process.

Several of these critiques were responded to specifically through phase IV, and the balance has been or is in the process of being responded to through adjustments in the planning process itself. Constructive evaluator comments relative to phase IV of the Furman program recommended that means be established for more precise, objective self-evaluation of faculty planning projects and the internal projects be evaluated by the steering committee for their accumulative effect on programs and the institution. The assessments of the fifty-nine planning activities were diverse, with many rated as highly successful and demonstrating identifiable behavioral changes among faculty as well as impact on students in the classroom. Others were noted for their potential rather than their immediate results, and still others were assigned marginal value. Perhaps the more interesting evaluation comment, particularly for its implications for and generalization to all programs of this nature, was the conclusion quoted from the final evaluation report: "The idea was a good one: to introduce strategies designed to encourage faculty participation in academic planning and decision making. . . . The idea was not fully realized, however, and perhaps could never be. Nonetheless, it resulted in a faculty development and institutional renewal program with unquestionably valuable outcomes. And if the project's strategies do not, for the greater part, warrant exact exportation to other higher education settings, still the fundamental ideas behind them do" (Hipps and Winstead, 1978, pp. 25–26).

Variations in Structure: Consistency in Process

As noted earlier, the order in which the elements of the planning process are introduced may vary with the readiness and sophistication of the institution and the primary change agent controlling their introduction. The elements of readiness include, but are not limited to, such internal conditions as organizational maturity, fiscal stability, leadership security and style, organizational self-image, trust level, institutional size, and dominance of either horizontal or vertical communication patterns and such external influences as economics, demographics, local values, constituent expectations, culture, and history. As these variables shift, so do planning and change strategies. One element in common to all of our efforts, wherever they are employed in higher education: we must work with and through people. And it is here that we can easily become snared in our own historical trap: the past tendencies of our universities to enshrine individual competition in the name of personal achievement can now create organizational paralysis when we are confronted with collectively transforming a commonly shared sensitivity into a program of inquiry, planning, and action (Maio and Buchtel, 1977).

Before we try to translate the above comments into, first, analyses of the three programs described earlier and, second, some generalizable principles of planning, it will be fruitful to review some assumptions.

At the beginning of this chapter we established the working definition of planning process by combining a standard definition with some elements of a human-action model of change, resulting in the collective ingredients restated as follows: systematic consideration of organizational goals and objectives; identification of programs; calculations and allocation of resources; identification of priorities and alternatives; program evaluation; identification of and working with human values, objectives, and goals; helping the members of the organization define or sense both their purpose and the organization's purpose; assisting the members of the organization to establish organizational norms consistent with the organizational goals.

The first five of these ingredients will be introduced as steps in that order in the planning and change process, with the next three ingredients being developed concurrently throughout the process. Since logic is more often a description of a desired course rather than an actual behavior, we can safely assume that it is not only rare, but suspect, if a planning process were to follow the described pattern. The three universities described here represented different emphases in structure; they shared common elements of actual and desired process. All three recognized the cross-disciplinary and cross-functional nature of the planning process; the key role of work groups or teams in the process; and the need for widespread participant awareness, openness, involvement, and acceptance (Buchtel, 1977). In addition to differing emphasis in structure, they differed in their points of entry into the planning process, in which of the essential ingredients they have covered to date, and which of the ingredients already existed to be assimilated in the process and which had to be initiated.

Akron: Emphasis on Process. The University of Akron began at the first step with a systematic consideration of its organizational goals and objectives. It then moved to develop and integrate the three human-action elements into the process obviously and deliberately through its team leadership program. Program identification was attempted almost simultaneously by the team leadership task forces and interns and the newly established Commission on Institutional Planning and Development. At this point, the trail begins to blur. Although the task forces and interns and the commission had official sanctioning to venture into program identification, the university as a composite human enterprise had not yet consented to this official sanction, and parallel paths of planning and change were in danger of being established. Responding to this danger, the task forces and interns have become a part of the commission; and the commission is building a wider base of participation.

Commission study groups are presently consolidating the existing information systems into one identifiable and responsive management information system to be coupled with the budgetary process (calculation and identification of resources); and the present approach to resource allocation through an "anarchy" form of trade-offs combined with priority decisions manifested through budget allocations is being replaced by bringing commission activities, management information systems, resource identification activities, and leadership priorities together in an organizational matrix form of constructive and calculated trade-offs. The identification of priorities and alternatives is being strengthened by increased confidence in commission and task force studies, retreat activities, and the potential of "forecast implications" that will be available through the recently established Institute for Futures Studies and Research. At the University of Akron, then, the emphasis is on process, with the ultimate structure probably taking the form of a matrix network of planning and change. During the transition, sound management of the enterprise is maintained by historical precedent. The balance between status quo and innovations in educational and social response will very likely shift with the movement along the planning continuum toward conscious fulfillment of each new ingredient. Akron's approach was believed appropriate for an established institution with a history of conservative management, in a relatively conservative community, and with a relatively new impatience to demonstrate its present academic strength and move rapidly into more programs responsive to social (urban) needs. It also reflects the concern of the leadership for the thoughts and involvement of the campus community and the human element in change.

Wichita State: Structure as Process. A similar analysis of Wichita State's planning approach would probably demonstrate that the structure was the process. That is, the sudden establishment of the criss-cross of task forces and committees within the institution was both a process and a structure for change. However, the establishment of this criss-cross after the traditional top leadership team determined the objectives might have been perceived by some with suspicion or as mixed signals. It was, in fact, a planning approach that was faithful to the history and expectations of the institution, that is, looking to a centralized leadership for direction and then working autonomously in teams to accomplish the goals. Referring to the basic elements in the development of a planning and change process, Wichita led off with identifying its program and then returned to identifying its goals and objectives. From there, Wichita appears to have exploded into all the other elements at the same time, with the least attention being given consciously to the human elements. Although, by their own admission, Wichita was almost inundated by its own explosion of activity, the results are emerging on the positive side of the ledger. Successful results have been reinforced by the leadership and the establishment of an organizational unit to continue the program.

Furman: Parallel Structure and Process. Furman appears to have followed the most logical sequence in the development of its planning approach, moving through each of the steps as though the sequence was based on the Furman model. However, conscious attention to involving the total constituency through the human-action steps came at the end of the series rather than as an integrated movement, as it might have been in an "ideal approach." There is little doubt that the smaller size of the institution and the lesser complexity of its programs contributed to this near-model sequencing. It is equally probable that the conscious predetermination of a classical plan, and the professional discipline of implementing it according to schedule while tuning it according to campus climate, were primary factors for success in this model.

Information Support System. The essential foundation of any planning process is reliable and current data about the organization that can serve as a resource for identifying troubles, diagnosing issues, monitoring trends, making decisions, and evaluating results. It should be clear already that Furman has a well-organized, informative support system integrated with its planning and change processes. What may not be so clear is that both Akron and Wichita State also have a supportive information system. However, the history and complexity of these two institutions have encouraged a decentralized information system. Means are now being pursued to link these systems formally with the planning and change process.

Planning and Change

Proper planning anticipates alternative possible and desired futures and tries to structure activities and assemble resources to achieve the desired futures. The step of identifying the organization's desired future as "goals and objectives" can become one of the major intimidations of a team inexperienced in planning but charged with the process. That is, they may believe they must have a definable, measurable goal to work from. In most cases, it is better (and more innovative) to start off with a general definition of a goal and then, based on mutual agreement and understanding, establish a goal that reflects available resources and energy and an ability to effect changes in a reasonable time period (Sikes, Schlesinger, and Seashore, 1974). At the same time, the expectations of the planning team and of the constituency at large should be assessed carefully and met as closely as possible so as to maintain a trust and confidence in the process. Both the Akron and the Wichita approaches walked a thin line in this regard, partly through their impatience to accomplish much in a little time and partly through tuning out the expectations of others. It is suspected that the Furman approach also walked a thin line in this regard by initially meeting the bureaucratic expectations more so than the academic expectations.

The planning process can be the change process as well. One convenient way of relating the two is to describe the change process as lower-order and higher-order change activities (Bergquist and Phillips, 1977; Lauderdale and Peterson, 1971; Sikes, Schlesinger, and Seashore, 1974). Lower-order change is any action that alters the outcome, but does not alter the way in which these outcomes are derived. For example, a lower-order change might influence a policy but will not change the way the decision was made nor the way related decisions will be made in the future. On the other hand, higher-order change influences both the outcome and the actual process, introducing new modes of thinking, behaving, and interacting. A successful planning process brings new modes of thinking, behaving, and interacting into the transcending realm of institutional planning. Therefore, a successful planning process is also a higher-order change action. However, implementation of the plans or actions resulting from the planning process must consciously identify lower-order or higher-order activities as the means of change. Generally, the lower-order change efforts are described as including capital infusion (resource-oriented, infusing [removing] massive amounts of resources into [from] identified areas of desired change); leadership or group dynamics (focus on improving the quality of leadership and of group functioning); and service coordination (identification and resolution of organization needs through the use of existing resources and the development of supplemental resources). Higher-order change efforts are generally described to include the pressure-group model (usually associated with unions, special interest, and other pressure groups); and the natural group model (identifying and increasing the natural relationships that already exist in the organization and realigning their direction). In my opinion, the leadership or group dynamic approach moves from a lower-order to a higher-order change in a college or university setting, as this approach also intervenes in the campus pressure-groups (faculty and student) and the natural-groups (organizational units and networks). Being aware of this, the planning group will, perhaps, be more sensitive to the realization that whatever the planning structure, it is also a change process. With this increased sensitivity, there should be fewer unanticipated outcomes—although they will always occur.

Caveats: Hindsights Offered as Foresights

Other caveats or alerts may be helpful to those who "plan on planning a planning process." First, most approaches to higher education planning are academically hierarchical by design, such as the Akron and Wichita approaches and phase IV of the Furman approach. Although the academic hierarchy organizational approach has many commendable features, it generally does not allow for participation from the external constituency, planning on an interdisciplinary basis, and planning and development by the administrative and service staff. These difficulties might be resolved by including a member of the community on the planning group and/or involving selected alumni or project sponsors in college and/or departmental groups; appointing a cross-representative task force to study and plan for interdisciplinary encouragement or a number of task forces along functional lines (for example, professionalism or urban involvement); and requiring planning efforts along administrative lines similar to those along academic lines, with the central planning group providing output from the academic planning group as indicators of long-range service needs.

Second, the fresh wave of newness that frequently accompanies a commitment to a planning effort often obscures the reality that a number of planning centers or influences are already operational on campus. Recognition of these existing centers and coordination of their planning inputs/outputs should be a consideration of the planning committee.

Third, the fallacy of "isolated taxonomies" is common when considering a planning process. That is, academic planning is considered exclusive of administrative or support service planning; planning, exclusive of development; or development, without planning. Although the balancing of all these factors in a total systematic approach to educational and organizational reform is mind boggling, it is essential to a successful effort.

Fourth, perhaps the most difficult tasks in the planned change process are objectively analyzing the formal organization and the informal networks, recognizing where they too must be changed, and effecting this change.

Fifth, the involvement of a wide constituency via a complex committee structure in the total planning effort over a rather lengthy period of time can detract or diffuse the authority of the president and the board. Leadership must be exerted from the beginning by the president's office. He or she must set forth the parameters and direction of the planning/change process; delegate authority to a central planning group, which will report to the president; and establish a realistic and enforced time schedule.

Finally, the person or persons who develop and monitor the planning process must have a realistic assessment of their own place and the place of their plans in the grander scheme of things.

Conclusion

The foregoing discussion set forth a model for the planning process that combines the measurable and structured mechanisms of management science with the considerations of organizational contingency and human sensitivities of organizational development. As such, developing and implementing a process and developing and effecting organizational change are almost one and certainly are interchangeable.

After a planning process is established, we should be aware of several facts. First, we do not plan certainty; we plan uncertainty. Second, there is no one approach that assures a close linkage between the collectively well thought out planning process and what actually happens because, third, in planning and change, we are trying to impose predictable expectations on unpredictable behaviors. Thus, the best a planning or change agent can hope for is to develop a process that will make it easier to herd the straying circumstances, organization flux, and shifting human behavior toward agreed-upon goals.

Bibliographical Essay

There is a growing number of published works concerned with planning in higher education, information systems, and the change process. There are some, although not as many, concerned with how two or more of these areas interrelate.

One of the more convenient references to help sort out the basics and the approaches to higher education planning is Richardson, Gardner, and Pierce (1977), which cites over forty works as it surveys the state of the art of institutional planning. Any advocacy stops with the support of the need for institutional planning, as the essay discusses supporting data; a synthesis of thought in the framework for planning; and a review of the types and uses of quantitative analytical tools, the implication of the program (real and apparent), and attitudes toward institutional planning. This document is particularly useful as an orientation handout to new members of a planning committee or to faculty and administrators who wish to obtain a quick, broad grasp of the field. *Higher Education Planning: A Bibliographic Handbook* (Halstead, 1979) is a comprehensive, annotated compendium of articles selected by experts in each of twenty-two topical areas and a number of subdivisions. Another useful reference in this genre is Staman (1978). A reference of a different nature is *Planning in Higher Education: A Manual for Colleges and Universities* (Millett, 1977), which keeps us in touch with the general yet comprehensive basics of the classical approach. Another influential reference, an earlier version of which is reflected somewhat in the model described for the University of Akron, is *Long-Range Planning: An Institution-Wide Approach to Increasing Academic Vitality* (Parekh, 1975), which is elegant in its straightforward nature and generalizability.

Higher education planning has to be within the context of higher education organization, governance, and change. Balderston (1974), Richman and Farmer (1974), Cohen and March (1974), Baldridge and others (1978), and Sayles (1976) provide the reader with both a heavy reading load and important and different approaches to understanding and interpreting higher education organizations and their dynamics. The context of organizational change is also provided in varying degrees in these volumes and articles. For more specific change contexts, see Section Four of Berquist and Phillips (1977), *Group and Organization Studies* (Jones and Pfeiffer), and Sikes, Schlesinger, and Seashore (1974).

Planning in the context of futures studies is an area growing rapidly both in publication and acceptance. Sandow (1971) lays the theoretical groundwork and some application for another useful volume, *A Futures Creating Paradigm: A Guide to Long-Range Planning from the Future for the Future* (1978).

Generally, case studies or "copies" of other universities' planning processes are useful when we want to see how much our own institution is ahead of or behind the field of practice. However, there are several case studies that are useful as models built from principles or paradigms described elsewhere. Two examples of this type of case study are *Planning for the Future —Handbook 1977– 78* (1977) and *Academic Planning at Indiana State University: Planning Matrix* (1978), both of which describe programs constructed from *A Futures Creating Paradigm* (1978) but demonstrating two derivations. Another instructive study is Kieft (1978), in which the planning processes and their development are described for West Virginia University, Western Washington University, Villa Maria College, and Kansas City Metropolitan Community Colleges and compared to an academic unit planning manual.

For state of the art and informational purposes, the series *New Directions for Institutional Research* (published by Jossey-Bass) and a subscription to *Planning for Higher Education* (published by the Society for College and University Planning) should satisfy most needs. In addition, to provide information on external, national trends and shifts relevant to institutional planning, the reader will also be interested in receiving the *Policy Analysis Service Reports* of the American Council on Education and the occasional papers published by the Aspen Institute for Humanistic Societies under the aegis of their Program in Education for a Changing Society.

References

Academic Planning at Indiana State University: Planning Matrix. Terre Haute: Indiana State University, 1978.

Ahlberg, C. D., and Christenson, D. D. *Report on Phase I, The W. K. Kellogg Founda-*

tion Leadership and Management Development Project at Wichita State University. Wichita, Kans.: Wichita State University, 1977.

Balderston, F. E. *Managing Today's University.* San Francisco: Jossey-Bass, 1974.

Baldridge, J. V., and others. *Policy Making and Effective Leadership: A National Study of Academic Management.* San Francisco: Jossey-Bass, 1978.

Bergquist, W. H., and Phillips, S. R. *A Handbook for Faculty Development.* (2nd ed.) Washington, D.C.: Council for Advancement of Small Colleges, 1977.

Buchtel, F. S. "Faculty and Administrator Development for Better Involvement in University Decision Making—An Actual Case." In *Proceedings, Improving the Process of Administration in Higher Education.* Academic administration workshop, ninth annual conference, American Institute for Decision Sciences, Chicago, 1977.

Cohen, M. D., and March, J. G. *Leadership and Ambiguity: The American College President.* New York: McGraw-Hill, 1974.

DeShon, D. S. "The W. K. Kellogg Foundation Program at the University of Akron: If We Had It To Do Over Again—Hindsight and Foresight." In *Proceedings, Improving the Process of Administration in Higher Education.* Academic administration workshop, ninth annual conference, American Institute for Decision Sciences, Chicago, 1977.

A Futures Creating Paradigm: A Guide to Long-Range Planning From the Future For the Future. Washington, D.C.: Resource Center for Planned Change, American Association of State Colleges and Universities, 1978.

Guzzetta, D. J. "Continuity, Change, and Challenge." Annual All-Faculty Remarks, September 27, 1974, the University of Akron.

Haas, R. M. "Integrating Academic, Fiscal, and Facilities Planning." *Planning for Higher Education,* 1976, 5, 2–5.

Halstead, D. K. (Ed.). *Higher Education Planning: A Bibliographic Handbook.* Washington, D.C.: National Institute of Education, U.S. Department of Health, Education and Welfare, 1979.

Hipps, G. M., and Winstead, P. C. *Faculty Development in Academic Planning: An Approach to Institutional Self-Renewal.* Greenville, S.C.: Furman University, 1978.

Jones, J. E., and Pfeiffer, J. W. *Group and Organization Studies,* The International Journal for Group Facilitators. University Associates, La Jolla, Calif. (subscription series).

Kieft, R. N. *Academic Planning: Four Institutional Case Studies.* Boulder, Colo.: National Center for Higher Education Management Systems, 1978.

Lauderdale, M., and Peterson, J. *Community Development.* Washington, D.C.: Education, Training, and Research Sciences Corp., 1971.

Lippitt, G. L., and Aurelio, J. *Final Evaluation Report, The University of Akron, W. K. Kellogg Foundation Program for the Development of Team Leadership at an Urban University.* Washington, D.C.: Project Associates, Inc., 1978.

Maio, E. A., and Buchtel, F. S. "The Importance of Team Leadership to the Urban University's Mission." Paper presented at National Invitational Conference, "Toward the Urban University." Northeastern Illinois University, Chicago, May 9–10, 1977.

Michael, D. N. *On Learning to Plan—and Planning to Learn: The Social Psychology of Changing Toward Future-Responsive Societal Learning.* San Francisco: Jossey-Bass, 1976.

Millett, J. D. (Ed.). *Planning in Higher Education: A Manual for Colleges and Universities.* Washington, D.C.: Management Division, Academy for Educational Development, Inc., 1977.

Ohio Board of Regents. *Planning/Universities.* Columbus: Ohio Board of Regents, 1973.

Ozbekhan, H. "Toward a General Theory of Planning." In B. Jantsch (Ed.), *Perspectives of Planning.* Paris: Organization for Economic Cooperation and Development, 1969.

Parekh, S. B. *Long-Range Planning: An Institution-Wide Approach to Increasing Academic Vitality.* New Rochelle, N.Y.: Change Magazine Press, 1975.

Planning for the Future—Handbook 1977–78. Menomonie: University of Wisconsin-Stout, 1977.

Richardson, R. C., Jr., Gardner, D. E., and Pierce, A. "The Need for Institutional Planning." *Research Currents.* Washington, D.C.: ERIC/Higher Education, American Association for Higher Education, 1977.

Richman, B. M., and Farmer, R. N. *Leadership, Goals, and Power in Higher Education: A Contingency and Open-Systems Approach to Effective Management.* San Francisco: Jossey-Bass, 1974.

Salloway, S. E, and Tack, M. W. "Comprehensive Planning: An Organizational Approach." *Planning for Higher Education,* 1978, 7 (2), 1–7.

Sandow, S. A. "The Pedagogy of Planning: Defining Sufficient Futures." *Futures,* 1971, *3* (4), 324–337.

Sayles, L. R. "Matrix Management: The Structure With A Future." *Organizational Dynamics,* 1976, *5*(2), 2–17.

Sikes, W. W., Schlesinger, L. E., and Seashore, C. N. *Renewing Higher Education from Within: A Guide for Campus Change Teams.* San Francisco: Jossey-Bass, 1974.

Staman, E. M. *A Catalogue on Planning in Higher Education: Organizations, Periodicals, Bibliographies.* Halifax, Canada: Society for College and University Planning, 1978.

The University of Akron. *Final Report, the W. K. Kellogg Foundation Program for the Development of Team Leadership at an Urban University.* Akron, Ohio: University of Akron, 1978.

Winstead, P. C. *Furman University's Management Planning Model for Liberal Arts Colleges.* Greenville, S.C.: Furman University, 1975.

Winstead, P. C. "Systematic Institutional Planning: Furman's Approach." Eleventh annual conference of the Society for College and University Planning, Washington, D.C., July 1976.

31

Nick L. Poulton

Strategies of Large Universities

During the past two decades, considerable effort has been directed toward the design and development of planning and management techniques to increase the level of rationality in postsecondary education decision making. The resulting literature contains many prescriptions for research and planning and a number of descriptions of experiences of single institutions, but little comparative evidence of the contributions planning and management techniques actually make to university functioning and decision making. This chapter compares the impacts of different master planning techniques, resource allocation efforts, and program review processes on central administrative operations in five research-oriented universities in order to offer research-based suggestions for improving the utilization of planning and institutional research in all universities. Previous chapters in this handbook discuss the methods and details of planning and in-

Note: Most of the material presented in this chapter was obtained through research conducted by the author in 1977 while at the University of Michigan with the support of funds provided by the Carnegie Corporation of New York. More details about the five universities described in it can be found in Lelong and others, 1980.

626

stitutional research techniques; this chapter emphasizes how these techniques change the kinds of decisions and the processes of university decision making, how they relate to the operating characteristics of the institution, and how the substance and process of these techniques and conditions of the institutional setting affect the use of planning and institutional research.

The three types of activity of interest—master planning, resource allocation, and program review—were selected for their respective association with the ends, means, and feedback components of the rational model of decision making. The five institutions described are the University of California, Berkeley; Colorado State University; the University of Minnesota; Stanford University; and West Virginia University. The four public schools are all land-grant institutions that offer a significant component of graduate education. Their planning activities reported in this chapter are outlined in Table 1 along with initiating conditions and primary outcomes of interest. Table 2 describes the specific activities at each university by identifying the major documents, planning processes, and coordinating and advisory groups involved.

Planning in Five Universities

All five universities except Stanford have had some experience with master planning, although Berkeley's experience at the time of this writing was limited to academic areas, whereas Colorado State and West Virginia had developed more comprehensive plans. Stanford and West Virginia provide two different examples of resource allocation activities; program review activities are best illustrated by Minnesota and Berkeley.

University of California, Berkeley: Academic Master Planning. Planning for higher education in the state of California has been an active concern of the state and the University of California system for more than twenty-five years. Through 1977, the Berkeley campus produced three major campus academic plans and several revisions. The 1957 plan grew from a concern on the Berkeley campus over the directions of growth during the 1960s. This plan established policies, principles, and criteria to guide this anticipated growth. It related the characteristics of the Berkeley schools, colleges, and departments to the demography of the state of California and the development of the Berkeley campus. The 1957 plan contained educational objectives and priorities and extrapolated enrollments. It made thirteen recommendations regarding enrollment balance and limits, admissions, student aid, staffing, administration, and facilities. Most of the substantive elements of the 1957 plan were implemented, but not in the detail projected, for the growth predictions soon became obsolete. However, the plan charted directions for academic development, diagnosed future problems, and identified policies that were to be needed.

The University of California system grew through the 1960s, but growth conditions for the Berkeley campus began to change by the mid 1960s. Campus enrollment approached its designed maximum, and increased funding was provided only for new students. Teaching assistant positions were reduced, and admissions/enrollment limits were imposed. Berkeley was projected to be a campus of relatively fixed size. Concerns for maintaining quality and flexibility within the campus increased. One response was the formation in 1965 of an academic plan steering committee of faculty and administrators charged to pro-

Table 1. Selected Planning Activities in Five Universities

Institution-Campus	Primary Activities	Initiating Conditions	Time of Initiation	Outcomes of Interest
University of California, Berkeley	Academic master plan Program review	Long history of planning activity; systemwide mandates	Master planning began in 1957, recent shifts in 1970 and 1974	Changed attitude to master planning; enrollment and faculty models; program review impacts
Colorado State University	Comprehensive master plan	Internally felt need for planned growth; legislative mandate	Recent phase began about 1971	Internal decisions on controlled growth; improved external image
University of Minnesota	Program evaluation	Internally felt need for evaluation; external grant	Effort began in 1972	Specific impacts across organizational units
Stanford University	Resource allocation Financial modeling	Budget deficits; internally felt need for revenue planning	Budget adjustments began in 1969	Specific revenue and budget plans; macromodeling; internal communications
West Virginia University	Master planning Resource allocation	Internally felt need for improved management	Current process began to develop in 1971	Integration of planning and budgeting

Table 2. Structure of Planning Activities in Five Universities

Institution-Campus	Documents	Processes	Advisory Groups	Coordinating Group
University of California, Berkeley	Revised academic plan 1969–1975 (1969) Campus academic plan 1974–1979 (1975)	Review of academic plan Enrollment planning Faculty renewal plan Program reviews	Committees of Academic Senate—Berkeley Division Graduate council	Assistant chancellor for budget and planning (and staff) Graduate division
Colorado State University	Pattern for the 1970s (six volumes, 1974)	Academic research and organization study[a] North Central Assoc. self-study[a]	(Task groups of two self-studies)	Office of university planning and budgets (and staff)
University of Minnesota	Toward 1985 and beyond (1971) Program review procedures (1975)	Individual program reviews Retrenchment and reallocation[a]	External review committees University review committees	Graduate school—policy and review committees
Stanford University	Budget protocols Operating budget guidelines (annual)	Operating budget cycle Budget adjustment program (BAP) Budget equilibrium program (BEP) Financial forecasting and equilibrium models	University advisory committee on budget planning (and two predecessors)	Vice-provost for budget and planning (and staff)
West Virginia University	Statistical profiles WVU organization Planning assumptions (annual)	Annual plan and operating budget cycle	University council on planning	Provost for planning (and staff)

[a]Single event, not a continuing process.

duce a new academic plan for the campus that would be a blueprint for the transition from extensive growth to a steady state in the 1970s. Three and one-half years were spent in producing the *Revised Academic Plan 1969–1975*. Individual units developed profiles, and the steering committee reviewed general policies with faculty committees and administrative officers. Detailed sections were produced through several interactions between departments and the steering committee as departmental aspirations were adjusted to fit within the stable campus profile. The plan was both a policy document and a detailed projection. It emphasized preserving the quality of existing programs and maintaining the flexibility to focus on advanced graduate education and scholarship. Key policy areas included the enrollment mix, the balance between liberal and professional education, the nature of graduate education, and the problems of undergraduate education. Detailed forecasts were developed for every college and department on enrollment levels, staffing levels, areas of future program development, and the processes of implementation and control.

The 1969 plan produced mixed results. The general policy statements, educational guidelines, and program directions were found to be useful; but changing circumstances again made the detailed forecasts for departments obsolete. Continuous academic planning did not materialize immediately, but staff support work on planning activities increased, and the analysis and discussion of major policy questions formed the basis for the next academic plan. One particular event moved several activities initiated for the 1969 plan into the mainstream of academic decision making. In 1970–71, the university systemwide administration reduced the staffing level for the Berkeley campus by 110 full-time-equivalent (FTE) faculty positions. The crisis forced the campus to refine its information and control of staff positions and prompted the adoption of a set of policies regarding faculty appointments. The crisis also emphasized the need for more enrollment and admission control and the need for more program review, both of which were proposed in the 1969 plan. But the planning activities found to be most useful were management processes such as enrollment controls, faculty renewal plans, and program reviews, not the detailed forecasts of enrollment, staff, and programs contained in the 1969 plan.

In the early 1970s, administration of the university system increased its interest in academic planning and appointed an advisory group representing all campuses to design an academic plan for the university system. This approach was approved by the regents in February 1974. The regents also mandated that each campus develop a campus academic plan that would complement the system plan; the total would become the plan for the entire University of California. The features of the 1974 plan were immense, and the schedule was extremely short. The campuses were given six months to respond. The scope of the campus academic plan included all instructional units, all organized research units, the library, and computing facilities. From the system perspective, the plan was designed to be a blueprint, an approach the Berkeley campus had twice before found to contain many pitfalls. Consequently, the Berkeley response was described as a "plan not to plan." It focused on the processes of faculty renewal planning, enrollment controls, and program review; and it included only those unit-level details minimally acceptable to the systemwide administration. Because of the short time to respond, the Berkeley draft was prepared centrally, drawing extensively from the 1969 plan. Individual units and key administrators all contributed to the document, but it was submitted as a draft with the qualification that it was contingent upon the review by faculty and administrative groups over a longer period of time. This response produced an underlying tension between the interests of the systemwide administration for developing a blueprint-oriented master plan and the interests of those on the Berkeley campus who wanted to move beyond a blueprint orientation and deal with the processes and tools that would allow the campus to maintain and use its resources flexibly.

The several different academic planning processes developed at Berkeley each served the needs of different people. The campus academic plan related more to the needs of campus administrators, such as the assistant chancellor for budget and planning. More detailed activities, such as the detailed program reviews conducted by the graduate division, were more significant to academic departments and operating units. The campus academic plan was more effective for presenting the total view of the campus and outlining general trends and parameters for campus change. It was not as meaningful for a department, for it seldom related to individuals in teaching situations. The periodic reviews of graduate programs and organized research units related much more to the activities of individuals, and they complemented the general trends presented in the campus academic plan by providing the basis for understanding detailed operations in a unit. The program review activity was also useful for identifying opportunities for change in departments, but the campus academic plan was not able to deal with this level of detail. Of the other planning processes, admission targets and enrollment controls were developed for specific student levels and individual graduate programs, whereas a campus enrollment ceiling was a parameter of the campus academic plan. The faculty renewal plan, based upon a faculty flow model, was useful to the chancellor's office for providing general guidelines on the number and kinds of faculty appointments advisable each year; but it did not assign faculty positions to specific departments.

Colorado State University: Comprehensive Master Plan. Colorado State University has been involved in developing a master plan since the late 1960s. In 1969, a concerted effort began that culminated in 1974 with a six-volume, comprehensive master plan titled *Pattern for the 70's* that covered the entire university. The climate for master planning began with the Colorado Commission on Higher Education, established in 1965. The commission developed as a strong coordinating board. It required long-range institutional plans, defined institutional roles within the state, approved facility plans, approved all new degree programs, and reviewed requests for the operating budget and capital construction. Prior to 1965, little planning activity had taken place at Colorado State University, and efforts to coordinate growth had been very limited. Requirements of the coordinating commission influenced thinking at Colorado State about how the university could retain control of its future direction. Statements of functions and goals had been prepared in 1966 and 1968, and a long-range space program was published in 1968. But these efforts had limited impact, for only a few administrative staff were actively concerned with the need for planning and coordinating growth.

In 1968, a new vice-president for academic affairs was appointed, followed by a new president in 1969. Both had been active in university administration at Colorado State. With these changes came an effort to improve the internal management practices of the university. A new faculty council code was adopted in 1968; and over the next two years, activities were directed toward developing departmental and college codes, a faculty evaluation system, departmental evaluation procedures, and personnel policies. Financial administration improved during the late 1960s, and an office of university planning and budget, which had the responsibility for developing management information and structuring the budget process for the university, was formed in 1969. Products developed by the National Center for Higher Education Management Systems were adopted, including the Resource Requirements Prediction Model (RRPM). All these efforts contributed to a climate where master planning could develop.

No single decision seems to have been made where the institution committed itself to developing a formal master plan. The concept was supported in principle by the executive officers, but internal advocacy came from key staff personnel. The first efforts at master planning in 1970–71 produced two documents that included goals and program plans for all academic and selected nonacademic areas, enrollment plans, an admissions philosophy, and a physical development plan. Most of this information was compiled by central staff personnel. During 1971–72, several events contributed to the completion of the comprehensive master plan. An intensive study of academic and research organization led to a refined statement of mission for Colorado State University. The institutional self-study for North Central Association reaccreditation produced detailed reviews of academic and support programs. The coordinating commission, the legislature, and the university agreed to a twenty-thousand FTE student maximum size for 1980. The felt need for a formal, well-integrated master plan for directing campus growth toward this maximum size grew considerably. The formal master planning document was drafted in 1973, then approved and published in October 1974.

Although faculty members were involved extensively with the academic research and organization study and the North Central self-study, the master plan was assembled by the office of university planning and budget using the products of these studies and the information available to that office. The completed master plan was intended to manage controlled growth, not accomplish retrenchment or reallocation. It included the mission statement; a prescribed enrollment growth pattern for each college and department; program plans for instruction, research, service, and support areas; a detailed physical development plan; and a five-year projection of resource requirements for each department produced by the RRPM simulation model.

The perceived results of the master plan were mixed, depending upon where a person was located in the organization. In general, most of the benefits were seen to accrue to central administrators and few to deans and department chairpersons. External needs for responding to the coordinating commission and legislature were met, but many internal needs for program development were not satisfied even though the master plan emphasized information on the internal operation of the university. Improved communication during the self-studies and the development of the master plan were more beneficial than the resulting products. Institutional goals and program directions were clarified, but little change occurred in resource allocation procedures. New program directions were limited, but the master plan was growth oriented and did not include criteria for reallocating resources. Through 1977, the master plan was not routinely updated, and funding conditions for the university became less optimistic. Significant changes in university operations were influenced by those parts of the master plan linked to ongoing processes, such as the annual adjustment of college admissions and enrollment targets and the longer-term development of physical facilities.

University of Minnesota: Program Review. The graduate school at the University of Minnesota has conducted detailed reviews of academic programs since 1972. This process evolved into a continuing activity where all graduate programs and most undergraduate programs are reviewed over a seven-year cycle. Thinking about program evaluation began in the late 1960s, and the university senate committee on resources and planning included program review in a planning document it published in 1971 titled *Toward 1985 and Beyond.* That document developed a rationale for program evaluation that was consistent with a number of other pressures at that time. The board of regents mandated all university units provide for evaluation in their constitution and by-laws. The university mission statement also stressed the need for evaluation. There were state pressures for more evidence of data-based planning and decision making. Simultaneously, there was a growing felt need on the part of administrators for more information for managing the institution.

The university response to a legislative funding crisis in 1971 helped focus the need for better program review information. In that year, the legislature provided no budget increases to cover inflation and program changes. The loss to the university was the equivalent of one hundred FTE positions in the base appropriation. The resulting retrenchment and reallocation process reduced budgets of university units to create a pool of funds for reallocation. Proposals for use of these funds were developed, and seven formal criteria for measuring and evaluating program contributions to the university mission were used. Although this process was developed as an alternative to uniform reductions, there was dissatisfaction with the negative tone of the process, the scarce evaluative data available for making program decisions, and the lack of time to do the necessary consultation.

In the fall of 1972, a new dean was appointed to the graduate school. This person had participated in drafting the retrenchment and reallocation criteria, was a respected faculty member, and became a very skilled administrator. The dean carried the felt need for more and better information to manage program quality and became an advocate for the program review process. The dean entered when the graduate school had just completed a reorganization into six divisional areas, each governed by a policy and review committee. The situation allowed for adjusting the graduate school function and role in the management of program quality. The program review process was modeled around many of the evaluative questions posed by the retrenchment and reallocation process. The design was developed into a grant proposal, and full funding was obtained. Program reviews began in the fall of 1972 with a relatively strong group of volunteer departments. Although fears were voiced by some faculty members and deans, the design was based upon considerable thought and experience with problems and felt needs. Consequently, much of the initial resistance began to decrease as the program review process unfolded. By 1974, the review process had been refined, and the joint review of graduate and undergraduate programs had become the standard approach. There were many changes in central administrative positions during this developmental period. But the process was oriented toward detailed features of the programs and departments being reviewed, and it did not require threatening commitments by central administration. The reviews were relatively productive and coincided with several central staff members' interests in developing program budgeting within central administration.

The review of an individual program or department required about one year and was accomplished using unit self-study and separate external and internal teams for each review. Program or department faculty members were charged with assembling an extensive and highly detailed profile of past activities, refining plans for the future, and reviewing the effectiveness of the means employed to achieve stated goals. Several national scholars were chosen to form the external reviewing committee to conduct a site visit and address questions of subject matter trends, quality of academic programming in the discipline, and quality of students with respect to national norms in the discipline. The university review committee appointed for the review monitored all stages and also concentrated on departmental organization and processes such as admissions and advising. It combined all sources of information, including its own independent study, and produced the written summary evaluation of the department and a set of recommendations. A review concluded with an implementation session involving the department chairperson, deans of the graduate school and the college, the vice-president, and central administrative staff.

The primary beneficiaries of the program reviews were the units that underwent review and the graduate school. The review provided the opportunity for structured introspection that did not normally take place, and it was able meaningfully to combine and communicate qualitative information with quantitative data. Goals were clarified within the department; bases for new faculty positions were better developed; priorities were addressed; and problem areas were identified. Changes often occurred even before the review cycle was complete. The graduate college used program review information to allocate limited resources for fellowships and research grants and to revise graduate school policies. Some college deans made similar use of the information. Central administrators became more knowledgeable of departmental situations, but there was no systematic process for routinely incorporating program review results into central administrative planning and decision making. The problems associated with program review included high workloads, unsystematic follow-up processes, greater emphasis on graduate than on undergraduate programs, inherently incomplete review cycles that often prevented comparison of situations using current information, and frustrations from unfulfilled expectations raised by a review.

Stanford University: Financial Planning. Stanford University has been involved in financial planning and forecasting activities since the early 1960s, when a forecasting technique was used for projecting the gross budget of the university ten years ahead. These activities changed in the late 1960s as budget deficits appeared unexpectedly, and Stanford University embarked on a systematic effort to bring the operating budget into balance and long-run equilibrium. The effort required eight years to achieve the desired objectives and involved the development of programs for universitywide budget base review, an annual budget protocol instrument, computer models for financial forecasting and budget equilibrium analysis, and internal communication mechanisms.

The late 1960s was a particularly difficult time for Stanford University. It was the site of vigorous student activism. Two major sources of income changed when enrollment stabilized and the real-dollar value of research funding stopped increasing. The provost position was vacant for one and one-half years; and a new president, appointed in 1968, resigned within two years. Nevertheless, financial managers pushed for immediate response to the unexpected 1968 deficit of approximately $1 million. The forecasting methodology was revised, and the resulting income and expenditure forecasts indicated an accumulating gap between income and expense totaling $2.5 million over the four years beginning in 1970. To close this gap, a budget adjustment program (BAP) was conceived and announced in October 1969. The program was directed by the vice-provost for budget and planning with the advice and consultation of a BAP advisory committee, a small group of faculty, students, and administrators. By the fall of 1970, further analysis indicated a $6 million gap over five years was a more appropriate target. Therefore, BAP began to make cumulative income and expenditure adjustments to restore budget balance by 1974 and to match the increasing rates of income and expenditure in order to maintain a balanced budget. The adjustments made during the first year of BAP totaled nearly $2 million.

Through BAP, budget development was placed in a five-year perspective. A budget protocol document was used to manage individual budget discussions with colleges and major divisions. A "relative severity of consequences" criterion was used to evaluate budget adjustment proposals. Both qualitative and quantitative information were combined when looking for improvements in activities. A norm of informed judgment was applied in making decisions. Considerable attention was given to communications and information flow to handle constituents' concerns, to combat mistrust and suspicion, and to provide a check on administrative judgment. The rational decision-making style advocated by the new provost, appointed in 1970, reinforced BAP implementation. A process for centralized faculty position control was developed, and analytical studies increased. The appointment of a new vice-provost for research brought a strong interest in computer modeling to planning and budgeting. In 1974, a large grant was secured from a private foundation to support the development of several computer models activities, including a long-range budget equilibrium model.

The five annual BAP cycles proceeded as designed for the first three years. The central budget staff and deans of the schools developed proposals where adjustments could be made; and these were reviewed by the BAP advisory committee before recommendations were made to the provost, the president, and the board of trustees. During the fourth year of BAP, in 1973–74, the scheduled deficit of $300,000 grew unexpectedly to $700,000. A recomputation of the 1974–75 situation indicated a $1.5-million deficit was unavoidable in the very year the budget was to be balanced. Hindsight indicated BAP goals had not gone far enough. Computer modeling efforts began to indicate a concept of budget equilibrium that involved trade-off relationships among elements of income and expense was necessary in order to manage the conditions affecting the budget. Consequently, BAP was replaced with the budget equilibrium program (BEP) in the fall of 1974. The goal was to achieve budget equilibrium between growth rates of income and expense by 1979–80. The basic criteria and approach to rational management developed during BAP were carried over into BEP. Emphasis was also placed on trade-offs between key financial variables and campus discussions regarding critical trade-off decisions. BEP utilized a refined long-range financial forecast and two computer models. A long-run equilibrium model was used to calculate a "new" gap of $10 million, and a transition to equilibrium model was used to design an approach to close that gap in three years. There was considerable surprise, dismay, and some distrust and suspicion when BEP was announced; so communication efforts were redoubled in order to dispel unfounded fears. The president appointed several task forces to study certain elements of the university budget in detail, such as university administration and support services, student support services and activities, the calendar and physical plant use, professorial rank and faculty development, and professional schools.

BEP proceeded according to design. Budget adjustments were identified, analyzed, and reviewed as they had been in BAP. Small surpluses were forecasted for 1977 to 1979. By 1978, the BEP adjustments were essentially completed. Following eight years of budget adjustments, the ultimate goal of budget equilibrium was achieved; and the gap had been closed. However, achieving equilibrium had created a new set of issues. The budget gap had been very useful as a symbol during the efforts to achieve equilibrium. But once the gap no longer existed, a new concept was necessary to emphasize the continuing effort needed to maintain equilibrium. Furthermore, the strategies and methods for maintaining equilibrium were not the same as those employed to achieve equilibrium. To avoid future deficits, additional studies were begun to analyze the economic context within which Stanford operates, the efficiency and effectiveness in the business and finance area using zero-based budgeting, and the most appropriate levels of centralization and decentralization in the administrative environment for sustaining individual unit initiative and effectiveness.

The financial planning models were macromodels, for they did not attempt to deal with data and information for any specific university unit. The focus was on aggregate, institutional-level variables, such as general categories of income and expense. The models dealt with a multiyear time horizon but also developed information for individual budget years within that time horizon. The long-range financial forecast was a "bottom-up" collection of many sources of information, including past trends, interviews with deans and administrative officers, external economic indicators such as the consumer price index, and individual judgments regarding the interrelationships of significant financial variables. The equilibrium models were "top-down" planning and decision-making tools for identifying a financial strategy for achieving budget equilibrium. The budget equilibrium model provided information on the magnitude of budgetary actions required, and the transition to equilibrium model developed alternative sets of year-by-year measures needed to reach financial equilibrium in a given number of years.

The annual process of producing an operating budget was managed through a budget protocol document that presented the parameters, boundaries, and criteria within which deans and directors were asked to present their budget proposals. The protocol was designed to define the centralized and decentralized components in the budget development process while simultaneously accommodating to appropriately different academic characteristics and administrative styles in the major operating units. The financial planning models contributed to this process by identifying the most critical financial planning variables and quantifying relationships and trade-offs between these financial variables. A firmer background was provided for the hard budgetary decisions required to maintain budget equilibrium. Furthermore, the relationships and products of the models provided a basis for discussion and communication on campus and raised the level of debate about hard issues. The entire budget process was an interplay among information developed through analytical studies, estimates and relationships highlighted through the financial models, detailed discussions of qualitative and quantitative aspects of specific proposals within the framework of the budget protocol, consultations with faculty advisory groups, and judgments made by deans, directors, and executive officers. Decisions that emerged were confirmed by the executive officers and the board of trustees. The results were then published and distributed to the faculty in a document called the *Operating Budget Guidelines*, which also contained descriptive and numerical background information.

Stanford rejected a blueprint-oriented approach to program and budget planning. Little emphasis was placed on formal statements of institutional goals and priorities. Instead, the emphasis was placed on centrally developed guidelines, parameters, and expectations for proposals to be developed by the operating units. Trade-offs between key budget variables provided the guidelines and parameters, and the budget protocol served as the instrument for top-down prompting of bottom-up planning. Some increased centralization was perceived in the budget-planning process, but the role of central administration in setting the boundaries was considered acceptable if subsequent decisions were seen to be based on informed judgment and rational principles.

By emphasizing quality arguments, informed judgment, and communication with university constituents, many benefits emerged, including an increase in the understanding of university problems and the roles of constituents in dealing with them, an increased trust and confidence in central administrative officers and staff, and improved quality of the governance processes. The need for both centralized and decentralized elements in budget decision making was established. Effective participation in budgeting then required an understanding and acceptance of this division of responsibility and a willingness to work within those boundaries. By building confidence in the people, processes, and rationale for decision making, there was greater acceptance of adverse situations and decisions. By discussing problems and alternatives widely and openly and validating the alternatives through consultation with advisory groups, the executive officers maintained the ability to make potentially divisive budget adjustments. The effectiveness of budget planning at Stanford depended as much upon the principles of administration as on the techniques of budget planning.

West Virginia University: Planning and Resource Allocation. Since the late 1960s, West Virginia University has maintained a concerted effort to develop a management style that integrates several planning activities with budget decision making. The management of resources by central administration has included the following elements: a planning process that provided information that expanded the bases for budget decision making; a planning office that coordinated, structured, and scheduled the planning and budgeting cycle; and a unique form of staff presidency that provided a supportive setting for integrating the products of planning with the decisions made at the central level.

The period prior to 1967 was one of rapid growth and diversification at West Virginia University. The central administration was organized along traditional hierarchical lines. Except for one planning committee effort that produced a report on master planning around 1963, planning existed largely in the thoughts of a few individuals; and little data were available for decision making. Budget development was based more on the prospects for funding from the state legislature than on systematically determined needs of the institution. Several people felt the need to improve institutional information base and management techniques to meet internal needs and to respond to requests from the state board of regents, established in 1969. A new president was appointed in 1967 and undertook to improve the administrative operations of the institution. This was done, however, by developing a specific form of administrative organization, the staff presidency. Presidential staff officers, called provosts, were assigned the responsibility for maintaining certain functions across the entire institution. Executive officers did not have line responsibility for specific units, and all major activity areas within the university reported to the entire staff presidency. Decision making was a group activity of the provosts chaired by the president. A post of vice-president for planning was created, and the university council on planning was formed. An information and analytical support capability was developed. A full-time institutional research office was established; a budget information system was developed; and an internal audit office was organized to conduct both compliance and management audits. Staff provosts were created as vice-presidents left the administration.

By 1971, an administrative team had been assembled; and the support data and analytical capability had improved. But the planning function and the role of the university council on planning were unclear. In the fall of 1971, a provost for planning was appointed who had served in a number of different positions in the university, including two years developing management information systems for central administration. The new provost brought a management by objectives orientation to the central administrative team and initiated a systematic collection and discussion of objectives for all university units. He undertook the tasks to organize, structure, and schedule an integrated process of budgeting and planning that included both the operating budget and capital improvements. The role and operations of the university council on planning were clarified.

Planning and budgeting at West Virginia University involved a set of planning documents and a two-year cycle for producing the annual plan and operating budget. The planning documents established a common base of knowledge and understanding for decision making. *WVU Organization* described the organizational structure and the conceptual and operational objectives of every academic and service unit in the university. *Planning Assumptions* contained ten-year assumptions for the university, and *Statistical Profiles* contained historical data. Information was organized along six facets: scope of mission, programs, staff, student body, sources of support, and facilities. These documents were maintained by the provost for planning and were updated periodically by the university council on planning and the provosts.

The annual plan and operating budget cycle began just over one year prior to the start of a budget year. The cycle had three phases: the budget request phase for developing the annual budget submitted to the board of regents; the operating budget phase, which brought the budget request within the dollars appropriated to the institution and produced an operating budget; and the operating budget year, during which adjustments were made to meet changing situations. The budget request phase began with the president's office staff review of university planning assumptions and a new ten-year enrollment forecast. Guidelines were developed and distributed to the deans and directors for the preparation of their budget request. The budget request package submitted by a dean or director to the president's office consisted of three parts: an annual report based upon unit objectives, a summary of unit strengths and weaknesses, and the specific budget request. All budget requests were given priorities within three categories: prior commitments, changes in continuing programs, and new programs. The dean or director determined these priorities, using whatever consultative or planning mechanism existed in a particular unit. The staff president analyzed budget requests. The financial information system provided options for program budgeting, a modified form of zero-based budgeting, or traditional line-item budget analysis. The president's office staff held individual budget conferences with each dean and director, made preliminary budget decisions, and then prepared the budget request for the board of regents. As the final appropriations became known, a "fine tuning" phase was conducted to review previous priority decisions, consider new proposals, and then fund as many top-priority items as the final appropriation would allow.

The planning documents were used during budget discussions with the operating units. The documents provided the general guidelines for considering budget requests. Over a period of time, as proposals from the units were reviewed and decisions were made, the relatively general statements of the planning assumptions and unit objectives acquired specific operating detail. In this way, the president's office staff translated the information contained in the planning documents into operational terms. If a budget request could not be justified by the existing statements of assumptions and objectives, the request would likely be returned and not considered until those assumptions and objectives had been changed. Within the staff presidency, the provost for planning and his staff coordinated the planning activities and maintained communications with the university council on planning and planning groups within individual operating units. As a member of the decision-making team, the provost for planning was the advocate for the established planning and budgeting processes and the application of information contained in the planning documents to appropriate decisions.

The university council on planning was the primary mechanism for involving students and faculty in the processes of central planning and decision making. The council and provost for planning also worked with operating units to help them develop analogous planning techniques. The president's office staff and the council itself interpreted the charge to the council as a charge not to do planning but to bring student and faculty perspectives of the longer-term context for the entire university to bear on current issues. This was done through the direct involvement of the council in developing the planning documents, reviewing the priorities for facility development and space utilization, and reviewing other proposals for their consistency with stated long-term assumptions and objectives. Over several years, there evolved a working relationship between the president's office staff and the university council on planning whereby the council was asked for substantive input on issues at an appropriate time where influence could be effective and the council met the expectation by being a knowledgeable sounding board as well as a source of ideas and information for the president's office staff. The university council on planning did not advocate a particular course of action. It influenced the criteria and the priorities upon which decisions were made. Consequently, the president's office staff gave considerable weight to the council's views and seldom contradicted them.

Planning and budgeting at West Virginia University served primarily the needs of central administration, and perceived benefits decreased as one moved to the department or program level. The planning and budgeting effort produced more systematic procedures for decision making; improved the data base and analytical capability for decision making; increased the integration of planning, budgeting, and program development; involved more units and participants in the planning and decision-making process; provided a model of integrated planning and decision making for other units of the university; and met the increased demands for information from both internal and external sources. All these results improved the administrative environment, but the process was oriented toward developing the total university budget and was conducted by the president's office staff. Individual units that provided a universitywide function or dealt with strategic issues benefited from the increased interaction and coordination available through the system. But the strong budget orientation was perceived as limiting the emphasis on program concerns of an academic unit when those concerns did not involve an immediate budget question. Not all program innovations involved budget adjustments, and hence there was some concern that the planning and budgeting system did not adequately support this kind of change. Concern existed over an undue emphasis on procedural elements at the expense of adequate consideration of the substance of proposals. By placing higher priority on prior commitments and existing programs, there was some fear that this structure of priorities would inherently maintain the status quo and limit institutional ability to adapt to changing pressures through new program development at the department level. However, the planning and budgeting system has proven to be durable; for in 1977, a new president reorganized the administrative structure by returning to line vice-presidents, but the planning and budgeting process was retained with little change.

Comparisons of Planning Practices

Two themes appear frequently in the following comments on planning activities and related outcomes. First, there are major distinctions between master planning and resource allocation techniques on the one hand and program review activities on the other that are based upon the inherent nature of the activities themselves. Second, impacts of planning are influenced by the administrative environment, particularly features such as openness, participation, and communication in university decision processes. These two themes are developed in the following selection of contributions and impacts users and participants felt were significant.

Presentation of Information. All planning activities provided new vantage points for systematic, structured introspection into university units and activities. Penetrating questions were asked; analyses were conducted; and information was held in ways that generated new ideas for improving the university and prompted intended actions sooner than before. Seldom was new information discovered. The primary asset was the organization of existing information in new ways that provided new insights. Consequently, the factual bases for decisions were clarified, and reasoned and informed value judgments were more easily made.

Characteristics of Planning Activities. Major distinctions emerged among the characteristics of different planning activities, as outlined in Table 3. Master plans and resource allocation techniques had a broad organizational scope and dealt with aggregate, largely quantitative information concerning the entire institution. In contrast, a program review was directed toward a single operating unit or academic program, even though all programs would be reviewed over several years. Review activities were tailored to individual situations and collected very detailed information, much of which was qualitative as well as quantitative in nature.

As described earlier in this chapter, a combination of several planning activities was present in each university. However, master plans, budget decisions, and program review recommendations were not always linked. For example, in cases where programs were reviewed, program recommendations were seldom included in master plans; and they did not influence budget decisions routinely. The inherently different nature of these activities, such as the departmental focus and detailed nature of information addressed through program review, as contrasted to the total organizational focus and aggregate nature of information utilized in master planning, seemed to account for this lack of closure. Depending upon the user's inclinations, program review results could influence resource allocation decisions; but these influences came intermittently because the budget was an annual function and program reviews cycled over many years.

The formal organization and administrative environment in each university were distinct and reflected the unique history of the institution and the influence of the individuals present. Hence, the organization of planning and the roles of participants depended upon several interrelated factors. A centrally located advocate/coordinator was an important figure. Each activity involved the direct or indirect participation of advisory groups composed typically of univer-

Table 3. Characteristics of Planning Activities

Characteristic	Master Plans	Resource Allocation Techniques	Program Reviews
Organizational focus	Total organization	Organization and major units	Single unit or program
Nature of issues	Mainly strategic	Mainly managerial	Operational and managerial
Time frame	Longer-term future	Shorter-term future	Past and future
Nature of information	Aggregate	Aggregate *and* detailed	Detailed
	Quantitative	Quantitative, *some* qualitative	Quantitative *and* qualitative
Process flexibility	Stable structure Stable content	Stable structure Variable content	Both variable to meet each situation

sity faculty, staff, and students. Top administration provided active support and leadership. Funds were committed to the development and operation of planning, and major grants from private foundations aided Minnesota and Stanford. Several communications channels were normally used to maintain participant involvement and constituent awareness.

Differential Utility to Users. Master plans and resource allocation techniques tended to be more the tools of the central administrator who had a primary concern for the entire institution. Central administrative personnel found master plans and resource allocation techniques systematized budget procedures, brought more information to bear on central policy decisions, increased decision makers' sensitivity to universitywide issues, and expanded the circle of participants that influenced decisions. The ability to capture information that described the entire institution at one point in time helped support trade-off decisions when allocating resources. However, departmental personnel did not necessarily find comprehensive master plans or resource allocation techniques of direct assistance in unit operations. A major concern at the departmental level was a perceived inability of centrally oriented plans to promote change within the departments. An individual program review never dealt with the entire institution, but it concentrated on the details of particular units. Therefore, a program review was of highest benefit to the unit undergoing review. It provided a rare opportunity for the unit to present its aspirations, needs, and problems to university administration, faculty, and colleagues in the discipline. Goals were clarified; a better basis was developed for faculty positions; and priorities and problem areas were recognized and approached more rationally and less emotionally. Program reviews seldom prompted major changes in institutional commitment toward a particular department or program, but they did support changes for improving the quality of academic programs and research.

The dean of a college or the director of a major university division found selected benefits from all the activities. Master plans and resource allocation techniques provided the guidelines, boundaries, and parameters within which the dean or director could manage. Depending upon their preferred management style, this was viewed as both an advantage and disadvantage. Program review reports supplemented a dean's knowledge of unit activities and trends in the discipline. Qualitative changes and shifts in priorities could be observed, and a unit's responsiveness to the recommendations of a program review indicated its health and vitality. Ultimately, perceived utility depended upon the match between the kinds and levels of information and issues addressed by an activity and the nature of issues of concern to a potential user.

Participants in Planning. All the activities studied had a central administrative focus, hence the functions of initiation and coordination were located in a central group and usually a specific individual who both advocated and coordinated the development of the process. These advocates/coordinators were strategically located as staff persons to key decision makers. They were very aware of the internal politics and the decision behavior of the executive officers. They usually headed an office of staff that provided the institutional research support for the planning activity. Wide participation was advocated, and almost all planning activities used a consultative/advisory group typically composed of faculty, staff, and students. Some groups performed specific tasks, such as the program review committees at Minnesota; whereas in other situations, such as Berkeley, faculty senate committees served in a consultative capacity.

Assembling an advisory group representing major constituents of the university was seldom a problem, but meaningful forms of participation were more difficult and required time to evolve. Advisory groups reacted to proposals prepared by administrative staff, reviewed and revised planning documents, conducted detailed investigations of specific issues, and provided an important communications channel. Advisory groups were not usually involved in initiating and coordinating a planning process. They typically reviewed process design as it was continually being developed and refined by the advocate/coordinator and associated support staff. Through review and consultation, the advisory groups communicated information to constituents and provided legitimacy for the planning activity from the view of constituents. This mutually supportive division of labor between administrative staff and advisory groups required time to evolve and depended upon the presence of an open operating style and mutual trust among participants. The members of advisory groups seldom viewed their role as actually making decisions. However, if a mutually recognized division of labor was present and it was apparent that continuing consultation influenced the design and substance of a planning process, then advisory group members seemed to be satisfied with their advisory role; and they perceived their efforts had influence on executive officers' decisions.

Participation levels among the three types of activities studied differed. The centrally oriented activities of master planning and resource allocation tended to have more limited involvement than the unit-focused activity of program review, which depended heavily on constituents. The roles of constituent groups in program reviews were well prescribed, and they were adjusted with experience and the requirements of individual reviews. The program review processes were highly participatory at both Berkeley and Minnesota. The nature of participation in master plans and resource allocation techniques tended to vary according to the administrative environment. Two examples that represent contrasting situations are Berkeley and Colorado State. Academic master planning at Berkeley took place in an environment that supported strong norms for faculty participation in all major campus issues. Most academic administrators were faculty members, who often return to teaching and research. Faculty members were directly involved in decisions on promotion and tenure. Consequently, all the planning activities on the Berkeley campus had strong elements of faculty participation even though those activities were coordinated by central administrative offices. The Colorado State setting was described as relatively centralized, and key decisions were said to be influenced most by top administrative officers. The master plan was developed primarily through administrative channels, with major contributions coming from academic deans. Faculty members were not directly involved in developing the master plan but did have an indirect input through the Academic Organization and Research Study and the North Central self-study that occurred concurrently. Faculty members had only limited opportunities to review and critique the master plan; whereas at Berkeley, they were involved in all elements of initiation, coordination, review, and even approval.

Importance of Communication. Institutions that had planning activities fairly well integrated with decision-making processes also had a heightened administrative awareness of the need for multichannel communication. There were realistic expectations for the effectiveness of various media. Direct personal contact was used to gain awareness of problems and acceptance of approaches and decisions for meeting those problems. The rhetoric employed while communicating became an important factor; for in order to gain visibility and commitment for action, planning activities were often described in terms of their total impact across the entire institution. If the importance and potential impact of planning activities were overstated, adverse reactions were likely; and expectations and fears were raised inappropriately. For in fact, actual adjustments in university operations came at the margins; and most university constituents perceived minimal, and often no direct impacts. The commitment to improve communication was often a reflection of a more fundamental attitude toward protecting institutional norms for openness and participation. In those institutional settings where these norms were highly regarded, administrative personnel consciously worked to avoid closing or reducing the lines of communication even in the face of concerns that the effort expended in preserving those links did not always seem to be worth the immediate benefits. Participating constituents did provide very useful ideas, if only infrequently; and administrative staff felt committed to being ready to receive and willing to act upon those ideas when they emerged.

Limits on Constituent Participation. Constituent involvement faced inherent limitations in all cases studied because constituents' time was limited, and planning tasks required the understanding of complex situations. Planning that was an integral part of the management process involved a complex, time-consuming set of tasks requiring the full-time commitment of administrative staff. The nature of the tasks was particularly complex if the activity covered the entire university. Typically, some faculty members were heavily involved. But they generally had full-time commitments in teaching and research and could normally devote little time to planning. The time required to become a knowledgeable and productive participant was great. Consequently, advisory groups tended to have a largely reactive role in the planning process. But in a case such as Stanford, where financial planning was an integral part of management, the advisory group role was not exclusively reactive and was supported by an element of mutual trust and confidence that all parties' interests would be treated fairly and equitably. These supportive attitudes seemed to develop in part through strong administrative staff attention to protecting the academic norms of openness and participation. Furthermore, the experience gained by an advisory group as it initially attempted to conduct detailed studies and analysis brought the realization that administrative staff had the time and expertise to provide analysis for the group and that staff and faculty shared many of the same attitudes and values.

All the universities were concerned with the very limited resources available to reward productive involvement in a planning activity. Participants were subject to several frustrations, and these placed additional pressures on coordination and communication in a planning process. The concern that programs or units would be reduced or eliminated was present in all cases, regardless of the nature of the activity; and the lack of resources to reward good planning by units reinforced these feelings. When meaningful participation did take place, the quality of arguments for resources improved; then expectations were raised for rewards based not only on the improved arguments, but simply on the expectation that a good faith effort deserved just rewards. Considerable frustration could appear, given the very few hard resources available. Program reviews are a case in point, for these reviews made very specific and well-documented recommendations for actions that were not placed in the context of the total institution within which deans and vice-presidents must act in allocating resources. Involvement in master planning and resource allocation processes generated other frustrations in addition to those regarding resources. Participants in these processes often felt they were not able to observe the results of their effort, given the scope and complexity of these activities and the typical involvement of a large number of people. Knowledge of the progress of recommendations, the basis upon which actions were taken, and the general influence of the participant's efforts was of constant interest to advisory groups. Because master planning and resource allocation processes often influenced decisions in subtle ways, faculty and advisory groups were seldom able to identify specific actions that resulted from their efforts. All these concerns indicated a strong need for effective internal communication between central administration and constituent groups.

Consequently, expanding participation through planning had the potential for expanding the level and extent of frustrated constituents. The combined problems of limited rewards, frustrated participants, and limited means of communicating with all members of the institution continually threatened the credibility of all the planning processes studied. Credibility was questioned most at the department level, regardless of how useful an activity was to central administrators for developing plans and adjusting the allocation of scarce resources.

Basis for Administrative Action. The ultimate contribution planning processes made to decision making was legitimizing the basis upon which university administrators took actions. Genuine openness and the sharing of information and problems identified through planning processes were means for maintaining the underlying elements of trust, confidence, and legitimacy upon which administrators were able to take action. Consequently, administrators were often able to act on very short notice and without prior consultation if those actions were consistent with previously developed and publicized principles. Actions were often precipitated spontaneously through program review. Individual faculty members and department chairpersons often adjusted operations within their control based upon the emerging conclusions of a review even before the review process had been completed. Where there was a fairly close match between the decision maker's needs, the kinds of information provided, and the level of issues a planning activity addressed, planning had higher potential for influencing decisions. Causality between decision needs, activity type, and administrative style did not seem to be a major issue, for all three elements evolved mutually. Planning processes evolved to meet specific needs and to incorporate a particular administrative style. Decision makers' perspectives changed to include important issues highlighted through the planning processes, for example, the need for increased communication and feedback to participating groups. And a need for mutually understood division of roles and functions in a decision-making process was the impetus for participants to become effectively involved in decision making.

Recommendations for Practice

This study of planning practices has indicated the problem of planning and institutional research in large universities is not the absence of ideal models for guiding the planning process or of information-processing techniques for providing information for decision making. The problem is the development of a strategy for moving university management toward a planning orientation in decision making where rational bases are provided for decisions and these bases accompany the decisions made. The life of a planning and institutional research advocate is complicated by many factors in a large university. The broad scope and wide diversity of activities present make integration, coordination, and internal communication particularly difficult. Planning and institutional research techniques exist in a continuing state of transition. Constituents and decision makers are usually unfamiliar with these techniques and their potential uses. Four topics that may help the practitioner organize thoughts while formulating a planning and institutional research strategy emerged from the research on planning practice.

First, the situation in an institution must be carefully diagnosed, for different planning and institutional research activities serve different needs and different users.

A productive match between user and activity necessitates an understanding of both. This requires identifying potential users and the decision questions they face and analyzing their decision-making orientation and information needs. Then planning processes and institutional research studies must be designed to contribute to the given situation. Unfortunately, the potential user may not be able to describe the desired product beyond the felt need for a different way of making decisions. Experience indicates directions for change are often learned through careful experimentation with different planning and institutional research projects. Hence, it is essential that techniques be tried, tested, and revised so people may learn from those experiences.

As more experience is gained with the design and implementation of "ideal models" of planning and institutional research practices, more realistic and more limited expectations usually emerge. For example, master planning as it is often practiced tends to be a singular effort with the "plan" as a primary product. The companion process for reviewing and revising the master plan on a regular basis is typically not given equal attention. Furthermore, early master plans tend to be very detailed, and these details quickly become obsolete as conditions change. What does persist are guidelines and boundaries that have been established for directing program and campus development. These must then be interpreted and applied to individual problems and situations. Some activities are needed to deal with major universitywide issues. Others are required to translate guidelines into daily practice, and still others are needed to serve the detailed problems of the department. For example, at the Berkeley campus of the University of California, the early "blueprint" view of academic master planning was discarded to such a degree that the response to a recently mandated master planning effort was called a "plan not to plan." However, general features of earlier plans do persist and underlie many decisions. Furthermore, a loose collection of program reviews, enrollment planning, and faculty renewal planning now exists; it complements the review of the campus academic plan. All these activities developed gradually over several years. Within this array are both centrally and decentrally oriented planning practices that meet the needs of many different users and the decentralized decision-making style of this particular university.

Second, much of planning and institutional research is communicating, educating, and evolving a mutually understood division of labor among participants.

A common principle underlying almost all planning and institutional activities is a commitment to constituent participation through direct involvement, observation, or communication. Implementing this principle requires careful attention. For those participants having a direct role, it is important that an effort be maintained to clarify the differing roles of all participants in a planning and decision-making process and that participants undertake responsibilities consistent with their time, interest, expertise, and primary assignment in the university. The capabilities of faculty, student, and staff participants should not be underestimated. For the participant who is primarily observing, it is most important to establish an open, collaborative style and not to demand specific products from these interactions. However, one must remain open to productive suggestions, for they may appear at any time and from any source. It is essential that constituents who implement decisions or are affected by them be provided with as much information as practical regarding the rationale for university actions, be those actions pleasant or painful. Unfortunately, this information seldom travels much beyond those directly involved. Nevertheless, the information must be available in routine fashion in order to maintain an attitude of openness, educate constituents, and help minimize fears and concerns about uncertain situations or potentially adverse decisions.

Third, the most effective planning and institutional research activities are those based upon principles that also guide the behavior of key decision makers.

This research has indicated that in some cases, planning activity appears to be an extension of the principles guiding administrative behavior and in other cases, the planning activity appears to be intervening to change those guiding principles. Furthermore, desirable outcomes are most prominent in those cases where planning principles and decision-making attitudes are compatible. This suggests planning advocates face considerably different administrative environments. In one case, the planning advocate is intervening to make major changes in the administrative environment. Typically then, decision makers' and participants' initial expectations are diverse. The underlying rationale for using planning products and integrating planning into decision making is poorly developed. Gaining commitment is required on two interfaces, with top administration and with constituent groups. Open communication channels need to be created. In contrast to this intervention situation, planning activities that extend from compatible management attitudes are guided by relatively consistent initial intentions. The underlying rationale is better developed. Gaining commitment is less complex and mainly directed toward constituent groups. The bases for open communications are likely to be present and need refinement, not creation. In these situations, administrators are likely to articulate the bases upon which they operate and the way planning and institutional research activities may contribute to decision making.

Fourth, plan on evolutionary planning. The study of individual university experiences indicates all facets of a planning situation evolve continuously. Obviously, the problems facing a university change as crises arise and dissolve, and they may divert attention away from the longer-range commitment to improve planning behavior. But other features also change. New people with different ideas, skills, and talents arrive. Organizational structures are revised. Felt needs change as different questions regarding university operation are asked and in turn raise new demands for information. Activities are adjusted to be more economical. Some initially intended activities are postponed or discarded as workloads expand. Images of university planning activity are transient, and rhetoric requires renewal in order to maintain visibility and sustain commitment to the longer-term goal of changed decision-making practices. Some of these changes are necessary; some are inevitable; and others are wholly unexpected. In any case, the nature and timing of key events, both intended and unintended, along with the conditions and people involved at given points, influence the outcomes of planning activity. Occasionally, unexpected events can be used to advantage. For example, a staffing reduction mandated for the Berkeley campus of the University of California provided an opportunity to use faculty renewal planning techniques that previously had been developed on an experimental basis. Unfortunately, these "constructive crises" are fortuitous coincidences that occur only when planning products are available for use. Hence, it is essential to experiment with projects so opportunities can be seized when they occur.

The primary products of planning and institutional research efforts are twofold: the improved ability to hold and analyze information and the improved bases for taking action. The evolution of planning and institutional research processes centers around three creative tensions: the match between the administrative environment as a target of change and the planning activity that prompts change, the mix of centrally oriented and decentrally oriented activities, and the mutual understanding of the division of roles among participants.

Bibliographical Essay

Allison (1971) describes three models for analyzing organizational decisions: the rational actor, organizational process, and governmental politics. Each model uses a different unit of analysis, is based on distinct organizing concepts, and looks at different evidence. Anthony (1965) identifies three management functions: strategic planning, management control, and operational control. Common management errors are described when practitioners fail to distinguish among them properly. Cohen and March (1974) describe eight models of governance and related administrative styles in academe, describe the university as an "organized anarchy," and discuss selected problems, including goal setting, planning, and organizational change. Schmidtlein (1974) develops a number of process and value orientations of two competing paradigms of decision making in an educational setting, the comprehensive/prescriptive paradigm and the incremental/remedial paradigm. Time and resource constraints are also discussed. The concept of loosely coupled systems is applied to educational organizations by Weick (1976); and many observations are offered that seem more appropriate to university decision making than those developed through rational, bureaucratic, or political models. Levine (1978) discusses organizational decline in relationship to current administrative theory and contrasts tactics used to resist or smooth decline. The university is one of several public organizations noted.

The critics of planning practices make several important points regarding the nature of the administrative environment. Cheit (1977) discusses several intended consequences of management systems that have not been fully met. Heim (1972) outlines a continuing conflict between traditional administrative styles of academic leadership and the more systems oriented attitudes required by most planning approaches. Wildavsky (1973) looks at failures of national planning efforts in developing countries and questions whether failure is integral to the very nature of planning. He discusses planning from many perspectives also applicable to a university setting.

There are many references that prescribe various planning strategies and describe case studies of actual university situations. Dror (1971) develops a structure for analyzing the environment of the planning process, the subject matter of the process, the planning unit, and the form of the plan to be produced. Friedmann and Hudson (1974) trace the historical development and discuss contributions and weaknesses of four major traditions of planning theory: philosophical synthesis, rationalism, organization development, and empiricism. Havelock (1973) is one example of a practitioner's guide to planning that is based on the research of dissemination and utilization of innovations. Kieft, Armijo, and Bucklew (1978) present a handbook for planning based on many of the products developed at the National Center for Higher Education Management Systems. Sturner (1974) has developed a guide to comprehensive action planning that draws on many of the concepts of organization development. Bergquist and Shoemaker (1976) present a typical rational planning cycle, beginning with institutional assessment and proceeding through clarifying goals, designing and implementing change efforts, and evaluating the results. They also present case studies of change efforts at three small private colleges, a nontraditional institution, and a university. Kieft (1978) also presents four case studies of planning, one each for a major research university, a regional state university, a small private college, and a metropolitan community college system. Very few studies are available on the actual outcomes and impacts of planning activities. However, several studies have been conducted in the field of evaluation research. Cox (1977) and Patton (1978) are two examples that provide observations on ultimate outcomes that are applicable to most planning activities.

The literature contains many items dealing with management information systems and quantitative techniques in planning and institutional research. Several recent additions provide useful summaries of practices and emerging results. Adams (1977) presents several views of current problems and rethinking of the integration of management information with decision making. Mason and Mitroff (1973) provide several thought-provoking directions for needed research on the use of management information systems. Hopkins and Schroeder (1977) and Lawrence and Service (1977) provide summaries of the utilization of quantitative methods such as simulation and analytical models.

References

Adams, C. R. (Ed.). *New Directions for Institutional Research: Appraising Information Needs of Decision Makers,* no. 15. San Francisco: Jossey-Bass, 1977.

Allison, G. *The Essence of Decision.* Boston: Little, Brown, 1971.

Anthony, R. N. *Planning and Control Systems: A Framework for Analysis.* Cambridge, Mass.: Harvard University Press, 1965.

Bergquist, W. H., and Shoemaker, W. A. (Eds.). *New Directions for Higher Education: A Comprehensive Approach to Institutional Development,* no. 15. San Francisco: Jossey-Bass, 1976.

Cheit, E. F. "Challenges Inherent in the Systematic Approach." In C. R. Adams (Ed.), *New Directions for Institutional Research: Appraising Information Needs of Decision Makers,* no. 15. San Francisco: Jossey-Bass, 1977.

Cohen, M. D., and March, J. G. *Leadership and Ambiguity: The American College President.* New York: McGraw-Hill, 1974.

Cox, G. B. "Managerial Style: Implications for the Utilization of Program Evaluation Information." *Evaluation Quarterly,* 1977, *1* (3), 499–508.

Dror, Y. *Ventures in Policy Sciences: Concepts and Applications.* New York: Elsevier, 1971.

Friedmann, J., and Hudson, B. "Knowledge and Action: A Guide to Planning Theory." *Journal of the American Institute of Planners,* 1974, *40* (1), 2–16.

Havelock, R. G. *The Change Agent's Guide to Innovation in Education.* Englewood Cliffs, N.J.: Educational Technology Publications, 1973.

Heim, P. "Management Systems and Budgeting Methodology: Do They Meet the Needs and Will They Work?" *NACUBO Studies in Management,* 1972, *2* (2).

Hopkins, D. S. P., and Schroeder, R. G. (Eds.). *New Directions for Institutional Research: Applying Analytic Methods to Planning and Management,* no. 13. San Francisco: Jossey-Bass, 1977.

Kieft, R. N. *Academic Planning: Four Institutional Case Studies.* Boulder, Colo.: National Center for Higher Education Management Systems, 1978.

Kieft, R. N., Armijo, F., and Bucklew, N. S. *A Handbook for Institutional Academic and Program Planning: From Idea to Implementation.* Boulder, Colo.: National Center for Higher Education Management Systems, 1978.

Lawrence, G. B., and Service, A. L. (Eds.). *Quantitative Approaches to Higher Education Management.* ERIC/Higher Education Research Report No. 4. Washington, D.C.: American Association for Higher Education, 1977.

Lelong, D. C., and others. "Planning in Higher Education." Unpublished manuscript, Institute of Higher Education, University of Texas System, Austin, 1980.

Levine, C. H. "Organizational Decline and Cutback Management." *Public Administration Review,* 1978, *38* (4), 316–325.

Mason, R. O., and Mitroff, I. I. "A Program for Research on Management Information Systems." *Management Sciences,* 1973, *19* (5), 475–487.

Patton, M. Q. *Utilization-Focused Evaluation.* Beverly Hills, Calif.: Sage, 1978.

Schmidtlein, F. A. "Decision Process Paradigms in Education." *Educational Researcher,* 1974, *3* (5), 4–11.

Sturner, W. F. *Action Planning on the Campus.* Washington, D.C.: American Association of State Colleges and Universities, 1974.

Weick, K. E. "Educational Organizations as Loosely Coupled Systems." *Administrative Science Quarterly,* 1976, *21* (1), 1–19.

Wildavsky, A. "If Planning Is Everything, Maybe It's Nothing." *Policy Sciences,* 1973, *4* (2), 127–153.

Name Index

Subject Index

A

Academic program evaluation: approaches to, 435–444; conducting of, 444–449; data analysis for, 442, 445–447; effectiveness of, 451–454; interpretation and review of, 434, 442–443, 447–448; for marketing purposes, 246–247; for multiple audiences, 443–445; planning of, 444–445; and planning, integrated, 450–451; system level, 449–451; team approach to, 441–443

Academic programs, 304–305; accreditation of, 106, 108; constituency planning participation in, 315, 317; and faculty utilization, 368–369; improvement of, 317–321; improving planning of, 321–324; information systems on, 518–520; inputs and outcomes of, 434–436; and institutional evaluation, 421; linkages in, 293; new, review and approval of, 450; new versus existing, 313, 315; planning cycles of, 312–313, 322; planning idea sources for, 311; planning styles for, 305–311; planning styles compared, 311–316; resource requirements

model for, 327–330; self-evaluation of, 441–444

Academy of Educational Development (AED): consortia study by, 100–101; planning model of, 140

Accountability: and academic freedom, 14; and budgeting process, 348; fiscal indicators of, 411; future state involvement in, 55–56; information systems for, 520–522; and program planning, 307; rise of, 13–14; and state coordination, 49–50, 52, 74–75, 87, 182–183, 196

Accreditation: and federal funding, 423–424; and institutional evaluation, 412–413; and institutional goals, 183–184; of programs, 106, 108; regional associations for, 97–99, 416–418; self-studies for, 415–418; states and, 53–54; voluntary associations for, 106–110

ACCTion Consortium, 102–103

Acquainter, The, 100, 109

Administration: in academic planning, 306, 309, 311, 313, 318; and administrative evaluation, 483–484; assignment review in, 385; costs of, 381–383; defined, 387; and faculty evaluation,